Jonas and Kovner's
Health Care Delivery
in the United States

9
edition

Anthony R. Kovner, PhD, is professor of health policy and management at the Robert F. Wagner Graduate School of Public Service at New York University, in New York City. He is trained in organizational behavior, health services management, and social and economic development. He received bachelor's and master's degrees from Cornell University, and his doctorate in public administration is from the University of Pittsburgh. Kovner is an experienced health care manager, having served as CEO of a community hospital, senior health care consultant for a large union, and manager of a group practice, a nursing home, and a large neighborhood health center. He is a board member of Lutheran Health Care and of Health Plus in Brooklyn, New York. He has carried out several funded research projects, most recently on factors associated with the use of management research in hospitals and health systems. He is author or editor of 9 books, 43 journal articles, and 24 case studies. He has directed several national demonstration programs funded by major foundations. Kovner was the fourth recipient, in 1999, of the Gary L. Filerman prize for educational leadership from the Association of University Programs in Health Administration.

James R. Knickman, PhD, is the first president and chief executive officer of the New York State Health Foundation (NYSHealth), a private philanthropy established with resources from Empire Blue Cross Blue Shield's conversion from a nonprofit to a for-profit corporation. Prior to joining NYSHealth, Knickman was vice president of research and evaluation at the Robert Wood Johnson Foundation (RWJF) in Princeton, New Jersey. There, he was responsible for external evaluations of RWJF national initiatives, developing research initiatives, and conducting internal programmatic analyses. Throughout his 14-year tenure at RWJF, Knickman led grant-making teams in clinical care for the chronically ill, long-term care, and population health. Between 1976 and 1992, Knickman served on the faculty of New York University's Robert F. Wagner Graduate School of Public Service. He serves on a wide range of advisory boards, including as chairman of the Robert Wood Johnson Health System in New Brunswick, New Jersey, and is a past board member of AcademyHealth in Washington, DC. He has published extensively and currently is an editorial board member for *The Milbank Quarterly* and *Inquiry*. Knickman received his BA from Fordham University and his PhD in public policy analysis from the University of Pennsylvania.

Jonas and Kovner's
Health Care Delivery
in the United States

9
edition

Anthony R. Kovner, PhD
James R. Knickman, PhD
Editors

Steven Jonas, MD, MPH, MS
Founding Editor

SPRINGER PUBLISHING COMPANY
New York

Springer Publishing Company, LLC
11 West 42nd Street
New York, NY 10036
www.springerpub.com

Acquisitions Editor: Sheri W. Sussman
Production Editor: Julia Rosen
Cover design: Mimi Flow
Composition: Apex CoVantage

08 09 10 11/ 5 4 3 2 1

Library of Congress Cataloging-in-Publication Data

Jonas and Kovner's health care delivery in the United States/Anthony R. Kovner, James R. Knickman, editors.—9th ed.
     p. ; cm.
  Rev. ed. of: Jonas & Kovner's health care delivery in the United States. 8th ed. c2005.
  Includes bibliographical references and index.
  ISBN 978-0-8261-2096-0 (hard cover : alk. paper)—ISBN 978-0-8261-2098-4 (soft cover : alk. paper) 1. Medical care—United States. I. Kovner, Anthony R. II. Knickman, James. III. Jonas, Steven. IV. Jonas & Kovner's health care delivery in the United States. V. Title: Health care delivery in the United States.
  [DNLM: 1. Delivery of Health Care—United States. 2. Health Policy—United States. 3. Health Services—United States. 4. Quality of Health Care—United States. W 84 AA1 J68 2008]
RA395.A3H395   2008
362.10973—dc22   2007043637

Printed in the United States of America by Bang Printing.

Contents

Part I: Perspectives

1 OVERVIEW: THE STATE OF HEALTH CARE DELIVERY IN THE UNITED STATES 2

James R. Knickman and Anthony R. Kovner

SUPPLEMENT: KEY CHARTS 13

Victoria Weisfeld

Part II: Providing Health Care

Part III: System Performance

Part IV: The Future

<AuQ1>

Part V: Appendices

Tables and Figures

Chapter 1

Chapter 2

Chapter 3

Chapter 15

Chapter 16

Chapter 17

Chapter 18

Foreword

It is ironic that health care, which occupies nearly one-sixth of the U.S. economy and affects us all, sooner or later, in the most intimate and important ways, remains *terra incognita* for so many of us. It is like the vast blank spaces in maps from the Middle Ages. The boldest, strongest, most confident layperson falls silent and tiptoes in the corridors of a hospital, sometimes bowing the head as the white-coated doctors stride by. We depend on health care, but in it we feel like strangers.

Each year, I am reminded that health care is a mystery to most as I begin to teach a Harvard College undergraduate course called *The Quality of Health Care in America,* which has become one of my annual projects. Forty or 50 young people, most of them in their senior year, join my coprofessors and me in a semester-long exploration of what health care achieves and what it fails to achieve. Most of these smart, interested students are ignorant of even the most basic patterns: the flow of patients, the flow of money, and the nature of the institutions that shape care. Few can describe Medicare, and even fewer know the difference between it and Medicaid. Terms such as *primary care, chronic disease, peer review, employer-based coverage,* and *evidence-based medicine* have only the vaguest referents in their minds. Most students assume at the outset that most of medical care is effective, efficient, scientifically grounded, and safe—despite the consistent testimony to the contrary in health services research and from the National Academies of Science. The minority who have had personal experiences of care—usually at the bedside of a grandparent or unfortunate friend—can, with the slightest encouragement, surface questions, concerns, and even outrage at flaws they saw; but most of these students assume, incorrectly, that their experience was the exception in a system that generally works well.

They know that health care costs too much; after all, that's in every morning newspaper. But they don't know why. They don't know where the money comes from, where it goes, or how efficiently it is used. They know little about international comparisons in either cost or quality, and they assume, like many Americans, that we have the best health care on Earth, which is wrong. They know that millions of us lack health insurance, but they don't know how many or why. They know that race and wealth are associated with unequal treatment and variation in health status, but they do not know how vast, unconscionable, and unnecessary those disparities are.

Some of these students will become doctors and nurses. The majority will enter other professions and callings. But, without exception, every one will encounter health care in ways that significantly affect their lives. There it will be, in the line on their paycheck stubs deducting the insurance premium and the Medicare tax; in their visits to the emergency department when they fall off their bicycles; in the answers they will seek when they or a loved one gets short of breath or loses weight; in the public debates among candidates; in the news about the labor-management negotiations; in the feature articles on fad diets; and in the editorials about malpractice reform, rationing, or the federal deficit.

Those who do become health care professionals will, of course, learn more about the system from inside. But their view, untended, will be myopic, local, and distorted. They will know that the lab report got lost, that the patients have been waiting too long, that the schedule is jammed, and that the Medicare fees got cut; but most of them won't know why any more than the laypeople do. They will be fish in water, who cannot understand water unless they get instruction.

This will not do. For a public so dependent on and concerned about the performance of health care, now and in the future, or for professionals and managers in health care so dependent on and concerned about the systems that make it possible for them to find meaning in their work, opacity about what health care is, how it works, what it comprises, and where it came from is paralyzing. It precludes reasonable expectations for change and effective action to make change. Ignorance about health care generates frustrated clinicians, angry patients, unaccountable politicians, and uninformed voters.

At its peak, the proper view—the proper knowledge—is a view of and knowledge about the system as a whole. That is neither inborn nor well-taught yet in U.S. health care. But that knowledge base is an essential precondition for progress.

This is what makes this textbook such a treasure. It is in very small company among available explications of the nature, components, history, stakeholders, dynamics, achievements, and deficiencies in a system of gigantic size and equally gigantic complexities. The editors are world-class scholars, and they have organized the writing of an equally distinguished squad of contributors. In their hands, many of the mysteries of health care dissolve into orderly and clear frameworks, and the most important dynamics become visible.

Making health care in the United States become what it should become is too important and too difficult a job to be left to any one stakeholder, profession, institution, or change agent. It affects all of us, and, somehow, sometime, we will need to find the will to act in concert to rebuild it—laypeople and professionals, hospitals and ambulatory care, payers and consumers, executives and the workforce, and more. Concerted effort will have to begin on a foundation of clear knowledge of the system we will work to change, and, to gain that knowledge, few resources are as valuable as the masterful and sweeping overview that these pages contain.

Donald M. Berwick, MD, MPP
President and CEO, Institute for
Healthcare Improvement

Organization of This Book

This text, *Jonas and Kovner's Health Care Delivery in the United States,* 9th edition, is organized into five parts: **Perspectives, Providing Health Care, System Performance, The Future,** and **Appendices.** The titles of these five parts can be formulated as answers to the following questions: How do we understand and assess the health care sector of our economy? Where and how is health care provided? How well does the health care system perform? Where is the health care sector going in terms of the health of the people, the cost of care, access to care, and quality of care? And what else do we need to know to answer the four previous questions?

Part I, Perspectives, is divided into an overview with supplemental charts and chapters on measuring health status, financing health care, public health, the role of government, and a comparative analysis of health systems in wealthy countries. Part II, Providing Health Care, contains chapters on acute care, chronic care, long-term care, health-related behavior, pharmaceuticals and medical devices, the workforce, and information management.

Part III, System Performance, includes chapters on governance, management, and accountability; health care quality; access to care; and costs and value. Part IV, The Future, projects what health care in the United States will look like over the short term. Three appendices in Part V contain a glossary, a guide to sources of data, and a list of useful health care Web sites.

This edition also includes an Instructor's Guide accessible online or in print for Professors' use only.

Contributors

Gerard F. Anderson, PhD, is a professor of health policy and management and professor of international health at the Johns Hopkins University Bloomberg School of Public Health, professor of medicine at the Johns Hopkins University School of Medicine, director of the Johns Hopkins Center for Hospital Finance and Management, and codirector of the Johns Hopkins Program for Medical Technology and Practice Assessment. He recently stepped down as the national program director for the Robert Wood Johnson Foundation sponsored program Partnership for Solutions: Better Lives for People With Chronic Conditions. Anderson is currently conducting research on chronic conditions, comparative insurance systems in developing countries, medical education, health care payment reform, and technology diffusion. He has directed reviews of health systems for the World Bank and USAID in multiple countries. He has authored 2 books on health care payment policy, published over 200 peer-reviewed articles, testified in Congress over 35 times as an individual witness, and serves on multiple editorial committees. Prior to his arrival at Johns Hopkins, Anderson held various positions in the Office of the Secretary, U.S. Department of Health and Human Services, where he helped to develop Medicare prospective payment legislation.

Donald M. Berwick, MD, MPP, is president, CEO, and cofounder of the Institute for Healthcare Improvement in Boston, Massachusetts. Dr. Berwick is a clinical professor of pediatrics and health care policy at the Harvard Medical School, and a pediatrician. An associate in pediatrics at Boston's Children's Hospital, he is also a consultant in pediatrics at Massachusetts General Hospital. Dr. Berwick is the author of *Escape Fire: Designs for the Future of Health Care* and co-author of the book, *Curing Health Care and New Rules.*

John Billings, JD, is associate professor of health policy and public service at New York University, teaching in the area of health policy. He is principal investigator on numerous projects to assess the performance of the safety net for vulnerable populations and to understand the nature and extent of barriers to optimal health for vulnerable populations. Much of his work has involved analysis of patterns of hospital admission and emergency room visits as a mechanism to evaluate access barriers to outpatient care and to assess the performance of the ambulatory care delivery system. He has also examined the characteristics of high-cost Medicaid patients to help in designing interventions to improve care and outcomes for these patients. As a founding member of the Foundation for Informed Decision Making, Billings is helping to provide patients with a clearer mechanism for understanding and making informed decisions about a variety of available treatments.

Carol S. Brewer, PhD, is an associate professor at the University at Buffalo School of Nursing and director of nursing at the New York State Area Health Education Center Statewide System. She has conducted nursing workforce research for over 13 years and has published and presented widely. Her current research uses her model of workforce participation to study the work participation of newly licensed registered nurses. This model accounts for Metropolitan Statistical Area differences and attitudes such as satisfaction and work family conflict. Her past research has utilized both secondary and primary data collection to examine a variety of nursing workforce issues. She has also conducted research focusing on the New York State supply of nurses and is responsible for the strategic planning for nursing workforce programs for the New York State Area Health Education Center (NYS AHEC) System. The NYS AHEC System focuses on recruiting, educating, and retaining the health care workforce for rural and underserved populations. Brewer also teaches graduate students about quantitative research methods and health care systems, policies, and ethics. She received her undergraduate degrees from Denison University (biology), Trenton State College (nursing), and a master's degree in nursing from the University of Knoxville, a master's degree in applied economics from the University of Michigan, and a PhD from the University of Michigan in nursing systems.

Joel C. Cantor, ScD, is director of the Center for State Health Policy and professor of public policy at Rutgers University. Cantor's research focuses on issues of health care regulation, financing, and delivery. His recent work includes studies of health insurance market regulation, access to care for low-income and minority populations, the health care safety net, and the supply of physicians. Cantor has published widely on health policy topics and serves on the editorial board of the policy journal *Inquiry*. Cantor serves frequently as an advisor on health policy matters to New Jersey state agencies; he currently serves as a member of the Governor's Commission on Rationalizing New Jersey's Health Care

System and chairs the New Jersey Mandated Health Benefit Advisory Commission. Prior to joining the faculty at Rutgers, Cantor served as director of research at the United Hospital Fund of New York and director of evaluation research at the Robert Wood Johnson Foundation. He received his doctorate in health policy and management from the Johns Hopkins University School of Hygiene and Public Health in 1988.

Carol A. Caronna, PhD, is an assistant professor in the Department of Sociology, Anthropology, and Criminal Justice at Towson University. She did her graduate work in sociology at Stanford University and, from 2000 to 2002, was a Robert Wood Johnson Scholar in Health Policy Research at the University of California, Berkeley School of Public Health (in collaboration with the University of California, San Francisco). Her work focuses on entrepreneurship, organizational identity, and institutional theory, with specific projects on the evolution of the health maintenance organization as an organizational form; mergers of secular and religious hospitals; and entrepreneurship in the nonprofit sector. In addition to being the coauthor of *Institutional Change and Healthcare Organizations: From Professional Dominance to Managed Care* (2000), she has published articles in *Social Science and Medicine, Journal of Health and Social Behavior,* and *Research in the Sociology of Organizations.*

Elaine F. Cassidy, PhD, is a program officer in research and evaluation at the Robert Wood Johnson Foundation, where she manages research and evaluation activities for the Vulnerable Populations portfolio. She also has been involved in grant-making for the Pioneer portfolio and the Addiction Prevention and Treatment targeted team. Her work and interests focus primarily on adolescent health and risk behaviors and on school-based interventions, particularly for children and adolescents living in low-income, urban environments. She is a former school psychologist and trained mental health clinician, who has provided therapeutic care to children and families in school, outpatient, and acute partial hospitalization settings. She holds a BA in psychology and liberal studies from the University of Notre Dame, an MSEd in psychological services from the University of Pennsylvania, and a PhD in school, community, and child-clinical psychology from the University of Pennsylvania.

Carol S. Chang, MPA, MPH, is a senior program director at the American Red Cross of Central New Jersey, where she oversees the chapter's emergency services, community services, and health and safety departments. Chang was formerly a program officer at the Robert Wood Johnson Foundation, where she worked with the public health team to develop and implement strategies to improve the performance, accountability, and visibility of governmental public health departments. Chang formerly worked with CARE-International to improve the food security of populations in Africa, Asia, Latin America, and the Caribbean. She earned MPH and MPA degrees from Columbia University.

Mary Ann Chiasson, DrPH, is an epidemiologist who joined the Medical and Health Research Association (MHRA) of New York City in 1999 as vice president for research and evaluation. MHRA is a not-for-profit organization that provides health and health-related services, conducts demonstration and research programs, and offers management services in order to improve community health and strengthen health policy. Before joining MHRA, Chiasson served for 9 years as an assistant commissioner of health at the New York City Department of Health with scientific and administrative responsibility for AIDS surveillance, AIDS research, and vital statistics and epidemiology. Chiasson's research interests include HIV transmission, women's reproductive health, and infant mortality. Her current research focuses on the Internet and high-risk sexual behavior among men who have sex with men. Chiasson is an associate professor of clinical epidemiology (in medicine) at the Mailman School of Public Health, Columbia University.

Penny Hollander Feldman, PhD, is vice president for research and evaluation at the Visiting Nurse Service of New York (VNSNY) and director of the VNSNY Center for Home Care Policy and Research. As center director, she leads projects focused on improving the quality, outcomes, and cost-effectiveness of home-based care, supporting informed policy making by long-term care decision makers, and helping communities promote the health, well-being, and independence of people with chronic illness or disability. Prior to joining VNSNY, Feldman served on the faculties of the Kennedy School of Government and the Department of Health Policy and Management at the Harvard School of Public Health, and she is currently associate professor in the Department of Public Health at Weill Medical College of Cornell University. The author of numerous publications, Feldman also has served on a variety of national committees shaping health care policy and practice, including the Institute of Medicine Committee on Improving the Quality of Long Term Care.

Steven A. Finkler, PhD, is professor emeritus of public and health administration, accounting, and financial management. He served for over 20 years as director of the specialization in health care financial management at New York University's Robert F. Wagner Graduate School of Public Service. He is an award-winning teacher and author.

He received a BS with joint majors in finance and accounting and an MS in accounting from the Wharton School at the University of Pennsylvania. His MA in economics and PhD in business administration were awarded by Stanford University. Finkler, who is also a CPA, worked for several years as an auditor with Ernst and Young and was on the faculty of the Wharton School before joining New York University. Among his publications are 18 books, including *Essentials of Cost Accounting for Health Care Organizations,* 3rd edition (with David Ward and Judith Baker), *Accounting Fundamentals for Health Care Management* (with David Ward), and *Financial Management for Public, Health, and Not-for-Profit Organizations* (2nd edition). He has published more than 200 articles in many journals, including *Hospitals and Health Services Administration, Healthcare Financial Management, Health Care Management Review, Health Services Research,* and the *New England Journal of Medicine.*

Ron Geigle is a strategist and communications expert on health policy issues, focusing on medical technology. In 1999, he founded Polidais, a policy analysis and public affairs company in Washington, DC, that provides research, policy positioning, and public affairs services for clients in the fields of health care, science, and technological innovation. Previously, Geigle served as the vice president of policy communications for the Advanced Medical Technology Association (AdvaMed). Prior to joining AdvaMed, he worked as a press secretary and legislative assistant in the U.S. Senate and House of Representatives and as a speechwriter for the chairman of a federal agency. He is a graduate of Harvard University and the University of Washington in Seattle.

Thomas E. Getzen, PhD, is professor of risk, insurance, and health management at the Fox School of Business, Temple University, and is executive director of iHEA, the International Health Economics Association, with 2,400 academic and professional members in 72 countries. He has also served as visiting professor at the Woodrow Wilson School of Public Policy at Princeton University, the Wharton School of the University of Pennsylvania, and the Centre for Health Economics at the University of York. His textbook *Health Economics: Fundamentals and Flow of Funds* (3rd edition, 2007) is used in graduate and undergraduate programs throughout the world. Getzen serves on the board of Catholic Health East, the ninth largest health care system in the United States, and on several other corporate and nonprofit boards. His research focuses on the macroeconomics of health, forecasting medical expenditures and physician supply, price indexes, public health economics, and related issues. Currently Getzen is at work on a model of long-term medical cost trends for use by the Society of Actuaries.

Marc N. Gourevitch, MD, MPH, is professor of medicine at the New York University (NYU) School of Medicine, where he is director of the Division of General Internal Medicine. Gourevitch's central research interests include integrating substance abuse care into general medical settings; defining system-congruent strategies for fostering behavior change and behavior-related chronic disease care; clinical epidemiology among drug users and other underserved populations; and pharmacologic treatments for opioid and alcohol dependence. He leads NYU School of Medicine's Fellowship in Medicine and Public Health Research, dedicated to enabling fellows and junior faculty to develop applied research skills to bring about advances in population health. Gourevitch received his medical degree from Harvard Medical School and completed his internship and residency in primary care internal medicine at Bellevue Hospital and the NYU School of Medicine.

Michal D. Gursen, MPH, MS, is a research analyst at the Center for Home Care Policy and Research at the Visiting Nurse Service of New York. At the center, Gursen works primarily on two projects: the AdvantAge Initiative and the Health Indicators in NORC Programs Initiative. Before coming to the center, she worked at the New York State Psychiatric Institute, where she studied psychoeducational interventions for people with mental illness. Prior to that, Gursen worked at Mount Sinai School of Medicine, where she researched psychosocial pathways leading to drug use. Gursen received her MPH in health policy and management with a concentration in effectiveness and outcomes research and an MS in social work from Columbia University. She holds a BA in psychology from Barnard College.

Kelly A. Hunt, MPP, is a senior program director at the New York State Health Foundation and has more than 14 years of experience that includes developing, managing, and funding health care policy analyses. As a research and evaluation officer at the Robert Wood Johnson Foundation (RWJF), she led the team responsible for the organization's Scorecard, an annual assessment of RWJF's impact; she was a member of a team developing a strategy to reduce racial and ethnic disparities in health care; and she oversaw demonstration programs to expand health insurance coverage, monitored a portfolio of health services research grants, and played a lead role in ensuring that the impact of RWJF's grant-making was carefully measured and disseminated. Previously, Hunt was a health and welfare consultant at Towers Perrin in New York City and a senior consultant at KPMG Peat Marwick. She is a coauthor on numerous health services research articles that have appeared in journals such as *Health Affairs, Health Services Research,* and *The Milbank Quarterly.* She holds a master's degree in public policy from Georgetown University.

Kelli A. Hurdle, MPA, is the associate director for clinical services in the Medicine Service Department at Bellevue Hospital Center. Her work centers on the development and evaluation of quality improvement and patient safety initiatives in the department. Before joining Bellevue in August 2005, Hurdle was a research assistant at New York University's Center for Health and Public Service Research. Prior to that, she worked at Cicatelli Associates, Inc., assisting health care organizations with program development and expansion, operations improvement, and capacity building. She received an MPA from the Robert F. Wagner Graduate School of Public Service at New York University and a BS degree from Villanova University.

Steven Jonas, MD, MPH, MS, is professor of preventive medicine, School of Medicine, and professor, Graduate Program in Public Health, at Stony Brook University (New York). He is a fellow of the American College of Preventive Medicine, the New York Academy of Medicine, the New York Academy of Sciences, and the American Public Health Association. He is editor-in-chief of the *American Medical Athletics Association Journal.* Over the course of an academic career that began in 1969, his research has focused on health care delivery systems analysis, preventive medicine and public health, and personal health and wellness. He has authored, coauthored, edited, and coedited over 25 books and has published more than 135 papers in scientific journals, as well as numerous articles in the popular literature. It was in the mid-70s that, having been given the opportunity to do so by Dr. Ursula Springer, he created *Health Care Delivery in the United States.*

Gary E. Kalkut, MD, MPH, is the vice president and senior medical director of Montefiore Medical Center in the Bronx, New York. Kalkut provides institutional clinical leadership for Montefiore's integrated delivery system that includes three hospitals with 1,100 beds and an ambulatory system with over two million visits in 2006, including 210,000 emergency department visits. He is also the chief medical officer of the Care Management Organization, which manages Montefiore's risk contracts. Kalkut is an infectious diseases physician and former medical director of the adult AIDS program at Montefiore. He received his medical degree at the Boston University School of Medicine and did his residency in internal medicine and fellowship in infectious diseases at Montefiore.

Roger Kropf, PhD, is a professor in the Health Policy and Management Program at New York University's Robert F. Wagner Graduate School of Public Service. Kropf is the author of three books on the application of information systems to health care management: *Strategic Analysis for Hospital Management* (with James Greenberg, 1984), *Service*

Excellence in Health Care Through the Use of Computers (1990), *Making Information Technology Work: Maximizing the Benefits for Health Care Organizations* (with Guy Scalzi, 2007). His current research is on how managers measure the benefits of health care information technology before approval, manage projects to assure they are on time and within budget, and obtain the desired benefits after implementation.

Laura C. Leviton, PhD, is a senior program officer of the Robert Wood Johnson Foundation in Princeton, New Jersey, and was a professor at two schools of public health. She collaborated on the first randomized experiment on HIV prevention and on two place-based experiments to improve medical care. In 1993, the American Psychological Association recognized her for distinguished contributions to psychology in the public interest. She has served on two Institute of Medicine committees dealing with public health topics and was appointed to the National Advisory Committee on HIV and STD Prevention of the Centers for Disease Control and Prevention. Leviton was president of the American Evaluation Association in 2000 and has coauthored two books: *Foundations of Program Evaluation* and *Confronting Public Health Risks.* She received her PhD in social psychology from the University of Kansas and postdoctoral training in research methodology and evaluation at Northwestern University.

Pamela Nadash, PhD, has most recently been a senior research associate at the Thomson Medstat Group, responsible for developing design options for a consumer-directed Medicare home health benefit and authoring papers highlighting promising practices in Medicaid home- and community-based services. She has also held research positions at the Center for Home Care Policy and Research at the Visiting Nurse Service of New York and at the National Council for the Aging. She is completing her PhD in public health and political science at Columbia University, conducting quantitative analyses of integrated and Medicaid-only managed long-term care programs.

Jennifer A. Nelson, MPH, is a biostatistician in the community epidemiology branch of the County of San Diego Health and Human Services Agency. She is a graduate of the Center for Population and Family Health at the Joseph L. Mailman School of Public Health of Columbia University. Before her work on communicable disease and vital statistics surveillance for the County of San Diego, she was a research associate in the Research and Evaluation Unit at the Medical and Health Research Association of New York City, Inc., where she worked on research projects relating to childhood obesity, reproductive health, and maternal and child health. Previous experience includes policy research at the National Center for Children in Poverty, health education and clinical assistance at a Planned Parenthood center, and health and nutrition education at a rural health clinic in West Africa as a Peace Corps volunteer.

C. Tracy Orleans, PhD, is senior scientist of the Robert Wood Johnson Foundation (RWJF). She has led or coled the foundation's public policy– and health care system–based grant-making in the areas of tobacco control, physical activity promotion, childhood obesity prevention, and chronic disease management. She led the foundation's health and behavior team and has developed and/or managed numerous RWJF national initiatives, including Addressing Tobacco in Health Care, Smoke-Free Families, Helping Young Smokers Quit, Bridging the Gap/Impact Teen, Substance Abuse Policy Research, Improving Chronic Illness Care, Prescription for Health, Active Living Research, and Healthy Eating Research. An internationally known clinical health psychologist, Orleans has authored or coauthored over 200 publications and has served on numerous journal editorial boards, national scientific panels, advisory groups (e.g., Institute of Medicine, National Commission on Prevention Priorities, U.S. Preventive Services Task Force), and as president of the Society of Behavioral Medicine.

Scott D. Rhodes, PhD, MPH, CHES, is associate professor in the section on health and society in the Department of Social Sciences and Health Policy, Division of Public Health Sciences, and in the section on infectious diseases in the Department of Internal Medicine. He also is an affiliate faculty of the Maya Angelou Research Center on Minority Health at Wake Forest University Health Sciences in Winston-Salem, North Carolina. Rhodes's research explores sexual health, HIV, and sexually transmitted disease prevention, obesity prevention, and other health disparities among vulnerable communities. Rhodes has extensive research experience with self-identifying gay and bisexual men and men who have sex with men; Latino immigrant communities; urban African American adolescents; persons living with HIV/AIDS; and men of color. He has broad experience in the design, implementation, and evaluation of multiple-level interventions; community-based participatory research; exploratory evaluation; the application of behavioral theory; lay health advisor interventions; sociocultural determinants of health; and Internet research.

Victor G. Rodwin, PhD, MPH, is professor of health policy and management at the Robert F. Wagner Graduate School of Public Service, New York University (NYU), and codirector (with Michael K Gusmano) of the World Cities Project, a joint venture of the Wagner School, NYU, the International Longevity Center-USA, and the Mailman School, Columbia University. Rodwin has written five books: *The Health Planning Predicament: Quebec, England, France and the U.S.* (1984), *The End of an Illusion: The Future of Health Policy in Western Industrialized Nations* (1984), *Public Hospital Systems in New York City and Paris* (1992), *Japan's Universal and Affordable Health Care: Lessons for the U.S.* (1994), and *Growing Older in World Cities: New York, London, Paris and Tokyo* (2006). Recent articles discuss French national health insurance and reform; infant mortality and income in four world cities; treatment of heart disease in these cities; and, most recently, avoidable hospital conditions in Manhattan and Paris, a study that illustrates a new approach to the comparative analysis of health systems. A member of the National Academy of Social Insurance since 1998, Rodwin received his MPH in social and administrative sciences and his PhD in city and regional planning from the University of California, Berkeley.

Thomas C. Rosenthal, MD, is professor and chair of the Department of Family Medicine at the University at Buffalo. He has been involved in health planning and workforce issues as a member of the New York State Rural Health Council and several committees of the Medical Society of the State of New York, including a task force to eliminate health disparities. He is the director of the New York State Area Health Education Center System and editor of the *Journal of Rural Health*. Rosenthal has published over 60 peer-reviewed articles and several monographs, and he edits a geriatric textbook, *Office Care Geriatrics*.

Michael S. Sparer, PhD, JD, is a professor of health policy at the Joseph L. Mailman School of Public Health at Columbia University. He spent 7 years as a litigator for the New York City Law Department, specializing in intergovernmental social welfare litigation. After leaving the practice of law, Sparer obtained a doctorate in political science from Brandeis University. Sparer is the editor of the *Journal of Health Politics, Policy and Law* and the author of *Medicaid and the Limits of State Health Reform*, as well as numerous articles and book chapters. In his writings, Sparer examines the politics of the U.S. health care system, with a particular emphasis on the nation's health insurance system as well as the ways in which federalism shapes policy.

Robin J. Strongin, MPA, a partner with Polidais LLC, brings 25 years of experience in health care policy, legislative analysis, and public relations. Prior to joining the firm in 2000, she was a senior research associate with the National Health Policy Forum at George Washington University. She formerly served as acting executive director and director of research for the Health Care Technology Institute. Her previous tenures with health and policy organizations include the National Leadership Coalition on Health Care and the Prospective Payment Assessment Commission (now the Medicare Payment Advisory Commission). She was selected as a presidential management intern and worked in the Office of Legislation and Policy of the Health Care Financing Administration (now the Centers for Medicare & Medicaid Services), in addition to serving in the Office of Congressman James J. Florio (D-NJ).

Bonnie J. Wakefield, PhD, RN, is director of health services research and development at the Harry S. Truman Memorial Veterans' Hospital in Columbia, Missouri. She holds appointments as associate research professor in the Schools of Nursing and Medicine at the University of Missouri. Wakefield's previous experience includes work as a staff nurse in critical care and development and implementation of successful staff development, patient education, and quality improvement programs in acute care settings. Her program of research focuses on patient safety in acute care settings and application of innovative telehealth strategies to improve health care delivery. She has completed two randomized controlled trials using home telehealth in patients with heart failure and comorbid diabetes and hypertension. She received her BSN from Bradley University and a PhD from the University of Iowa.

Douglas S. Wakefield, PhD, is director of the University of Missouri-Columbia Center for Health Care Quality and professor in the Department of Health Management and Informatics. He previously served as professor and head of the University of Iowa Department of Health Management and Policy from 1996 to 2005. His research interests are in patient care quality, safety, and value improvement. Wakefield's research has been funded from a variety of sources, including Agency for Healthcare Research and Quality (AHRQ), Health Resources and Services Administration, Robert Wood Johnson Foundation, Northwest Area Foundation, John Deere Health Foundation, and the Veterans Administration. Recently funded research includes three grants from AHRQ in which he is leading evaluations of the implementation of electronic health systems and computerized provider order entry systems in hospitals and is a co-investigator examining the value of health information technologies in rural settings.

Victoria Weisfeld, MPH, is a principal in NEW Associates, a strategic planning and communications consulting firm whose national clients include think tanks, foundations, and nonprofit organizations.

She combines her academic training in public health and journalism by helping health care organizations develop social marketing programs and disseminate information more effectively. An end-of-life communications program she developed, Last Acts, won the Public Relations Society of America's highest award. She also has developed and managed award-winning communications programs in community radio and public television outreach. She is a past president of the Communications Network in Philanthropy. Major employers were the Robert Wood Johnson Foundation in Princeton, New Jersey, and the Institute of Medicine in Washington, DC, where she wrote the initial draft of the seminal public health planning document, *Healthy People*. She serves on the board and advisory committees of several media organizations, as well as Family and Children's Services of Central New Jersey.

Victoria A. Wicks, MBA, is associate vice president of public policy for Sanofi-Aventis Pharmaceuticals. Wicks began her health care career in the managed care industry, holding positions in pricing, operations, product development, and medical affairs before becoming the senior vice president of marketing and sales for HIP, a 900,000-member plan in New York, then president and chief executive officer of a HIP Health Plan of New Jersey. She made the transition to the pharmaceutical sector at Roche Labs in marketing before moving to Aventis, now Sanofi-Aventis, in public policy. Wicks earned a BA from Bates College, Lewiston, Maine, where she currently serves on the board of trustees. She also received an MBA from the University of Massachusetts and has completed the Advanced Management Program at the Wharton School of the University of Pennsylvania.

PART ONE

Perspectives

1

Key Words

health care delivery	public health	market forces
quality improvement	healthy behavior	health workforce
financing	social determinants of health	engagement
access to care	health insurance	stakeholders
health technology	interest groups	

Overview: The State of Health Care Delivery in the United States

James R. Knickman and Anthony R. Kovner

Learning Objectives

- Understand defining characteristics of the U.S. health care system.
- Identify issues and concerns with the current system.
- Understand the dynamics that influence efforts to improve the system.
- Recognize the importance of engagement of stakeholders to the prospects of improving U.S. health care.

Topical Outline

- The importance of health and health care to American life
- Defining characteristics of the U.S. health care system
- Major issues and concerns facing the health sector
- Constraints that make change difficult in health delivery
- The key importance of leadership for a strong health care system

I

n this initial chapter, we present an overview of the U.S. health care delivery system. To set the stage for the in-depth looks at key aspects and components of the system in the chapters to follow, this overview describes the distinguishing characteristics of our health care system and how it is organized to meet the needs of 301 million Americans. It introduces the key challenges that face leaders of the health sector as they try to make it an ever-improving enterprise. And it discusses the social context shaping health care in the United States. A central theme is that efforts to improve the system require the engagement of stakeholders: frontline doctors and nurses, middle-level managers, patients, and consumers.

The health enterprise is one of the most important parts of the U.S. social system. Our nation cannot be strong or wealthy and citizens cannot lead fully productive lives without good health (Figure 1.1S in supplemental section at the end of this chapter). Each of us has helped loved ones face significant health challenges. We all know how "life as we know it" stands still in the face of a life-threatening or an activity-limiting illness. Most of us would sacrifice almost anything to restore the health of a loved one; some of us are willing to pay higher taxes to make sure that all Americans—friends, relatives, neighbors, strangers—have the health care services they need.

This special significance of health in our lives makes careers in the health sector so important and so attractive. People interested in the health sector have the chance to benefit people directly, while working to improve the operations of a complex social enterprise. The service sector is one of the fastest growing parts of the U.S. economy, and health services are perhaps its most challenging and interesting component.

Defining Characteristics of the U.S. Health Care System

The health care system in the United States encompasses a sprawling set of activities and enterprises. Using the word *system,* in fact, is a stretch, because in many ways the enterprise involves many actors working nonsystematically to achieve diverse aims. But, like the "hidden hand" that economists claim guides our general economic system, many fundamental forces keep individual actors working somewhat in tandem to produce and maintain health in our population.

Perhaps the first defining characteristic of the health enterprise is the distinction between activities directed at keeping people healthy and activities directed at restoring health once a disease or injury occurs. Keeping people healthy is the domain of the public health care system and the activities associated with behavioral health (Figure 1.2S). Public health (described in chapter 4) involves activities that work at the population level to keep us healthy: protecting the environment, making sure water supplies and restaurants and food are safe, and providing preventive health services, for example. Behavioral health (described in chapter 10) focuses on helping people make behavioral choices that improve or protect health: for example, not smoking, eating well, exercising, and reducing stress.

Once people become ill, the medical care sector takes over and delivers a wide variety of services and interventions to restore health. All too often, the medical care part of the system—which dwarfs the public health and behavioral health parts—ignores its potential to promote and maintain health (Figures 1.3S and 1.4S). One perplexing part of our health sector is that changing an individual's behavior has much greater impact on health and mortality than does spending money on medical care. Despite excellent research evidence documenting the importance of healthy lifestyles, we spend nine times more on medical care than on public health and behavioral health.

Additional defining features of the U.S. health care system include:

1. the importance of **institutions** in delivering care. Hospitals, nursing homes, community health centers, physician practices, and public health departments all are complex institutions that have evolved over the past century to meet various needs (discussed in chapters 7, 8, and 9). Each type of institution has its traditions, strengths, weaknesses, and a defined role in the health enterprise.
2. the role of **professionals** in running the system. Many different types of professionals make the system work, and each type has distinct roles (discussed in chapters 12 and 14). Physicians, nurses, administrators, policy leaders, researchers, technicians of many types, and business leaders focused on technology and pharmaceuticals all play essential roles.
3. developments in **medical technology, electronic communication,** and **new drugs** that fuel changes in service delivery. Over

the past 20 years, advances in technology and technique have exploded, making it possible to aggressively intervene to restore health in ways that were not dreamed of a generation ago (discussed in chapters 11 and 13). New techniques in imaging, electronic communication, pharmaceuticals, and surgical procedures are remarkable. These advances, however, have added costs to the system and have made health care unaffordable for a growing percentage of the U.S. population.

4. tension between "**caring**" and "**big business**" that shapes the system's culture. Americans are divided about whether they want a health care system that is more a social good, run by nonprofit organizations with benevolent missions, or whether they want health care to operate more like a big business, driven by market forces, profits, and efficiency. Many of the people who choose health care as a career are motivated at least in part by the potential to be a caring person. Yet, driving the system are many for-profit corporations—from pharmaceutical companies to medical device manufacturers, to insurance companies, to for-profit hospitals and nursing homes. Salaries are relatively high in the health sector, especially for physicians, administrators, and corporate executives. Although money clearly is an important shaper of the system, Americans want the caring aspect of health care to be central when they need services.

5. the dysfunctional **financing** and **payment** system. The U.S. health care system is expensive to maintain; we spent $1.988 trillion on health care in 2005—one out of every six dollars spent in the economy (discussed in chapter 3). Most people have health insurance to pay for services when they become ill, but some 45 million Americans do not. These uninsured (and the substantial number of underinsured) face tremendous financial risk if they become ill or injured. In addition, the way hospitals, physicians, and other providers are paid has become very complex because of the role of insurance. Remarkably, efficient, effective care is not rewarded. For example, fee-for-service payment systems reward unnecessary diagnostic tests and treatments; further, there is almost no reimbursement incentive for providers to adopt electronic communication or implement electronic patient records (discussed in chapter 13).

These defining characteristics make the health care system a dynamic part of our lives, a key part of our economy, and a constant source of contention in our political system (discussed in chapter 5). Addressing the challenges of this system is worth the effort and deserves the attention of the best and brightest of each generation.

Major Issues and Concerns

The defining characteristics of the health sector, described above, suggest the key challenges that have been the focus of health care leaders' attention in recent years. Briefly, they are:

1. **Improving quality:** Despite the large investments we make in the health care system, serious concerns about the quality of care have emerged in recent years (discussed in chapter 15 and shown in Figure 1.5S). Reliable studies indicate that between 44,000 and 98,000 Americans die each year because of medical errors. Other well-regarded studies show that fewer than half of people with mental health or substance abuse problems, asthma, or diabetes receive care known to be effective. Too often providers do not seem to have the knowledge or information they need to prescribe the correct treatment for their patients, even those with definite diagnoses. At times, people become lost in the large, cumbersome system we have constructed and do not receive the care they need. At other times, the lack of coordination between providers means that people receive duplicative and even counterproductive services.

2. **Improving access and coverage:** Too many Americans are uninsured, making care virtually unaffordable if they have a serious illness (discussed in chapter 16). People fail to get insurance coverage for many reasons, and political consensus about how to resolve this problem has not emerged over the past 20 years. Lack of coverage, however, is a peculiarly American problem. All other developed countries have public systems of insurance coverage or similar approaches to assuring that everybody can have the care they need (discussed in chapter 6). Many health leaders see the insurance challenge as the most important health issue facing our nation today. But even when people have insurance coverage, access to health care is not always easy. Many rural areas have shortages of health care professionals—especially doctors and dentists—and some services—especially specialist care, long-term care, and even hospital care (Figure 1.6S). Some services, such as mental health care, are woefully underfunded (Figure 1.7S). Immigrants face language barriers to getting effective care, and low-income groups, even when covered by public insurance programs, have a difficult time finding the services they need. As the country becomes more diverse, these types of access problems will become more acute (Table 1.1S).

3. **Keeping costs under control:** Expenditures on health care have been increasing much more quickly than expenditures in

the balance of the economy over the past 30 years (discussed in chapter 17). The explosion of expensive technology, the aging of the population, inflating salaries, and the growing prevalence of chronic conditions have made health care less and less affordable over time (Figure 1.8S). A key challenge is determining which new technology we can afford (and is worth the cost) and how to keep costs from growing too quickly. Cost increases clearly are at the heart of the access and coverage challenges outlined above. Unfortunately, leaders have not identified effective ways to keep costs under control. Reining in health care inflation remains one of the key challenges of the next 10 years—and not just for health care managers. The problem has become so acute that every sector of the U.S. economy has to be concerned about the impact of rising health care costs.

4. **Encouraging healthy behavior:** Avoiding illness and injury is the best way to keep health costs under control. Healthy behavior choices can help people avoid disease and injury. Using seat belts, getting preventive services, eating well, exercising, avoiding tobacco, and not using drugs or overusing alcohol are all central to health maintenance. It remains a challenge, however, to encourage healthy behavior. Most noticeably, we are in the middle of a disturbing obesity epidemic that has led to ever-increasing rates of diabetes and heart disease.

5. **Improving the public health care system:** We too often take for granted the safety of our water, food, and restaurants. And we fail to recognize the important roles the public health care system can play in preventive health, health education, environmental health, and prevention of bioterrorism. Perhaps because public health, when done effectively, is invisible (it *avoids* problems rather than fixes them), the United States has historically underinvested in public health. Making the case for better public health, providing adequate funding, and inspiring leading thinkers to take up public health careers is an ongoing challenge.

6. **Addressing social determinants of health:** Substantial inequalities in health status—rates of disease and death—exist across income groups, social classes, and ethnic groups. Given that most Americans believe we should have an equal opportunity approach to health maintenance, inequalities in health status are a key current challenge facing the health sector. In essence, however, the health care system can only help address inequalities to a certain degree. Some of the inequality is driven by social factors such as poverty and ineffective education systems.

7. **Strengthening the health workforce:** Recent years have seen acute shortages of nurses, primary care physicians, and long-term care providers (discussed in chapter 12). The health care system

must train and recruit the large and diverse cadre of workers that are needed to run health institutions. And *diverse* not only describes the number of roles within health care, but also the goal of achieving more ethnic and racial diversity in the workforce. Without talented and caring people agreeing to devote their careers to health services, the system cannot function.

8. **Encouraging more realistic expectations:** Consumers should expect and demand better quality and better efficiency from the delivery system. People also should recognize that their health is, to some degree, their own responsibility. To make this point, some analysts recommend that people should have to pay out of pocket for health problems caused by their own recklessness and should be rewarded for good health behavior. Some insurance companies already do this, offering lower premiums to people who do not smoke, are not obese, and have good driving records.

Prospects for Change and Improvement

Will the next generation of health care leaders make progress on the challenges facing the 21st-century health care system? Or will the system continue to provide excellent care to some and inefficient, ineffective care to others? The reality is that some Americans lead healthy lives, and others do not; some Americans receive excellent health care, while others do not.

Our sense is that the prospects for positive change are striking. Technology—applied creatively—offers numerous opportunities for improving how the system operates. The aging of our population—with baby boomers moving into the senior citizen category—is likely to create political pressure for improvements. Americans look abroad and see that other countries have solved these problems in different ways and, while there are complaints, are generally more satisfied with their health systems (Table 1.2S). And large investments in health services research have resulted in growing consensus about how to improve the delivery system.

The constraints we face in making progress toward improving the service system are political and economic. On the political side, sharp disagreements exist about how to create efficiency and effectiveness in the system. Some people favor market principles that rely on economic incentives, competition, and the laws of supply and demand to allocate health care resources. They believe the government is a negative force in assuring that the health care system operates effectively.

Other analysts, however, believe that health care is different than other economic commodities in ways that make market forces ineffective in logically allocating resources. These people believe that efficiency could be improved with government interventions, reliance on nonprofit systems, and more government financing of certain aspects of health care. Working our way through these fundamental differences in ideology is an essential part of the effort to improve our health care system.

Health care raises profound questions about what kind of country we want the United States to be. Is health or some part of health care a right, just like public education for grades kindergarten through 12? Or is health care a capitalistic endeavor, albeit one with a significant public sector component? Which kind of society do Americans want to live in?

Another constraining force that makes improvement difficult is that the current system rewards so many people employed in the health care sector with high salaries and other perks. Corporations and interest groups that benefit from the current system will lobby intensely against any change they see as threatening their stake in the system. Thus, some observers have thrown up their hands and concluded that it would be much simpler to design an effective health care system from scratch than to make the incremental changes needed to strengthen the current system.

The Importance of Engagement at the Ground Level

The health care system challenges are exciting. The two authors have had the privilege of working for many years in a range of professional roles and to have been part of numerous efforts to improve health care delivery in the United States. We have seen both successes and failures. We remain optimistic that pragmatism, flexibility, consensus building, and attention to objective, high-quality information can work to bring about positive change. We remain stimulated by the challenge and pleased that we made the choice of devoting our careers to helping our nation maintain a viable and effective health care system.

Certainly, we have observed that best practices are now being implemented across a wide range of domains affecting health and health care in the United States and worldwide. How do we speed the process of getting more of the system, more individual professionals, and more of our population engaged in best practices? Our text gives readers the information and some of the skills to do so.

The future of the U.S. health care delivery system will see improvements if committed and informed people choose to enter the field. It is our hope that this book provides a basis for future leaders to learn about the system and be stimulated to join the large cadre of professionals working to help Americans avoid preventable early death and serious illness and, if unavoidably sick and dying, to provide skillful care, compassion, and comfort.

Chapter 1 Supplement

Key Charts

Victoria Weisfeld

This short section of charts pulls together basic information on a number of subjects that cut across many of the other chapters of this book, such as the first two charts reporting good news and influences on health, and, conversely, it includes issues such as mental health and oral health that are not covered in detail in any of the remaining chapters. They help round out the vision of U.S. health care pursued in depth in the individual chapters. Each of the charts has an important story to tell that will help orient readers for the detail to come.

GOOD NEWS ABOUT THE
U.S. HEALTH CARE SYSTEM

The authors recognize that health care delivery in the United States is frequently presented as a glass half-empty story. People who work in health care are challenged (and sometimes frustrated) by the shortcomings in the system. Ironically, this is partly due to the tremendous accomplishments of the U.S. health care system. These advances make us long for more—to make access to care easier and cheaper, to overcome quality shortcomings, and, ultimately, to extend the benefits of better health to more Americans. Because we can see achievable goals, we want to reach them.

Before we ask readers to wade into many of the shortcomings of the system, consider the many accomplishments of the U.S. health system. Most important, dramatic improvements have been achieved in reducing death rates and increasing longevity. These benefits are largely due to the work of our health care and public health sectors in advocating reduced cigarette smoking; improving control of high blood pressure and other cardiovascular risk factors; greatly improved treatments of many types of cancer, HIV/AIDS, and other diseases; prevention of infectious disease; and improvements in the environment (reduced exposure to carcinogens and air pollution).

Figure 1.1S

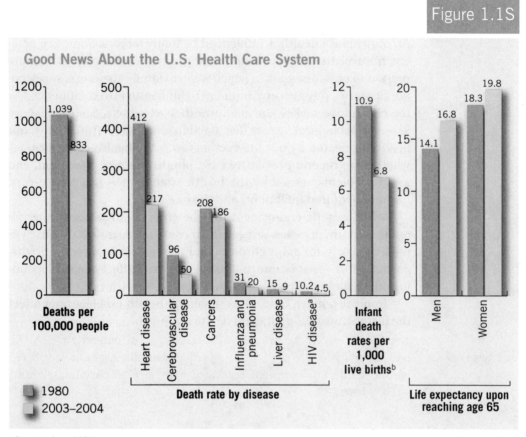

Good News About the U.S. Health Care System

Deaths per 100,000 people
- 1,039 (1980)
- 833 (2003–2004)

Death rate by disease

Heart disease: 412 (1980), 217 (2003–2004)
Cerebrovascular disease: 96 (1980), 50 (2003–2004)
Cancers: 208 (1980), 186 (2003–2004)
Influenza and pneumonia: 31 (1980), 20 (2003–2004)
Liver disease: 15 (1980), 9 (2003–2004)
HIV disease[a]: 10.2 (1980), 4.5 (2003–2004)

Infant death rates per 1,000 live births[b]
- 10.9 (1980)
- 6.8 (2003–2004)

Life expectancy upon reaching age 65

Men: 14.1 (1980), 16.8 (2003–2004)
Women: 18.3 (1980), 19.8 (2003–2004)

■ 1980
□ 2003–2004

[a] Data are from 1990.
[b] Data are from 1983.

Note. From U.S. Department of Health and Human Services, National Center for Health Statistics. (2006). *Health, United States, 2006, with chartbook on trends in the health of Americans,* Hyattsville, MD: Author. Retrieved from http://www.cdc.gov/nchs/data/hus/hus06.pdf#042

INFLUENCES ON HEALTH

An individual's health is influenced by many factors. Some are present from birth (genetic factors, congenital conditions), others are present in environments in which we live (family structure, socioeconomic status, physical environment). Our health also is influenced by the choices we make—our diet, whether we smoke, the exercise we get—the behavioral factors discussed in chapter 10. And, finally, our health is affected by our interactions with the health care system—whether we receive preventive care, obtain effective treatment, and avoid problems caused by the health system itself (medical errors, hospital-acquired infections, and the like).

While genetic endowment may be crucially important in developing certain diseases, especially those that manifest themselves relatively early, for many chronic conditions it can be merely a predisposing factor—that is, one that may or may not affect health, depending on what else happens to us over our life times.

Ironically, much of what we spend on health care does not affect the factors most influential on health status.

Figure 1.2S

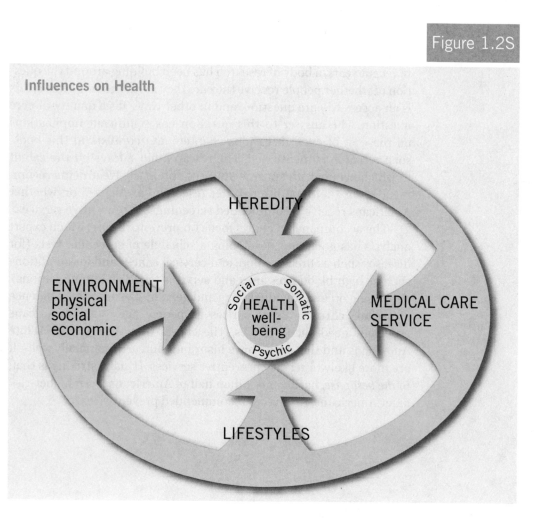

Influences on Health

HEREDITY

ENVIRONMENT
physical
social
economic

HEALTH
well-
being

Social

Somatic

Psychic

MEDICAL CARE
SERVICE

LIFESTYLES

GETTING THE PREVENTIVE CARE WE NEED

In recent years, a body of research has been building around the question of whether people receive the care they need. In some senses, this is an access-to-care question, and in other ways, it's a quality-of-care question. The answer to this question has significant implications on the cost of care. In various chapters and contexts in this book, such research is mentioned. The research has addressed the extent to which people with specific illnesses obtain the treatments recommended for their condition; other research has focused on whether Americans receive recommended screening and preventive services.

The accompanying charts focus on preventive care. Much expert analysis has gone into developing a schedule of screening tests (for diseases such as breast, colon, and cervical cancer and for conditions such as high blood pressure) and services (such as immunizations), depending on an individual's age and gender.[1] Because the incidence of serious chronic diseases rises as people age, older Americans especially need such services. The charts show clearly that White Americans and those who have insurance and are financially well-off are more likely to receive preventive services. Equally striking is that, *in the best case,* hardly more than half of Americans, even higher-risk older Americans, receive all recommended preventive care.

---

[1] See, for example, the work of the National Coordinating Committee for Clinical Preventive Services. Retrieved from http://www.ncbi.nlm.nih.gov/books/bv.fcgi?rid = hstat6.section.4491

Figure 1.3S

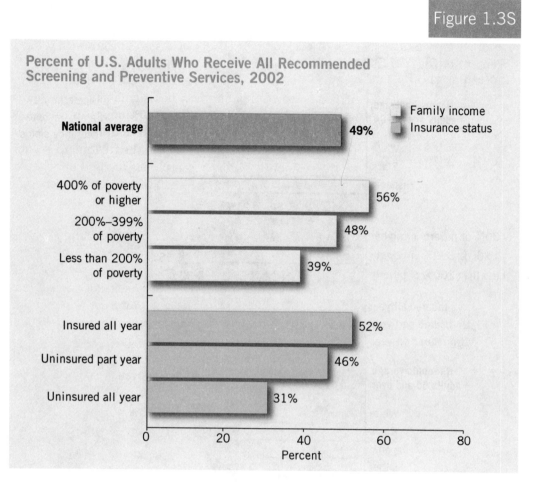

Percent of U.S. Adults Who Receive All Recommended
Screening and Preventive Services, 2002

National average — 49%

Family income
Insurance status

400% of poverty or higher — 56%

200%–399% of poverty — 48%

Less than 200% of poverty — 39%

Insured all year — 52%

Uninsured part year — 46%

Uninsured all year — 31%

Percent

Figure 1.4S

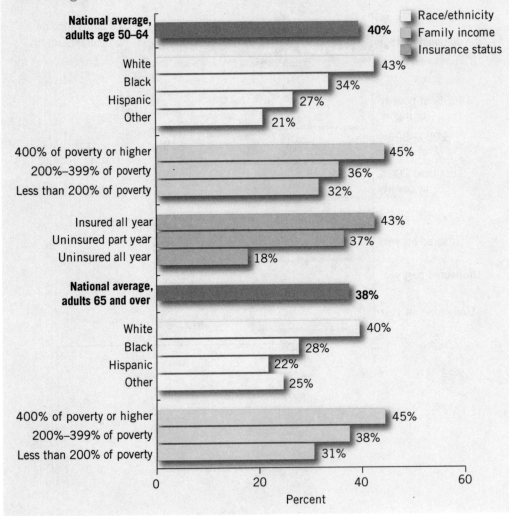

Percent of Older U.S. Adults Who Receive All Recommended Screening and Preventive Services, 2002

Note. From U.S. Department of Health and Human Services, Agency for Healthcare Quality and Research. (2002). *Medical expenditure panel survey.* Analysis by B. Mahato, Columbia University. Retrieved from http://www.meps.ahrq.gov/mepsweb/

THE CHANGING U.S. POPULATION

The racial and ethnic composition of the U.S. population is undergoing rapid change, and the nation's health system will need to adapt. First, different population groups have somewhat different patterns of illness. These differences are particularly pronounced in immigrant families who bring with them dietary and other habits of their home country. Thus, some of the differences recede with later generations, and the immigrants' grandchildren begin to experience disease patterns similar to those of the U.S. population in general—for better or worse. (Hereditary diseases linked to particular racial or ethnic groups do not evolve in this way. For example, Tay-Sachs disease continues to affect Eastern Europeans and Ashkenazi Jews almost exclusively, and sickle cell anemia remains primarily a disease of African Americans.)

Another way that population changes affect the health care system is around the question of health literacy. The U.S. health care system is extremely complex and—especially for people with limited resources in terms of insurance, income, education, or English—difficult to access. As more health care decisions and responsibilities are placed on consumers and as more post-hospital care takes place in the home environment, the situation can become acute for anyone who is not adequately helped to understand his or her role and supported in carrying it out. Again, the problems of health literacy are likely to be worse for immigrants and lessen as these individuals, or their children, begin to be more like the rest of the country.

Finally, while we call our nation a melting pot, social critics have suggested our society is less like tomato soup, every spoonful the same, and more like beef stew, with recognizable individual components. Some individuals are more comfortable dealing with other individuals like themselves and seek out health care professionals from their racial or ethnic group. For this reason, diversity in our health care workforce is important to good patient care; conversely, the many health professions facing shortages should look to the full spectrum of ethnic groups in order to expand the pool of new entrants. For people who do not speak English well, having a health professional who can speak to them in their language is an important—sometimes difficult to achieve—goal.

Table 1.1S	Current and Projected Makeup of the U.S. Population, 2000–2050					
Population Percentage	**2000**	**2010**	**2020**	**2030**	**2040**	**2050**
White	81.0	79.3	77.6	75.8	73.9	72.1
Black	12.7	13.1	13.5	13.9	14.3	14.6
Asian	3.8	4.6	5.4	6.2	7.1	8.0
Other	2.5	3.0	3.5	4.1	4.7	5.3
Hispanic	12.6	15.5	17.8	20.1	22.3	24.4
Non-Hispanic white	69.4	65.1	61.3	57.5	53.7	50.1

Note. From U.S. Census Bureau. (2004). *U.S. interim projections by age, sex, race, and hispanic origin.* Retrieved May 2007, from http://www.census.gov/ipc/www/usinterimproj

QUALITY VERSUS COSTS OF CARE

Americans might accept their higher costs of care if they believed their expenditures were buying them quality. But too many indicators suggest they are not. The landmark Institute of Medicine analyses of the quality of U.S. health care (*To Err Is Human*, 2000, and *Crossing the Quality Chasm*, 2001) are cited numerous times in this volume. If the average American is not aware of these academic assessments of health care problems, they have seen them in their own lives.

The public is not wrong about this issue. This chart shows how, for three major, common conditions of Americans over 65—heart attack, colon cancer, and hip fracture—average hospitalization costs vary by more than 50%, from just under $20,000 per case to well over $30,000. (Each dot on the chart represents a standardized hospital referral region.) Unfortunately, quality varies about as widely. The average quality (measured by survival after 1 year) was set at 1.0, and, naturally, many regions were under that average, and many were above.

If there were a relationship between the amount spent and the quality of care (survival) achieved, the dots on this chart would follow a slanted line—low expenditures and low survival, rising to higher expenditures and higher survival. In fact, we see a confusing picture. Many hospitals that spend less than the average demonstrate better outcomes, and this group includes several of the best-performing hospitals. By contrast, many hospitals that spend markedly more than the average have worse-than-average outcomes. (Note that these data have been adjusted to account for population differences—that is, sicker patients—in different hospital referral regions.)

Figure 1.5S

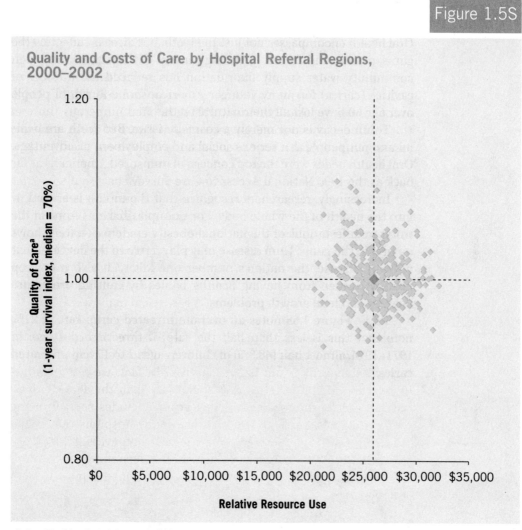

Quality and Costs of Care by Hospital Referral Regions, 2000–2002

[a] Indexed to risk-adjusted 1-year survival rate (median = 0.70) for Medicare patients with heart attack, colon cancer, and hip fracture.

Note. Fisher, E. & Staiger, D. Dartmouth College, Dartmouth atlas of health care team's analysis of data from a 20% national sample of Medicare beneficiaries. Cited in *Commonwealth fund national scorecard on U.S. health system performance.* (2006). Retrieved from http://www. commonwealthfund.org/publications/publications_show.htm?doc_id=401577.

ORAL HEALTH CARE

Oral health encompasses not just the teeth, but diseases affecting the gums, mouth, and throat, including cancers of these areas. Although community water supply fluoridation has reduced the number of cavities (caries) for many younger Americans, one-fourth of people over age 60 have lost all their natural teeth.

Tooth decay is not merely a cosmetic issue. Bad teeth are painful and put people at a serious social and employment disadvantage. Oral health needs were the top concern of uninsured Americans as far back as the 1995 National Access to Care Survey.[2]

Increasingly, researchers recognize that the mouth is a window into the health of the whole body. For example, diabetes—one of the worst manifestations of the national obesity epidemic—often shows up first in the gums. Gum disease may play a role in the development of heart disease, the nation's number one killer.[3] It also may keep healthy women from having healthy babies by causing premature delivery and fetal growth problems.

While Figure 1.6S notes an overall untreated caries rate of 22%, note that this is less than half the rate of three decades ago: in 1971–1974, almost half (48.3%) of children ages 2 to 17 had untreated caries.

---

[2] Mark L. Berk, Claudia L. Schur, and Joel C. Cantor, 1995, Data Watch: Ability to Obtain Health Care: Recent Estimates from the Robert Wood Johnson Foundation National Access to Care Survey. *Health Affairs, 14,* 139–146.

[3] People with severe gum disease are more likely to have had a heart attack, gum disease bacteria have been found in the linings of arteries, and animals with gum disease bacteria are susceptible to blockages in their arteries. See, for example, Sabine O. Geerts et al., 2004, Further Evidence of the Association Between Periodontal Conditions and Coronary Artery Disease, *Journal of Periodontology, 75,* 1274–1280; and Yong-Hee P. Chun et al., 2005, Mini-review: Biological Foundation for Periodontitis as a Potential Risk Factor for Atherosclerosis, *Journal of Periodontal Research, 40,* 87–95.

Figure 1.6S

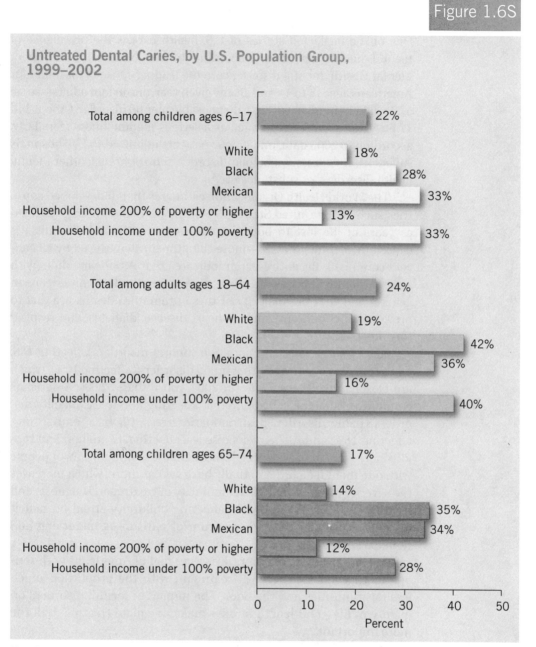

Untreated Dental Caries, by U.S. Population Group, 1999–2002

Total among children ages 6–17 — 22%

White — 18%
Black — 28%
Mexican — 33%
Household income 200% of poverty or higher — 13%
Household income under 100% poverty — 33%

Total among adults ages 18–64 — 24%

White — 19%
Black — 42%
Mexican — 36%
Household income 200% of poverty or higher — 16%
Household income under 100% poverty — 40%

Total among children ages 65–74 — 17%

White — 14%
Black — 35%
Mexican — 34%
Household income 200% of poverty or higher — 12%
Household income under 100% poverty — 28%

Percent (0, 10, 20, 30, 40, 50)

Note. From U.S. Department of Health and Human Services, Centers for Disease Control, National Center for Health Statistics. (2005). *National health and nutrition examination survey.* Analysis in the *Commonwealth Fund National Scorecard on U.S. Health System Performance,* 2006. Retrieved from http://www.cdc.gov/mmwr/preview/mmwrhtml/ss5403a1.htm

THE IMPACT OF MENTAL DISORDERS

One of the neglected stories of U.S. health care is the prevalence of mental health disorders. According to the National Institute of Mental Health, mental disorders are the leading cause of disability for Americans ages 15 to 44, and, in any given year, one in four adults—some 57.7 million Americans—has a diagnosable mental disorder. (About 1 in 17 has what would be classified as a serious mental illness.) Similarly, according to 2005 data, one in four patients admitted to U.S. hospitals suffers from depression, bipolar disorder, schizophrenia, other mental health disorders, or substance use.[4]

The World Health Organization estimates that in developed countries such as the United States, 15% of the burden of disease (defined as years of life lost to both premature mortality and disability) is caused by mental illnesses—more than the burden caused by all cancers combined. Recent research indicates that American adults with serious mental illnesses die about 25 years earlier than Americans in general and that the majority of these premature deaths are due to preventable conditions, such as heart disease, diabetes, and respiratory illnesses.[5]

The most serious and common mental disorders affecting U.S. adults are depression and other mood disorders (affecting 10%), which are closely linked to suicide (in 2004, more than 32,000 Americans committed suicide); schizophrenia, affecting about 1%; anxiety disorders (panic disorder, posttraumatic stress, phobias, and so on), affecting 18%; and Alzheimer's disease, affecting 4.5 million and rapidly increasing in prevalence. Comorbidity is common: 45% of people with one mental disorder actually have two or more, which increases the severity of effects and the complexity of treatment. Diagnosis and treatment of mental disorders affecting children—attention deficit disorder, hyperactivity, the spectrum of autism—is increasing and remains controversial.

Despite the large numbers, less than half of Americans with serious mental illnesses receive treatment, with the proportion much less for minorities and the poor. The impact of mental disorders on quality of life—and length of life—make adequate treatment all the more important.

---

[4] U.S. Department of Health and Human Services, Substance Abuse and Mental Health Services Administration, 2007, *Care of Adults With Mental Health and Substance Abuse Disorders in U.S. Community Hospitals, 2004.* Retrieved from http://www.ahrq.gov/data/hcup/factbk10

[5] J. Parks, D. Svendsen, P. Singer, and M. E. Foti (Eds.), 2006, *Morbidity and Mortality in People With Serious Mental Illness.* Alexandria, VA: National Association of State Mental Health Directors. Retrieved from http://www.nasmhpd.org/general_files/publications/med_directors_pubs/Tec hnical%20Report%20on%20Morbidity%20and%20Mortaility%20-%20Final%2011-06.pdf

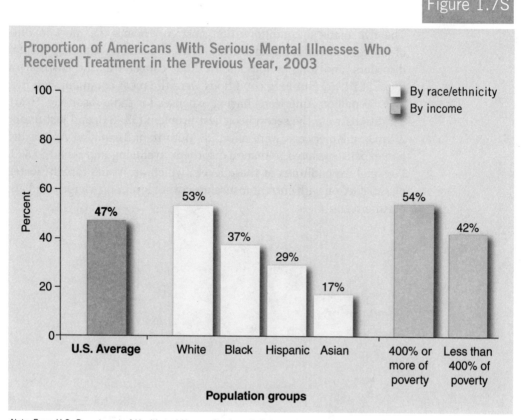

Figure 1.7S

Proportion of Americans With Serious Mental Illnesses Who
Received Treatment in the Previous Year, 2003

Note. From U.S. Department of Health and Human Services, Substance Abuse and Mental Health
Services Administration. (2003). *National survey on drug use and health.* Retrieved from http://oas.
samhsa.gov/2k6/mhTX/mhTX.cfm

COSTLY MEDICAL CONDITIONS

The five medical conditions that cost Americans the most in out-of-pocket expenditures are heart diseases, cancer, trauma, mental disorders, and lung conditions. In 2002, cancer was the costliest of these at $4,462, but lung conditions were the most common, with just over 50 million Americans having expenses for these disorders. Heart conditions were the second-costliest problem ($3,434), and just under 20 million Americans were affected. More than 31 million Americans had expenses related to mental disorders, averaging more than $1,500. Personal expenditures at these levels, which are rising rapidly, foster dissatisfaction with current insurance coverage among a large numbers of Americans.

Figure 1.8S

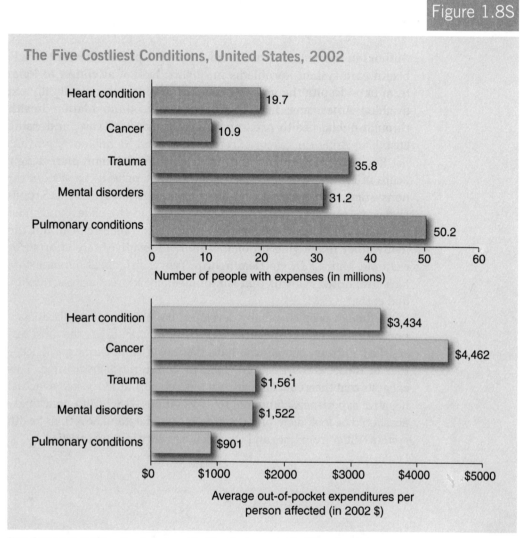

The Five Costliest Conditions, United States, 2002

Number of people with expenses (in millions)

- Heart condition: 19.7
- Cancer: 10.9
- Trauma: 35.8
- Mental disorders: 31.2
- Pulmonary conditions: 50.2

Average out-of-pocket expenditures per person affected (in 2002 $)

- Heart condition: $3,434
- Cancer: $4,462
- Trauma: $1,561
- Mental disorders: $1,522
- Pulmonary conditions: $901

Note. From Center for Financing, Access, and Cost Trends, Agency for Healthcare Research and Quality. (2002). *Household component of the medical expenditure panel survey,* HC-070. Retrieved from http://www.meps.ahrq.gov/mepsweb/

DISSATISFACTION WITH THE
U.S. HEALTH CARE SYSTEM

Authors in this volume have cited numerous problems with the U.S. health care system—problems in quality; lack of attention to long-term care despite the growing number of older, chronically ill, and disabled Americans; inadequate emphasis on population health through public health programs, lack of access to care, and rising costs.

For many Americans, the problems have become increasingly acute in recent years—so much so that they believe the system (or nonsystem, critics would say) must be completely rebuilt. U.S. policymakers, however, continue to tinker around the edges, and most national politicians focus on the issue of insurance reform, not the many other underlying problems. Some innovative state efforts (for example, Maine's Dirigo Health, http://www.dirigohealth.maine.gov) have attempted reforms that simultaneously address access, quality, and costs.

Although people in many developed countries express dissatisfaction with their nation's health care system, Americans are the most dissatisfied. Further, people who have the most health care experience—that is, those who are sicker—tend to be the most dissatisfied. This suggests that their concerns are not theoretical, but are based on actual negative experience, compared to expectations. U.S. health policymakers should be looking to other countries to understand how their health systems differ from ours and why their citizenry is more satisfied.

 International Perspectives on Health Systems, 2005

Percent Who Believe the Health Care System Should Be Completely Rebuilt	Canada	United Kingdom	Germany	United States
Overall	17	14	31	30
Among those who experienced a medical error	39	36	28	44
Among those who reported failures in coordination of care	31	33	34	44
Among those who avoided care because of cost	39	27	38	67

Note. From *Commonwealth Fund International Health Policy Survey of Sicker Adults.* (2005).
Retrieved from http://www.commonwealthfund.org/surveys/surveys_show.htm?doc_id=313115

2

Key Words

data

census

vital statistics

surveillance

demographic
characteristics

rates

numerator

denominator

morbidity

mortality

natality

infant mortality

crude and specific rates

age-adjusted and
age-standardized rates

incidence

prevalence

health status

provider- and patient-
perspective

utilization

ambulatory services

hospitalization

health services
utilization

program planning

Measuring Health Status

Mary Ann Chiasson and Steven Jonas

Learning Objectives

- List and characterize the major categories of data used to describe the people served and *not served* by the health care delivery system.
- List and characterize the major categories of data used to describe the health care delivery system and its activities.
- Describe the principal sources of health and health services data and state how and where to find them (using Appendix B as well as this chapter).
- Define the keywords listed on p. 34.

Topical Outline

- Data for health and health services: What are they? Why are they collected?
- How are health and health services data commonly organized and presented? What are the primary sources for the common data?
- Numbers and rates
- Primary defining characteristics of the U.S. population
- Vital statistics
- Morbidity and mortality
- Health status and health-related behavior
- Utilization of health services

Ahealth care system produces two things: treatments and information. Certainly, when it comes to trying to understand the health care system, a wealth of information is available regarding:

- Americans' health, diseases, disabilities, and risk factors.
- The health care services they need, versus what they actually receive, and the quality of those services.
- What they cost and who pays for them.
- The facilities and professionals that provide health care services.
- The overall scope of the nation's health care system, as a major component of the national economy.

Just as performance data and international comparisons are used in many other fields—from automobile production to agriculture to understanding the global economy—increasingly sophisticated ways of analyzing health care data enlighten and inform us about one of our economy's most important sectors. Performance data enable policymakers (at the macro level) and facility managers and health professionals (at the micro level) to plan for and target services and interventions and to measure their effectiveness.

> Increasingly sophisticated ways of analyzing health care data enlighten and inform us about one of our economy's most important sectors.

Information technology has revolutionized our access to data. Virtually all the numbers presented in this chapter are from national surveys and data collection systems, summaries of which are available on the Internet. They also are generally published in hard copy, usually annually. (See Appendix B for descriptions of principal data sources.) Because data collection and analysis can be lengthy processes, the most recent available data still may be several years old.

Commonly used data can be divided into five broad categories: census data, vital statistics data (births, deaths, marriages, and divorces), surveillance data, administrative data, and survey research data. These data can be obtained from a variety of sources and are collected for a variety of purposes. Most routinely used population and health data come from systems mandated by federal, state, or local law. For example, *vital statistics* systems record births, deaths, marriages, and divorces.

Population-based surveys collect detailed information on people's health, insurance status, use of health services, and health risks, through interviews with a relatively small sample of individuals chosen to be representative of the population. Data from interview surveys have been invaluable in linking behavior to health outcomes and in describing Americans' experiences with the health care system. Similarly, surveys are conducted with health care workers that provide information about the services they provide, the needs of their patients, and so on. Because many of the health care issues covered in surveys are not randomly distributed through the whole population, data from national surveys usually cannot be applied at the state or local levels, and data from state-level surveys, which are increasingly common, usually cannot be applied at the local level. Thus, while many *general* patient or provider characteristics can be described using readily accessible national sources, they do not necessarily reflect the situation with respect to *specific* populations.

This chapter focuses primarily on national data. The principal sources of the data presented are the National Center for Health Statistics (NCHS), the Centers for Medicare & Medicaid Services, the U.S. Census Bureau, the Bureau of Labor Statistics (for information on health care employment), and many other government agencies. Important health care data can be found in the regularly published *Statistical Abstract of the United States* and the compendium *Health, United States.* Detailed state and local vital statistics data are available from state health departments (see Appendix B).

Quantitative Perspectives

QUANTITATIVE DATA DESCRIBED

Populations can be described quantitatively in several ways, by size and demographic characteristics, direct measures of health and ill health, and utilization of health services. First, quantification can describe a population simply by the *number* of people and their demographic characteristics, such as age, sex, race, birthplace, geographic location, or such social characteristics as marital status, income, educational attainment, and employment. Some demographic characteristics, such as geographic location or age distribution, by themselves may indicate a population's relative disease risks. (Do many people live near water infested by mosquitoes carrying West Nile virus? Does the population include many infants or people older than 65?)

Second are *direct measures of health and ill health.* At present, characterizing the latter is easier than the former. Ill-health status is described by measures of mortality (death) and morbidity (sickness), either for the population as a whole—called *crude* rates—by cause, or by demographic characteristics of population segments (e.g., age, sex groups)—called *specific* rates. Disease-specific morbidity and mortality rates show the major health and illness problems known to affect the population. The distribution of crude and disease-specific mortality and morbidity rates by place, age, sex, ethnic group, and social characteristics shows which population subgroups are being affected by which diseases. The prevalence of behavioral risk factors such as smoking, sedentary lifestyle, and sun exposure suggests the kinds of interventions needed and likely future health care needs.

The third way to describe a population's health quantitatively is by the *utilization and quality of health services:* the kinds of services that are offered, by whom, and used by whom, under what circumstances, and to what effect. Utilization can be measured both quantitatively and qualitatively from the point of view of the consumer, the provider, or an external organization.

For example, physician-patient encounters can be reported in terms of how many physician visits the average patient makes in a year. The same set of events can be reported in terms of how many patient visits the average physician provides. The types and frequency of the visits and the outcomes of the services provided can be compared to national standards.

Patient-perspective data can indicate whether some population group—defined, for example, by social characteristics, ethnicity, or geography—overutilizes or underutilizes health services. Provider-perspective data describe the content and amount (workload) of physician and hospital services, in terms of provider characteristics (credentials, size, location, services offered, etc.). Taken together, these two perspectives can identify barriers to health care access, while the findings of accrediting organizations suggest quality and effectiveness of services provided.

In summary, describing health status and services quantitatively tells us how many of which kinds of people are at risk, which kinds of diseases and ill-health conditions they have, how those problems are distributed, who goes where for which health services, delivered by which types of providers, and, in some cases, the outcome of these services.

QUANTITATIVE DATA FACILITATE PROGRAM PLANNING AND EVALUATION

The second purpose of quantification in health care delivery is for *program planning and evaluation*. Descriptive data can reveal the existence of health or health services problems and aid in planning programs to solve them. These data inform utilization projections that are essential for program planning and cost estimation. Once new programs are under way, performance data are essential for evaluation, including whether the program is being used by the people for whom it was intended.

Although too often in the real world, program planning is not databased, some of the questions that should be asked in planning any new health services are:

> Descriptive data can reveal the existence of health or health services problems and aid in planning programs to solve them.

1. How many people live in the proposed service area, where, and what forms of transportation are available?
2. What are the age, sex, and marital status distributions?
3. What are the education levels, income, ethnicity, and languages spoken?
4. What is the sickness and health profile?
5. How is the population size and composition changing over time?
6. What are the financial resources, and what sorts of health insurance coverage does the population have?
7. What are the existing health care resources, where are they, and how are they used?
8. What do existing providers see as the unmet needs? How do they view the proposed service, and how will they relate to it?

QUANTITATIVE DATA ENABLE PERFORMANCE MEASUREMENT

With the advent of managed care and the increasing need to control health care costs, interest in performance has intensified, as has competition among providers and plans. The National Committee for Quality Assurance's (NCQA) Health Plan Employer Data and Information Set (HEDIS) clinical measures assess managed care quality and the HEDIS Consumer Assessment of Health Plans composite measures, which include patient satisfaction as well as provider ratings, relate to overall industry performance.

Numerous forms of health plan report cards have been developed to compare health plans and help consumers and purchasers make informed choices. NCQA assesses plan performance in five key areas: access and service, qualified providers, staying healthy (immunization and screening programs), getting better, and living with illness. Although interpreting report cards can be difficult, there are many potential benefits. As the practice patterns of health care providers are subject to greater public scrutiny, the overall level of care is likely to improve.

Understanding Numbers and Rates

Population, health status, and utilization data can be presented as both numbers and rates. A *number* is simply a count of conditions, individuals, or events. A *rate* has two parts: a numerator and a denominator. The *numerator* is the number of conditions, individuals, or events counted. The *denominator* is (usually) a larger group of persons, conditions, or events from among which the numerator data are drawn. Both numerator and denominator are stated, as in "number of deaths per 1,000 people." Rates customarily apply to a particular *time period.* For example, if one determined that 1,000 deaths occurred in a particular population during a year, 1,000 would be the numerator for the rate; if the whole population in which those deaths occurred is 100,000 (the denominator), the mortality *rate* for the population is 1,000/100,000 per year, equivalent, of course, to 10/1,000 or 1/100.

Usually a denominator is chosen that will make the rate a number of reasonable size, as long as the numerator will be one or larger. Thus, the less frequent the event being counted by the numerator, the larger the denominator must be. If an event is rare, as is true with certain causes of death, the *cause-specific mortality rate* might be, say, "2 deaths from [specific cause] per 1,000,000 per year."

Both denominators and numerators can be quite specific, as can their units. For example, in describing deaths from lung cancer that are caused by cigarette smoking, an age/cause-specific rate could be the number of deaths per year from lung cancer in men over age 45 who have smoked two or more packs of cigarettes per day for 20 years or more (the numerator), divided by the number of *all* men over 45 who have smoked two or more packs of cigarettes per day for 20 years or more (the denominator).

The units of the numerator and the denominator in health indices can be different. For example, in cause-specific mortality rates, the unit for the numerator is deaths by cause, while the unit for the denominator is the total number of persons in the population in question.

The numerator can be larger than the denominator. For example, in measuring total morbidity in a population, the number of diagnosed disease conditions may be greater than the number of people. The rate then is usually given with a denominator of one, for example, "In the population of a central African city there are 2.5 diseases per [one] person." This usage also occurs in utilization rates. For example, "The annual physician-visit rate in the United States is about six per person."

Rates are especially useful for measuring and describing changes over time, in everything from deaths to per capita health care expenditures. There are no hard and fast rules for data presentation, but the size of the denominator is crucial.

Health service utilization rates constitute a special group of rates. Usually they do not have customary numerators and denominators. For example, hospital-specific admission rates are commonly presented simply as a number per unit of time, as follows: "In 1997, the admission rate for hospital Y was 1,000 per month." One reason for using this formulation is that the sizes of the populations served by both institutional and individual providers are generally not known.

Census Data

The U.S. Constitution requires that a census be taken at least once every 10 years. The original purpose of the census was to apportion seats in the House of Representatives, and a census has been carried out every 10 years since 1790. Although every effort is made to accurately enumerate the U.S. population, the Census Bureau estimates that in 2000 there was a net overcount of approximately 1.3 million people. Counting inaccuracies varied by race/ethnicity. There was an estimated 1.13% overcount of non-Hispanic Whites and an estimated net undercount of 1.84% of non-Hispanic Blacks (Mulry, 2006). In addition to carrying out the decennial censuses, the Census Bureau makes interim population estimates on various parameters, based on information gathered from samples and a variety of other sources.

Births, deaths, immigration, and emigration are the four factors that produce changes in population size. During the 1970s and 1980s, the U.S. population grew about 10% per decade, followed by a 13% increase during the 1990s. Population growth is expected to decline to about 0.54% between 2040 and 2050.

Nevertheless, the mid-range U.S. population size projection for 2050 is still about 420 million, an increase of about 49% over the 2000 population. Even without taking into account the accompanying changes in the age composition of a population growing ever older, simple population size and growth rate will affect the demand for and utilization of health services. Census data from the past four decades document additional dramatic demographic changes in the U.S. population, which likewise have implications for health care. As a group, Americans are increasingly urban, better educated, and much more ethnically and racially diverse. Fewer are married, and more are imprisoned. But no population trend will affect health statistics and health care as much as growth in the over-65 population segment.

Vital Statistics

WHAT THEY ARE AND HOW THEY ARE COLLECTED

Data on births, deaths, fetal deaths, marriages, and divorces are termed *vital statistics*. These data are available from the NCHS. Birth and death data are probably the most commonly used indicators of the health status of a community. In the United States, state government (usually the health department) has primary responsibility for collecting these data through their vital registration systems. In addition, the District of Columbia and New York City are independent vital registration areas. State agencies frequently delegate the authority to process birth and death certificates to county or local health departments or local registrars.

Mortality was the first vital statistic to be collected annually in the United States. In 1900, 10 states and the District of Columbia voluntarily became the first "death registration states," carrying out that task and forwarding results to the federal government. Beginning in 1915, 10 states and the District of Columbia formed a "birth registration area." Fetal deaths have been counted since 1922. Since 1933, the birth and death registration area has included all of the states and the District of Columbia. A "marriage registration area" was first formed in 1957. By 1999, it included 42 states and the District of Columbia. The "divorce registration area" was established in 1958. By 1999, it covered 31 states and the Virgin Islands.

Until 1946, the Census Bureau assembled and reported on the nation's vital statistics. From 1946 to 1960, the work was performed by the Bureau of State Services of the U.S. Public Health Service; since 1960, NCHS, the Centers for Disease Control and Prevention (CDC), and the U.S. Department of Health and Human Services (DHHS) have carried out this function. Through cooperative activities of the states and NCHS, standard forms for data collection and model procedures for the uniform registration of vital events are developed. Certified copies of birth and death certificates are legal documents.

Birth certificates legally register births occurring in a state. Although the process varies slightly from state to state, in general, this record includes the newborn's name, date, time, and place of birth, and the mother's and father's name, address, date, and place of birth. This information appears on the birth certificate copy provided to the mother. The original certificate, retained by the state, also includes a confidential portion, containing extensive demographic and medical information on the mother and newborn, which may include a chronology of the birth, maternal medical and behavioral risk factors in the pregnancy, birth weight, and any abnormal conditions or congenital anomalies of the newborn. The facility where the birth occurs must complete the full form, and, thus, the health care system bears the responsibility for collecting and reporting birth data.

Similarly, death certificates register every death in the state where they occur. Again there is variation from state to state, but generally death certificates record extensive information about the decedent, including date, time, and place of death, name, age, sex, race/ethnicity, birthplace, usual occupation, and marital status. The certificate also provides a format for reporting causes of death. Generally, a licensed physician must pronounce death and certify the cause. The conditions reported on the certificate are coded by the state health department using a classification structure established in the *International Classification of Diseases (ICD), 10th Revision, Adapted for Use in the United States* (http://www.cdc.gov/nchs/about/otheract/icd9/abticd10.htm). These coding rules provide a template for the international standardization of mortality data and improve its usefulness by focusing on a single cause of death, called the *underlying cause of death.* The underlying cause and all other causes listed on the certificate together are designated the *multiple causes of death.* Unless otherwise specified, cause-specific mortality statistics refer to the underlying cause of death. (Preliminary U.S. death rates for 2004 are shown in Table 2.1.)

NCHS calculates vital statistics rates for the nation as a whole, using denominators based on the number of people counted by the Census Bureau on April 1 of each decennial year and on mid-year estimates for other years.

NATALITY

Natality data involve only live births. The U.S. *fertility rate* is defined as the number of births per 1,000 women ages 15 to 44 (women of child-bearing age). For 2004, the fertility rate increased slightly to 66.3 per 1,000 women 15 to 44, down from the post–World War II high of 123 per 1,000, reached in 1957 (NCHS, 2006). The *crude birth rate,* usually expressed as the number of live births per 1,000 population, was 14.0 per 1,000 in 2004. It likewise has steadily dropped from its post–World War II high of 25 per 1,000, reached in 1955. This was the peak of the baby boom, which extended from 1946 to 1964.

MORTALITY

Crude Death Rates

Mortality data reporting is required by law and is virtually complete. Death rates differentiated by age, ethnicity, and sex can be found in the *National Vital Statistics Reports, Vital Statistics of the*

Table 2.1	10 Leading Causes of Death, United States, 2004 (Preliminary)
Cause of Death	**Age-Adjusted Rates per 100,000 Population**
Heart diseases	217.5
Cancers	184.6
Cerebrovascular diseases (strokes)	50.0
Chronic lung diseases	41.8
Unintentional injuries (accidents)	36.6
Diabetes mellitus	24.4
Alzheimer's disease	21.6
Influenza and pneumonia	20.4
Kidney diseases	14.3
Septicemia	11.2

Note. From U.S. Centers for Disease Control. (2006). *National Vital Statistics Reports, 54*(19). p. 4.

United States, special studies published in NCHS's *Vital and Health Statistics,* Series 20, as well as the *Statistical Abstract* (again, refer to Appendix B).

Age-Adjusted Death Rates

In addition to crude death rates, age-adjusted (standardized) death rates are commonly used to compare relative mortality risk across groups over time. These constructed rates eliminate variability due to differences in the age composition of various populations. Statistically, an age-adjusted death rate is a weighted average of the age-specific death rates. Beginning with 1999 death data, the standard is based on the year 2000 population (Anderson & Rosenberg, 1998). Although the discussion of crude versus age-adjusted death rates may appear of interest only to statisticians, the following example illustrates the kinds of interpretation errors that can be made when mortality data are viewed by only one measure. For example, between 1979 and 1995, the U.S. crude death rate *rose* from 852.2/100,000 population to 880.0. Yet, during this time period, the age-adjusted death rate *dropped* from 577.0/100,000 to 503.9. The increase in the crude rate was due to the increasing proportion of the population in older age groups, which have higher death rates, not to a higher death rate across age groups.

Disease-Specific Mortality

Disease-specific causes of death are used to monitor prevention and treatment practices and programs. For most deaths, a physician must certify the death and determine its underlying cause. However, physicians have varying diagnostic styles, perspectives, and coding skills and may have little or no firsthand knowledge of the decedent's medical history. Furthermore, medical understanding and technical definitions of causes of death have changed over time.

For example, when someone dies from a heart attack that resulted from the complications of diabetes, is the cause of death diabetes or coronary artery disease? The physician must determine the immediate cause of death (in this example, most would say heart attack) and then sequentially list conditions leading to the immediate cause, lastly entering the underlying disease or injury that initiated the chain of events leading to death.

The leading causes of death generally evolve gradually, but several important shifts occurred in the past decade. AIDS is no longer among the leading causes because of the dramatic decline in mortality following the introduction of effective therapy in 1996. Alzheimer's disease unexpectedly appeared as a leading cause in 1999, when more than 10,000 additional deaths were attributed to it, compared to 1998. Initially this might suggest something of an epidemic, but closer examination of the data shows that the increase resulted from a change in ICD-10 that combined a previously separate category, presenile dementia, with Alzheimer's disease (Anderson, Minino, Hoyert, & Rosenberg, 2001).

Risk Factor–Specific Mortality

In the United States today, most deaths are caused by chronic diseases or conditions, such as injuries, in which environmental and personal risk factors are major causes. To highlight the significance of these factors, McGinnis and Foege (1993) took a different approach in analyzing the causes of U.S. deaths. They first identified the major nongenetic factors associated with various diseases; then, after an exhaustive review of the literature from 1977 to 1993, they attributed approximately half of all 1990 deaths to key risk factors, led by tobacco use (400,000 deaths) and diet/physical activity (300,000). Similarly, CDC investigators identified the causes of U.S. deaths in 2000. While smoking remained the leading cause, accounting for 18.1% of all deaths, poor diet and physical activity were a close second at 16.6% and may soon overtake smoking (Mokdad, Marks, Stroup, & Gerberding, 2004).

The picture arising from these analyses is particularly helpful in planning public health programs to prolong life, especially healthy life, by focusing on modifiable human behavior—cigarette smoking, eating patterns, physical activity—rather than on classic, medically oriented prevention, like treatment for hypertension. Indeed, mortality could be reduced more by lifestyle changes than through treatment of diseases or conditions that have already developed (McGinnis & Foege, 1993).

Infant Mortality

Deaths of live-born infants up to 1 year of age are captured by the *infant mortality rate*. It is usually calculated as an annual figure, based on the number of deaths (the numerator) divided by the number of live births in that year. Infant mortality relates to a variety of socioeconomic, environmental, and health care factors and is considered a fairly sensitive indicator of general health levels in a population. The most striking feature of the U.S. infant mortality rate is that, while it has consistently declined over the years, the rate for Blacks has consistently remained about double that for Whites. Detailed examinations of the relationships among ethnicity, other factors, and infant mortality are contained in *Vital and Health Statistics* (NCHS, 1992).

MARRIAGE AND DIVORCE

U.S. marriage and divorce rates have both declined over time (phenomena that may be related). Current detailed analyses of birth, marriage, and divorce statistics can be found in the *Vital and Health Statistics* Series 23, "Data From the National Survey of Family Growth," as well as in the *National Vital Statistics Reports.*

Morbidity

DEFINITIONS

Morbidity refers to sickness and disease. Like mortality, morbidity data can be expressed as either numbers or rates and can be cross-tabulated with a broad range of demographic characteristics. Morbidity data are extremely important in characterizing the health of a population. This is particularly so in a country like the United States, in which generally healthy living conditions and availability of medical treatment forestall death from many communicable and chronic diseases and injuries that might otherwise be fatal.

Morbidity data can be reported in terms of both incidence and prevalence. *Incidence* is the number of new cases of the disease during a particular time period, usually a year. For example, in 2002 there were about 42,000 new cases of AIDS reported in the United States (CDC, 2004).

Prevalence is the total number of cases in the population during a specified time period, or at one point in time *(point-prevalence)*. For example, by 2002, there were an estimated 857,516 total U.S. AIDS cases (both living and dead) since the first reports of AIDS in the early 1980s (CDC, 2004). The prevalence of living AIDS cases in 2002 was 384,906.

The list of significant nonfatal causes of ill health in the United States includes arthritis, low-back pain, the common cold, influenza, injuries, dermatitis, schizophrenia, and sexual problems (NCHS, 1999a, p. 5). Other diseases and conditions that may kill, but do so rarely, include sexually transmitted diseases other than AIDS, duodenal ulcers, and gall bladder disease.

> Morbidity is not nearly as simple to count and report as is mortality. . . . What is meant by the term *sickness*, and just when is a person "sick"? Who decides?

Morbidity is not nearly as simple to count and report as is mortality. Consider the following questions: What is meant by the term *sickness*, and just when is a person "sick"? Who decides? The physician? The patient?

The unknowns are compounded, because only infectious diseases are reportable in every state. Until the advent of antibiotics and vaccines, infectious diseases posed the greatest risk to the U.S. population. After several decades of complacency, new infectious agents (e.g., AIDS, Hantavirus, *E. coli* 0157:H7, hepatitis C, avian flu) and the resurgence of old threats (e.g., tuberculosis), together with concerns about antibiotic resistance and bioterrorism, have reignited interest in infectious disease surveillance.

As of January 2007, more than 50 infectious diseases were designated as *notifiable* at the national level (CDC, 2007). According to the CDC, notifiable diseases are those for which regular, frequent, and timely information regarding individual cases is necessary for prevention and control. States voluntarily report cases of these diseases, and their incidence appears in a weekly CDC publication called the *Morbidity and Mortality Weekly Report.* The CDC also publishes annual summaries of notifiable diseases, specific diseases, and disease categories (e.g., sexually transmitted diseases).

Surveillance for new cases of infectious diseases is both *passive* (health departments wait for reports from physicians) and, for more serious diseases such as AIDS, *active* (through routine review of laboratory logs and hospital and clinic charts). In general, however, surveillance relies on physicians. Unfortunately, physicians often fail to report certain diseases, even when legally required to do so. They may not want to take the time to complete the required paperwork, embarrass patients who have sexually transmitted diseases, or jeopardize the employment of patients with infections like tuberculosis. Many fail to report common childhood infections, considering them inconsequential, even though they may have serious consequences and may signal incomplete coverage by immunization programs.

Considerable controversy has been engendered by surveillance programs for several classes of infectious diseases (tuberculosis, sexually transmitted diseases, and AIDS), which require reporting the names of affected individuals to local and state health departments. This debate highlights the importance of privacy and confidentiality protections for all surveillance systems and for medical records in general.

Other diseases, events, and conditions of public health significance are reportable in at least some states; these include cancer, injuries, lead poisoning, childhood asthma, and congenital malformations. In recognition of cancer's rank as the second leading cause of U.S. deaths, Congress established the National Program of Cancer Registries in 1992 to either enhance existing registries or to implement them in 45 states, 3 territories, and the District of Columbia. No similar reporting requirements exist for many equally important disease categories, such as heart disease, diabetes, and stroke, to say nothing of very common and severe conditions such as arthritis and osteoporosis or lifestyle-related factors such as exercise, obesity, and cigarette smoking.

DATA ON MORBIDITY AND MORTALITY

Both providers and patients can be sources of morbidity data, and they provide quite different pictures of the same reality. Providers report morbidity by *diagnosis* and patients' *chief complaints*—that is, what they tell the physician the problem is. From that, the physician characterizes the problem as a specific condition or conditions that can be reported. Of course, patients don't usually tell their physician, "I think I've got diabetes mellitus," but rather reflect their own experience, with words such as, "I've been feeling kind of weak, I'm drinking a great deal of water and urinating a lot. Do you think maybe something's wrong?" This patient perspective can be captured in a population survey.

A partial picture of morbidity patterns can be drawn from a chief complaint profile for a population obtained from either source. One advantage of deriving information from a survey is that some people will never come to medical attention. Morbidity data are published regularly by NCHS and by CDC for reportable communicable diseases. NCHS data resources include:

- the National Health and Nutrition Examination Survey.
- the National Health Interview Survey (NHIS), which provides patient-perspective data for the utilization of ambulatory services.
- the National Hospital Discharge Survey (NHDS)—An example of provider-perspective data, it reports on hospital utilization by age and sex of patients, lengths of stay, diagnoses, and surgical and nonsurgical procedures.
- the National Ambulatory Medical Care Survey (NAMCS)—A continuing stratified random sample survey of private, nonfederal, office-based physicians, both allopathic and osteopathic, practicing in the contiguous United States, excluding anesthesiologists, pathologists, radiologists, and physicians engaged primarily in teaching, research, and administration. NAMCS morbidity data are collected from both patient and physician perspectives.
- the National Hospital Ambulatory Medical Care Survey.

Results of these surveys are published periodically in *Vital and Health Statistics, Advance Data,* and *Health, United States.* Together they constitute the National Health Care Survey. Series 1 of *Vital and Health Statistics* contains the general methodological and historical accounts of the whole endeavor; other series provide information from specific surveys.

In addition to national population-based surveys, individual states (e.g., California: http://www.chis.ucla.edu) and cities (e.g., New York City: http://www.nyc.gov/html/doh/html/community/community. shtml) are now routinely conducting health interview surveys with samples representative of local populations. Online systems that allow people to easily analyze and download data from these surveys are a boon to researchers, health planners, government officials, and the interested public.

Health Status and Health-Related Behavior

In 1979, the DHHS Office of the Assistant Secretary for Health (OASH) published the first national health status report, *Healthy People: The Surgeon General's Report on Health Promotion and Disease Prevention* (OASH, 1979). Subsequently, the OASH's Office of Disease Prevention and Health Promotion published *Promoting Health and Preventing Disease: Objectives for the Nation,* establishing 216 objectives to deal with 15 major diseases and conditions preventable with existing knowledge and techniques.

In 1991, the U.S. Public Health Service published the next comprehensive update for the program, *Healthy People, 2000,* which identified three broad goals: increasing the span of healthy life, reducing
health disparities, and achieving access to preventive services for
everyone. Subsequently, these reports have been updated and revised,
and the Public Health Service is currently working toward *Healthy
People, 2010* objectives. *Healthy People, 2010* is designed to achieve
two overarching goals: increase the quality and years of healthy life
and eliminate health disparities by gender, race/ethnicity, income
and education, disability, geography, and sexual orientation. The 2010
objectives, 467 in number, are being tracked by 190 data sources.

In support of the Healthy People effort, beginning in 1985 NCHS carried out a Health Promotion/Disease Prevention Survey as part of the
ongoing NHIS. This survey was repeated in 1990 and 1995, and some of
its questions have subsequently been incorporated into the NHIS and
other surveys. Results are published in *Vital and Health Statistics* Series
10, *Advance Data,* and the *Morbidity and Mortality Weekly Report.*

Since data from national surveys generally cannot be analyzed by
state, all states and the District of Columbia began participating in the
Behavioral Risk Factor Surveillance System in 1994, which uses telephone
surveys to monitor prevalence of personal health behavior such as smok-
ing at the state level. Data from this survey and the Youth Risk Behavior
Surveillance System, which surveys high school students, complement
NHIS data. CDC's National Center for Chronic Disease Prevention and
Health Promotion is responsible for both of these surveys. (See U.S.
Department of Health and Human Services, 2000, Vol. 2, for a complete
discussion of data sources that track progress toward the objectives.)

We're still left with the question, what is health? To follow the
lead of the World Health Organization, health is more than physical
health or absence of disease but includes mental and social well-
being, as well. Health encompasses the concepts of well-being and
even happiness. Some analysts are trying to capture these more elusive concepts as a truer measure of population health, and the NCHS's
National Health Interview Survey asks about feelings of sadness and
nervousness in addition to more standard questions about behavior,
such as smoking and physical activity.

Utilization and Cost of Health Care Services

The third quantitative perspective for viewing a population in terms
of health and ill health explores how the population uses the health

care delivery system and its impact on health status (Figure 2.1). As noted previously, in quantifying the utilization of health services, the same events can be counted from either the patient's or the provider's perspective. Because the results of the two types of counts are not always the same, one must distinguish carefully between the two.

Reliable utilization data are available primarily for services provided by licensed allopathic physicians (MDs) and doctors of osteopathic medicine (DOs), in licensed allopathic and osteopathic hospitals, and by licensed dentists.

In the United States, there is a substantial but unknown amount of complementary and alternative medicine (CAM) therapy provided by practitioners of chiropractic, naturopathy, homeopathy, massage therapy, acupuncture/acupressure therapy, and other holistic health practitioners. Data on these practitioners' activities are sparse, because they do not report visits, they are not surveyed, and payment for their services is only sporadically reimbursed by insurance companies (another common source of utilization data). However, population surveys suggest that more than 40% of all U.S. adults use

Figure 2.1

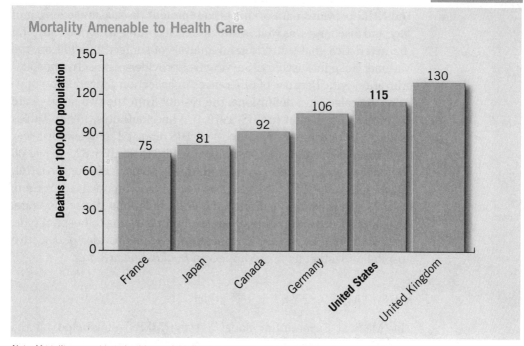

Mortality Amenable to Health Care

Note. Mortality amenable to health care is defined as deaths before age 75 that are potentially preventable with timely and appropriate medical care. From *Commonwealth Fund National Scorecard of U.S. Health System Performance.* (2006). Retrieved from http://www.commonwealthfund.org/publications/publications_show.htm?doc_id=401577

at least one alternative therapy, with an average annual visit rate among users of 7.6 (Eisenberg, et al., 1998). In 1997, as in 1990, there were more visits made to alternative therapists (629 million) than to primary care physicians (485 million), illustrating the importance of having a better understanding of how, why, and by whom CAM therapies are being used (Institute of Medicine, 2005).

AMBULATORY SERVICES

There are several sources of provider data on the utilization of ambulatory services. The most comprehensive is the National Ambulatory Medical Care Survey, usually reported upon in *Advance Data.* In addition to morbidity data, the NAMCS provides data on visits by age, race, sex, geographic region, metropolitan/nonmetropolitan living area, type of physician, and duration of visit. The other major source of provider-perspective data on use of ambulatory services is the American Hospital Association's (AHA) *Hospital Statistics,* published each summer, which reports hospital clinic and emergency department visits by such variables as number of beds in the hospital, its ownership, type, geographic region, and medical school affiliation.

INPATIENT SERVICES

The NHIS provides data on hospital inpatient days, average length of stay, and discharges, as well as utilization, according to various hospital characteristics, morbidity, and an analysis of surgery. In addition, the National Hospital Discharge Survey gives provider-perspective hospital utilization data. Because of differences in collection procedures, population sampled, and definitions, the results from the two surveys are not entirely consistent (NCHS, 1979, p. 1 and footnotes, 1999b, Tables 89 and 90). For example, for 1996, the NHIS reported significantly fewer discharges from short-stay hospitals than did the NHDS: 82.4 per 1,000 population for the former, compared with 102.3 per 1,000 for the latter. Again, AHA's *Hospital Statistics* provides data on inpatient utilization, describing hospitals by number of beds, admissions, occupancy rate, average daily census, and fiscal parameters according to hospital type, size, ownership, and geographic location. Certain provider-perspective hospital utilization data also appear in *Health, United States.*

MEDICAL EXPENDITURE PANEL SURVEY

The Medical Expenditure Panel Survey (MEPS) conducted by the Agency for Healthcare Research and Quality is a set of large-scale national surveys with two major components. The household component collects data for multiple years from a representative sample of families and individuals on the specific health services they use, how frequently they use them, the cost of these services, and how they are paid for. This component also includes interviews with the medical providers (doctors, hospitals, pharmacies, etc.) of the participants. The insurance component collects data from a sample of private and public sector employers on the cost and scope of health insurance held by and available to U.S. workers. Data are available on the MEPS Web site.

QUALITY OF CARE

Some data are available on the quality of health care. The most widely used measures are the NCQA HEDIS clinical measures that focus on some of the most serious and prevalent diseases and conditions. In addition, patient outcomes, including survival, can be measured for specific medical procedures. For example, New York has taken a leadership role in setting standards for cardiac surgery services, monitoring outcomes, and sharing performance data with patients, hospitals, and physicians (New York State Department of Health, 2000). Cardiac surgery mortality rates have plummeted since publication of the first survey in 1989.

Conclusion

An abundance of data concerning the U.S. population, its health, and how it uses the health care delivery system is collected and published in print and on the Internet. Ready access to data from multiple sources should not lull users into uncritically using and interpreting them, however. The reliability of the source and the collection methods must always be assessed. Additionally, even from reliable sources, data may not be consistent and will need thoughtful interpretation.

The federal statistical collection, reporting, and analysis systems have long been criticized. A 1979 study by the congressional Office of Technology Assessment (OTA) found "federal data collection activities . . . to be overlapping, fragmented, and often duplicative" (Office of Technology Assessment, 1979, p. iii).[1] In brief, the report recommended that a "strengthened coordinating and planning unit within HHS" be established that "would embody three basic characteristics: sufficient authority to impose decisions on agencies; the necessary statistical and analytical capabilities to conduct activities requiring technical expertise and judgement; and adequate resources to build a viable core effort" (OTA, 1979, p. 55).

---

[1] This report is still valuable to students of the federal data system and its users. It not only described data collection activities and the way they were organized and supervised, but also presented and analyzed all of the statutory authorities that establish those existing at the time (which happens to be almost all of those still in use).

The DHHS Data Council (http://aspe.hhs.gov/datacncl/) established in 1995 is the current iteration of a department-wide information systems committee. Its charge encompasses the OTA recommendations plus electronic information policy, including data standards, privacy, telemedicine, and enhanced health information for consumers. Near-universal access to the Internet and the widespread availability of high-speed computing capabilities have made the council's tasks simultaneously easier and more difficult. While these advances have greatly improved communication at all levels and expanded access to databases and the capacity to link multiple databases—a boon to health planners and researchers—they also have raised serious concerns about protecting the privacy and security of health-related information. In response, Congress enacted the Health Insurance Portability and Accountability Act of 1996, which has reshaped the way the health care industry collects, processes, stores, protects, and exchanges patient records. For the first time, national standards are mandated to protect the privacy of personal health records, and common standards are set for electronic transmission of patient information within the health care industry.

> Privacy and security concerns are likely to hold center stage among the many policy issues related to health care data collection and use.

Privacy and security concerns are likely to hold center stage among the many policy issues related to health care data collection and use, but other issues of importance include the utility and application of clinical trials methodology to the study of health outcomes; health services malpractice and malpractice litigation; technological and ethical matters arising from the use of electronic data collection and analysis; the decision-making process governing what is counted and what data are disseminated; cost/benefit analysis of health services interventions; government data collection requirements, utilization, and costs; and the impact of the Internet on health data requirements and availability.

There will always be gaps in our data collection systems. Nevertheless, we know a great deal about health, disease, and illness in the United States and about the functioning of our health care delivery system. But whatever the strengths and weaknesses of available health and health care data, this information means little unless it is put to proper use.

References

Anderson, R. N., Minino, A. M., Hoyert, D. L., & Rosenberg, H. M. (2001). Comparability of cause of death between ICD-9 and ICD-10: Preliminary estimates. *National Vital Statistics Reports, 49*(2). Hyattsville, MD: National Center for Health Statistics.

Anderson, R. N., & Rosenberg, H. M. (1998). Age standardization of death rates: Implementation of the year 2000 standard. *National Vital Statistics Reports, 47*(3). Hyattsville, MD: National Center for Health Statistics.

Centers for Disease Control and Prevention. (2004). HIV/AIDS surveillance report 2002. *Morbidity and Mortality Weekly Report, 14,* 1–40.

Centers for Disease Control and Prevention. (2006, June 28). *National Vital Statistics Reports, 54*(19), 4.

Centers for Disease Control and Prevention. (2007). Notice to readers: Notifiable infectious disease list and data presentation as of January 2007. *Morbidity and Mortality Weekly Report, 56,* 10.

Eisenberg, D. M., Davis, R. B., Ettner, S. L., Appel, S., Wilkey, S., Van Rompay, M., et al. (1998). Trends in alternative medicine use in the United States, 1990–97. *Journal of the American Medical Association, 280,* 1569–1575.

Institute of Medicine. (2005). *Complementary and alternative medicine in the United States.* Washington, DC: National Academies Press.

McGinnis, J. M., & Foege, W. H. (1993). Actual causes of death in the United States. *Journal of the American Medical Association, 270,* 2207–2212.

Mokdad, A. H., Marks, J. S., Stroup, D. F., & Gerberding, J. L. (2004). Actual causes of death in the United States, 2000. *Journal of the American Medical Association, 291,* 1238–1245.

Mulry, M. (2006). *Summary of accuracy and coverage evaluation for Census 2000.* Research Report Series (Statistics #2006–3). Washington, DC: U.S. Census Bureau, Statistical Research Division.

National Center for Health Statistics. (1979). *Health resources statistics: Health manpower and health facilities, 1976–1977* (DHEW Pub. No. PHS 79-1509). Hyattsville, MD: U.S. Government Printing Office.

National Center for Health Statistics. (1992). Infant mortality rates: Socioeconomic factors. *Vital and Health Statistics,* Series 22, No. 14.

National Center for Health Statistics. (1999a). Current estimates from the National Health Survey, 1994. *Vital and Health Statistics,* Series 10, No. 200.

National Center for Health Statistics. (1999b, September). *Health, United States, 1999, health and aging chartbook* (DHHS Pub. No. PHS 99-1232). Hyattsville, MD: Centers for Disease Control and Prevention.

National Center for Health Statistics. (2006, September 29). *National Vital Statistics Reports, 55*(1).

New York State Department of Health. (2000, September). *Coronary artery bypass surgery in New York State 1995–1997.* Albany, NY: Author.

Office of the Assistant Secretary for Health. (1979). *Healthy people: The surgeon general's report on health promotion and disease prevention* (DHEW Pub. No. PHS 70-55071). Washington, DC: U.S. Government Printing Office.

Office of Technology Assessment. (1979). *Selected topics in federal health statistics.* Washington, DC: U.S. Government Printing Office. Retrieved from http://govinfo.library.unt.edu/ota/Ota_5/DATA/1979/7916.PDF

U.S. Department of Health and Human Services. (2000, January). *Healthy people, 2010* (Conference edition in two volumes). Washington, DC: U.S. Government Printing Office.

3

Key Words

Financing Health Care

Kelly A. Hunt and James R. Knickman

Learning Objectives

- Quantify health care spending in the United States over time.
- Describe the major sources of health care spending.
- List and tabulate the major categories of services purchased.
- Differentiate between public and private spending and purchasing in addition to the categories of health plan types within the public and private system.
- Demonstrate an understanding of the extent to which health care spending is rising and the factors that contribute to such growth.
- Describe the major reimbursement mechanisms for health care services.
- Explain current policy issues in health care financing.

Topical Outline

- General overview of costs
- What the money buys
- How we pay for health care
- Reimbursement approaches
- Current policy issues in financing
- Conclusion

Health care is a complex set of services, and thus it is not surprising that the way we pay for health care is so complicated. At the heart of approaches to paying for health care are the complications caused by insurance. For most goods and services in our economy, simple prices can be set by suppliers—usually dictated by market forces—and then consumers choose whether to purchase a good or service at the offered price. Then there is a moment when a transaction occurs between supplier and purchaser, and money changes hands. Health insurance takes away this direct link between supplier and purchaser, because consumers pay for much of their health care through the intermediary of insurance. Insurers negotiate the price they will pay for services the insured person uses during the year. This price depends on many factors: market power, political considerations (since government is a major insurer), and concepts of fairness.

Many industrialized countries rely on public financing to pay for most health care. For example, Great Britain's National Health Service is subsidized by the national government, and Canada has a national health insurance system that pays for most health services (see chapter 6). In the United States, however, we rely on private financing mechanisms to pay for most health care and on government financing to fill in the gaps. An ongoing debate in U.S. politics focuses on whether what we do currently with private financing works adequately and fairly (see, e.g., Blendon, Young, & DesRoches, 1999; Davis & Schoen, 2003; Reinhardt, 2003).

The U.S. health care financing system has evolved continually since the large public financing programs, Medicare and Medicaid,[1] were implemented in the late 1960s. When the costs of health care began to increase rapidly in the 1970s—partly because of the expanding public and private insurance systems and partly because of expensive new health care technology—most insurers tried to

---

Acknowledgment: We are grateful for the research assistance of Kathryn Muessig.
[1] Medicare, signed into law July 30, 1965, as Title XVIII—Health Insurance for the Aged—of the Social Security Act, became effective July 1, 1966. It covered hospital services (Part A) and physician services (Part B). Medicare+Choice (informally called Part C, and now called Medicare Advantage), encouraging managed care enrollment, was added in 1997. Part D, covering prescription drugs and some preventive services, became effective January 1, 2006. Medicaid, or Title XIX of the Social Security Act, was signed into law the same date and is a federally aided, state-operated and -administered program that provides varying medical benefits for low-income individuals. In general, states establish eligibility rules, determine benefits, and set provider payments and administrative methods.

control rising costs by developing increasingly complex methods to reimburse hospitals, physicians, and other health care providers.

In the past, the impetus for innovations in health care financing has arisen from concerns about health care costs and efficiency, but, in recent years, payers have started to tie reimbursements to improvements in health care quality (see chapter 15), in the belief that higher quality care ultimately is less costly. A well-grounded understanding of health care financing is essential for people interested in improving many aspects of health care: quality, efficiency, fairness, access, and the viability of health care delivery organizations. This chapter focuses on (a) what the money devoted to health care buys, (b) where it comes from, (c) how health care providers are paid, and (d) current policy issues.

The Centers for Medicare & Medicaid Services (CMS),[2] part of the U.S. Department of Health and Human Services (DHHS), tracks national health care expenditures. According to CMS, the nation's health expenditures reached nearly $2 trillion in 2005, or just under 16% of the gross domestic product (Figure 3.1). These expenditures represent $6,697 per year of health spending for each individual in the United States—by far the highest spending rate in the world—and they are rising rapidly. (See chapter 6, Table 6.2, for a comparison of spending and health outcomes in different countries.)

What the Money Buys

CMS breaks health care spending into two major categories: *health services and supplies* and *investment*. Most spending in the health services and supplies category is for *personal health care*—$1.66 trillion in 2005 and projected to reach $3.2 trillion by 2015 (Table 3.1). Within personal health expenses, the four largest spending categories are for hospital care (by far), physician and clinical services, nursing home care, and prescription drugs. Together, they account for more than 80% of personal health care spending. The share of personal health expenditures paid by public sources has increased in recent years, driven by increased Medicaid expenditures for prescription drugs and expanded benefits (Kaiser Commission on Medicaid and the Uninsured, 2003).

---

[2] Formerly the Health Care Financing Administration, the agency was renamed CMS by DHHS Secretary Tommy Thompson in 2001, as part of a larger reform initiative. CMS is responsible for the administration and oversight of Medicare, and it works with the states to administer Medicaid and the State Children's Health Insurance Program. In addition, CMS has some regulatory responsibilities.

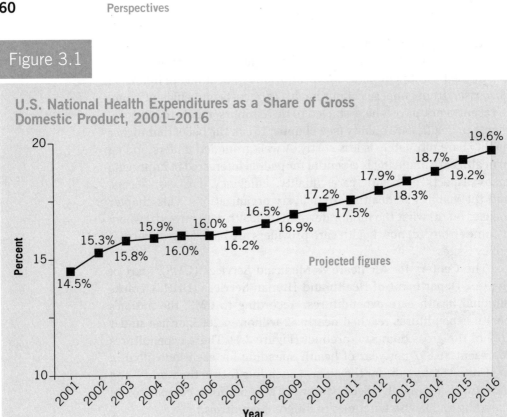

Figure 3.1

U.S. National Health Expenditures as a Share of Gross Domestic Product, 2001–2016

Note. From U.S. Centers for Medicare & Medicaid Services, Office of the Actuary, 2007. Retrieved April 5, 2007, from http://www.cms.hhs.gov/NationalHealthExpendData/downloads/proj2006.pdf

Table 3.1 U.S. National Health Expenditures (in Billions of Dollars), Selected Categories and Years, 1970–2015

Type of Expenditure	Actual			Projected	
	1970	2000	2005	2010	2015
Total national health expenditures	$73.1	$1,309.4	$1,987.7	$2,776.4	$3,874.6
Total of all personal health care	63.2	1,135.3	1,661.4	2,312.9	3,227.9
Hospital care	27.6	413.2	611.6	860.9	1,206.7
Physician and clinical services	14.0	290.3	421.2	577.1	774.9
Prescription drugs	5.5	121.5	200.7	291.5	453.6
Program administration and net cost of private health insurance	2.8	80.3	143.0	206.2	281.5

Note. 2005–2015 data are from U.S. Centers for Medicare & Medicaid Services, Office of the Actuary. (2007). Retrieved April 5, 2007, from http://www.cms.hhs.gov/NationalHealthExpendData/downloads/proj2006.pdf 1970 and 2000 data are from Levit, K., Smith, C., Cowan, C. et al. (2004). Health spending rebound continues in 2002. *Health Affairs, 23*(1). pp. 147–159.

How We Pay for Health Care

Americans pay for health care through a hybrid system that relies to some extent on direct payments by consumers, to a large extent on payments by private insurers and independent health plans, and—in the case of the poor, the elderly, the military, and some disabled Americans or war veterans—payments by the public sector. Private insurance is financed by individual and employer contributions that vary firm by firm and by individual.

As Figure 3.2 illustrates, in 2005, private insurance and individuals paid for just over half of all national health expenditures (55%), with the bulk of private payments coming from insurance ($694.4 billion, or 64% of all private payments) (Catlin, Cowan, Heffler, Washington, & the

Figure 3.2

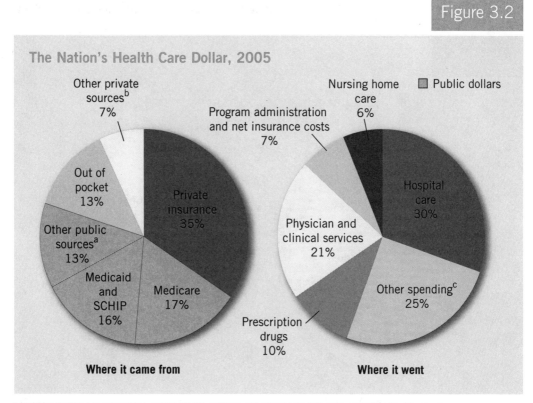

The Nation's Health Care Dollar, 2005

Where it came from

- Other private sources[b] 7%
- Out of pocket 13%
- Other public sources[a] 13%
- Medicaid and SCHIP 16%
- Medicare 17%
- Private insurance 35%

Where it went

- Nursing home care 6%
- Public dollars
- Program administration and net insurance costs 7%
- Hospital care 30%
- Physician and clinical services 21%
- Other spending[c] 25%
- Prescription drugs 10%

[a] Includes workers' compensation, public health, military and veterans health services, Indian Health Service, state and local hospital subsidies, and school health.
[b] Includes workplace health services, privately funded construction, and philanthropy.
[c] Includes dental services, other professional services, home health, durable medical products, over-the-counter medicines, public health, research, and structures and equipment.
Note. From U.S. Centers for Medicare & Medicaid Services, Office of the Actuary. (2007). Retrieved April 5, 2007, from http://www.cms.hhs.gov/NationalHealthExpendData/downloads/PieChartSources Expenditures2005.pdf

Health Accounts Team, 2007). Public funds paid for 45% of all health care spending, mostly under the Medicare program.

PUBLICLY FINANCED PROGRAMS

Medicaid

Medicaid originally was designed to assist recipients of public assistance—primarily single-parent families and the aged, blind, and disabled. Over the years, Medicaid has expanded to include additional groups and now covers poor children, their parents, pregnant women, the disabled and very poor adults (including those 65 and older). Much public attention is given to Medicaid's role in covering children's care, but, in reality, nearly 70% of its expenditures are for the one-quarter of enrollees who are elderly or disabled (Figure 3.3).

> Much public attention is given to Medicaid's role in covering children's care, but, in reality, nearly 70% of its expenditures are for the one-quarter of enrollees who are elderly or disabled.

Medicaid is administered by the states, and both the states and the federal government finance the program.

Figure 3.3

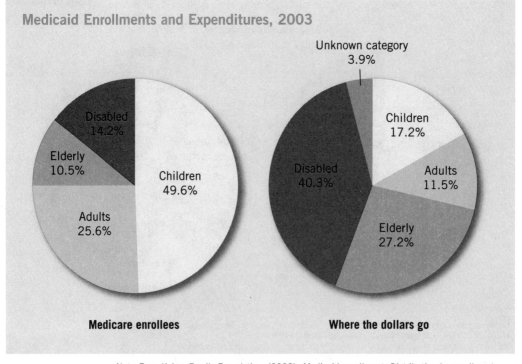

Medicaid Enrollments and Expenditures, 2003

Note. From Kaiser Family Foundation. (2003). *Medicaid enrollment: Distribution by enrollment group, FY 2003* and *Medicaid spending: Payments by enrollment group, FY 2003. State health facts.* Retrieved April 5, 2007, from http://www.statehealthfacts.org

Except for minimum mandatory benefits, the federal government gives states flexibility in implementing and administering Medicaid to best meet the needs of their residents. As a result, there are many seemingly arbitrary differences in eligibility and benefits across states. For example, while many states cover emergency dental treatment and dental care for children, fewer than half cover yearly dental exams and cleaning (American Dental Association, 2001; Kaiser Commission on Medicaid and the Uninsured, 2003). Rocky economic times often cause states to tighten Medicaid eligibility, enrollment standards, and benefits in order to reduce their budgets (see, e.g., Boyd, 2003; Holahan, Wiener, & Lutzky, 2002; and chapter 5).

A major change in Medicaid occurred when it adopted managed care in the early 1990s, but a number of problems undermined the hoped-for savings. Medicaid already paid providers rates below (sometimes significantly below) commercial levels and could not easily reduce them further; squeezing safety net providers that largely depended on Medicaid revenues would have jeopardized their financial viability; and, while managed care enrollment campaigns were targeted at low-income women and children, most Medicaid spending is for the elderly and disabled (Hurley & Somers, 2003). Congress made another significant change in the program in 1996, when welfare reform legislation for the first time de-linked welfare and Medicaid. Previously, people eligible for cash assistance were automatically eligible for Medicaid (Ellwood & Ku, 1998).

SCHIP

Congress passed the State Children's Health Insurance Program (SCHIP) as part of the Balanced Budget Act of 1997. Under SCHIP, the federal government provides states with just over $40 billion (over a 10-year period), generally to cover children not poor enough to be Medicaid-eligible and who are in families with incomes below 200% of the federal poverty line or with incomes up to 50 percentage points above the level currently determining Medicaid eligibility (U.S. Centers for Medicare & Medicaid Services, 2004). Like Medicaid, SCHIP is jointly financed by the state and federal governments, but the latter pays a higher percentage of program costs. State participation is voluntary, and implementation and administration are flexible. Some states introduce SCHIP as a stand-alone program, separate from Medicaid, while others blend the two.

Medicare

Medicare, administered by the federal government, originally targeted people 65 and over, but was quickly expanded to cover people with disabilities and severe kidney disease. To qualify, an individual had to be a U.S. resident for a specified number of years and have paid into the Social Security system. The entitlement was expanded in 1972 to allow people who did not meet the latter requirement to pay a premium for coverage. While enrollment in Medicare has doubled since its passage, annual expenditures have increased about 40-fold, making the federal government the nation's single largest payer of health care expenses.

Medicare has two parts: Part A, which is hospital insurance, and Part B, which is supplemental medical insurance covering outpatient care (see also chapter 5). The Balanced Budget Act of 1997 established the Medicare+Choice program, designed to build on existing Medicare managed care programs and expand options under Part B. In addition to giving Medicare beneficiaries more plan options, the law was supposed to bring savings. Ironically, enrollment in Medicare managed care was more rapid prior to passage of the legislation, although it continued to grow steadily until about 1999. After that, it declined for several reasons. First, a natural market phenomenon occurred—many managed care plans ceased offering Medicare+Choice because they could not or did not want to compete. At the same time, the government reduced payments, forcing seniors to pay higher premiums and out-of-pocket costs. Eventually, many managed care operators found the program unprofitable and pulled out of it entirely (Gold, 2001, 2003).

In the 1980s and 1990s, Medicare experienced a series of changes to its payment mechanisms, which show up as dips in the overall growth rate of national health expenditures. In the 1980s, Medicare started paying hospitals under a prospective payment system; by the 1990s, it had started paying physicians differently, too. The only other major change to the program before 2004 was the Medicare Catastrophic Coverage Act (1988), repealed within 2 years of passage because it was unpopular with seniors and interest groups.[3]

The Catastrophic Coverage Act repeal and the Clinton Health Reform debacle of the early 1990s curbed the political appetite for Medicare reform for a number of years. The issue finally came back when George W. Bush included a promise to add drug coverage to Medicare in his 2000 presidential campaign. This time the political stars were aligned, and Congress passed and the president signed into law the Medicare Modernization Act in December 2003. The Congressional Budget Office estimates the cost of this legislation at

---

[3] This legislation was designed to provide catastrophic financial protection to senior citizens, but many people the law was intended to protect already had supplemental insurance for catastrophic illness and were unwilling to accept a new tax to finance such coverage for the entire Medicare population. Also, many elderly did not understand this legislation, feared deductibles and coinsurance, and were satisfied with their current private insurance policies (Rice, Desmond, & Gabel, 1990).

$395 billion the first 10 years and over $1 trillion in each subsequent decade (Holtz-Eakin, 2004).

In addition to establishing a prescription drug benefit, the 2003 law included heavy subsidies for managed care plans, ostensibly to expand the availability of private insurance options for seniors. The law has many critics on both ends of the political spectrum. On one hand, critics say it is too complicated and leaves huge gaps in prescription drug coverage. They believe that the poorest and sickest beneficiaries may be worse off, because they will not be able to afford the new benefit or because the drugs they need may not be covered (Park & Greenstein, 2003). On the other hand, different critics say that because the subsidies afforded to private managed care plans are actually quite substantial, they will be able to fill the gap in drug coverage and offer better cost-sharing options, which will essentially force beneficiaries off traditional fee-for-service Medicare and into managed care (Butler & Moffitt, 2003; Park, Nathanson, Greenstein, & Springer, 2003). And they predict that these large subsidies will increase overall program costs. Finally, the legislation is criticized for introducing regressive changes in tax policy. Senior citizens and their advocates are a powerful political force, and they again may demonstrate their clout by forcing changes in the act once it has been implemented long enough to assess its impact on them.

Public Health

The United States spent $56.6 billion on the public health system during 2005—less than 4% of national health spending. Excluded from this total are the expenditures of state and local departments other than health that are responsible for health-related activities such as air and water pollution control, sanitation, and sewage treatment (Letsch, Levit, & Waldo, 1988). Also excluded are private expenditures on public health by employers and individuals. Projections suggest that this level of public health spending will be maintained. The relatively low level of government funding for public health, versus health insurance, deserves special attention, because state and local public health agencies are being asked to do much more to increase preparedness for threats that include bioterrorism and avian influenza.

Other Public Programs

In addition to Medicaid, SCHIP, and Medicare, the United States has a patchwork of government health care programs for special populations—active and retired military personnel, Native Americans, and injured and disabled workers. Historically, most health care needs of active-duty military personnel have been provided in military facilities, where retirees and families also could receive free treatment on a space-available basis. In 1966, Congress established the Civilian Health and Medical Program of the Uniformed Services (CHAMPUS), administered by the Department of Defense (DoD), as the military equivalent of a health insurance plan. It covered retirees and families of active-duty, retired, and deceased military personnel and partially reimbursed them for services from civilian health care providers. In the 1990s, the DoD overhauled the CHAMPUS program, now renamed TRICARE, to control costs and improve access. This overhaul introduced managed care into the system, which now serves more than eight million military personnel, retirees, and their dependents and survivors (Congressional Budget Office, 2003). Major complaints about the system are that the TRICARE provider network is inadequate, reimbursement rates are too low, and enrollee benefits are less generous than in employer-sponsored plans (Landers, 2003).

TRICARE spending almost doubled from 1988 to 2003, rising from $14.6 billion to $27.2 billion. Since the active-duty force dropped 38% during that same period, spending per active-duty service member nearly tripled—from $6,600 to $19,600. The same issues affecting health care costs nationally—greater use of technology, changes in utilization patterns, and higher medical prices—affect TRICARE, with these additions: a shift to accrual budgeting (where the cost of deferred compensation is reflected during a participant's working years) and an increasing number of retirees. Spending projections suggest TRICARE will cost $40 to $52 billion a year by 2020 (Congressional Budget Office, 2003).

The Veterans Health Administration operates the largest integrated health care system in the United States, providing primary care, specialized care, and related medical and social support services to U.S. veterans and their dependents (Veterans Health Administration, 2004). In fiscal year 2005, medical care accounted for $32.9 billion or 47% of total Veterans Administration spending (Department of Veterans Affairs, 2005).

In 1921, the Snyder Act established a program of health services for Native Americans, known today as the Indian Health Service and administered by the DHHS. Eligible are members of federally recognized Indian tribes and their descendants. The program's budget is approximately $3 billion annually, and it serves approximately 1.8 million of the nation's estimated 3.3 million American Indians and Alaska Natives (U.S. Department of Health and Human Services, 2004).

Workers' compensation is an insurance system intended to protect workers against the costs of medical care and loss of income resulting from work-related injury and, in some cases, sickness. Underlying workers' compensation is the premise that all accidents, regardless of fault, are the result of the risks of working in industry, and the employer and employee should share the burden of loss. Workers' compensation programs are operated by the states, each with its own authorizing legislation and requirements. The first such law was enacted in New York in 1910; by 1948, all states had a workers' compensation program.

PRIVATELY FINANCED HEALTH CARE

The private share of health care expenditures has been declining since the 1960s and even since the late 1980s, as Medicare, Medicaid, and other public sources of payments have increased. In 2005, the private share of the health care dollar was 55% or $1.1 trillion, paid out of pocket by patients and third parties. Third-party payers—mostly insurance companies—accounted for $694 billion of these private dollars. The share of payments made by private insurers increased steadily over most of the 20th century. Even in 1978, private insurance accounted for 21% of all payments, compared to 54% in 2002.

Insurance is a mechanism for sharing the risk of uncertain events across a large group of people who individually face approximately the same risk. In the early 20th century, when health care did not cost very much, insurance was unnecessary. However, costs rose rapidly after World War II as technology and medical knowledge expanded, and it became increasingly attractive to families to pay a fixed annual premium rather than face enormous medical bills in case of severe illness or injury.

In 2004, health expenditures for a nonelderly American hospitalized at least once during the year averaged over $12,000, which most people could not easily afford. But each year, only 6% of nonelderly Americans are hospitalized (Agency for Healthcare Research and Quality, 2004). Insurance spreads that 6% risk across the entire population; in essence, through our insurance premiums, we all help one another pay for expensive medical events.

Employer-Sponsored Versus Individual Health Insurance

During the Great Depression, hospitals found that most Americans could not afford to pay for their bills. The hospital industry, through the American Hospital Association, supported the growth of the first major health insurers: the Blue Cross plans in each state that pay for hospital care and the Blue Shield plans that pay for physician and other outpatient services. Over time these nonprofit insurers had to compete with for-profit insurance companies that emerged mostly during World War II, when unions began fighting for medical insurance to be part of employee benefits packages.

Growth in the health insurance market was a by-product of wartime wage and price controls; since wages were fixed, enhanced benefits packages were one way unions and employees could obtain increased compensation. It accelerated even more following the decision by the Internal Revenue Service that employers could take a tax deduction for the cost of health insurance provided to employees. The growing costs of health care would have led to increased private or public insurance eventually (the politics of why a public system did not emerge are discussed in chapter 5).

Over the next several decades, the employer-based health insurance system became increasingly entrenched. By the end of 2002, more than 64% of Americans received health insurance through their employer (Glied & Borzi, 2004). Although employer-based insurance dominates the private health insurance sector, a significant number of people must arrange and pay for health insurance on their own. The Employee Benefit Research Institute estimates that, in 2002, more than 160 million nonelderly Americans were covered by employment-based health benefits, and about 17 million purchased coverage for themselves and family members in the individual market (Fronstin, 2003).[4]

Some people work for employers that do not offer insurance, some are between jobs, some are ineligible for public insurance, and some are self-employed. These individuals must rely on the individual insurance market, where premiums are high and benefits less than generous. Employers can secure better, lower-cost coverage for several reasons: employed individuals tend to be in better health, reducing the risk and thus the cost to the insurer; risk can be spread across the group; and marketing and administrative costs are lower. The type of insurance employers' offer varies by the size of the workforce (Table 3.2).

COBRA

The Consolidated Omnibus Budget Reconciliation Act of 1985 attempted to reduce gaps in insurance coverage for individuals between jobs. It requires employers to extend health insurance benefits to former employees for up to 18 months. Depending on qualifying circumstances, coverage may be extended for a spouse or dependent children for up to 36 months. Employees generally pay the entire premium for the coverage, up to 102% of the cost of the plan (100% plus a possible 2% administrative fee) (U.S. Department of Labor, 2004). Although the cost of COBRA coverage may be high, it is still much less expensive than comparable coverage purchased in the individual market.

Managed Care

The biggest change in the privately financed portion of the U.S. health care system over the last three decades is the shift toward

---

[4] These numbers may vary slightly from other cited sources (such as Claxton et al., 2003) because they do not include the few insured, working elderly nor a selection of individuals who use multiple forms of health insurance.

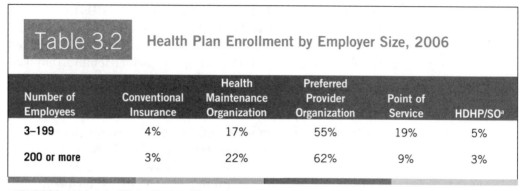

Table 3.2   Health Plan Enrollment by Employer Size, 2006

Number of Employees	Conventional Insurance	Health Maintenance Organization	Preferred Provider Organization	Point of Service	HDHP/SO[a]
3–199	4%	17%	55%	19%	5%
200 or more	3%	22%	62%	9%	3%

[a] HDHP/SO is a high-deductible health plan with a savings option.
Note. From Kaiser Family Foundation/Health Research and Education Trust. (2006). Survey of employer-sponsored health benefits. Retrieved from http://www.kff.org/insurance/7527/upload/7527.pdf

managed care that started in the late 1980s and took hold by the mid-1990s. Large businesses steered this shift, in an attempt to reduce insurance costs. Managed care plans structure and reimburse care differently than does conventional insurance. Very strict managed care plans, like health maintenance organizations (HMOs), use *capitated payments* and control which providers participate in their network. Capitated payments are fixed annual payments for each individual for whom the provider is responsible to provide care, regardless of the amount and kinds of services eventually needed. HMOs also require primary care physicians to be gatekeepers to other types of services, by requiring referrals for diagnostic tests and specialty care.

The theory was that capitation would encourage providers to think more carefully about the necessity of costly tests and procedures and that use of expensive specialists would be more controlled. Despite the limited reimbursement that capitation imposed, providers were expected to participate because of the potential for increased patient flow. For patients, in return for giving up the freedom to use whatever physician or hospital they chose, care would be more organized and specialist and primary care more effectively coordinated. HMOs generally act as both the insurer and the provider of services. However, HMOs use a range of approaches to actually providing services. Some employ physicians and own hospitals while others contract with networks of physicians and develop contracts with local hospitals. The best known HMO, Kaiser Permanente, uses a defined network of physicians and uses hospitals it owns to deliver services.

Managed care was very effective in reducing costs during the mid- to late 1990s. But, by the late 1990s, consumers had begun to push back on this type of insurance

> Managed care was very effective in reducing costs during the mid- to late 1990s. But, by the late 1990s, consumers had begun to push back on this type of insurance product.

product. They perceived many of the features of HMOs to be overly restrictive. They wanted to choose their own physicians, resented the specialty care gatekeeping and other "hassle factors," and demanded more choice in their plan options. They complained loudly to employers, who eventually moved toward offering less tightly controlled plans, which also were not capitated for providers. The potential to manage care had been there, but consumers did not like having their choices limited. This is in stark contrast to Medicaid managed care, which nationwide enrolls about two-thirds of Medicaid recipients (U.S. Centers for Medicare & Medicaid Services, 2005). Some states aggressively seek to increase enrollment of Medicaid recipients into capitated programs in an attempt to reduce spending.

Nowadays most consumers do not choose to enroll in HMO plans. Only in California and, to a lesser extent, the other West Coast states, do HMOs represent a significant share of the insurance and service delivery market. And, in many areas of the country—including most of the Eastern half—HMO penetration is minimal.

At the "liberal" end of the managed care spectrum are the rapidly growing *preferred provider organizations* (PPOs), which negotiate discounts with a list of physicians that they encourage plan members to use, for which they are rewarded with lower out-of-pocket costs (deductibles, co-pays, and coinsurance). Patients who go to an out-of-network provider often must pay the difference between the insurer's reimbursement rate and whatever the physician charges. By 2003, more than half of workers were enrolled in a PPO plan (Kaiser Family Foundation/Health Research and Educational Trust, 2003).

Consumer-Driven Health Care

An emerging issue in the private insurance market is *consumer-driven health care*. This is a strategy intended both to allow employees more choice in their health care decisions and to stabilize health care costs. The same theories that prompted capitated payments to providers, which were largely rejected, propel the idea behind consumer-driven health care. The design of consumer-driven plans varies, but essentially employers provide employees with a personal care account of a fixed amount in the form of a voucher, refundable tax credit, higher wages, or some other transfer of funds (Christianson, Parente, & Taylor, 2002; Gabel, Lo Sasso, & Rice, 2002). Employees choose their own services and providers, as well as manage their annual spending. Employees who use up all the funds in their personal care accounts are responsible for expenses up to a deductible, at which point wraparound or catastrophic coverage starts. The deductible establishes a minimum amount at which major medical expenses will be covered (e.g., $1,000).

Typically, employees can use their personal care account funds to purchase health care through an employer-sponsored intermediary, or, theoretically, they can purchase it on their own. Some intermediaries, such as Internet-based companies that give employees flexibility in choosing physicians and services, take on some of the sponsorship duties formerly borne by employers. They contract with networks of providers just like a PPO plan would; members can select providers who are in- or out-of-network. Other intermediaries allow employees to design their plans at a much more detailed level, allowing them to select co-payments and doctors to form a personalized network.

Consumer-driven health care is still a relatively new development, and, until recently, skeptics have doubted that it would become popular. However, in many industries the demand for labor has decreased since the late 1990s, and employers no longer need to offer generous health benefits to attract workers. The Internal Revenue Service has eased restrictions on tax-exempt health spending accounts funded by employers. The IRS now allows employees to roll over the unused portion of their spending account and maintain it with their employer even after leaving the company, a development that makes this health care financing model more attractive.

THE UNINSURED

Despite the size and scope of the U.S. system of private and public health insurance, it leaves some 46 million Americans uninsured. Even at the height of the economic boom of the late 1990s, the percentage of uninsured dropped only slightly. Because the uninsured generally cannot pay for care, they must rely on *"safety net" providers,* such as free clinics, federally qualified health centers, and hospital emergency departments. In 2001, people uninsured for at least part of the year received care valued at approximately $99 billion, of which about a third was *uncompensated* (i.e., not paid for out of pocket) (Hadley & Holahan, 2003). Lack of health insurance doesn't just affect people's ability to get health care. High medical debt is the leading cause of personal bankruptcy, the most common reason people lose their homes or cannot get a mortgage or rental property, and makes them unwilling to seek additional health services (Siefert, 2005).

> High medical debt is the leading cause of personal bankruptcy, the most common reason people lose their homes or cannot get a mortgage or rental property, and makes them unwilling to seek additional health services.

While more than 80% of Americans had some form of health insurance in 2002, and people who work for larger employers have more extensive coverage, some 16 million adults are seriously *underinsured,* which is defined as adults who are insured but report either (a) medical expenses amounting to 10% or more of income; (b) among low-income adults, medical expenses amounting to 5%

or more of income; or (c) health plan deductibles that take up 5% or more of income (Schoen, Doty, Collins, & Holmgren, 2005).

INSURANCE FOR SPECIALIZED SERVICES

Another form of uninsurance is lack of coverage for specific types of health care. The most significant services that generally are excluded from regular health insurance are long-term care services for the frail and disabled, dental care, vision care, and prescription drug coverage. When the insurance market was being developed six decades ago, these services were left out for various reasons, and they have never caught up. Long-term care is not covered in most insurance policies because it is generally considered a social service as much as a health care service. Even the Medicare program—specifically designed for the elderly, who are at highest risk of needing long-term care— excludes most forms of long-term care. Dental care and vision care were excluded because they are usually not the domain of physicians and hospitals. Prescription drugs are now the most anomalous exclusion, since today they are such an integral part of the service regimen for so many health problems, but 60 years ago, they were much less central to treatment and generally not very expensive.

In recent years, the insurance market has developed special policies that cover each of these types of services, sold separately from basic health care coverage. Medicare recently added a prescription drug benefit, and many employers now offer some form of prescription drug, dental, and vision care coverage, generally with high coinsurance rates.

Just 6 million U.S. elderly are covered by private long-term care insurance (Potter, 2003), which must be purchased before a person starts to become frail. This type of insurance has not spread widely, mostly because it's expensive relative to the resources of many elderly; an individual policy purchased at age 65 can cost $3,000 a year. If people enroll at an earlier age, annual premiums are lower, but most rarely think about the need for this type of coverage before at least their mid-50s. Many older Americans decide to take their chances and not purchase long-term care insurance because they don't believe they will ever need it. Some do not realize that Medicare doesn't cover long-term care. Others may know that, in most states, they can qualify for Medicaid coverage if they cannot pay for care and they end up spending all of their savings for care. However, in recent years, state governments—which pay a large share of Medicaid costs—have been seeking ways to reduce their responsibility to pay for the long-term care of people who could have purchased private coverage.

Researchers project that the percentage of people who depend on Medicaid coverage for long-term care will decline over the next

25 years (Knickman, Hunt, Snell, Alecxih, & Kennell, 2003). At the same time, they predict that the group of financially independent individuals who could afford most long-term care expenses with current income and savings will grow, as will the proportion of individuals who are neither Medicaid dependent nor financially independent. The latter is the group that tends to spend any savings they may have on health care costs if they have a catastrophic health event, ultimately becoming Medicaid-eligible.

Reimbursement Approaches

The complex U.S. system of reimbursements for health care involves both private and public payers, and changes in one side's approach have implications for the other. Fortunately, policymakers' skill in understanding the implications of reimbursement policies has improved markedly in recent years.

One feature noticeably lacking in most physician and hospital reimbursement approaches is a link to quality. Payment is based on delivery of services, but not necessarily the right services, delivered expertly. After much debate on this subject, and much verbal endorsement of quality care, some health plans are beginning to experiment with incentive payment programs intended to improve the content and effectiveness of services delivered (Strunk & Hurley, 2004; and chapter 15).

HOW DOCTORS ARE PAID

Physician services are a significant component of our national health care bill, accounting for more than one-fifth of all health care spending. Physicians typically work for themselves or in group practices, rather than as salaried employees in clinics, hospitals, laboratories, or other sites. That is to say that most are responsible for generating their own income. Further, they have a great deal of autonomy in caring for their patients. Their decisions and recommendations have a tremendous impact not only on their own incomes, but—because of the tests they order, drugs they prescribe, treatments they recommend, and referrals they make—they greatly influence the whole of health care spending.

The way public and private insurers reimburse physicians for care has changed a great deal in the past two decades. Traditionally, physicians were paid on a fee-for-service basis. They set their price and the patient or insurer paid it. Because insurers simply passed the costs along to employers in the form of higher premiums, which employers in turn built into the price of their products and services, no one had an incentive to keep fees down. Consumers usually did not pay directly for care, so did not pressure for lower prices, and insurers and employers lacked a framework for intervening. The fee-for-service system is often blamed for some of the rapid health care cost inflation since the 1960s, which eventually led to managed care on the one hand and to government regulation of reimbursement rates for Medicare and Medicaid on the other.

In recent years, net income for primary care doctors and most specialists has grown slowly, if at all, and, in some specialties, incomes have actually decreased. Still, medical schools continue to recruit highly qualified candidates, and major physician shortages—which might be expected if reimbursements were truly inadequate—have not occurred. Interestingly, in most areas of the country, physicians have not organized into large group practices, even though this might increase their ability to negotiate better rates.

Government Regulation of Physician Payment Rates

The federal Medicare program responded to price inflation in the late 1980s by developing a complicated set of fixed rates for specific physician services. The system, which covered a large number of services, is called the Resource-Based Relative Value Scale (RBRVS; Hsiao et al., 1988). The rates were determined through detailed research measuring the expected time and other resource inputs that physicians needed to deliver a specific service. A national advisory committee, now called the Medicare Payment Commission, which reports to Congress, guided the process. Physicians must accept the RBRVS rates if they want to serve Medicare patients, and most do.

Each state's Medicaid program also developed physician reimbursement rates, generally adopting the federal "take it or leave it" model. The Medicaid rates are often much lower than the Medicare rates for the same services, which may result in fewer physicians' accepting Medicaid patients. Only 21% of physicians were accepting new Medicaid patients in 2004, and 15% of physicians received no revenue through Medicaid (Cunningham & May, 2006). However, only 54% of primary care physicians were accepting most or all new Medicaid patients (Zuckerman, McFeeters, Cunningham, & Nichols, 2004).

Managed Care

Since the early 1990s, the concept of managed care, discussed earlier, has been private insurers' dominant paradigm for setting physician and hospital reimbursement rates. Currently, the most common approach is to develop a PPO made up of physicians who agree to accept discounted fees. In most markets, each insurer's preferred provider network includes a majority of the area's practicing physicians.

HOW HOSPITALS ARE PAID

Approaches to paying hospitals are similar to the approaches used to reimburse physicians. Medicare and Medicaid offer "take it or leave it" rates, often based on complicated formulas, while private insurers negotiate rates with hospitals individually. Insurers often permit managed care enrollees to use only certain hospitals. The current system has evolved substantially in recent decades; in the past, insurers, including Medicare, generally paid hospitals whatever they said their costs were, as long as costs were considered "reasonable." For many years, this unregulated approach fueled hospital cost inflation, especially when medical technology and new treatments began their rapid expansion. Today, many hospitals operate with small margins—many with negative margins—and must try to overcome shortfalls in government insurance payments with higher charges to private-paying patients (Table 3.3).

Diagnosis-Related Groups and Prospective Payment

In 1983, the federal government introduced a new hospital reimbursement system that dramatically altered the way it paid for Medicare beneficiaries' hospital care. The diagnosis-related groups (DRG) system set rates prospectively—that is, it said up front that it would pay a fixed amount for the hospital stay of a patient with a specific diagnosis and no more (with some outlier exceptions), no matter how much the patient's care eventually cost or how long the hospitalization. Fixed payments gave hospitals a powerful incentive to increase

Table 3.3	Hospital Financial Trends, 1980–2004, Adjusted for Hospitals' Outpatient Activities			
	1980	**1990**	**2000**	**2004**
Aggregate total hospital margins	3.6%	3.9%	4.6%	5.2%
Hospitals with negative total margins	25.7%	27.1%	32.0%	26.5%
Gross revenues from outpatient services	13%	23%	35%	36%
Expenses per hospital admission[a]	$1,851	$4,947	$6,668	$8,166
Payment-to-cost ratios: Medicare	96.5%	89.4%	99.1%	91.9%
Payment-to-cost ratios: private payers	112.9%	127.8%	115.7%	128.9%

[a] Adjusted for hospitals' outpatient activities.
Note. From American Hospital Association. (2006). *Trendwatch chartbook 2006.* Supplementary Data Tables. Retrieved from http://www.aha.org/aha/research-and-trends/health-and-hospital-trends/2006.html

efficiency, minimize unnecessary tests and services, and shorten patients' hospital stays.

In effect, the DRG system was a price system. From an economic perspective, the unusual aspect of the DRG system was that reimbursement rates were set by a "purchaser" rather than a "supplier," and they were set and have been revised not by market forces but by technical and sometimes political considerations.

DRG reimbursement rates are set according to different diagnoses and the resources normally required to treat them (i.e., the intensity of care required). Diagnoses are grouped, combining similar conditions and care needs; a price is set prospectively that reflects the average cost for that group. *Outliers*—patients who have unusually long hospital stays due to unexpected problems—generate extra payments. Each hospital receives DRG reimbursements based on the same formula, with some adjustment for local wages, costs, and other factors.

Per Diem Hospital Reimbursement

Few private insurers or state Medicaid programs have adopted the DRG payment approach and instead continue to negotiate per diem (daily) rates for hospital care. Medicaid programs often set their per diem rates prospectively and require hospitals to accept them. Private insurers in most parts of the country negotiate intensively with hospitals over rates. Insurers and hospitals alike use their market power to influence favorable rates. Insurers—especially if they cover a substantial share of a hospital's potential patient pool—have considerable clout if they can prevent their covered patients from using hospitals with higher rates, whereas hospitals have market power because many employers will not purchase insurance plans that do not include high-quality area hospitals in the network.

This negotiation environment more closely mirrors how prices are set in other markets involving large purchasers and producers (e.g., the market linking automobile manufacturers with the many companies that make auto parts). When the market works smoothly, both parties will come to agreements that push efficiency but leave the supplier—in this case, the hospital—with high enough reimbursements that it can achieve high quality care and stay financially viable.

Current Policy Issues

Most of this chapter describes the enormous amount the United States spends on health care, where the money goes, and how it is paid out. If left unchecked, U.S. health care expenditures are projected to constitute 20% of GDP by 2016. This statistic sounds daunting, but some experts wonder if it is really all that bad. The policy issue is: Can the United States afford these rapid expenditure increases? Or do they impede our ability to purchase other desired goods and services?

> If left unchecked, U.S. health care expenditures are projected to constitute 20% of GDP by 2016.

In purely economic terms, rising health care expenditures indicate a rising demand for health care services. But are we really gaining anything of value? Some economists argue that the nation can afford to spend more on health care if Americans place relatively more value on these services than on forgone non–health care purchases (Chernew, Hirth, & Cutler, 2003). If so, these researchers estimate that spending on non–health care goods and services would continue to rise over a long period of time, although the share of income growth devoted to health care would be larger than it has been historically. This is possible if health care spending rose slightly faster—their assumption was one percentage point—than the GDP. If health spending rose faster than that, then spending on non–health care goods and services would have to drop, rendering health care spending unaffordable. Cutler, Rosen, and Vijan (2006) more recently have estimated that increases in medical spending since 1960 have resulted in increased value in terms of life expectancy.

Other economists argue that allowing health care spending to increase unfettered is not desirable (Altman, Tompkins, Eilat, & Glavin, 2003). They argue that some growth in spending may be desirable, but that the way we spend our health care dollars is often wasteful and inefficient. Uncontrolled growth in health care spending will have a huge impact on employer-based coverage, as employers cut back on benefits, end coverage for retirees (who planned for retirement expecting it), or shift costs to employees.

RETHINKING THE STRUCTURE OF HEALTH INSURANCE

Increasing health care costs will inevitably affect the structure of the health insurance market—public, employment-based, and individual. On the public side, higher costs will force federal and state governments to make trade-offs among competing budget line items. Medicaid and SCHIP programs may have to scale back eligibility or tighten benefits, as is already happening in some states. As individuals covered by public programs receive benefits of lower value, and as fewer people are eligible for them, the demands on safety net providers will increase.

When private insurers face increased costs, they pass them on to employers, who in turn scale back benefit packages or shift costs to employees—again a phenomenon already occurring (Claxton, et al., 2003; Kaiser Family Foundation/Health Research and Educational Trust, 2003). These changes affect the value of these benefit packages, as Len Nichols (2004) described in congressional testimony: "Insurance differs in terms of the kind of financial protection it offers, in the potential for improvement to health it offers, and the humanity of the treatment when you contact the healthcare system." Ultimately, smaller employers may choose to stop offering health insurance altogether. Meanwhile, large employers have the additional option of tinkering with the design of their insurance packages, as they did in the managed care era of the 1990s and more recently with consumer-driven health plans.

VARIATIONS IN COSTS ACROSS MARKETS

Large variations in the use of and payment for health care services occur across local U.S. health care markets. For example, the frequency of cardiac bypass surgery varies by up to four times in different health care markets, from 3 procedures per 1,000 residents in Albuquerque, New Mexico, to more than 11 per 1,000 in Redding, California (Wennberg, Fisher, & Skinner, 2002). These variations are not explainable by differences in the local population or illness prevalence or severity. Instead, they are closely associated with the number of cardiac catheterization labs in different markets.

More recently, researchers have learned that more care is not better. Medicare expenditure data, analyzed by geographic region, indicate that spending more on health care did not give enrollees better access to care, better quality care, better health outcomes, or greater satisfaction with care (Fisher et al., 2003a, 2003b). In the regions that spent more on health care, money is being spent without benefit—in a word, wasted. If these dollars could be saved, they could be reallocated to more productive ends, including slowing the overall growth in health care costs.

> Researchers have learned that more care is not better.

CREATING REIMBURSEMENT INCENTIVES FOR QUALITY

Finally, we cannot talk about the implications of increases in health care spending without addressing the issue of quality of care. In 1999, the Institute of Medicine published a high-profile report—*To Err Is Human: Building a Safer Health System*—that described the failings of the U.S. health care system and outlined a strategy to improve the quality of care (Kohn, Corrigan, & Donaldson, 1999). One of the striking statistics from this report was the number of individuals who die every year due to medical error—estimated to be between 44,000 and 98,000.

In theory, health care purchasers could encourage higher quality care by paying for it. This is a deceptively simple idea, because there is still much debate over how to measure quality, and reimbursement mechanisms linked to quality are in early stages of development. The Center for Studying Health System Change recently reported widespread interest in designing payment incentives for quality: in 7 of the 12 communities center staff visit regularly, they found health plans attempting to figure out how to reward high-quality care (Strunk & Hurley, 2004). They found little standardization in the way plans measure quality, and basically they either provide bonuses or increase regular payments over a multiyear contract.

Analysts also are attempting to determine the business case for quality—that is, the actual financial return from purchasing better quality care on behalf of beneficiaries (Leatherman et al., 2003). The social case for quality care is easily understood, but it's much more complex to calculate savings achieved, particularly short-term savings.

Conclusion

The U.S. approach to financing health care has evolved steadily as the health services delivery system itself has evolved into the nation's largest service industry. Because of a sense that health care is different from other services, this evolution has been relatively uncontrolled and market oriented, even as the public sector expanded its role in paying for the care of poor and elderly Americans. In some ways, our nation's hodge-podge system does work: millions and millions of service transactions occur each year; and, for the most part, providers receive payments that keep them financially viable. But there are growing signs that the many shortcomings in our health care financing system may fracture the entire edifice.

First, health care expenditures continue to rise at rates that make most payers increasingly restive, even if some of these expenditures do actually produce patient benefits. Current financial incentives are not strong enough to force efficiency or encourage significant quality improvements.

Second, the current financing system leaves 45 million Americans uninsured and a substantial number underinsured. The nation's patchwork of safety net and charity care providers includes many institutions that teeter on the brink of insolvency.

Third, from a provider perspective, current financing approaches are far from ideal. While hospitals have had some ability to influence the rates received from private insurers, many physicians believe reimbursements are not adequate to support their increasingly complex practices.

Fourth, hospitals and physicians complain vigorously about the administrative burden of the current financing system. Rates and administrative rules vary among insurers, continuously change, and require substantial resources to handle paperwork, document costs, interact with payers, and collect payments owed. Some research suggests that the total cost to administer the U.S. health system far exceeds that of systems in other countries, such Canada and Great Britain (Himmelstein, Woolhandler, & Wolfe, 2004). While the U.S. system undoubtedly has many frustrating administrative complexities, estimating the administrative costs of the U.S. and Canadian systems is a challenging endeavor. Noted economist Henry Aaron (2003) takes these estimates to task explaining how difficult it is to estimate administrative costs accurately at a single point in time in a nation and then compare them to another nation.

Rising costs make the day ever-closer when problems in the financing of U.S. health care must be addressed. A key issue will be whether to attempt to fix the problems through marginal improvements and one at a time or to attempt to replace the current financing system entirely. This is a debate that needs to engage new thinkers, new leaders, and new researchers in the years to come.

References

Aaron, H. J. (2003). The costs of health care administration in the United States and Canada—Questionable answers to a questionable question. *New England Journal of Medicine, 349*(8), 801–803.

Agency for Healthcare Research and Quality. (2006). *Hospital inpatient services—Mean and median expenses per person with expense and distribution of expenses by source of payment: United States, 2004.* Medical Expenditure Panel Survey Component Data. Rockville, MD: Author.

Altman, S. H., Tompkins, C. P., Eilat, E., & Glavin, M.P.V. (2003, January 8). Escalating health care spending: Is it desirable or inevitable? *Health Affairs,* Web Exclusive, W3-1 to W3-7.

American Dental Association. (2001). *2000 survey of state dental programs in Medicaid.* Catalog Code #5M00. Chicago: Author.

American Hospital Association. (2006). *Trendwatch chartbook 2006.* Supplementary data tables. Retrieved from http://www.aha.org/aha/research-and-trends/health-and-hospital-trends/2006.html

Blendon, R. J., Young, J. T., & DesRoches, C. M. (1999). The uninsured, the working uninsured, and the public. *Health Affairs, 18*(6), 203–211.

Boyd, D. (2003). The bursting state fiscal bubble and state Medicaid budgets. *Health Affairs, 22*(1), 46–61.

Butler, S., & Moffit, R. (2003). Time to rethink the disastrous Medicare legislation. *Web Memo No. 370.* Washington, DC: Heritage Foundation. Retrieved June 4, 2004, from http://www.heritage.org/Research/HealthCare/wm370.cfm

Catlin, A., Cowan, C., Heffler, S., Washington, B., & the Health Accounts Team. (2007). National health spending in 2005: The slowdown continues. *Health Affairs 26*(1), 142–153.

Chernew, M. E., Hirth, R. A., & Cutler, D. M. (2003). Increased spending on health care: How much can the United States afford? *Health Affairs, 22*(4), 15–25.

Christianson, J. B., Parente, S. T., & Taylor, R. (2002). Defined-contribution health insurance products: Developments and prospects. *Health Affairs, 21*(1), 49–64.

Claxton, G., Holve, E., Finder, B., Gobel, J., Pickveign, J., Whitmore, H., et al. (2003). *Employer health benefits: 2003 annual survey.* Menlo Park, CA and Chicago: Kaiser Family Foundation/Health Research and Educational Trust.

Congressional Budget Office. (2003, September). *Growth in medical spending by the Department of Defense.* Retrieved June 16, 2004, from http://www.cbo.gov/showdoc.cfm?index=4520&sequence=0

Cunningham, P., & May, J. (2006). *Medicaid patients increasingly concentrated among physicians.* Tracking Report No. 16. Retrieved January 3, 2007, from http://www.hschange.com/CONTENT/866/

Cutler, D. M., Rosen, A. B., & Vijan, S. (2006). The value of medical spending in the United States, 1960–2000. *New England Journal of Medicine, 355*(9), 920–927.

Davis, K., & Schoen, C. (2003, April 23). Creating consensus on coverage choices. *Health Affairs,* Web Exclusive, W3–199 to W3–211.

Department of Veterans Affairs. (2005). Geographic distribution of VA expenditures for FY 2005. Retrieved January 3, 2007, from http://www1.va.gov/vetdata/docs/W-GDX-FY05(000).xls

Ellwood, M. R., & Ku, L. (1998). Welfare and immigration reforms: Unintended side effects for Medicaid. *Health Affairs, 17*(3), 137–151.

Fisher, E. S., Wennberg, D. E., Stukel, T. A., Gottlieb, D. J., Lucas, F. L., & Pinder, E. L. (2003a). The implications of regional variations in Medicare spending. Part 1: The content, quality, and accessibility of care. *Annals of Internal Medicine, 138,* 273–287.

Fisher, E. S., Wennberg, D. E., Stukel, T. A., Gottlieb, D. J., Lucas, F. L., & Pinder, E. L. (2003b). The implications of regional variations in Medicare spending. Part 2: Health outcomes and satisfaction with care. *Annals of Internal Medicine, 138,* 288–298.

Fronstin, P. (2003, December). Sources of health insurance and characteristics of the uninsured: Analysis of the March 2003 Current Population Survey. *Employee Benefit Research Institute,* Issue Brief 264.

Gabel, J. R., Lo Sasso, A. T., & Rice, T. (2002). Consumer-driven health plans: Are they more than talk now? *Health Affairs,* Web Exclusive. Retrieved July 20, 2004, from http://content.healthaffairs.org/cgi/content/full/hlthaff.w2.395v1/DC1

Glied, S. A., & Borzi, P. C. (2004). The current state of employer based health care. *Journal of Law, Medicine, and Ethics, 32,* 404–409.

Gold, M. (2001). Medicare+Choice: An interim report card. *Health Affairs, 20*(4), 120–138.

Gold, M. (2003, April 2). Can managed care and competition control Medicare costs? *Health Affairs,* Web Exclusive, W176–W188.

Hadley, J., & Holahan, J. (2003, February 12). How much care do the uninsured use, and who pays for it? *Health Affairs,* Web Exclusive, W66–W81.

Himmelstein, D. U., Woolhandler, S., & Wolfe, S. M. (2004). Administrative waste in the U.S. health care system in 2003: The cost to the nation, the states, and the District of Columbia, with state-specific estimates of potential savings. *International Journal of Health Services, 34*(1), 79–86.

Holahan, J., Wiener, J., & Lutzky, A. (2002, May 22). Health policy for low-income people: States' responses to new challenges. *Health Affairs,* Web Exclusive, W187–W218.

Holtz-Eakin, D. (2004). *CBO testimony estimating the cost of the Medicare Modernization Act.* Retrieved May 27, 2004, from http://www.cbo.gov/showdoc. cfm?index=5252&sequence=0

Hsiao, W. C., Braun, P., Dunn, D., Becker, E. R., Chen, S. P., Couch, N. P., et al. (1988). *A national study of resource-based relative value scales for physician services: Final report to the Health Care Financing Administration.* Publication 17-C-98795/1–03. Boston: Harvard University School of Public Health.

Hurley, R., & Somers, S. (2003). Medicaid and managed care: A lasting relationship? *Health Affairs, 22*(1), 77–88.

Kaiser Commission on Medicaid and the Uninsured. (2003, January). *Medicaid benefits: Services covered, limits, copayments and reimbursement methodologies for 50 states, District of Columbia and the territories (as of January 2003). Dental Services.* Retrieved June 17, 2004, from http://www.kff.org/medicaidbenefits/ dentalservices.cfm

Kaiser Family Foundation/Health Research and Educational Trust. (2003, May). *Trends and indicators in the changing health care marketplace, 2003.* Menlo Park, CA: Kaiser Family Foundation.

Kaiser Family Foundation/Health Research and Educational Trust. (2006). Employer health benefits: 2006 annual survey. Retrieved from http://www.kff.org/ insurance/ 7527/upload/7527.pdf

Kaiser Family Foundation, State Health Facts. *Medicaid enrollment: Distribution by enrollment group, FY 2003.* Retrieved April 5, 2007, from http://www. statehealthfacts.org

Kaiser Family Foundation, State Health Facts. *Medicaid spending: Payments by enrollment group, FY 2003.* Retrieved April 5, 2007, from http://www. statehealthfacts.org

Knickman, J. R., Hunt, K. A., Snell, E. K., Alecxih, L. M. B., & Kennell, D. L. (2003). Wealth patterns among elderly Americans: Implications for health care affordability. *Health Affairs, 22*(3), 168–174.

Kohn, L. T., Corrigan J. M., Donaldson, M. S., & Committee on Quality Health Care (Eds.). (1999). *To err is human: Building a safer health care system.* Washington, DC: National Academies Press.

Landers, P. (2003, March 31). Health care as war casualty: Reservists' families give up employer-paid insurance for coverage with big gaps. *Wall Street Journal,* B1.

Leatherman, S., Berwick, D., Iles, D., Lewin, L. S., Davidoff, F., Nolan, T., et al. (2003). The business case for quality: Case studies and an analysis. *Health Affairs, 22*(2), 17–30.

Letsch, S., Levit, K., & Waldo, D. (1988). National health expenditures, 1987. *Health Care Financing Review, 10*(2), 109–123.

Levit, K., Smith, C., Cowan, C., Sensenig, A., Catlin, A., Health Accounts Team. (2004). Health spending rebound continues in 2002. *Health Affairs 23*(1), 147–159.

Nichols, L. M. (2004, March 9). Myths about the uninsured. Testimony prepared for a hearing on the uninsured before the U.S. House of Representatives Committee on Ways and Means Health Subcommittee.

Park, E., & Greenstein, R. (2003). *Medicare agreement would make substantial numbers of seniors and people with disabilities worse off than under current law.* Washington, DC: Center on Budget and Policy Priorities. Retrieved June 4, 2004, from http://www.cbpp.org/11-18-03health.pdf

Park, E., Nathanson, M., Greenstein, R., & Springer, J. (2003). *The troubling Medicare legislation.* Washington, DC: Center on Budget and Policy Priorities. Retrieved June 4, 2004, from http://www.cbpp.org/11-18-03health2.pdf

Poisal, J. A., Truffer, C., Smith, S., Sisko, A., Cowan, C., Keehan, S., Dickensheets, B., & National Health Expenditure Accounts Projections Team. (2007, February 21).

Health spending projections through 2016: Modest changes obscure Part D's impact. *Health Affairs,* Web Exclusive, W242–W253.

Potter, A. (2003). *The evolution of long-term care insurance.* Windsor, CT: LIMRA International.

Reinhardt, U. (2003). The Medicare world from both sides: A conversation with Tom Scully. *Health Affairs, 22*(6), 167–174.

Rice, T., Desmond, K., & Gabel, J. (1990). The Medicare Catastrophic Coverage Act: A post-mortem. *Health Affairs, 9*(3), 75–87.

Schoen, C., Doty, M. M., Collins, S. R., & Holmgren, A. L. (2005, June 14). Insured but not protected: How many adults are underinsured? *Health Affairs,* Web Exclusive, W5–289 to W5–302.

Siefert, R. W. (2005). *Home sick: How medical debt undermines housing security.* Boston: Access Project. Retrieved from http://www.accessproject.org/adobe/home_sick.pdf

Strunk, B. C., & Hurley, R. E. (2004). *Paying for quality: Health plans try carrots instead of sticks.* Issue Brief No. 82. Washington, DC: Center for Studying Health System Change. Retrieved June 16, 2004, from http://www.hschange.com/CONTENT/675

U.S. Centers for Medicare & Medicaid Services. (2007). Overview: State Children's Health Insurance Program. Retrieved from http://www.cms.hhs.gov/LowCost HealthInsFamChild/

U.S. Centers for Medicare & Medicaid Services (2005). *Medicaid managed care penetration rates by state as of June 30, 2005.* U.S. Department of Health and Human Services. Retrieved July 2006, from http://www.cms.hhs.gov/medicaiddatasourcesgeninfo/downloads/mmcer05.pdf

U.S. Centers for Medicare & Medicaid Services, Office of the Actuary. (2007a). Retrieved April 5, 2007, from http://www.cms.hhs.gov/NationalHealthExpend Data/downloads/PieChartSourcesExpenditures2005.pdf

U.S. Centers for Medicare & Medicaid Services, Office of the Actuary. (2007b). Retrieved April 5, 2007, from http://www.cms.hhs.gov/NationalHealthExpend Data/downloads/proj2006.pdf

U.S. Department of Health and Human Services. (2004). *Indian Health Service Fact sheet.* Retrieved June 16, 2004, from http://www.ihs.gov/PublicInfo/Public Affairs/Welcome_Info/ThisFacts.asp

U.S. Department of Labor, Employee Benefits Administration. (2004). *Fact sheet: Consolidated Omnibus Budget Reconciliation Act of 1985.* Retrieved June 22, 2004, from http://www.dol.gov/ebsa/newsroom/fscobra.html

Veterans Health Administration. (2004). *Health benefits and services: General information.* Retrieved June 22, 2004, from http://www1.va.gov/health_benefits/page.cfm?pg = 1

Wennberg, J. E., Fisher, E. S., & Skinner, J. S. (2002, February 13). Geography and the debate over Medicare reform. *Health Affairs,* Web Exclusive, W96–W114.

Zuckerman, S., McFeeters, J., Cunningham, P., & Nichols, L. (2004, June 23). Trends: Changes in Medicaid physician fees, 1998–2003: Implications for physician participation. *Health Affairs,* Web Exclusive, W4–374 to W4–384.

4

Key Words

health
public health
World Health Organization
   (WHO) definition of
   health
prevention (primary,
   secondary,
   and tertiary)
population focus

determinants of health
public health infrastructure
core functions
assessment
policy development
assurance
cross-sector collaboration
state public health
   department

local public health
   department
categorical funding
essential services
health promotion
modifiable risk factor
social justice
utilitarianism
state public health laws

Public Health: Policy, Practice, and Perceptions

Laura C. Leviton, Scott D. Rhodes, and Carol S. Chang

Learning Objectives

- Contrast defining characteristics of public health and curative health care.
- Describe the federal, state, and local authority for public health law, regulation, and services.
- Identify issues and concerns with the current system.
- Identify ways to address current issues and concerns.

Topical Outline

- Defining characteristics
- Core functions of public health
- Federal agencies and activities
- State and local health department organization, law, and activities
- Challenges and opportunities for public health

his chapter introduces the policies, programs, and practices that constitute public health in the United States. Public health is defined by the Institute of Medicine (IOM) as "organized community efforts aimed at the prevention of disease and promotion of health" that focus "on society as a whole, the community, and the aim of optimal health status" (Institute of Medicine, 1988, pp. 39, 41). It is the science, practice, and art of protecting and improving the health and quality of life of communities and populations. Historically, public health focused on regulating and improving community sanitation and monitoring environmental hazards; today, the role of public health has expanded to include documenting and controlling communicable diseases, health promotion to encourage healthful behavior, and policy advocacy.

The first section of this chapter describes the distinctive goals and activities of public health. It describes the defining characteristics of public health that differentiate it from curative health care and outlines the core functions of public health. We then describe the complex network of laws, regulation, authority, and services involved. State, federal, and local government agencies, often called the *infrastructure,* are legally responsible for core public health functions (Institute of Medicine, 2003a). In addition, a wide variety of other public, private, and nonprofit organizations carry out responsibilities that affect the public's health. Finally, we turn to new developments and challenges for the future. Public health is in trouble. Health experts have warned about the system's disarray for close to 20 years. The challenges are formidable: the political and economic dominance of medical care; fragmented responsibility for achieving public health goals; widespread inattention and misunderstanding of public health's role; and, occasionally, a clash of values between public health and other social goals. Recently, some positive new developments show a better road ahead for public health.

Public Health Every Day

Imagine waking up and going through your morning routine. You slept 8 hours for a change, because health experts claim that lack of sleep causes stress and other health problems. You do wonder, though, whether the experts will claim something different next month. You wander into the bathroom and brush your teeth—they are still in your mouth thanks to adequate nutrition, the fluoride in your local water supply, and routine dental visits—and not because of the dental hygiene you learned in school, but rather the fear of bad breath. You rinse your mouth with water from the faucet knowing that it is safe to drink. Before the water ever reached your faucet, it was checked for heavy metals such as lead (which causes lower intelligence in children) and chemicals such as polychlorinated biphenyls, which cause cancer. When you flushed the toilet, you were sure that the waste would not get into the water supply and kill you.

You get your children ready for school; so far, they have all survived, never having had measles, diphtheria, polio, or other diseases that killed and maimed so many children in bygone days. The kids' breakfast includes cereal and pure pasteurized milk. (The kids talked you into buying the cereal they saw advertised on television. You looked at the nutritional label and thought the ingredients were okay.)

You open the newspaper to see that the authorities are monitoring a cluster of new flu cases—it looks as though a new influenza strain is spreading. The authorities reassure the public that the cluster is not avian flu, although the Europeans are reporting new cases in chickens. Your sister calls to announce she is going to have a baby! She is able to have children because she never got infected with a sexually transmitted disease, which is one cause of infertility. She is not aware that the toast she is eating is fortified with folic acid, the B vitamin that prevents birth defects.

The two of you also discuss your father. He needs to get his flu shot right away! The last time he got flu, he went to the hospital with pneumonia and could have died. Both of you are worried about him, because he is overweight, still smokes, and never exercises. Is a heart attack, diabetes, or stroke in his future? The odds are not in Dad's favor. Quit-smoking programs are available in the community without charge, so you agree that Dad's doctor should try suggesting them again. Too bad there are no sidewalks in Dad's neighborhood; he loves to walk, but there is too much traffic. Does the senior center have an exercise program that might appeal to him? You buckle the kids into their safety belts, confident that the car's design will protect you and your family from injury. When you get to your job, you see an updated sign that reads: "607 days without an accident at this worksite."

> Public health affects the lives of Americans profoundly, but more often than not it is invisible to them.

Public health affects the lives of Americans profoundly, but more often than not it is invisible to them.[1] Table 4.1 lists some of the organizations, public policies, and activities that underlie the protections described in this scenario.

---

[1] This scenario was adapted from a brochure for state legislators that describes the value of public health at a level anyone can appreciate (Hooker & Speissegger, 2002).

Table 4.1   Public Health Protection Every Day

Public Health Issue	Federal Responsibility	Other Responsibility
Guidance and Education		
Sleep	NIH, CDC, SAMHSA, OSHA (shift workers)	Popular press, medical care providers, schools
Nutrition	FDA, USDA, ODPHP	Schools, medical care, nutritionists, and dieticians
Dental hygiene	CDC, NIH, Surgeon General	State and local health departments, schools, dental and medical care
Healthy weight	ODPHP, NIH, CDC	Popular press, medical care, state and local health departments, American Heart Association, AARP
Communicate risk of new infectious diseases	CDC, USDA, Homeland Security	State and local health departments, World Health Organization
Smoking	ODPHP, NIH, CDC	Popular press, medical care, state and local health departments, the courts, American Heart Association, American Lung Association
Physical activity	ODPHP, NIH, CDC	Popular press, medical care, state and local health departments, American Heart Association, AARP, urban planners, YMCA, YWCA, Sierra Club
Seat belts	ODPHP, CDC, NHTSA	State and local health departments, schools, medical care, popular press
Law and Regulation		
Public Health Issue	Federal Responsibility	Other Responsibility
Fluoridation		State law, county and municipal codes
Drinking water	EPA, FEMA	State and local health departments, state and local departments of environment, municipal water authority/sanitary districts
Childhood immunization	DHHS regulation (standing orders to immunize)	State health codes (reportable disease) and immunization requirements
Food labeling, pure milk	FDA, EPA	State inspection programs (some)
Reproductive health—STD control		State health codes (reportable diseases)
Folic acid	FDA	

Table 4.1 *(Continued)*

Law and Regulation		
Public Health Issue	**Federal Responsibility**	**Other Responsibility**
Seat belts		All state transportation laws
Car safety	NHTSA, other U.S. Department of Transportation	State laws
Safety at work	OHSA	State laws and agencies
Prevent or contain new infectious diseases	CDC, USDA, Homeland Security	State and local health departments

Services		
Public Health Issue	**Federal Responsibility**	**Other Responsibility**
Nutrition	USDA, HHS (various)	State agencies, school districts, food pantries
Dental care	CMS, HRSA	State agencies, school districts, dentists
Immunization	CMS, HRSA	State agencies, local health departments, school districts, medical providers
Reproductive health—STD control	CDC (training, guidance, lab oversight)	State and local health departments, medical care, family planning and other nonprofit organizations, medical care, pharmacies (condoms)
Folic acid	USDA (WIC)	State and local health departments, medical care, pharmacies
Healthy weight		Medical care, private and nonprofit organizations (e.g., Weight Watchers™)
Smoking	HHS (various)	American Cancer Society, American Heart Association, American Lung Association, state and local health departments, medical care, private organizations (SmokeEnders™), pharmacies (nicotine replacement)
Physical activity		Senior centers, American Heart Association, AARP, YMCA, YWCA, parks and recreation department, Sierra Club
Prevent or contain new infectious diseases	HRSA, CDC, USDA	State and local health departments, state and local emergency management departments, World Health Organization, hospitals, Red Cross

Who Is in Charge of Public Health?

The responsibility for public health and the infrastructure to make it work are divided among many agencies across all levels of government. Nongovernmental organizations also share responsibility for public health: professional associations, businesses and corporations, private and nonprofit organizations. Table 4.1 illustrates the diffused responsibility for public health, although a comprehensive list of protections would consume the rest of this chapter. Public health law, regulation, and organizational practice are like snowballs rolling downhill, gathering new layers over time. At least four general reasons account for the complexity and diffuse responsibility of public health in the United States:

- Decentralized governmental authority
- Our tendency to create problem-specific infrastructure and policies
- A general reliance on private and nonprofit entities
- The large size of the public health–related domain

The first factor that makes the public health field so complex is our country's pattern of decentralized government; in the Constitution, states are given responsibility for public health, except where specified by federal law. How much responsibility the states in turn share with local government varies a great deal across and within states, and rests with diverse agencies, boards of health, and municipal codes.

Second is the distinctive American tendency, first recognized in 1839, to design laws, policies, and associations that are problem-specific, rather than general (de Tocqueville, 2001). For example, individual diseases receive special legal recognition, and new federal programs are created to deal with them. Diverse federal departments deal with such health problems as assuring pure food and drugs, monitoring and controlling infectious diseases, providing guidance to prevent chronic diseases, improving traffic safety, and assuring a healthy place to work. Political interests also cause fragmented responsibility. For example, in response to the meat industry, the U.S. Department of Agriculture (USDA) inspects meat products, while the Food and Drug Administration (FDA) inspects most other foods; the USDA inspects frozen lasagna if it has meat in it, but the FDA inspects vegetarian lasagna.

A third, also distinctively American, approach is the heavy reliance on nonprofit organizations, rather than government, to achieve public health goals. Yet nonprofit organizations in the United States also tend to be issue-specific. For example, the American Heart Association, the Planned Parenthood Federation of America, the Environmental Defense Fund, the American Foundation for AIDS Research, and local AIDS service organizations each arose to meet a specific health-related need.

The fourth cause of diffused responsibility lies in the broad definition of health goals and debates over what should be done to achieve them. The World Health Organization defines health as more than the absence of disease. Health is "a state of complete mental, physical and social well-being" (World Health Organization, 1978). Well-being is achieved, for example, when children perform well in school and do not fear neighborhood violence, when physical and mental functioning is maintained well into old age, and when people have a better quality of life. Social, behavioral, and environmental forces have by far the largest role to play in determining health status. But where, then, do we draw the line between health goals and other societal goals? Should we draw such a line? Who has responsibility, and for which goals? There is no correct answer to these questions, but there are superior ways for public health leadership to meet their challenge. One that we will discuss at length in this chapter is cross-sector collaboration.

Defining Characteristics of Public Health

Three key assumptions distinguish public health from the health care delivery systems discussed elsewhere in this text: (a) a healthy population is in the public interest; (b) health is strongly determined by community and societal-level forces; and (c) working at a collective or community level, these forces can be marshaled to improve a population's health.

A HEALTHY POPULATION IS IN THE PUBLIC INTEREST

The Health of Populations

Public health focuses on the *health status of entire populations,* not just individuals. It is concerned with the incidence, prevalence, and distribution of health problems, as described in chapter 2. In using these indicators, public health aims to identify health problems and improve them through action at a community or collective level. This aim is well justified by past successes. Most of the increased life expectancy seen in the 20th century was not caused by curative medical care, but by pervasive improvements in sanitation and nutrition—classic public health arenas (Institute of Medicine, 1988).

> Most of the increased life expectancy seen in the 20th century was not caused by curative medical care, but by pervasive improvements in sanitation and nutrition—classic public health arenas.

Public health also takes action on the *health risks of the whole population.* The focus on populations discards the idea that only sick people need care and other people can be ignored. Rather, a continuum of risk exists for many diseases and injuries in the population as a whole (Institute of Medicine, 2003a). For example, the average American has a one in three chance of a serious motor vehicle accident in his or her life time (National Highway Traffic Safety Administration [NHTSA], 1997). Public health efforts try to reduce injuries, not only for the groups at highest risk—for instance, drunk drivers—but for everyone at risk—that is, people who ride in cars. Everyone is protected by laws requiring seat belts and child restraints, not just people with poor driving records. In the same way, public health takes action to address Americans' risk of heart disease. Public health intervenes with entire populations to reduce cholesterol and high blood pressure, encourage physical activity and smoking cessation, and help people maintain healthy weight (U.S. Department of Health and Human Services, 2000a).

The Public Interest Justification

Since ancient times, people have sought collective means to protect themselves when faced with plague, famine, and environmental disaster (Fee & Fox, 1988; Rosen, 1993). Prevention became increasingly effective through science and technology in the 19th century, when bacteriology emerged as a discipline and cities created clean water and sanitation systems (Duffy, 1992). In that era, public health was justified mostly on utilitarian grounds: the greatest good for the greatest number. Healthy people were a more productive workforce and better able to defend the nation (Rosen, 1993).

Today, the justification for public health has changed. In 1978, the World Health Organization formally redefined health as a human right, and identified public health as a means to achieve social justice. Some Americans question whether social justice is a legitimate public health concern. In truth, a blend of utilitarian and social justice arguments support most public health services today, and too much attention to the one argument can obscure the other. For example, many health departments provide medical care to the poor. But is this strictly a way to achieve social justice? It is also utilitarian if it produces healthy children, better able to learn, and a healthy work-force. Even when a public health department provides medical care, it is promoting health and preventing disease—for example, when it immunizes children and promotes healthy pregnancies. Such medical services benefit all of society in the long run.

Some writers question whether collective action and community benefit jeopardize individual liberty (Leviton, Needleman, & Shapiro, 1997). Public health policy and practice are usually a balance between individual freedoms and collective benefits. For example, health departments have police powers to control infectious disease, but they need to do so without appearing to abuse this power.

Finally, some may question whether public health is a good use of tax money. Public health agencies at all levels of government reflect the mixed economy of the United States. They address some market failures of both curative and preventive care. A case in point is the treatment and prevention of sexually transmitted diseases (STDs), which are highly infectious, widespread, and dangerous. Chlamydia and gonorrhea are especially dangerous for women and often have no symptoms (Eng & Butler, 1997). Many private providers do not routinely screen for STDs and thus greatly underdiagnose them. Private providers have neither authority nor resources to identify and treat an affected patient's sexual partners, which is the key to preventing the patient's reinfection and the infection of additional people. Because STDs are a clear and present danger to the community, health departments can require treatment and will confidentially notify sexual partners. Readers may find this topic distasteful, but health departments have to take responsibility for these dangerous diseases in a realistic, objective way. Public health services often involve jobs that nobody else wants.

HEALTH IS STRONGLY DETERMINED BY COMMUNITY AND SOCIETAL-LEVEL FORCES

Determinants of Health

McGinnis and Foege (1993) established that a fairly short list of behav-ioral and environmental forces cause about half of all avoidable deaths (see chapter 2 for more information on these risk factors). The Institute of Medicine (2003a) revised that figure upward to 70% after reviewing evidence on a broader range of health determinants. Health care ser-vices (mostly doctor and hospital services) are not the primary ways to avoid such deaths, and they make a fairly small contribution to avoid-ing mortality overall. Yet health care services account for an estimated 95% of federal health expenditures, even though effective public health interventions would do much more to improve health (McGinnis, Williams-Russo, & Knickman, 2002). "It then follows that the nation's heavy investment in the personal health care system is a limited future strategy for promoting health" (Institute of Medicine, 2003a, p. 21).

Figure 4.1 portrays health determinants as a series of concentric circles, each at increasing distance from the innate characteristics of the individual at the core. Similarly, some writers describe a chain of events influencing health, in which "upstream" forces, such as policies and environmental conditions, can affect "midstream" forces, such as behavior and other disease precursors. Although medical treatment can address upstream and midstream factors, it is primarily a "downstream" force, focused on remedy for a specific disease or injury. Public health, by contrast, typically seeks to affect upstream and midstream factors. As Kreuter and Lezin (2001, p. 4) note:

> Both a focus on the individual and a focus on populations are important in order to achieve improvements in health. A population health approach stimulates us to consider a different and broader set of options for improving and sustaining health—not to replace a focus on individuals, but to complement and support it.

Challenges for Public Health Policy

A focus on these broader determinants raises several questions. How far upstream should the public health mission extend? Which of the many upstream, midstream, or downstream forces should be its focus? Should the intervention consist of law, regulation, partnerships with community leaders, collaboration with other private or nonprofit organizations, specific services, guidance and education, or a combination of these?

Green and Kreuter (1999) provide a useful framework to evaluate where and how public health might intervene. Decision makers need to consider the *importance* of a particular force (How big an effect does it have on health status?), its *prevalence* (How commonly does it affect the population?), and its *modifiability* (How feasible is it to change this force?). Most important, decision makers should want to know *how effective* the changes are likely to be, for improving health outcomes and quality of life. Public health funds are very limited, and difficult choices must be made about funding priorities. Yet with notable exceptions, the public health field has been slow to adopt evidence-based practice or the analysis of effectiveness and cost-effectiveness (Fielding & Briss, 2006; Leviton & Guinan, 2003).

COMMUNITY AND COLLECTIVE INTERVENTIONS WILL IMPROVE HEALTH

Disease Prevention and Health Promotion

At the *individual* level, the focus of prevention is on probabilities: reducing one's chances (risk) of disease. At the *population* level, the

Figure 4.1

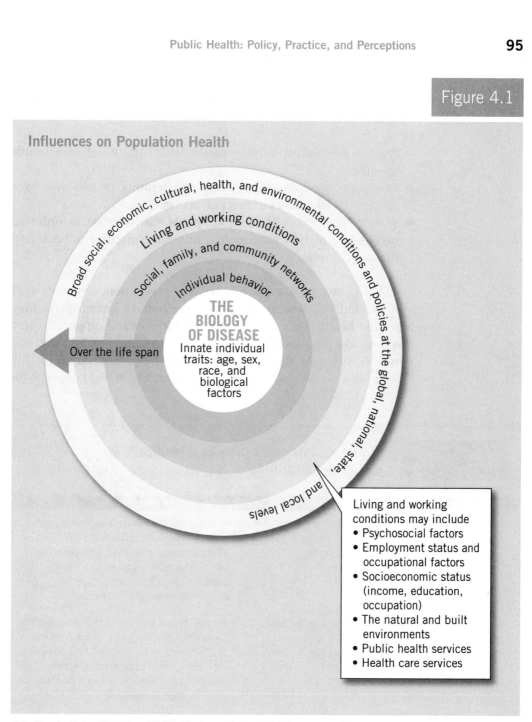

Influences on Population Health

Broad social, economic, cultural, health, and environmental conditions and policies at the global, national, state, and local levels

Living and working conditions

Social, family, and community networks

Individual behavior

THE BIOLOGY OF DISEASE

Innate individual traits: age, sex, race, and biological factors

Over the life span

Living and working conditions may include
- Psychosocial factors
- Employment status and occupational factors
- Socioeconomic status (income, education, occupation)
- The natural and built environments
- Public health services
- Health care services

Note. From Institute of Medicine. (2003). *The future of the public's health in the 21st century.* Washington, DC: National Academy Press. p. 52.

reduced risk for individuals translates into percentages or proportions: that is, a lower rate of preventable diseases and injuries. The reduced burden of disease and injury is the nation's return on investment in prevention.

The U.S. Preventive Services Task Force (1996) uses three long-accepted categories to describe the full array of potential preventive interventions:

- *Primary prevention,* helping people avoid the onset of a health condition.
- *Secondary prevention,* identifying and treating people who have developed risk factors or preclinical disease.
- *Tertiary prevention,* treating an established disease in order to restore the highest functioning, minimize negative impact, and prevent complications.

These categories, especially tertiary prevention, obviously spill over into individual medical care delivery, but at a systems level, they are public health issues. Providers need guidance and support to carry them out. We can see the differences in Table 4.2 for heart disease and stroke. Notice that successful prevention for an individual (in this case, a person who might have a heart attack or stroke) depends on

Table 4.2	Differences Between Individual Medical Care and Public Health Role	
	Individual Medical Care	**Public Health Role**
Primary prevention	Encourages patients to maintain healthy weight, be physically active, and not smoke	Works to establish bike and walking paths, works to eliminate trans fats from foods, offers smoking quit-lines, advocates for smoke-free public spaces and higher cigarette taxes, provides prevention guidelines to medical care providers
Secondary prevention	Regular checkups for detection and treatment of high blood pressure, elevated cholesterol, and other risk factors	Mounts public service campaigns about the importance of controlling blood pressure and "knowing your number" for cholesterol, provides guidelines to medical care providers on diagnosis of blood pressure and hypercholesterolemia
Tertiary prevention	Medical treatment to save the heart muscle after a heart attack or prevent complications from stroke, treatment of atherosclerosis, cardiac rehabilitation and medication to restore function and prevent recurrence	Provides guidelines to medical care providers, creates widespread awareness of the symptoms of heart attack and stroke and the need to seek help quickly, provides CPR training, provides automated external defibrillator machines in public places and worksites, establishes effective emergency systems, sponsors patient support groups

the widespread availability of prevention services at a *population* level. In this sense, even planning for the rapid deployment of ambulances becomes a public health issue. Planning and developing prevention services requires a public health problem-solving approach, described in the next section.

Health promotion works to achieve the WHO definition of health as being more than the absence of disease. It is defined as "the combination of educational and environmental supports for actions and conditions of living conducive to health" (Green & Kreuter, 1999). Health promotion often focuses on prevalent types of behavior, termed *behavioral risk factors* or *lifestyle factors,* that promote or impair health (see chapter 10). Preventable risks and unhealthy behavior that can be changed are called *modifiable risk factors.* An important resource for public health, *Healthy People 2010,* provides a comprehensive review of modifiable risk factors, effective strategies, and public health objectives for the nation (U.S. Department of Health and Human Services, 2000a). The priority areas for these public health objectives are presented in Table 4.3. Disease prevention and health promotion are rarely completely effective, because there are no "magic bullets" for most health problems. A residual group of people will continue to fall prey to illness and injury. For example, heart attacks still occur, even with all the best primary and secondary prevention strategies that are currently in place.

> Disease prevention and health promotion are rarely completely effective, because there are no "magic bullets" for most health problems.

Prevention strategies vary in their effectiveness, cost-effectiveness, and public acceptability. Combining several strategies can have a cumulative benefit. Motor vehicle injury presents a case in point: safer roads and cars and stiffer penalties for drunk driving helped reduce the rate of injury and deaths, but air bags still make a major additional contribution. Even with all these protections, driver and passenger behavior—such as the use of seat belts and child restraints—still matter. Using seat belts prevents 45% of fatalities that would otherwise occur, 50% of severe injuries (60% in light trucks), and 16% of minor injuries (NHTSA, 1997).

Universal and Targeted Prevention

Universal prevention means that everyone receives the interventions equally, while *targeted prevention* involves identifying and serving people at higher risk of disease or injury. When they are possible, universal approaches are often more effective to improve the health of populations. The case of traffic safety illustrates these approaches. People who drive while intoxicated are clearly at highest risk of injury, and targeting drunk drivers has improved road safety generally. However, universal protections, such as seat belts, air bags, and safer vehicles contribute much more to reducing traffic fatalities and

Table 4.3   *Healthy People 2010 Focus Areas*

Healthy People 2010 is a comprehensive set of national disease prevention and health promotion priorities and objectives for the first decade of the 21st century. It was created by scientists both inside and outside of government, with the overarching goals of increasing quality and years of healthy life and eliminating health disparities in the following 28 areas:

1. Access to quality health services	15. Injury and violence prevention
2. Arthritis, osteoporosis, and chronic back conditions	16. Maternal, infant, and child health
3. Cancer	17. Medical product safety
4. Chronic kidney disease	18. Mental health and mental disorders
5. Diabetes	19. Nutrition and overweight
6. Disability and secondary conditions	20. Occupational safety and health
7. Educational and community-based programs	21. Oral health
8. Environmental health	22. Physical activity and fitness
9. Family planning	23. Public health infrastructure
10. Food safety	24. Respiratory diseases
11. Health communication	25. Sexually transmitted diseases
12. Heart disease and stroke	26. Substance abuse
13. HIV	27. Tobacco use
14. Immunization and infectious diseases	28. Vision and hearing

Note. Retrieved from http://www.healthypeople.gov

injuries, because they help everyone, even those who never encounter a drunk driver (NHTSA, 1997).

People at the highest risk of disease or injury are an important focus for public health when the risk is prevalent and when there are effective means to identify and treat them. For example, a national campaign in the 1970s led to improved identification and treatment of people with high blood pressure. This, in turn, greatly reduced premature death and disability from cardiovascular disease (U.S. Centers for Disease Control and Prevention, 1999). However, an initial goal was to make sure that providers screened *all* their patients for high blood pressure, a universal strategy with a population focus.

In many cases, targeting those at highest risk can reduce the overall burden of disease and injury in the population. For example, prevention of HIV has shifted from raising awareness in the entire population, to a three-tiered approach. The first priority is to identify individuals already infected with the human immunodeficiency virus (HIV), in order to give them early treatment, reduce their viral load to forestall progression to the full-blown disease known as AIDS, and encourage them to avoid infecting others. The second priority targets individuals whose behavior puts them at high risk of HIV infection through unprotected sex or needle-sharing. Finally, the third priority is to create continued awareness of the need for prevention in the population at large (Janssen, Holtgrave, Valdiserri, Shepherd, & Gayle, 2001).

Core Functions of Public Health

The other defining characteristic of public health is its distinctive approach to problem solving for population-level health issues. This approach involves three core functions: assessment of health problems, policy development to take action on those problems, and assurance that the proposed actions are taken (Institute of Medicine, 1988).

DEFINITION OF CORE PUBLIC HEALTH FUNCTIONS

Assessment

The statistical tools basic to public health assessment were described in chapter 2. This chapter, by contrast, describes what decision makers and practitioners do with these statistics in their *assessment of public health problems:* their prevalence, their severity, and their causes. Public health agencies have the primary responsibility for a number of data-gathering and analysis activities: surveillance of population health status, monitoring of disease trends, and analysis of the causes of those trends. However, they do not carry out these functions by themselves. They are highly dependent on people and institutions that provide the information. For example, health care providers are required by law to report new cases of certain infectious diseases—AIDS, anthrax, botulism, measles, malaria, STDs and tetanus, to name a few. Maintaining a high level of cooperation with these providers is essential.

With the advent of electronic health records, shared databases, high-speed computing and connectivity, public health surveillance and analysis is undergoing profound changes. These improvements are timely in light of the need for rapid responses to potential bio-terrorism, the need to pinpoint and analyze outbreaks of infectious diseases, and containment of virulent new infectious diseases, such as avian influenza and Severe Acute Respiratory Syndrome (SARS) (Institute of Medicine, 2003a, 2003b). Even with new technology, however, public health surveillance will only be as good as the information that others provide.

Policy Development

The second core function is to *create and advocate for solutions* to achieve public health goals. Policy development activities can be formal or informal. Formal policy development includes devising laws and regulations to protect the public, as in the case of environmental protection; funding and reimbursement for specific services such as child immunizations; and setting guidelines or standards for services such as laboratory testing for infectious diseases. The informal policy development process is also important. Public health organizations do not have the legal authority, financial capability, or personnel to address all health problems by themselves. Realistically, public health agencies need to engage other organizations, community leaders, and professionals in planning and problem solving. In many instances, these other organizations have the ability to affect a public health outcome—in promoting worker safety or building bicycle paths, for example—even without direct involvement of a public health agency.

Assurance

This third core function involves *enforcement of policy,* as in the case of sanitation inspections in restaurants or nursing homes; *ensuring proper implementation* of necessary services, as in the supervision of home visits to new mothers in disadvantaged communities; and *adequate crisis response,* as when public health plays a role in emergency preparedness. (As described below, many public health departments take on a special assurance function—direct health care provider—to assure that indigent Americans get health care.)

Again, however, public health organizations cannot assure by themselves that all the relevant activities are accomplished and accomplished well. For example, local health departments are helped a great deal when people who live and work in their area voluntarily comply with health and safety codes. Similarly, at the national level, the Occupational Safety and Health Administration cannot protect workplace safety everywhere, constantly. Workplace inspections and prosecution of violators are costly, labor intensive, and not very frequent; voluntary compliance is essential. Likewise, the Department of Agriculture cannot thoroughly inspect every last chicken for salmonella and other problems—resources are too limited and legal challenges too easy (Institute of Medicine, 2003c). When public health agencies collaborate with business, other organizations, and public agencies, assurance is often more effective.

PUBLIC HEALTH PROBLEM SOLVING: AN EXAMPLE

The following example, concerning the birth defect spina bifida, illustrates the cyclical problem-solving approach used in public health (Figure 4.2). Different types of assessment, policy development, and assurance issues emerge as public health professionals:

1. define the health problem (in this case, spina bifida), its magnitude, and nature
2. identify causes and protective factors
3. develop and test intervention strategies
4. implement the interventions
5. evaluate the impact of the interventions
6. revisit and refine these activities.

Figure 4.2

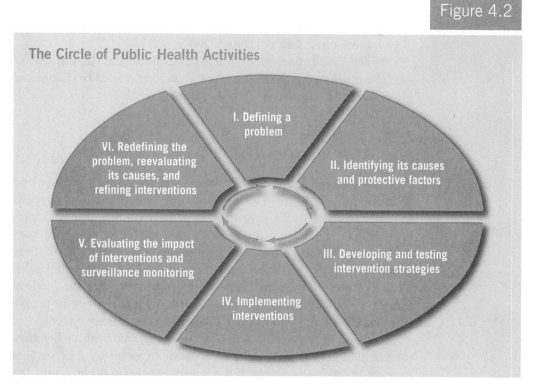

The Circle of Public Health Activities

I. Defining a problem

VI. Redefining the problem, reevaluating its causes, and refining interventions

II. Identifying its causes and protective factors

V. Evaluating the impact of interventions and surveillance monitoring

III. Developing and testing intervention strategies

IV. Implementing interventions

Note. From U.S. Department of Health and Human Services. (2001). *The Surgeon General's call to action to prevent and decrease overweight and obesity.* Rockville, MD: Author. p. 3. Last revised January 11, 2007.

1. ***Define the problem:*** Spina bifida is a neural tube defect[2] that, in its most severe form, leads to leg paralysis, bowel and bladder control problems, and, without treatment, mental retardation. Spina bifida affects between 1,500 and 2,500 U.S. infants every year—approximately 1 in every 2,000 live births (*Assessment*).

2. ***Identify causes:*** The March of Dimes (2004) projects that up to 70% of spina bifida cases can be prevented if women take enough folic acid (a B vitamin) before and during pregnancy. Folic acid is most effective in promoting healthy neural tube development when taken before pregnancy and during the critical first weeks. For this reason, the March of Dimes recommends that, even before they become pregnant, women take a multivitamin with 400 mg of folic acid every day and eat foods rich in folic acids (*Policy Development*).

3. ***Develop and test interventions:*** Unfortunately, women may not know they are pregnant until it is too late, and the defect has developed. Also, foods that naturally contain folic acid may not be readily available to the poor (*Assessment*). One alternative is to fortify common foods with folic acid (*Policy Development*).

4. ***Implement the interventions:*** Since 1998, enriched cereal, pasta, flour, and bread products have been required to include folic acid (*Assurance*).

5. ***Evaluate their impact:*** After this requirement was introduced, one study found a decrease of 19% in neural tube defects *(Assessment)* (March of Dimes, 2004).

6. ***Revisit and refine:*** Many scientists believe that the amount of folic acid in grain products is not enough and want to change the regulation to increase it *(Policy Development)*.

CORE FUNCTIONS: OVERLAP OF ROLES AND RESPONSIBILITIES

The public health focus on populations and prevention overlaps and complements the focus of health care delivery systems. This happens in several ways. Health care delivery systems often deal with prevention, but at the individual level. Many public, private, and non-profit organizations recommend, require, or train providers to deliver preventive services. In these ways, other entities are doing public health work. Conversely, many public health departments are the medical provider of last resort, providing standard medical services for people who cannot obtain them through the health care delivery system.

Health care delivery systems also overlap public health when they use population health indicators. For example, an insurance company may study the health status of the lives it covers (in other words, the

---

[2] Neural tube defects occur early in pregnancy, when the neural tube, which eventually develops into the spine and brain, does not form properly.

population of families that pay for coverage). Whether it does so in the public interest or to save money is irrelevant. When such private-sector interests are in line with public health goals, then alliances become possible to achieve those goals. Alliances across sectors and interests have successfully tackled issues ranging from infection control to improving the quality of preventive services, to problem solving around migrant health, to teen pregnancy prevention (Leviton et al., 1997).

These overlaps may seem confusing, but the key to understanding public health is that, in the United States, *no single organization or governmental agency has complete responsibility for public health goals.* Medicine, government, insurance companies, employers, researchers, schools, and many other organizations and individuals are working toward public health goals whenever they focus on prevention and population health.

> Medicine, government, insurance companies, employers, researchers, schools, and many other organizations and individuals are working toward public health goals whenever they focus on prevention and population health.

Governmental Authority for Public Health

FEDERAL AUTHORITY AND INFRASTRUCTURE

Although the states have constitutional authority to implement public health, a wide variety of federal programs and laws assist them. Many federal agencies have primary responsibility for public health, and most are involved in other issues as well.

U.S. DEPARTMENT OF HEALTH AND HUMAN SERVICES

The U.S. Department of Health and Human Services (DHHS) is the principal federal agency for assuring health and providing essential human services. All of its agencies have some responsibility for prevention. Through 10 regional offices, the DHHS coordinates closely with state and local government agencies. The DHHS funds these agencies, as well as private sector and nonprofit organizations, to provide a variety of services. In the **DHHS Office of the Secretary,** there are two units important to public health:

- The **Office of the Surgeon General** of the United States. The Surgeon General is appointed by the president and has the primary duty to provide leadership and authoritative, science-based recommendations about the public's health. For example, the Surgeon General's 1964 report that smoking causes cancer stimulated most of the work eventually leading to the dramatic decline in smoking in the United States. More recent Surgeon General's reports have addressed AIDS, suicide, obesity, and oral health. The Surgeon General has titular responsibility for the 6,000 commissioned officers of the Public Health Service, who have positions throughout the DHHS and also may be assigned to universities or state and local health departments.

● The **Office of Disease Prevention and Health Promotion (ODPHP).** ODPHP has an analysis and leadership role for health promotion and disease prevention. ODPHP produced *Healthy People 2010*, the latest in a series of reports on important health objectives for the nation that have both broad consensus and a scientific basis.

Public Health Service

The eight health agencies of the DHHS are organized under the Public Health Service (PHS) as follows:

● The **Centers for Disease Control and Prevention (CDC)** is the lead federal agency that develops and implements disease prevention and control, environmental health, and health promotion/health education activities. The CDC is an authoritative source of information and guidance for state and local health departments. A hallmark of the CDC's approach is the promotion of health through strong community partnerships in the United States and abroad. Working with state governments and other partners, the CDC manages a health surveillance system to monitor and prevent disease outbreaks (including bioterrorism), implements strategies for both infectious and chronic disease prevention, and maintains national health statistics. Working with the World Health Organization, the CDC guards against international disease transmission and has U.S. personnel stationed in more than 25 foreign countries.

● The CDC director also administers the **Agency for Toxic Substances Disease Registry (ATSDR),** which helps prevent exposure to hazardous substances from waste sites that appear on the U.S. Environmental Protection Agency's National Priorities List. ATSDR creates toxicological profiles of chemicals at these sites.

● The **National Institutes of Health (NIH)** constitute the world's premier medical research organization and comprise 27 institutes and centers. The NIH supports more than 35,000 research projects on diseases such as cancer, Alzheimer's disease, mental illness, arthritis, and HIV/AIDS. Much of the basic science and clinical research supported by NIH is directly or indirectly relevant to prevention, and epidemiological (population-level) studies into the causes and risk factors for disease are often generously funded. The NIH also conducts some population-level prevention programs and demonstration projects, but the agency faces a challenge when it comes to translating its research into practical services for wide-spread public health application.

- The **Food and Drug Administration (FDA)** assures the safety of all food except for meat and poultry; all prescription and non-prescription drugs; blood products, vaccines, and tissues for transplantation; medical equipment and devices that emit radiation, including microwave ovens; animal drugs and feed; and even cosmetics. New products that are designed to treat human conditions or diseases must be evaluated by FDA reviewers for safety and effectiveness before they are made available to consumers. Products can be as simple as a toothbrush or a nonprescription analgesic and as complex as a state-of-the-art excimer laser or the latest drug to treat HIV. To be approved, these products must meet FDA's rigorous standards, and they must continue to meet them while on the market.

- The **Health Resources and Services Administration (HRSA)** helps build the health care workforce through many training and education programs. It also helps prepare the nation's health care system and providers to respond to bioterrorism and other public health emergencies. Through the Bureau of Maternal and Child Health, the HRSA administers a variety of programs to improve the health of mothers and children. Working with the CDC, it coordinates HIV prevention and treatment for people living with HIV/AIDS.

- The **Substance Abuse and Mental Health Services Administration (SAMHSA)** works to improve the quality and availability of substance abuse prevention, addiction treatment, and mental health services. SAMHSA provides funding through block grants to states to support substance abuse and mental health services and helps to improve substance abuse prevention and treatment through the identification and dissemination of best practices. SAMHSA also monitors the extent of substance abuse in American society.

- The **Agency for Healthcare Research and Quality (AHRQ)** supports research on health care systems and quality, including ways to introduce more preventive services into primary care. It houses the U.S. Preventive Services Task Force, an independent panel that reviews evidence on the effectiveness of clinical preventive services and develops recommendations for primary care and preventive practice.

- The **Indian Health Service (IHS)** provides health services to federally recognized American Indian and Alaska Native tribes. IHS is the principal federal health care provider and health advocate for native people, and its goal is to raise their health status to the highest possible level.

Other DHHS Agencies

- Readers may find it odd that the **Centers for Medicare & Medicaid Services (CMS)** appears in a list of agencies that affect public health. However, CMS plays a vital role in primary, secondary, and tertiary prevention through its reimbursement (or not) of preventive services and its influence on state Medicaid and SCHIP programs. Through its policies, the CMS can determine whether health care providers get paid for routine mammograms and adequate prenatal care, for example, and, through its initiatives to "pay for quality," the CMS can require that the most effective and cost-effective prevention practices become widely used.

- The **Administration for Children and Families (ACF)** is not a health agency, but it is responsible for approximately 60 programs that promote the economic and social well-being of children, families, and communities. Many of these programs are strongly linked to prevention and to population health, or they incorporate prevention into their services. The ACF administers the state-federal public assistance program called Temporary Assistance for Needy Families (TANF), the national child support enforcement system, and the Head Start program. ACF provides funds to help low-income families pay for child care, supports state foster care and adoption assistance programs, and funds programs to prevent child abuse and domestic violence.

- The mission of the **Administration on Aging (AoA)** is to promote the dignity and independence of older people and to help society prepare for an aging population. AoA is not a health agency, but it is part of a federal, state, tribal, and local partnership called the National Network on Aging. This network consists of 56 State Units on Aging, 655 Area Agencies on Aging, 243 tribal and native organizations, and more than 29,000 local community-service organizations. Ranging from primary prevention activities in senior centers to tertiary prevention through adult day care centers, AoA activities promote health by promoting successful aging.

Other Federal Agencies

A variety of other federal agencies have important roles in promoting population health:

- The **Veterans Health Administration (VHA)** is part of the Department of Veterans Affairs, the second largest cabinet-level agency. VHA is available to serve the needs of the nation's approximately 26 million military veterans. As a major provider of health care, the VHA, like the CMS, provides preventive services.

- The **U.S. Department of Agriculture (USDA)** was created to help America's farmers and ranchers, but today it also focuses on prevention and the health of populations. It is responsible for the safety of all meat, poultry, and egg products. Through its Food and Nutrition Service, the USDA leads the federal antihunger effort and promotes good nutrition through the Food Stamp, School Lunch, School Breakfast, and the Women, Infants, and Children (WIC) programs. The USDA sets nutrition guidelines and publicizes its food guidance system. It is a research leader in everything from human nutrition to new crop technologies. It works with state cooperative extension services in both urban and rural areas to educate the public on nutrition, sanitation, health education, and family life (e.g., parenting skills). The USDA brings adequate housing, modern telecommunications, and safe drinking water to rural U.S. communities. Finally, the USDA plays a vital role in environmental health through the National Forest Service, new technologies to minimize the use of pesticides, and conservation of soil and water on private land.

- The **Environmental Protection Agency (EPA)** is an independent agency that develops and enforces environmental regulations for many aspects of the environment, including clean air and water, keeping food free of pesticide contamination, preventing and cleaning up contaminated sites, handling hazardous materials, and much more. The EPA delegates monitoring and enforcement to states and tribes, and about half of the EPA's budget supports state environmental programs. Where national standards are not met, EPA has legal authority to enforce them and impose penalties. It supports research, assessment, and education to improve decision making about environmental issues and works with a wide variety of private, nonprofit, state, and local organizations on voluntary programs and research.

- The **National Highway Transportation Safety Administration (NHTSA),** an agency within the U.S. Department of Transportation, is responsible for preventing death, injury, and economic loss due to motor vehicle crashes. This is accomplished by setting and enforcing safety performance standards for motor vehicles. Grants to state and local governments support local highway safety programs, including reducing the threat of drunk drivers and promoting the use of seat belts, child safety seats, and air bags.

- The **Occupational Safety and Health Administration (OSHA),** an agency of the U.S. Department of Labor, sets and enforces standards for the safety and health of workers, encourages continual workplace safety improvements; partners with state health and safety organizations, business, and labor to create safer work environments; and provides training, outreach, and education on health and safety.

● Several other federal agencies have duties relevant to public health: for example, the Department of Housing and Urban Development (to provide clean and safe places to live), the Department of Homeland Security (to prevent and coordinate response to terrorist attacks and natural disasters), the Consumer Product Safety Commission (enforcing the Poison Prevention Packaging Act and getting unsafe products off the market), the Federal Bureau of Investigation (enforcing the Federal Anti-Tampering Act), the Department of Transportation (enforcing the Sanitary Food Transportation Act), and even the U.S. Postal Service (enforcing laws against mail fraud, with respect to the sale of ineffective or dangerous drugs and supplements).

Federal and State Relations

Although the 10th Amendment to the U.S. Constitution gives the states primary responsibility for public health, states must constantly interact with these federal agencies. For example, the DHHS provides substantial support directly to state health departments in the form of block grants for maternal and child health and preventive services, and to state agencies for child welfare services, substance abuse, and mental health. The CDC provides grants and cooperative agreements to states, cities, and community-based organizations for HIV prevention and for chronic disease control. The USDA provides health departments with direct support for WIC services and nutrition education. The EPA provides direct resources to the states for environmental management. Most of these funding streams are *categorical*—that is, the funding is intended for specific categories of people or special purposes. Congress authorizes categorical funding to address a specific health problem such as preventing AIDS or infant mortality. However, categorical funding limits states' flexibility to deliver a range of relevant services with available resources. Even the block grants, which aim to give states flexibility in the use of funds, are still relatively narrow in purpose.

Both the state and federal governments have strengths and resources to respond to the concerns of the country's citizens. States and localities are closer to the communities that they serve and often better understand local conditions and how these affect services. Meanwhile, the federal government generally has greater resources and scientific expertise for tackling large and complex health threats. The CDC, for example, leads the investigation of serious disease outbreaks such as SARS. The federal government also becomes involved when health threats cross state borders, even though its intervention can sometimes increase confusion about which public health agency is responsible for which actions and services. In the crisis situations most likely to trigger federal intervention, clear lines of authority and communication are obviously essential.

Sometimes state and local public health standards and services exceed federal regulations or guidelines. Sometimes states cannot comply with federal regulations, such as EPA pollution standards, and the federal government must step in. In other cases, a national guideline is recommended, not regulated. When a state cannot meet the recommended guideline, the federal government may provide technical assistance and financial support. However, federal intervention can sometimes undermine the already fragmented provision of public health services within states and local communities.

STATE AND LOCAL AUTHORITY AND INFRASTRUCTURE

Power and Position of State Public Health Departments

The 50 states vary greatly on how they define and delegate public health authority and responsibility. States enacted public health statutes over time to respond to specific diseases or health threats. These laws are fragmented and badly out of date (Gostin, 2000; Institute of Medicine, 1988; 2003a, 2003b). For example, some state laws have separate sections for specific communicable diseases, instead of standard approaches to address infectious disease in general. This leaves them with no standards for addressing new infectious diseases, such as SARS or the West Nile virus. Some state public health statutes do not reflect advances in public health practice and constitutional law, or they neglect important safeguards for privacy and due process and against discrimination. Inconsistencies between states create problems when diseases and emergencies cross state lines, as they would in the event of bioterrorism.

> Inconsistencies between states' public health laws create problems when diseases and emergencies cross state lines.

The state health officer directs the department of public health and may report directly to the governor or to an officer in the governor's cabinet. The health department's position in the chain of command affects the power of its director and the quality of the services it manages. In 2005, 29 state public health departments were freestanding, while 21 were bureaus within a larger umbrella department (Beitsch, Brooks, Menachemi, & Libbey, 2006). Umbrella departments combine public health with other health-related programs such as Medicaid, human services and welfare, mental health and substance abuse, or environmental management. Medicaid and public assistance programs, being among the costliest state programs, tend to garner most of a governor's attention.

The way various health-related programs are organized affects how well public health activities can be coordinated. For example, environmental protection is often located outside the health department, in which case conservation, wilderness preservation, or litigation around toxic spills may head that agency's agenda. This situation often leaves less opportunity for effective interaction with the health department, even though it must monitor potential health consequences of environmental exposures.

Organization of State and Local Public Health Departments

A 2005 survey classified the way that the states share power between state and local public health departments (Beitsch et al., 2006). Thirteen states have *centralized* public health powers whereby state law assigns both general and specific public health responsibilities to a comprehensive department of health. In the centralized approach, there are no autonomous local public health departments, only satellite offices around the state. Centralized departments are responsible for the administration of public health care, the control of communicable diseases, population-focused health promotion, and environmental health. Even within the centralized model, other agencies will have a role in public health.

Twenty-one states use a *decentralized* approach in which the state public health agency does not directly perform public health services and minimally regulates local and municipal services. The state delegates public health authority and direct responsibility to local communities, which are often the first to be affected by public health challenges. Often this means that municipalities create a board of health and a local health department. In the decentralized approach, citizens expect both formal and informal community leaders to offer public health solutions and provide services.

Sixteen states take a hybrid approach to the distribution of public health powers; they use either a *mixed* or a *shared authority* model. These states share public health functions between the state and local governments. For example, the state legislature may assign primary responsibility for certain functions to the state department of health, while delegating other specific functions to local governments. The local public health authorities enjoy independence from state control over their assigned responsibilities, but on some matters they must defer to the state department of health.

The National Association of County and City Health Officials (NACCHO) Web site (www.naccho.org) offers further detail on the range of organizational arrangements, responsibilities, and authority of local health departments. One reason that state-local health department arrangements are so varied is simply historical. The first public health agencies were formed in the early 1800s and were primarily city-based. The next wave occurred later in the 19th century when state health agencies began to form. Finally, throughout the 20th century, county health departments developed. One can see the effects by comparing older states to states that were admitted to the union more recently: New Jersey has hundreds of municipal and county-level health agencies, while Oregon has 24 county health departments.

Essential Public Health Services

State responsibilities for public health generally include disease and injury prevention, sanitation, controlling water and air pollution, vaccination, isolation and quarantine, inspection of commercial and residential premises, food and drinking water standards, extermination of vermin, fluoridation of municipal water supplies, and licensure of physicians and other health care professionals. However, the activities and services provided vary widely across states and localities. In the face of this variation, public health professionals agree that all health departments should provide the 10 essential services listed in Table 4.4. The ability of every health department to do so is questionable. Most are seriously understaffed. Staff skills in many local health departments are weak. Large numbers of the most experienced professionals are on the verge of retirement (Gebbie & Turnock, 2006). Well-trained personnel are needed to replace them, and an adequate supply is in some doubt. Departments with under-trained staff cannot be expected to establish effective partnerships with other organizations, particularly those in the highly profession-alized health care sector. The erosion of resources, workforce competencies, and leadership are all issues that public health needs to address. The way they are doing so is the subject of the final section of this chapter.

Public Health Departments as the Provider of Last Resort

Beginning in the mid-1970s, many state and local health departments shifted their resources away from infectious disease control (and other traditional public health initiatives) and increased their efforts to become direct providers of primary and preventive care for the underserved. As a result, health departments have become an increasingly important part of the medical safety net for people who have limited options for care. By the late 1980s, for example, 92% of local health departments were immunizing children, 84% were providing other child health services, and nearly 60% were offering prenatal care services. At the same time, many health departments provide large amounts of specialty care services, especially to populations underserved by the traditional medical community. For example, many county health departments provide mental health services.

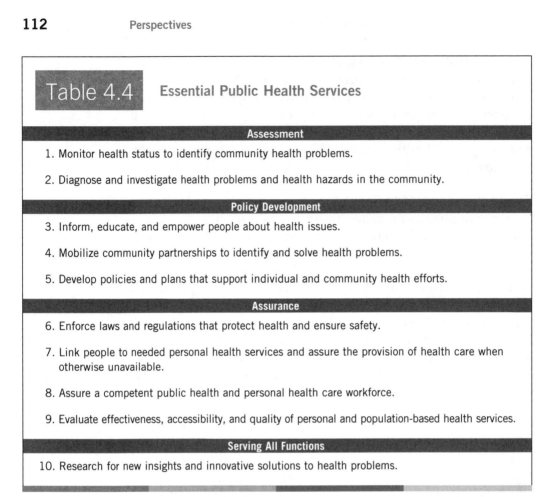

Table 4.4	Essential Public Health Services
Assessment	
1. Monitor health status to identify community health problems.	
2. Diagnose and investigate health problems and health hazards in the community.	
Policy Development	
3. Inform, educate, and empower people about health issues.	
4. Mobilize community partnerships to identify and solve health problems.	
5. Develop policies and plans that support individual and community health efforts.	
Assurance	
6. Enforce laws and regulations that protect health and ensure safety.	
7. Link people to needed personal health services and assure the provision of health care when otherwise unavailable.	
8. Assure a competent public health and personal health care workforce.	
9. Evaluate effectiveness, accessibility, and quality of personal and population-based health services.	
Serving All Functions	
10. Research for new insights and innovative solutions to health problems.	

Note. Abstracted from Institute of Medicine. (2003a). *The future of the public's health in the 21st century.* Washington, DC: National Academy Press.

Most treat STDs. Still others care for people with AIDS (Wall, 1998). As demographic trends in the United States change, public health departments have been challenged and constitute the major provider of services to meet the health needs of non–English speaking immigrants, such as Latinos (Rhodes et al., 2007).

The emphasis on direct-care services was prompted by the growing number of people without health insurance and by the growing number of communities in which the local health department was the only or at least the primary source of care for the medically indigent. At the same time, however, the growing emphasis on direct-care services meant fewer resources for activities to improve the health of *populations.* This shift prompted concern among many public health leaders. The public health department seemed to be retreating from its core mission (population-based activities) just as the nation was experiencing an epidemic of public health problems.

Challenges and Opportunities

In order to maintain public protections and make further progress, public health must overcome three daunting challenges. It must improve the infrastructure of health departments. It must better communicate its value to the public and engage the wide variety of organizations that are so vital to carrying out its goals. And it must restore both leadership and effective advocacy. This section describes some positive new developments for public health.

IMPROVING THE INFRASTRUCTURE

Throughout this chapter, we have illustrated how the public health infrastructure—the capacity of public health agencies to carry out their essential functions—is in trouble. This can lead to absurd situations. We know an infectious disease physician who was bitten by a bat, but her health department could not test the bat for rabies. Another colleague dialed the state health department hot line one evening during the anthrax crisis, and the state epidemiologist answered the phone because no one else was available. These represent serious infrastructure flaws. But several recent developments provide hope for improvement.

Improving Public Health Competencies and Organizational Effectiveness

There has been considerable movement to upgrade the competence of individual public health workers. Performance standards have emerged both for individuals and agencies. It is believed that these help public health to be better accountable for its activities and effectiveness. Demonstrating accountability is believed to be critical to gain and maintain essential resources for public health.

Working with national public health organizations such as NACCHO and the Association of State and Territorial Health Officials (ASTHO), the CDC developed the National Public Health Performance Standards Program (U.S. CDC, 2004). One section of the program provides guidance on the specific competencies needed for jobs in public health laboratories, informatics, and environmental health technology. The performance standards may eventually become requirements. Already they provide the basis for voluntary certification in several states, as well as a plan for national voluntary accreditation of local health departments (Gebbie & Turnock, 2006). Meanwhile, they help to clarify what is expected of workers who provide public health services. The standards may also help to motivate improvements by identifying and publicizing gaps in the infrastructure.

Schools of public health are vital to many of the country's public health functions. However, only a relatively small percentage of today's health department employees have an advanced public health degree. The existing workforce needs to be upgraded through new continuing education programs, management academies, and certificate programs. The curriculum in schools of public health is moving toward a focus on community problems, required experiences in public health practice, and subject matter that, in general, makes closer contact with the realities and needs of public health agencies (Institute of Medicine, 2003a).

The Robert Wood Johnson Foundation–funded Turning Point initiative was an effort to transform the U.S. public health system into a more effective, community-based, collaborative, and responsive system. Begun in 1997, Turning Point operated through state and local partnerships in selected states and through several collaborative working groups. In particular, a performance measurement collaborative worked to assess and monitor agency performance using the CDC standards. Turning Point also initiated important work on public health law and on cross-sector collaboration, described below.

In 2002, NACCHO began a process to define what people in any community can reasonably expect local health departments to provide, regardless of where they live. As of this writing, the process is still under way. The Operational Definition aims to develop a shared understanding of public health, and thus promote consistency and accountability of local health departments. The Operational Definition uses the framework of the 10 essential services listed in Table 4.4, and will be the basis for local health department standards for a planned national system of public health agency accreditation.

An important national development is the movement toward the accreditation of state and local governmental public health departments. Public health agencies are not currently subject to national standards or reviewed by an external accrediting body. However, there is consensus on the need for such accreditation. A national accreditation system for public health could provide benchmarks for continuous quality improvement practices, establish a mechanism for accountability, and strengthen the credibility of public health agencies. By 2004, several states had already begun their own accreditation or performance assessment systems. These states include Michigan, Washington, North Carolina, Illinois, New Jersey, Ohio, and Florida. In 2006, both ASTHO and NACCHO endorsed the recommendations of a joint Exploring Accreditation Project for a voluntary national accreditation program and committed to moving forward with implementation (http://www.exploring accreditation.org).

New Responsibilities for Public Health

Since the anthrax attacks in 2001, public health agencies have faced the added responsibility of protecting the public against bioterrorist threats and other public health emergencies, such as pandemic influenza. In a normal flu season, influenza takes the lives of about 37,000 people in the United States and between 250,000 and 500,000 worldwide (http://www.pbs.org/wgbh/rxforsurvival/series/diseases/influenza.html). Up to 50 million Americans get the flu each year, and 200,000 Americans are hospitalized (National Foundation for Infectious Diseases, 2006). Influenza costs the U.S. economy about $12 billion annually in direct medical costs and loss of productivity (Garrett, 2005). Although the annual toll is significant, influenza has the potential to become far more lethal, because the viruses can mutate rapidly into new strains. Three times during the 20th century, new flu strains have generated pandemics causing high death rates and great social disruption. In 1918, an estimated 1 billion people had influenza worldwide. Between 40 and 50 million died in 18 months—several times the total number of deaths in all of World War I. In the United States alone, 550,000 lost their lives to the disease. Subsequent pandemics were much milder, but the consequences were still significant. An estimated 2 million people died in 1957 and 1 million in 1968 (Center for Infectious Disease Research & Policy, 2007).

Experts agree that another flu epidemic is not only inevitable, but also likely to happen soon. A severe form of human influenza—one that attacks not just the respiratory system but every tissue of the body—can originate in birds, chickens, and pigs. Avian flu was not known to strike humans, but in 1997, the H5N1 avian flu strain successfully made this cross-species leap. If a strain evolves that can spread from human to human, the virus could spread rapidly, possibly reaching all continents in less than 3 months. Because most people will have no immunity to the pandemic virus, infection and illness rates will be high. The World Health Organization (2005) estimates 2 million to 7.4 million possible deaths.

Public health systems are the cornerstone of pandemic preparedness and response. Public health surveillance systems must be able to pick up unusual clusters of cases and signal the first instances of human-to-human transmission at the earliest possible moment. Vaccines are the single most important intervention for preventing influenza morbidity and mortality, during both seasonal epidemics and pandemics. Public health departments play a critical role in developing and implementing vaccination strategies, including important logistics and monitoring functions. Further, public health departments must now be skilled in risk communications to give the public clear messages. They must coordinate with other local, state, and federal public health entities as well as health care, law enforcement, Red Cross, business, and other community partners. They must share information electronically across jurisdictions and levels of government. This requires investment in new information technology, not only for likely pandemics but for other emergencies and disasters as well (Lurie, Wasserman, & Nelson, 2006).

New Resources for Public Health

The anthrax attacks vividly highlighted public health's shortfalls and led both the public and policymakers to pay renewed attention to it. With the possibility of additional biological, chemical, or radiological attacks fresh in mind, Congress appropriated much more funding to the CDC and state health departments to prepare. This influx has permitted some improvements—enabling new hires, upgrades to the Health Alert Network, and improved informatics. According to ASTHO, this additional funding has indeed strengthened the overall public health infrastructure, in addition to fortifying the country against terrorism (Steib, 2004). At the same time, funding for other essential functions has not kept pace, and the nation's capacity to respond effectively to a biological or chemical attack remains one of the most important unknowns of the 21st century (Lurie et al., 2006).

Improved Public Health Statutes

The Turning Point initiative developed a Model State Public Health Act that takes a systematic approach to establishing authority and implementing public health responsibilities. As of October 2006, the Model Act has been introduced in whole or in part through 110 bills or resolutions in 33 states, of which 44 have passed. An update and summary of the Model Act can be found at http://www.publichealthlaw. net/Resources/Modellaws.htm#TP. The act is divided into nine articles that address current and future health threats. It posits that a public health law should include:

- modern surveillance techniques and reporting practices
- epidemiologic investigations in response to specific outbreaks or high rates of diseases or conditions among subpopulations
- testing and screening for existing and emerging conditions
- immunization for vulnerable populations, including children and others at risk of disease transmission
- responsible and respectful use of quarantine and isolation, where warranted, in cases of communicable conditions.

While the Model Act addresses inconsistencies within a state, other improvements are needed for problems that cross state lines. Currently, the states and localities have mutual aid agreements and laws that permit government personnel to work across state borders during emergencies. However, incompatible state privacy laws could be a serious problem in the event of bioterrorism or natural disasters such as Hurricanes Katrina and Rita. In those instances, Gulf Coast residents from at least three states were evacuated to every state of the union, where they were served by emergency personnel brought in from still other states. The DHHS Office of Civil Rights, which administers HIPAA, the nation's primary health information primacy law, has developed a tool to help sort out conflicting privacy standards (http://www.hhs.gov/ocr/hipaa/decisiontool), but imagine trying to use this tool in an emergency!

Finally, a Model State Public Health Emergency Powers Act has been introduced in whole or in part through 171 bills or resolutions in 44 states. Thirty-eight states have passed a total of 66 bills or resolutions that include provisions from or are closely related to the Act (http://www.publichealthlaw.net/Resources/Modellaws.htm#MSEHPA). Among other features, the act requires a comprehensive plan for coordination of services and logistics in public health emergencies, authorizes quarantine, provides for disposal of human remains and infectious materials, and facilitates coordination among jurisdictions and levels of government (Speissegger & Runyon, 2002).

PUBLIC RELATIONS FOR PUBLIC HEALTH

True public relations means relating effectively and constructively to the public, and it is possibly the most important competency for public health. Public health needs to build a constituency that understands its value. Creating coalitions, gaining allies to address public health problems, effective advocacy, and managing a multicultural workforce requires skill in interpersonal relations, not technical expertise (Nelson & Essien, 2002).

Effective communication about public health issues is a key competency that needs much more attention (Institute of Medicine, 2003a, 2003b). The general public does not understand what public health is, often supposing it refers to programs for the poor. Nor do terms such as *disease prevention* or *health protection* do much better in conveying what public health is all about. Public health professionals have difficulty articulating the importance of their work and the issues it addresses. For example, when they talk about infrastructure, they too often assume that outsiders know what the term means concretely and why it is so important.

The public—and policymakers—react to specific problems and crises. They do not see the disease and death that has been prevented. And when an eroded infrastructure hinders crisis response—such as when the 2001 anthrax episode overwhelmed many public health

> The public—and policymakers—react to specific problems and crises. They do not see the disease and death that has been prevented.

laboratories or after Hurricane Katrina, when even such a basic function as handling the dead broke down—they do not understand why the problem is not solved quickly. Another reason for policymaker inattention may be that formally recognized public health programs have such small federal budgets compared to entitlement programs such as Medicare and Medicaid or the research program of the National Institutes of Health. With this in mind, how can public health develop an effective public constituency?

Public Health Flashpoints

Public health goals can sometimes conflict with other social or political agendas. The most prominent example in recent decades has been the prevention of AIDS. Because men who had sex with men were the first group known to contract AIDS, policy support for its prevention was slow in coming, and many social conservatives expressed the belief that "gays deserved AIDS" (Shilts, 1987). Public views certainly did not change when injection drug users started to contract AIDS. In fact, opposition to dealing with the epidemic remained high, even when HIV began to affect women and infants. Indeed, throughout history, people have blamed outsiders ("dirty foreigners") for epidemics of infectious disease and believed that personal character flaws caused illnesses such as tuberculosis (Fee & Fox, 1988). Even today, blaming the victim is a surprisingly common reaction to a range of public health problems.

The very methods of public health can conflict with other definitions of the public interest. For example, although using condoms is one of the few effective ways to prevent HIV/AIDS, social conservatives are unwilling to promote condom use because it appears to sanction sex outside of marriage. Similar objections have been raised regarding a new vaccine to prevent infection with the sexually transmitted human papilloma virus, which can cause cervical cancer. To be most effective, the vaccine should be administered to young women before they are sexually active, and, again, social conservatives oppose it on the grounds that it would promote sexual activity.

Fluoridation offers another case in point with a surprising political twist. Originally, opposition to community water fluoridation came from right-wing groups who believed fluoridation was a communist plot. Today, opposition comes from small, but vocal segments of the antigovernment, alternative medicine, and environmental movements. Over one-third of the U.S. population does not have fluoridated water, and whether to fluoridate—or keep fluoridating—is being loudly debated in many communities. Yet fluoridation is the single most cost-effective way to achieve oral health and one with decades of demonstrated safety (National Academy of Sciences, 2006; U.S. DHHS, 2000b).

Building and Maintaining Public Trust

Public health practitioners sometimes tend to be authoritarian and paternalistic, especially when they stress science and technology while ignoring collaboration and democratic process. This tendency weakens their connections to grassroots groups and local leadership. The last years of the 20th century heightened public awareness of the need for a new form of leadership in public health—one that engages people on their own terms to engender trust and cooperation. For example, the populations most at risk of AIDS had no reason to trust authority figures, and often were not seen in health care systems until it was too late. It was imperative for public health leadership to engage the grassroots leadership that was most trusted by people at risk. It was imperative to approach people where they live and congregate, to give them the message of AIDS prevention through people they trusted and saw every day (Leviton & Guinan, 2003). Similar challenges arose in the environmental movement. Over time, the EPA learned to work with communities affected by toxic contaminants. But in the early days, it did not listen to the public about their concerns, did not provide the information they needed, or gave them incomprehensible techno-babble that enraged community leaders (Leviton et al., 1997). Bureaucratic ways of doing business were simply not effective when people had legitimate concerns.

The most difficult lesson for public health came from the Tuskegee Syphilis Study (Jones, 1993). In 1932, 600 poor African American men in Macon County, Alabama, became syphilis research subjects without their knowledge, when the Public Health Service and the Tuskegee Institute began a study of the natural course of syphilis, offering the men free medical care. Of 600 subjects, 339 had syphilis but were left untreated for up to 40 years, even though a penicillin cure became available in 1947. As many as 100 of the men died of syphilis before a public outcry and a federal advisory panel's recommendations halted the study in 1972. Along with the Nuremberg Code on medical experiments, this episode led Congress to require a wide variety of new protections for human research subjects. In 1997, President Bill Clinton offered an official public apology to the Tuskegee Study's eight survivors and participants' families. However, public health—and the health care system more generally—has never fully regained African Americans' trust.

More Effective Communication

Public health professionals are addressing the challenges of public relations in a variety of creative ways. The organization Research! America (www.researchamerica.org) has conducted polls on public awareness of public health over the past few years, and, thanks in part to its media advocacy, there is a growing understanding of what public health is. NACCHO and ASTHO have generated materials to explain public health in a more engaging way (NACCHO, 2006). To improve communication about specific health risks and strategies, the CDC has developed *CDCynergy,* a computer-based tool to improve practitioners' communication about health risks, disease, and public health activities. Materials for improved communication are updated constantly at the CDC Web site (http://www.cdc.gov/communication/cdcyenergy.htm), but the field still has a long way to go.

Effective Policy Voices

ASTHO and NACCHO offer important tools to their membership to increase effectiveness in state and local policy and politics. **Research! America** presents a toolkit for advocates to engage Congress and state lawmakers in support of public health. Professional organizations such as the American Public Health Association attempt to convey the importance of the public health mission and to advocate for needed changes.

The Trust for America's Health (2006a) is emerging as an especially vigorous and articulate champion. The trust advocates passionately for attention to specific health problems—what Americans generally respond to—tying these issues to the need for better public health infrastructure. Advocacy in public health generally has a two-fold purpose. It can be aimed at strengthening the public health infrastructure through resources and reorganization, but it can also aim to achieve goals outside the formal agency structure. For example, advocacy led to increased taxes on cigarettes and bans on smoking in public places and is generating new state and local policies to increase the school physical education requirement, bring recess back into the school day, and require healthier offerings in school cafeterias (Trust for America's Health, 2006b).

A positive national development is the growing number of state-level public health institutes (PHIs). These institutes are outside state government and can accept private funds and implement ideas much more quickly than health departments. PHIs also are more flexible than state bureaucracies. Institute staff can advocate vigorously for public health programs and funding, whereas state employees have limits. PHIs can sometimes offer a credible, neutral, third-party voice on issues and can convene all the interested parties to address a broad health problem and implement a multisector strategy. In general, health departments are quite positive about PHIs and see their value (Institute of Medicine, 2003b).

Local public health departments have always connected to grassroots leadership and other public services in order to solve collective problems. However, their leadership abilities for cross-sector collaboration are now being cultivated as never before, in what has become known as the collaborative leadership approach. For example, Colorado's data on health status were reported by race and ethnicity for the first time in 2001, leading residents to realize that the state's African Americans had an overall life expectancy that was 4 years less than Whites. The state's Turning Point program began working with communities to build awareness of health disparities. Together, they advocated for a more diverse public health workforce and developed a Citizen's Advisory Commission on Minority Health. In 2004, Colorado formed an Office of Health Disparities within the state health department to continue work on this issue.

Collaborative leadership means understanding where public health shares common goals with other interest groups and building coalitions based on those common interests. For example, the state health officer of Nevada managed to fluoridate the entire state through collaborative leadership, finding an effective advocacy partner in the Junior League of Nevada. Its members testified about devastating oral health problems among the state's children and were effective in a way that public health statistics were not (Association of State and Territorial Dental Directors, 2002).

Shared Interests and Shared Resources

Throughout this chapter, we have attempted to show the many ways in which a wide variety of organizations take on the public health role when they focus on populations. This approach means that other interests can be aligned with the public health mission. For example, walkable communities can appeal to both real estate developers and public health advocates. Across the nation, public health professionals are now working with city planners, the police, real estate developers, and others, reframing suburban sprawl as an issue that has consequences for people's health. Likewise, employers and public health advocates alike see advantages to having health promotion and disease prevention programs in the workplace (Leviton, 1989).

In the same way, public health organizations are now participating more effectively in emergency preparedness, because they can show where the public health interest is aligned with national defense and preparation for natural disasters. Unbelievably, some of the emergency preparedness exercises that preceded Hurricane Katrina did not even consider the health care needs that might arise. In the process of discussing improved disaster planning, public health officials have been able to show the relevance of their work to a wide range of public interest problems. Through this type of coalition building at all levels, public health finally can leave the sidelines. Sometimes it must lead, and sometimes it must follow, but most often, we will find public health walking hand-in-hand with its many partners.

References

Association of State and Territorial Dental Directors. (2002). *Proven and promising practices for state and community oral health programming: Passage of the fluoridation bill in Nevada.* New Bern, NC: Author. Retrieved November 21, 2007, from http://www.astdd.org/bestpractices/pdf/DES31002NVfluoridationbill.pdf

Beitsch, L. M., Brooks, R. G., Menachemi, N., & Libbey, P. M. (2006). Public health at center stage: New roles, old props. *Health Affairs, 25,* 911–922.

Center for Infectious Disease Research & Policy. (2007). *Pandemic influenza.* Minneapolis, MN: Author. Retrieved November 21, 2007, from http://www.cidrap.umn.edu/cidrap/content/influenza/panflu/biofacts/panflu.html

de Tocqueville, A. (2001). *Democracy in America.* New York: Signet.

Duffy, J. (1992). *The sanitarians: A history of American public health* (Reprinted ed.). Urbana, IL: University of Illinois Press.

Eng, T. R., & Butler, W. T. (Eds.). (1997). *The hidden epidemic: Confronting sexually transmitted diseases.* Washington, DC: National Academy Press.

Fee, E., & Fox, D. M. (1988). *AIDS: The burdens of history.* Berkeley: University of California Press.

Fielding, J. E., & Briss, P. A. (2006). Promoting evidence-based public health policy: Can we have better evidence and more action? *Health Affairs 25,* 969–978.

Garrett, L. (2005). The next pandemic? *Foreign Affairs, 84,* 3–23.

Gebbie, K. M., & Turnock, B. J. (2006). The public health workforce, 2006: New challenges. *Health Affairs, 25,* 923–933.

Gostin, L. (2000). *Public health law: Power, duty, restraint.* Berkeley: University of California Press.

Green, L. W., & Kreuter, M. (1999). *Health promotion planning: An educational and ecological approach.* New York: McGraw-Hill.

Hooker, T., & Speissegger, L. (2002). *Public health: A legislator's guide.* Denver, CO: National Conference of State Legislators. Retrieved from http://www.ncsl.org/programs/health/publichealth.htm

Institute of Medicine. (1988). *The future of public health.* Washington, DC: National Academy Press.

Institute of Medicine. (2003a). *The future of the public's health in the 21st century.* Washington, DC: National Academy Press.

Institute of Medicine. (2003b). *Who will keep the public healthy? Educating public health professionals for the 21st century.* Washington, DC: National Academy Press.

Institute of Medicine. (2003c). *Scientific criteria to ensure safe food.* Washington, DC: National Academy Press.

Janssen, R. S., Holtgrave, D. R., Valdiserri, R. O., Shepherd, M., & Gayle, H. D. (2001). The serostatus approach to fighting the HIV epidemic: Prevention strategies for infected individuals. *American Journal of Public Health, 91,* 1019–1024.

Jones, J. H. (1993). *Bad blood: The Tuskegee Syphilis Experiment* (New and expanded ed.). New York: Free Press.

Kreuter, M., & Lezin, N. (2001). *Improving everyone's quality of life: A primer on population health.* Seattle, WA: Group Health Community Foundation.

Leviton, L. C. (1989). Can organizations benefit from worksite health promotion? *Health Services Research, 24,* 159–189.

Leviton, L. C., & Guinan, M. E. (2003). HIV prevention and the evaluation of public health programs. In R. O. Valdiserri (Ed.), *Dawning answers: How the HIV/AIDS epidemic has helped to strengthen public health.* Oxford: Oxford University Press.

Leviton, L. C., Needleman, C. E., & Shapiro, M. (1997). *Confronting public health risks: A decision maker's guide.* Thousand Oaks, CA: Sage.

Lurie, N., Wasserman, J., & Nelson, C. D. (2006). Public health preparedness: Evolution or revolution? *Health Affairs, 25,* 935–945.

March of Dimes. (2004). Spina bifida. *Quick references and fact sheets.* Retrieved March 15, 2004, from http://www.marchofdimes.com/professionals/6811224.asp

McGinnis, J. M., & Foege, W. H. (1993). Actual causes of death in the United States. *Journal of the American Medical Association, 270,* 2207–2212.

McGinnis, J. M., Williams-Russo, P., & Knickman, J. R. (2002). The case for more active policy attention to health promotion. *Health Affairs, 22,* 78–93.

National Academy of Sciences. (2006). *Fluoride in drinking water: A scientific review of EPA's standards.* Washington, DC: National Academy Press.

National Association of County and City Health Officials. (2006). *Shelter from the storm: Local public health faces Katrina.* Washington, DC: Author.

National Foundation for Infectious Diseases. (2006). *Influenza.* Retrieved November 21, 2007, from http://www.nfid.org/influenza

National Highway Traffic Safety Administration. (1997). *Compendium of traffic safety research projects, 1987–1997.* Retrieved July 28, 2004, from http://www.nhtsa.dot.gov/people/injury/research/COMPEND2.HTM

Nelson, J. C., & Essien, J. D. K. (2002). *The public health competency handbook: Optimizing individual and organizational performance for the public's health.* Atlanta, GA: Emory University. Retrieved from http://www.naccho.org/GENERAL810.cfm-7k

Rhodes, S. D., Eng, E., Hergenrather, K. C., Remnitz, I. M., Arceo, R., Montaño, J., & Alegría-Ortega, J. (2007). Exploring Latino men's HIV risk using community-based participatory research. *American Journal of Health Behavior, 31,* 146–158.

Rosen, G. (1993). *A history of public health* (Expanded ed.). Baltimore: Johns Hopkins University Press.

Shilts, R. (1987). *And the band played on: Politics, people and the AIDS epidemic.* New York: St. Martin's Press.

Speissegger, L., & Runyon, C. (2002). *The Model State Emergency Health Powers Act: A checklist of issues.* Denver, CO: National Council of State Legislatures.

Steib, P. A. (2004). Federal funding key to public health preparedness. *ASTHO Report, 12*(2), 1, 5.

Trust for America's Health. (2006a). *F as in fat: How obesity policies are failing in America.* Washington, DC: Author.

Trust for America's Health. (2006b). *Ready or not? Protecting the public's health from disease, disasters, and bioterrorism.* Washington, DC: Author.

U.S. Centers for Disease Control and Prevention. (1999). Achievements in public health, 1900–1999: Decline in deaths from heart disease and stroke—United States, 1900–1999. *Morbidity and Mortality Weekly Report, 48,* 649–656.

U.S. Centers for Disease Control and Prevention. (2004). *The National Public Health Performance Standards Program.* Atlanta, GA: Author. Retrieved July 30, 2004, from http://www.cdc.gov/programs/partnr07.htm

U.S. Department of Health and Human Services. (2000a, November). *Healthy People 2010: Understanding and improving health* (2nd ed.). Washington, DC: U.S. Government Printing Office. Stock Number 017-001-001-00-550-9.

U.S. Department of Health and Human Services. (2000b). *Oral health in America: A report of the Surgeon General.* Rockville, MD: Author.

U.S. Department of Health and Human Services. (2001). *The Surgeon General's call to action to prevent and decrease overweight and obesity.* Last revised January 11, 2007. Rockville, MD: Author.

U.S. Preventive Services Task Force. (1996). *Guide to clinical preventive services* (2nd ed.). Washington, DC: U.S. Department of Health and Human Services.

Wall, S. (1998). Transformations in public health systems. *Health Affairs, 17,* 64–80.

World Health Organization. (1978). Declaration of Alma-Ata. International Conference on Primary Health Care, Alma-Ata, USSR, 6–12 September. Retrieved November 21, 2007, from http://www.who.int/hpr/NPH/docs/declaration_almaata.pdf

World Health Organization. (2005). *Ten things you need to know about pandemic influenza.* Retrieved November 21, 2007, from http://www.who.int/csr/disease/influenza/pandemic10things/en/index.html

5

Key Words

government
regulation
Medicare
Medicaid
Child Health Insurance
    Program

Employee Retirement and
    Income Security Act
    (ERISA)
public hospitals
The uninsured

The Role of Government in U.S. Health Care

Michael S. Sparer

Learning Objectives

- Review the evolution of government's role during the course of U.S. history.
- Describe the roles of the federal, state, and local governments in the U.S. health care system.
- Examine the key issues and options on the current health policy agenda.

Topical Outline

- The government as payer: The health insurance safety net
- The government as regulator
- The government as health care provider
- Key issues on the health care agenda

Government is deeply entrenched in every aspect of the U.S. health care system. The federal government provides tax incentives to encourage employers to offer health insurance to their employees; provides health insurance to the poor, the aged, and the disabled; and operates health care facilities for veterans. State governments administer and help pay for Medicaid, regulate private health insurance and medical schools, license health care providers, and operate facilities for the mentally ill and developmentally disabled. Local governments own and operate public hospitals and public health clinics and develop and enforce public health codes.

Even with this extensive agenda, government officials seem certain to add new tasks and new programs to it. The nation is engaged in an ongoing debate over whether government should guarantee health insurance to the nearly 45 million people who are currently uninsured. Federal and state officials are engaged in an equally controversial debate over the rise of managed care and the extent to which government should regulate that industry. And the aging of the baby boom generation prompts many to suggest that the nation needs to do more to develop an adequate and affordable system of long-term care.

The goal of this chapter is to provide an overview of government's role in the health care system. The chapter is divided into three sections. First is a discussion of government as a payer for health care services. The theme is that government provides health insurance to many of those who are not covered by the employer-sponsored private health insurance system. The section describes the evolution of the private system, the gaps in that system, and the government's efforts to aid those outside of the private system. Second is a summary of government as regulator of the health care system. The focus is on state and federal efforts to enact patient protection legislation. Third is a discussion of government as a provider of health care. The section reviews the health systems operated by the three levels of government: the Veterans Administration facilities run by the federal government, the institutions for the mentally ill operated by the states, and the public hospitals and public health clinics owned and administered by local governments.

The Government as Payer:
The Health Insurance Safety Net

For much of U.S. history, the national government and the states were minor players in the nation's health and welfare systems. The nation's social welfare system was shaped instead by the principles that governed the English poor law system. Social welfare programs were a local responsibility, and assistance was provided only to those who were outside the labor force through no fault of their own (the "deserving poor"). National welfare programs were considered unwise and perhaps even unconstitutional. The main exception was the Civil War pension program, which provided federal funds to Union veterans, but even this initiative was administered and implemented at the local level.

Lacking federal or state leadership (and dollars), local governments tried to provide a social and medical safety net. The most common approach was to establish almshouses (or shelters) for the indigent aged and disabled. A medical clinic often provided health care to almshouse residents. These clinics eventually evolved into public hospitals, offering services to the poor without charge. Generally speaking, however, the clinics (and hospitals) provided poor-quality care and were avoided by people who had any alternative. Similarly, the few private hospitals then in operation were charitable facilities that served only the poor and the disabled. These hospitals, like their public counterparts, represented only a small and rather disreputable portion of the nation's health care system.

Most 19th-century Americans instead received health care in their homes, often from family members who relied on traditional healing techniques. At the same time, an assortment of health care providers—physicians, midwives, medicine salesmen, herbalists, homeopaths, and faith healers—offered their services as well. Generally speaking, these providers charged low fees and families paid out of pocket, much as they would for other commodities. As the 19th century drew to a close, two developments fundamentally changed the nation's health care marketplace. First, allopathic physicians (MDs) won the battle for primacy among health care providers. Americans increasingly believed that medicine was a science and that physicians were best able to deliver high-quality care. The status and prestige accorded to physicians grew, while the role of alternative medicine providers declined.

> The emergence of a physician-dominated health care system was accompanied by a second pivotal factor—the dramatic growth in the size and the status of the U.S. hospital industry.

The emergence of a physician-dominated health care system was accompanied by a second pivotal factor—the dramatic growth in the size and the status of the U.S. hospital industry. Indeed, the nation's stock of hospitals grew from fewer than 200 in 1873 to 4,000 (with 35,500 beds) in 1900, to nearly 7,000 (with 922,000 beds) by 1930 (Annas, Law, Rosenblatt, & Wing, 1990). This growth was prompted by several factors. Advances in medical technology (antiseptics, anesthesia, X rays) encouraged wealthier people to use hospitals, eliminating much of their prior social stigma. The number of nurses expanded dramatically, as nurses evolved from domestics to trained professionals, and hospital-based nurses worked hard to improve hospitals' hygiene. The growing urbanization and industrialization of American life produced an increasingly rootless society, less able to rely on families to care for their sick at home. Finally, the medical education system began to require internships and residencies in hospitals as part of physician training, which put a cadre of trained doctors working full-time in these facilities.

As the hospital industry grew, so too did the costs of care. By the mid-1920s, there was growing recognition that middle-income Americans needed help in financing the rising costs of hospital care and increasingly high-tech medicine. The onset of the Great Depression made the situation more problematic. Efforts to create systems of health insurance were the result (see chapter 3 for more on the early history of private health insurance).

General optimism combined with demonstrable advances in medical technology after World War II engendered confidence that the medical system would in time conquer nearly all forms of disease. This perception prompted the federal government (through the National Institutes of Health) to funnel billions of dollars to academic medical researchers. And with federal dollars so readily available, medical schools soon emphasized research, and medical students increasingly chose research careers. Around the same time, Congress enacted the Hill-Burton Program, which provided federal funds to stimulate hospital construction and modernization. The policy assumption was that all Americans should have access to the increasingly sophisticated medical care rendered in state-of-the-art hospital facilities.

As the employer-sponsored health insurance system grew, so too did concern about people who were unable to access such coverage (such as the aged, the disabled, and the otherwise unemployed). For many years, liberal politicians had argued without success in favor of government-sponsored health insurance. President Harry Truman had even posited that health insurance was part of the Fair Deal that all Americans were entitled to. However, neither Truman nor his liberal predecessors ever came close to overcoming the strong opposition to national health insurance from doctors, businessmen, and others who viewed it as un-American and socialistic. By 1949, mainstream Democrats had abandoned their visions of universal insurance and proposed instead that the Social Security (retirement) system be expanded to provide hospital insurance for the aged, reasoning that the elderly were a sympathetic and deserving group, and hospital care was the most costly sector of the health care system.

Conservatives opposed the plan, arguing that it would give free coverage to many people who were neither poor nor particularly needy. They argued instead that government's role is to provide a safety net to the deserving poor who are unable to access employer-sponsored coverage. The result was an amendment to the Social Security Act in 1950 that, for the first time, provided federal funds to states willing to pay health care providers to care for welfare recipients. Interestingly, this "welfare medicine" approach passed with bipartisan support (Sparer, 1996). For liberals, this was an acceptable, albeit inadequate, first step, but at least some poor people finally could obtain services. Conservatives went along because a medical safety net for the poor would undermine arguments for a more comprehensive health insurance program and because responsibility for the program was delegated to state officials.

In 1960, newly elected President John F. Kennedy revived the effort to enact hospital insurance for the aged. Congress responded by enacting the Kerr-Mills Program. This program distributed federal funds to states that were willing to pay health care providers to care for the indigent aged, expanding the welfare medicine model. Congress later opened the program to covering the indigent disabled. These initiatives again deflected support from the president's broader social insurance proposal.

The political dynamic evolved considerably by 1965. President Lyndon B. Johnson and the Democrats controlling Congress were enacting various laws designed to turn the United States into a "Great Society." This seemed an opportune time to renew the effort to enact national health insurance. Even longtime opponents of health insurance expansions expected Congress to enact a plan far more comprehensive than Kerr-Mills. President Johnson followed the path set by Truman and Kennedy and again proposed hospital insurance for the aged. At the same time, various Republican legislators, citing the nation's oversupply of hospitals, and desiring to return to a physician-centered delivery system, recommended that Congress enact physician insurance for the aged. And the American Medical Association (AMA), hoping once again to scuttle the social insurance model, urged Congress simply to expand Kerr-Mills.

As Congress debated these various proposals, Congressman Wilbur Mills, powerful chair of the House Ways and Means Committee and an aspiring presidential candidate, convinced his colleagues to enact all three expansion initiatives. The president's proposal for hospital insurance for the aged became Medicare Part A. The Republican proposal for physician insurance for the aged became Medicare Part B. The AMA's effort to expand Kerr-Mills became Medicaid. And the government, for the first time, became a true health insurance safety net for those unable to access employer-sponsored coverage (Marmor, 2000).

MEDICAID

Medicaid is not a single national program, but a collection of 50 state-administered programs, each providing health insurance to low-income state residents. Each state initiative is governed by various federal guidelines, and the federal government then contributes between 50% and 78% of the cost (the poorer the state, the larger the federal contribution). In 2005, the various Medicaid programs covered roughly 55 million Americans at a cost of more than $305 billion (Kaiser Family Foundation, 2007a).

Given its decentralized structure, state officials have considerable discretion to decide who in their state receives coverage, what benefits they receive, and how much providers are paid. One not surprising result is that states such as New York have more generous eligibility criteria than do poorer states like Alabama or Mississippi. Interestingly, however, there are stark contrasts even among the larger states. New York, for example, spent more than $7,500 per enrollee in 2004, while California spent only $2,054 (Kaiser Family Foundation, 2004b).

During the late 1980s, Congress for the first time imposed rules designed to increase state coverage. In 1988, it required states to cover pregnant women and infants with family income below 100% of the poverty line. Previously states typically covered this group only if family income was around 50% of the poverty level. The next year, Congress required states to cover pregnant women and children under age 7 whose family income was below 133% of the poverty level. Then, in 1990, Congress required states to phase in coverage for all children younger than 19 with family income below 100% of the poverty level. As a result of these mandates, the number of children on Medicaid nearly doubled between 1987 and 1995, and the total number of recipients increased from roughly 26 million to nearly 40 million.

Medicaid expansions were the nation's main strategy for reducing the ranks of the uninsured. Concomitantly, the Medicaid price tag grew from $57.5 billion in 1988 to $157.3 billion in 1995. State officials blamed this increase on the federal mandates. Federal regulators disputed the claim and suggested that the states themselves were largely responsible for the increase in Medicaid costs, citing accounting techniques through which states shifted state-funded programs into their Medicaid budget (thus drawing down additional federal dollars). Hence, there was significant intergovernmental tension (Holahan & Liska, 1997).

During the early 1990s, President Clinton, a former state governor and a critic of Medicaid mandates, stopped considering Medicaid the linchpin in efforts to reduce the number of uninsured. Recognizing that many uninsured people are in families where the husband or wife works full- or part-time, he proposed instead to require that employers offer health insurance to their employees. The Clinton administration's proposal for national health insurance failed, but the shift away from federal Medicaid mandates persisted. Instead, federal officials became more lenient in approving state requests for waivers from federal Medicaid rules, giving states additional flexibility and autonomy.

Two trends dominated Medicaid policy during most of the 1990s. First, states used their expanded discretion to encourage or require beneficiaries to enroll in managed care delivery systems. Between 1987 and 1998, the percentage of enrollees in Medicaid managed care increased from less than 5% to more than 50%, from fewer than 1 million to more than 20 million. Second, the growth in the number of Medicaid beneficiaries ended, and a slow decline in the number of enrollees began. The most convincing explanation for the enrollment decline was federal welfare reform, enacted in 1996. Before then, beneficiaries enrolled in Aid to Families with Dependent Children were automatically enrolled in Medicaid. Thereafter, those on welfare needed to apply separately for Medicaid, as did those no longer entitled to welfare but still eligible for Medicaid. Millions did not know they were Medicaid eligible, the administrative hurdles deterred others from applying, whereas still others were dissuaded by the stigma attached to receiving public assistance. For all of these reasons, between 1995 and 1997, the number of adult Medicaid beneficiaries declined 5.5%, and the number of child beneficiaries declined 1.4%.

During the late 1990s, state and federal officials undertook a major effort to increase Medicaid enrollment. One strategy was to simplify the eligibility process (shortened application forms, mail-in applications, and more eligibility-determination sites). A second strategy was to simplify eligibility rules (eliminating assets tests and ensuring 12 months of continuous eligibility). A third strategy was to expand outreach and education—increasing marketing activities and encouraging community-based institutions to educate and enroll. These efforts succeeded. Beginning in mid-1998, Medicaid enrollment began to increase again, a trend that has continued into 2007.

The growth in enrollment, along with higher costs for prescription drugs, services for people with disabilities, and long-term care, has

> The growth in enrollment, along with higher costs for prescription drugs, services for people with disabilities, and long-term care, has led to escalating Medicaid costs in the last few years.

led to escalating Medicaid costs in the last few years. At the same time, state tax revenues declined precipitously in the early 2000s. The ensuing budget crises prompted Medicaid cost-containment efforts in every state. The most popular option was an effort to control the rising cost of pharmaceuticals, either through leveraged buying (purchasing pools) or limits on access (formularies). Other Medicaid cost-containment strategies have included freezing or cutting provider reimbursement, reducing benefits (such as dental and home care), cutting eligibility, increasing co-pays, and expanding disease management initiatives.

MEDICARE

Like Medicaid, Medicare was enacted in 1965 to provide health insurance to segments of the population not generally covered by the mainstream employer-sponsored health insurance system. And like Medicaid, Medicare has become a major part of the nation's health care system, providing insurance coverage to nearly 37 million persons over the age of 65 and to roughly 7 million of the young disabled population, at a total cost of just over $374 billion (Kaiser Family Foundation, 2007c).

In other respects, however, Medicare differs significantly from its sister program. Medicare is a social insurance program, providing benefits to the aged and the disabled regardless of income, whereas Medicaid is a welfare initiative, offering coverage only to those with limited income. Medicare is administered by federal officials and the private insurers they hire to perform particular tasks, whereas Medicaid is administered by the states following federal guidance. Medicare is funded primarily by the federal government (plus beneficiary co-payments and deductibles), whereas Medicaid is funded by the federal government and the states without any beneficiary contribution. Medicare has a relatively limited benefit package that excludes much preventive care, long-term care, and, until 2003, prescription drugs outside of the hospital and the oncologist's office, whereas Medicaid offers a far more generous set of benefits.

Medicare has three separate parts, with different funding sources and eligibility requirements. Medicare Part A covers inpatient hospital care. It is financed by a 2.9% payroll tax (1.45% paid by the employer and 1.45% paid by the employee). All beneficiaries automatically receive Part A coverage. Medicare Part B, in contrast, is a voluntary program, providing coverage for outpatient care for beneficiaries who choose to pay a $98 monthly premium (starting in 2007, individuals with annual income over $80,000 pay a higher, income-based premium). Some 95% of beneficiaries choose to enroll. The balance of the Part B bill is paid by general federal revenues. Medicare Part D, enacted in late 2003, also is a voluntary program, in which private health plans offer different levels of prescription drug coverage to beneficiaries.

Prior to 1994, the revenue contributed to the Part A Trust Fund exceeded the program's expenses, and the fund built up a significant surplus. Beginning in 1994, expenses began to exceed revenue, the surplus was used to pay bills, and it began to shrink. Alarmed Medicare experts predicted that the surplus would be gone by the early 2000s, that the Trust Fund would be unable to pay its bills, and that Medicare would slide into bankruptcy. In response to this crisis, Congress in 1997 enacted a broad effort to reduce Medicare costs, mainly by cutting provider reimbursement. The legislation also contained provisions designed to encourage beneficiaries to enroll in managed care (described in chapter 3). While the managed care initiative had only mild success, enrolling only about 11% of Medicare beneficiaries, the effort to cut Medicare spending was remarkably successful. In 1998, Medicare spending declined for the first time in the program's 33-year history.

The rapid shift in the economics of Medicare prompted an equally rapid change in its politics (Oberlander, 2003). No longer were politicians claiming that the program was about to go bankrupt. No longer was there talk of greedy providers overcharging and generating excess profits. No longer was there an intense effort to enroll beneficiaries in managed care. There were instead three competing views about how to respond. One camp emphasized the need to undo some of the cuts in provider reimbursement, another focused on the importance of expanding the benefits package, and still another argued against new spending measures, whether on behalf of providers or beneficiaries. This last group—the fiscal conservatives—proposed that any surplus remain in the Trust Fund to be used in years to come.

Faced with these options, Congress chose in 1999 to undo some of the cuts in provider reimbursement. Provider organizations argued that the prior cuts in reimbursement were unnecessarily endangering the financial health of thousands of doctors and hospitals. Even supporters of the cuts conceded that the extent of the reductions was far greater than expected. As a result, Congress reduced the impact of the cuts by $16 billion over the following 5 years and $27 billion over the following 10 years. In 2000, Congress passed another giveback initiative, this time delivering to providers $35 billion over 5 years and $85 billion over 10 years.

Following the provider giveback legislation, newly elected President George Bush and Congress took up the issue of prescription drug coverage and enacted Medicare Part D. Under this legislation, beneficiaries can receive outpatient drug coverage through a managed care plan or, if they wish to stay in fee-for-service Medicare, through a private prescription drug plan. In most communities, seniors can choose between dozens of plans, some of which offer limited coverage for a small monthly premium, while others offer more generous benefits for a higher premium. The average monthly premium is $25, in exchange for which the beneficiary has a $265 deductible, after which the plan pays 75% of drug costs up to $2,400 and 95% of the costs beyond $3,850 (the beneficiary pays 100% of the costs between $2,400 and $3,850).

The Medicare drug legislation was extraordinarily controversial and partisan. President Bush and leading Republicans note that the legislation, expected to cost $410 billion over its first 10 years, is the largest public insurance expansion since Medicare was first enacted, and that it will provide significant coverage to millions of seniors. Leading Democrats, while supporting the goals of the legislation, complain that the initiative gives too little to needy seniors and too much to health maintenance organizations, big business, and the pharmaceutical industry. Several of the continuing controversies are described in the last section of this chapter.

President Bush's prescription drug plan was designed, in part, to revive the effort to encourage beneficiaries to enroll in managed care. Medicare managed care enrollment had been sagging largely because of declining health plan interest. In 1998, for example, more than 6 million Medicare beneficiaries were enrolled in 346 health plans. By early 2004, only 4.6 million were enrolled in 145 plans (Kaiser Family Foundation, 2004a). Health plans said the main reason they exited the program was inadequate reimbursement. However, several studies suggested that Medicare was actually losing money on the managed care initiative, since its capitation rates were set high, based on the health care experience of the average client in a particular community, while the typical managed care enrollee was healthier and less costly than average (Kaiser Family Foundation, 2004a).

In an effort to reverse the decline in health plan participation and to advance the goals of privatization and competition, the Bush administration proposed that the new drug benefit be delivered exclusively by managed care plans. While the legislation as enacted does not go so far, it does dramatically increase health plan capitation rates in an effort to encourage plans to get back in the game. In 2004, for example, average monthly capitation rates increased almost 11%, and in some communities, rates went up by more than 40% (Kaiser Family Foundation, 2007b). As a result, plans have begun aggressively marketing to beneficiaries, and, by early 2007, there were 8.3 million Medicare managed care enrollees (Kaiser Family Foundation, 2007b).

RECENT EFFORTS TO HELP THE UNINSURED

Over the last decade, the number of Americans without health insurance has grown from roughly 35 million to approximately 45 million—more than 15% of the nation's population. Millions more are underinsured, with high out-of-pocket medical expenses. Most of the uninsured (more than 80%) are in families with a full- or part-time worker, and most of these workers are self-employed or employed by small businesses. States with a strong industrial and manufacturing base are likely to have fewer uninsured, while states with large numbers of immigrants and a service-based economy are likely to have more. In Iowa, Massachusetts, and Wisconsin, for example, less than 10% of the population is uninsured; while in California, Louisiana, and Texas, the percentage hovers between 20% and 25%.

Rather remarkably, the dramatic increase in the nation's uninsured population began in the mid-1990s—an era of unprecedented economic growth, low unemployment, and relatively small rises in health care costs—then accelerated during the economic downturn of the early 2000s. Much of the increase in the uninsured population also occurred during a time when the Medicaid rolls were expanding dramatically. The best explanation for the rise in the number of uninsured is the decline in the number of Americans with employer-sponsored private health insurance. Between 1977 and 2004, the percentage of Americans under age 65 with employer-sponsored coverage dropped from 66% to 61% (Clemens-Cope, Garrett, & Hoffman, 2006).

> Rather remarkably, the dramatic increase in the nation's uninsured population began in the mid-1990s—an era of unprecedented economic growth, low unemployment, and relatively small rises in health care costs—then accelerated during the economic downturn of the early 2000s.

The decline in employer-sponsored coverage is due to several factors. Many employers have increased the share of the bill that the employee must pay, prompting some employees to abandon their coverage. Other employers are eliminating coverage for spouses and children or phasing out retiree health coverage. Still others are hiring more part-time workers and outside contractors, thereby avoiding the need to even offer health insurance. At the same time, much of the recent job growth is in the service sector of the economy. These jobs are notoriously low paying and rarely provide health insurance.

In response to these trends and to media and political attention to the problems of the uninsured, state and federal officials tried during the early 1990s to enact new programs for the uninsured (Brown & Sparer, 2001; Sparer, 2003). These proposals generally sought to require employers to provide health insurance to their employees (and to use public dollars as a safety net for those outside the labor market). The idea was to retain and reinvigorate the employer-sponsored health insurance system. By the mid-1990s, however, the various employer mandate proposals (including the plan proposed by President Bill Clinton) had disappeared, defeated by vehement opposition from the business community. Business opponents argued that the mandate would be too costly and would force employers to eliminate jobs.

Following the collapse of the employer mandate strategy, policymakers (especially at the state level) enacted a host of efforts designed to make health insurance more available and more affordable in the small group and individual insurance markets. These reforms focused on three problems in the health care system. First, employers in the small business community often cannot afford to provide health insurance to their employees. These employers lack the market clout to negotiate a good deal, particularly given the high administrative costs associated with insuring a small group. Second, the self-employed and employees of small businesses generally earn too little to purchase health insurance in the individual market. Third, people with a high risk of catastrophic medical costs are often excluded from the individual insurance market regardless of their ability to pay.

Many of these state initiatives required insurers to guarantee coverage to segments of the small business community. Others encouraged small businesses to join state-run or state-administered purchasing alliances. Still others allowed insurers to sell no-frills insurance policies, presumably at a lower cost than the more comprehensive packages states often mandate. Taken together, however, the various state mandates have had only a modest impact on the number of uninsured (Robert Wood Johnson Foundation, 2007), while generating significant political controversy, especially from healthy younger workers who complain about paying higher rates to subsidize the older and the sicker and from insurance companies threatening to exit reform-minded states.

By the late 1990s, state and federal policymakers had shifted their focus away from the insurance reforms that had been disappointing up to that point, and toward programs that expanded health insurance for children. Several factors explained the trend. Children are considered a deserving group; there is bipartisan agreement that youngsters should not go without health care services because their parents cannot afford to pay. Children are a relatively low-cost population. In 1993, for example, the average child on Medicaid cost just under $1,000, whereas the typical aged recipient cost over $9,200, and disabled recipients' costs averaged just under $8,000. Child health initiatives are consistent with the political agendas of both Republicans and Democrats. Republicans, along with many moderate Democrats, support insurance expansions as a counterbalance to other social welfare cutbacks. For example, families that move from welfare to work continue to need help obtaining health insurance for their children.

At the same time, liberal Democrats, still reeling from the defeat of national health insurance proposals, saw health insurance for children as an incremental step on the path to universal health coverage.

Given this bipartisan support, Congress enacted the State Child Health Insurance Program (SCHIP). States can use SCHIP funds to liberalize their Medicaid eligibility rules, to develop a separate state program, or to create a combination of the two. The main advantage to using the funds to expand Medicaid is administrative simplicity for both the client and the state. This is especially so for families in which some children are eligible for Medicaid and others for SCHIP. At the same time, there are several advantages to creating a separate state program:

- Enrollment can be suspended when the dollars are spent, unlike with Medicaid, which is an entitlement program.
- The state has more discretion when developing the benefit package.
- It can impose co-payments and premiums, which generally are not allowed under Medicaid.
- Beneficiaries and providers may be more likely to participate because the new program lacks the stigma associated with Medicaid.

By all accounts, early efforts to enroll children into SCHIP were disappointing. By the end of 1999, roughly 1.5 million youngsters were enrolled in the program, far fewer than predicted. The low enrollment was due to several factors. Large numbers of eligible families did not know they were eligible. Others were deterred by the complicated application processes. Still others were dissuaded by the stigma often associated with government insurance programs. And the premiums and other cost-sharing requirements clearly discouraged others. As a result, by the end of 2000, 38 states had not spent their full allotment of federal SCHIP dollars. Funds not expended in these states were reallocated to the dozen other participating states.

Beginning in early 2000, however, SCHIP enrollment began to rise significantly. By the end of the year, there were roughly 3.3 million enrollees—nearly double the number from the prior year—and by 2005, there were more than 6 million enrollees. Policymakers attribute the turnaround to improved outreach and education initiatives and to simplified processes for eligibility and enrollment. There was rare bipartisan support for expanding SCHIP, and in early 2001, federal regulators authorized several states to use SCHIP dollars to cover parents as well as their children. SCHIP even "dodged the first budget ax" in 2002, when state budget crises forced cutbacks in numerous other programs (Howell, Hill, & Kapustka, 2002).

Despite the growth in public insurance programs like SCHIP, the number of uninsured keeps rising. At the same time, there is renewed interest among policymakers in developing a comprehensive reform. Several states—most notably Massachusetts, Maine, and Maryland—have enacted important reforms. Other states and federal officials continue to tinker with more incremental strategies to aid the uninsured. While there are countless proposals and plans, the long list of options can be divided into four basic categories.

First, policymakers can focus on the millions of Americans who are eligible for public coverage but who are not enrolled because of a lack of knowledge, complicated application processes, a perceived stigma, concerns about immigration status, or the cost of premiums. To reach this population, policymakers can focus on outreach and education, as well as simplifying the application process. Second, lawmakers can expand eligibility for public insurance, either incrementally (via a modest Medicaid or SCHIP expansion) or comprehensively (perhaps by expanding Medicare to cover all Americans). Third, policymakers can continue the long-standing effort to make health insurance more affordable, especially for the small business community, both by encouraging lower-cost insurance—such as high-deductible policies that can be combined with a health savings account—and by providing subsidies for the purchase of such coverage, most often through tax credits. Fourth, legislators can mandate expanded private coverage. In 2006, for example, Massachusetts enacted an individual mandate, under which state residents are generally required by law to have health insurance. Other states continue to focus on employer mandates. Maryland, for example, enacted a law requiring large corporations (such as Wal-Mart) to spend a percentage of their revenue on health benefits for employees. While the courts found that the mandate violated federal law, other states (and some federal policymakers) still feel the employer mandate is the best policy option.

The Government as Regulator

One of the key issues in contemporary health politics is the extent to which the states and the federal government should regulate the managed care industry. Between 1997 and 2000, for example, 35 states enacted laws designed to protect patients enrolled in managed care. In 1999, both the U.S. Senate and the House of Representatives passed their own versions of a managed care bill of rights, and the effort to resolve differences between the two bills became a bitter partisan battle. During the 2000 presidential campaign, George Bush and Al Gore debated vigorously over the content of a good patient protection act, both claiming to be fully in favor of the concept. While the issue slid off the political agenda during the early 2000s, a Supreme Court decision in mid-2004 limiting patients' right to sue their HMO could generate renewed interest in legislative action, though there is little evidence so far of such a trend.

The focus on patient protection during the late 1990s was prompted by a consumer backlash against managed care. Interestingly, however, the proposed federal legislation, if enacted, would represent an important policy shift, because there is little precedent for federal regulation of the health insurance industry. At the same time, state legislators, while more accustomed to regulating private insurers (as well as other sectors of the health care industry) complained that their efforts are undermined by a federal pension law (the Employee Retiree Income and Security Act [ERISA], see below) that restricts state regulatory authority. These officials urged Congress to repeal or amend ERISA and thereby allow the states far greater regulatory autonomy.

States have traditionally dominated regulations of all aspects of the nation's health care system, although the federal government regulates some of the public health aspects of the health care system (see chapter 4). States supervise the nation's system of medical education, license health care professionals, and oversee the quality of care delivered by health care providers. States administer the workers' compensation system, which provides benefits to workers injured on the job, and states govern consumer-protection efforts, such as those that hold providers accountable through, for example, medical malpractice litigation. Beginning in the 1920s, the states also began to regulate the nation's private health insurance system, establishing capitalization and reserve requirements, regulating marketing and enrollment activities, and (in some states) establishing the rates paid by insurers to various providers, especially hospitals.

> States have traditionally dominated regulations of all aspects of the nation's health care system.

Prior to the 1960s, state insurance departments rarely exercised their regulatory power, imposing few substantive requirements on insurance companies. Liberal critics complained that the relationships among providers, insurers, and regulators were far too cozy. Providers—especially hospitals—charged high rates, insurers paid the bill with few questions asked, regulators did little to make sure that insurance companies were adequately capitalized, and they did even less to guarantee that clients were treated fairly. In response, several states imposed new administrative requirements, most of which dealt with health plan finances, benefit packages, and marketing practices. In the mid-1960s, for example, New York regulated the rates that hospitals could charge insurers. About the same time, states also imposed tougher capitalization and reserve requirements.

Over the next two decades, states required insurers to cover certain medical services—from mental health to chiropractor visits—in every insurance package they issued. Indeed, there are now more than 1,000 of these benefit *mandates*. For example, 40 states require that insurers cover alcohol treatment services, 39 require coverage for mammography, and 29 require mental health coverage.

The states' ability to regulate health insurers was limited, however, in 1974, when Congress enacted the Employee Retiree Income and Security Act. ERISA was intended primarily to prevent unfair denial of pensions to employees.[1] But the law also contains a provision that prohibits states from regulating employee benefit programs unless the law is part of the "traditional" state regulation of insurance, a provision that has led to endless confusion, controversy, and litigation.

Consider, for example, the convoluted legal reasoning that governs state efforts to require insurers to cover certain medical services. The courts have ruled that these laws apply to coverage provided by a traditional insurance company (like Blue Cross or Prudential) but not by a company that *self-insures* (that is, bears the risk of employee medical costs itself, hiring insurers simply to process claims and manage utilization). Following the same reasoning, the courts have held that companies that self-insure are exempt from state capitalization and reserve requirements, state taxes imposed on insurers, and all other state regulations. Thus, self-insured plans do not have to comply with state laws that provide patient protections—for example, appeals processes when care is denied, access to the hospital emergency room or certain medical specialists, or bans on censoring what doctors can say to their patients.

To be sure, companies that self-insure are required to adhere to federal regulatory requirements: ERISA simply exempts them from state regulation. But federal officials have generally steered clear of imposing any such requirements. As a result, self-insured companies are more or less unregulated; the states cannot regulate them, and the federal government rarely does. Not surprisingly, this legal quirk is a strong incentive for firms to self-insure. By the mid-1990s, more than 70% of large firms offered self-insured plans to their employees (Dranove, 2000), and more than 56 million Americans were covered by self-insured health plans.

ERISA also makes it extremely difficult for subscribers to sue their health plan. Consider, for example, the situation in which an individual claims she was injured when her health plan wrongfully

---

[1] The law requires that pension plans be adequately funded, that investing requirements be reasonable, and that companies provide employees with understandable information about their pension programs.

refused to authorize needed care. The woman seeks to sue the health plan for negligence. Prior to ERISA, she could have initiated such a lawsuit in state court and demanded damages to cover the cost of the denied services, as well as compensation for the injury and the unnecessary pain and suffering endured. She might also have won punitive damages (intended to punish the health plan for its wrongful behavior). But because of ERISA, the woman cannot bring her case to state court (unless she is a government employee, is in a government-funded health plan, or buys health insurance in the nongroup market). She must instead proceed in federal court under a very different set of rules. Yet, in her federal action, the most the woman could win would be the cost of the wrongfully denied care; she could not win compensation for pain and suffering, nor could she win punitive damages.[2]

Until recently, ERISA was viewed as a barrier to suits against health plans for poor care delivered by an affiliated doctor. During the late 1990s, however, several states, led by Texas, enacted laws designed to overcome this barrier and to permit such cases to proceed in state court. The courts have consistently distinguished these "poor quality of care" cases from "wrongful denial of care" cases and so far have permitted them to proceed.[3] Patients' right to sue their managed care plan thus depends on the source of their health insurance and the nature of the claim. In June 2004, the Supreme Court upheld this unwieldy and unfair set of rules, deciding that only Congress could remedy the inequity and that it could do so only by amending ERISA (*Aetna Health, Inc., vs. Davila,* 2004).

The regulatory vacuum became especially controversial during the mid-1990s as a consumer backlash arose against much of the managed care industry. Congress was pressured either to amend ERISA and allow state regulation of the self-insured or to enact federal consumer protection legislation. The effort to amend ERISA faces significant political opposition. Sponsors of self-insured plans, especially multistate employers and labor unions, are well organized and influential. Their lobbyists argue that the goal of the law is to avoid

---

[2] The impact of the ERISA barrier is also illustrated by the case of *Goodrich vs. Aetna.* Mr. Goodrich was a government prosecutor in California, suffering from stomach cancer, whose request for surgical relief was wrongfully denied and delayed (even though Aetna's own doctors were in favor of the procedure). After Goodrich died, his estate brought a lawsuit in state court seeking damages for the wrongful denial of care. The jury awarded his estate $4.5 million in actual compensatory damages and $116 million in punitive damages (Johnston, 1999). Rather remarkably, however, had Goodrich not worked for the government, his estate would have had to proceed in federal court and could have collected a maximum of roughly $400,000 (the cost of the surgical procedure).

[3] Whether the health plan is then held liable for the malpractice of the provider depends on the relationship between provider and plan. Staff model HMOs, which exercise close oversight of their salaried doctors, are more likely to be liable than are independent practice associations, with their large and loosely controlled provider network.

inconsistent state regulations that would undermine the efficient administration of their organizations.

Congress, however, has begun to experiment with federal consumer protection legislation and may move further in this direction. In 1996, for example, it enacted a federal law modeled after state laws guaranteeing new mothers the right to spend at least 48 hours in the hospital following the birth of a child. The next year, Congress enacted the Health Insurance Portability and Accountability Act, which seeks to make health insurance more available to the self-employed and to those who work in small companies.

The Government as Health Care Provider

Each of the three levels of government owns and operates large numbers of health care institutions. The federal government provides care to veterans through the massive Veterans Affairs health care system, the Veterans Health Administration (VHA). The states care for developmentally disabled individuals in both large institutional facilities as well as smaller group homes. And local governments own and operate acute care hospitals and public health clinics that provide a medical safety net for the poor and the uninsured.

THE VETERANS HEALTH ADMINISTRATION

The VHA is required to offer health care to veterans and their dependents. There are approximately 70 million Americans now eligible for these services (25 million veterans and 45 million dependents or survivors of deceased veterans). To serve this population, the VHA owns and operates 163 hospitals, 134 nursing homes, more than 800 outpatient clinics, and 206 readjustment counseling centers. These facilities are divided into 22 integrated service networks nationwide. In 2000, more than 3.6 million people received care in one of these facilities, at a cost of more than $19 billion.

The VHA system is an integral part of the nation's system of medical education. Nationally, 107 medical schools and 55 dental schools use VHA facilities to train students and residents. Indeed, more than 50% of the nation's physicians have received part of their education and training in the VHA system.

In recent years, the VHA system has engaged in a wide-ranging initiative to improve the quality of care provided in its facilities. It created the National Center for Patient Safety (NCPS) to lead efforts to reduce the number of medical errors. The NCPS program is considered so innovative and important that it was recently a finalist in the Innovations in American Government Program sponsored by the Ford Foundation and the Kennedy School of Government at Harvard University.

The issue of medical errors received national attention when the Institute of Medicine reported that an estimated 44,000 to 98,000 persons die each year because of medical errors. Much of the usual effort to reduce medical error focuses on individual wrongdoing: If only Dr. Jones had operated on the right leg; or if only Nurse Smith had given the right medication. Hospitals and other providers too often respond to medical errors by trying to identify and punish the "culprit," while policymakers press for a practitioner data bank that will list the providers guilty of committing them. The NCPS takes a different approach. It focuses on finding the root cause of the error, which is a much more effective strategy for preventing future errors. For example, if a medication error is due to unclear labeling of drugs, it is better to fix the label than punish the individual who misread it. In the NCPS system, health care staff members are encouraged to report "close calls" as well as "adverse events." In the past, no one was likely to report or investigate such near-misses. The nurse would be too embarrassed and the system too uninterested. The goal now is to encourage these reports, ensuring that they are completely confidential; a small team seeks out the root cause of the problem; and a plan of action is created to make a similar error less likely in the future.

A major strategy in VHA quality improvement efforts has been widespread implementation of information technology. Over the past few years, it has spent hundreds of millions of dollars on an electronic medical records system, bar-coded medication administration, and computerized physician order entry. One result is that, in August 2005, after Hurricane Katrina, the VHA could quickly retrieve the health records for Gulf Coast evacuees scattered around the country, while the civilian health system remained in chaos for weeks and months (Markle Foundation et al., 2006). Relaxed eligibility requirements combined with a growing reputation for quality care has increased demand for VHA services.

STATE FACILITIES FOR THE MENTALLY ILL

Prior to the 1860s, government's role in caring for the mentally ill was handled locally, part of the safety net provided to the so-called deserving poor. (Many mentally ill people did not come to the attention of public authorities. Families, embarrassed by the presence of a mentally ill relative, kept them at home, out of sight, in sometimes appalling conditions.) Perhaps the most common strategy utilized by county governments was to house the indigent insane in almshouses or shelters for the poor. Many of those who were severely ill were locked in local jails. But by the mid-19th century, several counties had also established hospitals for mentally ill people, though little treatment was offered even in the best of them. The goal instead was to warehouse mentally ill people and separate them from the rest of society.

Dorothea Dix and other reformers slowly persuaded nearly every state legislature to assume responsibility for people with mental illnesses and to construct state hospitals for their care. State mental hospitals generally were located in remote rural communities. Reformers believed that patients were more likely to improve in a quiet and serene environment, which accorded with communities' desire to put the mentally ill "out of mind, out of sight." State mental hospitals were extraordinarily large, some with as many as 2,000 patients. In 1920, the nation's 521 state hospitals had an average bed capacity of 567. In contrast, the nation's 4,013 general hospitals at that time had an average bed capacity of only 78 (Starr, 1982).

By the turn of the 20th century, state governments had emerged as the primary providers of care for those with mental illnesses and behavioral disorders. Behavioral health became the only health problem with a separately financed and managed treatment system, and state governments assumed responsibility for the entire system (Hogan, 1999). The system grew exponentially, as county governments transferred many noncriminal people still under their jurisdiction, such as the old and the senile, to state facilities (thereby transferring the cost of their care as well). By 1959, roughly 559,000 patients were housed in state mental hospitals across the country (Katz, 1989).

Beginning in the 1960s, a new generation of reformers challenged the conditions in many state institutions. They contended that patients were warehoused rather than treated, were kept isolated from families and friends, and often were brutalized by staff or other patients. At the same time, medical researchers were developing a host of new drugs that enabled large numbers of patients to cope, more or less, in the community. Perhaps most important, the federal government began funding community-based mental health services, while restricting federal funding for inpatient psychiatric services. Medicaid, for example, prohibited coverage for inpatient care in psychiatric institutions for people between the ages of 22 and 64, while providing coverage for a host of mental health services in community settings. Similarly, Congress provided direct funding to help establish a system of community mental health centers.

For all of these reasons, state governments began a massive effort to discharge patients from state hospitals and to divert others from admission. This policy, however, has not been a complete success. Although people with mental illness are no longer subjected to overcrowded and poor-quality institutions, large numbers of them cannot find housing or services in the community and end up homeless and inadequately treated. State officials' most popular strategy for addressing these new problems is to delegate responsibility for the indigent mentally ill to managed care plans specializing in behavioral health. It remains to be seen whether the managed care revolution will solve the long neglect of our mentally ill citizens, yet it is quite clear that state governments will continue to have the overall responsibility for their care.

LOCAL GOVERNMENT AND THE SAFETY NET FOR THE POOR

Scattered throughout the United States are more than 1,500 public general hospitals, nearly all of which are owned and operated by local governments. More than two-thirds are small (fewer than 200 beds), located in rural communities, and have low occupancy rates (generally well below 50%). Many of the urban institutions, in contrast, are quite large and have high occupancy rates. For example, the 100 largest urban public hospitals average nearly 600 beds and have an occupancy rate of roughly 80%. Indeed, the average big-city public hospital is three times the size of the typical, non-government-owned facility, has four times as many inpatient admissions, provides five times as many outpatient clinic visits, and delivers seven times as many babies.

Urban public hospitals also treat a disproportionately high percentage of the poor and uninsured. In 1991, nearly 50% of their patient population was on Medicaid, 25% was uninsured, and only 12% had private insurance. Generally, these institutions treat a sicker, more difficult population than do most of their commercial or nonprofit counterparts. These are the providers of last resort, treating the homeless mentally ill, the babies addicted to cocaine, and the victims of violence.

> Urban public hospitals are the providers of last resort, treating the homeless mentally ill, the babies addicted to cocaine, and the victims of violence.

Local governments also fund and administer more than 3,000 public health departments. Each of these departments makes an effort, at least to some degree, to assess the public health needs of the community, develop policies that address those needs, and assure that primary and preventive health services are provided to all (see chapter 4).

Key Issues on the Health Care Agenda

Health care policymakers are grappling with a host of difficult issues, ranging from the uninsured to the long-term care system to how best to serve those with special needs (such as mental illness or substance abuse). In this section, three such issues are identified, and the key options on the policy agenda are summarized.

THE UNINSURED

Policymakers need to make a series of decisions about the nation's uninsured population. Should government target its dollars on further expanding the various public insurance initiatives? How can government encourage those who are eligible but not enrolled in public programs to sign up? Is it wiser to spend public dollars providing tax credits and other incentives to encourage uninsured people to purchase their own private insurance policies? Are there other ways to help the uninsured, and if so, are they politically and financially feasible?

Early in the 2008 presidential campaign, the leading candidates for the Democratic nomination all proposed comprehensive efforts to aid the uninsured. Hillary Clinton and John Edwards, for example, proposed that all Americans be required to have health insurance (a so-called individual mandate) and that the federal government offer an affordable insurance alternative for those unable to access or afford private insurance. Barack Obama offered a similar proposal, though his individual mandate proposal covered only children. All of the Democratic candidates also proposed significant expansions in current public insurance programs (such as Medicaid and SCHIP) and a range of initiatives designed to slow the rise in health care expenditures.

The 2008 Republican presidential candidates generally disparaged the Democratic approach as too focused on public insurance, with too many government mandates, and costing too much money. The Republicans instead suggested a focus on market-based solutions, such as consumer choice health plans, health savings accounts, and expanded competition in the individual insurance market. Former New York City Mayor Rudolph Giuliani, for example, proposed providing individuals with a large tax credit with which to purchase insurance in the individual market. The Republican candidates' proposals are consistent with President Bush's long-standing proposals to aid the uninsured.

MEDICARE AND PRESCRIPTION DRUGS

Even before the enactment of the Medicare prescription drug coverage law in 2003, more than 75% of Medicare beneficiaries had some coverage for the cost of prescription drugs, either from a retiree health plan, a managed care plan, a Medi-gap policy, Medicaid, or a state-financed pharmaceutical assistance program. Nonetheless, with drug costs rising rapidly, with more than 10 million seniors having no drug coverage whatsoever, and with health plans and large companies scaling back the scope of their drug coverage, the political pressure to produce Medicare drug coverage was irresistible.

Over the next several years, policymakers will undoubtedly revisit some of the more controversial elements of the recent drug legislation. These are among the key issues sure to resurface:

- The law's provision requiring that prices be set by marketplace negotiations between pharmaceutical companies and health plans and barring Medicare officials from negotiating rates with the drug companies.
- The provision of $71 billion in subsidies to companies that retain retiree coverage in order to convince them not to scale back retiree health coverage. (Retiree health plans now provide drug coverage to roughly one-third of all Medicare beneficiaries.)
- Treatment of *dual-eligibles* (that is, people on both Medicaid and Medicare), who previously received drug coverage from Medicaid, but under the new law are covered by the less generous Medicare benefit.
- Higher rates paid to managed care plans and the imposition of income-based premiums on people with annual income above $80,000.
- The so-called donut hole, which requires beneficiaries to pay a large percentage of their drug costs.
- Failure of insurers (and Medicare, for that matter) to provide adequate and accurate information about plan costs and coverage to people who call their toll-free numbers (U.S. Government Accountability Office, 2006a, 2006b).

REGULATING THE MANAGED CARE INDUSTRY

The concept of a national patient protection act has bipartisan congressional support, and both the House and Senate enacted bills on this issue in 1999. However, sharp differences exist between the political parties and between the two houses on how best to achieve the goal. Two key issues dominate the debate. First, the House of Representatives and most liberals want the national law to apply to everyone with private health insurance (roughly 158 million Americans), whereas the Senate and the Republican leadership want the bill to cover only those 56 million or so in self-insured health plans and thus not covered by state patient protection laws.

Second, the more expansive House proposal allows consumers to bring lawsuits to state courts against managed care plans for the denial or delay of needed treatment. In these state court proceedings, injured parties could receive compensation for pain and suffering as well as punitive damages designed to punish especially malicious acts. The Senate bill would allow lawsuits only in federal court, if at all, with limited rights to compensation for pain and suffering and without any right to punitive damages.

References

Aetna Health, Inc., *vs.* Davila, 542 US 200. (2004).

Annas, G., Law, S., Rosenblatt, R., & Wing, K. (1990). *American health law*. Boston: Little, Brown & Co.

Brown, L. D., & Sparer, M. S. (2001). Window shopping: State health reform politics in the 1990s. *Health Affairs, 20,* 50–67.

Clemens-Cope, L., Garrett, B., & Hoffman, C. (2006). *Changes in employee health insurance coverage, 2001–2005*. Washington, DC: Kaiser Commission on Medicaid and the Uninsured.

Dranove, D. (2000). *The economic evolution of American health care*. Princeton, NJ: Princeton University Press.

Hogan, M. (1999). Public sector mental health care: New challenges. *Health Affairs, 18,* 106–111.

Holahan, J., & Liska, D. (1997). The slowdown in Medicaid growth: Will it continue? *Health Affairs, 16,* 157–163.

Howell, E., Hill, I., & Kapustka, H. (2002). *SCHIP dodges the first budget ax*. Urban Institute, Assessing the New Federalism. Policy Brief A-56. Washington, DC: The Urban Institute.

Johnston, D. (1999, January 21). $116 million punitive award against Aetna. *New York Times,* C1.

Kaiser Family Foundation. (2004a). *Medicare advantage fact sheet*. Menlo Park, CA: Author.

Kaiser Family Foundation. (2004b). *State health facts*. Menlo Park, CA: Author.

Kaiser Family Foundation. (2007a). *The Medicaid program at a glance*. Menlo Park, CA: Author.

Kaiser Family Foundation (2007b). *Medicare advantage fact sheet*. Menlo Park, CA: Author.

Kaiser Family Foundation. (2007c). *Medicare at a glance*. Menlo Park, CA: Author.

Katz, M. (1989). *The undeserving poor*. New York: Pantheon Books.

Markle Foundation, American Medical Association, Gold Standard, et al. (2006). *Lessons from KatrinaHealth*. Retrieved from http://www.markle.org/downloadable_ assets/katrinahealth.final.pdf

Marmor, T. (2000). *The politics of Medicare* (2nd ed.). New York: Aldine de Gruyter.

Oberlander, J. (2003). *The political life of Medicare*. Chicago: University of Chicago Press.

Robert Wood Johnson Foundation. (2007). *The state of the states.* Princeton, NJ: Author. Retrieved from http://www.rwjf.org/files/publications/other/StateoftheStates 2007.pdf

Sparer, M. S. (1996). *Medicaid and the limits of state health reform.* Philadelphia: Temple University Press.

Sparer, M. S. (2003). Leading the health policy orchestra: The need for an intergovernmental partnership. *Journal of Health Politics, Policy and Law, 28,* 245–270.

Starr, P. (1982). *The social transformation of American medicine.* New York: Basic Books.

U.S. Government Accountability Office. (2006a). *Medicare Part D: Prescription drug plan sponsor call center responses were prompt, but not consistently accurate and complete.* GAO-06-710. Retrieved from http://energycommerce.house.gov/Press_ 109/GAO.report.06-710.pdf

U.S. Government Accountability Office. (2006b). *Medicare. Communications to beneficiaries on the prescription drug benefit could be improved.* GAO-06-654. Retrieved from http://www.gao.gov/new.items/d06654.pdf

6

Key Words

health systems

national health insurance (NHI)

national health service (NHS)

inputs and outputs

outcomes

inefficiency in the allocation of resources

direct versus indirect third-party payment

comparative analysis

policy learning

world cities

Comparative Analysis of Health Systems Among Wealthy Nations

Victor G. Rodwin

Learning Objectives

- Identify key elements of health system models.
- Understand conceptual and methodological issues in the analysis of health systems.
- Identify common problems of health systems and policy across wealthy nations.
- Highlight key features and issues in the French, Canadian, and British health systems.
- Analyze the U.S. health system from a comparative perspective.
- Examine the uses of comparative analysis in learning from abroad.

Topical Outline

- The evolution of health systems and policy in wealthy nations
- Overview of health system models
- Comparative analysis of health systems
- Common problems of health care organization and policy in three nations
- The U.S. health system in comparative perspective
- New approaches to comparative analysis health systems abroad
- Concluding observations

W indows can sometimes be mirrors. A look at health systems abroad—particularly in nations at similar levels of economic development—can enable us to develop a better understanding of our health system in the United States. We tend to be ethnocentric in our views of health care organization and policy. Despite differences in the organization and financing of their health care systems, however, most health policy-makers in other wealthy nations share a number of common problems with their counterparts in the United States. First, how should they decide—or explicitly not decide—what proportion of gross domestic product (GDP) should be devoted to health and welfare? Second, how should they agree on appropriate criteria for allocating health and social service expenditures? Third, how can they implement established policies through regulation, promotion of competition, budgeting, or reimbursement incentives directed at health care providers? This chapter provides a historical context, an overview of health system models, and a broader framework within which to compare the health systems facing these universal questions. Cross-national comparisons of health systems can provide a useful perspective for understanding our own system and expanding our vision of what is possible.

The Evolution of Health Systems and Policy in Wealthy Nations

Over the course of the 20th century, national governments have gradually extended their role over the financing and organization of health care services. What was once largely the responsibility of the family, philanthropy, religious institutions, and local governments has largely been taken over by national and subnational governments—a trend that has accompanied the rise of the welfare state (De Kervasdoué, Kimberly, & Rodwin, 1984). This evolution has affected all wealthy, industrially advanced nations that form the majority members of the Organisation for Economic Co-operation and Development (OECD).[1]

I wish to thank Jin Liu for assistance including updating the OECD data and preparing the tables for this chapter.

[1] In this chapter, wealthy nations are defined as the top two-thirds of all OECD members, measured in terms of gross domestic product per capita, in 2002 U.S. dollars, after adjusting for the relative

The pattern of increasing government expenditure and intervention in the health sector became more pronounced in the decades following World War II, to the point where few people could claim not to have benefited from many dimensions of this government largesse. Even in the United States, where conservatives have resisted this trend, who could claim not to have benefited—directly or indirectly—from hospitals that were granted tax-exempt status or other government subsidies, health professionals who were trained with government grants, medical research that was financed by the federal government, private health insurance that was tax deductible to an employer, or a host of public health programs, including Medicaid and Medicare?

The growth of government involvement in health care systems characterized OECD nations during the great boom years of health sector growth (the 1950s and 1960s), when governments encouraged hospital construction and modernization, workforce training, and biomedical research. It has continued since the 1970s, when the goals shifted more toward rationalization and cost containment. As we begin the 21st century, public and other forms of collective private financing—for example, health insurance—have become the dominant sources for funding health care, and public expenditure on health care has become the largest category of social expenditure as a share of GDP, after social security payments. Furthermore, governments, including the U.S. government, have increasingly broadened the scope of their intervention to encompass new regulatory functions (see chapter 5).

> As we begin the 21st century, health insurance has become the dominant source for funding health care, and public expenditure on health care has become the largest category of social expenditure in OECD nations.

These trends are so powerful that they have affected the way we conceptualize health care systems. Indeed, the comparative study of health systems is dominated by attention to the role of the nation state. Thus, in this chapter, we first provide an overview of health system models across OECD nations. Next, we review some general issues raised by the comparative analysis of health systems. To provide further context for some health system models that are important for the United States—France, Canada, and Great Britain—we also review some common problems of health care organization and policy in these nations. Finally, we analyze the U.S. health system from a comparative perspective; examine the uses of comparative analysis for Americans, in learning from abroad; and present some new and promising approaches to the comparative analysis of health systems.

---

purchasing power of the currencies in these nations. This definition encompasses all OECD members except Greece, Portugal, Korea, Czech Republic, Hungary, Slovak Republic, Poland, Mexico, and Turkey.

Overview of Health System Models

Whether one's image of a health system is private and market-based—as in the United States and Switzerland—or public and state-controlled—as in Great Britain and Scandinavian nations—or at some intermediary point along such a continuum—as in France, Canada, and Japan—it is possible to make some useful distinctions with respect to the financing and organization of health services. Table 6.1 classifies components of health systems by distinguishing the sources of health care financing (in the columns) and organizational arrangements (in the rows).

The four principal sources of financing to pay for health services are (a) *government*—general revenue funds from the fiscal tax system; (b) *social security/national health insurance*—funds from compulsory payroll taxes through the social security system; (c) *private insurance*—funds raised through voluntary premiums assessed by private health insurance companies; and (d) *out of pocket*—funds from individual patient payments. There are, of course, other minor sources of health care financing, particularly for capital expenditures. These include direct employer contributions and philanthropic funds.

Table 6.1   Health System Components: Organizational Arrangements and Sources of Financing

Organization Type	Sources of Financing			
	Government	Social Security/NHI	Private Insurance	Out of Pocket
Public	Veterans Administration	Medicare pays for patient in a public hospital	Private insurer pays for patient in a public hospital	Patients pay for their own care in a public hospital
Private nonprofit/ quasi-governmental	Medicaid pays for patient in a nonprofit hospital	Medicare pays for patient in a nonprofit hospital	Private insurer pays for patient in a nonprofit hospital	Patients pay for their own care in a nonprofit hospital
Private for-profit	Medicaid pays for patient in a for-profit hospital	Medicare pays for patient in a for-profit hospital	Private insurer pays for patient in a for-profit hospital	Patients pay for their own care in a for-profit hospital

The organizational arrangements in Table 6.1 refer to the supply of health services: public, private not-for-profit, or private for-profit. Within these categories, many distinctions may be added. For example, in the United States, some publicly capitalized organizations (row 1) are national (the Veterans Administration); others are subnational (state mental hospitals); and many are local (municipal hospitals). Likewise, the not-for-profit category may include a variety of quasi-public organizations—for example, hospital trusts in Britain. The for-profit form of organization, an important subcategory in the United States, would include investor-owned hospitals and managed care organizations (MCOs). Indeed, the growth of large investor-owned MCOs distinguishes the health system of the United States from that of most other OECD nations.

In summary, Table 6.1 highlights components of the U.S. health system that are characterized by specific relationships among organizational arrangements and sources of health care financing. This matrix may be used as a framework for cross-national comparative analysis of health systems.

NATIONAL HEALTH SERVICE SYSTEMS

National health service (NHS) systems—such as those in Great Britain, Sweden, Norway, Finland, Denmark, Portugal, Spain, Italy, and Greece—are typically traced back to Lord Beveridge, the British economist who wrote the blueprint for that country's NHS immediately following World War II. Such systems are characterized by a dominant share of financing derived from taxes (see Table 6.1, column 1). Likewise, their systems of hospital provision were dominated by public-sector organizational forms (row 1) that are now coming to resemble quasi-public organizations in Great Britain (row 2). These general characteristics do not preclude other forms of financing (columns 2, 3, and 4), nor do they preclude a significant mix of other associated organizational forms. Indeed, some of the most interesting differences among NHS systems revolve around the extent to which they combine a different mix of columns and rows. For example, the relative size of private financing and provision is much higher in Italy and Spain than it is in Sweden or Denmark.

Another distinguishing characteristic of NHS systems is their tendency to rely largely on budgets to allocate government resources in the health sector and control total health care expenditures. National health insurance systems, by contrast, have had a more open-ended reimbursement system for health care providers, but this distinction is rapidly blurring as NHI systems are increasingly under pressure to operate within budget limits.

NATIONAL HEALTH INSURANCE SYSTEMS

National health insurance (NHI) systems—such as those in France, Germany, Belgium, Luxembourg, and Japan—are typically traced back to Chancellor Otto von Bismarck, who established the first NHI program for salaried industrial workers in Germany in 1883. NHI systems tend to be characterized by a dominant share of financing from Table 6.1, column 2. Canada is an exception to this pattern because the dominant share of financing is from general tax revenues. Likewise, NHI systems of provision are characterized by a more balanced public-private mix than in NHS systems. Once again, these general characteristics do not preclude the contributions of other forms of financing (columns 1, 3, and 4), nor do they preclude having a dominant share of public hospitals in nations such as France and Germany (row 1).

As with NHS systems, NHI systems are characterized by significant variation in their financing and organizational arrangements. For example, the share of French health care expenditures that is financed from general tax revenues (column 1) has increased beyond 40%. Likewise, the relative share of proprietary hospital beds ranges widely across NHI systems from none in Canada to 26% in France.

OTHER HEALTH SYSTEM MODELS

Although this chapter focuses on health systems of wealthy nations, it should be noted that Table 6.1 can be used to classify health systems around the world. Developing nations still finance most of their health care expenditures from out-of-pocket payments (Table 6.1, column 4), although experiments are under way to develop systems of mutual aid through voluntary private health insurance (Dror & Preker, 2002). Also, with regard to contagious diseases such as HIV/AIDS that have what economists call negative externalities, public and private international health care financing has increased tremendously (for example, the several global AIDS initiatives). Likewise, in the independent states of the former Soviet Union—so-called transitional economies—out-of-pocket payments usually are more than half of all health care expenditures. The same is true in China and India. In Latin American nations, by contrast, although there are few systems of universal NHI coverage, social security financing based on payroll taxes (row 2) covers an important share of health care expenditures.

AN EMERGING PARADIGM

In all the columns and rows of Table 6.1, it is hard to locate any existing health system within any one category. Because of the enormous pluralism of the United States, components of its health system are within each category. Among most OECD nations, which include Japan and the United States, no existing systems actually correspond to the pure NHI and NHS models. In fact, most health systems in wealthy nations have converged along the lines of what Hurst (1992) calls the contractual model. This model indicates that there is an important dimension missing in Table 6.1—the relationships between health care purchasers and health care providers. Chernichovsky (2002) analyzes this emerging paradigm in relation to what he calls the "organization and management of care consumption."

> What is important in the comparative analysis of OECD health systems—beyond the question of how to finance health services or how to achieve the right balance between public and private organizational arrangements—is how to allocate available resources to achieve the best results.

The contractual model and the new organization and management functions suggest that what is important in the comparative analysis of OECD health systems—beyond the question of how to finance health services or how to achieve the right balance between public and private organizational arrangements—is how to allocate available resources to achieve the best results. This challenge raises issues of health system performance, governance, accountability, consumer control, management of care, and overall integration of health services across the full continuum of care.

Comparative Analysis of Health Systems

Comparative analysis of health systems in wealthy OECD nations has resulted in a large and growing literature that provides profiles and improves our understanding of health care systems abroad. Three stages may be distinguished in the evolution of such research (Dumbaugh & Neuhauser, 1979), all of which are apparent in contemporary studies of health systems abroad. The first stage dominated the field until the mid-1960s and continues today in the form of "travelogues" written by physicians returning from overseas tours. During the second stage, researchers described health systems from a variety of perspectives—often with hopes of promoting health care reform. During the third stage, analysts have attempted to make the comparison of health systems into a kind of social science. This type of analysis focuses largely on explaining variations across health systems on the basis of received theories within such disciplines as anthropology, sociology, political science, and economics.

The social science approach to the comparative analysis of health systems has some of the defects of its virtues. To achieve a rigorous study design, it classifies data on health systems, formulates hypotheses, and tests them against available evidence. Economists, for example, focus on cross-sectional comparisons of health services utilization and expenditures, thus narrowing the scope of research questions and eroding the ideals shared by stage-two scholars, who were more motivated by the pragmatic concerns of improving health care delivery in their countries. Social scientists tend to display more interest in the theoretical concerns of their disciplines than in social change. Nevertheless, some excellent studies have been produced that have raised some conceptual and methodological issues that remain at the center of comparative health systems research. These will be touched on in subsequent sections of this chapter.

CONCEPTUAL ISSUES

The concept of a *health system* is critical in efforts to compare health care financing and organization across nations. There is yet no fully satisfactory definition of this concept, for it is difficult to agree on both the boundaries of the system and on a definition of health. Blum (1981) provided a graphic model of health, which suggests that health care services are merely one input to health among three others— heredity, behavior, and environment (Mokdad, Marks, Stroup, & Gerberding, 2000) and have since estimated that behavioral factors account for roughly half of all deaths in the United States. Viewing the concept of a health system at a macrosociological level, Field (1973) proposed the following formal definition: A health system is "that societal mechanism that transforms generalized resources . . . into specialized outputs in the form of health services" (p. 768). He added that "the 'health system' of any society is that social mechanism that has arisen or been devised to deal with the incapacitating aspects of illness, trauma, and (to some degree) premature mortality . . . the five D's: death, disease, disability, discomfort, and dissatisfaction" (p. 772). Anderson (1972) outlined more concretely the "boundaries of a relatively easily defined system with entry and exit points, hierarchies of personnel, types of patients"—in short, what he calls "the officially and professionally recognized 'helping' services regarding disease, disability and death" (p. 22).

Another approach to the concept of a health system is to define it implicitly by postulating a causal model of it. Thus, De Miguel (1975) outlined four subsystem levels that influence health status: individual, institutional, societal, and environmental. Such an approach allows one to analyze a health system by investigating the effects of a hierarchy of independent variables on the dependent variable, health status. It also raises questions about the most effective levels at which to effect system change.

METHODOLOGICAL ISSUES

A key issue of method in comparative health systems research involves the selection of two or more health systems that allow the analyst to hold some variables constant while manipulating experimental ones. With respect to the performance of a health system, for example, how does one evaluate health system outcomes among different systems characterized by different patterns of financing, organization, and access? Quasi-experimental research designs suggest matching two health systems on all but a few policy-related factors. But such matching, let alone a real experiment, is rarely feasible in policy research.

One response to this difficulty has been to match health systems on at least some criteria (e.g., levels of economic development and health resources) and then to call for in-depth studies of contrasting cases (Elling & Kerr, 1975). Another response has been to use the language of natural experiment and view most similar systems as laboratories in which to assess the effects of alternative policy options at home (Marmor, Bridges, & Hoffman, 1978). A more recent response has been to adopt a modular approach that examines, systematically and sequentially, diverse components of health systems—for example, needs, inputs, the delivery process, and health system outcomes (Ellencweig, 1992).

A second methodological issue in the social science approach to comparative health systems research is whether the descriptive studies and data collected during stages one and two (previously described) are actually comparable. If they are not, this casts great doubt on the utility of the comparisons. Even if they are, qualifications usually must be given.

The most difficult issues in evaluating health system performance involve specifying the relationship between the elements of a health system (inputs and outputs) and their impact on health status (outcomes). But how does one disentangle the effects of health services on health from the effects of improvements in social services, income security, education, and transportation, not to mention individual behavior or the social and physical environments? This question raises the problem of devising indicators of health status. It also explains why, in his comparative study of the United States, Sweden, and England, Anderson (1972) found it impossible to attribute differences in the usual health indices of morbidity and mortality to patterns of health care organization in these countries.

Although there has been some progress on this score over the past 35 years, it remains extraordinarily difficult to evaluate the performance of health care systems, for this requires measurable indicators of health system inputs and outputs and development of health status indicators to measure outcomes. The World Health Organization

(WHO) published a study of health system performance in which member health systems were ranked on the basis of eight measures (WHO, 2000). The results are controversial and suffer from grave methodological problems (Coyne & Hilsenrath, 2002; Navarro, 2002). Nonetheless, the temptation to rank health care systems has encouraged a search for the best health care system, which has become the holy grail of comparative health system performance studies. What is missing, however, in this approach is any effort to compare and understand health systems with respect to their cultural context, values, and institutions.

LEARNING FROM ABROAD

Comparative studies of health systems and policy are sparse. Most often, they describe an innovation or an experience in a health care system abroad; only rarely do they interpret or evaluate this experience based on a common analytic framework (Marmor, Freeman, & Okma, 2005). Exceptions to this general rule are of interest because they have contributed at least three ideas with implications for how we might learn from health systems abroad.

First is the idea of evolutionary progress in health systems. Roemer (1977) described the evolution of health systems as a march toward a health ideal characterized by increasing shares of public expenditure on health services and increasing government control over the health care sector. Medical sociologists Field (1973) and Mechanic (1976) argued that health systems in Western industrialized nations are converging on similar paths. Unlike Roemer, Field and Mechanic were not convinced that this trend necessarily implies progress.

The second idea, the notion of public policy learning, is methodological. For example, the most-similar-systems approach views health systems as laboratories in which to assess the effects of alternative policy options at home. Examples of this approach include Evans's (1984) book on health economics in Canada, as well as Marmor's (1994) analyses of the Canadian experience. The most-similar-systems approach is also highlighted in Glaser's (1991) studies of health policy in Western Europe and Canada. These studies are distinctive, however, in that they begin with the premise that the U.S. health care system has many problems and that the policies and experiences of Western Europe and Canada can shed light on and provide a useful range of solutions for the United States.

The third idea focuses on understanding either determinants of health policies or at least their effects. Leichter (1979), for example, analyzed the determinants of health policies in Britain, Germany, Japan, and the former Soviet Union. Similarly, Hollingsworth (1986), Immergut (1992), and Tuohy (1999) have attempted to relate differences in structure, performance, and policy among such nations as the United States, France, Germany, Britain, and Canada.

The idea of evolutionary progress in the development of health systems suggests that the United States can predict and learn about future policy issues by studying nations whose systems are more advanced, bringing foreign solutions to bear on American problems. Finally, the idea of using comparative analysis to understand the determinants and effects of health policies abroad can assist us in evaluating alternative policy options at home.

> The idea of evolutionary progress in the development of health systems suggests that the United States can predict and learn about future policy issues by studying nations whose systems are more advanced, bringing foreign solutions to bear on American problems.

There is, however, an important caveat to these views. The ideas briefly discussed above—indeed, most of the literature in comparative health policy—often minimize or overlook the substantial problems faced by health systems abroad. An alternative, problem-oriented approach reverses this emphasis. For example, another way to think about learning from health systems abroad is to begin with the recognition that most countries, irrespective of their particular health system, face common, serious problems with regard to efficiently allocating scarce health care resources and making access to them equitable. The OECD and the World Bank have published important comparative studies that reflect this approach (see References at the end of this chapter). With this approach, there are at least three ways of viewing the problems.

Economists emphasize the problem of inefficiency in the allocation of health care resources. They point out that cost containment should not be confused with allocative efficiency in the use of health care resources, and they study the possibilities for obtaining more value for the money spent on health care. This applies not only with regard to improving health status but also with respect to altering input mixes in the provision of health services that take advantage of cost-effective treatment settings (e.g., ambulatory surgery) and personnel (e.g., nurse practitioners).

Public health and medical care analysts criticize the lack of integration among primary, secondary, and tertiary levels of care. They have called for redistributing resources away from hospitals to community-based ambulatory care services and public health programs, inasmuch as the allocation of resources within health regions has been notoriously biased in favor of more costly technology-based medical care at the apex of the regional hierarchy (Fox, 1986). This allocation pattern weakens institutional capability for delivering primary care services and exacerbates the separation of primary, secondary, and tertiary levels of care, thus making it difficult for providers to assure that the right patient receives the right kind of care, in the right place, and for the right reason.

Consumers have noted the inflexibility of bureaucratic decision-making procedures and the absence of opportunities for exercising what Hirschman (1970) calls "voice" in most health care organizations. Indeed, the problem of control and how it should be shared among consumers, providers, managers, and payers is at the center of most criticisms leveled against the current structure of health systems in industrialized nations. In all of these systems, decisions about what medical services to provide, how and where they should be provided, by whom, and how often are separated from the responsibility for financing medical care.

Common Problems of Health Care Organization and Policy in Three Nations

Drawing on the problem-oriented approach presented above, this section analyzes common problems with regard to the efficient allocation of and equitable access to scarce health care resources in three OECD nations: France, Canada, and Britain (see Table 6.2). These nations are far smaller than the United States in terms of population. They have slightly lower gross domestic product per capita and spend less on health care as a percentage of GDP. In the aggregate, they deliver more hospital bed days and doctors' consultations per capita. With respect to health outcomes, measured against most traditional health indicators, they appear to be better off. All of them have lower infant mortality rates, higher life expectancy at birth, and (except for the United Kingdom) higher life expectancy at age 65.

The health systems of all three nations deserve to become better known in the United States, because they represent models that have been invoked in U.S. efforts to achieve health care reform. France is a prototype of a traditional European employment-based NHI system; Canada represents 12 different examples, from its various provinces and territories, of a newer NHI system operating in a federal institutional structure that resembles more closely that of the United States; Britain is the model par excellence of an NHS operating under a highly centralized government authority.

FRANCE

The French health system combines national health insurance with solo, office-based, fee-for-service private practice in the ambulatory care sector and a mixed hospital care sector of which two-thirds of

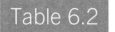

Table 6.2 — Health System Characteristics and Outcomes: France, Canada, United Kingdom, and United States

	Year	France	Canada	U.K.[a]	U.S.
Health System Characteristics					
Health expenditures as a percent of gross domestic product	2004–2005	10.5%	9.9%	8.5%	15.3%
Per capita health expenditures in $US (purchasing power parity)	2004	$3,159	$3,165	$2,508	$6,102
Public expenditures on health as a percentage of total health expenditures	2004–2005	78.4%	69.6%	87.1%	44.7%
Percentage of national health expenditures spent on administration and insurance	2003	1.9%	2.6%	3.3%	7.3%
Health Outcome Characteristics					
Infant mortality per 1,000 live births	2002–2004	3.9	5.3	5.1	7.0
Life expectancy (females) at age 65	2002–2003	21.4	20.8	19.1	19.8
Life expectancy at birth (males)	2003–2004	76.7	77.4	76.2	74.8
Mortality preventable by health care (deaths per 100,000 population)	1998	75	92	130	115

[a] OECD data are for the United Kingdom (England, Scotland, Wales, and Northern Ireland). However, when the Northern Ireland data are excluded, the figures are very similar to those for Great Britain (England, Scotland, and Wales).
Note. Most information is from OECD data released October 2006 and retrieved from http://www. oecd.org/document/16/0,2340,en_2649_34631_2085200_1_1_1_1,00.html National expenditures on administration and insurance from OECD 2005 data; U.S. infant mortality rates from K. D. Kochanek & J. A. Martin. *Supplemental analyses of recent trends in infant mortality.* Retrieved from http://www.cdc.gov/nchs/products/pubd/hestats/infantmort/infantmort.htm

all acute beds are in the public sector and one-third are in the private sector. Physicians in private practice and in private hospitals are reimbursed according to a negotiated fee schedule. Roughly 30% of all physicians select the option to extra-bill beyond the negotiated fees that, for the remaining 70% of physicians, represent payment in full (Rodwin et al., 2006). They may do so as long as their charges are presented with "tact and measure," a standard that has never been legally defined but which has been found, empirically, to represent a 50% to 100% increase in the negotiated fees. Public hospital physicians work on a part-time or full-time salaried basis. Private hospitals used to be reimbursed through a negotiated per diem fee, but in the late 1990s, they gradually moved to a case-mix reimbursement system. Before 1984, public hospitals were reimbursed based on a retrospective, cost-based, per diem fee; since then, they have received prospectively set "global" budgets adjusted for patient case-mix.

Although the French NHI was rated first in terms of overall efficiency and fairness by the 2000 World Health Organization study of health system performance, it still has several problems. From a public health point of view, there is inadequate communication between full-time salaried physicians in public hospitals and solo-based private practice physicians working in the community. General practitioners in the fee-for-service sector (roughly half of French physicians) have informal referral networks to specialists and public hospitals, but there are no formal institutional relationships that assure continuity of medical care, disease prevention and health promotion services, post-hospital follow-up care, and, more generally, no systematic linkages and referral patterns between primary, secondary, and tertiary services.

From an economic perspective, problems of economic efficiency remain. On the demand side, two factors encourage consumers to increase their use of medical care services: uncertainty about the results of treatment and the availability of universal and comprehensive insurance coverage. To reduce the risk of misdiagnosis or improper therapy, physicians are always tempted to order more diagnostic tests. Since NHI covers most of the cost, there is no incentive—for either physicians or patients—to balance marginal changes in risk with marginal increases in costs. This results in excessive and often inappropriate use of services.

On the supply side, fee-for-service reimbursement of physicians provides incentives for them to increase their volume of services to raise their income. Likewise, case-based reimbursement of private hospitals provides incentives to increase patient admissions as long as revenues exceed costs. The imposition of global budgets in 1984 eliminated this problem for the French public hospitals. The move toward using case-mix indicators in setting public hospital budgets and negotiating per diem fees for private hospitals also have weakened the incentives to increase hospital services. However, the budgets for public hospitals represent a blunt policy tool—one that tends to support the existing allocation of resources within the hospital sector and possibly jeopardizes the quality of public hospital services. Hospitals relatively easily can receive an annual budget to maintain ongoing activities, but only with great difficulty can receive additional compensation for higher service levels, institutional innovation, or improvements in the quality of care. Since 1996, even with prospectively set budgets for public as well as private hospitals, these institutions naturally have sought to maximize the level of their annual allocations and to resist budget cutbacks.

In summary, under French NHI, providers have no financial incentives to achieve savings while holding quality constant or even improving it; nor are there incentives—in public hospitals, for example—to increase service activity in exchange for more revenues. Therefore, consumers have few incentives, other than minimal co-payments, to be economical in their use of medical care. Also, there are no incentives to move the French system away from hospital-centered services toward new organizational forms that encourage teamwork among general practitioners, specialists, and hospitals and greater responsiveness to emerging market demands.

In 1996, as part of a broader reform of the social security system, Prime Minister Alain Juppé attempted the most far-reaching reform of the French health sector since 1958 (Le Pen & Rodwin, 1996). The central state's supervisory role over the national health insurance system was reinforced. In addition, the French Parliament was made accountable for health expenditures. It was required to set a global expenditure target for total health care expenditures reimbursed by the NHI and to set budget targets for each of France's 21 regions. To advise Parliament in this new responsibility and assist the Ministry of Health in overseeing the health system, a number of new institutions were created: the National Committee on Public Health, a National Agency for Hospital Accreditation, and Quality and Regional Agencies for hospital planning and control.

Although President Jacques Chirac dissolved Parliament shortly after the national strikes in protest of the social security reforms, almost all of the health care reforms were maintained by the social-ist government of Prime Minister Lionel Jospin. Since then, Prime Minister Jean-Pierre Raffarin fine-tuned the Juppé reform and created a High Authority for Health to replace the National Agency on Hospital Accreditation and Evaluation. This authority is charged with developing medical guidelines for physicians in private practice, which the NHI funds have the discretion and authority to enforce. The problems identified earlier are still not resolved, and the reforms are still not entirely implemented. But the French central government is increasingly intervening to modernize and rationalize the health care system, which suggests an emerging French model of state-led managed care (Rodwin & Le Pen, 2004).

CANADA

Under Canadian national health insurance, although coverage for pre-scription drugs is far less generous than in France (only two provinces have a program to cover prescription drugs), most provinces have no co-payments for any covered hospital or medical service (Deber, 2003). Thus patients pay no portion of their medical bills and have first-dollar coverage for a comprehensive package of hospital and medical services. Physicians in ambulatory care are paid predominantly on a fee-for-service basis, according to fee schedules negotiated between physicians' associations and provincial governments. All physicians must accept these fees as payment in full. In contrast to France, where most physicians in public hospitals are salaried, most physicians in Canadian hospitals are paid on a fee-for-service basis, as in the United States.

Canada has few private, for-profit hospitals. Most acute-care hospitals are private, nonprofit institutions. But their operating expenditures are financed through the NHI system, and most of their capital expenditures are financed by the provincial governments. In the United States, among advocates of NHI, Canada's health system has often been depicted as a model that could save almost $300 billion in U.S. administrative (insurance) costs and increase coverage (Woolhandler, Campbell, & Himmelstein, 2003). Its financing—through a complex shared federal and provincial tax revenue formula—is more progressive than the European NHI systems that are financed through payroll taxes. Perhaps more important, Canadians' health status is high by international standards. Finally, compared to the United States, Canada has achieved notable success in controlling the growth of health care costs. What, then, are the problems?

Health care providers perceive Canada's successful cost-containment program as a crisis of underfinancing. Physicians complain about low fee levels. Hospital administrators complain about draconian budget control. And other health care professionals say that the combination of a national physician surplus and excessive reliance on physicians prevents an expansion of their roles.

Although Evans (1992) contends that Canadian cost-control policies cannot be shown to have jeopardized the quality of care, providers and administrators alike claim that there has been deterioration since the imposition of restrictive prospective budgets. Leaving aside the issue of quality, the Canadian system faces the same economic efficiency issues that France does: no incentives for the hospital, the physician, or the patient to be economical in the use of health care resources. On the demand side, taking urgent care as an example, patients have few incentives to use community health centers rather than rush directly to the hospital's costly emergency room. On the supply side, citizens are allowed to view physicians and hospitals as essentially a free service at their disposal, again with no incentive to economize in their use. Nor does the system create incentives to use less skilled health care professionals as substitutes for physicians or hospital-based services, which would encourage organizational innovations in health care delivery. These problems are common to all health systems, but they are especially acute in a system characterized by concentrated political interests—health care providers on the one hand and a single payer on the other—that tend to support the status quo. Providers organized in strong associations have strong monopoly power, which they use to defend their interests; the monopoly power of sole-source financing (NHI) keeps provider interests in check, but at the cost of not encouraging new forms of medical practice, such as hospital-physician partnerships and health centers.

Stoddard (1984) characterized the problems of the Canadian health system as "financing without organization," and this is still a fundamental problem. In his view, Canadian provinces "adopted a 'pay the bills' philosophy, in which decisions about service provision— which services, in what amounts, produced how, by whom and where—were viewed as the legitimate domain of physicians and hospital administrators" (p. 3). The reason for this policy is that provincial governments were concerned about maintaining a good relationship with providers, though this concern has not avoided tough negotiations and periodic confrontations. But there have been only limited efforts to devise new forms of medical care practice—for example, health maintenance organizations (HMOs) or new institutions to handle long-term care for the elderly. The side effect of Canadian national health insurance has been to support the separation of hospital and ambulatory care and to reinforce traditional organizational structures.

As in France, there are, in essence, two strategies for managing the Canadian health system and making needed adjustments. The first involves greater regulation on the supply side: stronger controls on hospital spending, more rationing of medical technology, and more hospital mergers and eventually closures. The second involves increased reliance on market forces on the demand side: various forms of user charges such as co-payments and deductibles now advocated as a form of privatization. The former will control health care expenditures in the short run, but it fails to affect practice styles, because it does not evaluate levels of service provision and therapies prescribed with respect to likely patient benefit.

The more effective the first strategy turns out to be, the more likely it is to exacerbate confrontations between providers and the state and jeopardize health service delivery. As for the second strategy, it focuses on consumer demand and neglects the issue of supply-side efficiency. It provides no mechanism by which consumer decisions can signal providers to adopt more efficient practice styles. Moreover, to the extent that it has been used, it has raised the level of patients' out-of-pocket expenditures in a system originally intended to eliminate these costs.

Between these two strategies, there is increasing recognition among Canadian policymakers that the health sector requires significant reorganization. In Ontario, in 1996, the Health Services

Restructuring Commission (HSRC) was formed; in Quebec, the federation of general practitioners (GPs) formed a task force on the reorganization of primary care. Both of these efforts reinforced a trend toward integrated health systems and the use of gatekeepers in primary care. In Ontario, the main accomplishment of HSRC was to devise a seven-point plan to restructure the balance of resources among hospitals and community health services. In Quebec, the main accomplishment of the task force also was limited to planning for needed reforms. The Canadian system has been remarkably resistant to organizational reform, in practice.

Throughout the 1990s, the major Canadian health policy battles were fought over the problem of funding health services. Hospital budget cuts held per-capita public spending on health care roughly constant from 1992 to 1997, but total health care spending, as a percent of GDP, fell by a full percentage point (Naylor, 1999). Meanwhile, the combination of hospital cuts and escalating drug costs eroded public confidence in the system. But in the spring of 2000, contentious meetings between provincial health ministers and federal officials resulted in a deal to restore federal cash payments for health care and other social welfare services.

From 2000 to 2004, the federal government agreed to provide $1 billion (Canadian) to purchase medical equipment in hospitals and $800 million (CA) to support projects that reform the delivery of primary care services (Kondro, 2000). The strings attached to this deal commit the provinces to develop a formulary for prescription drugs and to produce annual report cards on the performance of their respective systems. Thus, the pressure is still on to produce some organizational reform and hold the supply side more accountable to those paying the bill (Rominow, 2002).

GREAT BRITAIN

Many models of a national health service exist in Europe, ranging from decentralized systems in Sweden, Norway, Finland, and Denmark to more centralized systems in Spain, Greece, Portugal, and Italy. Because the British NHS is one of the oldest and most thoroughly studied models, it stands as an exemplar. It is financed almost entirely through general tax revenues and is accountable directly to the central government's Department of Health and Social Security (DHSS) and Parliament. Access to health services is free of charge to all British subjects and to all legal residents. Despite universal entitlement, health expenditures in Great Britain represent only 8.4% of the gross domestic product—about half the rate of spending in the United States (see Table 6.2).

Although the NHS is cherished by most Britons, there are nevertheless some serious problems concerning both the equity or access and efficiency of resource allocation in the health sector. With regard to equity (defined as equal care for those at equal risk), in 1976, the Resource Allocation Working Party (RAWP) developed a formula for narrowing inequities in the allocation of NHS funds among regions (Townsend & Davidson, 1982). The formula was one of the most far-reaching attempts to allocate health care funds, because it incorporated regional differences in health status based on standardized mortality ratios (DHSS, 1976). Some progress was made in redistributing the aggregate NHS budget along the lines of the RAWP formula in the 1980s. It was eventually eliminated in the 1990s, and substantial inequities remain from the point of view of both geographic distribution and social class.

> Although the National Health Service is cherished by most Britons, there are nevertheless some serious problems concerning both the equity or access and efficiency of resource allocation in the health sector.

With regard to efficiency, the problems are even more severe, because NHS resources are extremely scarce by OECD standards. Perhaps because there are fewer health care resources in Britain than in the rest of Western Europe or the United States, the British have been more aggressive in weeding out inefficiency than have wealthier countries. And because the NHS faces the same demands as other systems to make technology available and to care for an increasingly aged population, British policymakers recognize that they must pursue innovations that improve efficiency. But there have been numerous obstacles: opposition by professional associations; difficulties in firing and redeploying health care personnel; and the institutional separation between hospitals, general practitioners, and community health programs.

The tripartite structure of the NHS has, since its establishment in 1948, been a source of inefficiency:

1. Regional Health Authorities (RHAs) had been responsible (until the mid-1990s) for allocating budgets to districts and hospitals. Hospital-based physicians, known as "consultants," are paid salaries from these budgets, with distinguished clinicians receiving "merit awards"; and all consultants have the right to see a limited number of private, fee-paying patients in so-called pay beds within their service units.

2. Outside the RHA budget (until the mid-1990s) were the Family Practitioner Committees (FPCs) responsible for paying general practitioners, ophthalmologists, dentists, and pharmacists. These are now called Primary Care Trusts from which GPs are reimbursed on a capitation basis, with additional remuneration coming

from special "practice allowances" and fee-for-service payments for specific services (e.g., night visits and immunizations).

3. Separate from both the RHAs and the FPCs are the local authorities, which are responsible for the provision of social services, public health services, and certain community nursing services.

This institutional framework has created perverse incentives—for example, to shift borderline patients from GPs to hospital consultants, to the community, and back to the hospital. Until the reforms introduced by the Thatcher government in 1991, GPs had no incentive to minimize costs and could even impose costs on RHAs by referring patients to hospital consultants or for diagnostic services. NHS managers could shift costs from the NHS to social security by sending elderly hospitalized patients to private nursing homes. And consultants could shift costs back onto the patient by keeping long waiting lists, thereby increasing demand for their private services. As in France and Canada, neither patients nor physicians in Britain directly bear the cost of the decisions they make; the taxpayers pay the bill.

Four strategies—all of them inadequate—have attempted to deal with this problem. The first came promptly with the arrival of the first Thatcher government in 1981. After cautious attempts to denationalize the NHS by promoting a shift toward NHI and privatization, the conservative government backed off when they realized that such an approach would not merely provoke strong political opposition but also would increase public expenditure and therefore conflict with its budgetary objectives. Instead, the strategy was confined to encouraging competition and creating limited market incentives. To begin with, the government allowed a slight increase in private pay beds within NHS hospitals; it introduced tax incentives to encourage the purchase of private health insurance and the growth of charitable contributions; and it encouraged local authorities to raise money through the sale of surplus property, outsourcing to the private sector such services as laundry, cleaning, and catering.

The second response was the Griffiths Report (1983), which resulted in yet another reorganization. Roy Griffiths, the former director of a large British department store chain, introduced the concept of a general manager at the department (DHSS), regional, district, and unit levels. This manager was presumably responsible for the efficient use of the budget at each NHS level. In summary, the report observed, in a sentence that has since become well known, "If Florence Nightingale were carrying her lamp through the corridors of the NHS today, she would almost certainly be searching for the people in charge" (Griffiths, 1983, p. 12). The problem is, however, that, following the Griffiths Report, the tripartite structure of the system remained largely unchanged, and the general managers had very little information about least-cost strategies across the structure that could produce improvements in health status.

The third attempt to improve efficiency tackled the problem of rising drug costs (Maynard, 1986). In April 1985, the government limited the list of reimbursable drugs and reduced the pharmaceutical industry's rate of return. These measures helped contain the costs of the formerly open-ended drug budget within the NHS, but there is no evidence that they had any impact on the efficiency of resource allocation—for example, substituting prescription drugs for hospital care.

Finally, the fourth and most significant reform aimed at improving NHS efficiency, announced in a government white paper titled *Working for Patients* (1989), was the National Health Service and Community Care Act passed in 1990. The white paper proposed a range of significant changes, all of which attempt to create "internal markets" within the public sector, by giving providers incentives to treat more patients and having "money follow patients"—meaning that hospital specialists who treat more patients would generate increased income flow to their hospitals. On the demand side, the government proposed that, instead of operating as monopoly suppliers of services, district health authorities be required to purchase services for the patients they serve. On the supply side, the government proposed that NHS hospitals be given the option to convert from purely public status to that of independent, self-governing trusts. Also, the government proposed that general practitioners be given the option to serve as "fundholders" for their enrolled patients and thereby serve as purchasers on their behalf for basic specialty and hospital services.

In July 1990, Regional Health Authorities were streamlined and Family Practitioner Communities were transformed into new Family Health Service Authorities (FHSAs), with stronger management over primary care. In 1996, the districts were merged with the FHSAs into roughly 80 Health Authorities and placed under a new National Health Service Executive with eight regional offices. The Health Authorities were supposed to function as integrated purchasing coalitions, thereby strengthening the role of internal markets in the allocation of health resources. These reforms shifted the balance of power between GPs and hospital specialists, encouraged innovation in primary care, promoted greater cost consciousness, and raised administrative costs (Smee, 2000).

Following Tony Blair's election as prime minister in 1994, the New Labour Party's "third way" reforms focused more on collaboration and less on competition, but the new policy retained the major elements of the internal market reforms noted above. The purchaser-provider split was retained, albeit with more emphasis on cooperation between purchasers and providers. All GPs have been brought into budget-holding primary care trusts, thus adding important elements of managed care to the NHS. The former GP fundholders have now been largely absorbed by primary care trusts, and the Health Authorities are losing their former purchasing role as they become increasingly responsible for providing a framework for Primary Care Group accountability (Dobson, 1999). This fusion of a range of financing and care-provision functions represents the emergence of managed care in Great Britain. Finally, as in France and Canada, the British NHS has made efforts to improve quality of care and practice standards. The National Institute for Clinical Effectiveness is setting standards, and the Council for Health Improvement will enforce them (Le Grand, 1999).

In retrospect, it is no exaggeration to suggest that the history of the British NHS is largely a story of successive organizational reforms to improve the efficiency of resource allocation and equity of access within the health care sector. An additional and more recent goal has been to increase responsiveness of health care providers to consumers. Nonetheless, most astute observers of the NHS concur that even the most radical reforms under Prime Ministers Margaret Thatcher and Tony Blair have had limited effects on the basic structure and problems of the system (Klein, 1998). The fundamental tension between the ideological push to introduce market mechanisms and the need for central control to preserve political accountability has remained intact. Moreover, the institutional power of central control appears to have the upper hand.

The U.S. Health System in Comparative Perspective

How does the U.S. health care system measure up in comparison to the health systems in France, Canada, and Great Britain? To answer this question, we review the ways in which the U.S. health system differs from and resembles that of other OECD nations. We examine this issue from the perspectives of two characteristics that typically distinguish the United States from Western Europe and Canada: (a) the structure of health care financing and organization and (b) values and popular opinion.

THE STRUCTURE OF HEALTH CARE FINANCING AND ORGANIZATION

The prevailing image of the U.S. health care system is one of a privately financed, privately organized system with multiple payers. These characteristics derive, in large part, from the absence of a publicly mandated national health insurance program. In comparison with other wealthy OECD nations, the U.S. government's share of health care expenditures is the lowest (44.7%). At the same time, the United States has the highest annual per capita health care expenditures—public and private combined ($6,102 in 2004).

Organizational arrangements for health care in the United States are noted for being on the private end of the public-private spectrum (see Table 6.1). In comparison with Western Europe, the United States has one of the smallest public hospital sectors. In the organization of ambulatory care, U.S. private fee-for-service practice corresponds to the norm in NHI systems. However, the absence of a national health insurance program in the United States has resulted in a system of multiple payers, a more pluralistic pattern of medical care organization, and more innovative forms of medical practice—for example, multispecialty group practices, HMOs, ambulatory surgery centers, and preferred provider organizations (PPOs).

> The absence of a national health insurance program in the United States has resulted in a system of multiple payers, a more pluralistic pattern of medical care organization, and more innovative forms of medical practice.

The United States also differs from wealthy OECD nations with regard to the ways in which health resources are used. For example, the United States is among the OECD countries with the lowest number of acute care hospital beds per 1,000 population. Yet the United States is not less likely to hospitalize patients than other nations; instead, Western Europe or Canada lack a strong nursing home industry and provide some portion of long-term care services in hospitals. The United States also differs from other OECD nations in having the lowest number of bed days per 1,000 population (700). This reflects a combination of low hospital admission rates and short lengths of stay in acute care hospitals.

Noteworthy points of similarity between the United States and other OECD nations can be found in the broad structure of health care financing and provider reimbursement. From the point of view of both consumers and providers, the essential feature of modern health care systems is the central role of third-party payment, by either government or health insurers. On the financing end, all health systems are supported primarily either by general revenue taxes or by payroll deductions in the form of compulsory taxes or voluntary health insurance premiums. On the payment end, the magnitude of third-party payments dwarfs the out-of-pocket payments by consumers.

For consumers, what matters with regard to health care financing is not the relative public and private mix but rather the relative portion of *direct* versus *indirect* third-party payment. To emphasize that the larger portion of health care financing in the United States is private is misleading, because both public and private health care financing are forms of third-party payment. They accounted for 78% of personal health expenditures in 2002, leaving consumers with direct out-of-pocket contributions equal to 14% of total health expenditures. The OECD does not routinely compare consumers' out-of-pocket payments to total personal health expenditures. However, available data on this important indicator suggest that the United States is not as different from France, Canada, and Britain as commonly believed.

The popular image of a high-cost private health care system in the United States is misleading and incomplete. Despite a notable but small investor-owned hospital sector, a dominant investor-owned managed care sector, and the *relatively* small size of the public sector in the United States, in comparison with OECD nations, the public sector plays an important role in the U.S. health care system—in providing both outpatient (ambulatory) care and hospital services.

With regard to ambulatory care, there is a maze of special federal programs and a network of local government services largely for the poor. The services are provided either in county or municipal hospital emergency rooms, in local health departments, or in nonprofit community health centers receiving significant public financing from federal, state, and local governments. As for hospitals, almost 30% of all U.S. hospitals are owned and operated by government entities (American Hospital Association, 2000). These include the federal Veterans Health Administration hospitals; marine and military hospitals; and state, county, and municipal hospitals. Although the Medicaid program was intended to bring the very poor into mainstream medicine (i.e., into the private sector), county governments continue to finance care for the "medically indigent" either through private providers or directly in public hospitals. These hospitals are a major source of care not only for Medicaid recipients, but also for more than half of the poverty population not eligible for Medicaid.

In sum, there are distinctive characteristics of health care financing and organization in the United States alongside striking points of similarity with Western European nations and Canada. The distinctive characteristics of the U.S. health care system include the absence of a national health insurance program, a preference for institutional flexibility, and innovative forms of medical care organization. The points of similarity—the coexistence of both public and private care providers and third-party payment—are structural features that the U.S. health system shares with most other OECD nations.

AMERICAN VALUES AND POPULAR OPINION

Nineteenth-century liberalism still colors Americans' perceptions of equity, the proper role of government, and citizenship. These perceptions represent a range of values and popular opinions that distinguish the United States from Western Europe and Canada.

American attitudes about health care equity were formed more than a century ago, as the country became populated by successive waves of immigrants to urban centers. During this period, the concept of the "truly needy" emerged (Rosner, 1982). Many Americans adopted a sense of responsibility and came to these newcomers' aid, but those with harsher attitudes, inspired by social Darwinist notions, distinguished between the truly needy and the "undeserving" or "unworthy" poor. Whereas in Western Europe broadly based socialist parties viewed poverty as an outcome of the economic system, in the United States there was an inclination to regard poverty as an individual problem, even a moral failing. Hence, the greater attention to *equality of opportunity* in the United States as compared with *equality of results* in the more left-leaning European social democracies.

The United States has a history of antigovernment attitudes compared to Western Europe and Canada. Suspicion regarding excessive government authority and the assertion of individual liberties is a pervasive American value—a value that also makes many Americans averse to tax increases. American perceptions of citizenship also contrast strikingly to Western European ones. In the United States, individualistic values on the one hand and social and ethnic heterogeneity on the other have resulted in "fractionalized understandings of citizenship" (Klass, 1985). In Western Europe and Canada, citizenship connotes solidarity and universal entitlements. No wonder Western Europe and Canada have largely succeeded in covering all of their citizens under some form of national health insurance, and the United States has not.

Americans generally dislike the idea of universal entitlements. As Reinhardt (1985) observed, when Americans face a trade-off between establishing tax-financed entitlements and leaving the uninsured on their own, they tend to choose the latter. It would be misleading, however, to draw any conclusions about how generous Americans are or how much social welfare they provide based only on this one tendency. In contrast to Western Europe and Canada, Americans promote redistribution policies through local assistance, charitable giving, private philanthropy, and indirect subsidies to the voluntary sector via tax exemptions. Such fragmentation of responsibility results in millions of poor Americans falling through the system's cracks.

Clearly, the United States differs from Western Europe and Canada with regard to values and popular opinion. But how important are these differences?

THE USES OF INTERNATIONAL COMPARISONS

Given the ways in which the health sector in the United States resembles that of Western Europe and Canada and the ways in which it is exceptional, can cross-national comparative analysis actually provide us with useful lessons? If the United States is truly exceptional in the health sector, then it can be argued that there is little to learn. Countries often rely on this "assumption of uniqueness" to reject other countries' ideas and approaches (Stone, 1981). To the extent that the United States is like other nations, however, a case can be made for drawing lessons from their experience.

For example, there is a widely shared belief among American policymakers that a national program providing for universal entitlement to health care would result in runaway costs. To counter this argument, advocates point to the nations—especially Canada and France—that entitle all of their residents to a high level of health services while spending less than the United States on administration and on care. Britain's national health service, although typically considered a "painful prescription" for the United States (Aaron & Schwartz, 2005), nevertheless assures first-dollar coverage for basic health services to its entire population and, as we have seen, spends less than half as much money per capita as does the United States.

Great Britain, France, and Canada have produced some of the leading physicians and hospitals in the world. Judging by various measures of health outcome, they are in the same league as, or better than, the United States (see Table 6.2). Meanwhile, the United States has high uninsurance rates and spends more for health care than any other industrially advanced nation (see chapter 3).

Should we, therefore, adopt a Western European or Canadian model of health care financing and organization? Or should we maintain our present system and recognize that it is a manifestation of American exceptionalism—that is, of the ways in which the United States is fundamentally different from most OECD nations? Both of these responses are probably inadequate. The second "we're different" response insulates us from the experience of other nations. It smacks of ethnocentrism, makes us conservative, and thereby supports the status quo. The first response—that we should adopt a Western European or Canadian model—errs in the other direction, by relying too heavily on the experience of those nations, whose systems have flaws, too. Moreover, it disregards some health care delivery models in the United States—for example, innovations that promote health services integration in the Veterans Health Administration (Oliver, 2007) and those of prepaid multispecialty health maintenance organizations, such as Kaiser Permanente.

> Virtually no one in Canada or Western Europe views the U.S. health care system as a model to emulate.

Virtually no one in Canada or Western Europe views the U.S. health care system as a model to emulate. Even under the government of Prime Minister Margaret Thatcher there was no significant challenge to the principle of a national health service in Britain (*Working for Patients*, 1989). Nor is there any question about eliminating national health insurance in such countries as

France, Canada, Germany, Belgium, or the Netherlands. Nevertheless, a number of fashionable American themes have drifted north to Canada and across the Atlantic to Western Europe. In the context of the problems identified earlier—inefficiency in the allocation of health care resources, lack of continuity between levels of care, and the absence of consumer voice in most health care organizations—the concept of a managed care organization, in combination with elements of market competition, has a certain appeal to policymakers in other countries. Since an MCO is, by definition, both an insurer and a provider of health services, it establishes a link between the financing and provision of health services. Because its managers have a budget to care for an enrolled population, they have powerful incentives to provide needed services cost-effectively and maintain quality to minimize disenrollments.

The idea of introducing MCOs or similar kinds of health care organizations into national systems that provide universal entitlement to health care in many ways resembles the U.S. experience of encouraging Medicare beneficiaries to enroll in Medicare+Choice (see chapter 5). This idea involves two reforms. It spurs policymakers to combine regulatory controls with competition on the supply side; and it encourages them to design market incentives for both providers and consumers of health care.

To the extent that the insertion of MCOs into NHI or NHS systems represents an American "solution" to *foreign* problems, it may provide a way in which Canada and Western Europe could learn from the United States. It may also, paradoxically, have more practical implications for the United States than attempting to adapt a European NHI system into the U.S. context. For example, the insertion of MCOs into NHI or NHS systems might provide insights on how managed care and universal coverage could be combined in the United States sometime in the future.

New Approaches to Comparing Health Systems

Beyond serving as a mental exercise, viewing one's own system with a reflective telescope, and speculating about ways that useful policy lessons may be derived from comparative analyses, what more can be gained from comparative studies of different health systems? The field is moving in two promising directions: (a) comparison of disease-specific treatment patterns and outcomes across nations and (b) comparison of health systems and outcomes across cities.

Both directions represent responses to important gaps in existing comparative research on health systems.

LIMITS TO EXISTING DATA

The Limits of OECD Data

As shown in Table 6.2 and the analysis of OECD data on the United States, in comparative perspective, we spend more on health care than any other nation, yet we rank nowhere near the top in key health measures such as life expectancy at birth or infant mortality. Further analysis of OECD data indicates that the higher spending and lower aggregate use of health services in the United States are explained by the much higher average prices for medical goods and services (Anderson, Reinhardt, Hussey, & Petrosyan, 2003). Beyond this important conclusion, however, aggregate OECD data are insufficient to make any claims about average productivity and quality of medical treatments provided in the United States compared to other countries. Unfortunately, the OECD's extensive database on inputs, spending, and health status outcomes does not include information on the outcomes of medical treatments for common conditions.

The Limits of Cross-National Comparisons

In addition to the limits of the OECD database, questions may be raised about whether the nation state is the most appropriate organizational unit for comparing the performance of health systems—particularly with respect to the U.S. system, where there is great geographic variation in population composition, provider practice patterns, dominant financing approaches, health services organization, and public-/private-sector roles. Because we live in a more urbanized world, some researchers are looking to the city as a useful unit of analysis for understanding the health sector (Vlahov & Gallea, 2002). Yet most health services research—both in the United States and among international organizations, such as the United Nations, the World Health Organization, and the OECD—continues to assume that nations remain the most relevant units of analysis for assessing the performance of health systems and health policy.

First, there are enormous variations in health and health system performance within nations, between urban and rural areas, large and small cities, depressed and prosperous ones, and even within cities (Andrulis & Goodman, 1999; Center for Studying Health System Change; New York City Department of Health and Mental Hygiene, 2004; Wennberg & Gittelsohn, 1973).

Second, it is exceedingly difficult to disentangle the relative importance of health systems from other factors affecting health, including the sociocultural characteristics and neighborhood context of the population whose health is measured (Ellen, Mijanovich, & Dillman, 2001). It is even more difficult to do so at a level of aggregation such as the nation state, where important health policy decisions are made.

Third, despite the rise of the welfare state, even in the most centralized nations, the solutions to many health and social policy problems elude national and state governments. Some of the most challenging problems—care for vulnerable older people, those with severe mental illnesses, the most economically disadvantaged and the uninsured—fall into a kind of residual category that is handed down to local governments, with city governments bearing a disproportionate share of responsibility (Rodwin & Gusmano, 2005).

Responding to these shortcomings of cross-national comparisons, exciting new research is being developed, as described below.

COMPARISON OF HEALTH SYSTEMS AND OUTCOMES ACROSS CITIES

A number of efforts are under way to examine health systems and outcomes across cities. One of the best known is the World Health Organization's Healthy Cities Project, a movement to promote population health in cities throughout the world (Aicher, 1998). Although this project aimed largely at sensitizing local authorities to the health implications of different urban policies, current efforts to evaluate diverse city programs may result in valuable, more fine-grained data on the social and economic factors affecting population health, as well as on the role of health systems.

In Europe, the Mégapoles Project (Bardsley, 1999), which focused on the socially disadvantaged, represents an innovative attempt to combine research and practice by collecting a database on the major capital cities of Europe, their health systems, and population health status. Along with the compilation of comparative data across these cities, the project has initiated study groups of health and social service professionals to search for relevant innovations in the areas of services for older people and youth. Although this project is the most well-developed attempt to compare the health of city residents, it is limited in that the choice of cities was driven by political criteria. European capitals such as Vienna and Oslo are so much smaller than London that it is questionable whether they really can learn from one another.

The World Cities Project (Rodwin & Gusmano, 2002) represents a new approach to the comparison of health systems of cities because it explicitly compares the health systems and health status of the urban core of the four largest cities in the OECD nations: New York, London, Paris, and Tokyo (see Figure 6.1). The urban core as a unit of analysis provides a frame for focusing cross-national comparisons on

Figure 6.1

Urban Cores of Four Largest Cities of Organisation for Economic
Co-operation and Development in World Healthy Cities Project

Urban Core and First-Ring Populations (millions)

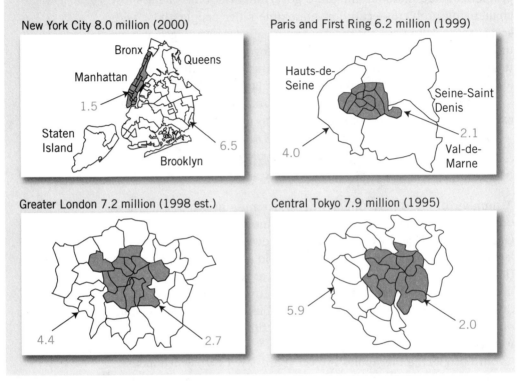

New York City 8.0 million (2000)

Bronx
Queens
Manhattan
1.5
Staten Island
Brooklyn
6.5

Paris and First Ring 6.2 million (1999)

Hauts-de-Seine
Seine-Saint Denis
2.1
4.0
Val-de-Marne

Greater London 7.2 million (1998 est.)

4.4
2.7

Central Tokyo 7.9 million (1995)

5.9
2.0

a more coherent and discernible set of health system characteristics. For example, Manhattan, Paris, Inner Tokyo, and Inner London have similar concentrations of teaching hospitals, medical schools, physicians, and acute care hospital beds. This project illustrates how a comparative analysis, structured by similar units of analysis, can highlight striking similarities and differences for further investigation. All four urban cores have economies based on services and information, closely tied to national and international transactions. They also are centers of culture, media, government, and international organizations. And their residents are some of the wealthiest and some of the poorest members of their respective nations.

A major focus of this ongoing project is to explore the how the cities' health systems and neighborhood characteristics affect two outcomes: the use of health services and health status. So far, it has resulted in comparative analysis of several specific issues—aging and long-term care, patterns of infant mortality, patterns of coronary artery disease, and patterns of avoidable hospital conditions (Gusmano, Rodwin, & Weisz, 2006). By comparing these issues in cities that share many characteristics (size, density, share of foreign-born, income disparities), but differ in the financing and organization of their health systems and degree of income inequalities and neighborhood segregation, it is possible to generate and test hypotheses on why these cities differ from one another along a range of indicators.

COMPARISON OF DISEASE-SPECIFIC TREATMENT PATTERNS AND OUTCOMES

In response to the limits of the OECD data, another line of significant work is now under way in a subset of OECD nations focusing on specific diseases and drawing on individual-level data related to specific health conditions. For example, the McKinsey Healthcare Productivity Project compared the management of diabetes mellitus, cholelithiasis (gallstones), lung cancer, and breast cancer in Germany, the United Kingdom, and the United States (Garber, 2003; McKinsey Global Institute, 1996). Also, the OECD itself has launched the Aging-Related Diseases Project, in which an impressive team of economists has attempted to link treatments with outcomes by collecting comparative data on ischemic heart disease, stroke, and breast cancer (Moise & Jacobzone, 2003).

Do such studies yield valid findings across OECD nations? Not yet. But others are in progress, as well. The Commonwealth Fund's International Working Group on Quality Indicators collected data in Australia, Canada, New Zealand, England, and the United States for 21 indicators, such as rates of 5-year cancer survival, death within 30 days after acute myocardial infarction and stroke, breast cancer screening, and asthma mortality (Hussey et al., 2004). In her commentary on this study, McGlynn (2004) concluded that there is no perfect health system, because each country outdoes its counterparts along some of the key performance indicators used to rank health care systems.

Conclusion

The new approaches to comparing health systems noted in this chapter have not yet yielded robust results on the relative performance of different health care systems. At this stage, these approaches are presented to provide a sense of new directions in the field of international comparative analysis. What, then, can be learned from the experience of wealthy nations in covering their population for the risks of falling ill?

Although careful studies of selected nations suggest that there is no perfect health system, it is possible to draw three conclusions from the evidence presented in this chapter. First, in striking contrast to the United States, the experience of other wealthy nations suggests that there need not be financial barriers to health care access. To be sure, there will always be social, geographic, and other barriers, but virtually all financial barriers have been eliminated in Bismarckian NHI systems such as in France and Canada and in Beveridgean NHS systems such as Great Britain. Second, there are many ways to achieve universal coverage. Not all NHI systems are the same, as demonstrated by the comparison of France and Canada. Nor are all NHS systems the same, which could be demonstrated by comparing Scotland, Wales, and England within Great Britain or by comparing Great Britain's NHS system with those of Italy, Spain, or Scandinavia. Third, although universal coverage matters a great deal, providing it does not solve many of the other problems health systems face: inefficiency in the allocation of health care resources; the lack of integration among primary, secondary, and tertiary levels of care; and uneven quality and bureaucratic decision making.

Beyond these generalizations, there is little doubt that comparative research on health systems in wealthy nations could be helpful to health policymakers and managers in the United States who seek to draw lessons from experiences abroad. The challenge is to teach policymakers and managers how to assess critically the kinds of comparative studies that will no doubt be invoked in the coming years as we contemplate, once again, how to reform the U.S. health care system. Will consumers of comparative health systems research succumb to the temptations of ranking systems based on a limited number of measurable performance indicators? Or will they ask the important questions about the importance of values, which indicators can properly be compared, what data are reliable, and how can these factors be understood in the political, economic, and institutional context of diverse nations?

References

Aaron, H., & Schwartz, W. (2005). *Can we say no? The challenge of rationing health care.* Washington, DC: Brookings Institution.

Aicher, J. (1998). *Designing healthy cities: Prescriptions, principles, and practice.* Malabar, FL: Krieger.

American Hospital Administration. (2000). *Hospital statistics.* Chicago: Author.

Anderson, O. (1972). *Health care: Can there be equity? The United States, Sweden, and England.* New York: Wiley.

Anderson, G., Reinhardt, U., Hussey, P., & Petrosyan, V. (2003). It's the prices, stupid: Why is U.S. spending so much higher? *Health Affairs, 22*(3), 89–105.

Andrulis, D., & Goodman, N. (1999). *The social and health landscape of urban and suburban America.* Chicago: AHA Press.

Bardsley, M. (1999). *Health in Europe's capitals.* Project Mégapoles. London: Director-ate of Public Health, East London and the City Health Authority. Retrieved from http://www.lho.org.uk/Download/Public/8016/1/projmega_3.pdf

Blum, H. (1981). *Planning for health.* New York: Human Sciences.

Center for Studying Health System Change. Design and Methods for the Community Tracking Study. Retrieved March 20, 2007, from http://www.hschange.com/index.cgi?data=01

Chernichovsky, D. (2002). Pluralism, choice, and the state in the emerging paradigm in health systems. *Milbank Quarterly, 80,* 5–40.

Coyne, J., & Hilsenrath, P. (2002). The world health report 2000. *American Journal of Public Health, 92,* 30–33.

Deber, R. (2003). Health care reform: Lessons from Canada. *American Journal of Public Health, 93,* 20–24.

De Kervasdoué, J., Kimberly, J., & Rodwin, V. (Eds.). (1984). *The end of an illusion: The future of health policy in Western industrialized nations.* Berkeley: University of California Press.

De Miguel, S. (1975). A framework for the study of national health systems. *Inquiry, 12,* 10.

Department of Health and Social Security. (1976). *Sharing resources for health in England: Report of the Resource Allocation Working Party.* London: Her Majesty's Stationery Office.

Dobson, F. (1999). Modernizing Britain's national health service. *Health Affairs, 18*(3), 40–41.

Dror, D., & Preker, A., (2002). *Social reinsurance: A new approach to sustainable community health financing.* The World Bank/International Labour Office. Retrieved from http://books.google.com/books?hl=en&lr=&id=nX5WLYimInAC&oi=fnd&pg=PR13&dq=Preker,+A.,+%26+Dror,+D.+(2002).+Social+reinsurance:+A+new+approach+to+sustainable+community+health+financing.+&ots=Ub7Jhh_o7j&sig=nooXvRBqXNZz-C04f9nEk5Z1MGQ#PPT1,M1 IL/World Bank

Dumbaugh, K., & Neuhauser, D. (1979). International comparisons of health services: Where are we? *Social Science and Medicine, 221,* 13B.

Ellen, I., Mijanovich, T., & Dillman, K. (2001). Neighborhood effects on health: Exploring the links and assessing the evidence. *Journal of Urban Affairs, 23,* 391–408.

Ellencweig, A. (1992). *Analyzing health systems: A modular approach.* New York: Oxford University Press.

Elling, R., & Kerr, H. (1975). Selection of contrasting national health systems for in-depth study. *Inquiry* (Suppl. 12), 2.

Evans, R. (1984). *Strained mercy: The economics of Canadian health care.* Toronto: Butterworths.

Evans, R. (1992). Canada: The real issues. *Journal of Health Policy, Politics and Law, 17*(4), 739–763.

Field, M. (1973). The concept of "health system" at the macrosociological level. *Social Science and Medicine, 7,* 763–785.

Fox, D. (1986). *Health policies, health politics.* Princeton, NJ: Princeton University Press.

Garber, A. (2003). Comparing health care systems from the disease-specific per-spective. *A disease-based comparison of health systems: What is best at what cost?* Paris: Organisation for Economic Co-operation and Development.

Glaser, W. (1991). *Health insurance in practice: International variations in financing, benefits, and problems.* San Francisco: Jossey-Bass.

Griffiths, R. (1983). *NHS management inquiry.* London: Department of Health and Social Security.

Gusmano, M., Rodwin, V., & Weisz, D. (2006). A new way to compare health systems: Avoidable hospital conditions in Manhattan and Paris. *Health Affairs, 25,* 510–520.

Hirschman, A. (1970). *Exit, voice and loyalty.* Cambridge, MA: Harvard University Press.

Hollingsworth, J. (1986). *A political economy of medicine: Great Britain and the United States.* Baltimore: Johns Hopkins University Press.

Hurst, J. (1992). *The reform of health care: A comparative analysis of seven OECD countries.* Paris: Organisation for Economic Co-operation and Development.

Hussey, P., Anderson, G., Osborne, R., Feek, C., McLaughlin, V., Miller, J., & Epstein, A. (2004). How does the quality of care compare in five countries? *Health Affairs, 23*(3), 89–99.

Immergut, E. (1992). *Health politics: Interests and institutions in Western Europe.* New York: Cambridge University Press.

Klass, O. (1985). Explaining America and the welfare state: An alternative theory. *British Journal of Political Science, 15,* 427–450.

Klein, R. (1998). Why Britain is reorganizing its National Health Service—Yet again? *Health Affairs, 17*(4), 111–125.

Kondro, W. (2000). Canada's ministers agree on health package. *Lancet, 356,* 1011.

Le Grand, J. (1999). Competition, cooperation, or control? Tales from the British National Health Service. *Health Affairs, 18*(3), 27–39.

Leichter, H. (1979). *A comparative approach to policy analysis: Health care policy in four nations.* Cambridge, UK: Cambridge University Press.

Le Pen, C., & Rodwin, V. (1996). Le plan Juppé: Vers un nouveau mode de régulation des soins. [The Juppé plan. Toward a new form of health regulation.] *Droit Social, 9*(10), 859–862.

Marmor, T. (1994). *Understanding health care reform.* New Haven, CT: Yale University Press.

Marmor, T., Bridges, A., & Hoffman, W. (1978). Comparative politics and health policies: Notes on benefits, costs, limits. In D. Ashford (Ed.), *Comparing public policies.* Beverly Hills, CA: Sage.

Marmor, T., Freeman, R., & Okma, K. (2005). Comparative perspectives and policy learning in the world of health care. *Journal of Comparative Policy Analysis, 7*(4), 331–348.

Maynard, A. (1986). *Annual report on the National Health Service.* New York: Center for Health Economics.

McGlynn, E. (2004). There is no perfect health system. *Health Affairs, 23*(3), 100–102.

McKinsey Global Institute. (1996). *Health care productivity.* Washington, DC: McKinsey Consulting.

Mechanic, D. (1976). The comparative study of health care delivery systems. In D. Mechanic (Ed.), *The growth of bureaucratic medicine: An inquiry into the dynamics of patient behavior.* New York: Wiley.

Moise, P., & Jacobzone, S. (2003). Population ageing, health expenditure and treatment: An ARD perspective. In Organisation for Economic Co-operation and Development, *A disease-based comparison of health systems: What is best at what cost?* Paris: Author.

Mokdad, A., Marks, J., Stroup, D., & Gerberding, J. (2000). Actual causes of death in the United States. *Journal of the American Medical Association, 291,* 1238–1245.

Navarro, V. (2002). Can health care systems be compared using a single measure of performance? *American Journal of Public Health, 92*(1), 31–34.

Naylor, C. D. (1999). Health care in Canada: Incrementalism under fiscal duress. *Health Affairs, 18*(3), 9–26.

New York City Department of Health and Mental Hygiene. (2004). *Take care New York.* Available at www.nycdoh.gov

Oliver, A. (2007). Veterans Health Administration: American success story? *Milbank Quarterly, 85*(1), 5–35.

Reinhardt, U. (1985). Hard choices in health care: A matter of ethics. In L. Etheredge (Ed.), *Health care: How to improve it and pay for it.* Washington, DC: Center for National Policy.

Rodwin, V., & Gusmano, M. (2002). The world cities project: Rationale, organization, and design for comparison of megacity health systems. *Journal of Urban Health, 79*(4). Retrieved from http://www.ilcusa.org/projects/research

Rodwin, V., & Gusmano, M. (Eds.). (2005). *Growing older in world cities: New York, London, Paris and Tokyo.* Nashville, TN: Vanderbilt University Press.

Rodwin, V., & contributors. (2006). *Universal health insurance in France: How sustainable?* Washington, DC: Embassy of France. Retrieved from http://www.nyu.edu/wagner/health/universal.pdf

Rodwin, V., & Le Pen, C. (2004). French health care reform. *New England Journal of Medicine, 351,* 2259–2261.

Roemer, M. (1977). *Comparative national policies for health care.* New York: Marcel Dekker.

Rominow, R. (2002). *Commission of the future of health care in Canada.* Retrieved from http://www.healthcarecommission.ca.gov

Rosner, D. (1982). Health care for the "truly needy": Nineteenth-century origins of the concept. *Milbank Memorial Fund Quarterly: Health and Society, 60,* 355.

Smee, C. (2000). United Kingdom. *Journal of Health Politics, Policy and Law, 25,* 945–951.

Stoddard, D. (1984, May). *Rationalizing the health care system.* Paper presented at the Ontario Council Conference, Toronto.

Stone, D. (1981). *The limits of professional power: National health care in the Federal Republic of Germany.* Chicago: University of Chicago Press.

Townsend, P., & Davidson, N. (Eds.). (1982). *Inequalities in health: The Black report.* London: Penguin.

Tuohy, C. (1999). *Accidental logics: The dynamics of change in the health care arena in the United States, Britain, and Canada.* New York: Oxford University Press.

Vlahov, D., & Gallea, S. (2002). Urbanization, urbanicity, and health. *Journal of Urban Health, 79*(Suppl. 1), S1–S11.

Wennberg, J. E., & Gittelsohn, A. (1973). Small area variations in health care delivery. *Science, 182,* 1102–1108.

Woolhandler, S., Campbell, T., & Himmelstein, D. (2003). Costs of health care administration in the United States and Canada. *New England Journal of Medicine, 349,* 768–775.

Working for patients. (1989). London: Her Majesty's Stationery Office.

World Health Organization. (2000). *The World Health Report 2000. Health systems: Improving performance.* Geneva, Switzerland: Author. Retrieved from http://www.who.int/whr/2000/en

Providing Health Care

7

Key Words

Acute Care

Marc N. Gourevitch, Carol A. Caronna,
and Gary E. Kalkut

Learning Objectives

- Provide an overview of acute care sites and practitioners.
- Describe the historical development of acute care in the United States.
- Differentiate between ambulatory and primary care.
- Describe the role of emergency services in the spectrum of acute care.
- Describe types of hospitals and health systems involved in acute care.
- Discuss changes and challenges facing acute care providers.

Topical Outline

- History of acute care
- Kinds of acute care: ambulatory, primary, emergency, specialty
- Hospitals in the United States, kinds of acute care hospitals, and hospital systems
- Current issues in acute care

cute care can be defined as the diagnosis and treatment of active or acute medical conditions in a hospital or ambulatory setting. Acute care spans a range that includes an outpatient visit for treatment of a sore throat to hospitalization for emergency neurosurgery. Acute care is delivered in hospitals, physician offices, emergency departments, urgent care centers, freestanding surgical centers, hospital outpatient clinics, and community health centers. Doctors, nurses, physician assistants, and nurse practitioners may provide acute care. Over several decades, an increasing proportion of acute care has moved to outpatient settings driven by financial incentives, advances in medical technology, and physician and patient preferences. This trend has implications for patient access, cost of care, regulatory oversight, and medical providers, including the role of the acute care hospital in contemporary health care delivery. This chapter explores the current spectrum of acute care in the United States and the challenges facing acute care delivery.

The History of Acute Care

The history of acute care can be divided into several stages of development. Prior to the mid- to late 1870s, "the family, as the center of social and economic life in early American society, was the natural locus of most care for the sick" (Starr, 1982, p. 32). Family members, usually women, were responsible for treating illnesses using medicinal herbs, medical almanacs, and knowledge from oral tradition. Physicians and lay healers treated paying patients in their homes, even for surgery. Hospitals were used to care for, but not cure, the more seriously ill and the poor. Of the approximately 180 hospitals in the United States in the 1870s, most were simply poorhouses, staffed by untrained nurses, and typically serving people of a certain religion, age, or ethnic group.

Advances in biomedical science and technology in the late 1800s led to more effective medical means of cure and intervention. In the early 1900s, hospitals evolved into the medical facilities we are familiar with today, where doctors treat patients for specific illnesses and diseases. Improvements in hygiene and techniques for asepsis and surgical anesthesia prompted surgery to move from the home to the hospital. As demands for admission increased, hospitals limited their patients to those with acute care (versus long-term care) needs and sought contacts with physicians in the community to fill their beds with acute care patients. The availability of more sophisticated equipment in medical facilities and the desirability of consulting with other doctors about serious cases also encouraged the move of acute care from the home to medical offices and hospitals. By 1909, there were more than 4,300 hospitals in the United States (Stevens, 1971). By the 1920s, most home care was limited to first aid and everyday hygiene.

In the 1920s and 1930s, doctors generally were solo practitioners, treating patients in their offices and the hospitals where they had privileges. Some doctors practiced in clinics—in rural and poor areas that lacked hospitals or in private group practices in urban areas, such as the Mayo Clinic in Minnesota and the Palo Alto Medical Clinic in northern California (Starr, 1982). Industrial workers at remote sites often received acute care at hospitals and clinics owned and staffed by their employers, such as railroads, shipyards, and construction firms. Although they were unusual at the time, many of these early clinics and industrial health plans served as models for managed care organizations and integrated health care systems formed in the latter part of the 20th century.

> Many of the early employee clinics and industrial health plans served as models for managed care organizations and integrated health care systems formed in the latter part of the 20th century.

The World War II era brought significant changes to the world of acute care. New developments, such as the introduction of widespread antibiotic use in 1943, markedly improved survival from certain infections. Health insurance became more widespread. Labor unions obtained health insurance benefits for many workers, which fostered the expectation that health insurance should be linked to employment, and the health insurance industry developed rapidly after World War II. The 1946 Hill-Burton Act provided federal funds for hospital construction and brought hospitals to underserved areas. In the 1960s, the introduction of Medicare and Medicaid provided federally funded health insurance for Americans who lacked an employment relationship—namely, the elderly and the poor. Concerns about whether there would be enough doctors to meet the population's needs led to increased funding for medical training and the establishment of new health care occupations, including nurse practitioners and physician assistants.

In the 1970s, more and more Americans had access to health care and insurance, and insurers reimbursed doctors on a fee-for-service basis. These factors led to an escalation of medical costs, which was of particular concern to the federal government. Starting in the 1980s, federal legislation created a prospective payment system for hospitalizations under Medicare. Instead of fee-for-service reimbursement, hospitals were allowed a set payment per hospitalization, depending on the patient's diagnosis. The private insurance industry eventually adopted strategies for cost containment, such as capitation and discounted contracts with preferred providers. Because early models of managed care saved money by reducing hospital admissions and lengths of stay, government programs and insurance companies adopted managed care strategies—including utilization review and prior authorizations—that encouraged physicians to limit hospitalizations. As a consequence of these financial pressures—plus safer anesthesia, less invasive surgical techniques, and other technologies—the delivery of acute care became more and more likely to be provided on an outpatient basis.

Kinds of Acute Care Today

In today's environment of financial constraints and managed care, acute care is still provided in familiar settings, but patients are likely to be cared for by nurse practitioners and physician assistants in addition to primary care physicians. Rather than practice by themselves, doctors are more likely to have formal, legal links with other doctors, hospitals, and integrated health care systems. Patients today may see a health care provider at a clinic, doctor's office, outpatient facility owned by a hospital or group of doctors, or at a hospital, or they may communicate with a provider via telephone or Internet. Decisions about where to provide acute care are made based on how it can be delivered most efficiently and cost-effectively. Hospital stays are minimized, and patients may be prepared for surgery, undergo rehabilitative therapy, and receive follow-up care in outpatient settings or even at home.

AMBULATORY CARE

Ambulatory care covers health care services provided on an outpatient basis, requiring no overnight hospital stay. It is provided by many types of health care professionals in a broad range of settings and includes primary care, emergency care, and ambulatory subspecialty care (including ambulatory surgery). Several themes shape the face of ambulatory care today, reflecting the intense pressures of cost containment in the health care industry. Because care is generally more expensive to provide in inpatient than in outpatient settings, recent trends in ambulatory care reflect efforts to prevent hospitalization. When patients

> Because care is generally more expensive to provide in inpatient than in outpatient settings, recent trends in ambulatory care reflect efforts to prevent hospitalization.

are hospitalized, efforts are made to reduce the length of their stay and hasten their transition to an ambulatory care setting. To reduce patients' overall use of acute care services, health plans have launched initiatives in chronic disease management and delivery system integration. All of these trends have contributed to the growth of outpatient care relative to inpatient care. Efforts to decrease hospital length of stay and to shift many surgical procedures to the ambulatory setting mean that some ambulatory settings are caring for very sick patients.

Ambulatory Care Statistics

In the United States, 1.1 billion ambulatory care visits were made in 2004 to physicians' offices, hospital outpatient departments, and hospital emergency departments, with a mean of 3.8 such visits per person (U.S. Department of Health and Human Services, 2004). Of these ambulatory care visits, 82% were to physicians' offices, 8% to hospital outpatient departments, and 10% to hospital emergency departments. The frequency of physician office visits varies by age, gender, race, and socioeconomic status (see Figure 7.1). Rates for women were higher than for men (4.4 visits versus 3.3 visits per year), primarily reflecting a marked difference in the 18- to 44-year-old category. Physician

Figure 7.1

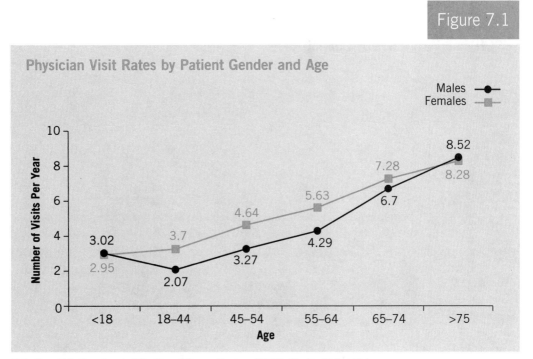

Physician Visit Rates by Patient Gender and Age

Males ●
Females ■

Note. From U.S. Department of Health and Human Services. (2003). *Health, United States.* Washington, DC: U.S. Government Printing Office. p. 260.

office visit rates increased with age, with highest rates (8.3 per year) among those 75 years and older. Sharp differences in the pattern of ambulatory care utilization between Whites and Blacks were evident (see Figure 7.2). Whites visited physicians' offices (particularly specialists' offices) more often than Blacks, yet Blacks used emergency department services at nearly double the rate of Whites (0.69 versus 0.35 visits per year, respectively). Stated differently, emergency department visits comprised 17.7% of total ambulatory care visits for Blacks, compared with 8.9% for Whites.

Differences in utilization rates between rich and poor persist, although they have diminished in recent years. In 1964, 59% of poor and 74% of nonpoor families reported a physician visit within the last year, compared to rates in 1998 of 80% and 86%, respectively (U.S. Department of Health and Human Services, 1995, Table 77; U.S. Department of Health and Human Services, 2000, Table 71). In 2005, 12.2% of poor Americans did not receive medical care due to cost, compared to 3.2% of Americans who weren't poor (U.S. Department of Health and Human Services, 2007). Utilization of ambulatory care appears to be more strongly determined by insurance status than by income bracket, however. Lack of health insurance for children under

Figure 7.2

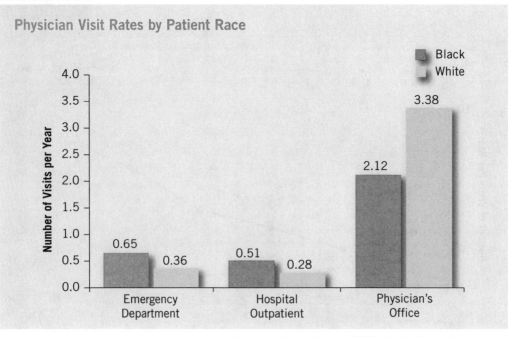

Physician Visit Rates by Patient Race

Note. From U.S. Department of Health and Human Services. (2003). *Health, United States.* Washington, DC: U.S. Government Printing Office. pp. 260–261.

age 6, the group most in need of immunizations and psychosocial, neurological, and behavioral assessments, is a particular problem.

Organization of Ambulatory Care Services

There are two major categories of ambulatory care. Most ambulatory care is delivered in physician offices by individual physicians either in solo practice or who have organized themselves into partnerships or private group practices. The second category may be thought of as care organized and delivered under the auspices of institutions. This category includes ambulatory care provided in hospital-based outpatient clinics, walk-in centers, and emergency departments; hospital-sponsored group practices and health promotion centers; freestanding "surgi-centers" and "urgi"- or "emergi-centers"; health department clinics; neighborhood and community health centers; organized home care; community mental health centers; school and workplace health services; and prison health services.

PRIMARY CARE

Primary care signifies a relationship between a patient and clinician that is longitudinal and that both patient and clinician view as the patient's principal source of general outpatient medical care. The Institute of Medicine (1996) defines primary care as "the provision of integrated, accessible care services by clinicians who are accountable for addressing a large majority of personal health care needs, developing a sustained partnership with patients, and practicing in the context of family and community" (p. 1). Embedded within this definition are the concepts of longitudinal care characterized by continuity with a single provider and a comprehensive approach to patients' multiple medical needs. Also implicit in this definition is the notion of primary care provider as coordinator of patients' care, ranging from subspecialist referrals to social service assistance. Primary care is thus one type of ambulatory care a patient may receive. A person seeking medical care directly from various subspecialists as the need may arise, but who has no principal ongoing relationship with any of them, would be using ambulatory care but not primary care.

Primary Care Providers

Primary care is provided by four principal categories of professionals: physicians, nurse practitioners (NPs), physician assistants (PAs), and nurse-midwives. The physician specialties typically considered providers of primary care are general internal medicine, family practice, pediatrics, geriatrics, and, for many women patients, obstetrics/gynecology. Other specialist and subspecialist physicians also can provide primary care. For example, a cardiologist who sees a patient in her office following hospitalization for a first heart attack may become the patient's primary care physician. In this case, the cardiologist might care for the patient's various medical problems over time, or at least maintain awareness of the care the patient is receiving from other physicians, with a view toward ensuring that the patient's overall care is comprehensive and coordinated. Over the last two decades, the percentage of primary care visits provided by generalists (general internists, family practitioners, and pediatricians) has declined (from 57% in 1980 to 51% in 2000), relative to that provided by specialists (U.S. Department of Health and Human Services, 2003, Table 84).

Nurse practitioners, physician assistants, and nurse-midwives are gaining in importance as primary care providers. Although they follow a different educational path than do physicians, there is substantial overlap in their capabilities in many ambulatory primary care settings. NPs and PAs typically have the skills to perform an estimated 75% of the services that physicians provide for adults and 90% of services provided to children (Scheffler, 1996).

Sites for the Provision of Primary Care Services

Primary care in the United States is provided in a number of settings, with private physician offices continuing to be the most common. In recent years, community-based and hospital-based primary care clinics have expanded their primary care capabilities in response to the increased numbers of people eligible for subsidized health insurance through Medicaid managed care and State Children's Health Insurance Plans. Academic medical centers (teaching hospitals closely aligned with medical schools) also have been aggressive in expanding primary care operations into surrounding communities in order to maintain their traditional patient base, to invigorate education of medical students and physicians in training, and to support clinical research.

EMERGENCY CARE

The United States has developed a complex and comprehensive system of emergency care, ranging from the national 911 emergency response system to hospital-based emergency services, which has been bolstered by the emergence of emergency medicine as a formally recognized medical specialty. Most U.S. hospitals, including more than 93% of community hospitals, provide emergency department services (American Hospital Association, 2006). Although designed to care for the acutely ill or injured patient, emergency departments also serve as a major source of

> Although designed to care for the acutely ill or injured patient, emergency departments also serve as a major source of walk-in services for less sick patients.

walk-in services for less sick patients. Many physicians in practice who are affiliated with a specific hospital will use its emergency department (ED) as a resource-rich setting in which to assess patients with serious problems that may lead to inpatient admission or whose evaluation requires equipment or diagnostic imaging facilities not available in the physician's office. Similarly, extended care facilities such as nursing homes and chronic disease hospitals may use the emergency services of a nearby acute care facility to evaluate a patient with a sudden change in medical status. Emergency services are, therefore, not only a major source of admissions to hospitals, but also an important interface between the worlds of ambulatory and inpatient medicine.

Patients often err in over- or underinterpreting the gravity of symptoms they are experiencing. Most patients reporting to an emergency service believe they need immediate attention. Others know they do not have an urgent or emergent problem, but simply use the emergency service because it is the most convenient source of care available. Although emergency department visits are not particularly costly, there is broad consensus that it is a poor place to obtain general primary care, because many important elements of care (e.g., continuity of care with a single provider, preventive health screenings and immunizations) receive little or no attention there. At the same time, emergency department visits may signal that primary care settings have missed opportunities to prevent exacerbations of chronic medical conditions such as asthma, congestive heart failure, diabetes, and vaccine-preventable, acute infections such as influenza and certain common types of pneumonia.

In fact, many hospitals have developed walk-in care centers to relieve emergency departments from having to assess and treat patients with conditions that do not demand immediate attention. Business motives in developing such centers include concentrating the attention of more costly emergency department staff and equipment on cases more likely to result in hospital admissions (the financial lifeblood of most hospitals), and competing with freestanding walk-in services or urgi-centers for ambulatory care volume. Such centers are often open evening and weekend hours and offer after-hours telephone consultations. Nevertheless, EDs remain a common point of contact with the health care system for a large number of people with no regular source of care. Recognizing this, some EDs have developed programs to provide brief public health-oriented preventive health interventions, such as HIV testing with risk reduction counseling or childhood immunizations. Such innovative programs embody the tension between a public health outreach paradigm and the need to optimize the efficiency and fiscal viability of resource-intense hospital-based settings.

SPECIALTY CARE

Specialty care, as distinct from general primary care, is care given by physicians who have received additional training in a specific area of expertise (e.g., endocrinology, pediatric cardiology). Specialty care is practiced and delivered by physicians in a broad array of disciplines and delivered in diverse settings. Primary care providers refer patients to specialists for evaluation or treatment of conditions that require particular expertise. Thus, while most primary care clinicians are comfortable treating patients with disorders of the thyroid gland, many would refer such patients to an endocrinologist for initial evaluation and for additional consultation when changes in the treatment regimen appeared indicated. Patients often choose to bypass generalist physicians and go directly to a specialist. This route has become less common, however, because managed care financially penalizes self-referral.

Surgical ambulatory care consists of surgical procedures performed on nonhospitalized patients. From 1995 to 2005, ambulatory surgeries rose from 51.5 to 59.0 per 1,000 persons, while inpatient surgeries fell from 37.1 to 34.1 per 1,000 persons (American Hospital Association, 2007). In 2005, 63% of all surgeries were performed on an outpatient basis. This reflects a marked change from 1980, when only 16.4% of surgery was performed on an outpatient basis (U.S. Department of Health and Human Services, 1995, Table 90), and demonstrates the growth of acute care provision in outpatient settings. This shift can be attributed to improved technology, economic pressures, and the demands of both patients and third-party payers.

Imaging procedures (e.g., traditional X rays, ultrasound, computerized tomography [CT scans], and magnetic resonance imaging [MRI]) can be performed in a variety of settings, including ambulatory imaging facilities located in hospitals or community health centers, large multispecialty group practice, or freestanding facilities. Some primary care physicians and a growing number of subspecialist physicians—including gastroenterologists, urologists, orthopedists, and cardiologists—perform imaging procedures in their offices.

Hospitals in the United States

Although the majority of acute care visits take place in doctors' offices, hospitals play an important role in delivering acute care, in both inpatient and outpatient settings. This section gives an overview of acute care hospital types, services, and structures, with an emphasis on the ways hospitals have adjusted to the changing environment of acute care.

In 2005, there were 4,936 community hospitals in the United States, with more than 802,000 beds (American Hospital Association, 2007). Of the $1.9 trillion spent on health care in 2004, hospital costs accounted for 30%. Most U.S. hospitals are nonprofit or are owned by local, state, or federal governments (see Table 7.1). As the total number of hospitals decreased in the last 20 years, more than 600 state and local government hospitals and 300 nonprofit hospitals have closed, while the number of investor-owned hospitals has increased slightly. Hospitals of different ownership types vary with regard to several characteristics. The average length of stay at state and local government hospitals is higher than average for hospitals generally, while the average length of stay for investor-owned hospitals is lower. State and local government hospitals have almost double the number of outpatient visits compared to investor-owned hospitals, but they have similar numbers of patient admissions. Expenses at nonprofit hospitals are almost $100 a day higher, on average, than for other types of hospitals.

Several significant changes have occurred in hospital utilization in the last 20 years (see Table 7.2). The increased demand for inpatient care is reflected in the recent trend of rising hospital admissions. In 2005, there were more than 35 million hospital admissions, a 14% increase over 1994—the year managed care brought admissions to their lowest point in many years. However, on a per capita basis, the number of hospital admissions per 1,000 population has held steady since 1993, fluctuating around 117 to 119. This compares to the much higher rate of 159.5 in 1980. Thus, the higher number of admissions in part reflects growth in the U.S. population. The aging of the population is another important driver of increased demand for hospital services, although lack of access to timely ambulatory care also plays a role. A consequence of the relatively abrupt increase in inpatient

Table 7.1 Community Hospital Ownership

Ownership	1985	1995	2005
Nonprofit	3,349	3,092	2,958
State and local government	1,578	1,350	1,110
Investor owned	805	752	868
Total	5,732	5,194	4,936

Note. From American Hospital Association. (2007). *Hospital statistics, 2007.* Chicago: Healthcare InfoSource. Community hospitals are defined by the AHA as all nonfederal short-term general and special hospitals whose facilities and services are available to the public.

 Community Hospital Utilization Data by Decade

	1985	1995	2005
Number of hospitals	5,732	5,194	4,936
Beds (thousands)	1,001	873	802
Patient admissions (thousands)	33,449	30,945	35,239
Births (thousands)	3,521	3,765	3,988
Outpatient visits (thousands)	218,716	414,345	584,429
Average length of stay (days)	7.1	6.5	5.6
Average daily census (thousands)	777	548	540
Full-time employees (thousands)	2,997	3,714	4,257
Expenses (adjusted per inpatient day)	$460.19	$967.69	$1522.42
Gross outpatient revenues (percentage of all revenues)	16%	33%	37%

Note. From American Hospital Association. (2007). *Hospital statistics, 2007.* Chicago: Healthcare InfoSource. Community hospitals are defined by the AHA as all nonfederal short-term general and special hospitals whose facilities and services are available to the public.

demand nationally has been greater hospital crowding with longer waits for services, including emergency department care and ancillary testing.

Demand for hospital outpatient services has grown steadily. In 1985, there were 218 million outpatient visits to acute care hospitals; by 2005, this number had increased to 584 million (American Hospital Association, 2007). These outpatient visits contributed to increasing percentages of gross revenues for acute care hospitals, from 16% in 1985 to 33% in 1995 to 37% in 2005.

TYPES OF ACUTE CARE HOSPITALS

Acute care hospitals may have different types of ownership, and many hospitals are now part of multihospital and integrated health care systems.

Teaching Hospitals

Approximately 400 major hospitals or health care systems in the United States are members of the Council of Teaching Hospitals and Health Systems. To qualify as a member, a hospital must have an affiliation agreement with a medical school and demonstrate a commitment to graduate medical education by participating in at least four residency training programs. According to the Association of American Medical Colleges (2004),

> Teaching hospitals are providers of primary care and routine patient services, as well as centers for experimental, innovative and technically sophisticated services. Many of the advances started in the research laboratories of medical schools are incorporated into patient care through clinical research programs at teaching hospitals.

Teaching hospitals are among the largest hospitals in the country; they may be private or government supported; and they provide a disproportionate share of uncompensated care compared to other hospitals. Teaching hospitals are often in large urban centers and may be part of an academic medical center, with close ties to a medical school, including physicians on staff who hold an academic appointment and teach medical students or residents in training.

Montefiore Medical Center (MMC) is an example of a teaching hospital that is part of an academic medical center. It comprises two acute care adult hospitals and a children's hospital, all in the Bronx, the poorest of New York City's five boroughs. It is the principal training venue for medical students at the Albert Einstein College of Medicine and sponsors residency programs in 63 medical specialties with more than 865 trainees, making it one of the largest medical training programs in the country. Including patient visits in its emergency departments, MMC had nearly 2 million ambulatory visits in 2003. Inpatient volume reached 68,000 discharges in 2006, with total clinical activity that has grown by approximately 33% in the past decade. In 2006, MMC had a surplus of just over 1% on total revenues of $2.2 billion.

In a market characterized by an unfavorable payer mix dominated by government insurance, rising costs, and declining payments, MMC's strategy has been based on expanding its primary care network with over 20 community ambulatory practices throughout its service area staffed by MMC-employed physicians. MMC also has invested over $150 million in its business and clinical information systems since 1995 to integrate provider information across its extensive delivery system and to gather clinical data for quality improvement initiatives. MMC has demonstrated that medication errors have decreased by 80% because of the introduction of computerized physician orders and a pharmacy information system. MMC is implementing bar-coding of patient identification bracelets during medication administration to ensure that drugs are not given to the wrong patient—the most common medication error identified at the center.

Montefiore Medical Center can be considered both a teaching hospital in a large academic medical center and a community hospital that has made health care delivery to Bronx residents a component of its business strategy and a central element of its mission. Many urban teaching hospitals replicate this hybrid status, serving as primary care community providers while offering tertiary care and clinical research to a broad regional or national patient base.

Public Hospitals

Public hospitals receive financial support from local, state, or federal government beyond the patient care reimbursement they receive from Medicaid and Medicare. The National Association of Public Hospitals and Health Systems (NAPHHS) has more than 100 member hospitals in 30 states and includes public hospitals in our largest cities, such as Bellevue in New York, Cook County in Chicago, and LA County in Los Angeles. NAPHHS categorizes its members into three models of governance: direct operation by local or state governments, operation by a separate public entity such as the Health and Hospitals Corporation in New York City, or ownership and operation by a not-for-profit corporation, usually with a contractual relationship with the local government.

Public hospitals are larger on average than other hospitals in their market area and typically have about twice the number of discharges. All have increasingly busy emergency departments and ambulatory clinics, providing more than 35 million ambulatory visits (NAPHHS, 2007). Public hospitals are considered "safety net" hospitals, because they provide significant services to uninsured, underinsured, or other vulnerable populations and offer services to all—regardless of ability to pay—as part of their mission or legal mandate. NAPH hospitals, which constitute only 2% of the nation's hospitals, provide one-quarter of all uncompensated care nationally. State and local subsidies contributed nearly 14% of NAPH hospitals' support, and, when combined with Medicare and Medicaid payments, total government support is 69%.

Public hospitals play unique roles in the neighborhoods they serve. They typically offer community outreach and health education programs directed at minority communities. Their emergency rooms are busy, often serving as municipal trauma centers and as home bases for local 911 systems. They have become an invaluable component of local disaster preparedness, working with public health departments. Public hospitals are also training facilities, turning out more than 15% of U.S. medical and dental residents.

The hospitals of the Bureau of Health Services in Cook County, Illinois, exemplify the role of the public hospital. The mission of the Cook County Bureau of Health Services is to provide a comprehensive program of quality health care, with respect and dignity, to the residents of Cook County, regardless of their ability to pay. The Bureau of Health comprises two acute care hospitals, a chronic care and rehabilitation facility, 30 community and school-based ambulatory care sites, and a correctional health service. Its emergency departments are among the busiest in the country; they provide tertiary care clinical service in many specialties, including state-of-the-art imaging technology. The Bureau of Health Services has developed centers of excellence that address inner-city health issues across its care continuum, including asthma, violence prevention, lead poisoning, maternal health, and cancer treatment and prevention.

Cook County Hospital was established in 1866 to provide care to indigent residents of Chicago after the city's Board of Commissioners recognized that the medical care provided at its poorhouse was inadequate. Cook County Hospital grew to 3,400 beds, established a school of nursing, and became an important academic medical center that trained generations of physicians. In December 2002, a new $600 million hospital, named for the current president of the Cook County Board of Commissioners, John H. Stroger, Jr., replaced the facility built in 1914. The new Cook County Hospital has 464 beds, including 80 intensive care (ICU) beds, 58 neonatal ICU beds, and an 18-bed burn unit. Reflecting the growing importance of ambulatory care, 40% of this 1.2-million-square-foot building is devoted to ambulatory care services. For fiscal 2004, the Cook County Bureau of Health Services appropriated $460 million for the Stroger Hospital and projects $390 million in revenue from its operation. Eighty-seven percent of the hospital's revenues come from state and federal programs.

Rural Hospitals

A hospital is designated as rural if it is located in a city of less than 50,000 or a total metropolitan population of less than 100,000. Of the 4,936 U.S. hospitals in 2005, there were 2,009 (41%) classified as rural. The number of rural hospitals has declined by less than 1% since 1998, a closure rate identical to metropolitan area hospitals. Despite the slight decline in the number of rural hospitals, admissions have risen 5.5% since 1998. The average rural hospital has 79 beds compared to 236 for hospitals in metropolitan areas; 74% of rural facilities have fewer than 100 beds.

Rural hospitals are under significant clinical, financial, and regulatory pressures to meet current standards of medical practice. The demographics of rural America are changing, and many locales are losing population. Those who stay tend to be older and poorer, and, increasingly in many counties, Hispanic immigrants. Medical care's increasing dependence on expensive technologies can magnify the disparities in services offered by smaller hospitals and add to the difficulties rural hospitals have in attracting and retaining skilled providers. However, telemedicine (audio and video communication with physicians in larger medical centers) gives local providers a new kind access to specialist consultations. A recent study at the University of Washington showed that telemedicine resulted in better care, according to referring and consulting physicians, compared to phone consultation; it resulted in a change in management in 64% of cases and was satisfying to patients who did not have to travel long distances (Norris, 2002). More widespread availability of broadband Internet access in rural communities is critical to expanding the utility of telemedicine.

An example of a rural hospital with telemedicine capabilities is the Haxtun Hospital in Haxtun, Colorado. Founded in the 1960s, the Haxtun Hospital District serves a 300-square-mile area of western Philips County, with a population of roughly 2,500 residents. The 15-bed, critical access hospital has a Colorado level 4 trauma classification with staff trained in trauma life support and trauma nursing. Its services include emergency medicine, surgery, obstetrics, and imaging. CT scan and MRI services are provided by a mobile unit. In 1989, the Haxtun Hospital District became a member of the High Plains Rural Health Network, which connects 18 rural hospitals, two urban hospitals, and a secondary referral center located in Colorado, Kansas, Nebraska, and Wyoming. In 1995, the network received a grant from the Office of Rural Health Policy to develop a telemedicine network; in 2001, it received an additional grant from the U.S. Department of Agriculture Rural Utilities Service, Distance Learning and Telemedicine Program. These grants allowed the network to create direct video and radio links between emergency room staff and board-certified emergency room specialists at two urban facilities. Teleconferences with urban providers enable the rural physicians to decide whether to provide treatment locally or transport emergency patients to urban hospitals.

The Balanced Budget Act (BBA) of 1997 reduced Medicare payments to all hospitals by $119 billion (11.4%) from 1998 to 2004, including a $15 billion reduction for rural hospitals. The Balanced Budget Refinement Act of 1999 restored about 13% of these cuts for rural hospitals. Part of the BBA, the Medicare Rural Flexibility Program, allowed Medicare to certify some rural hospitals as critical access hospitals, if the facility was the sole source of inpatient care in a community. Critical access hospitals are reimbursed on a cost-based schedule instead of a standard case rate, a much more generous payment method. Additionally, the Medicare Reform Act of 2003 increased reimbursement to rural health facilities by $25 billion, including a premium for telemedicine, and expanded ambulance services in rural counties. Despite these enrichments, rural hospitals will likely require additional federal subsidies to make technology investments and to cover operating costs in order to maintain financial viability.

Multihospital and Integrated Health Care Systems

Most hospitals are integrated into their communities through ties with area physicians and other health care providers, clinics and outpatient facilities, and other practitioners. Almost half of the nation's hospitals also are tied to larger organizational entities: multihospital and integrated health care systems, networks, and alliances. A *network* is a group of hospitals, physicians, other providers, insurers, or community agencies that work together to deliver health services. *Multihospital systems* include two or more hospitals owned, leased, sponsored, or contract managed by a central organization. An *alliance* is a formal organization, usually owned by shareholders or members, that works on behalf of its individual members in the provision of services and products (most commonly, group purchasing) and in the promotion of activities and ventures. The same hospital can participate in more than one of these categories.

In 2005, there were 369 multihospital or integrated health care systems in the United States. The majority were not-for-profit, including religious (55) and secular (244) systems. Sixty-five systems were investor-owned, and five were operated by the federal government (Departments of the U.S. Navy, U.S. Air Force, U.S. Army, Veterans Administration, and the Bureau of Indian Affairs). Investor-owned systems tend to have more, but smaller, hospitals than nonprofit systems and generally own or manage hospitals in more parts of the nation. Many of the large for-profit systems have headquarters in the South, particularly in Tennessee and Texas. Secular nonprofit systems tend to be smaller and more regional.

Kaiser Permanente is an example of an integrated health care system. As one of the nation's first health maintenance organizations (HMOs), Kaiser Permanente operates under the principles of prepaid insurance, physician group practice, preventive medicine, and the organized delivery of services—putting as many services as possible under one roof. The Kaiser Permanente Medical Center in Oakland, California, typifies the system's integration of medical care. Several large physician office buildings are situated in the same complex as an acute care hospital, several laboratories, and several pharmacies. Members in the Oakland area receive all of their medical care at the same medical center, which employs a full range of practitioners, including both generalists and specialist physicians. If a patient's doctor orders a medical test, the patient walks to the appropriate testing center located within the complex. The logistics of hospitalizing patients or using sophisticated medical equipment are simple and routine. Referrals to specialists are handled within the system.

In addition, the complex is served by public buses and a free shuttle to and from the nearest subway station. A Kaiser health plan member conceivably could be treated for all health care needs at the Oakland medical center, from birth to death.

Kaiser Permanente serves members in several regions: California, Oregon/Washington, Hawaii, Colorado, Georgia, Ohio, and the District of Columbia metropolitan area. The integrated system consists of three separate entities: the Kaiser Foundation Health Plan, Inc., which provides insurance; Kaiser Foundation Hospitals and Subsidiaries, which manages hospitals and medical office buildings; and the Permanente Medical Groups. The Health Plan and Hospitals organizations contract exclusively with each region's Permanente Medical Group to provide medical care for its members. Nationwide, Kaiser Permanente had 8.4 million members as of December 2005.

Another example of an integrated health care system is the federal Department of Veterans Affairs (VA). The hospitals and ambulatory programs of VA make it the largest health care delivery system in the country. There are 25 million veterans currently alive in the United States who are potentially eligible for health care benefits; family members of disabled veterans and survivors of veterans are also eligible. VA care is not free to beneficiaries, but costs are usually limited to co-payments. The extent of coverage depends on congressional appropriations, with a priority list of covered beneficiaries that targets fully or partially disabled veterans. Eligibility can change annually, depending on the level of funding.

VA hospitals have been referred to as an unrecognized component of the national health care safety net (Wilson, 1997). The majority of VA patients have no private insurance and a high burden of chronic disease, psychiatric illness, substance abuse, and physical disability. VA hospitals have been reorganized over the past decade and now enjoy a reputation for higher quality care that takes advantage of a sophisticated national hospital information system.

SERVICES AND STRUCTURES OF ACUTE CARE HOSPITALS

Hospitals are diverse in their governance, organization, mission, and relationships to their communities. They also vary by organizational structure and the scope of services delivered. All hospitals, however, must adhere to the standards of an organization called the Joint Commission in order to receive reimbursement from Medicare, Medicaid and private insurance (see chapter 15 for more information on the Joint Commission).

The medical care delivered in hospitals ranges from well patient health maintenance to organ transplantation. Most hospitals provide emergency care, outpatient surgery, CT scanning, and outpatient services. Just over half of acute care hospitals have MRI capabilities and oncology services. A third to a quarter provides primary care, HIV/AIDS services, coronary angioplasty, hospice care, and open heart surgery. And a fifth or less provides angioplasty, infertility services, alcohol and drug treatment, or organ transplants. As the practice of medicine has grown increasingly dependent on sophisticated technology for routine diagnosis and treatment, even smaller acute care hospitals must own or have access to expensive equipment and services. At the same time, biomedical progress has driven large, tertiary care facilities, particularly university-affiliated ones, to offer cutting-edge treatments and research protocols available only in select centers across the country.

> As the practice of medicine has grown increasingly dependent on sophisticated technology for routine diagnosis and treatment, even smaller acute care hospitals must own or have access to expensive equipment and services.

Certain principles characterize all hospitals. Physicians determine who is admitted and direct care during the hospital stay. Other licensed health professionals—particularly nurses but also respiratory therapists, physical therapists, social workers, pastoral caregivers, and technicians—provide service components that are critical to patients' recovery. Physicians are primarily organized along the lines of the medical specialties. The larger the hospital and hospital network and the more specialized the medical services, the greater the number of separate medical departments. Departments found in most hospitals include internal medicine, surgery, pediatrics, obstetrics/gynecology, psychiatry/neurology, radiology/diagnostic imaging, pathology, anesthesiology, family medicine, and emergency medicine. Other more specialized medical departments tend to be organized around organs and organ systems—for example, ophthalmology (eye); otolaryngology (ear, nose, and throat); urology (male sexual/reproductive system and the urinary tract of males and females); orthopedics (bones and joints); and so on.

Hospital diagnostic and therapeutic services, which may be attached to one of the medical departments, include laboratory services (usually directed by the department of pathology); electrocardiography (directed by cardiology); electroencephalography (neurology); radiography (radiology); pharmacy; clinical psychology; social service; inhalation therapy (anesthesiology); nutrition as therapy; physical, occupational, and speech therapy (rehabilitation medicine, if present); home care; and medical records, among others. Nonclinical services include finance, facilities and equipment, human resources, and management.

Physicians relate to hospitals in different ways. Attending physicians on the hospital staff, who are not salaried, often conduct much of their business in private offices they own or rent. These physicians may admit patients to more than one hospital and may compete with the hospital for patients or customers. Other physicians may be salaried or paid by the hospital, according to the amount of hospital work they do. These physicians often see patients or provide diagnostic services in offices that are provided by the hospital. Some hospitals employ physicians to provide primary care in competition with other physicians who are attending or with local nonhospital-affiliated practitioners. Other hospitals contract with physician groups to provide emergency care or subspecialty services on hospital premises or in satellite centers. Some physicians maintain their own practices distinct from the hospital but also receive a part-time salary from the hospital for administrative work.

Shortell (1985) has conceptualized four models of organization among physicians and hospitals: traditional (departmental), divisional, independent-corporate, and parallel. Under the *traditional* model, although each department retains relevant medical specialists, it does not provide the support services required by the physician to provide care, such as nursing, housekeeping, dietary, and clerical staff. Physicians are not a part of the hospital chain of command, as are nurses or assistant administrators. In hospitals, this is referred to as a *dual authority structure.* Most physicians are not hospital employees. Many physicians do not see themselves as primarily responsible to hospital administration but function rather as independent medical practitioners who must practice according to medical staff bylaws, rules, and regulations.

The *divisional* model is characterized by the placement of functional support services within medical divisions, which are organized along departmental lines. Each division, such as medicine or physical medicine, includes many of the support services, such as nursing and clerical (and sometimes dietary and medical records and other services) it needs to perform its tasks. Each medical division leader is responsible for management, including financial management, of both medical and support services.

Under the *independent-corporate* model, the medical staff becomes a separate legal entity that negotiates with the hospital for its services in return for receiving support services. An independent group of physicians provides medical services to the hospital, under contract. The *parallel* model involves the creation of a separate organization to conduct certain activities that are not handled well by the formal hospital organization. Certain physicians are selected to participate in a parallel organization for a certain percentage of their time, to work on important problems, and to report back to the formal structure. Some of these physicians would have positions in the formal structure as well.

Physicians and other clinicians practicing in hospitals have their own staff organization, with bylaws, rules, and regulations that must be approved by the hospital's governing board (see also chapter 14).

Medical staff bylaws specify procedures for election of medical staff officers by their membership. The officers are given authority under the bylaws to enforce rules and regulations. The officers delineate privileges and recommend disciplinary action when necessary through the committee structure. They enforce the bylaws and must oversee the committee structure and submit reports of medical staff activities to the governing board.

There are numerous medical staff committees in the hospital, some of which may include nonphysicians, particularly nurses, as members. The executive committee, if there is one, coordinates all activity, sets general policies for the medical staff, and accepts and acts upon recommendations from the other medical staff committees. The joint conference committee, if present, acts as a liaison between the medical staff and the governing board in deliberations over matters involving medical and nonmedical considerations. The credentials committee reviews applications by physicians to join the medical staff and considers the qualifications of education, experience, and interests before making recommendations for appointment to the executive committee, which will then make recommendations for appointment to the governing board. In some hospitals, the joint conference committee is also involved in this process.

Through the initiative of the Joint Commission, the medical staff (and the board) is increasingly structured to place higher priority on clinical quality improvement and patient care outcomes. Medical staff committees can be structured in various ways to accomplish this. Commonly, there is an overall medical staff committee concerned with clinical quality improvement as well as various subcommittees, such as infection control and quality improvement. In some cases, what were formerly medical staff committees have become hospital-wide committees, as physicians and others have realized that improvement of clinical performance rests increasingly on the teamwork of physicians, other clinicians, and support staff—not on physicians alone.

Many hospitals have hired salaried medical directors and quality improvement review teams. When physicians admit patients to the hospital, in most instances they are free to order whatever tests or treatments they deem necessary. Thus, a physician basically determines the amount of services used and the consequent costs of patient care. Physicians have every reason to want the best possible hospital setting in which to practice medicine, especially when it is provided at little personal cost to them.

Although the physician is technically a guest in the hospital, the hospital is responsible for the care its staff renders to patients on a physician's orders. Hospitals are legally responsible and, to the extent that hospital negligence is involved, financially responsible for the care provided by their entire professional staff, including physicians.

Therefore, many hospitals require physicians to have malpractice insurance as a condition of staff membership.

Current Issues in Acute Care

Delivering acute care requires consideration of numerous challenging issues in the ever-evolving health care delivery system. This section addresses such elements of today's acute care as team-based care, patient-centered care, physician training, access to care, and costs of care, as well as future challenges for acute care. (A lengthy description of pay-for-performance is included in chapter 15.)

TEAM-BASED CARE

In the primary care setting, pressures on providers to maximize the number of patients they see in a day are often at odds with pressures to provide comprehensive services to patients with complex needs. Apportioning tasks between members of a primary care team is one solution to this tension. For example, a diabetic with morning headaches might spend 10 minutes with the doctor for insulin dose adjustment, then 20 minutes with the on-site nutritionist for an assessment and brief intervention regarding late-night snacking. Such arrangements play to the strengths of each team member, meet patients' needs, enable physicians to maintain productivity, and do not compromise quality of care.

Team-based care plays a central role in the inpatient setting as well, where management of a patient with an acute medical condition (e.g., a heart attack) associated with a chronic condition (e.g., nicotine dependence) is enhanced by involving an interdisciplinary provider team. This is especially true as hospitalists manage an increasing proportion of hospitalized patients across the country. (*Hospitalists* are physicians whose practice is confined to hospital-based acute care, with expertise in the inpatient management of acute illness, use of care pathways, and efficient use of hospital services to optimize the quality and safety of care while minimizing length of stay and unnecessary utilization of resources.) Team-based care allows primary care physicians to partner with hospitalists to care for their patients across settings.

Advantages to such divisions of labor include time savings for office-based primary care providers by eliminating frequent trips between office and hospital and the quality, efficiency, and safety that can derive from having hospital-based specialists manage the increasingly complex course of an acute illness that requires inpatient treatment. Links between care provided in chronic (e.g., nursing homes) and acute care settings are similarly enhanced by coordinated, cross-site team-based care.

The principal disadvantage to such divisions of labor—the potential lack of continuity of care—can be overcome by having systems for efficient communication among team members. Team-based care is thus gaining acceptance as a strategy for enhancing the efficiency, quality, and continuity of care in diverse care settings. The growing reach of electronic medical information systems facilitates interdisciplinary team management and coordination and gives multiple caregivers ready access to a single consolidated medical record.

PATIENT-CENTERED CARE

In the highly complex world of medical care, it has become too easy to forget the central reason for the system's existence: the patient. Too often, patients' preferences regarding their care are not elicited or, worse, are ignored. While some decisions may be best left to the provider team (e.g., which antibiotic to use), others (how aggressively to treat a cancer) require careful consideration of the patient's views. Most readers will be able to identify an experience with the medical system in which advice given felt at odds with their preferences. To be effective, much medical care requires the patient's engagement in treatment, whether in taking a medication regularly and as prescribed, adhering to dietary advice, participating in physical therapy following surgery, or defining the goals of care at the end of life. Patients are much more likely to be engaged in their care when their preferences and goals are helping to drive the process.

> In the highly complex world of medical care, it has become too easy to forget the central reason for the system's existence: the patient.

With the goal of refocusing the health care delivery system on putting patients first, a movement to advance patient-centered care has recently gained momentum. The Institute of Medicine (2001) has recognized patient-centered care as a central goal toward which health systems must strive as they are redesigned around principles of quality and safety. Patient-centered physician-guided care is the centerpiece of the American College of Physicians' blueprint for the future of primary care. Early experiments have found that when patients participate more fully in decision making, one result is a significant reduction in more aggressive treatments. A component of patient-centered care is giving patients Internet access to elements of their electronic medical records. Online appointment scheduling, e-mail consultations with physicians, and other services enabled by Internet access will become more widespread as services are designed around patients'—rather than health professionals'—needs.

CHANGES IN PHYSICIAN TRAINING

Each year, approximately 12,000 residents complete training in generalist specialties (internal medicine, family medicine, and pediatrics) in the United States. It is this group of individuals that will effect lasting changes in care delivery in diverse settings. Already, changes in health care delivery have had a substantial impact on the thinking of leaders in medical education. In the early 1990s, the majority of medical school deans overseeing residency education were concerned about the impact of managed care on their training programs. But by 1997, their emphasis was on how to teach the "new medicine" to residents, not based on cost of care concerns but based on the best interests of patients.

New requirements for the accreditation of residency training programs exemplify this shifting approach. Now residents must have experience in providing continuity of care for patients in community-based settings, not just in hospital-based outpatient clinics. Primary care residency programs' formal curriculum must include training in biomedical ethics, medical-legal issues, cost management of health care, and the responsibility of health care providers for an entire population of individuals. As a result, physicians entering practice today will have some knowledge of the trends and forces shaping the world in which they will practice.

Starting in July 2003, all accredited U.S. residency programs have been required to adhere to work-hour standards—an 80-hour work week, no more than 24 hours of continuous work time, one full day off per week, and at least 10 hours off between work shifts. This schedule represents a significant restructuring of postgraduate medical education. Previously, no uniform work hour standards existed, and work weeks in excess of 100 hours were common. Multiple studies have demonstrated that sleep deprivation among resident physicians impairs cognitive performance and is associated with increased patient care errors. In response to fewer work hours by residents, hospitals have increased their reliance on physician extenders, such as physician assistants, and on attending physicians to deliver patient care formerly provided by residents. While few doubt that reduced work hours benefits patient care and medical education, some critics—including current trainees—have voiced concerns about problems with continuity of care and an erosion of medical professionalism in training programs due to reduced work hours.

ACCESS TO CARE

Approximately 45 million Americans lack health insurance coverage, a tremendous barrier to their ability to access comprehensive medical care services. An additional 16 million Americans are underinsured, which means they lack enough financial protection to cover medical expenses. Access is limited for millions of others because of where they live, the language they speak, their inability to read, and a host of other reasons.

The provision of care to under- or uninsured persons is a major financial strain for acute care facilities. In 2004, the financial impact on nonfederal community hospitals of delivering uncompensated care was estimated at $40.7 billion. For some hospitals, the costs of caring for uninsured or underinsured individuals are partially offset by federal Disproportionate Share Hospital funds. These cover a modest portion of unreimbursed care for hospitals designated as safety nets based on their volume of low-income Medicare and Medicaid patients. In 2006, an Institute of Medicine report recommended that Congress increase reimbursements to the large safety net hospitals.

Barriers to accessing health care are also experienced by many persons who have health insurance. The underinsured, like the uninsured, receive less ambulatory and inpatient care than the fully insured and seek medical help in more advanced stages of illness and injury. Access to care for the insured is impacted by rising out-of-pocket costs for premiums, deductibles, and co-payments, as well as reduced benefits. Strategies to enhance access in this group can include community outreach, health education in schools and on the job, and enhancing cultural sensitivity and linguistic capability among front-line providers.

Solving the challenge of ensuring ready access to primary health care for all will require sophisticated understanding of the impact on medical costs and the lost productivity of not having such access—as well, in the end, as sustained political will.

COSTS OF ACUTE CARE

The cost of both inpatient and ambulatory care has risen significantly over the past decade. In 2005, U.S. spending on health care increased 6.9% and reached nearly $2 trillion. Most projections forecast continued growth of health care spending as the population ages, new and expensive pharmaceuticals continue to be introduced, and ever-new technology becomes available for diagnosis and treatment. Cost containment is a central issue in acute care today because of pressure from payers, led by the federal government, and from consumers paying more in insurance premiums and out-of-pocket expenses.

Health insurance premiums and deductibles increased nearly 6% a year in the last decade. In 2005, Americans spent $249.4 billion on out-of-pocket health expenditures. In addition to growing costs,

> Comparing patients with similar health status, patients in higher spending areas of the country receive more care, have more frequent physician visits, have more tests and minor procedures, and use more specialty and hospital services than patients in lower spending areas—with no effect on health outcomes or patient satisfaction.

geographic variation in acute care utilization poses a challenge to practitioners and payers. A number of studies and federal reports have found that, comparing patients with similar health status, patients in higher spending areas of the country receive more care, have more frequent physician visits, have more tests and minor procedures, and use more specialty and hospital services than patients in lower spending areas. This increased utilization has no effect on health outcomes or patient satisfaction. Higher spending areas tend to have a predominance of specialists and more services available. Geographic variation in the price of services also impacts the cost of acute care.

Cost containment strategies have focused on reimbursement mechanisms, clinical practice, and more active oversight of resource utilization. For example, prepayment for health care (capitation) was designed to transfer financial risk to managed care companies and their providers, with the associated incentive to contain costs. Although credited with slowing the rise of health care spending in the last decade, the financial benefits of this model have not been sustained as providers and patients became dissatisfied with restrictions on choices. Complicating the equation are evolving requirements by accrediting organizations such as the National Committee for Quality Assurance, demanding that HMOs adhere to screening and prevention guidelines. In turn, many HMOs have required that practitioners listed on their panels adhere to these standards. Clinical practice variability—diverse approaches by different doctors to managing similar problems—has thus come under scrutiny as a challenge to containing costs, particularly as evidence-based best practices are promoted as a central element of quality improvement.

Delivering procedurally oriented medical services in ambulatory settings, including surgical and imaging procedures, can save money by avoiding the high fixed costs of hospitals. Other approaches to cost containment in ambulatory care include preventive services, delivery of care by nonphysician providers (e.g., physician assistants or nurse practitioners), shared decision making among physicians, and more advanced disease management practices. One solution to geographic variation in utilization is to increase access to primary care in high spending areas. Standardization of insurance forms and payment protocols can reduce ambulatory care billing costs, as can collecting payments up front rather than billing for care on a per-episode basis. Encouraging the use of generic drugs through tiered co-payment structures has become a standard practice to reduce costs for both insurers and patients.

Health information technology (IT) is one strategy purported to improve care, reduce wasteful and redundant treatments, prevent medical errors, and reduce administrative costs. Some studies claim that systems such as electronic medical records and computerized physician order entry with decision support could create savings of up to $80 billion a year, though few data demonstrating actual costs saved from such approaches are yet available. In addition, the question of who should pay for health IT—which could cost more than $400 billion to build on a national scale—makes it difficult to persuade government, providers, payers, and patients that this investment is needed.

At the patient level, much remains to be learned regarding the cost-effectiveness of interventions that promote healthful behavior and healthy outcomes, such as improving literacy, fostering healthy diets, increasing exercise, and stopping smoking.

Future Challenges

Effective, evidence-based care of populations or panels of patients offers the potential to improve health outcomes and reduce costs. For example, administering influenza vaccine to an entire population of elderly patients should decrease the seasonal number of hospital admissions for pneumonia and other influenza-related complications, while improving the health status of vaccine recipients. Early recognition and management of slowly progressive diseases, as achieved by screening for breast, prostate, or colon cancer or by maintaining tight control of diabetes, offers great potential to improve patients' health as well as decrease the costs of their care. Wellness programs aimed at decreasing the incidence of obesity, heart disease, or smoking-related illnesses will become standard features of the care offered by primary care providers, either directly or indirectly, to their populations of patients. Early detection of conditions that currently have no, or only minimally effective, treatments, such as Alzheimer's disease, will become more important as our ability to treat them improves. Integrating provider teams and information systems that span ambulatory and inpatient settings will begin to make improvements in acute care delivery a realizable goal.

References

American Hospital Association. (2006). *Trendwatch chartbook 2006: Trends affecting hospitals and health systems.* Prepared by The Lewin Group, Inc., for the American Hospital Association. Retrieved from http://www.aha.org/aha/research-and-trends/trendwatch/

American Hospital Association. (2007). *Hospital statistics*. Chicago: Healthcare InfoSource.

Association of American Medical Colleges. (2004). *Teaching hospitals*. Retrieved from http://www.aamc.org/teachinghospitals.htm

Institute of Medicine. (1996). *Primary care: America's health in a new era*. Washington, DC: National Academy Press.

Institute of Medicine. (2001). *Crossing the quality chasm: A new health system for the 21st century*. Washington, DC: National Academy Press.

National Association of Public Hospitals and Health Systems. (2007, January). Addressing disparities and serving diverse patient populations. *Research Brief*. Retrieved from http://www.magnetmail.net/images/clients/NAPH/attach/01_2007_Research_Brief.pdf

Norris, T. E., Hart, G. L., Larson, E. H., Tarczy-Hornoch, P., Masudo, D. L., Fuller, S. S., et al. (2002). Low-bandwidth, low-cost telemedicine consultations in rural family practice. *Journal of the American Board of Family Practice, 15*(2), 123–127.

Scheffler, R. M. (1996). Life in the kaleidoscope: The impact of managed care on the U.S. health care workforce and a new model for the delivery of primary care. In K. D. Yordy, K. N. Lohr, & N. A. Vanselow (Eds.), *Primary care: America's health in a new era* (pp. 312–340). Washington, DC: National Academy Press.

Shortell, S. M. (1985). The medical staff of the future: Replanting the garden. *Frontiers of Health Services Management, 1*(3), 3.

Starr, P. (1982). *The social transformation of American medicine*. New York: Basic Books.

Stevens, R. (1971). *American medicine and the public interest*. New Haven, CT: Yale University Press.

U.S. Department of Health and Human Services. (1995). *Health, United States*. Washington, DC: U.S. Government Printing Office.

U.S. Department of Health and Human Services. (2000). *Health, United States*. Washington, DC: U.S. Government Printing Office.

U.S. Department of Health and Human Services. (2003). *Health, United States*. Washington, DC: U.S. Government Printing Office.

U.S. Department of Health and Human Services. (2004). *Ambulatory medical care utilization estimates for 2004*. Retrieved February 22, 2007, from http://www.cdc.gov/nchs/products/pubs/pubd/hestats/estimates2004/estimates04.htm

U.S. Department of Health and Human Services. (2007, January). *Summary health statistics for the U.S. population: National Health Interview Survey, 2005*. Vital and Health Statistics, Series 10, Number 233.

Wilson, K. (1997). The VA healthcare system: An unrecognized national safety net. *Health Affairs, 16*, 200.

8

Key Words

chronic condition

chronic care

care coordination

activity limitations

Chronic Care

Gerard F. Anderson and James R. Knickman

Learning Objectives

- Quantify cost and prevalence of chronic conditions.
- Identify the overlap between chronic conditions and activity limitations.
- Recognize the problems faced by people with chronic conditions.
- Explore some of the options to change the delivery system to better meet the needs of people with chronic conditions.
- Examine changes that will be necessary to allow delivery systems to change.

Topical Outline

- Definition of and prevalence of chronic conditions
- Chronic conditions and activity limitations
- The cost of chronic care
- Insurance coverage and chronic care
- Dissatisfaction
- The evolving health care system
- Personal empowerment
- The Chronic Care Model
- Payment, coverage, information systems, medical education, and biomedical research
- Conclusion

I

ronically, the U.S. health care system is best organized to address acute events such as heart attacks and major traumas (epitomized by the portrayals in the NBC television show "ER"), yet most of the demand for medical care services is for treatment of chronic conditions such as asthma, diabetes, hypertension, Alzheimer's disease, congestive heart failure, and depression. In 2004, chronic conditions prompted most doctor visits, inpatient hospital and nursing home stays, drugs prescribed, and other health services used. Chronic conditions were responsible for more than three-quarters of health care spending. Yet, despite this enormous financial outlay, because the health care system remains oriented to acute care, people with chronic conditions often do not receive appropriate treatment. The result is much unnecessary suffering and more disability, at much higher-than-necessary financial cost.

The 131 million Americans with one or more chronic conditions encompass the entire spectrum of ages, income levels, and geographic regions. Many people with chronic conditions also have activity limitations. In the next several decades, both the cost and the prevalence of chronic conditions are projected to increase. By 2030, almost half of all Americans will have one or more chronic conditions. These numbers alone suggest why the health care system should be oriented to treating people with chronic conditions; however, clinical data as well as the perceptions of the public, clinicians, and policymakers suggest that the current system is not meeting their needs.

Consider, for example, the case of a patient we will call Mary B. She is a 78-year-old Medicare beneficiary with diabetes, coronary heart disease, asthma, and hypertension, and is in the initial stages of Alzheimer's disease. She sees at least six doctors and numerous other health care providers who treat these various conditions. However, since her doctors and other providers don't customarily communicate with one another, each one will develop a treatment protocol for Mary B. without knowing what the other ones are doing. As a result, she will have duplicate tests, unnecessary and redundant work-ups, advice from one clinician that contradicts the advice of another, preventable hospitalizations and nursing home stays, and other services that increase health spending and lower the quality of care for Mary B. At least one time during the year she is likely to arrive at the pharmacist only to be told that the prescription she is trying to fill could cause an adverse drug reaction with other medications she is taking. A time-consuming, expensive, and frustrating situation for any patient, in Mary B.'s case, because of her decreasing mental function, this lack of coordination and information-sharing is a nightmare. In this chapter, we will explore that nightmare further and provide some suggestions about what needs to change in many aspects of the health system in order for it to meet the needs of today's patients.

Definition of and Prevalence of Chronic Conditions

Chronic conditions are broadly defined as illnesses or impairments that are expected to last a year or longer, limit what one can do, or require ongoing medical care. By this definition, an estimated 131 million Americans (46% of the U.S. population) had a chronic condition in 2005. This number is projected to increase to 161 million Americans (49% of the population) by 2030. Other definitions of chronic conditions and other projection methods produce slightly different numbers, but all of the estimates agree that 40% to 50% of the U.S. population has at least one chronic condition.

Figure 8.1 shows common chronic conditions in the United States across all age groups in 2000. Hypertension (high blood pressure) is the most common, occurring in more than one in four Americans and becoming much more prevalent with age. More than half of all people over age 65 have hypertension. When several different chronic mental health conditions (depression, schizophrenia, dementia, etc.) are combined, they form the second most common chronic condition, occurring in all age groups.

Not all chronic conditions have the same impact on individuals. They vary considerably in how much they limit what one can do and the amount and type of ongoing care required. For example, people with diabetes have a wide range of limitations and treatment regimens. Some need to only monitor their blood glucose daily, while others become blind or lose their mobility. In its early stages, Alzheimer's disease can cause people to momentarily forget names or other details, but eventually the condition may completely deprive them of memory.

As people age they are more likely to develop a chronic condition (Figure 8.2). For example, heart disease and Alzheimer's disease are much more common among the elderly. Even so, approximately one in five children ages 18 or under has a chronic condition. This compares to four in five people over age 65. Given the increasing average age of the U.S. population, this relationship will become increasingly

Figure 8.1

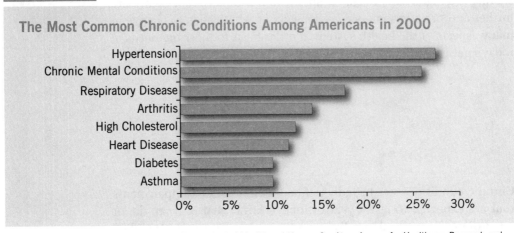

The Most Common Chronic Conditions Among Americans in 2000

Note. From U.S. Department of Health and Human Services, Agency for Healthcare Research and Quality. (2002). *The medical expenditure panel survey.* Washington, DC: U.S. Government Printing Office.

evident as the baby boomers begin to pass age 65 and the proportion of the population over 65 increases from 12.7% in 2000 to a projected 20.0% in 2030.

Most clinical and media attention focuses on one chronic condition at a time. It is difficult to pick up a newspaper without reading a report of a new way to prevent or treat, for example, hypertension, diabetes, depression, or asthma. Yet, half of all people with a chronic condition have more than one. People with multiple chronic conditions are the heaviest users of medical care services, are the most expensive to treat, and have the most problems with the medical care system.

> Half of all people with a chronic condition have more than one.

Consider Mary B. again, with her five specialists as well as a primary care physician. If she is hospitalized (a one-in-three chance), she will see even more doctors and other health professionals. If she enters a nursing home (a 40% chance), she will encounter a completely different set of providers. On average, she will fill one prescription per week. There is no easy way for all these doctors and other clinicians to communicate with each other regarding Mary B.'s conditions. It is unlikely that the clinicians treating her will be using an electronic medical record that might make information-sharing easier. Because of her initial stages of Alzheimer's, she is unable to remember what all the doctors have told her. If she has a family, one of members (most likely a daughter) may intervene and attempt to coordinate her care. This could literally become a full-time job.

Figure 8.2

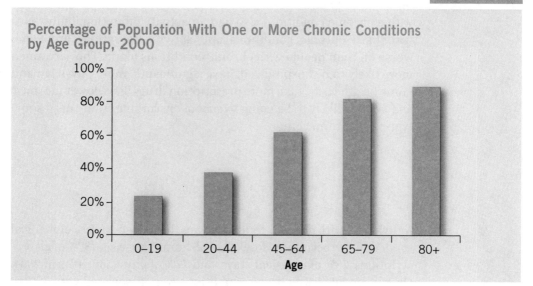

Percentage of Population With One or More Chronic Conditions by Age Group, 2000

Note. From U.S. Department of Health and Human Services, Agency for Healthcare Research and Quality. (2002). *The medical expenditure panel survey.* Washington, DC: U.S. Government Printing Office.

The prevalence of multiple chronic conditions also increases with age. Approximately one in three children with one chronic condition has at least one more. In adults ages 18 to 64, approximately two in three who have one chronic condition have another. But after age 65, almost 90% of people who have one chronic condition have multiple ones. The percentage of Americans with multiple chronic conditions is projected to increase from 22% in 2000 to 26% in 2030.

Chronic Conditions and Activity Limitations

Individuals with chronic conditions may also have activity limitations. There are many different ways to define activity limitations, each producing a different estimate of the number of people affected. For the purpose of calculating the overlap between chronic conditions and activity limitations, the following definitions are used. A *chronic condition* is an illness or impairment that is expected to last a year or longer, limits what one can do, or requires ongoing medical care. People with *activity limitations* need help or supervision with one or more activities of daily living or instrumental activities of daily living. (See chapter 9.)

By these definitions, 125 million Americans had a chronic condition in 2000. Of these, approximately 92 million had a chronic condition but no activity limitation. However, 33 million Americans (one in four with a chronic condition) also had an activity limitation. Individuals with both chronic conditions and activity limitations are much worse off than people with chronic conditions alone. They are much more likely to be hospitalized, have significantly more physician and home health visits, take more prescription drugs, have lower incomes, and are less likely to be going to school or working. Many need some type of long-term care.

Paying for Chronic Care

Individuals with chronic conditions are the heaviest users of medical services. They accounted for 96% of all home care visits, 87% of all prescriptions, 78% of inpatient stays, and 72% of physician visits in 2004. Overall, people with chronic conditions were associated with 78% of all medical care expenditures in 2004. As the prevalence of chronic conditions increases in the next several decades, these percentages will likely increase. In addition to the medical expenditures, much of the cost burden for people with chronic care is borne by families who provide informal care, as described in chapter 9.

As shown in Figure 8.3, in 2004, two-thirds of Medicare expenditures were for beneficiaries with five or more chronic conditions. Clearly, the greatest potential for cost savings and quality improvement in Medicare—and in the nation's health care system as a whole—is among the 23% of Medicare beneficiaries who have five or more chronic conditions. The Medicare program recently initiated a series of demonstrations that will test various models for identifying people most likely to benefit from various interventions and the types of interventions that are most likely to be successful with them. One of the most important comparisons will be between disease management models that utilize outside groups to help beneficiaries manage their care and models that incorporate care management practices directly into the doctor's office.

> The greatest potential for cost savings and quality improvement in Medicare—and in the nation's health system as a whole—is among the 23% of Medicare beneficiaries who have five or more chronic conditions.

Insurance status is a strong predictor of the percent of health spending associated with chronic conditions. Almost 100% of Medicare spending is for beneficiaries with one or more chronic conditions, and more than 80% is for beneficiaries with multiple chronic conditions. This is true for Medicare beneficiaries with supplemental insurance (also known as Medigap), people dually eligible for both

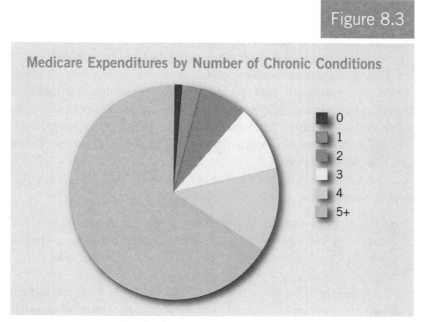

Note. From U.S. Centers for Medicare and Medicaid Services. (1999). *Medicare standard analytic file.* Baltimore, MD: U.S. Government Printing Office.

Medicare and Medicaid coverage, and those with only Medicare coverage. More than 80% of private health insurance spending and Medicaid spending (not including those dually eligible) is for people with one or more chronic conditions. The uninsured are least likely to spend money on chronic illnesses for several reasons: they are younger and therefore less likely to have a chronic condition, and they tend to postpone care until they need to go to the emergency room or the hospital. Nevertheless, almost two-thirds of all medical care spending for the uninsured is for people with a chronic condition, and more than 40% is for people with multiple chronic conditions. Because health care spending usually increases with the number of chronic conditions a person has, uninsured individuals with multiple chronic conditions are likely to have high out-of-pocket costs and insufficient care.

Dissatisfaction With the Current System

Individuals with chronic conditions report considerable difficulty obtaining the services necessary to improve or maintain their health status. The American public overwhelmingly recognizes that people with chronic conditions do not have access to adequate health insurance coverage or to appropriate medical services. The level of dissatisfaction is much lower with respect to acute care services.

Health insurance remains oriented toward acute episodes, but Americans recognize that even people with health insurance, if they have chronic conditions, have problems accessing health care services. For example, almost three in four believe that people with chronic conditions have difficulty obtaining access to primary care and specialty physicians.

Three health insurance practices cause the most problems for people with chronic conditions:

- Some services are not covered by some insurance plans. One example is transportation to medical care providers—a critical problem for people too sick or too disabled to drive or take public transportation.
- The criterion of "medical necessity" is used to deny payment even when the service is covered. For example, a person who needs ongoing rehabilitation after a stroke may find that insurance won't cover treatment after a set number of weeks. Or coverage of a specific service is denied because it won't actually improve the insured person's condition. This definition of medical necessity makes sense in acute care situations, but may not in chronic care, where maintaining function or health status is often the goal.
- Cost-sharing is a third common problem. To prevent excessive or unnecessary treatment, insurers generally require beneficiaries to bear some portion of the cost of their care, through deductibles, coinsurance, or co-payments. Again, this makes sense in an acute care context, but cost-sharing can create a substantial financial burden for people with multiple chronic conditions who must go to multiple doctors repeatedly.

Given these practices, Mary B. may have difficulty getting Medicare to pay for treatment for her Alzheimer's disease, because she is unlikely to improve. In fact, her condition is likely to deteriorate. (As a result, many doctors code chronic conditions as something else in order to be paid. For other professional services, such as physical therapy, this subterfuge may not be as easy.)

With her five chronic conditions, Mary is likely to have more than 30 doctor visits, 2 hospitalizations, and 50 prescriptions during a year. If each of these services requires a $10 co-pay, she will have $820 in out-of-pocket medical expenses for the year, not counting services she needs for which there is no coverage at all. If she must go into a nursing home, the annual cost could exceed $80,000. In

2000, people like Mary, with five or more chronic conditions, generally spent more than $10,000 annually out-of-pocket for health services.

Further, care coordination is needed to help maximize the benefit from physicians and other providers patients do see. Mary B.'s proposed new treatment for diabetes could conflict with her ongoing treatment for congestive heart failure. Her endocrinologist should work with her cardiologist to resolve any treatment discontinuities. Currently, who arranges this and how the information is shared is left completely to chance. It is unlikely that there is an electronic medical record that all her physicians can access. Appropriate care coordination is unlikely to happen. Good coordination would involve physicians and other health professionals working in acute care, long-term care, and rehabilitation settings developing a coordinated care plan.

In a national survey of the American public, more than 60% of caregivers of people with serious chronic conditions reported that they received conflicting medical advice from different providers. More than half of people with serious chronic conditions and their caregivers reported that they received different diagnoses for the same set of conditions. Almost half of Americans with multiple chronic conditions went to a pharmacy last year only to be told that the prescription they were having filled could adversely interact with other medications they were taking. In a recent survey, physicians reported that they found it difficult to coordinate care for people with chronic conditions and recognized that poor care coordination was leading to adverse outcomes, such as unnecessary hospitalizations and nursing home stays (Mathematica Policy Research, 2001).

Other research is beginning to document the adverse outcomes generated by lack of care coordination. For instance, one study found that, over the course of a year, 7 out of 1,000 Medicare beneficiaries with one chronic condition will have a preventable hospital stay, whereas, among those with five chronic conditions, 95 out of 1,000—almost 1 in 10—will have a preventable hospitalization (Wolf, Starfield, & Anderson, 2002). The number rises to 261 per 1,000 among those with 10 or more chronic conditions. Unnecessary hospitalizations not only increase health care spending, they also reduce health care quality. At a cost of more than $6,000 per hospitalization, the potential savings from reducing or eliminating unnecessary hospitalizations are considerable. If the number of duplicative tests and the probability of having an adverse drug reaction due to drug interactions also can be reduced, the potential savings from better care coordination are enormous.

The Evolving Health Care System

The evolution of the U.S. health care system in the 20th century reflected the changing demographics, mortality, and morbidity of the U.S. population. During the first half of the century, the health care system emphasized treating infectious diseases, reflecting the impact of destructive epidemics such as the Spanish influenza outbreak of 1918–1919. Smallpox, typhoid, cholera, tuberculosis, and other infectious diseases drove the design and implementation of the health care system. This era culminated with the successful development of a variety of vaccines and improved public sanitation and environmental standards that greatly reduced illness and death from infection.

After World War II, a new era began. The health care system shifted its focus to the treatment of acute illnesses—trauma, heart attacks—and the use of improved surgical techniques. It evolved the delivery, financing, educational, and biomedical research systems to support this emphasis on acute, episodic care, and treatment for these conditions has improved dramatically in the last 60 years.

By the turn of the new century, a third transformation had begun. Some of the successful treatments of acute conditions (severe birth defects, stroke) had enabled the survival of people who, in the past, would not have lived. Many of them need ongoing—sometimes lifelong—treatment. Some diseases—such as HIV/AIDS and some cancers—that used to be in the acute care category are now treatable on a long-term, chronic basis. Other socioeconomic and environmental changes have enhanced longevity generally, and, by living longer, individuals acquire chronic conditions along with their gray hair. This growing prevalence of chronic conditions necessitates yet another health care transformation—one that will require significant changes in personal responsibility, too. We group these changes into three categories: patient empowerment, major reforms to the health care delivery system, and other system reforms.

PERSONAL EMPOWERMENT

Individuals, clinicians, and policymakers can undertake health care activities that would help prevent chronic conditions. A number of studies have shown that most chronic conditions are preventable—or at least better managed—by changes in personal behavior (quitting smoking, better nutrition, more exercise). Other studies have shown that specific interventions can successfully promote these behavior changes. A key factor is the support and encouragement of one's physician. It takes persistent attention to motivational issues to help people avoid the first, second, or tenth chronic condition.

However, even if many new chronic illnesses were prevented or postponed, it is still necessary to help those who already have them. The first step is *personal empowerment.* The personal empowerment movement began among people with disabilities, many of whom require long-term care services. Publicly funded programs began to subsidize personal assistance programs, covering everything from bathing and dressing to shopping and housekeeping, acknowledging the need to provide direct support for people with long-term health problems. The programs also allowed recipients to arrange and supervise their own services, a feature known as *consumer direction.* A number of factors have led to this growing empowerment, among them legal direction (such as the Supreme Court's 1999 Olmstead decision and the Americans with Disabilities Act), aggressive advocacy of disability rights groups, and cost considerations.

A number of programs have been designed to foster personal empowerment for people with chronic conditions. For example, the Robert Wood Johnson Foundation has operated a program with state Medicaid agencies titled "Cash and Counseling." It gives people who meet Medicaid criteria for nursing home eligibility (health status as well as income and asset requirements) the option to receive cash benefits instead of services, and they can use the cash in conjunction with counseling to purchase services on their own and remain in their homes. Findings from this program suggest that people are more satisfied with services when they can purchase what they think they really need. And they appear to be doing well in maintaining their ability level.

Growing awareness of the importance of patient activation has expanded to include people with chronic conditions. Providers have begun to recognize the importance of making people with chronic conditions partners in their care. One example of this type of consumer-directed care was developed by Hal Holman and colleagues at the Stanford Patient Education Research Center, in what they call the Health Partners approach to care. This system relies on provider-patient interaction beyond the traditional acute care–oriented hospital and doctors' office settings. It engages patients by informing them of the nature of their conditions and what they can do to improve their quality of life. As Holman says,

> Providers have begun to recognize the importance of making people with chronic conditions partners in their care.

> a one-on-one interaction between doctor and patient was an appropriate management tool when acute disease was the dominant problem. This works with something like a broken leg or a bout of pneumonia that is new to the patient. But with chronic disease, we should be exploring a new model, because patients have time to become "smart" about what's happening. (Medical Staff Update, 2000, p. 1)

THE CHRONIC CARE MODEL

The patient empowerment model pioneered by Holman represents an important departure from traditional patient care, but it does not address the need to reorient health care providers toward caring for people with chronic conditions. Edward Wagner and his colleagues at Group Health of Puget Sound in Seattle, Washington, have developed a Chronic Care Model that integrates various aspects of the provider-patient interaction, shown in a simplified version in Figure 8.4. There are six components of the Chronic Care Model that can lead to better care for people with chronic conditions:

- *Community programs* can play an important supporting role. Nutrition and exercise classes at senior centers, for example, can reinforce healthy behavior and provide opportunities for socialization.

Figure 8.4

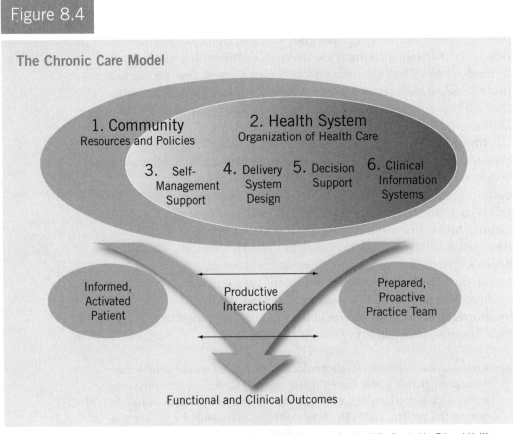

The Chronic Care Model

Note. From The Improving Chronic Illness Care Program, Seattle, WA, directed by Edward H. Wagner, Group Health Cooperative of Puget Sound. Retrieved from http://www.improvingchroniccare.org/change/model/components.html

- The *organization of the overall health system* is critical. Currently, the health care system is designed to be reactive—performing when people are injured or sick—and should evolve to one that is proactive, focused on keeping people as healthy as possible.
- A crucial aspect is the patient's own *self-management.* Patients who properly take care of themselves can minimize complications, symptoms, and disabilities. Engendering a sense of personal responsibility for health outcomes encourages people to assume the central role in their care. Using established programs to provide basic information, emotional support, and strategies for living with chronic conditions is an important part of self-management support. Care decisions must be based on clearly established guidelines rooted in clinical research, and these guidelines need to be explained to people so they understand the principles underlying their care and can make fully informed choices.
- The *health care delivery system design* should integrate chronic care guidelines into reminders, feedback, and standing orders for practitioners to make them more evident as clinical decisions are made. To this end, involving supportive specialists in primary care is an increasingly common part of chronic care. Keeping providers focused on maintaining health rather than restoring it requires a combination of case management, aggressive follow-up, and ensuring that information is relayed to patients in ways that are compatible with their culture and background.
- The fifth and sixth components of the Chronic Care Model—*decision support* and *clinical information systems,* respectively—are inextricably linked. Managing chronic care effectively requires access to information not only on individual patients, but on populations as well. A comprehensive clinical information system helps providers issue timely reminders about needed services and allows for an individual patient's health care data to be followed easily and effectively. Population-level data can point to groups needing additional attention and aid in monitoring the performance of particular providers and, thereby, support quality improvement efforts. Access to these data allows providers to develop evidence-based guidelines for their practices and to share them with their patients, so that they can understand the principles underlying their care.

The Chronic Care Model emphasizes that patients who are informed about their conditions and who assume an active role in managing their care, working in tandem with providers who are prepared and supported with time and resources at their disposal, are likely to have more productive health care interactions and better health outcomes (Bonomi, Wagner, Glasgow, & Von Korff, 2002). For example, acute episodes for people with diabetes or asthma decrease when engaged patients work closely with proactive providers. These patient-physician interactions are not restricted to face-to-face encounters, but may be telephone conferences, group visits, or e-mail exchanges.

In an ideal world, Mary B. would find a delivery system that allows her to participate in the decision-making process about her care. She would know her different clinicians, and they would openly communicate with her and with each other. And the community in which she lives would be supportive of her—and her family caregiver's—needs. The next question is how this optimistic scenario can be supported and sustained. This will require reform in other parts of the health care system.

OTHER SYSTEM REFORMS

Individuals can assume greater personal responsibility and be given information to help them manage their behavior and treatment. Delivery systems can improve the way they provide care. However, it will be difficult to sustain these activities if other components of the health care system are not oriented toward prevention or the delivery of ongoing, chronic care. In this final section, necessary changes to the payment system, coverage policy, information systems, medical education training, and biomedical research are briefly outlined.

Payment System Reforms

The current fee-for-service payment system encourages episodic care and cost-shifting among individual facilities or providers and across different payers. Many experts have acknowledged that managed care systems should be ideal for promoting the integrated delivery systems that good chronic care ultimately requires. However, enrollment in staff model and other health maintenance organization models that stress care coordination are on the decline due to the complexity of managing these organizations, the difficulty of recruiting physicians to work in them, and the reluctance of many individuals—especially those without chronic conditions—to enroll.

Less restrictive health plans that operate through exclusive provider networks rarely have patient information or payment systems that foster care coordination. Their information systems do not allow clinicians to communicate with each other, particularly when enrollees seek care from several networks or groups. Often health plan providers, if they are in a capitated system, are capitated within their own specialty spheres and are responsible only for the utilization of their own services. As a result, they have no need to be aware of the services their patients are using outside their specialty (or office) and, indeed, may have the perverse incentive (from a quality or care point of view) to refer a patient to many other providers, so that the costs of treatment are not charged against the fixed payment they received. Insurers and managed care plans faced with rising program costs are reluctant to pay for expensive infrastructure, such as information systems, or extra services, such as care coordination.

If there is a desire to change the way care is practiced, financial incentives at the practitioner level also will need to change. One approach is to adopt the clinical care manager model. In this model, a patient with multiple chronic conditions who is having difficulty self-managing care would designate a clinician as clinical care manager. This physician would receive a monthly administrative payment to compensate for the additional office staff time required to take on this role. The purpose of this model is to assign the task of treatment coordination to a single clinician and reimburse accordingly. The ultimate responsibility for treatment—and, therefore, resource utilization—would rest with this physician. At present, most physicians are not trained to take on this role, although they could hire individuals to perform this function. However, if payment were tied to process and outcome standards, the field would respond over time.

> If there is a desire to change the way care is practiced, financial incentives at the practitioner level also will need to change.

Under this model, Mary B., with her five chronic conditions, would qualify for a clinical care manager whom she (or her caregiver) would select. Perhaps the clinical care manager would receive $100 per month to help her manage her care and to coordinate services and share information with other clinicians.

Coverage Reforms

Three improvements in health insurance coverage would greatly aid people with chronic conditions. First, certain benefits should be added to insurance policies to cover the kinds of special services needed by people with chronic conditions. Second, the medical necessity criterion should be clarified to allow claims for services that preserve the health status of a chronically ill individual. Third, coinsurance should be restructured so that people with multiple chronic conditions do not face overwhelming financial burdens.

Clinical Information Systems

Information systems need to become more common that allow one clinician to know what tests, treatments, and medications a patient has received from other clinicians—each of them treating a different condition or symptom. Electronic medical records systems allow access to such a common set of data, and the Veterans Health Administration (VHA) already has this type of system in operation. Within the VHA, physicians know how other physicians are caring for a patient and can easily share laboratory results and radiologic images. Information systems that allow communication across clinicians and providers could improve quality of care, reduce unnecessary hospitalizations, eliminate duplicative tests, decrease the amount of contradictory advice, and lower medical care costs.

Medical Education Reforms

Diagnosing and treating problems in isolation is not appropriate for patients with multiple chronic conditions. Clinicians will need to learn to work with others—physicians and nonphysicians alike—to treat this growing category of patients and work with their family caregivers. This will require a relatively fundamental change in how doctors are trained, especially for care in the outpatient setting.

Advances in Biomedical Research

Biomedical research will need to operate differently. Currently, most clinical trials exclude people with multiple chronic conditions. Practicing physicians, therefore, cannot be sure whether a drug, device, or procedure will help or harm their patients.

This array of issues is likely to be addressed only when stresses in the health care system force a rethinking of our approach to insurance coverage and health care delivery more generally. Because the Medicare program spends two-thirds of its budget on people with five or more chronic conditions, the Medicare program is a logical place to start thinking about the policies and strategies that would encourage more appropriate payment and coverage practices, physician training, and biomedical research standards. Already, Medicare is involved in substantial efforts to introduce electronic health records (Anderson, 2005).

International Trends

Other countries also are becoming interested in better chronic care. The World Health Organization and the World Bank have recently published studies showing the significant burden of chronic conditions in lower- and middle-income countries. They have published studies showing the cost-effectiveness of certain interventions. Among industrialized countries, Australia, the United Kingdom, and Germany have recently instituted a series of programs that reflect their growing concern with chronic diseases. Better care for people with chronic conditions has become an international concern.

Conclusion

In the coming years, the U.S. health care system will have to focus on better ways to manage care for people with chronic conditions, especially multiple chronic conditions. Substantial reform is needed if the 125 million Americans with one or more chronic conditions are to receive the kinds of services that will improve their functioning and participation in society, as well as their quality of life. At the same time, the individuals affected and their families will need to know a great deal more about their own personal health care responsibility, how the medical care system is organized, and how to make sure they receive the services they require.

References

Anderson, G. (2005). Medicare and chronic conditions. *New England Journal of Medicine, 353,* 305–309.

Bonomi, A. E., Wagner, E. H., Glasgow, R., & Von Korff, M. (2002). Assessment of chronic illness care: A practical tool for quality improvement. *Health Services Research, 37,* 791–820.

Mathematica Policy Research Inc. (2001). *National Public Engagement Campaign on Chronic Illness—Physician Survey, Final Report.* Princeton, NJ: Author.

Medical Staff Update. (2000). Fact file, questions and answers. Interview with Joseph R. Hopkins and Halsted R. Holman. *Stanford Hospital and Clinics, 24*(2), 1–3.

Wolf, J. L., Starfield, B., & Anderson, G. (2002). Prevalence, expenditures, and complications of multiple chronic conditions in the elderly. *Archives of Internal Medicine, 162,* 2269–2276.

9

Key Words

long-term care
chronic health conditions
activities of daily living
instrumental activities of
    daily living
formal and informal services/
    paid and unpaid caregivers
nursing homes
home- and community-based
    services (HCBS)

home care
home health care
certified home health agency
    (CHHA)
hospice services
adult day care
respite services
assisted living facilities
continuing care retirement
    communities (CCRCs)

financing mechanisms—
    public/private financing;
    integrated long-term
    and acute care financing;
    private LTC insurance
access
quality
consumer choice

Long-Term Care

Penny Hollander Feldman, Pamela Nadash,
and Michal D. Gursen

Learning Objectives

- Define the key components of long-term care (LTC) and discuss the factors that contribute to need and demand for service.
- Describe the principal users of and the principal sources of payment for LTC.
- Discuss the differences and similarities between individual and societal-level goals for the LTC system.
- Distinguish among the principal paid providers of LTC and the populations they serve.
- Identify the major cost, quality, and access issues in LTC and discuss the strengths and weaknesses of alternative policy options.

Topical Outline

- Introduction to long-term care
- Long-term care needs and demands
- U.S. spending on LTC and its financing
- The goals of long-term care
- Who supplies long-term care
- Challenging issues
- Conclusion

T

Nearly every American will encounter the need for long-term care, either for themselves or a loved one. The rapidly increasing cost of long-term care is one of the largest expenses facing states and their spiraling Medicaid budgets. We need to change the culture of long-term care to help our seniors age healthier and our states more efficiently provide the dignified care our citizens deserve.

—*Dirk Kempthorne, former Chair, National Governors Association*

he need for long-term care (LTC) is growing. The U.S. population is aging, and the fastest population growth is among the *oldest old*—those people 85 years or older who are most likely to be affected by chronic, disabling conditions. Moreover, technological advances are enabling virtually everyone with a disabling condition—young or old—to live longer. Today, hardly any human, no matter how handicapped or disabled, is beyond some rehabilitation. As a result, family caregivers, community service providers, health care experts, policymakers, and consumers of care are struggling daily to identify the kinds of services and supports that will optimally address the challenges of those who live with disability.

All too often, the public equates LTC with care in a nursing home or another institution. However, LTC is a broad constellation of services provided in diverse settings to a heterogeneous population with many different needs. *Supportive services* form the core of LTC. These services include personal assistance with basic daily activities such as bathing, eating, walking, or going to the toilet. In the LTC literature, such activities are commonly referred to as *activities of daily living* or ADLs. Supportive services also include help with household chores and related activities such as shopping, cooking, managing money and paying bills, or traveling to and from one's home. In the LTC literature, these activities are commonly referred to as *instrumental activities of daily living* or IADLs.

> Family caregivers, community service providers, health care experts, policymakers, and consumers of care are struggling daily to identify the kinds of services and supports that will optimally address the challenges of those who live with disability.

In addition, millions of individuals with chronic disabling conditions also require ongoing medical monitoring and intervention to control the symptoms and progression of their disease. Others require rehabilitative services to recover physical or mental function or to delay a decline. Still others may benefit from *palliative care,* which addresses physical, mental, spiritual, and social needs of patients and caregivers. (Although palliative care is most commonly associated with the decision to give up active medical treatment in the last weeks, days, or hours of life, a number of experts are seeking to incorporate palliative care principles in the LTC continuum.) This chapter uses *a broad definition of LTC that encompasses a range of supportive, rehabilitative, nursing, and palliative services provided to people—young or old—whose capacity to perform daily activities is restricted due to chronic disease or disability.* Table 9.1 outlines the range of services included in our definition of LTC and provides examples of each. LTC may be provided in institutions, congregate settings, or individual homes or apartments to people of all ages suffering from physical and mental disabilities.

Long-Term Care Needs and Demands

The nation's 9.5 million individuals in need of long-term care differ considerably in the severity of their limitations and their need for assistance. Some individuals may require direct hands-on

 **Table 9.1**   Range of Long-Term Care Services

Type of Service	Example
Housekeeping and other support for instrumental activities of daily living	Cleaning, cooking, laundry, shopping, home maintenance, financial management
Companionship and social support	Visiting, calling, counseling, advising, case management
Transportation	Arranging, accompanying, providing transportation and escort services
Personal care	Hands-on, supervision of, or standby assistance with activities of daily living (bathing, dressing, walking, transferring, feeding, toileting)
Nursing and health care procedures	Assessment, care planning, promotion of optimum health status, including recovery from acute illness and relief of symptoms
Rehabilitative services	Exercises and programs to improve or restore functioning (motion, speech, bowel, bladder)
Palliative care	Comfort care, symptom management, and medication management at the end of life
Care management	Planning and arranging appointments, equipment, transportation, and provider communication

Note. Adapted from Kane, R. A. (1999). Goals of home care: Therapeutic, compensatory, either, or both? *Journal of aging and health, 11.* pp. 299–321, Tables 2 and 3.

assistance or supervision to meet their basic daily needs; for others, special equipment or training can enable them to function relatively independently. Disability can be present from birth, it may occur as the result of injury or disease, or it may manifest itself as a part of the aging process. Most older Americans are generally healthy, but as people age, they do become more dependent. They are at increased risk of the chronic diseases of old age—arthritis, hypertension, heart disease, diabetes, and hearing, vision, and cognitive impairments. They require help with tasks such as cleaning, shopping, and preparing meals. They also become more reliant on others for transportation and for assistance in activities of daily living. In 2003, adults 85 or older were more than seven times as likely as adults ages 65 to 74 to need personal assistance with activities of daily living (U.S. Centers for Disease Control and Prevention, 2004).

The demand for LTC is expected to grow in the coming years as both the absolute numbers and the proportion of older people in the population increase. The most significant growth will be among people 85 or older, who are at highest risk for disability and institutionalization. Exponential growth of the older population will almost certainly increase the number of Americans with serious chronic conditions and related functional impairments. However, a number of recent studies suggest that increased demand for LTC may not be directly proportionate to increases in absolute numbers, because today's older Americans tend to be less disabled than those of 10 or 20 years ago. For example, from 1989 to 1999, the number of people 65 and older who reported any need for assistance rose from 6.6 to only 6.8 million—1.5 million fewer than would have been expected had disability rates stayed at the 1984 level (Gibson et al., 2003).

Costs and Financing of Long-Term Care

Determining what proportion of U.S. health care expenditures is spent on LTC is difficult, because the national chart of health accounts does not clearly separate out LTC dollars. Moreover, the federal figures do not take into account the enormous value of unpaid LTC services provided by family, friends, and neighbors. Many estimates of formal (i.e., paid) LTC spending in the United States simply sum expenditures for nursing home and home health services—some $158 billion in 2004. But not all care provided by home health agencies and nursing homes is long-term care. Virtually all home health agencies and many nursing homes also serve short-stay patients. Furthermore, LTC is provided by a wide variety of other organizations, such as local housekeeping agencies, aide registries, and meal delivery programs, as well as community-based residences, including "board and care" homes, assisted living facilities, and many others. LTC expenditures in these settings are not captured in the formal health accounts. In addition, in 2004, the economic value of unpaid caregiving was estimated at $306 billion—nearly twice the annual cost of nursing home and home care combined (Arno, 2006).

The three major sources of financing for formal LTC services are Medicaid, Medicare, and personal out-of-pocket spending. Medicaid covers proportionately more nursing home than home health care, while Medicare covers proportionately more home health than nursing home care. Although between them, Medicaid and Medicare cover about 60% of LTC spending, private out-of-pocket payments for LTC are quite substantial (33%). Private health insurance covers less than 5% of all LTC spending (see Figure 9.1).

Medicaid, the federal-state entitlement program that covers medical and other health-related services for selected low-income Americans, is the one national program with a clear mandate to cover long-term care (see chapter 5). States are free to regulate the supply of nursing home beds and to determine rates of payment for Medicaid residents. However, federal rules are quite explicit with regard to eligibility for nursing home coverage: states must cover nursing home care for disabled individuals 65 and older with income up to three times the limit—$623 per month in 2007—of the federal Supplemental Security Income program (U.S. Centers for Medicare & Medicaid Services, 2007). Individuals may qualify for Medicaid by spending down their income and assets as a result of their institutionalization. In turn, they must contribute all of their income to their nursing home care, except for a small personal needs allowance determined by the state. In 2005, Medicaid covered 44% of all nursing home expenditures (Catlin, Cowan, Heffler, Washington, & National Expenditure Accounts Team, 2007), and Medicaid was the principal source of coverage for about two-thirds of current nursing home residents.

Under federal guidelines, state Medicaid programs are required to cover home health care ordered by a physician for people who are eligible for skilled nursing services. Under the "optional" category, programs also may choose to cover personal care. In 2002, 32 states offered personal care as an optional Medicaid benefit, at a total cost of

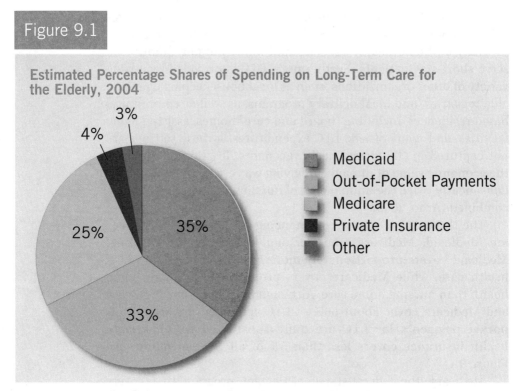

Figure 9.1

Estimated Percentage Shares of Spending on Long-Term Care for
the Elderly, 2004

3%
4%

25%   35%

33%

Medicaid
Out-of-Pocket Payments
Medicare
Private Insurance
Other

Note. Excludes informal care. From U.S. Congressional Budget Office. (2004). *Financing long-term
care for the elderly.* Retrieved from http://www.cbo.gov/ftpdoc.cfm?index=5400&type=1

$5.5 billion; by 2005, personal care expenditures reached $8.6 billion
(Burwell, Sredl, & Eiken, 2004, 2006).

In addition, states may apply for a federal waiver that allows
them to cover a broad array of medical and supportive home- and
community-based services (HCBS) to selected subgroups of people
who would otherwise require nursing home care. States can limit
the number of people who receive HCBS services, thus avoiding the
potential financial cost of an open-ended entitlement. In 2005, spending on HCBS waiver programs was $22.7 billion, nearly three times
the amount spent in 1997; most of this spending was for people with
developmental disabilities.

The Medicare program, which pays for skilled nursing home
care[1] and home health services needed on a part-time or intermittent basis, was originally intended to provide a finite, postacute care
benefit. Nevertheless, during the 1990s, the Medicare home health
benefit became an important source of LTC funding, fueled by an
open-ended fee-for-service payment system and a federal court case

---

[1] For up to 100 days after a hospitalization for people who need continued nursing or therapy
services.

that relaxed the rules for home care eligibility. To constrain rapidly growing costs, Congress mandated a new Medicare home health prospective payment system, which resulted in dramatic decreases in short-run outlays. Medicare home health spending plummeted from a 1997 high of $18 billion to about $7.5 billion in 2003 (U.S. Department of Health and Human Services, 2003). By 2005, however, Medicare home health expenditures were up to $17.9 billion, demonstrating spectacular growth over a 2-year period (Catlin et al., 2007).

Over this period, there also was a dramatic increase in the share of all home care services funded by Medicaid and other state and local programs, which may explain why analyses of the early impact of the home health prospective payment system found no clear evidence of harm to beneficiaries. By 2005, federal and state Medicaid dollars accounted for $15.5 billion of total U.S. home health expenditures or 32.6% of the total, while Medicare's $17.9 billion accounted for 37.7% (Catlin et al., 2007).

Given the limits of both Medicaid and Medicare LTC coverage, it is not surprising that out-of-pocket payments constitute a significant share of spending for both nursing home residents and HCBS users. In 2005, out-of-pocket payments accounted for $37.4 billion or 22% of total nursing home and home health expenditures (Catlin et al., 2007). The bulk of these payments covered the costs of nursing home care, as individuals contributed to the high costs of those institutions—more than $75,000 a year on average for a private room (MetLife, 2006). These costs can deplete personal assets, and, by spending down, residents become eligible for Medicaid.

Purchase of private LTC insurance policies has grown rapidly. The industry claimed an 18% increase for each year between 1987 and 2001 (Coronel, 2003). Much of this growth is likely due to an increased availability of policies through employers. The federal government made long-term care insurance available to its employees in 2002. Nevertheless, private health insurance payments still covered only 7.5% of nursing home expenditures in 2005 (Catlin et al., 2007)—a share predicted to rise to 17% by 2020 (U.S. Congressional Budget Office, 2004).

Because annual premiums for LTC insurance are expensive—from $1,000 to $2,300 at age 65 or $4,200 to $7,000 at age 79—policies tend to be bought by more affluent individuals.[2] The future importance of private insurance as a vehicle for covering LTC costs is uncertain; however, some experts estimate that, over the next 20 years, 10% to 20% of retirees could have sufficient financial resources to purchase such policies (Tilly et al., 2000).

---

[2] Premium ranges depend on whether the policy includes inflation protection or a nonforfeiture benefit.

The Goals of Long-Term Care

We have discussed what LTC services are, who needs and gets them, and how they are financed. The goals of LTC, however, are less straightforward, primarily because LTC is not an end in itself but rather a means to multiple ends, depending on whose perspective is being considered. Table 9.2 lists some LTC goals expressed from the point of view of the individual consumer and from a broader societal perspective. These goals matter, because it is the balancing of individuals' and society's goals that determines the shape of LTC services. In some cases, societal and individual goals correspond well. For example, both aim to facilitate individual choice. But they can conflict when it comes to decisions about the financing and delivery systems.

Virtually every individual goal embodies an element of subjective judgment.[3] For example, the definitions of *comfort, health, autonomy,* and *choice* will vary from individual to individual and, for any one individual, will vary over time. Some of the individual goals are *therapeutic goals* in that they entail an effort to achieve measurable improvement—or forestall measurable deterioration—in an individual's physical, psychological, or social health. Others are *compensatory goals* in that they aim to compensate for an individual's functional impairments by facilitating comfort, safety, and autonomy despite disability.

The list of societal goals also contains much subjectivity and many potential contradictions. For example, the terms *adequate, equitable, acceptable,* and even *cost-effective* are all subject to widely different interpretations depending on the discipline, philosophy, politics, socioeconomic status, or institutional vantage point of those defining the terms.

Providers of Long-Term Care

UNPAID CAREGIVERS

The vast majority of long-term care in the United States is provided by family, friends, neighbors, and other unpaid caregivers. Unpaid care provided by these individuals is usually referred to as *informal care.* However, many advocates object to the term *informal,* which seems to belie the amount of time, effort, organization, and coordination dedicated to the task.

---

[3] Much of the following discussion of goals is adapted from Feldman (1999).

Table 9.2	Individual and Societal Goals for Long-Term Care

Individual	Societal
Meet needs for care and assistance	Provide an adequate level of services to meet basic needs
Ensure comfort, safety, and freedom from pain	Target those most in need
Remain at home as long as possible in the face of disability and dependence	Promote the efficient production of cost-effective services
Maximize function; prevent or delay deterioration of functional abilities	Maximize individual responsibility
Access services readily	Promote a fair and equitable distribution of services
Maintain and improve physical, psychological, and social health and well-being	Provide comprehensive services
Improve self-knowledge and self-care abilities	Encourage reliance on informal systems of family-provided care
Maximize independence, autonomy, and individual choice	Facilitate consumer choice
Receive highest quality care	Ensure acceptable quality of services
Find information easily	Integrate and coordinate services
Minimize out-of-pocket costs	Contain costs to government and taxpayers

Most experts would agree that family care is undervalued in our society. First, there has been no official governmental effort—comparable, for example, to the national health accounting system—to calculate the dollar value of unpaid services. An estimate of family caregiving in New York State found that family members provided an average of 22 hours of care per week, worth between $7.5 and $11.2 billion per year (Farberman et al., 2003). Second, despite an abundant literature on caregiver burden and stress, systematic efforts to provide information, training, support, and respite to family caregivers are quite recent and not well funded. The range of short-term respite services—which may be supplied at home, in adult day centers, or in institutions (e.g., nursing homes, hospitals, or foster care homes)—varies across states and suffers from limited funding.

> Family members provide an average of 22 hours of care per week, worth between $7.5 and $11.2 billion per year.

The undervaluing of family care is all the more remarkable given nearly universal acknowledgment that the availability of families willing to care for their loved ones is probably the pivotal factor in preventing or postponing nursing home placement, and thereby considerably limits government's financial responsibility for the institutional care of indigent elders. Although lawmakers continue to propose a variety of initiatives, including tax deductions, tax credits, and federal appropriations that would support informal caregiving, only one significant initiative has been approved. Through the Older Americans Act, Congress funded a National Family Caregiver Support Program to establish support networks providing information about the availability of support services for family caregivers and assistance in gaining access to them, individual counseling to help make decisions and solve problems, respite care, and supplemental services. Funding for this program rose from $125 million in its first year (2001) to $155.2 million in 2003.

PAID CAREGIVERS

Since the Medicare and Medicaid programs were signed into law in 1965, the supply of LTC services has been heavily influenced by the primary payer of those services—government. The two major types of organizations that have evolved to provide LTC in the United States are home care agencies and nursing homes. Many more people receive home care than nursing home care, although expenditures for the latter are much higher, due to the more complicated range of services provided and the inclusion of housing costs in the nursing home payment. In addition, a small but growing number of individuals receive LTC services in adult day centers, while many more are being served by a large and growing number of alternative community-based residential settings, such as assisted living facilities, board and care or adult family homes, and—for the very affluent—continuing care retirement communities and life-care communities.

Home Care Agencies

In 2004, more than 7,500 home health care agencies were certified by Medicare to provide medically related services for its beneficiaries (National Association for Home Care, 2007), while a larger but unknown number—generally unlicensed—provided nonmedical personal care, housekeeping, or chore services (including, for example, meal delivery) in individual homes and congregate residential settings. Medicare-certified home health agencies (CHHAs) provide skilled nursing, rehabilitation, and home health aide services to individuals in their place of residence to promote, maintain, or restore health or to maximize independence while minimizing the effects of disease and disability. Individuals receiving Medicare services from CHHAs must be homebound and demonstrate medical necessity for intermittent, part-time, skilled nursing or therapy services ordered by a physician. State Medicaid programs' home health eligibility rules often match Medicare's, although care recipients must meet a state's definition of indigence to be eligible for service.

Since the introduction of the Medicare program, the home health industry has changed considerably in both composition and size. Although community-based visiting nurse associations were historically the predominant provider of home health services, both hospital-based and proprietary agencies are important parts of the industry today. Multiple and complex reasons have contributed to the changing composition of CHHAs. However, the responsiveness of the proprietary sector to changes in Medicare entitlement and payment policy has played a significant role.

Among the array of LTC services, home health services touch the greatest number of people. Most home health patients enter care after a hospitalization, and approximately a third have just had a surgical or diagnostic procedure. Insofar as home health care focuses on helping patients learn how to better self-manage complex chronic conditions such as diabetes, heart failure, or chronic lung disease, it is generally viewed as an economical way to prevent unnecessary hospitalizations or rehospitalizations.

Hospice Services

Hospice care is a program of palliative care for terminally ill individuals, as well as support to their families and other loved ones. Hospices are staffed by interdisciplinary teams that include physicians, nurses, medical social workers, therapists, clergy, and counselors, complemented by volunteers, who develop and implement a coordinated plan of care that is sensitive to the personal and cultural values of individual care recipients and their families. The main goals of palliative care, which need not be confined to formal hospice programs, are to sustain the highest quality of life attainable through the control of pain and symptoms and to maintain care recipients' independence, comfort, and dignity through the period of terminal illness, whatever its length.

Medicare has significantly shaped the hospice industry. Since it began funding hospice services in 1983, it has become the primary source of hospice financing, and providers, patients, and program expenditures have increased dramatically. The Medicare hospice benefit encompasses a wide range of medical and palliative services, including medications, medical supplies, and hospitalization if necessary. Medicare hospice expenditures rose from $205.4 million in 1989 to more than $6.7 billion in 2004 (Hospice Association of America, 2006), while the proportion of Medicare beneficiaries who died while enrolled in hospice grew from fewer than 1 in 10 to more than 1 in 5 (Campbell, Lynn, Louis, & Shugarman, 2004).

The Medicare program certified more than 2,800 U.S. hospices in 2005. Among Medicare-certified hospices, about 57% are freestanding, mostly nonprofit organizations. Approximately 23% are owned and operated by home health agencies (both nonprofit and proprietary), 19% are hospital-based, and less than 1% are operated by nursing homes (Hospice Association of America, 2006).

Medicare hospice services are generally viewed as cost-effective. A recent study found hospice to be cost-neutral to cost-saving for people who die of cancer, but cost-adding for those who die of other causes (Campbell et al., 2004). In part, this is because declines for cancer patients are relatively predictable, and, increasingly, patients are enrolled near the end of that decline; by contrast, the trajectory of other illnesses, such as congestive heart failure, is much more erratic. The study concluded that, even though in some cases hospice care might cost Medicare somewhat more than conventional care, its quality-of-life benefits for both patients and caregivers might well merit those greater costs.

Nevertheless, several barriers have prevented expansion of palliative care. These include Medicare's eligibility rules, which require a life expectancy of 6 months or less (although patients theoretically may be recertified as having a 6-month prognosis multiple times); the lack of systematic training of physicians in palliative care principles; and the widespread perception on the part of both professionals and families that opting for palliative care means abandoning hope. Hospice services are a humane and compassionate way to deliver health care and supportive services to the terminally ill, and some of these obstacles eventually may give way to wider financing and broader acceptance.

Nursing Homes

U.S. nursing homes are diverse in ownership, size, services, and populations served. The federal government defines *nursing homes* as facilities with three or more beds that routinely provide nursing care services (Gabrel, 2000). They may be freestanding or distinct units of larger facilities or chains.

The nursing home industry is heavily dependent on Medicare and Medicaid reimbursement, which requires facilities to meet federal standards enforced through annual inspections and complaint investigations conducted by the states. Approximately 80% of nursing homes are certified by both Medicare and Medicaid and another

16% by one of the two programs, while just 2% operate with state licensure only (Jones, 2002). All employ paid staff to provide basic medical and personal care to address the long-term needs of frail residents.

Over the last 20 years, U.S. nursing homes have experienced significant changes in the services they provide and the populations they serve. Where the sole purpose of many institutions was once to provide a permanent residence for frail individuals (especially elders) to live out the last years of their lives, nursing homes today serve a more varied population. Many facilities provide medically intensive, rehabilitative services to patients who stay for a short time only, and a number have added special care units for patients with special needs (e.g., Alzheimer's disease, AIDS, brain injury, ventilator dependency, or hospice care). Nursing home residents are typically the oldest old, and the average age of nursing home residents has been rising. The two most important predictors of whether an individual enters a nursing home are lack of a spouse and greater disability.

The future need for nursing home beds in the United States will depend on a number of factors, including demographic changes (the rapidly aging U.S. population), patterns of marriage and disability, public and private financing policies, and the availability of care alternatives. Projecting future nursing home use based on past utilization patterns must be done cautiously to avoid overestimates. In the mid-1970s, for example, the nursing home population grew at a 4.8% annual rate. By the early 1980s, however, this rate had fallen to 1.7%, and in the late 1980s to early 1990s, it dropped even further, to about 0.4% per year. This drop occurred even though the average annual increase in the size of the older population remained roughly constant (2.7%). Improvements in older Americans' health almost certainly played a part, as did the increasing longevity of men who are available to support their wives at home. Finally, the rapid growth in alternative approaches—such as assisted living and home monitoring technology—suggest that elders' LTC needs will increasingly be met outside of nursing homes.

Adult Day Services

Adult day services are community-based group programs that are becoming an important component in the overall mix of home and community-based LTC options. In 2002, 3,407 centers operated across the country, mostly in more densely populated areas. Partners in Caregiving (2003) estimated that nearly 4,000 additional adult day centers are needed in urban areas and almost 1,500 in rural areas. These programs, most of which are nonprofit (78%), provide a variety of health, social, and other support services in a protective setting during any part of a day, but for less than 24 hours. The aim is not to supplant, but rather to support, informal caregivers, especially those who work during the day. Normally, clients visit adult day centers for a full day a few days a week.

Adult day health services (21% of all centers) are *medical model* centers that seek to provide a full array of health and health-related services. Adult day *social model* centers (40% of all centers) provide a range of nonmedical support services. The remainder (39%) combines features of the other two. Nearly all adult day centers provide some types of therapeutic activities (97%) and personal assistance—help with meals, walking, and toileting; most provide meals (84%) and social services (82%). Among the other services provided, 74% are health-related services, 70% medication management, 68% transportation, 64% help with bathing and grooming, 47% nursing, 28% rehabilitation therapy, 12% medical services, and 7% provide hospice.

In 2002, adult day centers charged an average of $46 a day—although costs on average were $56 per day per client—making subsidies an important part of center financing. Public programs accounted for 38% of revenues, while private-pay participants accounted for a little over a third (35%). Another 14% of centers' funding came from nonoperating revenue such as grants and donations. The final 13% came from other operating revenue, including managed care. Despite (or perhaps because of) this array of funding sources, 44% of centers reported a deficit in 2002.

Quality control for adult day centers is still under development. Currently, about three-quarters of them are licensed or certified by their state, while the rest either operate in states where certification and licensure do not exist or are not required. In addition, although centers can be accredited through the Commission on Accreditation of Rehabilitation Facilities, relatively few are currently accredited or plan to apply for accreditation.

Community-Based Residential Alternatives to Institutional Care

Many adults experiencing or anticipating some disabling condition are seeking noninstitutional residential settings that will allow them to live independently but will provide necessary assistance with personal care, meals, and other household activities. Community-based residential care and assisted living facilities provide housing, food, supervision or protective oversight, and personal assistance. These residential nursing home alternatives are marketed, reimbursed, and regulated under various labels and definitions across and within states. Their labels include *board and care, adult family homes, personal care homes, assisted living facilities,* and many others. Even the single category of assisted living can encompass a wide range of residential settings-with-services, depending on whether a state chooses to license these facilities and how it defines their essential features.

Ardent proponents of homelike settings argue that the defining features of assisted living should be private rooms and bathrooms, lockable doors, and individual cooking facilities or appliances. In addition, they say that facilities should have available a range of services, including assessment and care planning, personal care, medication assistance, the option of three meals per day, 24-hour staffing, and access to nursing services. However, a recent survey of facilities that self-identified as assisted living facilities suggests that the great majority do not fit this model.

Depending on the state and the services provided, residential care settings may or may not be licensed. Thus, an estimate of their numbers is necessarily imprecise. One study estimated that there were approximately 36,000 *licensed* residences for older adults in the United States in 2002, with approximately 910,000 beds (Mollica, 2002). Other sources have estimated that more than a million people over 65 reside in some kind of community residential setting (American Association of Homes and Services for the Aging [AAHSA], 2000b). Although current residents of alternative settings are less disabled, on average, than nursing home residents, they often have significant disabilities. One national survey found that almost one-fourth of residents received help with at least three ADLs, and approximately one-third had moderate to severe cognitive impairments (Hawes, Rose, & Phillips, 1999).

Some community residential facilities are designed to be like small family homes; others may house up to 1,000 individuals in semi-private rooms; while others, such as many assisted living facilities, are apartmentlike residences with private bathrooms, cooking facilities, and lockable doors. The services provided range from light housekeeping to assistance with medications or activities of daily living to daily nursing care.

The cost of living in a residential care facility ranges from a few hundred dollars to more than $3,000 per month, based on the services available. Some charge an all-inclusive rate for housing and all other services. Others use a basic/enhanced model that provides a predefined group of services (including housing) for a flat fee and charge extra for all other services. A third group uses a fee-for-service model. Finally, a fourth service-level model charges residents a fixed fee based on a predetermined level of care (AAHSA, 2000a).

While individuals' monthly Supplemental Security Income or Social Security payments may be sufficient to cover the room and board costs in low-price, low-service facilities, they usually won't cover the costs of facilities located in expensive urban areas or those offering a great many services or amenities. Assuming that savings can be realized by diverting individuals in need of LTC from nursing homes to less costly residential settings, many states have begun to fund the nonhousing costs of alternative community care settings through Medicaid's home- and community-based programs. Even so, these settings receive most of their revenue from out-of-pocket payments by residents or family members. For those with private LTC insurance, it may cover some costs.

State efforts to expand residential LTC options have been tempered by concerns about quality of care and periodic budget crises. One particular area of concern is what happens to individuals as they grow more frail and disabled. Will they be discharged as soon as their care needs increase, preventing them from aging in place? (Many board and care homes and assisted living facilities reject applicants with wheelchairs, incontinence, cognitive impairments, behavioral problems, or who need their medications dispensed to them.) Or, will they *not* be discharged to a more intensive setting if their needs outstrip what a community residence can provide?

Continuing Care Retirement Communities

Continuing care retirement communities (CCRCs) are a type of community residential care facility that explicitly addresses the resident retention issue. This model offers more than one level of care, ranging from independent living in a housing or apartment complex, to assisted living, to nursing home care on site. Among the services offered by CCRCs are meals, transportation, social services, and nursing services, as well as recreational and educational activities. In addition, many CCRCs are equipped with amenities such as banks, barber shops, fitness centers, and gardening facilities.

The Continuing Care Accreditation Commission, an independent, third-party accreditation system acquired in 2003 by the Commission on Accreditation of Rehabilitation Facilities, estimated that, in 2004, approximately 2,500 CCRCs were in operation nationwide, mostly in Pennsylvania, California, Florida, Illinois, and Ohio. The number of CCRCs increased about 75% from 1996 to 2000, with a corresponding increase in the number of residents, from 350,000 to 625,000 (AAHSA, 2000b).

Residents can choose from a variety of coverage options and payment plans. They can choose coverage for unlimited access to specified health services or opt for a fee-for-service plan. Similarly, residents can rent their housing unit or purchase it. Most CCRCs are costly and not widely affordable. In 2004, entrance fees, which may be fully or partially refundable, ranged from $38,000 to $400,000, depending on the size of the living unit. Monthly fees ranged from $650 to $3,500, although additional fees could be required depending on the payment plan (Medicare.gov, 2007). Because many CCRCs are relatively new, questions have been raised about their financial viability and their capacity to provide intensive nursing care to residents who will eventually require it. Thus, they are not viewed as a mainstream solution to the demand for affordable community-based residential care facilities.

Challenging Issues

Containing costs, promoting access, and assuring quality of needed services—the classic triumvirate of U.S. health care policy problems—pose many challenges for current and future LTC policymakers. On the cost side, LTC looms as a large and growing component of health care expenditures, particularly of overstressed state budgets. On the access side, the institutional bias of the LTC system has limited development of and access to affordable community-based alternatives to nursing home care. Furthermore, reliance on Medicaid and personal savings as the two main sources of LTC financing means that many people forgo necessary or beneficial services until the need becomes urgent, when they risk impoverishment if they avail themselves of LTC. Meanwhile, the future availability of an adequate range of LTC services (including the necessary infrastructure for home-based services) is uncertain. Finally, on the quality side, increased regulation has yielded some measurable improvements in nursing home care—the principal target of improvement efforts. Nevertheless, serious quality issues remain for all service settings.

> Long-term care looms as a large and growing component of health care expenditures, particularly of overstressed state budgets.

CONTAINING COSTS WHILE IMPROVING ACCESS

For many years, policymakers—particularly state policymakers—have been concerned about the rising costs of long-term care, a concern that will heighten as the disabled and elderly population increases. In general, states have employed three broad strategies to control LTC expenditures: substituting private or federal dollars for state dollars; shifting the cost control burden to providers by controlling nursing home bed supply or cutting provider payment rates; and attempting to reform the health care delivery system through some combination of integrating acute and LTC services and increasing the availability of HCBS alternatives to institutional care.

The first strategy includes the creation of incentives for individuals to purchase private LTC insurance—for example, by allowing purchasers to keep more assets than generally allowed in order to qualify for Medicaid when their insurance benefits run out. It also includes "musical chairs" initiatives designed to shift as many LTC costs as possible from state Medicaid budgets to the federal Medicare program.

The second, *provider burden,* strategy—based on the assumption that "a bed built is a bed filled"—includes the use of state certificate of need laws to control the building of nursing beds. It also includes tight reimbursement controls.

The third strategy, system reform, has two variants. One type of experiment involves people eligible for both Medicare and Medicaid (*dual eligibles*) who are placed into managed care programs that cover primary, acute, and long-term care, funded by consolidating Medicare and Medicaid funding streams. The second variant involves using a host of state incentives to foster the growth of HCBS and community-based residential care options.

None of the three strategies has produced unmitigated, resounding success, although several show promise—notably, system reforms that focus on pooling financing for long-term, primary and acute care services. Advocates of this approach argue that integrated funding for dual eligibles not only will be less expensive, but also will make services more effective and efficient. Several models have received widespread attention.

● The Arizona Long Term Care System (ALTCS) is a statewide program that capitates Medicaid acute and LTC services, which are generally provided alongside but not financially integrated with Medicare-covered services. Although outside evaluators agree that ALTCS has saved money, there is some disagreement about whether these savings are attributable to the effective management of LTC services or to the program's restrictive eligibility requirements (Sparer, 1999; Weissert, 1997).
● In PACE, the Program of All-Inclusive Care for the Elderly, Medicare and Medicaid premiums are pooled to finance a staff-model HMO that focuses on elderly health issues and relies heavily on multidisciplinary care management teams to coordinate and provide services, including a rich package of LTC benefits. Although the PACE sites provide excellent care and do appear to save money (White, 1998), so far they have been successful only on a very small scale. By the end of 2004, some 90 PACE sites across the country cared for approximately 9,000 individuals (U.S. Congressional Budget Office, 2004).

Uncertainty about the cost-savings potential of Medicare-Medicaid integration stems from the difficulty of implementing it, which has limited the amount of experimentation. States must strike agreements with the federal government (waivers are needed), and managed care entities must work with unfamiliar patient populations, providers, and services. Such difficulties have motivated a number of states—for example, New York, Texas, and Wisconsin—to test less comprehensive but nevertheless ambitious models.

Meanwhile, a body of evidence suggests that state-initiated system reforms aimed at increasing the availability of HCBS can serve more individuals without significantly raising total LTC costs. For 20 years or more, the LTC literature has been replete with articles debating the potential financial impact of increasing the availability of HCBS. Experience in Oregon, Washington, and Colorado now suggests that expansion need not increase total LTC costs if entry to nursing homes is tightly controlled and a variety of lower cost residential care and home-based service options are targeted to those most in need of supportive care (Alecxih, Lutzky, Corea, & Coleman, 1996).

Accordingly, states are increasingly focusing on developing home and community-based alternatives to nursing homes. In fact, spending on HCBS has increased much faster than spending on nursing home care. From 1990 through 2002, the compound annual rate of growth for Medicaid-funded HCBS services was 24%, while the rate of growth for nursing homes was 8.2%. Even so, HCBS expansion is uneven among states, and most Medicaid dollars for LTC continue to go to nursing homes.

ASSURING QUALITY IN LONG-TERM CARE

Assuring quality in LTC is an inexact science. In nursing homes, the attempt to assure quality has resulted in a welter of monitoring requirements and complicated regulations, which address everything from the width of hallways to the length of time between residents' meals. Despite what many consider significant over-regulation, many nursing homes nevertheless deliver substandard care. Meanwhile, alternatives to micromanagement are comparatively untested. Although one would hope that the mistakes of nursing home regulators can be avoided in some of the newer alternative residential settings, such as assisted living facilities, little consensus exists as to how this can be accomplished.

The landmark Nursing Home Reform Act of 1987 sought to upgrade the quality of nursing home care by instituting a broad set of regulatory changes aimed at improving resident assessments, rights, care processes, staffing, inspection procedures, and the enforcement of inspection findings. Nevertheless, a report by the General Accounting Office (2003) concluded,

> The proportion of nursing homes with serious quality problems remains unacceptably high, despite a decline in the incidence of such reported problems. Actual harm or more serious deficiencies were cited

for 20 percent or about 3,500 nursing homes during an 18-month period ending January 2002, compared to 29 percent for an earlier period. (p. 1)

Monitoring nursing homes to enforce the standards laid down by law is a joint responsibility of state and federal government. This includes regular surveys to evaluate compliance with regulations and measures to assure that shortcomings are rectified. Nursing homes out of compliance may be subject to monetary penalties, state-assigned substitute management, staff training in problem areas, and required correction of deficiencies in specified time intervals. The ultimate sanction is when Medicare or Medicaid withdraws certification and payment.

Investigations of the effectiveness of these quality enforcement mechanisms routinely turn up serious flaws. The understatement of quality problems has been attributed at least in part to the inability or unwillingness of surveyors to detect and document problems. Their unwillingness may in turn be attributable to concern that imposing heavy fines or closing an institution could make things worse for residents.

As part of a recent Nursing Home Quality Initiative (NHQI), the federal government launched a new Web site, *Nursing Home Compare* (http://www.medicare.gov/NHCompare/home.asp), which provides nursing home quality indicators for all Medicare- and Medicaid-certified nursing homes in the country. The hope is that consumers will use such information to choose among providers, thereby fostering improved quality through market mechanisms. The indicators are derived from assessment data (referred to as the Minimum Data Set) that nursing homes routinely collect at specified intervals during residents' stays and include measures such as percent of residents with moderate to severe pain, percent with pressure sores, and percent who have deteriorated in their ability to perform activities of daily living. The Web site also incorporates quality information from other sources, including state surveys. Yet, consumers may be unable to act readily on the quality indicators, given limited nursing home bed availability in some areas and the crisis situation that often precipitates a nursing home placement. Moreover, the indicators omit important aspects of quality, such as residents' self-reported quality of life or self-perceived psychological and social well-being.

A new "culture change" movement explicitly addresses these aspects of nursing home quality (Miller & Mor, 2006). The last decade has seen the emergence of a national network of nursing homes, labor unions, foundations, and others committed to radical change in nursing home values and practices. A central tenet of the movement is that institutional care must be deinstitutionalized to the maximum extent possible and that a humane physical and social environment must be created to support each resident's life, dignity, and autonomy.

- One early example was The Eden Alternative™, which emphasizes that nursing homes should be viewed as "habitats for human beings rather than facilities for the frail and elderly."
- Another example is the Green House Project developed in Tupelo, Mississippi, in 2003. This homelike model reconfigures the structure of nursing homes with multiple clusters of small houses or apartments—each with a shared, open kitchen and a private room and bath for each resident. As a result of a successful evaluation of this model, the Robert Wood Johnson Foundation has provided funding to create over 100 Green Houses across the United States over the coming years (Hsu, 2006).

Nevertheless, how rapidly or widely the culture change movement will influence the nursing home industry is still an open question.

For the foreseeable future, care at home will be the preference of individuals in need of LTC services, and many elders say they would rather die than live permanently in a nursing home (Mattimore et al., 1997). But home care, too, presents a series of quality assurance challenges. First and most obvious, care delivered at home is difficult to observe and supervise. Second, the quality and outcomes of home care are significantly influenced by a wide variety of difficult-to-control factors, such as the physical environment and family circumstances of the person needing care. Third, even among Medicare-certified home health agencies, most services are provided by paraprofessional aides whose training requirements are minimal and whose supervision may be the responsibility of professionals who work for a separate agency or organization. In addition, workplace injuries, heavy workloads, and low wages among aides often result in burnout and turnover, which create discontinuities in care and affect the morale of remaining staff.

Because home care is funded through a patchwork of federal, state, and local programs, the regulatory regimen differs considerably among programs and across locales. To address quality issues in Medicare-funded home health, the federal government has launched a Home Health Quality Initiative (http://www.cms.hhs.gov/quality/hhqi/)—similar to the NHQI described earlier—which provides comparative information on the patient outcomes achieved by Medicare CHHAs across the country. As in the NHQI, consumers can access a Web site (http://www.medicare.gov/HHCompare) containing a range of information based on a standard patient assessment mandated by the federal government and regularly administered. Among the published indicators are the percentages of patients who improve at bathing and walking, who experience less pain, and so on. Like the Nursing Home Quality Indicators, these are intended to inform consumer choice. However, their impact may turn more on the ways that providers use them to inform their internal quality improvement efforts than on the choices made by consumers.

Quality problems also exist in assisted living facilities, where a lack of federal regulation has resulted in wide variations, making them difficult to compare and assess. Facilities vary in size, cost, privacy, staff-resident ratio, and available services. States may set their own standards for licensure, staffing, physical design, and resident population characteristics, but there is little consensus on what those standards should be. On one side are providers and some consumer advocates concerned about excessive regulation and fearing that the homelike atmosphere of these facilities will be lost if nursing home–like regulations are implemented. On the other side are policymakers and consumer advocates who are more focused on safety and quality of care than innovation.

CHOICES FOR LONG-TERM CARE CONSUMERS

Today in the United States, there is wide agreement that consumers should have significant choice regarding their long-term care arrangements. This argument is made on the grounds of ethical, psychological, and quality considerations. The consumer-directed movement in long-term care arose out of resistance to the medicalization of everyday life for people with chronic or disabling conditions. Consumers pointed out that the role of medical professionals in their daily affairs could be reduced, particularly given the low-tech nature of many LTC services. They felt that, regardless of age, they should be able to take responsibility for and control those aspects of services they feel capable of managing. In their view, the role of professionals is to assist users of LTC services in assessing and managing their own care, not in determining what they need when.

> The consumer-directed movement in long-term care arose out of resistance to the medicalization of everyday life for people with chronic or disabling conditions.

Consumer choice first requires that the conditions for choice exist. At a minimum, this means that consumers are considered the primary decision makers regarding the services they receive, unless they choose to delegate that responsibility; a range of service options is available to them; information about these options is available; and they participate meaningfully in service allocation and systems design (National Institute on Consumer-Directed Long-Term Services, 1996). Some distinguish between *consumer-directed care,* when consumers take responsibility for all aspects of care, including hiring, firing, training, supervising, and evaluating their own caregivers, and *consumer-centered care,* when care managers aim to involve consumers and incorporate their preferences into care plans. In one form or another, consumer choice is relevant to all LTC recipients, including those with developmental disabilities, mental illnesses, and cognitive impairments such as Alzheimer's disease.

Inevitably, respecting consumers' choice involves trade-offs with professional judgments and may, in some cases, compromise patients' safety, but family members and service providers are often uncomfortable with this. Service providers are also concerned about their potential liability for any adverse events. However, advocates of consumer choice argue that it is an individual's right—in LTC as it is in other areas of life—to take risks in order to lead a preferred lifestyle. Furthermore, several recent studies have found that consumer outcomes such as reduction in unmet needs, occurrence of care-related problems, and satisfaction with services are as good or better among people served by consumer-directed programs as among comparable groups receiving usual care (Benjamin & Fennell, 2007; Foster, Brown, Phillips, Schore, & Carlson, 2003).

Currently, efforts to increase choice in long-term care are hampered by the institutional bias of the LTC system, which limits the options available for those who need care and ignores their preference for care at home. A number of federal initiatives and the U.S. Supreme Court's 1999 Olmstead decision have encouraged the development of consumer-directed options nationwide. The decision in *Olmstead vs. L.C.* confers a duty on states to serve people with disabilities in the "most integrated setting"—that is, a setting that "enables individuals with disabilities to interact with non-disabled persons to the fullest extent possible" (http://www.hhs.gov/ocr/olmintro.htm). President Bush's New Freedom Initiative is an effort to remove barriers to community living for people of all ages with disabilities and long-term illnesses. A recent report details the initiative's key accomplishments and future plans to increase access to education, employment, and community life through the use of technology (White House Domestic Policy Council, 2004).

FUTURE FINANCING FOR LONG-TERM CARE

Policy experts agree that significant additional resources will be required to meet the future LTC needs of the U.S. population. They also generally agree that the need for LTC is an *insurable risk*—that is, an uncertain occurrence that carries with it substantial, even catastrophic, financial consequences for individuals, but affects a relatively small and predictable proportion of the total population. Such events make a strong case for insurance mechanisms that spread the risk of financial loss across a large group of people. But considerable disagreement exists on the policy options that should be pursued (Feder, 2001; Miller & Mor, 2006).

At one extreme are those who believe that LTC should first and foremost be the responsibility of government, financed by a social insurance mechanism that provides universal benefits and spreads the risks and costs across the public at large. Wiener, Illston, and Hanley (1994), for example, have recommended a social insurance model that would provide LTC coverage for all who need services, regardless of income. The insurance would pay for home- and community-based care options, along with nursing home care. Because social insurance programs are costly, financing would derive from several sources, including federal taxes, state sources, and recipients.

At the other extreme are those who believe that paying for LTC should be primarily a private responsibility, that public policy should focus on improving the market for purchase of private LTC insurance, and that government's role in direct financing of services should be limited to providing a safety net for the truly destitute. Policies that might improve the market for private LTC insurance include standardizing private policies, allowing consumers to supplement Medicaid benefits with private coverage, and expanding the tax deductibility of LTC insurance premiums (U.S. Congressional Budget Office, 2004).

In between are those who argue out of principle or pragmatism for approaches that combine public and private dollars and accommodate both insurance and welfare mechanisms. Recognizing the high costs of private LTC insurance policies, Chen (2003), for example, proposes a system consisting of social insurance, private insurance, and personal savings. In this model, the social insurance component would be funded by diverting a small portion of Social Security benefits and would provide a basic level of coverage to everyone. Private insurance—or Medicaid, in the case of indigent individuals in need of LTC—would then supplement this basic provision.

Enacting LTC financing reform has proved more successful in other countries than in the United States. For example, in 1994, Germany instituted mandatory, universal social insurance for long-term care that covers both community-based and institutional care. Benefits, which people can receive as cash or services, are financed by a premium set at 1.7% of salary, paid jointly by German employees and employers (Cuellar & Wiener, 2000). Similarly, in 2000, Japan introduced a universal LTC insurance program that covers both institutional and community-based care, half of which is paid through general revenue and the other half through premiums levied on those over age 40 (Campbell & Ikegami, 2000). Japan's move is surprising for a country with strong social norms regarding family care and a reputation for lagging as a welfare state, but its experience may show how major demographic shifts can move policy.

For the time being, however, domestic LTC financing reform appears to be stalled. For a brief period during the Clinton administration's health care reform initiative, publicly financed LTC insurance was on the policy agenda, along with national health insurance. But since 1993, LTC insurance has received little attention except from a few ardent advocacy groups. Although LTC is a necessary service, it has been largely ignored by those not directly needing care. Some say that, because the health care system is focused on cure rather than on care, LTC has low status. Others argue that the drawbacks of expanding publicly financed LTC outweigh the benefits, because increased public spending would diminish personal responsibility and worsen future fiscal problems. Still others argue that social attitudes about disability at the end of life prevent us from thinking hard about the need for care and facing up to the problems involved in providing it. All of these arguments doubtless contain a grain of truth. However, the growing need for services will make confronting these hard issues ultimately unavoidable.

Conclusion

This chapter has reviewed key facts about long-term care: what it is, who receives it, who provides it, and who pays for it. The most important fact, however, is that *our nation has an increasing number of people who will need LTC services and our current system is unprepared to meet the demand in ways that consumers would prefer and will need.* This chapter also has covered some of the pressing issues around service provision and the challenges involved in financing and assuring quality of services—none of which are likely to be resolved soon.

References

Alecxih, L. M., Lutzky, S., Corea, J., & Coleman, B. (1996). *Estimated cost savings from the use of home- and community-based alternatives to nursing facility care in three states.* Washington, DC: AARP.

American Association of Homes and Services for the Aging. (2000a). *Assisted living.* Washington, DC: Author.

American Association of Homes and Services for the Aging. (2000b). *Continuing care retirement communities.* Washington, DC: Author.

Arno, P. S. (2006). *Economic value of informal caregiving: 2004.* Care Coordination & the Caregiver Forum, Department of Veteran Affairs, National Institutes of Health, Bethesda, MD.

Benjamin, A. E., & Fennell, M. L. (2007). Putting consumers first in long-term care: Findings from the cash & counseling demonstration and evaluation. *Health Services Research, 43*(1), Part II.

Burwell, B., Sredl, K., & Eiken, S. (2004, May). *Medicaid long-term care expenditures in FY 2003.* Memorandum. Cambridge, MA: Medstat.

Burwell, B., Sredl, K., & Eiken, S. (2006, July). *Medicaid long-term care expenditures in FY 2005*. Memorandum. Cambridge, MA: Medstat.

Campbell, D. E., Lynn, J., Louis, T. A., & Shugarman, L. R. (2004). Medicare program expenditures associated with hospice use. *Annals of Internal Medicine, 140,* 269–277.

Campbell, J. C., & Ikegami, N. (2000). Long-term care insurance comes to Japan. *Health Affairs, 19*(3), 26–39.

Catlin, A., Cowan, C., Heffler, S., Washington, B., & the National Health Expenditure Accounts Team. (2007). National health spending in 2005: The slowdown continues. *Health Affairs, 26*(1), 142–153.

Chen, Y. (2003). Funding long-term care: Applications of the trade-off principle in both public and private sectors. *Journal of Aging and Health, 15*(1), 15–44.

Coronel, S. (2003). *Long-term care insurance in 2000–2001*. Washington, DC: Health Insurance Association of America Center for Disability and Long-Term Care.

Cuellar, A. E., & Wiener, J. M. (2000). *Can social insurance for long-term care work? The experience of Germany*. Washington, DC: Urban Institute.

Farberman, H. A., Finch, S. J., Horowitz, B. P., Lurie, A., Morgan, R., & Page, J. (2003). A survey of family care giving to elders in New York State: Findings and implications. *Care Management Journals, 4*(3), 153–160.

Feder, J. (2001). Long-term care: A public responsibility. *Health Affairs, 20*(6), 112–113.

Feldman, P. (1999). "Doing more for less": Advancing the conceptual underpinnings of home-based care. *Journal of Aging and Health, 11*(3), 261–276.

Foster, L., Brown, R., Phillips B., Schore J., & Carlson, B. L. (2003). *Does consumer direction affect the quality of Medicaid personal assistance in Arkansas?* Princeton, NJ: Mathematica Policy Research.

Gabrel, C. S. (2000). An overview of nursing home facilities: Data from the 1997 national nursing home survey. In *Advance Data from Vital and Health Statistics* (No. 311). Hyattsville, MD: National Center for Health Statistics.

General Accounting Office. (2003). *Nursing home quality: Prevalence of serious problems, while declining, reinforces importance of enhanced oversight*. (GAO-03–561). Washington, DC: U.S. Government Printing Office.

Gibson, M. J., Freiman, M., Gregory, S., Kassner, E., Kochera, A., Mullen, F., et al. (2003). *Beyond 50.03: A report to the nation on independent living and disability*. Washington, DC: AARP Public Policy Institute. Retrieved from http://www.research.aarp.org/il/beyond_50_il.html

Hawes, C., Rose, M., & Phillips, C. D. (1999). *A national study of assisted living for the frail elderly: Results of a national survey of facilities* (prepared for the U.S. Department of Health and Human Services, Assistant Secretary for Planning and Evaluation). Beachwood, OH: Myers Research Institute.

Hospice Association of America. (2006). *Hospice facts and statistics*. Retrieved from www.nahc.org/hospicefs06.pdf

Hsu, C. (2006, June 19). The greening of aging. *U.S. News & World Report*. Retrieved from http://www.usnews.com/usnews/biztech/articles/060619/19leader.htm

Jones, A. (2002). The national nursing home survey: 1999 summary. National Center for Health Statistics. *Vital and Health Statistics, 13*(152), 1–116.

Mattimore, T. J., Wenger, N. S., Desbiens, N. A., Teno, J. M., Hamel, M. B., Liu, H., et al. (1997). Surrogate and physician understanding of patients' preferences for living permanently in a nursing home. *Journal of the American Geriatrics Society, 45*(7), 818–824.

Medicare.gov. (2007). Types of long-term care. Retrieved from http://www.medicare.gov/LongTermCare/Static/CCRC.asp?dest = NAV%7CTypes%7CTypes%7CCCRC

MetLife Mature Market Institute. (2006, September). *The MetLife market survey of nursing home & home care costs.* Retrieved from http://www.metlife.com/WPSAssets/21052872211163445734V1F2006NHHCMarketSurvey.pdf

Miller, E., & Mor, V. (2006). *Out of the shadows: Envisioning a brighter future for long-term care in America.* Providence, RI: Brown University Report for the National Commission for Quality Long-Term Care.

Mollica, R. (2002). *State assisted living policy: 2002.* Portland, ME: National Academy for State Health Policy.

National Association for Home Care. (2007). Basic statistics about home care. Retrieved from http://www.nahc.org/04HC_Stats.pdf

National Institute on Consumer-Directed Long-Term Services. (1996). *Principles of consumer-directed home and community-based services.* Washington, DC: National Council on the Aging.

Partners in Caregiving. (2003). *National study of adult day services, 2001–2002.* Winston-Salem, NC: Partners in Caregiving: The Adult Day Services Program, Wake Forest University School of Medicine.

Sparer, M. S. (1999). *Health policy for low-income people in Arizona.* Washington, DC: Urban Institute.

Tilly, J., Goldenson, S., Kasten, J., O'Shaughnessy, C., Kelly, R., & Sidor, G. (2000). *Long-term care chart book: Persons served, payors, and spending.* Washington, DC: Congressional Research Service.

U.S. Centers for Disease Control & Prevention. (2004). *Early release of selected estimates based on data from the January–September 2003 National Health Interview Survey.* Retrieved from http://www.cdc.gov/nchs/about/major/nhis/released200403.htm#12

U.S. Centers for Medicare & Medicaid Services. (2007). *2007 SSI FBR, resource limits, 300% cap, break-even points, spousal impoverishment standards.* Baltimore, MD: U.S. Department of Health and Human Services, Centers for Medicare & Medicaid Services.

U.S. Congressional Budget Office. (2004). *Financing long-term care for the elderly.* Washington, DC: Congress of the United States. Retrieved from http://www.cbo.gov/ftpdoc.cfm?index=5400&type=1

U.S. Department of Health and Human Services. (2003). *2003 CMS statistics.* CMS Publication No. 03445. Washington, DC: U.S. Department of Health and Human Services.

Weissert, W. G. (1997). Cost savings from home- and community-based services: Arizona's capitated Medicaid long term care program. *Journal of Health Politics, Policy, and Law, 22*(6), 1329–1357.

White, A. J. (1998). *The effect of PACE on costs to Medicare.* Cambridge, MA: Abt Associates.

White House Domestic Policy Council. (2004). *The president's New Freedom Initiative for people with disabilities: The 2004 progress report, executive summary.* Washington, DC: White House Domestic Policy Council. Retrieved from http://www.whitehouse.gov/infocus/newfreedom/toc-2004.html

Wiener, J. M., Illston, L. H., & Hanley, R. J. (1994). *Sharing the burden: Strategies for public and private long-term care insurance.* Washington, DC: Brookings Institution.

10

Key Words

behavioral risk factors	obesity	paradigm shift
prevention	health disparities	social ecological models
tobacco use	patient self-management	health care quality
risky drinking	stages of change	improvement
diet and physical activity	clinical practice guidelines	chronic care model

Health-Related Behavior

C. Tracy Orleans and Elaine F. Cassidy

Learning Objectives

- Describe the contributions of personal health practices (e.g., tobacco use, risky drinking, physical activity, diet, obesity) to individual and population health status.
- Describe how strategies for changing individual and population health behavior have evolved, and identify the targets and characteristics of effective interventions.
- Summarize new clinical and community practice guidelines for health behavior change.
- Describe how strategies for improving the delivery of primary care health behavior change interventions have evolved, and identify the targets and characteristics of effective interventions.
- Summarize new models and prospects for addressing behavioral risk factors through national health care quality improvement efforts.

Topical Outline

- Behavioral risk factors: overview and national goals
- Changing health behavior: individual-oriented and population-based interventions for achieving national health objectives
- Changing provider behavior: provider-oriented and system-based interventions for achieving national health care quality objectives

H ealth care professionals, who live in a world in which often-heroic efforts are needed to save lives, can easily believe that medical care is the key instrument for maintaining and assuring health. This chapter explains, however, that behavioral choices—how we live our lives—are the key instruments that determine Americans' health and well-being. To some extent, the task of helping people choose healthy lifestyles falls into the realm of behavioral psychology and sometimes social marketing. However, emerging theories of how to encourage healthy lifestyles include major roles for medical providers. Therefore, clinicians, health care payers, managers of provider organizations, and health care policymakers need to understand the dynamics of behavioral choices that affect health.

This chapter begins with a brief overview of the major behavioral risk factors that contribute to the growing burden of preventable chronic disease in the United States—tobacco use, alcohol abuse, sedentary lifestyle, and unhealthy diet, related obesity, and overweight. It then describes the extraordinary progress that has been made over the past three decades to help adults modify these risk factors by intervening both at the individual level—with educational and behavioral treatments that can be delivered in clinical settings—and at the broader population level—with environmental and policy changes that help to support and maintain healthy behavior. Theoretical advances (e.g., social learning theory, stage-based and social ecological models) have led to a paradigm shift in understanding the need for broad-spectrum, multilevel ecological approaches, and new science-based clinical and community practice guidelines have developed to guide them. Similarly, multifaceted efforts have been successful in encouraging clinicians to use proven health behavior change protocols in their interactions with patients. Many parallels can be drawn between what we have learned about ways to promote health through individual behavior change and what we have learned about improving health care quality through provider behavior change. Significant progress made in both areas has created unprecedented potential for breakthrough improvements in national health status and health care quality.

The four leading behavioral risk factors—tobacco use, alcohol abuse, sedentary lifestyle, and unhealthy diet—together accounted for more than 900,000 deaths in 2000.

Behavioral Risk Factors:
Overview and National Goals

Acute and infectious diseases are no longer the major causes of death, disease, and disability in the United States. Today, chronic diseases—coronary heart disease, cancer, diabetes, asthma, and cancer—are the leading causes of death and disease. Given the continued aging of the population, both the prevalence and costs of chronic illness care will continue to rise. Yet, much of the growing burden of chronic disease is preventable. More than a decade ago, McGinnis and Foege (1993) estimated that 50% of mortality from the 10 leading causes of death was attributable to behavior that causes or complicates chronic disease. A more recent analysis by Mokdad, Marks, Stroup, and Gerberding (2004) confirmed this estimate, finding that the four leading behavioral risk factors—tobacco use, alcohol abuse, sedentary lifestyle, and unhealthy diet—together accounted for more than 900,000 deaths in 2000. Moreover, research findings over the past two decades have established that modifying these risk factors leads to improved health and quality of life and to reduced health care costs and burden (Institute of Medicine, 2000; Orleans, Ulmer, & Gruman, 2004).

Today, almost 90% of Americans report that they have at least one of these risk factors, and 52% report two or more, with the highest prevalence of individual and multiple behavioral risks occurring in low-income and racial and ethnic minority groups (Coups, Gaba, & Orleans, 2004; Institute of Medicine, 2000). Given these statistics, it is not surprising that half of the leading health indicators tracked by *Healthy People 2010,* which sets forth the nation's primary objectives for promoting longer, healthier lives and eliminating health disparities, relate to healthy lifestyles (U.S. Department of Health and Human Services, 2000a). Selected indicators for tobacco use, alcohol abuse, physical activity, diet, and obesity are shown in Table 10.1.

TOBACCO USE

Tobacco use causes more preventable deaths and diseases than any other behavioral risk factor, including 435,000 premature deaths from several forms of cancer, heart, and lung disease (Mokdad et al., 2004), and it accounts for annual health care costs of $75 billion. Smoking represents the single most important modifiable cause of poor pregnancy outcomes, accounting for 20% of low–birth weight deliveries, 8% of preterm births, and 5% of perinatal deaths. For infants and young children, parental smoking is linked to SIDS, respiratory illnesses, middle ear infections, and decreased lung function, with

Table 10.1 Selected *Healthy People 2010* Objectives: Behavioral Risk Factors

	Baseline[a] (%)	2010 Goals (%)
Tobacco use		
Cigarette smoking		
Adults (18 years and older)	24	12
Adolescents (grades 9 through 12)	35	16
Exposure to secondhand smoke		
Children (6 years and younger)	27	10
Alcohol misuse/risky drinking		
Proportion of adults who exceed guidelines for low-risk drinking	72 (women); 74 (men)	50
Binge drinking		
Adults (18 years and older)	16.6	6
Adolescents (12 to 17 years)	7.7	2
Deaths from alcohol-related auto crashes	5.9	4
Physical activity		
Regular moderate physical activity		
Adults (18 years and older)[b]	15	30
Adolescents (grades 9 through 12)[c]	27	35
Vigorous physical activity (at least 3 days per week for 20 minutes)		
Adults (18 years and older)	23	30
Adolescents (grades 9 through 12)	65	85
Diet and overweight (older than age 2)		
Proportion of people eating at least two servings of fruit daily	28	75
Proportion of people eating at least three servings of vegetables (at least one of which is dark green or orange) daily	3	50

Table 10.1 *(Continued)*	Baseline[a] (%)	2010 Goals (%)
Proportion of people eating at least six servings of grain products (at least three being whole grains) daily	7	50
Overweight and obesity		
Obesity among adults (aged 20 years and older)	23	15
Overweight and obesity among children and adolescents (aged 6 to 19)	11	5

[a] Baseline data extracted from sources between 1988 and 1999.
[b] At least 30 minutes per day.
[c] At least 30 minutes 5 or more days per week.
Note. From U.S. Department of Health and Human Services. (2000b). *Healthy people 2010: Understanding and improving health.* Washington, DC.

annual direct medical costs estimated at $4.6 billion. Quitting, even after 50 years of smoking, can produce significant improvements in health and health care utilization.

Although the adult smoking prevalence rate has dropped 40% since the first Surgeon General's report in 1964, nearly one in four adults still smokes, with the highest rates (33%) in low-income populations (U.S. Public Health Service, 2000). Rates of smoking during pregnancy also have dropped in the past decade, but in 1999 12% of women reported that they smoked during pregnancy. Each day, more than 3,000 children and teens become new smokers, 30% of whom will become addicted (U.S. National Center for Health Statistics, 1999). Also, 28% of high school and college students and 33% of young adults not attending college smoke cigarettes. Nearly 8 million Americans, mostly adolescent and young adult males, report using smokeless tobacco, which is linked to oral cancer, gum disease, and tooth loss. In addition, 27% of children age 6 and younger are exposed to harmful environmental tobacco smoke at home, and 37% of nonsmoking adults are exposed at home or in the workplace (U.S. Centers for Disease Control and Prevention, 2006).

ALCOHOL USE AND MISUSE

Alcohol abuse or misuse includes alcohol dependence and risky or harmful drinking. About 5% of the U.S. adult population meets the criteria for alcoholism or alcohol dependence, and another 20% engages in harmful or risky drinking, defined as drinking more than

1 drink per day or 7 drinks per week for women, more than 2 drinks per day or 14 drinks per week for men, periodic binge drinking (five or more drinks on a single occasion), drinking and driving, or drinking during pregnancy (Whitlock, Polen, Green, Orleans, & Klein, 2004). Approximately 40% of college students and young adults engaged in binge drinking from 1975 to 2002—a rate well above the *Healthy People 2010* goal of 6% (Johnston, O'Malley, & Bachman, 2003). Alcohol misuse is most common in young adults, particularly among White and Native American men. Moderate levels of alcohol use in adults (below those defined as risky) have been linked to modest health benefits, such as lowered risk for heart disease (Whitlock et al., 2004).

Alcohol misuse is associated with 60% to 90% of cirrhosis deaths, 40% to 50% of auto-related fatalities, and 16% to 67% of home and work injuries (McGinnis & Foege, 1993) and with fetal alcohol syndrome. It caused an estimated 85,000 deaths in 2002 (Mokdad et al., 2004). The total annual costs of alcohol misuse— including costs related to health care, lost wages, premature death, and crime—were estimated at $185 million in 1998 (U.S. National Institute on Alcohol Abuse and Alcoholism, 2001). The health benefits of treating of alcohol dependence are well established, and the U.S. Preventive Services Task Force (USPSTF; 1996) found that brief behavior change interventions to modify risky drinking levels and practices produced positive health outcomes detectable 4 or more years later.

PHYSICAL ACTIVITY

The health risks associated with physical inactivity and sedentary lifestyle are numerous. They include heart disease, Type 2 diabetes, stroke, hypertension, osteoarthritis, colon cancer, depression, and obesity (USPSTF, 2003b). Engagement in physical activity helps maintain healthy bones, muscles, joints, and weight, and it is associated with positive psychological benefits. Physical activity has been shown to reduce feelings of anxiety and depression and promote feelings of well-being. U.S. medical costs associated with sedentary lifestyle were estimated at nearly $76.6 billion in 2000.

Healthy People 2010 guidelines recommend that adults and adolescents engage in moderate physical activity (such as walking or biking) for at least 30 minutes at least 5 days a week and that they engage in vigorous physical activity that promotes the development and maintenance of cardiorespiratory fitness 3 or more days per week for 20 or more minutes per occasion. As shown in Table 10.1, most American adults and adolescents do not follow these recommendations. The populations most at risk for inactivity include those with lower income and education levels, those living below the poverty line in all racial and ethnic groups, members of several racial/ethnic minority groups (e.g., African Americans, Hispanics), and those with disabilities (Powell, Slater, & Chaloupka, 2004).

DIET

In conjunction with sedentary lifestyle, unhealthy eating is linked to an estimated 400,000 deaths each year in the United States (Mokdad et al., 2004). Together, inactivity and unhealthy diet are associated with 25% to 30% of cardiovascular deaths, 30% to 35% of cancer deaths, and 50% to 80% of Type 2 diabetes cases (McGinnis & Foege, 1993). They also have contributed jointly to a surge in overweight and obesity that has reached epidemic proportions over the last 20 years, particularly within low-income and minority populations.

Four of the 10 leading causes of death—coronary heart disease, some cancers, stroke, and Type 2 diabetes— are associated with unhealthy diet. The relationships between dietary patterns and health outcomes have been examined in a wide range of observational studies and randomized trials with patients at risk for diet-related chronic diseases. The majority of studies suggest that people consuming diets that are low in fat, saturated fat, trans-fatty acids, and cholesterol and high in fruits, vegetables, and whole grain products containing fiber have lower rates of morbidity and mortality from coronary artery disease and several forms of cancer (USPSTF, 2003a). Moreover, dietary change has been found to reduce risks for many chronic diseases, as well as for overweight and obesity (USPSTF, 2003b).

> Four of the 10 leading causes of death—coronary heart disease, some cancers, stroke, and Type 2 diabetes—are associated with unhealthy diet.

Dietary Guidelines for Americans age 2 and older recommend 3 to 5 daily servings of vegetables and vegetable juices, 2 to 4 daily servings of fruits and fruit juices, and 6 to 11 daily servings of grain products, with no more than 30% of total calories from fat and 10% from saturated fat (USPSTF, 2003a). But, as Table 10.1 shows, enormous gaps exist between the recommended guidelines and actual diets for American children and adults. The diets of more than 80% of Americans, especially those in low-income populations, do not meet these guidelines (Powell et al., 2004; USPSTF, 2003a).

OBESITY

As poor dietary habits and physical inactivity have become endemic, national obesity rates have soared. Nearly 70% of all American adults are overweight or obese—up from 12% just one decade ago (Mokdad et al., 2004). This trend is alarming, given the strong links between obesity and many chronic diseases. Total expenditures related to overweight- and obesity-related problems were estimated at nearly $92.6 billion in 2002 (Finkelstein, Fiebelkorn, & Wang, 2003)—a number that is likely to rise unless effective interventions are put in place. New findings show that even modest weight loss (e.g., 5% to 10% of body weight) over a period of 12 to 24 months can reduce these risks and prevent the onset of diabetes among adults with impaired glucose tolerance (Tuomilehto et al., 2001).

Even more alarming is the prevalence of overweight and obesity among children and adolescents (ages 6 to 19), which has increased significantly over the past two decades (Ogden et al., 2006). Like adults, overweight youth are at risk for coronary heart disease, hypertension, certain cancers, and even Type 2 diabetes early in life (Freedman, 2002). The highest and fastest rising rates of childhood obesity are seen among children and adolescents of African American or Latino descent and children (particularly girls) from low-income backgrounds—making efforts to reach these groups a public health priority.

Changing Health Behavior

The landmark Institute of Medicine report, *Health and Behavior*, published 25 years ago, was one of the first scientific documents to convincingly establish the links between behavioral risk factors and disease and to identify the basic biopsychosocial mechanisms underlying them. It recommended intensified social and behavioral science research to develop interventions that could help people change their unhealthy behavior and improve their health prospects. This section presents a broad overview of the research that has ensued, which has attempted to close the gap between what we know and what we do when it comes to adopting healthy lifestyles.

A BRIEF HISTORY OF BEHAVIOR CHANGE INTERVENTIONS

Early behavior change efforts in the 1970s and 1980s relied primarily on public education campaigns and individually oriented health education interventions. They were guided by the Health Belief Model and similar theories (the Theory of Reasoned Action, the Theory of Planned Behavior) that emphasized the cognitive and motivational influences on health behavior change. This type of intervention strategy sought to raise awareness of the harms of unhealthy behavior versus the benefits of behavior change (e.g., Glanz, Rimer, &

Lewis, 2002; Whitlock, Orleans, Pender, & Allan, 2002). These cognitive/decisional theories were based on a "rational man" model of human behavior change, with an underlying premise that people's intentions and motivations to engage in behavior strongly predict their actually doing so (i.e., "if you tell them, they will change"). Because raising health risk awareness and motivation was a primary goal, the doctor–patient relationship was seen as a unique and powerful context for effective health education.

In fact, both population-level and individual clinical health education efforts based on these theories achieved initial success. For instance, tens of thousands of smokers quit in response to the publication of the first U.S. Surgeon General's Report on Smoking and Health in 1964 and the multiple public education campaigns that followed. By the mid-1980s, most U.S. smokers said they wanted to quit and were trying to do so, mostly for health reasons. Recent findings confirm that physician advice can be a powerful catalyst for health behavior change—boosting the number of patients who quit smoking for at least 24 hours or who made some changes in their diet and activity levels (Kreuter, Cheda, & Bull, 2000). But a growing body of research found these successes to be modest—the interventions were important and perhaps *necessary* for changing people's health knowledge, attitudes, and beliefs, as well as broader social norms, but *not sufficient* to produce lasting behavior change. Cumulative findings have made it clear that people need not only motivation but also new skills and supports to succeed in changing deeply ingrained health habits (Whitlock et al., 2002).

These findings spurred the development and testing of expanded multicomponent, cognitive-behavioral treatments designed not only to (a) raise perceptions of susceptibility to poor health outcomes and benefits of behavior change but also to (b) teach the skills required to replace ingrained unhealthy habits with healthy alternatives and to (c) help people make changes in their natural (home, work, social) environments that will aid in successfully establishing and maintaining new behavior. *Social learning theory,* which emphasized interactions between internal and external environmental influences on behavior, provided the primary theoretical basis for this evolution, and it remains the dominant model for effective cognitive-behavioral health behavior change interventions.

Lifestyle change interventions derived from social learning theory combined education and skills development. They included techniques such as modeling and behavioral practice to help people learn not just why but *how* to change unhealthy habits. For instance, they taught effective self-management and behavior change skills, such as goal-setting, self-monitoring, and stress management skills for people who had relied on smoking, eating, or drinking as coping tactics. They taught skills for re-engineering the person's immediate environments, replacing environmental cues and supports for unhealthy behavior with new cues and supports for healthy ones (e.g., removing ashtrays, replacing unhealthy high-calorie foods with healthy alternatives, finding exercise buddies, and avoiding high-risk events, such as office parties at which risky drinking was expected). Another principle was that problem solving should start with helping people set realistic, personal behavior change goals and go on to address the unique barriers and relapse-temptations they face. The expectation was that setting and meeting achievable goals would lead to heightened self-efficacy and confidence in the ability to succeed. Finally, new social learning theory treatments taught patients to take a long-range perspective, viewing repeated attempts over time as part of a cumulative learning process rather than as signs of failure.

Effective multicomponent treatments were initially delivered and tested in multisession, face-to-face group or individual clinic-based programs, typically offered in clinical or medical settings and usually led by highly trained (e.g., MD, PhD) professionals. Results were extremely encouraging, with substantial behavior change—for example, smoking quit rates as high as 40%—maintained 6 to 12 months posttreatment. However, participants were typically self-referred or recruited based on high readiness or motivation for change, and thus represented a small fraction of those who could benefit. And treatment costs were high. The next push was to distill core elements of this treatment approach into lower-cost formats with much wider reach. These formats included paraprofessional-led worksite clinics, self-help manuals and programs, and brief primary care counseling. Absolute treatment effects were smaller—for example, 20% long-term smoking quit rates—but potential population impacts were much greater: only 5% to 10% of smokers might ever attend intensive clinics, but a brief effective tobacco intervention reaching the 70% of U.S. smokers who saw their primary care physicians each year would double the nation's annual quit rate.

Development of the *stages-of-change model* in the mid-1980s accelerated the shift from individual to population intervention models and has had a profound, lasting impact on the design and delivery of health behavior change programs. Studying how people went about changing on their own, Prochaska and DiClemente (1983) discovered that health behavior change was a multistage process:

- *Precontemplation*—not planning to change behavior; behavior is not seen as a problem.
- *Contemplation*—seriously planning to change behavior within next 6 months, weighing the pros and cons, and building supports and confidence.

- *Preparation*—plans to change are imminent; small initial steps are taken.
- *Action*—active attempts are made to quit smoking, drink less, become more active, or change to a healthier diet and to sustain changes for up to 6 months.
- *Maintenance*—change is sustained beyond 6 months.
- *Relapse*—the individual returns to any earlier stage and begins to recycle through the earlier stages.

Different skills and knowledge and different types of treatment were needed to help people in each stage; motivational and educational interventions were helpful to people in precontemplation and contemplation stages, and active cognitive-behavioral interventions were needed for those in preparation, action, and maintenance stages. Moreover, many population surveys found that, at any given time, the vast majority of people (80%) are in the precontemplation and contemplation stages, which helped to explain why so few enrolled in weight loss or quit smoking clinics, even when these were free and accessible.

The stages-of-change model has been successfully applied to each of the behavioral health risks covered in this chapter as well as to other risks (e.g., cancer screening adherence, sun protection). It also has been used to help people with multiple risk factors make progress in changing several at the same time (Prochaska et al., 2007). This model helped propel a shift away from one-size-fits-all approaches to individualized, stage-tailored strategies that could be effectively applied to entire populations—in communities, worksites, and health care settings—assisting people at *all* stages of change, not just the motivated volunteers in action stages, but also those needing motivation and support to reach action stages. It stimulated the development and wider use of effective motivational interventions for clinical settings, especially motivational interviewing, which seeks to help people strengthen their determination to change behavior (Emmons & Rollnick, 2001).

Originating as they did in the study of successful self-change, stages-of-change models fueled a burgeoning movement toward low-cost self-help tools and treatment formats. Some tools capitalized on computer-based and interactive communication technologies to design and deliver print materials, interactive video, Web-based, and telephone interventions that could fit not only the individual's stage of change but also address many other variables important for tailoring treatment methods and improving treatment outcomes—for example, degree of nicotine addiction, unique behavior change assets, barriers, and cultural norms (Glasgow, Bull, Piette, & Steiner, 2004).

A final force in the evolution from individual to population-based approaches was the emergence of *social marketing strategies,* which apply the concepts and tools of successful commercial marketing to the challenge of health behavior change. Basic marketing principles and methods—including market analysis, audience segmentation, the use of focus groups—played an especially important role in the development of culturally appropriate communication and intervention strategies for reaching underserved and high-risk, low-income and racial/ethnic minority populations for whom the prevalence of behavioral health risks is highest (e.g., Maibach, Rothschild, & Novelli, 2002). For instance, social marketing strategies have been used to tailor a state-of-the-art self-help quit smoking guide to the needs of African American smokers and to develop messages for Black radio stations that promoted the use of the guide as well as free telephone quit-line counseling. Results included a higher quit-line call rate and a higher quit rate among African Americans receiving the tailored guide, versus a generic one.

> Social marketing strategies apply the concepts and tools of successful commercial marketing to the challenge of health behavior change.

THE ROLE AND IMPACT OF PRIMARY CARE INTERVENTIONS

The progress in health behavior change research and treatment described above sets the stage for the development of brief, individually oriented, primary care health interventions that could be widely offered to all members of a practice, health plan, or patient population. These efforts were based on a strong rationale for primary care interventions to address behavioral health risks. Over 80% of American adults report having a usual source of care, visiting their doctor's offices on average about three times each year. Patient surveys have repeatedly found that patients expect and value advice from their providers about diet, exercise, and substance use and are motivated to act on this advice (Kreuter et al., 2000; Stange, Woolf, & Gjeltema, 2002). Similarly, most primary care providers describe health behavior change advice and counseling as an essential part of their role and responsibilities. The unique extended relationship that is the hallmark of primary care provides multiple opportunities over time to address healthy behavior in a "string of pearls" approach, capitalizing both on teachable moments—for example, introducing physical activity or diet counseling when test results show elevated cholesterol levels—and a therapeutic alliance that often extends beyond the patient to include key family members. This vision has prompted a tremendous amount of work to identify brief, effective interventions that could be integrated into routine practice.

In the *minimal contact* primary care counseling interventions that were distilled from the successful multicomponent models, the physician was seen as the initial catalyst for change, providing brief motivational advice, social support, and follow-up, with referral to other staff members or community resources for more intensive assistance. Stage-based and social marketing approaches held the potential to reach and assist entire populations of patients, including those not yet motivated for change and those in underserved and high-risk groups. Computer-based, patient-tailored, and population-targeted interventions provided new ways to reduce provider burden. And the emergence of managed care as the dominant health care model brought new incentives and demands for population-based preventive clinical services and more centralized systems for delivering them.

Progress in developing effective minimal-contact, primary care interventions occurred first in the area of smoking cessation, culminating in the development of an evidence-based practice-friendly intervention model now known as the 5 *A*s: Ask, Advise, Agree, Assist, Arrange Follow-up (U.S. Public Health Service, 2000). The 5 *A*s model was developed through a review and meta-analysis of hundreds of controlled studies and has been widely promoted through government-approved clinical practice guidelines. The model was found to be effective when used by a variety of health care providers (physicians, nurses, dentists, dental hygienists), with as few as 2 to 3 minutes of in-office provider time.

The model starts with *asking* about tobacco use. Then, provide *advice* aimed at raising personal quitting motivation and self-efficacy and offer help. The *agree* step starts with assessing patient readiness to quit and goes on to establish a goal and quitting plan. For those not ready to quit, *assistance* includes a recommended motivational intervention; for those who are ready to quit, *assistance* combines brief behavior-change counseling with FDA-approved pharmacotherapy, such as nicotine gum, patch, nasal spray or inhaler, or bupropion hydrochloride (Zyban, unless contraindicated). Behavioral counseling was found to be most effective when provided through multiple formats—self-help materials and face-to-face or telephone counseling—and there is a clear dose-response relationship between the amount of counseling and quit rates. Effective follow-up *arrangements* include planned visits, calls, or contacts to reinforce progress, adjust the quitting plan to better meet individual needs, or refer for more intensive help. One-year quit rates for patients receiving these interventions are typically two to three times higher than the 7% quit rates among people who try quitting on their own. In fact, the Centers for Disease Control and Prevention and Partnership for Prevention found the 5 *A*s intervention to be one of the two most effective and cost-effective of all evidence-based clinical preventive services (Coffield et al., 2001).

The 5 *As* model was recently adopted by the U.S. Preventive Services Task Force as a unifying conceptual framework applicable to addressing *all* behavioral health risks, including risky drinking, physical activity, diet, and obesity. In most cases, the USPSTF found that counseling interventions could produce clinically meaningful, population-wide health improvements that were sustained for at least 6 to 12 months. Although there are many common elements, the specific intervention components and intensity of recommended strategies vary from behavior to behavior, as does their effectiveness with unselected versus high-risk patients. Primary care providers may intervene more forcefully with healthy patients when they are known to be at high risk for a particular chronic disease, and patients at high risk may feel more vulnerable and motivated to act on the advice and assistance they receive.

The first step is always to *assess,* not only the relevant behavior (using a standard health risk appraisal or brief screening that can easily be administered in a busy practice setting) but also the individual factors that are helpful in tailoring the intervention, such as medical and physiologic factors, motives, barriers, patient's stage of change, social support, and cultural values. Based on this information, ideally with reference to the patient's immediate health concerns and symptoms, the clinician provides brief, personalized *advice,* expressing confidence in the patient's ability to change and soliciting the patient's thoughts about the recommended changes. The next critical step is to negotiate and *agree* on a collaboratively defined behavior change goal and treatment plan, which commonly includes practical problem solving to *assist* the patient in addressing personal change barriers, building social support, developing a more supportive immediate social and physical environment, and securing adjunctive behavior change resources[1] and pharmacologic aids, such as nicotine replacement. The final step is to *arrange* follow-up support and assistance, including referral to more intensive or customized help.

These new guidelines provide unprecedented scientific support for the USPSTF assertion that "the most effective interventions available to clinicians for reducing the incidence and severity of the leading causes of disease and disability in the U.S. are those that address patients' personal health practices" (1996, p. iv). However, several important limitations and gaps must be noted. The greatest

---

[1] Adjunctive resources can include face-to-face counseling from medical or community-based programs, telephone counseling, tailored or generic self-help materials, and Web-based and other interactive tools that are personally tailored to a patient's gender, age, racial/ethnic or cultural group, health status or condition, stage of change, and other relevant variables. They can be used before, during, and after the office visit.

limitation is the lack of long-term maintenance following successful behavior change for 12 months or longer. This is not surprising, given that patients return to the environments that shaped and supported their unhealthy lifestyles and choices. Higher maintenance rates were achieved in clinic-based programs that offered extended booster or maintenance sessions, providing ongoing social support and behavior change assistance, or in those that helped patients create an enduring "therapeutic micro-environment" to shield them from unhealthy influences—for example, implementing an in-home smoking ban, arranging for the delivery of recommended diet foods, or arranging ongoing behavior change buddies.

Researchers and policymakers agree that current major research and evidence gaps include:

- Too few studies to develop and test primary care interventions for children and adolescents, for any of the behavioral risk factors discussed in this chapter (tobacco, alcohol, physical activity, diet, obesity).
- Similarly, too few studies to develop and test behavior change interventions for underserved populations, especially those in low-income and racial/ethnic minority groups.
- Except for obesity, little is known about how best to address multiple behavioral risk factors in the same individual or population.
- And, despite growing evidence that effective chronic illness care often revolves around helping patients change the behavioral risks that cause or complicate their disease, formal evidence reviews and recommendations, such as those issued by the USPSTF, have focused mainly on primary prevention in healthy populations.

MULTILEVEL MODELS FOR POPULATION-BASED HEALTH BEHAVIOR CHANGE

The shift to population-based models of health promotion and disease prevention was prompted by several factors:

- the success of effective, brief, and intensive interventions based on social learning theory, which gave greater prominence to environmental factors in healthy and unhealthy behavior;
- the emergence of new stage-based and social marketing models for population-wide interventions; and
- the disappointing reach and long-term effectiveness of even the most successful cognitive-behavioral treatments.

The lackluster performance of the old, individual treatment approach was especially apparent when contrasted with new evidence from public health research showing far-reaching and lasting health impacts from environmental and policy changes that eliminated the need for individual decision making. A prime example is the development of safer roads and more crashworthy automobiles, combined with shifts in laws and norms regarding seatbelt use and drinking and driving, which collectively produced a dramatic decline in auto-related deaths and injuries.

With the stage well set, the final push for a change in approach came in the 1990s with the development of *social ecological models* of health behavior. These models integrate behavioral science with clinical and public health approaches. They redefined what the targets of successful health interventions need to be—not just individuals but also the powerful social contexts in which they live and work. And they emphasized that a person's health behavior is affected by multiple levels of influence: interpersonal factors (e.g., physiologic factors, knowledge, skill, motivation), social factors (e.g., social-cultural norms, supports, and networks), organizational and community factors, broader environmental influences, and public policies. Proponents of the ecological model recommended multi-level strategies that address all these levels of influence (Institute of Medicine, 2000). Specifically, they proposed that educational and clinical interventions to improve the motivation, skills, and supports for behavior change at the individual level (e.g., for permanently quitting smoking or risky drinking, or adopting and maintaining healthier activity and eating patterns) would be more successful when policies and influences in the wider environment supported healthy behavior through, for example, clean indoor air laws and access to safe and attractive places to walk or bike and healthy, affordable food choices.

A strong proponent of the ecological approach, McKinlay (1995) proposed a template for more effective population health promotion strategies that linked individual-level, clinical health behavior change strategies with broader, population-level health promotion efforts, including upstream policy and environmental interventions. The model McKinlay proposed (see Table 10.2) recommended interventions across a broad spectrum of factors, linking downstream individual clinical approaches with midstream interventions aimed at health plans, schools, worksites, and communities with upstream macro-level public policy and environmental interventions strong enough to subvert or redirect countervailing societal, economic, and industry forces. In essence, McKinlay argued that success in achieving lasting population-wide health behavior change required a "full court press."

In a review of the past three decades of progress in population health promotion, the most recent Institute of Medicine (2000)

Table 10.2	The Population-Based Intervention Model

Downstream Interventions	Midstream Interventions	Upstream Interventions
Individual-level interventions aimed at those who possess a behavioral risk factor or suffer from risk-related disease. Emphasis is on changing rather than preventing risky behavior.	Population-level interventions that target defined populations in order to change and/or prevent behavioral risk factors. May involve mediation through important organizational channels or natural environments.	State and national public policy/ environmental interventions that aim to strengthen social norms and supports for healthy behavior and redirect unhealthy behavior.
☐ Group and individual counseling	☐ Worksite and community-based health promotion/disease prevention programs	☐ National public education/ media campaigns
☐ Patient health education/ cognitive behavioral interventions	☐ Health plan–based primary care screening/intervention	☐ Economic incentives (e.g., excise taxes on tobacco products, reimbursement for effective primary care, diets, and extensive counseling)
☐ Self-help programs and tailored communications	☐ School-based youth prevention activities	☐ Policies reducing access to unhealthy products (e.g., pricing, access, labeling)
☐ Pharmacologic treatments	☐ Community-based interventions focused on defined at-risk populations	☐ Policies reducing the advertising and promotion of unhealthy products and behavior

Note. From McKinlay, J. B. (1995). The new public health approach to improving physical activity and autonomy in older populations. In E. Heikkinen (Ed.), *Preparation for aging,* New York: Plenum. pp. 87–103.

report on health and behavior reached the same conclusion. It used McKinlay's broad-spectrum, multilevel model for describing the balance needed between the dominant clinical and individually oriented approaches to disease prevention, on one hand, and the population-level approaches addressing the generic social and behavioral factors linked to disease, injury, and disability, on the other. Observing that "it is unreasonable to expect that people will change their behavior easily when so many forces in the social, cultural and physical environment conspire against such change" (Institute of Medicine,

"(I)t is unreasonable to expect that people will change their behavior easily when so many forces in the social, cultural and physical environment conspire against such change."—Institute of Medicine

2000, p. 2), the authors recommended population-based health promotion efforts that:

- use multiple approaches (e.g., education, social support, laws, incentives, behavior change programs) and address multiple levels of influence simultaneously (i.e., individuals, families, communities, nations)
- take account of the special needs of target groups (i.e., based on age, gender, race, ethnicity and social class)
- take the long view of health outcomes, because changes often take many years to become established
- involve a variety of sectors in society that have not traditionally been associated with health promotion efforts, including law, business, education, social services, and the media (Institute of Medicine, 2000, p. 6).

The last three decades of progress in national tobacco control, hailed by some as one of the greatest public health successes of the second half of the 20th century, is the example most often used to illustrate the power and promise of ecological approaches for health intervention (Warner, 2000). In response to comprehensive tobacco control programs and policy changes in health care settings, worksites, schools, and communities in all 50 states, U.S. smoking rates have dropped markedly. The multilevel and broad spectrum interventions have included changes in laws and regulations (clean indoor air laws, worksite smoking bans, changes in minimum age of purchase laws, advertising regulation, increased public and private insurance coverage for tobacco dependence treatment); economic disincentives (increases in tobacco prices and cigarette excise taxes); effective mass communication and counter-advertising campaigns; and increased access to effective quit smoking interventions (widening access to nicotine replacement through over-the-counter products, the proliferation of national, state, and health plan quit lines). Although major disparities in tobacco use and its addiction remain, regressive tobacco tax and price increases have proved especially effective in certain high-risk and underserved populations—including adolescents, pregnant women, and low-income smokers. Telephone quit lines have expanded the reach of evidence-based individual counseling to traditionally underserved low-income and minority populations.

Reflecting the growth in research evaluating the population impacts of midstream and upstream interventions for tobacco control, the Centers for Disease Control and Prevention (CDC) Task Force for Community Preventive Services now conducts systematic evidence reviews for community-based and policy interventions to change health behavior similar to the reviews conducted by the

USPSTF for downstream clinical interventions. Based on its review of the evidence for 14 different interventions, the CDC recommends

- smoking bans and restrictions to reduce exposure to environmental tobacco smoke;
- tax and price increases and mass media campaigns to reduce the number of youth who start smoking and to promote cessation; and
- patient telephone quit-line support, as well as a number of health care system interventions,[2] also to increase cessation.

Similar ecological models have been described and proposed for each of the other major behavioral risk factors discussed in this chapter—including risky drinking, physical activity, dietary behavior change, and obesity. And, in 2005, the CDC Community Preventive Services Task Force developed guidelines to promote better health among community members. These guidelines initially concentrated on physical activity and obesity (CDC, 2005).

There is a great sense of urgency about the need to identify evidence-based full-court press strategies that can halt the nation's current obesity epidemic (Mokdad et al., 2004). The dramatic rise in the prevalence of overweight and obesity among youth and adults over the past several decades is primarily due to environmental and economic changes affecting behavior on both sides of the *energy balance equation:* that is, the amount of energy (calories) used versus the amount consumed. The cumulative effects of technology—such as automobile-dependent transportation, more sedentary jobs, and less recreation—along with changes in lifestyles in typical suburban environments, which limit the places to which adults and children can walk, have reduced the amount of physical activity in everyday life. At the same time, increased access to low-cost, sugar-laden, and high-fat foods and beverages, larger portion sizes, increased restaurant use, an exodus of grocery stores and other sources of fresh fruits and vegetables from cities to suburbs, and the rising cost of fresh fruits and vegetables relative to soda and snack foods have helped to promote excessive caloric intake, especially in low-income and racial/ethnic minority populations.

Rapid progress is being made in understanding the environmental and policy factors that affect physical activity and in identifying promising multilevel, broad-spectrum interventions. The CDC Community Preventive Services Task Force reviewed research on interventions and found evidence for recommendations spanning the full McKinlay model. These include *downstream* health behavior change programs that increase social supports for physical activity and exercise (e.g.,

---

[2] Health system interventions include provider reminder systems plus provider education and reducing out-of-pocket costs for effective cessation therapies.

walking clubs); *midstream* requirements for school physical education classes that increase the time students spend in moderate or vigorous physical activity and "point of decision" prompts on elevators and escalators that encourage people to use nearby stairs; and *upstream* efforts to create, or increase, access to safe, attractive, and convenient places for physical activity (e.g., parks, trails, bike lanes, sidewalks), along with informational outreach to change knowledge and attitudes about the benefits of and opportunities for physical activity.

These recommendations sparked a study of socioeconomic differences in access to community sports areas, parks, swimming pools, beaches, and bike paths, which found predicted disparities in facilities, favoring the wealthy over people in low-income and minority communities (Powell et al., 2004). A set of CDC physical activity recommendations was issued in 2005, addressing transportation and land use policies ranging from zoning guidelines to improved federal, state, and community projects for walking and bicycling. Together, these guidelines provide an unprecedented science-based blueprint for multisector efforts by professionals in public health, urban planning, transportation, parks and recreation, architecture, landscape design, public safety, and the mass media to close the gaps between recommended and actual physical activity levels for children and adults and to address pervasive environmental disparities.

As we learned from the success of tobacco control, highly credible scientific evidence can persuade policymakers and withstand the attacks of those whose interests are threatened. But the difficulty of implementing effective broad-spectrum approaches should not be underestimated. Powerful political barriers include the sale, promotion, and marketing of unhealthy products, industry lobbying, limited public support for healthy public policies, and inadequate funding for and enforcement of effective policies and programs. For example, youth tobacco and alcohol access laws have been poorly enforced, the Tobacco Master Settlement Agreement funds have been used to reduce state budget deficits rather than for evidence-based tobacco control, and farming of unhealthy crops continues to be subsidized. Creating a favorable political climate requires advocacy in order to instill broad public pressure and support for change, clear and well-communicated evidence of public demand and support for change, and evidence of the beneficial health and economic impact of proposed programs and policies.

With respect to special needs populations, systematic surveillance can monitor the prevalence of both behavioral risk factors and effective programs and policies. Such surveillance systems, which already exist for tobacco control and are rapidly developing for physical activity, establish a national baseline that makes it possible to assess the effects of specific interventions and to evaluate important local, state, and national intervention efforts. Finally, while some events and political changes may create opportunities for rapid change, as did the Tobacco Master Settlement Agreement, a long-term view is essential. Most successful health promotion and social change efforts have required decades of hard work.

Changing Provider Behavior

One of the most basic measures of national health care quality is the extent to which patients receive recommended, evidence-based care. Now that evidence-based government guidelines exist for primary care interventions to help patients modify the major behavioral risks for preventable death and chronic diseases, putting these guidelines into practice has become an important objective for national health care quality improvement efforts. The Institute of Medicine's (2001) report *Crossing the Quality Chasm* set forth a bold national agenda for improving health care quality across the full spectrum of care from prevention to acute and chronic illness and palliative care, including health behavior change. A follow-up report (Institute of Medicine, 2003) selected health behavior change interventions for tobacco and obesity as 2 of the top 20 priorities for national action.

CLOSING THE GAP BETWEEN BEST PRACTICES AND USUAL CARE

Despite strong evidence for behavioral prevention in primary care, there are gaps between recommended and actual care, which are consistently greater than those for other evidence-based medical treatments and procedures (Glasgow, Orleans, Wagner, Curry, & Solberg, 2001). For instance, in a study of the quality of outpatient health care for U.S. adults, McGlynn and colleagues (2003) found that U.S. adults, on average, received about *half* the recommended medical care they needed overall, and even less—only 18%—of the lifestyle screening and counseling services they needed. It is safe to say that most patients who could benefit from health behavior change counseling, especially those from low socioeconomic groups and with racial/ethnic minority backgrounds, are not receiving it. In most studies, patients receive only the first two of the five *As*— *assessment* and *advice*.

- **Tobacco use.** Only 50% to 60% of current smokers report being asked about tobacco use or report being advised to quit, and only about half report any assistance (counseling, pharmacotherapy) or follow-up (Orleans & Alper, 2003). Brief primary care tobacco use counseling has been ranked the single highest priority clinical preventive service that is received by fewer than half of the patients who need it (Coffield et al., 2001).

- **Alcohol use.** Only 10.5% of adults seen in primary care settings were screened for alcohol misuse and referred for treatment when alcohol-dependent (McGlynn et al., 2003).
- **Physical inactivity and unhealthy diet.** In a 1992 survey, 40% of internists and 30% of nurse practitioners reported routinely assessing the physical activity levels of their patients, but only about half of each group reported developing physical activity plans for them (Francis, 1999). A 1997 survey found that only 42% of adult patients reported receiving advice from their primary care providers to increase their activity levels (Eden, Orleans, Mulrow, Pender, & Teutsch, 2002). Data from the 2000 National Health Interview Survey found that, among adults who had seen a doctor in the past 12 months, only about a quarter reported receiving physician advice on diet (25%) and activity (21%) (Honda, 2004). And in a 1999–2000 survey of U.S. adults, 33% reported past-year medical advice to eat more fruits and vegetables, and 29% reported receiving advice to reduce their fat intake (Glasgow, Eakin, Fisher, Bacak, & Brownson, 2001).
- **Obesity.** Fewer than half (42%) of obese adults (body mass index [BMI] of 30 or greater) surveyed in 1996 reported that their primary care provider had advised them to lose weight. Patients who were sicker (with diabetes, for example), had higher BMIs, and were better educated were more likely to report receiving weight loss advice (Galuska, Will, Serdula, & Ford, 1999).

Early efforts to improve provider adherence to recommended clinical practices mirrored early efforts to boost patient adherence to recommended health practices. These efforts employed individually focused educational strategies, including educational materials and continuing medical education (CME) to change provider motivation, knowledge, attitudes, and self-efficacy. This was true for evidence-based clinical practice guidelines generally and for prevention and behavior change guidelines specifically. These efforts, like the parallel patient-focused efforts, achieved modest success. Systematic evidence reviews conducted in the 1990s found that most educational approaches, including traditional CME, were of little effectiveness; more interactive and skills-based educational efforts that used principles of adult learning and were consonant with the principles of social learning theory (including modeling by respected peer "opinion leaders") were somewhat effective; and multicomponent interventions that addressed the multiple intrapersonal and environmental barriers to provider adherence, especially system barriers, were most effective. Reflecting on these findings and foreshadowing the paradigm shift that was to follow, was the following observation:

> The faith that education can induce change in physicians' practices assumes that doctors' decisions are based on rational behavior and that poor decisions are simply the result of inadequate information. Give physicians information that is adequate and they will change their behavior. This is reasonable, but it does not work in practice. (Greco & Eisenberg, 1993, p. 559)

The limited success of "if you tell them, they will change" educational strategies drew greater attention to the many system-level barriers to guideline adherence, including the pressure of time (in the face of more urgent medical issues), inadequate office supports, a lack of provider and patient resources, and missing financial incentives. Follow-up studies confirmed that clinician training was most effective when combined with efforts to create office supports to prompt, facilitate, and reward the delivery of preventive interventions, especially behavioral counseling, and that the most successful interventions were not one-size-fits-all, but tailored to the unique barriers present in any particular office practice.

MULTILEVEL APPROACHES FOR IMPROVING THE DELIVERY OF EFFECTIVE CLINICAL INTERVENTIONS

Collectively, these findings led to a shift in understanding what the targets of interventions to change *provider* health care practices need to be. Crabtree, Miller, and Stange (2001) introduced a *practice ecological model* to describe the need to address not just the behavior of individual providers, but also the powerful effects of the health care systems in which they practice. They and other proponents of a broader view of health care improvement emphasize the need for *broad-spectrum* strategies addressing *multiple* levels of influence: downstream intrapersonal/individual provider-level factors; midstream interpersonal/practice team, office microsystems and health plan influences; and upstream macro-level health care systems and policies. The Institute of Medicine's (2001) *Crossing the Quality Chasm* report proposes a charter for national health care quality improvement, as follows: "The current care systems cannot do the job. Trying harder will not work. Changing systems of care will" (p. 4). The report went on to recommend a fundamental re-engineering of the nation's health care system—moving from a system designed

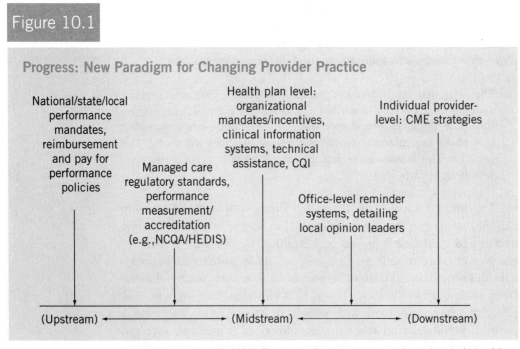

Figure 10.1

Progress: New Paradigm for Changing Provider Practice

Note. From McKinlay, J. B. (1995). The new public health approach to improving physical activity and autonomy in older populations. In E. Heikkinen (Ed.), *Preparation for aging*, New York: Plenum. pp. 87–103.

primarily to support and pay for the delivery of reactive acute illness care to one that would support and pay for the planned proactive (and behavioral) care needed to manage and prevent chronic disease.

Several thorough reviews have identified effective systems supports and policy changes needed to improve the preventive care provided by clinicians (see Figure 10.1). Again, work in the area of tobacco has led the way. The CDC reviewed research on the effectiveness of multiple interventions (e.g., provider training/feedback, organizational, administrative, and reimbursement changes) to improve the delivery of primary care tobacco interventions. It recommended reducing patient co-payments for proven tobacco dependence treatment services and establishing reminder systems to help providers identify patients who use tobacco products and prompt them to implement the 5 *A*s (e.g., chart stickers, stamps including tobacco use as a "vital sign," medical record flow sheets, checklists). The CDC recommended provider training through CME seminars, lectures, videos, and written materials for providers and patients, in conjunction with reminder systems. Similarly, training plus office supports significantly improve the delivery of screening and counseling for unhealthy diet and risky drinking (USPSTF, 2003a, 2003b; Whitlock et al., 2004).

In response to these findings, it has been said that "an ounce of prevention takes a ton of office system change." Until recently, we lacked a coherent model for what this "ton of change" included. Filling this void, Wagner and colleagues reviewed the research on effective chronic illness care and prevention and devised a model for the multiple interlocking systems supports required for effective planned, proactive chronic illness care—the Chronic Care Model (see chapter 8 and Figure 8.4). This model appears to apply equally to the *prevention* as to the *treatment* of chronic disease, both of which require helping patients to change the behavioral risk factors that cause or complicate chronic conditions.

The six key elements of the Chronic Care Model can be implemented at the level of the office practice or the larger health care delivery system. Each of the elements includes interventions that are planned rather than reactive; patient centered and informed by individually relevant patient data; proactive, involving scheduled outreach and follow-up; and population-based—that is, focused on an entire panel of patients with a specific behavioral risk factor, disease, or condition and not just individuals who seek care. Prevention and treatment of chronic conditions similarly require regular (nonsymptom-driven) screening and counseling for health behavior change, involve ongoing planned care with proactive follow-up, depend on active patient involvement in decision making and adherence, and require links to supportive community resources and services (Glasgow, Eakin, et al., 2001).

The Chronic Care Model was recently used to describe an organization-wide initiative at Group Health Cooperative of Puget Sound that integrates screening and treatment for tobacco use with routine primary care. This successful plan applied all six model elements as follows:

- *Health care organization*—health plan leaders made reducing tobacco use their top prevention priority, provided financial and other incentives to providers (including hiring dedicated clinic counselors), and eliminated patient co-payments for counseling.
- They used *clinical information systems* to create a registry of the tobacco users enrolled in the health plan, track their use of treatment resources and programs, and generate proactive telephone quit-line calls for patients and feedback reports for providers.
- *Decision support tools* included extensive provider training, ongoing consultation, automated patient assessment and guideline algorithms, and reminder tools.
- *Practice redesign and self-management support* included self-help materials and a telephone quit-line to deliver counseling and pharmacotherapy without burdening the provider.
- *Community resources and policies* included referral to community and worksite quit smoking clinics and related healthy lifestyle

change programs, focused on stress management, exercise, and weight loss, as well as support for worksite smoking cessation campaigns and smoking restrictions and expanded state funding for tobacco prevention and control programs.

This integrated "full-court press" dramatically reduced the prevalence of smoking among plan members, from 25% in 1985 to 15.5% in 1993, and led to substantial reductions in (former) smokers' inpatient and outpatient health services utilization.

The Chronic Care Model provides a unifying approach to health care quality improvement that cuts across different types of health behavior and chronic conditions. It promises to provide a more efficient, sustainable, and cost-effective approach to health care quality improvement. This is especially the case given the development of several successful continuous quality improvement (CQI) techniques for putting Chronic Care Model–based system changes into place. Promising midstream CQI techniques involve testing office system changes to find ways to eliminate the barriers there and strengthen the supports for recommended care, often through a series of "rapid cycle" (plan-do-study-act) improvement efforts (Chin et al., 2004).

Successful collaborative CQI interventions have been delivered through learning collaboratives involving multiple health care teams from different organizations who meet and work over a 12- to 18-month period with faculty experts in CQI techniques and in the type of care targeted for improvement (e.g., treating diabetes, tobacco dependence, obesity). Individual practice-level, Chronic Care Model–based improvements involve planning, implementing, evaluating, and refining changes in individual practices. These collaboratives have substantially increased the proportion of patients—including the most disadvantaged patients—who are receiving evidence-based care and for whom individual behavior change plans were developed and implemented (Chin et al., 2004).

Effective individual practice consultation models for CQI also have been developed. The best example comes from the STEP-UP (Study To Enhance Prevention by Understanding Practice) trial conducted by Goodwin and colleagues (2001). This randomized, controlled trial tested a brief practice-tailored approach to improving preventive service delivery, emphasizing improving rates of health habit counseling. Intervention practices received a 1-day practice assessment, an initial practice-wide consultation, and several brief follow-up visits to assess and address practice-specific factors related to improving the delivery of preventive services. All interventions were delivered by a specially trained nurse facilitator who helped practices identify promising changes and presented a menu of tools for implementing them (e.g., reminder systems, flow sheets, patient education materials, clinical information systems), including a practice improvement manual. This brief CQI intervention resulted in significant improvements at 6 and 12 months that were maintained at a 24-month follow-up. Improvements in behavioral counseling services were especially dramatic. The investigators attributed these lasting results to the maintenance of the practice and system changes that were made—changes that may have been easier to institutionalize because they were tailored to the unique characteristics of each practice.

The STEP-UP trial has furnished compelling evidence that even a brief tailored intervention can increase providers' and practices' abilities to help their patients adopt healthier lifestyles, despite competing demands and pressures and meager reimbursement. The parallels between the STEP-UP and individual health behavior change counseling and maintenance are striking. The same issues are important for individual behavior change and practice-level provider behavior change—that is, using practice *assessment* and feedback; *advising* on strategies to address the barriers and opportunities in each practice; *agreeing* on a mutually negotiated, achievable, and specific action plan tailored to each practice's resources, problems, and readiness for change; *assisting* with tools and ongoing incremental problem-solving strategies; and *arranging* for follow-up support and resources to refine and maintain successful improvements.

In the long run, just as upstream macro-level societal and policy change is needed to sustain individual behavior change, upstream macro-level health system and policy change will be needed to support and spread the kinds of midstream and downstream changes that can improve care in office practices and health plans. Such changes include quality performance measurement and public reporting; "pay-for-performance" initiatives that reward providers based on the quality of care they offer; and improved information technology to support care improvement. Some research has found that providers were more likely to offer health behavior change counseling when a portion of their capitation payment depended on their doing so. And providers in physician organizations were found to be more likely to offer proven health promotion services if their performance measures were publicly reported or they received public recognition or economic benefit from doing so, and if they had greater clinical information technology capacity (McMenamin et al., 2004).

> Just as upstream macro-level societal and policy change is needed to sustain individual behavior change, upstream macro-level health system and policy change will be needed to support and improve care in office practices and health plans.

Conclusion

Health-related behavior represents a prime target for improving national health and health care. Never have we known more about the importance of addressing the lifestyle factors and behavior that pose the most serious threats to Americans' health, produce the greatest demands on our health system, and contribute most to health care costs. The growing burden of chronic disease, a national epidemic of obesity, and escalating health care costs—at a time when health care spending already is growing faster than the U.S. gross domestic product—make establishing a stronger preventive orientation in the nation's health care and public health systems an urgent priority. Never have we known as much about how to motivate, support, and assist individuals to make lasting lifestyle changes or how to support and assist health care professionals to deliver evidence-based behavioral preventive care. The tremendous parallel gains made in what we have learned about the processes, principles, and paradigms both for effective health promotion for individuals and effective health care quality improvement for providers have created unprecedented potential for positive change. The stage is set for breakthrough improvements in national health status and health care quality, but realizing this potential depends entirely on how we use this newfound understanding. "Knowing is not enough; we must apply," said Goethe. "Willing is not enough; we must do."

References

Chin, M. H., Cook, S., Drum, M. L., Jin, L., Guillen, M., Humikowski, C. A., et al. (2004). Improving diabetes care in Midwest community health centers with the health disparities collaborative. *Diabetes Care, 27*(1), 2–8.

Coffield, A. B., Maciosek, M. V., McGinnis, J. M., Harris, J. R., Caldwell, M. B., Teutsch, S. M., et al. (2001). Priorities among recommended clinical preventive services. *American Journal of Preventive Medicine, 21*(1), 1–9.

Coups, E. J., Gaba, A., & Orleans, C. T. (2004). Physician screening for multiple behavioral health risk factors. *American Journal of Preventive Medicine, 27*(2), 34–41.

Crabtree, B. F., Miller, W. L., & Stange, K. C. (2001). Understanding practice from the ground up. *Journal of Family Practice, 50*(10), 881–887.

Eden, K. B., Orleans, C. T., Mulrow, C. D., Pender, N. J., & Teutsch, S. M. (2002). Does counseling by clinicians improve physical activity? A summary of the evidence for the U.S. Preventive Services Task Force. *Annals of Internal Medicine, 137*(3), 208–215.

Emmons, K. M., & Rollnick, S. (2001). Motivational interviewing in health care settings: Opportunities and limitations. *American Journal of Preventive Medicine, 20,* 68–74.

Finkelstein, E. A., Fiebelkorn, I. C., & Wang, G. (2003, May 14). National medical spending attributable to overweight and obesity: How much, and who's paying? Retrieved from http://content.healthaffairs.org/cgi/content/full/hlthaff. w3.219v1/DC1

Francis, K. T. (1999). Status of the year 2000 health goals for physical activity and fitness. *Physical Therapy, 79*(4), 405–414.

Freedman, D. S. (2002). Clustering of coronary heart disease risk among obese children. *Journal of Pediatric Endocrinology and Metabolism, 15*(8), 1099–1108.

Galuska, D. A., Will, J. C., Serdula, M. K., & Ford, E. S. (1999). Are health care professionals advising obese patients to lose weight? *Journal of the American Medical Association, 282*(16), 1576–1578.

Glanz, K., Rimer, B. K., & Lewis, F. M. (2002). Theory, research, and practice in health behavior and health education. In K. Glanz, B. K. Rimer, & F. M. Lewis (Eds.), *Health behavior and health education: Theory research and practice* (3rd ed., pp. 22–39). San Francisco: Jossey-Bass.

Glasgow, R. E., Bull, S. S., Piette, J. D., & Steiner, J. (2004). Interactive behavior change technology: A partial solution to the competing demands of primary care. *American Journal of Preventive Medicine, 27*(25), 80–87.

Glasgow, R. E., Eakin, E. G., Fisher, E. B., Bacak, S. J., & Brownson, R. C. (2001). Physician advice and support for physical activity: Results from a national survey. *American Journal of Preventive Medicine, 21*(3), 189–196.

Glasgow, R. E., Orleans, C. T., Wagner, E. H., Curry, S. J., & Solberg, L. I. (2001). Does the Chronic Care Model serve also as a template for improving prevention? *Milbank Quarterly, 79,* 579–612.

Goodwin, M. A., Zyzanski, S. J., Zronek, S., Ruhe, M., Weyer, S. M., Konrad, N., et al. (2001). A clinical trial of tailored office systems for preventive service delivery: The Study to Enhance Prevention by Understanding Practice (STEP-UP). *American Journal of Preventive Medicine, 21,* 20–28.

Greco, P. J., & Eisenberg, J. M. (1993). Changing physicians' practices. *New England Journal of Medicine, 329*(17), 1271.

Honda, K. (2004). Factors underlying variation in receipt of physical advice on diet and exercise: Applications of the behavioral model of health care utilization. *American Journal of Health Promotion, 18*(5), 370–377.

Institute of Medicine. (2000). *Promoting health: Intervention strategies from social and behavioral research.* B. D. Smedley & S. L. Syme, Eds. Washington, DC: National Academy Press.

Institute of Medicine. (2001). *Crossing the Quality Chasm: A new health system for the 21st century* (R. Briere, Ed.) Washington, DC: National Academy Press.

Institute of Medicine. (2003). *Priority areas for national action: Transforming health care quality. Quality Chasm* series. K. Adams & J. M. Corrigan, Eds. Washington, DC: National Academy Press.

Johnston, L. D., O'Malley, P. M., & Bachman, J. G. (2003). *Monitoring the future: National survey results on drug use, 1975–2002: Vol. 2. College students and young adults.* (NIH Pub. No. 03–5376). Bethesda, MD: National Institute of Drug Abuse.

Kreuter, M. W., Cheda, S. G., & Bull, F. C. (2000). How does physician advice influence patient behavior? *Archives of Family Medicine, 9*(5), 426–433.

Maibach, E. W., Rothschild, M. L., & Novelli, W. D. (2002). Social marketing. In K. Glanz, F. M. Lewis, & B. Rimer (Eds.), *Health behavior and health education* (3rd ed., pp. 437–461). San Francisco: Jossey-Bass.

McGinnis, J. M., & Foege, W. H. (1993). Actual causes of death in the United States. *Journal of the American Medical Association, 270,* 2207–2212.

McGlynn, E. A., Asch, S. M., Adams, J., Keesey, J., Hicks, J., DeCristofaro, A., et al. (2003). The quality of health care delivered to adults in the United States. *New England Journal of Medicine, 348*(26), 2635–2645.

McKinlay, J. B. (1995). The new public health approach to improving physical activity and autonomy in older populations. In E. Heikkinen (Ed.), *Preparation for aging* (pp. 87–103). New York: Plenum.

McMenamin, S. B., Schmittdiel, J., Halpin, H., Gillies, R., Rundall, T. G., & Shortell, S. M. (2004). Health promotion in physician organizations: Results from a national study. *American Journal of Preventive Medicine, 26*(4), 259–264.

Mokdad, A. H., Marks, J. S., Stroup, D. F., & Gerberding, J. L. (2004). Actual causes of death in the United States, 2000. *Journal of the American Medical Association, 291*(10), 1238–1245.

Ogden, C. L., Carroll, M. D., Curtin, L. R., McDowell, M. A., Tabak, C. J., & Flegal, K. M. (2006). Prevention of overweight and obesity in the United States: 1999–2004. *Journal of the American Medical Association, 295,* 1549–1555.

Orleans, C. T., & Alper, J. (2003). Helping addicted smokers quit. In S. L. Isaacs & J. R. Knickman (Eds.), *To improve health and health care* (Vol. 6, pp. 125–148). San Francisco: Jossey-Bass.

Orleans, C. T., Ulmer, C., & Gruman, J. (2004). The role of behavioral factors in achieving national health outcomes. In R. G. Frank, A. Baum, & J. L. Wallander (Eds.), *Handbook of clinical health psychology: Vol. 3. Models and perspectives in health psychology.* Washington, DC: American Psychological Association.

Powell, L. M., Slater, S., & Chaloupka, F. J. (2004). The relationship between community physical activity settings and race, ethnicity, and socioeconomic status. *Evidence-Based Preventive Medicine, 1*(2), 135–144.

Prochaska, J. O., & DiClemente, C. C. (1983). Stages and processes of self-change of smoking: Towards an integrative model of change. *Journal of Consulting and Clinical Psychology, 51,* 390–395.

Prochaska, J. O., Velicer, W. F., Rossi, J. S., Redding, C. A., Greene, G. W., Rossi, S. R., et al. (2007). Impact of simultaneous stage-matched expert system interventions for smoking, high fat diet and sun exposure in a population of parents. *Health Psychology, 12,* 170–178.

Stange, K. C., Woolf, S. H., & Gjeltema, K. (2002). One minute for prevention: The power of leveraging to fulfill the promise of health behavior counseling. *American Journal of Preventive Medicine, 22*(4), 320–323.

Tuomilehto, J., Lindstrom, J., Eriksson, J. G., Valle, T. T., Hamalainen, H., Ilanne-Parikka, P., et al. (2001). Prevention of Type 2 diabetes mellitus by changes in lifestyle among subjects with impaired glucose tolerance. *New England Journal of Medicine, 344*(18), 1343–1350.

U.S. Centers for Disease Control and Prevention. (2005). Physical activity: Guide to community preventive services. Retrieved February 14, 2007, from http://www.thecommunityguide.org/pa

U.S. Centers for Disease Control and Prevention. (2006). Tobacco information and prevention source (TIPS). *Secondhand smoke: Fact sheet.* Retrieved December 3, 2007, from http://www.cdc.gov/tobacco/data_statistics/Factsheets/Secondhand Smoke.htm

U.S. Department of Health and Human Services. (2000a). *Healthy People 2010* (2nd ed., Vol. 1). Washington, DC: Author.

U.S. Department of Health and Human Services. (2000b). *Healthy People 2010: Understanding and improving health.* Washington, DC: Author.

U.S. National Center for Health Statistics. (1999). *Healthy People 2000 Review, 1998–1999.* Hyattsville, MD: Public Health Service.

U.S. National Institute on Alcohol Abuse and Alcoholism. (2001, January). *Economic perspectives in alcoholism research: Alcohol Alert No. 51.* Washington, DC: Author.

U.S. Preventive Services Task Force. (2003a). Behavioral counseling in primary care to promote a healthy diet: Recommendations and rationale. *American Journal of Preventive Medicine, 24*(1), 93.

U.S. Preventive Services Task Force. (2003b). Screening for obesity in adults: Recommendations and rationale. *Annals of Internal Medicine, 139*(11), 930–932.

U.S. Preventive Services Task Force. (1996). *Guide to clinical preventive services* (2nd ed.). Baltimore: Williams & Wilkins.

U.S. Public Health Service. (2000). *Treating tobacco use and dependence: A clinical practice guideline.* AHRQ Publication No. 00–0032. U.S. Department of Health and Human Services. Retrieved from http://www.ahrq.gov

Warner, K. E. (2000). The need for, and value of, a multi-level approach to disease prevention: The case of tobacco control. In B. D. Smedley & S. L. Syme (Eds.), Institute of Medicine, *Promoting health: Intervention strategies from social and behavioral research* (pp. 417–449). Washington, DC: National Academy Press.

Whitlock, E. P., Orleans, C. T., Pender, N., & Allan, J. (2002). Evaluating primary care behavioral counseling interventions: An evidence-based approach. *American Journal of Preventive Medicine, 22*(4), 267–284.

Whitlock, E. P., Polen, M. R., Green, C. A., Orleans, C. T., & Klein, J. (2004). Behavioral counseling interventions in primary care to reduce risky/harmful alcohol use by adults: A summary of the evidence for the U.S. Preventive Services Task Force. *Annals of Internal Medicine, 140*(7), 557–568.

11

Key Words

clinical trials	research and development	payment
drug	formulary	user fees
pharmacogenomics	rebates	premarket approval
generics	pharmaceutical	value
Medicare prescription drug	pharmacy benefit	evidence
legislation	manager	innovation
prescription	reimportation	Food and Drug
patents	coverage	Administration

Pharmaceuticals

Robin J. Strongin, Ron Geigle, and Victoria A. Wicks

Learning Objectives

- Compare and contrast the U.S. pharmaceutical industry.
- Understand the drug discovery and development processes.
- Describe the FDA drug approval processes.
- Understand the difference between drugs and biologics.
- Describe the Medicare Part D drug benefit.
- Analyze pharmaceutical marketplace dynamics.
- Highlight landmark legislation.
- Describe the growing focus on value in drugs.

Topical Outline

- Discovery and development
- Research and development: the price of innovation
- Patents and generics
- Pharmaceutical marketplace dynamics
- The Medicare Prescription Drug, Improvement and Modernization Act of 2003
- Medicare coverage and payment
- Private sector coverage, payment, and cost control
- The value of medical technology
- Conclusion

Prescription drugs are integral to the U.S. health care delivery system. They have revolutionized the prevention, diagnosis, and treatment of disease. But the price tag of this medical progress is staggering—not only in terms of dollars, but in the degree of risk companies must take and the complex responsibilities they must bear as they balance safety on the one hand with experimental development on the other.

The U.S. pharmaceutical industry invests billions of dollars in research and development (R&D). It is regulated by the U.S. Food and Drug Administration (FDA) and, for many patients, represents a critical lifeline to better health. Currently, the industry faces challenges in both the private and public sectors of the marketplace, as coding, coverage, payment, and reimbursement decision making require increasingly sophisticated levels of analysis and greater proof of both medical benefit and cost-effectiveness. The industry also faces the troubling reality that not all individuals who need these products are able to access them—because of insurance denials, affordability, or politics.

Although an impressive number of drug discoveries occur in smaller life sciences and pharmaceutical companies, the majority of successfully marketed drugs are products of large, multinational drug firms—where the infrastructure, experience, capital, and vast resources necessary to finance and market innovation are more plentiful. By contrast, the medical device industry comprises many small and start-up companies. In this industry, scientists work side by side with practicing physicians to create, modify, and improve new and existing technologies. Often these companies partner with larger companies to bring these products to market.

With scientific advances, a number of exciting new therapies are on the horizon. Some of these are drugs; some are devices. Some are a combination of both, while still others are defining entirely new technologies. Genomics, nanotechnology, robotics, information systems, vaccines, and pharmacogenomics all hold the promise of further breakthroughs in medical science.

Pharmaceuticals

DRUG DISCOVERY AND DEVELOPMENT

In 1928, a Scottish bacteriologist inadvertently left a culture of staphylococci uncovered in his London laboratory. A mold grew in the culture. He later noticed that a space had formed between the bacteria and the mold and realized that something in the mold was destroying the bacteria. Alexander Fleming named his discovery penicillin. Although the process of drug discovery today can still be as serendipitous, it is not haphazard. The discovery and subsequent development of new drugs occur within a structured framework and require heavy investments of time and resources.

The Preclinical Phase

Drug discovery and development consists of both a preclinical and a clinical phase. In the preclinical phase, chemists must learn how to make the candidate drug in quantity, while ensuring that the substance is stable. A company usually files one or more patent applications at this time and begins toxicological tests as well as short- and long-term animal testing. Depending on the outcomes of these tests, a manufacturer must then decide whether to begin the clinical phase of R&D, which evaluates the safety and effectiveness of the drug in humans. Before a company can begin U.S. clinical trials, it must submit an Investigational New Drug (IND) application to the FDA for approval.

The Drug Approval Process: Testing for Safety and Efficacy

The regulatory process begins when an IND is submitted to the FDA. The FDA does not investigate new drugs or conduct any trials. Rather, it reviews the manufacturing process and analyzes the chemical, preclinical, and clinical data submitted by the company.

Phase I Trials. INDs are in effect 30 days after submission to the FDA, unless they are placed on clinical hold—typically, as a result of a safety concern. If not, a manufacturer can proceed with its clinical trials, continuing its animal studies at the same time. In Phase I trials, initial human safety studies are conducted. These generally involve between 20 and 100 healthy volunteers. Phase I studies are designed also to determine the metabolic and pharmacologic actions of the drug in humans.

The objective in this phase is to provide information on toxicity and to identify potential side effects. The drug is administered at very low doses, much below the dose that had an effect in the animal studies. If no side effects occur, the dose is gradually increased until a dosage range—establishing toxic levels—is determined.

All research involving FDA-regulated products must be reviewed by an institutional review board before human testing can begin. These review boards, known as IRBs, exist in research institutions, academic health centers, and hospitals. They are made up of experts and lay persons whose job it is to make certain that participants are well informed and willing to participate before the studies get under way.

Phase II Trials. Phase II trials are controlled efficacy studies, which attempt to determine optimal dosage levels and to detect short-term side effects. They tend to be double-blinded, randomized controlled trials. In a randomized controlled trial, patients are randomly assigned to (1) a treatment group, which receives the experimental drug, or (2) a control group, which receives a placebo, standard treatment, or no treatment. This phase takes approximately 2 years to complete and involves a few hundred patients. The term *double-blinded* means that neither the patient nor the researcher knows who is receiving which treatment, a procedure intended to eliminate bias.

> One of the most difficult aspects of clinical trials involves the selection of clinical endpoints—that is, whether the study should focus on intermediate endpoints, such as changes in biochemical, physiological, or anatomical parameters, or look for effects on mortality, morbidity, or quality of life.

One of the most difficult aspects of clinical trials, which usually occurs during Phase II, involves the selection of clinical endpoints—that is, whether the study should focus on intermediate endpoints, such as changes in biochemical, physiological, or anatomical parameters, or look for effects on mortality, morbidity, or quality of life. These decisions are critical and have enormous impact on the development process. Testing treatments for AIDS provides a good example, in that a number of drugs being developed today are not necessarily designed to cure AIDS, but rather to relieve symptoms of the disease. The issue of endpoint selection is key in developing drugs to treat chronic, degenerative diseases, too.

Phase III Trials. Until recently, most of the drugs that make it to Phase III had a very good chance of going to market. But, in fact, the FDA approved only 18 new drugs in 2006—the lowest number in almost 8 years. During Phase III, which takes from 1 to 3 years, the drug is typically studied in 2,000 to 3,000 human subjects having the relevant disease or condition, in order to analyze long-term safety, efficacy, and toxicity. Also occurring at the same time as Phases II and III—although not part of the trials—are efforts by chemists and engineers to scale up to produce, as efficiently as possible, large quantities of the compound.

Expedited Drug Reviews: Treatment INDs. For patients with serious or immediately life-threatening diseases, the drug approval process presents a difficult dilemma. On the one hand, the lengthy approval process is designed to ensure that new drugs are safe and effective. On the other hand, if a new drug appears to be a promising treatment for a terminal illness, time is crucial. The FDA has responded by developing stopgap mechanisms to enable physicians to use an investigational new drug for desperately ill patients, provided there is no comparable or satisfactory alternative.

New Drug Applications. At the completion of Phase III trials, the company summarizes its study findings, as well as the formulation and chemistry of the drug, quality control procedures, and manufacturing processes, and submits a new drug application (NDA) to the FDA. Once the FDA approves this application, the manufacturer may market the new drug *for the specific indications that the FDA approved.* However, the FDA does not regulate the practice of medicine. Physicians can, therefore, prescribe a drug for off-label uses not sanctioned by the FDA and frequently do so. (Companies can conduct new rounds of trials to support such additional uses of the drug, if they wish.)

Phase IV. Phase IV consists of postmarketing studies and takes place over the life of a drug. The main objective is to examine long-term safety and effectiveness and includes the reporting of adverse drug reactions to the FDA. In addition to the submission of adverse reaction reports by manufacturers and health professionals, large-scale, randomized controlled trials may also be conducted—often by such agencies as the National Heart, Lung, and Blood Institute rather than the sponsor—to amass additional data. Phase IV activities are a much larger part of the drug approval process in Europe, where the philosophy is to get a product to market sooner and then monitor it more closely.

Increasing New Drug Approvals for Adults and Children

Analysts studying the pharmaceutical industry follow the FDA's record regarding how long it takes and how many new drugs are approved over a given time. One of the most meaningful indicators is the number of new molecular entities (NMEs) annually approved by the FDA. NMEs are defined as compounds that have not previously been marketed in the United States. The FDA also approves new drug applications for products that are not new molecular entities. Tracking NME approvals provides analysts with a good indication of the pharmaceutical industry's level of innovation.

Accelerated review times have been bolstered by the passage of two key pieces of federal legislation. The first, entitled the Prescription Drug User Fee Act (PDUFA), which Congress passed in 1992, authorized the FDA to collect user fees from pharmaceutical companies, which are used to hire more drug reviewers and to improve the computer infrastructure necessary to hasten the review process. In exchange, the FDA was required to meet annual performance targets. In 1997, when the PDUFA legislation was to sunset, Congress passed the Food and Drug Administration Modernization Act (FDAMA). Among other things, the FDAMA provided for an additional 5 years of user fee legislation and expanded PDUFA's emphasis on faster approval times to stimulate further pharmaceutical R&D. PDUFA was again up for reauthorization in 2007 and has been passed as the FDA Amendment Act (FDAAA, Public Law 110-85). As part of this new law, the agency is slated to receive increased funding to expedite the drug review process. Regulations are still pending on additional features, such as new drug safety provisions.

Another important element of FDAMA was the creation of the *pediatric exclusivity provision*—the aim of which was to stimulate research on drugs for children. The legislation provides a pharmaceutical manufacturer or sponsor with an additional 6 months of marketing exclusivity for the drug product in exchange for pediatric study data. Another effort to encourage pharmaceutical research in the pediatric field resulted in the April 1999 Pediatric Rule, which stipulates that applications for new active ingredients, new indications, new dosage forms, new dosing regimens, and new routes of administration must contain a pediatric assessment unless the sponsor (manufacturer) has obtained a waiver or deferral of pediatric studies.

RESEARCH AND DEVELOPMENT: THE PRICE OF INNOVATION

Drug products in the early part of the 20th century consisted mainly of patent medicines, home remedies, and folk cures. The sophisticated, science-based pharmaceutical industry that exists today did not start to develop until the 1930s, when the first sulfa drug was introduced. This discovery set the stage for the development of penicillin, which ushered in the "age of antibiotics" that lasted from the late 1930s until the early 1950s. The biotechnology industry, born in the late 1970s, moved the industry even further along with advances involving monoclonal antibodies, cell culture, and genetic modification, among others.

In many ways, companies today are being forced to rethink their R&D portfolios. The nature of R&D is changing, as our understanding of disease and therapy is undergoing a profound shift. Scientists today realize that many diseases are actually a collection of several different diseases, each with a unique molecular cause. As the secrets of genomics are unveiled, new miracle products (drugs may no longer be the correct term) will become available. Already new medicines account for 40% of the increases in Americans' life expectancy.

Sophisticated new tools, such as computer modeling, 3-D computer-visualization techniques, combinational chemistry, and X ray crystallography, have greatly improved the process of discovery. Nevertheless, pharmaceutical R&D remains a costly—and risky—business:

- In 2005, U.S. pharmaceutical companies spent $51.3 billion in research and development.
- It costs an average of $850 million to discover and develop one new medicine.

- It takes on average 10 to 15 years from the time a drug is discovered in the laboratory until it reaches patients.
- In the 1990s, the United States surpassed Europe as the leading site for pharmaceutical R&D (Accenture, 2007).

Research and development efforts constitute only part of a company's risk. The ability to recoup the company's research investments is another. For that to occur, patent protection is the life preserver.

PATENTS AND GENERICS

Patent protection is essential for companies investing in pharmaceutical R&D. Unlike many other technological advances, a drug product, once discovered, is relatively easy to reproduce. Without the period of market exclusivity that patents provide, companies would not have the opportunity to recoup their R&D investments. The 20-year clock starts ticking when a patent is filed with the U.S. Patent and Trademark Office; however, because of the length of the testing period, the effective patent life—that is, the time from FDA marketing approval to loss of patent protection—averages 11 to 12 years.

> Without the period of market exclusivity that patents provide, companies would not have the opportunity to recoup their R&D investments.

Some argue that patents provide companies with a monopoly, a barrier to market entry for competing products. Another side of that argument is as follows:

> Patents do not grant complete monopoly power in the pharmaceutical industry. The reason is that companies can frequently discover and patent several different drugs that use the same basic mechanism to treat an illness. The first drug using the new mechanism to treat that illness—the breakthrough drug—usually has between one and six years on the market before a therapeutically similar patented drug (sometimes called a me-too drug) is introduced. (Congressional Budget Office, 1998, p. xi)

As the future of medical research changes, patent policy will face interesting challenges. For example, the area of genetic research has raised significant issues, such as what is patentable (that is, are gene sequences bona fide inventions?). While the future of patenting and biotechnology is still unfolding, past patent legislation and regulation affect today's pharmaceutical market. This is true both domestically and abroad, where patent piracy costs the industry hundreds of millions of dollars each year, despite various protections agreed to in the North American Free Trade Agreement and the General Agreement on Tariffs and Trade.

The 1984 Drug Price Competition and Patent Term Restoration Act

More than half of the prescriptions filled annually are for generic drug products. These substitutes typically enter the market priced at 70% to 80% of the cost of the relevant brand-name drug, dropping to 40% or less as the market becomes more competitive (Employee Benefits Research Institute, 2004).

Domestically, the prescription drug market was radically altered with the passage of the 1984 Drug Price Competition and Patent Term Restoration Act, "intended to strike a balance between promoting innovation (by guaranteeing makers of brand-name drugs a certain number of patent years) and ensuring that consumers have timely access to lower-cost generic medicines (by guaranteeing makers of generic drugs that those patents would eventually end)" (Serafini, 2000, p. 548). The Greater Access to Affordable Pharmaceuticals Act of 2001 further eased the ability of quality generic equivalent products to enter the market sooner.

Since the 1980s, the use of generics has continued to increase. Along with the passage of the two federal measures, state drug-product substitution laws allowing pharmacists to dispense a generic even when the physician specifies a brand-name drug, and the active promotion of generic substitution by government health programs and private health plans have all spurred an increase in generic sales. As a result, the Generic Pharmaceutical Association (GPhA) projects global sales of generic drugs to rise from $29 billion in 2003 to $49 billion in 2007. Beyond 2004, GPhA expects generic drug sales to increase an average of 14% per year. A number of factors contribute to the increase in their growth, not the least of which are patent expirations on major brand-name drugs. According to GPhA, patents of several "blockbuster" drugs will expire soon, including drugs worth $27 billion with patents expiring in 2007 and drugs worth $29 billion expiring in 2008.

Generic Equivalence

The FDA uses three terms to describe generic drug products: pharmaceutical equivalence, bioequivalence, and therapeutic equivalence.

- *Pharmaceutical equivalence:* Drug products are considered pharmaceutical equivalents if they have the same active ingredient(s), the same dosage form, and are identical in strength to the brand-name product. Even if a generic has a different color, a different taste, or comes in a different shape or package, the FDA considers the product to be equivalent if it meets the same standards for strength, quality, purity, and identity as the branded product.

- *Bioequivalence:* A generic drug is considered bioequivalent if it is absorbed in the bloodstream at the same rate and extent as the brand-name drug.
- *Therapeutic equivalence:* A generic drug is considered therapeutically equivalent to the comparable brand when the FDA determines the generic is safe and effective, pharmaceutically equivalent, and bioequivalent.

The growing number of biologic products (for example, human growth hormone) are difficult to produce, and the FDA currently has no mechanism for measuring the equivalency of biological products and therefore, no mechanism for approving generic biologicals for market. The overall effect of this regulatory gap on the market, on competition, and on price, sales, and health care expenditures remains to be seen.

MARKETPLACE DYNAMICS

There is no single pharmaceutical marketplace. There is no single price for a specific drug product. There are multiple customers, distribution channels, prescription drug reimbursement systems, purchasing arrangements, pricing methodologies, marketing techniques, and cost-control tools. This makes the economics of the pharmaceutical marketplace extremely complex: the companies range in size from newly merged behemoths to very small one-product start-ups; some manufacturers are multinational, others are domestic, and still others are foreign companies seeking to do business in the United States.

Changes and trends that consumers see include: products once requiring prescriptions are now being sold over the counter; more and more products are being marketed directly to them; and a large number of top-selling products have or are due to come off patent very soon, enabling consumers to purchase generic versions at a greatly reduced cost.

Drug Expenditures

Three factors have contributed to the recent increases in U.S. pharmaceutical costs: *unit cost inflation, utilization* (increases in the absolute number of prescriptions), and *intensity* (availability of new drug technologies and the therapeutic mix—substituting newer, higher-cost products for older, less-expensive products, including generics). The best evidence suggests that while pure price inflation has played a relatively small role, especially on existing (older) prescription drug products, utilization growth has played a major role in the overall increases (Brandeis University/Schneider Institute for Health Policy, 2000).

Fueling the increase in prescription drug utilization is the explosion of direct-to-consumer (DTC) advertising by the pharmaceutical companies. One study reported that "the 10 drugs most heavily advertised directly to consumers in 1998 accounted for $9.3 billion or about 22 percent of the total increase in drug spending between 1993 and 1998" (National Institute for Health Care Management, 1999, p. iii). The study found that, in 1998, pharmaceutical companies spent $8.3 billion promoting their products in the United States, of which approximately $1.3 billion was spent on DTC advertising and $7.0 billion on advertising and detailing (visits) to health care professionals.

> Fueling the increase in prescription drug utilization is the explosion of direct-to-consumer (DTC) advertising by the pharmaceutical companies.

Other nonprice factors explaining the growth in total drug expenditures include demographic changes (a growing elderly population, changing chronic disease prevalence patterns); the growth in third-party drug coverage, which tends to increase demand; record sales of new products; new product formulations; changing mix of products used; patient noncompliance; and inappropriate prescribing.

Prescription Drug Pricing: Multiple Markets, Multiple Prices

Pricing alone does not account for the total growth in drug expenditures. But it does play a role, especially for newer products. As external market forces change, companies' internal pricing strategies also change.

Defining and comparing pharmaceutical prices is complicated and not always consistent—many terms are used to refer to prices, and many methodologies are employed to derive them. Among the variety of factors considered are the relative commercial success of the agent; the prices, product features, and past actions of the competition; specific patient characteristics; the economic and social value of the therapy; the decision-making criteria of prescribers and those who influence that decision; company needs in terms of market position, revenue, and other considerations; the current and anticipated insurance reimbursement environment; company abilities, including available budgets and willingness to support the product; and the type of manufacturer supplying the drug (Kolassa, 1997).

Three basic pricing strategies designed to maximize competitive edge are:

- *Premium:* The product, anticipating little direct competition, is priced above prevailing levels to maximize profits. Prilosec®, the first proton pump inhibitor, was priced in this manner.
- *Parity:* The product is viewed as only incrementally different from current competitors and its price is set roughly equivalent to its competitors' prices. The nonsedating antihistamine Claritin® and

the ACE inhibitor Accupril® were priced at parity to the market leaders at the time they launched. This strategy is often accompanied by tactical discounts and rebates.

- *Penetration:* A product is viewed as equal to, or slightly inferior to, current or anticipated offerings and is priced below prevailing levels in hopes of gaining market share with its low price or making it harder for anticipated future competitors to enter the market. Generics generally employ this strategy (Kolassa, 1997).

Manufacturers choose a pricing method depending on internal strategies, external forces, distribution channels, and specific purchasers. The price a manufacturer sets always changes as the product makes its way through the distribution chain and onto the negotiating table. It is not unusual for one specific product to be priced differently in different markets, thereby creating an array of prices for the same product. For example, people with prescription drug insurance will almost always pay less, because volume discounts have been negotiated on their behalf. Similarly, different government programs negotiate a variety of prices based on various legislative and regulatory requirements.

International Comparisons

Over the years, analysts have made many cross-national drug pricing comparisons. But conclusions must be drawn carefully. Because markets, demographics, and values vary, currency values fluctuate, and medical practices and economic circumstances also vary, it is almost impossible to substitute one country's pricing methods for another's. Nevertheless, for many reasons, price differentials between products purchased in the United States and other countries are often substantial, although generics are generally cheaper in the United States. Because the United States is one of the few countries without government price controls for prescription drugs, many global pharmaceutical companies are building U.S. research facilities to take advantage of a more favorable economic environment.

Cost-Control Tools

Prescription drug benefits, once viewed as a relatively small expenditure by employers and purchasers, have grown and now come under tighter cost control. While the clinical benefits of many of these new products are significant, their high prices sometimes place a heavy burden on payers and patients. In addition to the more traditional cost-control methods—formularies (a limited drug menu), generic substitution, prior authorization, beneficiary cost-sharing (i.e., the recent move by most third-party plans to triple-tiered co-pays), prescribing and dispensing limits, drug utilization review, disease management, and the use of mail service pharmacies for maintenance drugs—additional cost control tools are being utilized, as described below.

Pharmacy Benefit Managers. By acting as intermediaries between pharmaceutical manufacturers and third-party payers (that is, employers, managed care organizations, labor unions, and state-funded pharmaceutical assistance programs for the elderly), pharmacy benefit managers (PBMs) administer prescription drug benefits. In addition to offering their core services—claims processing, record keeping, and reporting programs—PBMs offer customers a wide range of services, including drug utilization review, disease management, consultative services, and Internet fulfillment. PBMs also assist clients with establishing their benefit structure. Options for plan design include developing and maintaining a network of pharmacy providers, providing prescriptions by mail, and developing and maintaining a drug formulary. In an effort to save plan sponsors money, PBMs negotiate with pharmaceutical manufacturers for rebates on products selected for the formulary (Strongin, 1999).

Negotiated Discounts. Negotiating discounts for pharmaceuticals is a common practice. PBMs and managed care plans, for example, negotiate discounts in exchange for the ability to increase market share, while some federal government agencies (for example, the Veterans Health Administration, the Public Health Service, and the Indian Health Service) mandate discounts.

Drug Interchange Programs. The use of various drug interchange programs, such as generic substitution, therapeutic substitution (which requires pharmacists to give patients chemically different, less-costly drugs that may accomplish the same objective as the ones their doctors prescribe), and step therapy (which requires doctors to prescribe lower-cost drugs whenever possible. If they prove ineffective, physicians can prescribe more expensive medications)—has sparked a good deal of controversy. At issue is the question of whether these programs compromise patients' access to necessary therapies.

Other Initiatives—Reimportation. One of the more controversial cost-control tools used by individuals, states, and other purchasers is the importation and reimportation of pharmaceutical products. Proponents of this approach are urging the federal government to find a way to bring cheaper drugs safely into the country, while opponents say the practice is potentially dangerous and will ultimately erode the nation's drug development pipeline.

Private and Public Prescription Drug Markets

What is the effect of these cost-control measures on the overall cost and quality of health care? Americans spent over $188 billion on prescription drugs in 2004, slightly more than 10% of the country's entire health care bill. Annual growth in prescription drug spending, which had been at the 10% to 15% level since 2000, declined to 8.2% between 2003 and 2004 (U.S. Government Accountability Office [GAO], 2006).

In 2005, drug companies spent less on direct-to-consumer advertising ($4.2 billion) than on promotion to physicians ($7.2 billion) or on R&D ($31.4 billion) (U.S. GAO, 2006). DTC has many detractors, and the GAO concluded that it increases prescription drug spending and utilization and that it can have both positive and negative effects on consumers.

More than three in five Americans fill at least one prescription annually, and more than half of those older than 75 fill more than 15 prescriptions (including refills) annually. The pharmaceutical market can be broken down into two broad categories: private markets and government programs. The private marketplace includes retail (such as traditional drugstore chains, mass merchandisers, independent pharmacies, supermarket pharmacies, and mail order pharmacies), wholesale, hospital, managed care organizations, and providers (such as clinics, long-term care facilities, including nursing homes, outpatient facilities and physician offices), and the Internet. The federal government spends billions of dollars each year providing pharmaceutical products to beneficiaries through its Federal Employees Health Benefits Program, Department of Veterans Affairs (VA), Medicaid, and various public health programs. Until 2003, however, the Medicare program was noticeably absent from this list.

Medicare Prescription Drug, Improvement, and Modernization Act of 2003

On December 8, 2003, President George W. Bush signed landmark legislation that created a voluntary Part D drug benefit for Medicare beneficiaries that began in January 2006 (described in chapters 3 and 5). To take advantage of the existing competitive market in health care, the new Medicare drug benefit is being delivered through a variety of private risk-bearing entities under contract with the U.S. Department of Health and Human Services. Drug benefits are provided through stand-alone prescription drug plans or comprehensive plans run by Medicare managed care programs.

Results from the first year of implementation (2006) showed significant competition between plans and overall satisfaction among the 22.5 million Medicare beneficiaries who have enrolled. (Nearly 16 million Medicare beneficiaries have some other form of creditable drug coverage, such as through employer-based retiree plans or the Veterans Administration.) As of 2007, most plan offerings deviated from the standard benefit design, offered benefits without an up-front deductible, and required co-payments. Most plans retained the legislation's coverage gap (the so-called donut hole), in which beneficiaries fall if they incur annual costs for drugs above a certain amount. In that "hole," they can be responsible for 100% of their prescription costs until they have paid $3,850 out of pocket (in 2007) for drugs on their plan's formulary. Estimates vary, but in 2007, approximately four million beneficiaries are expected to be affected.

Implementation of the Medicare prescription drug benefit had a mixed impact on the pharmaceutical industry. Although the introduction of insurance coverage increased access for the roughly 10 million beneficiaries who did not otherwise have coverage, sales increases were highly dependent on the individual manufacturer's product portfolios. Those with drugs heavily utilized by seniors saw sales increases; others saw only marginal impact. At the same time, Medicare Part D made the federal government the largest customer for pharmaceutical manufacturers and brought with it a significant increase in government regulation, including a movement toward price transparency. Medicare Part D drug pricing will be a major political issue for the newly elected Democratic majority in Congress.

The VA's Federal Supply Schedule

In 1999, federal purchasers using the federal supply schedule (FSS) administered by the Department of Veterans Affairs (VA) spent more than $1.5 billion on prescription drugs. The VA negotiates FSS contracts with individual manufacturers according to a set statutory and regulation framework. The Veterans Health Care Act of 1992 established a mandatory federal ceiling price (beyond those of the FSS) on a manufacturer's sales of "innovator" medicines. The FSS generally limits annual increases in any pharmaceutical price over the life of a contract (typically 5 years). For noninnovator, multiple-source drugs, price is negotiated and is never higher than that paid by other customers.

Medicaid Rebates

The Omnibus Budget Reconciliation Act of 1990 (OBRA) established the Medicaid rebate program. In exchange for having their products reimbursed (that is, on Medicaid's formulary), pharmaceutical manufacturers rebate part of the price to the states. Additionally, a penalty is imposed when drug prices exceed the rate of inflation. OBRA 93 and the Deficit Reduction Act changed the pricing schedule of single-source and innovator multiple-source drugs approved by the FDA.

Patient Assistance Programs

To address public concerns about access to needed medications, U.S. pharmaceutical manufacturers offer patients free drug programs that are primarily coordinated through their physicians' offices. In 2004, over 22 million prescriptions were filled through patient assistance programs. Critics maintain that these efforts are inadequate to meet the needs of the more than 45 million uninsured Americans.

Biologic Products

The biotech drug and vaccine industry continues to expand. New indications approved by the FDA increased from 7 in 1994 to 40 in 2004. In 2006, there were more than 300 biotech drug products and vaccines in clinical trials, targeting more than 200 diseases, including various cancers, Alzheimer's disease, heart disease, diabetes, multiple sclerosis, AIDS, and arthritis.

Biologics, in contrast to drugs that are chemically synthesized, are derived from living sources (such as humans, animals, and micro-organisms). Most biologics are complex mixtures that are not easily identified or characterized, and many biologics are manufactured using biotechnology. Biological products often represent the cutting-edge of biomedical research and, in time, may offer the most effective means to treat a variety of medical illnesses and conditions that at present have no other treatments available.

Medical Devices:
Brief Overview

The medical device industry operates much like the pharmaceutical industry. Medical devices are used in many of the same settings, by the same kinds of practitioners, undergo FDA premarket regulation, and—like drugs—seem to be in a constant state of innovation and evolution.

Yet medical devices are an industry unto themselves, with a unique character. Medical device–producing firms are often much smaller than pharmaceutical companies; their financing is less pre-dictable and flows in different patterns; and the products undergo a distinctive form of innovation that is highly interactive with, and dependent upon, medical practitioners.

Many complex policy issues influence medical device develop-ment and innovation, from how the Food and Drug Administration regulates medical products to how insurance companies decide whether to pay for particular technologies. But underscoring virtually all of these issues is a clear and unmistakable policy question: to what extent do medical devices improve patient health and offer value to patients, consumers, and medical providers? How well companies answer this question factors heavily into whether their products, and their companies, succeed.

Patients and consumers encounter medical devices every day—in hospitals, physician offices, outpatient clinics, and other treatment settings. Medical devices are the instruments that doctors and nurses use to diagnose or treat a medical condition or injury. Devices can range from relatively simple products—such as surgical gloves, tongue depressors, eyeglasses, or hearing aids—to highly sophisticated treatment technologies—such as cardiac defibrillators, fiber optic surgical instruments, or artificial joints—as well as diagnostic products like CT scanners, blood testing equipment, or ultrasound machines. All products in the industry—as well as the device and diagnostic industry itself—are generally referred to as *medical technology*.[1]

SIZE OF THE DEVICE MARKET

Developing and marketing medical technology is a financially robust industry. Industry sources predicted that the U.S. medical device market would reach $86 billion by the end of 2006 (close to $220 billion worldwide) and grow an additional 10% in 2007 (PharmaMedDevice, 2007). The median net income, or profit margin, from 1998 to 2002 was 18% for device companies and 14% for supply firms—well above the average in U.S. industry as a whole.

> Industry sources predicted that the U.S. medical device market would reach $86 billion by the end of 2006 (close to $220 billion worldwide) and grow an additional 10% in 2007.

Many device companies are quite small. Of the 6,000 firms in the industry, some 5,000 have fewer than 50 employees and are responsible for 10% of overall industry sales (Lewin Group, 2000). In contrast, many of the large firms are multinational corporations, some with more than 100,000 employees. In fact, the top 2% of large companies generate almost half of sales in the industry. Device markets are also generally much smaller than those of the pharmaceutical industry. While an individual pharmaceutical product could easily generate annual revenues topping $1 billion, no device product achieves revenues on that scale.

INTENSIVE COMMITMENT TO RESEARCH AND DEVELOPMENT

Much of the device industry's success can be attributed to the rapid pace of innovation, reflected, in part, by its strong commitment to research and development. R&D spending as a percentage of medical

---

[1] This term is also used frequently to encompass all medical interventions, including devices, pharmaceuticals, and medical procedures. In this chapter, however, *medical technology* refers only to medical devices and diagnostic products.

device industry sales increased from 5.4% in 1990 to 11.4% in 2002. That brings the industry's R&D investment in line with the percentage invested by the pharmaceutical industry—and well above that of most other sectors (AdvaMed, 2004).

The most R&D intensive companies produce laboratory tests and related diagnostic products, followed by firms making surgical and medical instruments. Another R&D standout is the small company sector generally. Companies with sales under $5 million in 2002 spent 343% of sales on R&D, while those with sales between $5 million and $20 million invested 39% (AdvaMed, 2004). Although such companies might employ only a handful of workers, they are often powerhouses of innovation—taking on projects that larger companies find too risky—and are often responsible for some of the most dramatic advances, including angioplasty catheters, artificial hips, mechanical heart valves, intravenous pumps, and blood glucose monitors.

Small medical technology firms nevertheless are highly vulnerable. They must negotiate the complex regulatory and payment requirements, which takes time and money. They also depend on funding from venture capital firms, which may be available—or not—depending on many factors, not the least of which is the time required for regulatory approval and return on investment in a new product. Large companies have little trouble raising capital, relying on cash from their own operations or turning to public equity or debt offerings when necessary. Since 1994, such companies have performed well ahead of the Standard & Poor's 500 index.

Acquisitions are common in the industry, a reflection of two forces: first, the need among larger firms to expand financial clout and product breadth and, second, the need among smaller firms for the marketing and regulatory expertise of larger firms, along with their financial resources.

DIALOGUE OF INNOVATION

Another defining characteristic of the medical device industry is its unique process of innovation. Whereas the traditional model of innovation—proceeding from concept, to prototype, to production, to market adoption—certainly occurs with medical technology, the process tends to be more dynamic, interactive, and unpredictable, because a vast amount of innovation occurs *after* medical devices reach the market and are used in real-world care by clinicians.

There is a kind of "dialogue of innovation" between clinicians and manufacturers, whereby medical technologies undergo near continuous improvement and adjustments—perhaps adding a new capacity, speed, or use for another patient group—as clinician experience grows and they see new possibilities and applications. Although breakthrough innovation often occurs, innovation in medical device technology is more typically marked by incremental change. Examples include improvements in the materials, design, and fixation of artificial hips; the power source, size, and capability of cardiac pacemakers; and the decreased size and increased functionality of fiber optic endoscopes.

One of the effects of this process is short product life—sometimes a few months to a few years—making the role of patents much less important than they are for new drugs. Over time, generations of incremental change can translate into major transformation in a product line. A good example is the implantable cardiac defibrillator, which can correct life-threatening and often fatal heart arrhythmias. Originally introduced in the late 1980s, the device required open-chest surgery, general anesthesia, and a 12-day hospital stay. The mortality associated with surgery was about 4%, with hospital costs in the range of $100,000. Over the past two decades, multiple iterations have resulted in a device that is now one-sixth the size of the early versions, lasts three times as long, and treats a number of additional conditions. Open-chest procedures are no longer required, and some implants can be performed on an outpatient basis. The mortality associated with the operation is now well under 1%.

Another important aspect of device innovation is that the ultimate value of a product in improving patient care often does not become clear until the product is well along in the process of incremental change. Angioplasty was introduced in the early 1980s as a less-invasive alternative to coronary artery bypass surgery. Only after multiple generations of incremental improvements and growing physician experience did the technology become the primary method for reestablishing blood flow in blocked arteries.

THE VALUE OF MEDICAL TECHNOLOGY

Since the late 1990s, the medical device industry has accelerated its efforts to underscore the economic, not just the clinical, value of its products, by identifying and then quantifying the economic benefit from health improvements—such as allowing workers to get back to work sooner, reducing disabilities, creating new efficiencies in health care delivery, and providing lower-cost treatments. The industry also is working to identify the economic value of better health. In some areas, such as improvements in treating cardiovascular disease and low–birth weight babies, strong cases can be made that the benefits from medical technology, on average, far exceed their costs (Cutler & Huckman, 2002). In early 2004, AdvaMed cosponsored a report with other major medical groups that calculated the economic value of health improvements over the past two decades. The report found that each additional dollar spent on health care between 1980 and 2000 produced health gains valued at $2.40 and $3.00. Regarding the four major diseases studied, the report found that, in the 20-year period,

- Mortality from heart attack was cut in half.
- Stroke deaths were reduced by a third.
- Mortality from breast cancer declined 20%.
- Diabetes management led to a 25% reduction in serious complications, such as blindness, kidney failure, and stroke (MEDTAP International, 2004).

The leading trade association for the medical imaging industry, the National Electrical Manufacturers Association, introduced a Web site in 2004 that uses peer-reviewed literature to identify the economic and clinical value of imaging technologies. The Web site, www.medicalimaging.org, shows how imaging detects disease early, enables less invasive therapies, introduces efficiencies in health care delivery, and improves worker productivity. For example, the site presents evidence that medical imaging eliminates half the futile surgeries for lung cancer and that imaging-guided breast biopsies cost a third of what surgical biopsies do and take half the time.

Despite the growing availability of evidence of this type, balancing the cost, quality, and access equation for both pharmaceutical and medical device products continues to be an ongoing challenge for everyone—regulators, payers, and providers of health care, industry, and, most importantly, patients.

Conclusion

It is difficult to say whether Americans pay too much—or too little—for their prescription drugs. Industry critics maintain that prices and profits are too high and cite price discrimination (selling the same drugs for less to large purchasers), drug prices out of proportion to the cost of production, and a lack of price competition among companies as chief abuses. Members of the pharmaceutical industry and some in academia, in response, point to the industry's extremely high R&D costs and increases in quality of life from reduced mortality and morbidity. They point out that drug treatments are less expensive for a number of diseases, such as ulcers and asthma, than are surgery and hospitalization. And they suggest that, in order to measure more accurately the *value* of pharmaceutical products, decision makers should move away from "silo budgeting"—that is, analyzing prescription drug cost expenditures without accounting for total health care offsets.

The highly innovative and dynamic medical devices industry continues to generate significant innovations and clinical successes. With an aging U.S. population, demand for these products will clearly increase. R&D investments continue to be strong, along with industry revenues and earnings. Successful companies will be those that can marshal the evidence, pinpoint value, and offer cost-effective technologies.

References

Accenture. (2007). *The pursuit of high performance through research and development, understanding pharmaceutical research and development cost drivers.* Retrieved December 10, 2007, from http://www.phrma.org/files/Accenture%20R&D%20Report-2007.pdf

AdvaMed. (2004). *The medical technology industry at a glance.* Retrieved December 10, 2007, from http://www.advamed.org/NR/rdonlyres/0A261055-827C-4CC6-80B6-CC2D8FA04A33/0/ChartbookSept2004.pdf

Brandeis University/Schneider Institute for Health Policy Prescription Drug Analysis Group. (2000). *Prescription drug policy: Background paper for the Princeton Conference.*

Congressional Budget Office. (1998, July). *How increased competition from generic drugs has affected prices and returns in the pharmaceutical industry.* CBO Papers. Retrieved from http://www.cbo.gov/ftpdoc.cfm?index=655&type=0&sequence=0

Cutler, D. M., & Huckman, R. S. (2002, October). *Technological development and medical productivity: Diffusion of angioplasty in New York State.* Working Paper 9311, National Bureau of Economic Research.

Employee Benefits Research Institute. (2004, January). *Prescription drugs: Recent trends in utilization, expenditures, and coverage.* EBRI Issue Brief No. 265.

Kolassa, E. M. (1997). *Elements of pharmaceutical pricing.* United States. Pharmaceutical Products Press: Binghamton, NY.

The Lewin Group. (2000). Outlook for medical technology innovation: Will patients get the care they need? Report 1: *The state of the industry.* Prepared for the Advanced Medical Technology Association.

MEDTAP International. (2004). *The value of investment in health care: Better care, better lives.* Bethesda, MD. Retrieved from http://www.medtap.com/Products/HP_FullReport.pdf

National Institute for Health Care Management. (1999). *Factors affecting the growth of prescription drug expenditures.* Washington, DC: Author.

PharmaMedDevice. (2007). http://www.pharmameddevice.com

Serafini, M. W. (2000, February 19). No easy prescription on no-name drugs. *National Journal,* 548.

Strongin, R. (1999, October 27). *The ABCs of PBMs.* National Health Policy Forum Issue Brief No. 749. Retrieved December 10, 2007, from http://www.nhpf.org/pdfs_ib/IB749_ABCsofPBMs_10-27-99.pdf

U.S. Government Accountability Office. (2006, November). Report to Congressional Requestors, "Prescription drugs: Improvements needed in FDA's oversight of direct-to-consumer advertising" (GAO-07-54).

12

Key Words

health workforce	advanced practice nurse	allied health
health professionals	nurse practitioner (NP)	full-time equivalent (FTE)
supply	physician	certification
demand	graduate medical education	licensure
need	international medical school	
registered nurse (RN)	graduate	

The Health Care Workforce

Carol S. Brewer and Thomas C. Rosenthal

Learning Objectives

- Recognize the factors that influence the supply and demand of health care workers.
- Recognize the difficulties in estimating the future demand and supply of health care workers.
- Describe the types of health care workers in the United States.
- Identify some of the major issues facing clinicians, managers, and health care policy makers about the health care workforce.
- Analyze policy options to influence the size, distribution, and training of the health care workforce.

Topical Outline

- Supply and demand factors
- Types of health care workers
- Medical practice
- Nursing practice
- Other health care workers
- Allied health professionals
- Issues
- Keeping current about the health care workforce
- Conclusion

M

any changes have occurred in the U.S. health care system over the last 10 years, with a dramatic impact on the number and types of workers needed and where and how they will practice. Health care professionals are evaluating their roles and relationships within the health care system and with other workers. Education and regulatory systems are responding and evolving as well.

Over the last 50 years, health care employment has consistently grown at a faster rate than overall employment in the U.S. economy. From 1983 through 2002, the number of people working in health care occupations increased 58% (U.S. Census Bureau [USCB], 2003), and, from 2000 to 2004, the number of people working in health care occupations increased 13.2%; total U.S. employment increased only 1.7% in the same 4-year period (USCB, 2006). Even during economic recessions, health care employment has risen. The health care workforce is large and diverse, and health services are labor intensive. This is true whether the services are provided in hospitals, nursing homes, or physicians' offices.

> Over the last 50 years, health care employment has consistently grown at a faster rate than overall employment in the U.S. economy.

Analysis of staffing patterns typical of health maintenance organizations in the 1990s led to predictions that the country would have an oversupply of various health care personnel. Failure of managed care to become dominant and the rising demand for health care created by an aging population have reversed these projections. Modern health care programs focusing on technical and specialized health interventions, such as cardiovascular treatment, also have created a need for additional health care personnel, at least in some categories.

In 2004, the 13.8 million people in the health occupations were 9.9% of the total U.S. workforce—a 1% increase over 2000. This number does not include the many affiliated workers in information technology, secretarial, janitorial, and other occupations who work in health care settings. The U.S. Bureau of Labor Statistics (BLS) projects that health care employment will rise more than 33.5% by 2014. The health occupations account for more than half of the projected top 20 fastest-growing occupations. The BLS also predicts that, between 2004 and 2014, more new jobs (1.9 million, or 21.1% of all new jobs) will be created in the health services sector than in any other U.S. industry.

Health care professionals and other health care workers are most often employed in hospitals (41%), nursing homes (21%), and physician offices (16%) (see Table 12.1). Although hospitals employ the largest number of patients, they are one of the smallest types of health care employers—only 1.9% of all employers. The largest type of health care employer is physician offices.

Many health personnel work in non–health care settings—for example, physicians teach in medical schools, pharmacists work for drug manufacturers, and nurses work in schools. Counting members of the health workforce can be difficult, and different government agencies count them in different ways. Some count workers by the number of people who work in a particular setting or occupation (e.g., state licensing boards count the number of licensed practitioners); some take into consideration how much they work (full-time or part-time, with two part-time workers making one full-time equivalent, or FTE, worker); and some, notably the U.S. Department of Labor, by the number of paychecks or jobs. Thus, if an employer substitutes part-time workers for full-time workers, Department of Labor data might show an increase in the number of jobs, even though the FTEs remained the same. Nor is the number of licenses a foolproof method of estimating the number of workers,

Table 12.1	Percent Distribution of Wage and Salary Employment and Establishments in Health Services, 2004	
Establishment Type	**Percentage of Establishments**	**Percentage of Employment**
Hospitals	1.9	41.3
Nursing and residential care facilities	11.6	21.3
Physician offices	37.0	15.5
Dental offices	21.0	5.7
Home health care services	3.0	5.8
Offices of other health practitioners	18.7	4.0
Outpatient care centers	3.2	3.4
Other ambulatory health care services	1.5	1.5
Medical and diagnostic laboratories	2.1	1.4

Note. From Bulletin 2601, U.S. Department of Labor, Bureau of Labor Statistics. (2007). *The 2006–2007 career guide to industries.* Retrieved from http://www.bls.gov/oco/cg/print/cgs035.htm

because many inactive professionals maintain their licenses, and many are licensed in several states.

Supply and Demand Factors

Five factors influence supply and demand in the health care workforce: demographics, education, the health care delivery system, the economic system, and context. The contextual factors—U.S. culture, government, and political system—help determine the range of options within which we can find solutions to workforce issues. These five factors interact in complex ways to produce the aggregate supply and demand for health care workers. If they are in balance, we have *market equilibrium*—that is, there are enough workers wanting the jobs employers have, at the wages they are offering (Table 12.2).

Historically, we have seen disequilibrium in one or more health workforce markets. Policy makers tend to worry most about workforce shortages, but sometimes the country has had too many of a particular group of workers. Because doctors and nurses are the largest of the health professions and the best organized politically, they are often the focus of labor supply policy. An economic factor that has strongly influenced workforce policy in recent decades is the evolution in managed care from 1993 to 2000. Managed care had many effects discussed elsewhere in this text, and one of them was to flatten income growth for nurses and physicians. Physicians still are among the nation's highest paid professionals, but the average net income from the practice of medicine declined an inflation-adjusted 7% from 1995 to 2003, and primary care physician income declined 10%, as a result of additional reimbursement changes (Tu & Ginsberg, 2006).

A 1995 Pew Health Professions Commission report pointed out that managed care organizations in California used fewer physicians and nurses than did providers elsewhere. It predicted that managed care would cause both professions to be oversupplied and recommended reducing the number of educational programs. The study was repeated in 2004 with similar findings—the physician to population ratio was 22% to 37% lower in three very large managed care organizations than in the rest of the country (Weiner, 2004). However, there are a number of problems in applying the findings of this analysis to the overall health care workforce. Except for Medicaid and Medicare health maintenance organizations (HMOs), HMOs care for a population that has at least one employed family member. HMO families tend to be younger and healthier than the population as a whole. HMO enrollees therefore require fewer health services than older and

 **Table 12.2**   Health Workers in Selected Occupations per 100,000 U.S. Population, 2004

Occupation	Number per 100,000 Population	Occupation	Number per 100,000 Population
Registered nurses	802.0	Nurse practitioners	42.04
Licensed practical nurses	239.3	Physician assistants	7.88
		Dental hygienists	53.9
Dentists	59.4	Podiatrists	6.13
Chiropractors	29.14	Opticians	22.32
Optometrists	7.83	Pharmacy technicians	105.68
Pharmacists	77.02	Social workers	158.27
Psychologists	33.52	Occupational therapists	29.53
Physical therapists	49.45	Respiratory therapists	32.10
Speech-language pathologists and audiologists	34.8	Medical and clinical laboratory technologists and technicians	101.32
Emergency medical technicians and paramedics	65.06	Dietitians and nutritionists	16.28
Medical records and health information technicians	53.43	Radiologic technologists	62.01
Nuclear medicine technologists	5.92	Nursing aides, orderlies, and attendants	475.05
Home health aides	212.64		

Note. From The New York Center for Health Workforce Studies. (2006). *The United States health workforce profile.* Rensselaer, NY: Author. Retrieved from http://chws.albany.edu

disabled citizens. Further analysis, taking into account the aging of the baby boom generation and the increased severity of hospitalized patients' illnesses—and the many new and advanced intensive services available to treat them—has resulted in projections of an impending shortage of physicians, nurses, rehabilitation and long-term care workers, hospital pharmacists, and others (Association of American Medical Colleges [AAMC], 2007).

The current alarm regarding potential workforce shortfalls is driven by projected increases in demand for services, exacerbated by the aging of the workforce. Nursing is a prime example. The average age of registered nurses (RNs) was 46.8 years in 2004 and continues to rise. Only 16.6% of nurses were under age 35 (Spratley, Johnson, Sochalski, Fritz, & Spencer, 2004). Already, according to an American Hospital Association (2006) report, 118,000 RNs are needed to fill vacant positions nationwide. In 2000, the nursing shortage was estimated at 6% nationally, but, by 2020, it is expected to grow to 29% unless demand decreases or supply can be greatly increased. Although the absolute number of U.S. nurses is expected to grow until 2011, after that, the number of nurses who are retiring will exceed the number entering the profession (U.S. Department of Health and Human Services, 2002). However, a study using 2005 data found that, due to increased numbers of people entering nursing at older ages—in their late 20s and early 30s—the shortage may be moderated, although it will not be eliminated (Auerbach, Buerhaus, & Staiger, 2007).

The average age of workers in many other health professions tends to be older, too, in part because of lengthy training and in part because many individuals enter the health professions (excluding medicine) mid-career. At the same time, not enough younger people are entering health professions for various reasons. Women—the mainstay of many health occupations—have many more career options today. Prospective students find characteristics of the health care delivery system, such as 24-hour and holiday staffing, unappealing; and shortages of health profession faculty at colleges limit the number of students in educational programs.

MEASURING SUPPLY

If students make health career choices in response to current shortages, their decisions are not reflected in the workforce supply until they graduate several years later—a classic lagging indicator.

Two fairly sensitive indicators of changes in the supply of health care workers are admission and enrollment figures for educational programs. Data supplied by accrediting organizations may vary across organizations. For example, in nursing, the American Association of Colleges of Nursing (AACN) and the National League for Nursing keep statistics that differ somewhat. Also, if students make health career choices in response to current events (shortages), their decisions are not reflected in the workforce supply until they graduate 2 to 8 years later (depending on the discipline)—a classic lagging indicator.

Workforce productivity also affects supply. Younger and female health professionals tend to work fewer hours and select work settings that allow more flexibility in scheduling than do older or male professionals. For example, more women are becoming pharmacists (and working fewer hours), and more men are becoming nurses (and working longer hours). Male nurses are 5.7% of the RN workforce and tend to be younger (Spratley et al., 2004). More male than female nurses are employed (88% versus 81%) (Spratley, Johnson, Sochalski, Fritz, & Spencer, 2001). The proportion of women physicians increased from 10% in 1975 to 27.2% in 2005 (AAMC, 2006b), and the proportion will continue to increase since women made up nearly 50% of medical school classes in 2005. Women physicians tend to work in salaried positions with predictable work hours, are more likely to choose non-surgical specialties and retire earlier, and are less likely to work in rural areas.

Periodically, certain medical specialties, such as primary care physicians, psychiatrists, or specific subspecialists, are deemed to be in short supply. However, assessing whether the nation has a sufficient number of particular types of physicians—or other health care professionals, for that matter—depends on how health care is organized and financed. In 1975, a third of all U.S. physicians were in primary care specialties (internal medicine, family practice, pediatrics, and general practice). In 2003, 40.8% were in primary care (U.S. Bureau of Labor Statistics, 2006–2007), but a decline can be predicted, because there was a 41% drop in family medicine residents from 1999 to 2005 (Brotherton, Rockey, & Etzel, 2005). This decline is attributed to decreasing reimbursement for primary care. The U.S. primary care physician–population ratio is lower than that of other countries, such as Canada, Great Britain, and Germany, where more than half of physicians are in primary care specialties. These countries have established a concept of medical homes, where the patient is expected to identify with and maintain a continuity relationship with a primary provider. Citizens visit their primary care physicians more often, knowing that they will be referred for specialty care if needed. As a result, fewer specialized procedures are performed (Lasser, Himmelstein, & Woolhandler, 2006). Implementing similar patterns would alter the balance of need and services in U.S. health care.

PHYSICIAN SUPPLY

The supply of physicians in the United States has increased steadily since the 1950s but still lags behind many developed countries. The physician–population ratio increased from 169 nonfederal physicians per 100,000 people in 1975 to 288 per 100,000 in 2002—a 70% increase (Pasko & Smart, 2003). In 2004, according to the Organisation for Economic Co-operation and Development (2006), the United States was tied with Denmark in 16th place globally, with 2.4 doctors per 1,000 people. Countries that rank higher have up to 4.9 physicians per 1,000. About one in four U.S. physicians graduated from a medical school in a foreign country (now called an international medical graduate) (AAMC, 2006a).

One of the more hotly debated recent health workforce policy issues has been physician workforce planning. At the core of the debate is how to encourage the production of a physician workforce that can best meet the health care needs of the nation. The debate has been fueled by a lack of agreement as to whether the current and projected supply is adequate to meet the nation's needs as well as whether the marketplace, without specific government interventions, will produce the appropriate number, mix, and distribution of physicians. The federal Council on Graduate Medical Education (COGME), by statute, advises the Department of Health and Human Services and Congress on physician workforce issues. Even COGME has produced greatly varying predictions of the physician workforce over the past two decades.

Factors that will increase the demand for physicians are the evolution of managed care to an approach with fewer restrictions and greater access, the aging of the baby boom generation, the general growth in the nation's population, expansion of the economy, and the increase in women physicians (who, because of family demands, typically work fewer hours). Demand will also increase if insurance coverage is extended to some of the 46 million people in the United States who are currently uninsured. Factors that could reduce demand are the growing supply of physician extenders and some new technologies that may make physicians' work more efficient—although most new medical technologies actually increase demand.

Physicians and other practitioners, who control the ordering of tests, procedures, referrals, and treatments, generate demand for many other services and therefore have an enormous impact on health care costs and demand. Specialists order more tests and procedures per patient than primary care physicians. Much of this is to be expected, since specialists should be seeing cases that are difficult to diagnose or that require specific treatments, surgeries, or interventions. For example, in the United States, 89% of physician visits by patients with chronic lung disease are to a primary care physician (family physician, general internist, or pediatrician); similarly, 94% of asthma visits and 89% of visits for anxiety or depression are made to primary care physicians (Green, Lanier, & Yawn, 2001). By contrast, the few patients who are seen by specialists are usually diagnostically or therapeutically more complicated. In countries with health care systems that are more reliant on primary care than the United States, citizens have more physician visits but fewer tests and procedures than do Americans. Virtually all the difference across countries in health care expenditures can be explained by practice patterns in primary versus specialty care (Rosenthal, Fullerton, Andreassen, & Veneri, 1997).

In the United States, specialists are paid nearly twice as much as primary care physicians. Medical students are predictably inclined to select specialties that are more highly paid. High payments also encourage specialists to see patients more often. As a result, more than 20% of the care provided by doctors in some overpopulated specialties could be provided by lower-cost primary care physicians (Starfield & Lemke, 2005). In England and Canada, specialists generally make 20% to 30% more than do primary care physicians, roughly half of all residencies are in primary care, and competition for primary care residency positions is high.

When seeking primary care, patients expect convenient, reliable, effective treatment by someone they trust who will be empathetic and pay attention to their physical and environmental needs. They are less concerned about continuity of care than about being shepherded smoothly to sources of specialty care. In 2006, 86% of Americans were able to identify a usual place to go for medical care, a "medical home" (U.S. Department of Health & Human Services, National Center for Health Statistics, 2007).

The U.S. physician workforce remains less diverse than that of the population as a whole. Historically, about 3% of all U.S. bachelor degree graduates apply to U.S. medical schools, 55% of whom were biology majors. In 1994, 83% of African American biology majors from America's top universities applied to medical school. Although the number of African American biology majors graduating from universities increased 96% from 1994 to 2004, the percent applying to medical school decreased to 44% in 2004. As a result, the absolute number of African Americans applying to medical school remained essentially the same: 746 versus 775. Hispanic Americans showed a slight decrease in medical school applicants from 1994 to 2004. Over the same decade, among Whites, the proportion of biology majors applying to medical school dropped from 41% to 27% (Garrison, 2006). Increased opportunities in other fields, academic competition, and increased dissatisfaction of physicians with their career choice have dampened interest in medical school for men in all groups, but not for women.

It is unclear how increased use of the Internet and e-mail communication will impact demand for physician services. A 2005 survey of Florida primary care physicians indicated that 16% had used e-mail to communicate with patients (Brooks & Anderson, 2005). A survey of 200 patients from two family physician practices revealed that 68% had access to e-mail, and 80% of those would feel comfortable communicating health issues that way. One barrier is that only 42% of these patients were willing to pay for e-mail consultations. Surprisingly, 65% of patients with e-mail addresses indicated that these had changed less often than either their street address or their phone number. As expected, availability of the Internet was affected by socioeconomic factors, with poorer patients having less access (Virji et al., 2006).

All evidence suggests that the United States needs more physicians. Procedural specialties, such as dermatology, radiology, and gastroenterology will experience continued demand, as will primary care and psychiatry. How the numbers will balance will greatly depend on the continued evolution of the U.S. health care system.

In addition, primary care practice is changing. Not only has the number of primary care tasks grown exponentially, but physician performance is being measured, monitored, and reimbursed according to the ability to perform these tasks reliably and consistently. One research team has published several provocative studies assessing the impact of the proliferation of practice guidelines; in part, this research was done in response to criticisms that primary physicians are failing to follow various evidence-based practices. The researchers based their studies on a hypothetical 2,500-patient panel, matched to the U.S. population for age, gender, and prevalence of 10 common chronic diseases. (Note that rural practices are usually much larger than 2,500.) Given this population, the researchers concluded that it would require 3.5 hours each working day to care for the chronic disease patients whose conditions were well controlled and 10.6 hours to care for the estimated number with uncontrolled disease. To deliver all recommended preventive services to the practice's patients would require an *additional* 7.4 hours per day (Ostbye et al., 2005; Yarnall et al., 2003). This does not take into account short-term illnesses such as colds and flu, minor injuries, and the myriad other medical complaints with which primary care practitioners are presented daily.

Excessive demands contribute to long waiting times and a growing proportion of patients reporting that they cannot schedule appointments on a timely basis. As a result, emergency departments are overflowing with patients who do not have access to primary care. Many patients with diabetes, hypertension, and other chronic conditions may not receive adequate clinical care, partly because half of all patients leave their office visits without having understood what the physician said in a hurried visit (Roter & Hall, 1989).

These factors add up to an unsurprising result: fewer U.S. medical students are choosing careers in primary care (American College of Physicians, 2006). Between 1997 and 2005, the number of U.S. graduates entering family practice residencies dropped by half. Because family physicians are the only specialty to distribute geographically in ratios identical to the population, this trend further aggravates geographic disparities. Fixing primary care requires improved models of primary care practice (microsystem improvement) and reform of the larger health care system

> Fixing primary care requires improved models of primary care practice (microsystem improvement) and reform of the larger health care system (macrosystem reform).

(macrosystem reform). Fortunately, microsystem improvement is taking place. Many primary care practices have instituted policies to reduce appointment delays and implement chronic care management models effecting improvements in process and outcomes. Unfortunately, with the exception of a recent increase in relative value unit assignments by Medicare, which will increase primary care reimbursement, little activity is evident at the macrosystem level, and few payers adequately reimburse primary care services.

NURSING SUPPLY

The major source of data about the registered nurse workforce is the Health Resources and Services Administration's (HRSA) quadrennial National Sample Survey of Registered Nurses. The most recent survey (2004) reports that the United States had 2.9 million registered nurses, about 2.4 million (83%) of whom were employed in nursing, and 58% of whom worked full-time. The National Council of State Boards of Nursing (NCSBN) reported a somewhat larger total—about 3.1 million licensed RNs, a number that includes duplicate licenses.

Estimates from the 2004 national survey show wide variation across states in the ratio of employed RNs to the general population. California (the state with the lowest ratio) had 590 RNs per 100,000 population, whereas New Hampshire (the state with the highest ratio) had 1,283 per 100,000, and the completely urban District of Columbia had 2,093 per 100,000. The national average was 825 per 100,000. In 2006, the United States ranked ninth worldwide; other developed countries have up to 1,490 nurses per 100,000 (OECD, 2006).

The homogeneity of the nursing workforce has been a concern for the nursing field, other health professions, and the government for many years. In 2004, about a third of all Americans were of minority race or ethnicity, and this percentage is expected to continue to increase. However, only about 12% of RNs were minorities, and 88% were White, non-Hispanic. Nationally, Asians constitute a disproportionately large share of the nursing workforce, but the Asian component does not necessarily reflect the nationalities of the Asian population in local communities. This issue is important not because we should expect—or desire—an exact nurse-to-patient ethnicity match, but because it indicates that a large pool of potential nurses remains relatively untapped, and because it reflects on the overall cultural competency of our health care institutions. The percentage of men, another minority group in nursing, was 5.7% in 2004, a slight increase from previous years.

Cyclical shortages and surpluses of registered nurses occurred during the 20th century. This reflects a number of factors, including the lag in response of prospective students and the educational system to changes in health care demand. Severe nursing shortages in the late 1980s prompted a significant rise in average salaries for registered nurses, which in turn led to an increase in the number of nursing students in the early 1990s. At the same time, reacting to higher RN salaries and shortages, as well as pressure to reduce costs from managed care, health facilities increasingly sought ways to substitute lower-cost personnel for RNs (Brewer & Kovner, 2001). Throughout the late 1990s, enrollment in nursing education programs fell.

In 1998, analysts observed the first signs of another nursing shortage, and the projected shortfall is substantial—more than a million nurses by 2020. This shortage is deemed more serious, more long-lasting, and more difficult to remediate than those of the past, even though wages and enrollments are rising. A major reason is the shortage of nursing faculty: AACN's 2006–2007 report on nursing enrollments found that 30,709 qualified nursing applicants were turned away from baccalaureate programs in nursing in 2007. According to the schools, the top reason for not accepting all qualified students into these programs continues to be insufficient faculty (71%), as well as insufficient clinical teaching sites, classroom space, clinical preceptors, and budgets (Rosseter, 2006).

The stress, hours, and physical demands of patient care, particularly in hospitals and nursing homes, may lead some nurses to leave health facilities, particularly hospitals, where the shortage is felt most keenly (American Hospital Association, 2006; Brewer, Feeley, & Servoss, 2003). With a full economy and increased job opportunities on the business side of health care, nurses can find good jobs outside of direct patient care.

GEOGRAPHIC DISTRIBUTION OF HEALTH PROFESSIONALS

Another major issue for the health care workforce is its uneven distribution, with persistent shortfalls in rural and urban underserved areas. Rural areas typically do not have large employers offering insurance benefits, and the reimbursement rates of Medicaid and Medicare may be too low to attract doctors, dentists, and nurses to these areas.

The distribution of the workforce results from the complex interplay of supply and demand factors discussed previously. Scholarships are available for primary care practitioners (physicians, nurses, and physician assistants) who agree to work for a time in underserved areas, and loan repayment programs are available for physicians as well as various mental health practitioners, social workers, and dental hygienists. But many graduates want to practice near where they were educated, typically in urban areas, rather than move to rural or underserved locales. Counties and regions designated as federal medically underserved areas and health professions shortage areas (HPSAs) become eligible or receive preference for more than 30 federal programs. The Department of Health and Human Services establishes these designations for rural or urban areas, population groups, or medical facilities (AAMC, 2007). Approximately 30 million people live in these shortage areas.

Approximately 20% of Americans live in rural communities, but only 11% of physicians practice there. Between 2000 and 2005, the number of U.S. FTE physicians and residents in clinical practice grew 7%; 38% of these physicians worked in primary care specialties (Table 12.3). Nonmetropolitan counties with large towns (10,000 to 25,000) and attractive economies have seen the biggest increase in physicians per 100,000 (U.S. DHHS, Health Resources and Services Administration, 2007). In a recent survey of rural hospital CEOs in the Midwest, 86% reported a physician shortage in their communities; 64% indicated a shortage of family physicians. Other heavily recruited specialties included obstetrics-gynecology, general surgery, orthopedic surgery, general internal medicine, cardiology, and psychiatry. In addition, other health professionals were in short supply and being recruited: registered nurses (91%), pharmacists (64%), and nursing aides (46%)

Table 12.3	Characteristics of the U.S. Physician Supply		
Physician Characteristics	**Data Year**	**Number of Physicians**	**Percentage**
Total number in clinical practice	2005	764,400	100.0
Number in primary care	2005	292,100	38.2
African American	2004	20,653	2.3[a]
Hispanic	2004	27,935	3.2[a]
Asian	2004	73,152	8.3[a]
Women	2004	235,627	26.6[a]

[a] Base is 884,974 and includes physicians not in clinical practice.
Note. Total and *primary care* are from U.S. Department of Health and Human Services, Health Resources and Services Administration. (2006). *HRSA—Physician supply and demand: Projections to 2020.* Retrieved from http://bhpr.hrsa.gov/healthworkforce/reports/physiciansupplydemand/default.htm. *Minorities* are from Minority Affairs Consortium, American Medical Association. (2006). Chicago. Retrieved from http://www.ama-assn.org/ama/pub/category/12930.html. *Women* are from American Medical Association. (2006). Chicago. Retrieved from http://www.ama-assn.org/ama/pub/category/print/12928.html

(Glasser, Peters, & MacDowell, 2006). Despite these shortages, most rural residents rely on urban areas for limited amounts of care. On average, they travel only a few minutes more for primary care but frequently must travel three times further for specialty care or when undergoing specific procedures (Chan, Hart, & Goodman, 2006).

One way to improve the distribution of physicians across the geographic continuum would be to prepare rural students better for competing in the medical school application process. Of those practicing in a rural site, 32% graduated from a rural high school, as compared with 11% of practitioners in nonrural communities. Similarly, physicians who graduate from high schools in a census tract with a higher proportion of minorities tend to practice in higher-minority communities (Hughes et al., 2005). Including some residency training experiences in rural communities also increases the likelihood a physician will practice in a rural area (Rosenthal, 2002). Another approach has been to increase the backup available to rural physicians, who are truly on call 24 hours a day, 7 days a week, 365 days a year—especially if they are the only physician in the community, they generally work longer hours and see more patients than their urban counterparts.

This lack of interest in rural practice is attributed to perceptions of lower income and slower income growth, professional isolation, and longer work hours for primary care physicians (Bodenheimer, 2006). The lower physician-to-population ratio in rural areas reflects, in part, the minimum population base needed to financially support a physician practice. Family physicians need a population base of about 3,000 in order to support a practice; by contrast, neurosurgeons need a population base of about 100,000 to generate enough cases to enable maintenance of specialty skills. The J-1 visa waiver process has encouraged more international medical graduates to settle in rural locales. However, many do not stay beyond the 2- to 3-year service requirement. Although women are more likely to choose primary care specialties, they are less likely to locate in rural communities (Larson et al., 2003).

Although generally well accepted by patients, one early study, conducted in 2000–2001, indicated that telemedicine was not cost-effective for providing medical specialist consultations for underserved communities if demand for these networks is low (de la Torre, Hernandez-Rodriguez, & Garcia, 2004). Internationally, all countries with significant rural populations struggle to assure access for rural communities. In the United States, it would take 3,500 additional physicians to achieve a ratio of 1:3,000 in health professions shortage areas (Larson et al., 2003). The Association of American Medical Colleges (2007) has recommended an increase of 1,500 physicians in the National Health Service Corps program to address this need.

Once thought to be a solution to the challenge of physician maldistribution, nurse practitioners and physician assistants have distributed themselves geographically similar to physicians (Lin, Burns, & Nochajski, 1997). About 20% of NPs and 18% of PAs practice in rural communities.

Types of Health Care Workers

Within the health care workforce are hundreds of professions, sub-specialties, and occupations with educational requirements ranging from a high school degree to doctoral and professional degrees. Details about some of these professions can be obtained from the Web sites listed at the end of this chapter.

Regulation of health professionals is a state responsibility. Each state has its own legal definition of the practice of each profession and the scope of activities in which it may engage. States can require registration, licensure, or certification, or all of these. In addition, states are responsible for approving educational programs and curricula and for maintaining information about the professions and registry lists used for research on the health care work force. States are reluctant to give up their oversight function to national governing or licensing bodies.

> Each state has its own legal definition of the practice of each health profession and the scope of activities in which it may engage.

Often a professional discipline is based on a defined scope of practice, and a particular professional is licensed to practice the full discipline. However, parts of the professional's practice may be delegated to less highly trained people—such as licensed practical nurses, radiology technicians, and dental hygienists—who may or may not be licensed. Unlicensed occupations are not subject to much regulation, although their educational programs may be accredited. If these health workers provide patient care, they generally work under the supervision of a licensed health professional.

The economic concept of *labor substitution* holds that if costs (e.g., wages per hour) increase for one profession or occupation, the demand for it decreases, and the demand for less costly substitutes increase. Licensing requirements and other government regulations can prevent employers from substituting less costly health care workers. Professional organizations generally put up a vigorous political fight to keep lower-paid professionals from competing with their members or obtaining direct insurance reimbursement for their services. Turf battles of this kind have occurred between anesthesiologists and certified registered nurse anesthetists and between dentists and dental hygienists, among others. Still, related professionals often must work together, each using the full scope of their practices in the care of their patients, in which case demand for one can create a demand for the complementary profession. Contemporary education and practice models have focused on developing these mutually supportive aspects of health care practice under the rubric of *interdisciplinary* or *collaborative care,* but strong separate traditions of education and practice have limited these efforts to only moderate success.

Medical Practice

American medicine has been undergoing a major transformation. Changes in the health care system are challenging physicians and transforming their traditional role in health care, from being the dominant, controlling force, to being one member of a team of players. The increased use of nurse practitioners, physician assistants, and other health care professionals is facilitating greater collaboration and cooperation among health care professionals. Physicians still play a central role in determining the type of care provided, admitting patients to health facilities, ordering tests, prescribing drugs and treatments, and making referrals to specialists or other providers, but now they generally share the responsibility and oversight with other professionals and managed care organizations.

Two types of physicians dominate in the United States: allopathic (MD) and osteopathic (DO). *Allopathic medicine* is "a system of medicine based on the theory that successful therapy depends on creating a condition antagonistic to or incompatible with the condition to be treated" (Slee & Slee, 2004). By contrast, *osteopathic medicine* "emphasizes a theory that the body can make its own remedies, given normal structural relationships, environmental conditions, and nutrition. It differs from allopathic primarily in its greater attention to body mechanics and manipulative methods in diagnosis and therapy" (Slee & Slee, 2004).

UNDERGRADUATE MEDICAL EDUCATION

The majority of the nation's allopathic and osteopathic medical schools are part of academic medical centers, most of which include a tertiary hospital. In the past decade, the number of allopathic schools has held steady at 125 (with 17,370 first-year enrollment in 2006), while the number of osteopathic schools grew from 17 in 1996 to 23 in 2006 (with 3,908 first-year enrollment in 2005). Medical school usually requires 4 years following baccalaureate education. The first 2 years are usually classroom instruction with introduction of patient interviewing and physical diagnosis skills. The second 2 years are primarily clinical—that is, working with patients, with close supervision. This aspect of medical training has been centered within hospitals, resulting in extensive experience in acute, highly technical care, but more and more schools are attempting to increase the time spent in outpatient settings. Only in recent years has curriculum been expanded to include cultural competencies.

After graduation, allopathic and osteopathic physicians have the same legal scope of practice in their respective states and take the same U.S. Medical Licensing Examination for basic science knowledge, clinical knowledge, and clinical skills. The final examination is taken after the first year of postgraduate work, usually while the physician is serving in a hospital residency program, and every state requires it before awarding a license to practice. Consensus on the appropriate size of the physician pipeline—that is, size of medical school enrollment and number of residency slots—does not exist.

Despite high tuition and a lengthy education period, medical education is still highly sought after, and applicants exceed available slots by more than 2 to 1, according to data from the Association of American Medical Colleges (2006c). Enrollments at allopathic schools were relatively stable from 1980 to 2005 at about 16,000 each year, but they increased 2.2% in 2007, and an AAMC survey of medical school deans predicts them to go higher over the next 5 years. Five new allopathic medical schools are on the drawing boards for opening in the next 5 years, in response to an AAMC recommendation for a 30% increase in medical school enrollment by 2015 (AAMC, 2006a).

The percentage of allopathic matriculants who are underrepresented minorities (14.7% in 2006) has increased, and the percentage for women (49.3%) held nearly constant since 2003. African American matriculants increased slightly, by 8% of a relatively small number, and Hispanic matriculants increased by 11%. Among osteopathic students in 2005–2006, 8.6% were from underrepresented minority groups, almost 16% were Asian and Pacific Islanders, and 49% were women (American Association of Colleges of Osteopathic Medicine. 2007).

The failure of U.S. medical schools to enroll underrepresented minorities consistent with their proportion of the total population has implications for equity, access, and quality of health care. Much energy has been directed at this problem, but insufficient progress has been made. Underrepresented minority physicians are more likely to practice in underserved communities, serve underserved populations, and be attuned to their patients' cultural and social norms, which can be critical in diagnosis and effective treatment.

Even though physicians can anticipate higher-than-average incomes once they begin practice, in 2005, more than 85% of medical students graduated with debts averaging more than $113,000 (AAMC, 2006b). Further, there is a lengthy postgraduate training period, during which salaries are relatively low, whereas most loans come due in the second year of postgraduate training. These are additional factors that discourage young physicians from choosing the relatively lower-paid specialties.

In 2000, the National Board of Medical Examiners began developing a clinical skills exam to be taken in conjunction with Part 2 of the United States Medical Licensure Exam. The clinical skills exam requires that students be observed interacting with standardized patients in a performance exam offered in several sites around the country. (*Standardized patients* are trained actors who portray patients during an interview and physical examination with a medical student or physician trainee. They realistically depict patient interactions, discuss their symptoms, and answer questions.) This exam is an attempt to improve the evaluation of the medical student in the areas of patient care, professionalism, and interpersonal and communication skills. Some medical schools have increased the use of standardized patients, computerized patient simulators, and other types of clinical experiences to prepare their students for this added testing.

GRADUATE MEDICAL EDUCATION

To obtain a state license to practice and to be recognized by the profession as fully prepared, a physician must complete at least 1 year of supervised, practical clinical experience, through graduate medical education (GME). Most often this year is part of a hospital-based residency training program that qualifies the physician to become board-certified in a specialty, such as family medicine, internal medicine, pediatrics, or surgery. After residency, a physician may further subspecialize. For example, after a 3-year residency in internal medicine, a physician may choose to undergo 2 additional years of residency training in cardiology, gastroenterology, or several other subspecialties. Teaching hospitals offer residents an opportunity to see a wide range of patient conditions, and, in many cases, teaching hospitals are where medical schools and their faculty also are located, in which case they are collectively termed academic medical centers.

GME is funded largely by Medicare ($7.9 billion in direct and indirect payments in 2004). GME programs have major influence on the number and types of physicians available in a region and are a major source of revenue for teaching hospitals. Because residency reimbursement is so hospital-oriented, training tends to be focused on the kinds of patients and procedures found in hospitals. This strengthens training in the procedure-focused specialties such as surgery but does not improve preparation for outpatient, longitudinally focused primary care specialties. As more medical services shift to ambulatory settings, there is a growing effort to provide more training outside of hospitals. Analysts have encouraged developing methods of reimbursing GME that would support this greater variety of training locations.

Allopathic residency programs are accredited by the Accreditation Council for Graduate Medical Education, a private national body that establishes standards and assesses individual residency program performance against those standards. Osteopathic internship and residency programs are accredited by the American Osteopathic Association.

U.S. residency programs accept graduates of U.S. and overseas medical schools alike. International medical graduates may be U.S. or foreign citizens. In 2005, 26.4% of the 101,291 residents in training in the United States were international medical graduates (AAMC, 2006b). This percentage is about the same as it was in the 1970s and varies considerably by state and specialty, as more popular residencies attract higher proportions of U.S. medical graduates. To be admitted into a residency program, an international medical graduate must be certified by the Educational Commission for Foreign Medical Graduates, which requires a passing score on the United States Medical Licensure Exam parts 1 and 2 and a clinical skills exam.

As medical innovations develop, specialties such as medical genetics and hospitalists develop. The growth of the hospitalist role has been particularly interesting and resulted from cost pressures on hospitals, growing concerns about patient safety, and decreasing primary care inpatient volume. In addition, hospital administrators believe hospitalists are effective in controlling costs—particularly important for patients insured under fixed-payment plans. Hospitalists also provide inpatient coverage for physicians, particularly when residents are in short supply (Pham, Devers, Kuo, & Berenson, 2005).

Nursing Practice

The nursing workforce includes a variety of practitioner types and skill levels—from unlicensed nursing assistants to doctorally prepared nurse researchers. Together, they constitute the largest group of health care workers.

REGISTERED NURSES

Nursing is often described as the diagnosis and treatment of human responses to health problems. Each state Board of Nursing defines and interprets the authority and scope of practice of registered nurses practicing in its state. All states require that prospective registered nurses attend an approved educational program and take a national licensing exam, the National Council Licensure Examination for RNs. In 2004, according to the National Council of State Boards of Nursing (NCSBN), 87,171 first-time U.S. candidates took the exam, and 85.3% passed; also taking the test were 18,278 foreign-educated first-time candidates, 58.2% of whom passed. The number of test-takers in both groups increased from 2003 to 2004, with the number of foreign-educated nurses taking the exam tripling since 1999.

OTHER NURSING PERSONNEL

Licensed practical nurses (LPNs) and licensed vocational nurses (LVNs) work under the supervision of RNs or physicians and perform such caregiving tasks as administering medications and changing dressings. LPNs/LVNs also must pass a national examination in order to be licensed by their states. In 2004, the NCSBN reports that 62,112 candidates took the exam, 80% of whom passed.

Additional nursing personnel include a variety of unlicensed assistive personnel, such as nurse aides, assistants, orderlies, and technicians. These personnel also work under the supervision of RNs and perform simple tasks such as taking vital signs and providing comfort measures such as bathing and changing linens. These occupations are not licensed by the states, although federal Medicare and Medicaid regulations require that nursing assistants who work in long-term care facilities must complete a specified educational program and pass a written and practical test. In addition, Medicare-certified home health agencies must hire certified home health aides. Some states have specific educational requirements for some of these categories of workers. More than half of the states have regulations or guidelines for RNs who supervise them.

NURSING EDUCATION

One of the most confusing aspects of the nursing profession is the variety of programs for educating nurses. Unlike medicine and most other health care professions, which have consistent educational requirements, nursing offers the student a number of options. Students can attend a 2-year college program conferring an associate's degree, a 3-year hospital-based (diploma) program, or a 4-year college program culminating in a bachelor of science in nursing. At the graduate level, nursing offers 2-year master's degree programs and multiyear doctoral programs. The American Nurses Association and some other groups recommend a bachelor's degree as the minimum preparation needed for carrying out the complex nursing tasks required in today's health care environment. However, all state boards of nursing accept any of these programs as appropriate preparation for the RN licensing examination.

Both the National League for Nursing and the AACN accredit nursing programs and collect data on programs, admissions, enrollments, and graduations. Neither organization has complete data, making it difficult to reliably track students in the educational pipeline. Accreditation standards do not specify course requirements, so curricula vary widely from school to school, and transfer of nursing course credits is extremely difficult. Fewer nurses today are prepared in the hospital-based diploma programs that were popular several decades ago. In 1980, 63% of licensed RNs had received their initial nursing education in a diploma program; in 2004, the figure was 18%. Meanwhile, baccalaureate education is on the rise: in 1980, 17% of RNs had baccalaureate degrees, compared to 34% in 2004 (Spratley et al., 2004).

Enrollments and graduations have fluctuated over the years. Total enrollments in baccalaureate nursing programs decreased each year from 1994 to 2000, but have increased since then, by 13% from 2004 to 2005, and by 7.6% in 2006 but only 5% in 2007 (AACN, 2007). HRSA predicts that the United States must graduate approximately 90% more nurses between now and 2020 in order to meet projected demand (Biviano, Fritz, Spencer, & Dall, 2004).

> The United States must graduate approximately 90% more nurses between now and 2020 in order to meet projected demand.

Educational requirements for other nursing personnel, such as licensed practical nurses and nursing assistants, vary by state and employment setting. Practical nurse education, usually 1 year long, occurs in high schools, hospitals, community colleges, or vocational schools. Training takes from a few hours to 6 months or more.

GRADUATE NURSING EDUCATION

Registered nurses with baccalaureate degrees can earn master's degrees in advanced clinical practice, teaching, and nursing administration/management. Most graduate students choose to focus on advanced clinical practice and usually focus on a practice area, such as adult health, maternal-child health, psychiatric-mental health, or community health. Specific programs include content ranging from nursing informatics, to home health care management, to geriatrics. Enrollment of nurses in master's programs declined steadily until 2001, but has increased since, by an average of 2,283 students per year. However, because many of these students are part-time, the number of graduates has increased by only 143 per year, on average. The paucity of master's-level graduates is especially problematic because this is the pool from which new faculty will emerge.

Nursing offers three types of doctoral degrees. The ND (doctor of nursing) is similar to the MD in that it is the first professional degree, building on the earlier undergraduate education and preparing the student to take the state RN licensing exam. The DSN and DNSc are professional doctorates that prepare the nurse for advanced clinical practice. The PhD is a research degree, with requirements similar to the PhD in other fields; it requires extensive preparation in a narrow field and a dissertation. Total enrollment of students in nursing doctoral programs has increased slowly but steadily by about 30 additional students per year; in 2002, just over 3,500 students were enrolled in doctoral programs. Of these, 93.3% were women, and 14.4% were minority students (AACN, 2003).

EMPLOYMENT SETTINGS

In 2004, about 56% of RNs worked in hospitals, 15% in public health or community health care of various types, and 12% in ambulatory care settings, while 6% worked in nursing homes, which are largely staffed by LPN/LVNs. More than 15% of RNs hold more than one job (Spratley et al., 2004). *Staff nurses* is the term used to describe nurses who typically work in direct patient care, with individuals who are acutely ill (as in a hospital), chronically ill or recovering from illness (as in a home setting or skilled nursing facility), or are well but requiring preventive care (as in a health department or managed care organization).

When adjusted for inflation, average salaries for RNs were relatively flat from 1992 to 2000, but increased 12.8% from 2000 to 2004 (Spratley et al., 2004). Because of the current nursing shortage, inflation-adjusted salaries have been rising. RN salaries vary by geographic area, setting, position, education, and experience. In 2006, the median salary for registered nurses ranged from $44,200 in Iowa to $69,000 in California (*America's Career Infonet*, 2004). Detailed information about a variety of occupations (including nursing), educational requirements, and income is available in the *Occupational Handbook* of the Bureau of Labor Statistics.

Mid-Level Professionals

The term *mid-level professional* generally refers to physician assistants and advanced practice nurses (including nurse practitioners). These two practitioner levels have developed to fill the need for medical care in rural and other areas where physicians are lacking, as well as to provide services that are theoretically less expensive than those provided by a physician. Physician assistants practice under the direct supervision of physicians who remain legally responsible for the care they deliver. By contrast, advanced practice nurses collaborate with physicians as required by state law but practice on their own license and are legally responsible for the care they provide. Three key legal issues for mid-level practitioners are (1) the degree to which they can diagnose and prescribe treatment independent of a physician's oversight, (2) whether they can prescribe medications, and (3) whether they can be directly reimbursed by insurance. Without these legal rights, it is difficult to establish an independent practice, and most mid-level practitioners are salaried.

ADVANCED PRACTICE NURSES

In 2004, there were more than 240,000 advanced practice nurses (APNs) in the United States who were certified as clinical nurse specialists, nurse practitioners, nurse midwives, or certified registered nurse anesthetists. *Clinical nurse specialists* have advanced degrees and skills in a particular area, such as mental health, cancer, or women's health, and they often practice in acute care settings. *Nurse practitioners* perform an expanded nursing role and diagnose and manage most common and many chronic health problems, often in primary care settings. In most states they can prescribe medicines, although their scope of practice—including whether they must have a collaborating relationship with a physician—varies across states. *Nurse midwives* provide pre-, intra-, and postpartum care, family planning services, and routine gynecological care, as well as care for newborns. *Nurse anesthetists* administer anesthesia. Numerous studies affirm that nurse practitioners provide cost-effective health care equal in quality to that provided by physicians, at substantially lower educational cost.

Educational requirements for advanced practice nurses differ considerably from state to state. Most, but not all, require a master's degree and by 2015 will require a DNP. (This increase in educational requirements comes about in response to the growth of other professional doctorates, as well as the increased clinical expertise, and academic and practicum hours required for effective practice.) Laws related to prescribing pharmaceuticals are inconsistent. Some states allow advanced practice nurses (clinical nurse specialists and nurse practitioners) to prescribe without physician collaboration or authorization; other states require that they have a practice arrangement with a physician; still other states do not allow them any prescribing privileges; and some states limit prescribing authority to central sites or formularies (preapproved lists of drugs that are acceptable to insurance companies or institutions). Reimbursement policies have been liberalized in the last 10 years, so that APNs have little difficulty obtaining reimbursement for services.

PHYSICIAN ASSISTANTS

Likewise, states regulate the practice of physician assistants (PAs). Although technically they operate under a physician's direct supervision, that does not necessarily mean on-site supervision, and in most states the amount of authority delegated to a PA is a decision between the physician and the PA. Both the demand for and supply of PAs have been increasing rapidly. PAs can expand access to primary care and improve physician productivity, both of which are crucial with the expansion of managed care. PAs can substitute for physicians or replace hospital residents in hospitals.

Sixty-four percent of PAs are women, 88% are White, and their mean age is 41. The largest proportion of them (44%) is employed by single or multispecialty physician group practices; another 13% are employed by solo physician offices; and 23% are employed by hospitals. Only 15% currently report working in nonmetropolitan areas, a decline of 4% from 2003. Their median total income in 2006, including productivity or other bonuses, was $82,223 (American Association Physician Assistants, 2007). As the effectiveness and efficacy of PAs are demonstrated in more and more specialty areas, they may be drawn away from primary care.

The physician assistant is a relatively new profession. The first PA education program was established by Duke University Medical Center in 1965, in part to allow an opportunity for medics who had gained clinical experience in the Vietnam War to practice in the health care field. In 1971, with the passage of the Comprehensive Health Manpower Act, federal financial support became available and contributed to the rapid expansion of PA training programs. Most programs require applicants to have previous health care experience and some college education. Programs are about 26 months in length and are located in different types of academic settings. Most PAs are educated at the bachelor's level, but 35% have a master's degree (AAPA, 2007).

Other Health Care Workers

DENTISTS

In 2006, doctors of dental surgery or the equivalent and doctors of dental medicine held approximately 150,000 dentistry jobs. About one-third are self-employed. Dentists are educated in 56 U.S. schools of dentistry. In 2001–2002, women were 15.6% of the total dentistry workforce and 37.5% of new graduates (Sinkford, Valachovic, & Harrison, 2003). Like doctors and nurses, dentists' average age is increasing. A 4% growth in the total number of dentists is expected by 2012, and most new jobs will result from the need to replace retiring dentists.

In 1999–2000, 2.2% of active dentists and less than 5% of dental students were African American; 2.8% of active dentists and 5.3% of dental students were Hispanic. Dental medicine has been slow to embrace community-based training. More than half of dental seniors spent less than 4 weeks on extramural clinical rotations (not in a dental school clinic). As for many other health professions, geographic distribution of practicing dentists is uneven, with too few practicing in inner-city and rural areas.

PHARMACISTS

Pharmacists today do not merely fill prescriptions; they also provide customers with information and education about the drugs they are taking and possible drug interactions. Pharmacists held about 230,000 jobs in 2006. About 61% of them work in community pharmacies that are either independently owned or part of a drugstore chain, grocery store, department store, or mass merchandiser. Others work in hospitals, clinics, or drug companies. All states require pharmacists to be licensed. Pharmacists supervise pharmacy technicians, who provide assistance in filling prescriptions and other tasks.

By 2006, all 89 U.S. pharmacy education programs were granting the degree of doctor of pharmacy (PharmD), a 4-year program that requires 2 years of college prior to admission. PharmDs must pass the licensure examination of a state board of pharmacy. Pharmacy was one of the first professions to confer a doctoral degree without requiring a bachelor's degree first. Pharmacists can specialize in pharmaceutics and pharmaceutical chemistry (physical and chemical properties of drugs and dosage forms), pharmacology (effects of drugs on the body), toxicology and pharmacy administration by obtaining a master's degree or doctoral degree in pharmacy and through residency programs.

PODIATRISTS

The nation's 13,000 podiatrists provide a wide range of medical and surgical services to diagnose, treat, and prevent foot conditions. There are seven 4-year podiatric medical schools in the United States that grant the DPM degree, and most states require a postdoctoral residency program of at least a year. Most podiatrists are solo practitioners, although more are entering partnerships with other podiatrists, orthopedic groups, or other health practitioners. Median annual earnings of salaried podiatrists were $94,400 in 2004.

Allied Health Professionals

The American Medical Association lists over 6,700 programs in 65 disciplines that can be considered allied health—that is, "health care practitioners with formal education and clinical training who are credentialed through certification, registration, and/or licensure" (U.S. Department of Health and Human Services, 1999). Technicians supervised by other professionals, such as pharmacy technicians, usually are considered allied health professionals.

Allied health occupations are among the fastest growing in health care, but the exact number of allied health professionals is difficult to estimate. They include a wide range of occupations—dental hygienists, dietetic technicians, occupational therapists, clinical laboratory workers, operating room technicians, medical transcriptionists, speech-language pathologists, audiologists, and many, many others. Women predominate in most of the allied health professions and, in most of them, are 75% to 95% of the workforce. New allied health occupations develop in response to the shortage or high cost of other professionals. Education and training is not always standardized, and little is known about the implications for patient outcomes of substituting allied health personnel for more highly trained professionals (U.S. Department of Health and Human Services, 1999). Standards for licensure, registration, or certification vary by profession and state. Several of the more common allied health professions are described briefly below.

PHYSICAL THERAPISTS

Physical therapists (PTs) provide services that help restore function, improve mobility, relieve pain, and prevent or limit permanent physical disabilities among patients suffering from injuries or disease. There were 155,000 PT jobs in 2004, but this number is greater than the number of therapists, because PTs commonly hold more than one job. For example, some work part-time in private practice and part-time in a health care facility. Most physical therapists (about two-thirds) work either in hospitals or in the offices of other health practitioners. They also work in home health, nursing homes, outpatient care, and physician offices. In 2004, they earned about $61,000. They also supervise physical therapy technicians who assist patients in completing exercise and therapeutic regimens.

Of the 205 accredited PT educational programs in 2004, 94 offered master's degrees and 111 offered doctoral degrees. The Commission on Accreditation in Physical Therapy Education requires programs to offer degrees at the master's level and above, although the recommended degree is the clinical doctorate.

CHIROPRACTORS

Chiropractic medicine is a system of diagnosis and treatment based on the concept that health and disease are related to nervous system function, that disease is due to nervous system irritation, and that health can be restored by removing the irritation. Chiropractors treat problems of the musculoskeletal system (particularly the spine) and neurological system holistically and with manipulation. They do not use drugs or surgery, but they do use diagnostic tests such as radiographs. Chiropractors are educated in 4-year programs, which follow at least 2 years of undergraduate education. There were 15 chiropractic education programs and 2 independent chiropractic institutions accredited by the Council on Chiropractic Education in 2006. Their graduates are eligible for licensure in all 50 states. In 2004, chiropractors held approximately 53,000 jobs, earning a median income of $69,910. Demand for alternative health care by consumers is expected to result in steady growth in this profession. Geographic imbalances exist in this profession, although many chiropractors do practice in small communities.

OPTOMETRISTS

Optometrists are licensed to diagnose eye disorders, provide selective eye treatments, and, in some states, prescribe a limited range of drugs. Optometrists held about 34,000 jobs in 2004. Educated at one of the 17 accredited schools of optometry, students have 4 years of professional training following undergraduate school. Optometrists provide many of the same nonsurgical services as ophthalmologists (who are medical doctors), usually at a lower cost. As state governments consider an increased scope of practice for optometrists, and managed care encourages use of lower-paid professionals, predictably, conflicts have arisen between optometrists and ophthalmologists.

ALTERNATIVE PRACTITIONERS

Alternative practitioners include naturopathic physicians, homeopaths, practitioners of acupuncture and other Asian therapies, as well as traditional healers from a variety of cultures, such as the Hispanic *curandero*. (Chiropractors also are considered alternative practitioners.) Several states now license alternative health care providers. The National Center for Complementary and Alternative Medicine, established in 1998, is dedicated to evaluating healing practices and determining their effectiveness. This federal center has categorized alternative medicine into seven types, according to the approach to treatment: mind-body medicine, alternative medical systems, lifestyle disease and prevention, biologically based therapies, manipulative and body-based systems, biofield, and bioelectromagnetics. Alternative therapies are well accepted by the general public and account for a significant part of health care spending. In addition, some insurance plans cover certain alternative services, primarily in response to consumer demand.

Health Care Workforce Issues

INTERNATIONAL MIGRATION OF HEALTH WORKERS

The World Health Organization's Global Health Workforce Alliance (http://www.who.int/workforcealliance/en/) estimates that there are 59.2 million full-time paid health workers worldwide, about two-thirds of whom provide direct services. The rest are engaged in support, research, and management. Enormous diversity exists in the proportions of workers to population—from 2.3 workers per 100 people in Africa to 24.8 per 100 in the Americas (in aggregate). Demographics, emigration, and epidemiological events such as HIV/AIDS, as well as limited funding for training have created worldwide shortages. Some 57 countries have critical shortages of an estimated 2.4 million doctors, nurses, and midwives, with sub-Saharan Africa and Southeast Asia having the largest shortfalls.

International migration of health workers from poorer to richer countries has become a sensitive international policy problem. Data on health workers' migration is confined mostly to doctors and nurses and indicate that better pay, safer environments, the opportunity to upgrade qualifications and skills, and family-related matters are major "pull" factors for emigration. "Push" factors include poor living conditions, inadequate work facilities, and heavy workloads. Positive aspects of emigration are the remittance money immigrants send home to families and their increased skills if they return home. Some countries such as the Philippines actively encourage emigration because of the remittances amounting to billions of dollars. Filipino nurses are 76% of the foreign nurse graduates in the United States. Negative aspects are the resource losses to the country of origin and threats to its health care system, just as resources are becoming available to address HIV/AIDS and improve immunization coverage. For example, 13% of Ghana's nurses and 29% of its doctors work abroad; similarly, 7% of South Africa's nurses and 37% of its doctors work abroad.

The recruitment agencies that have proliferated to take advantage of the desire to emigrate have been criticized for contributing to donor country shortages and unethical operations. Nor do they help foreign professionals cope in their new country, where they may have to deal with cultural and social isolation, lack of information about their rights, and unequal work conditions. However, looming shortages of health workers in developed countries continue to make overseas recruitment attractive, despite the ethics of taking workers from countries that desperately need them. The ability of U.S. health services to absorb large numbers of international graduates has fueled recommendations that U.S. training programs be expanded to enable more U.S. citizens to become health care professionals.

PUBLIC POLICY CHALLENGES

The proliferation, overlap, and duplication among health care occupations, doctoral creep in graduate education, educational variation across health occupations, appropriate staffing ratios in hospitals, and need for more health professionals in rural and other underserved areas are all important health workforce policy problems. State governments have traditionally regulated professional licensure, while national professionally controlled organizations accredit and credential many of the occupations and their training programs. There has been no accepted federal government role for determining standards and accountability for health professions education or utilization or for developing a coherent response to the migration of health professionals.

States are responsible for regulating educational programs and providing publicly funded educational programs. However, state budgetary constraints may make it difficult to respond to market opportunities. For example, the bricks-and-mortar costs of expanding clinical labs makes expanding clinical programs very expensive. Centralized workforce policy, which is common in Europe and many other countries, has not been politically acceptable in the United States.

The health care marketplace has never been a free market in the economic sense, and it is unclear how fast and to what degree it would respond to imbalances, if left alone. State and federal legislators respond to workforce shortages by developing programs such as the Nurse Re-Investment Act of 2002, which established scholarships, loan forgiveness, and training and career-ladder programs. Some government programs are designed to attract people into health care or into certain underserved areas. For example, Area Health Education Centers are federally funded programs designed to address recruitment, retention, and distribution of health care workers, particularly in rural and other medically underserved areas. Similarly, the National Health Service Corps is a federal program that reduces medical student debt burden in exchange for service in a designated underserved area. Some states also provide funds for these purposes. Educational loan repayment and scholarship programs are the primary policy tools used in these programs, but funding varies depending on the congressional budgeting process. Despite the wide variety of such programs, they have not been able to solve the access problems of rural and some urban areas that remain chronically underserved, although possibly the situation would be worse without them. The private sector—notably, foundations such as the Robert Wood Johnson Foundation and Pew Charitable Trusts—also has established demonstration programs and centers for studying workforce problems and potential remedies.

Another problem is the lack of agreement on data and analyses needed across the workforce. Workforce data collection and analyses are highly variable from state to state and among occupations. Recent reductions in HRSA funding have virtually eliminated support for five regional Centers for Health Workforce Research. Census Bureau information can be used for some occupations, and the Bureau of Labor Statistics collects information about jobs and wages and makes regular forecasts. Much essential information used by government forecasters is collected by private organizations that provide accrediting or other services. Occupations (such as nursing assistants and aides) that are not represented by an organization that has the resources to collect data—no matter how essential to the system—are difficult to study or plan for. Finally, workforce analyses are performed by various researchers or private subcontractors using different methodologies, some of which may not be transparent or rigorous or yield comparable results.

Development of workforce policy is hindered by a lack of agreement on what is an adequate workforce. We do not have well-defined standards for access, staffing, or appropriate health professional-to-population ratios. For example, the complex definition of rural geographic areas complicates the assessment of the distribution of the workforce into rural areas (U.S. Department of Agriculture, 2003). Currently, health professional shortage areas primarily reflect physician shortages, and a comparable designation process has not been developed for all health professions. Medicare allows higher reimbursement in HPSA-designated rural areas, and rural health clinics may receive enhanced payments as well, but some communities are too small to support economically viable medical practices.

INTERDISCIPLINARY AND COLLABORATIVE EDUCATION AND PRACTICE

Most health care professionals today are educated in discipline-specific professional schools, health facilities, or divisions of colleges and universities. Although students in a variety of programs may attend the same institution, rarely do they take courses together, share the same faculty, or participate in joint clinical teaching. When professions perpetuate this type of fragmentation, patients suffer. Optimal care requires extensive collaboration and interdisciplinary teamwork among health care personnel—doctors, nurses, social workers, physical therapists, pharmacists, nutritionists, aides, and even nontraditional caregivers such as acupuncturists and massage therapists.

In recognition of the complexity and multiple dimensions of healing, an increasing number of health professions are trying to incorporate collaborative practice in their training and education programs. Many problems arise because of a lack of professional guidelines and curriculum models; controversies over core curricula; faculty resistance; faculty workload; and possible effects on enrollment, accreditation, and licensure requirements.

Despite some movement toward interdisciplinary collaboration, friction will arise regarding the degree to which professions can substitute for each other in the workplace. In some cases, allied health workers can partially substitute for more highly educated professionals, sometimes in new or extended roles created by employers looking to cut costs. Professional competition spills over into the legislative and regulatory arenas, when different groups argue for or against an expanded scope of practice for a particular occupation or profession. Medicaid and private insurance reimbursement policies can become another battleground. Regrettably, few studies have been made of the impact on patient outcomes of permitting different occupations to perform specific activities, or of the effects of changing how health professions and occupations interact. Thus, the debates among professions are often merely self-interested rather than substantive policy discussions, and they have a negative effect on the promotion of interdisciplinary, collaborative care.

> Scope-of-practice debates among professions are often merely self-interested rather than substantive policy discussions, and they have a negative effect on the promotion of interdisciplinary, collaborative care.

Conclusion

A continuing concern for the health care workforce is having adequate numbers of health care professionals as the demographics of the workforce and the U.S. population change. Historically, shortages of workers in any one field have fundamentally altered professional scope of practice in that field and have caused permanent alterations in how health care workers interact.

Current rapid changes in the U.S. health care delivery system will undoubtedly lead to changes in the roles and relationships of health professionals. Managed care and the growing use of information technologies will simultaneously require and enable greater collaboration. Some of these changes will mean greater supervision and management of health professionals by people outside their specific discipline, and some health professionals may resist this inevitable oversight. New relationships and new definitions of professionalism may be needed.

Issues regarding scope of practice, prescriptive authority, and reimbursement are likely to continue to be troublesome. As health care moves increasingly from the hospital to the community, greater coordination of patient care and professional cooperation will be required, with specific patient circumstances determining who should be the primary caregiver or coordinator.

Lastly, a workforce research agenda is needed. Basic research describing health care occupations is often provided by various organizations, but there is no common understanding of what data need to be collected. We also need to evaluate the effectiveness of existing workforce programs that address misdistribution, recruitment, and retention, and to assess the roles of allied and alternative health workers.

References

American Academy of Physician Assistants. (2007). *Data and statistics.* Retrieved December 11, 2007, from http://www.aapa.org/research/

American Association of Colleges of Nursing. (2007). *Enrollment growth slows at U.S. nursing colleges and universities in 2007 despite calls for more registered nurses.* Retrieved December 11, 2007, from http://www.aacn.nche.edu/Media/NewsReleases/2007/enrl.htm

American Association of Colleges of Osteopathic Medicine. (2007). *2006 annual report on osteopathic medical education.* Chevy Chase, Maryland. Retrieved April 4, 2007, from http://www.aacom.org/resources/bookstore/2006statrpt/Pages/default.aspx

American College of Physicians. (2006). *The impending collapse of primary care medicine and its implications for the state of the nation's health care.* Retrieved January 5, 2007, from http://www.acponline.org/hpp/statehc06_1.pdf

American Hospital Association. (2006). *Prepared to care: The 24/7 role of America's full service hospitals.* Chicago: American Hospital Association Press.

America's Career InfoNet. (2004). *Salary data.* Retrieved January 9, 2007, from http://www.acinet.org/acinet/default.asp

Association of American Medical Colleges. (2006a). *AAMC statement on the physician workforce.* Washington, DC: Author. Retrieved January 11, 2006, from http://www.aamc.org/workforce/workforceposition.pdf

Association of American Medical Colleges. (2006b). *Medical student education: Cost, debt, and resident stipend facts.* Washington, DC: Author. Retrieved January 9, 2007, from http://www.aamc.org/students/financing/debthelp/factcard06.pdf

Association of American Medical Colleges. (2006c). U.S. medical school enrollment continues to climb. *Press Release,* October 18. Washington, DC: Author. Retrieved

April 4, 2007, from http://www.aamc.org/newsroom/pressrel/2006/apps_entrants 2006.pdf

Association of American Medical Colleges. (2007). *Workforce.* Washington, DC: Author. Retrieved January 5, 2007, from http://www.aamc.org/workforce

Auerbach, D. I., Buerhaus, P. I., & Staiger, D. O. (2007). Better late than never: Workforce supply implications of later entry into nursing. *Health Affairs, 26*(1), 178–185.

Biviano, M., Fritz, M. S., Spencer, W., & Dall, T. M. (2004). *What is behind HRSA's projected supply, demand, and shortage of registered nurses?* Washington, DC: U.S. Department of Health and Human Services, Health Resources and Services Administration, Bureau of Health Professions, National Center for Health Workforce Analysis. Retrieved from http://bhpr.hrsa.gov/healthworkforce/reports/behindrnprojections/index.htm

Bodenheimer, T. (2006). Primary care—will it survive? *New England Journal of Medicine, 355*(9), 861–864.

Brewer, C. S., Feeley, T. H., & Servoss, T. J. (2003). A statewide and regional analysis of New York state nurses using the 2000 national sample survey of registered nurses. *Nursing Outlook, 51*(5), 220–226.

Brewer, C. S., & Kovner, C. T. (2001). Is there another nursing shortage? What the data tells us. *Nursing Outlook, 49*(1), 20–26.

Brooks, B. A., & Anderson, M. A. (2005). Defining quality of nursing work life. *Nursing Economics, 23*(6), 319–326.

Brotherton, S. E., Rockey, P. H., & Etzel, S. I. (2005). US graduate medical education, 2004–2005: Trends in primary care specialties. *Journal of the American Medical Association, 294*(9), 1075–1082.

Chan, L., Hart, L. G., & Goodman, D. C. (2006). Geographic access to health care for rural Medicare beneficiaries. *Journal of Rural Health, 22*(2), 140–146.

de la Torre, A., Hernandez-Rodriguez, C., & Garcia, L. (2004). Cost analysis in telemedicine: Empirical evidence from sites in Arizona. *Journal of Rural Health, 20*(3), 253–257.

Garrison, G. (2006). *Closing the gaps in the medical school applicant pool.* Washington, DC: American Association of Medical Colleges. Retrieved November 20, 2006, from http://www.aamc.org/newsroom/pressrel/2006/growing_gap_facts.pdf

Glasser, M., Peters, K. D. H., & MacDowell, M.D.H. (2006). Rural Illinois hospital chief executive officers' perceptions of provider shortages and issues in rural recruitment and retention. *Journal of Rural Health, 22*(1), 59–62.

Green, L. A., Lanier, D., & Yawn, B. P. (2001). The ecology of medical care revisited. *New England Journal of Medicine, 345*(16), 1211–1212.

Hughes, S., Zweifler, J., Schafer, S., Smith, M. A., Athwal, S., & Blossom, H. J. (2005). High school census tract information predicts practice in rural and minority communities. *Journal of Rural Health, 21*(3), 228–232.

Larson, E. H., Johnson, K. E., Norris, T. E., Lishner, D. M., Rosenblatt, R. A., & Hart, L. G. (2003). *State of the health workforce in rural America: Profiles and comparisons.* Seattle, WA: WWAMI Rural Health Research Center.

Lasser, K. E., Himmelstein, D. U., & Woolhandler, S. (2006). Access to care, health status, and health disparities in the United States and Canada: Results of a cross-national population-based survey. *American Journal of Public Health, 96*(7), 1300–1307.

Lin, G. E., Burns, P. A., & Nochajski, T. H. (1997). The geographic distribution of nurse practitioners in the United States. *Applied Geographic Studies, 1*(4), 287–301.

Organisation for Economic Co-operation and Development. (2006). *Health employment, practicing physicians density per 1000 population (head counts).* Retrieved January 9, 2007, from http://www.oecd.org

Ostbye, T., Yarnall, K. S., Krause, K. M., Pollak, K. I., Gradison, M., & Michener, J. L. (2005). Is there time for management of patients with chronic diseases in primary care? *Annals of Family Medicine, 3,* 209–214.

Pasko, T., & Smart, D. (2003). *Physician characteristics and distribution in the US.* Chicago: American Medical Association Press.

Pham, H. H., Devers, K. J., Kuo, S., & Berenson, R. (2005). Health care market trends and the evolution of hospitalist use and roles. *Journal of General Internal Medicine, 20*(2), 101–107.

Rosenthal, N. H., Fullerton, H. N., Jr., Andreassen, A., & Veneri, C. M. (1997). Evaluating the 1995 BLS projections. *Monthly Labor Review, 120*(9), 3–4.

Rosenthal, T. C. (2002). Rural graduate medical education: An idea, challenged. *Family Medicine, 34,* 293–294.

Rosseter, R. J. (2006). *Nursing shortage fact sheet.* Washington, DC: American Association of Colleges of Nursing. Retrieved December 12, 2006, from http://www.aacn.nche.edu/Media/FactSheets/NursingShortage.htm

Roter, D. L., & Hall, J. A. (1989). Studies of doctor-patient interaction. *Annual Review of Public Health, 10,* 163–180.

Sinkford, J. C., Valachovic, R. W., & Harrison, S. (2003). Advancement of women in dental education: Trends and strategies. *Journal of Dental Education, 67*(1), 79–83.

Slee, D. A., Slee, V. N., & Schmidt, H. J. (2008). *Slee's Health Care Terms, Fifth Edition.* Sudbury, MA: Jones & Bartlett.

Spratley, E., Johnson, A., Sochalski, J., Fritz, M., & Spencer, W. (2001). *The registered nurse population: Findings from the National Sample Survey of Registered Nurses (NSSRN).* Research Triangle Park, NC: Research Triangle Institute.

Spratley, E., Johnson, A., Sochalski, J., Fritz, M., & Spencer, W. (2004). *Preliminary findings: 2004 National Sample Survey of Registered Nurses.* Research Triangle Park, NC: Research Triangle Institute. Retrieved from http://bhpr.hrsa.gov/health workforce/reports/rnpopulation/preliminaryfindings.htm

Starfield, B., & Lemke, K. W. (2005). Comorbidity and the use of primary care and specialist care in the elderly. *Annals of Family Medicine, 3*(3), 215–222.

Tu, H. T., & Ginsberg, P. B. (2006). *Losing ground: Physician income, 1995–2003.* Tracking report no. 15. Washington, DC: Center for Studying Health System Change. Retrieved January 5, 2007, from http://www.hschange.com/CONTENT/851

U.S. Census Bureau. (2003). *Statistical abstracts of the United States, 2003* (123rd ed.). Washington, DC: U.S. Government Printing Office.

U.S. Census Bureau. (2006). *Annual estimates of the population by sex, race and Hispanic or Latino origin for the United States: April 1, 2000 to July 1, 2005.* National Population Estimates—Characteristics. Washington DC: Author. Retrieved December 12, 2006, from http://www.census.gov/ipc/www/usinterimproj/

U.S. Department of Agriculture, Economic Research Service. (2003). *Briefing room: Measuring rurality: New definitions in 2003.* Washington, DC: Author. Retrieved January 5, 2007, from http://www.ers.usda.gov/Briefing/Rurality/NewDefinitions

U.S. Department of Health and Human Services, Health Resources and Services Administration. (1999). *Building the future of allied health: Report of the implementation task force of the national commission on allied health.* Rockville, MD: Bureau of Health Professions.

U.S. Department of Health and Human Services, Health Resources and Services Administration. (2002). *Projected supply, demand, and shortages of registered nurses: 2000–2020.* Rockville, MD: Author. Retrieved from http://www.ahca.org/research/rnsupply_demand.pdf

U.S. Department of Health and Human Services, Health Resources and Services Administration. (2006). *Physician supply and demand: Projections to 2020.* Rockville, MD: Author. Retrieved January 5, 2007, from http://bhpr.hrsa.gov/healthworkforce/reports/physiciansupplydemand/default.htm

U.S. Department of Health and Human Services, National Center for Health Statistics. (2007). Percentage of persons of all ages with a usual place to go for medical care: United States, 1997–September 2006. *Early release of selected estimates based on data from the January–September 2006 National Health Interview Survey* (Figure 2.1, p. 11). Rockville, MD: Author.

U.S. Department of Labor, Bureau of Labor Statistics. (2004). *Career guide to industries.* Washington, DC: Author. Retrieved January 12, 2007, from http://stats.bls.gov/oco/cg/cgs035.htm

U.S. Department of Labor, Bureau of Labor Statistics (2007). *Occupational outlook handbook.* Washington, DC: Author. Retrieved from http://www.bls.gov/oco/cg/print/cgs074.htm

Virji, A., Yarnall, K. S., Krause, K. M., Pollak, K. I., Scannell, M. A., & Gradison, M., et al. (2006). Use of email in a family practice setting: Opportunities and challenges in patient- and physician-initiated communication. *BioMed Central Medicine, 4,* 18.

Weiner, J. P. (2004). Prepaid group practice staffing and US physician supply: Lessons for workforce policy. *Health Affairs, 23*(2), W43–W59.

Yarnall, K. S., Pollak, K. I., Ostbye, T., Krause, K. M., & Michener, J. L. (2003). Primary care: Is there enough time for prevention? *American Journal of Public Health, 93,* 635–641.

13

Key Words

information technology
clinical quality
service quality
wireless
computerized physician order
   entry (CPOE)
electronic medical record
   (EMR)

outsourcing
data repositories
picture archiving and
   collection systems
Health Insurance Portability
   and Accountability Act
   (HIPAA)
decision support

personal digital assistants
   (PDAs)
return on investment (ROI)
authorization
authentication
regional health information
   organizations (RHIO)
interoperability

Information Management

Roger Kropf

Learning Objectives

- Identify why collecting and using information is important to patients, clinicians, and payers.
- Illustrate how information technology can help improve the quality of medical care and prevent injury and deaths.
- Show how technology can increase patient satisfaction.
- Provide examples of how information technology can help reduce or control the increase in health care costs.
- Describe some of the issues that face providers and some of the options for dealing with them.

Topical Outline

- Why is managing information important in health care?
- Improving clinical quality through information technology
- Information technology benefits for patients
- Speeding adoption of health care information technology
- Issues: cost of technology, who will pay, federal role, lack of standardization, winning clinician acceptance and support, assuring confidentiality

Enormous advances in medical knowledge, technology, and the training of health care professionals have been made in the last 100 years. We know more and have better tools for preventing, finding, and curing disease. Yet the management of the tremendous volumes of information the health care system generates has not changed nearly as much and lags behind developments in many other industries. Physicians, nurses, and other clinicians still write on pieces of paper that are then filed. When information is needed, someone goes and finds that paper (or tries to) and brings it to the clinician. If a bank operated that way, tellers would be writing checking account balances in a huge ledger, which would have to be retrieved every time a customer wanted to withdraw money.

Adopting health care information technology (HIT) should be relatively easy, since the technology is an increasingly common feature of our everyday lives. But it hasn't happened yet. In 2005, approximately 24% of physicians used electronic health records in the ambulatory setting (see Figure 13.1; Burt, Hing, & Woodwell, 2006). Fewer than 5% of hospitals had the technology (called computerized physician order entry or CPOE) to allow physicians to enter orders directly into a computer for transmission to the laboratory, pharmacy, or other units (Cutler, Feldman, & Horwitz, 2005; Jha et al., 2006). This laggardly performance is a serious concern for all of us, because accurate application of medical knowledge saves lives, and errors cost lives—and dollars.

The cost of technology, disagreement on who should pay, the perceived lack of information on the benefits, a lack of standardization that makes implementation costly and difficult, resistance by clinicians, and concerns about security and patient confidentiality are all frequently mentioned as obstacles to adoption of health information technology.

IMPROVING CLINICAL QUALITY

The medical chart of a typical hospital patient contains dozens, if not hundreds, of pieces of paper, including reports of laboratory tests, orders for drugs, and notes written by nurses and doctors. Paper records may lead to oversights and errors that can have serious or fatal consequences. Some of the handwriting is hard to read. Nurses and physicians must decide how to interpret new information that arrives (test results, therapists' assessments, and the like) and must

Figure 13.1

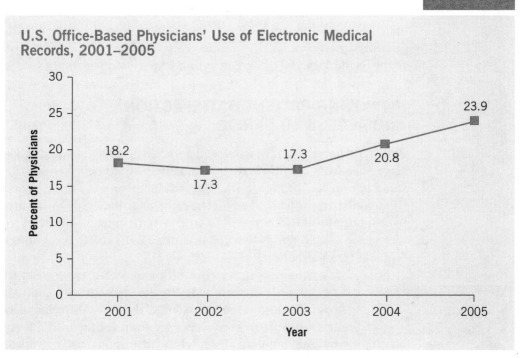

U.S. Office-Based Physicians' Use of Electronic Medical Records, 2001–2005

Note. The trend is significant (p < .05). Includes nonfederal, office-based physicians who see patients in an office setting. Excludes radiologists, anesthesiologists, and pathologists. From U.S. Centers for Disease Control and Prevention, National Center for Health Statistics. (2007). *National ambulatory medical care survey, 2001–05*. Washington, DC: Author.

search out any additional information they need in order to respond appropriately. Clinicians who are called in for a consultation about the patient may not have access to the entire record.

In contrast, computerized medical records can be designed to make information easy to find; the text is legible; graphics convey information efficiently. From the main record, a large amount of additional information may be accessible about a patient—such as X rays—or a record of all the medications the patient is taking. Links also may exist to general information about the patient's condition, relevant clinical trials, and so on. When information is posted to the chart that requires action, the patient's nurse or physician can be alerted automatically. The chart can be searched. Clinicians in different locations can view all the information they need to see.

Electronic medical records (EMRs) represent only one application of information technology that offers the potential to improve the quality of health care. For the patient, this can mean shorter hospital stays and fewer physician visits, a faster recovery and fewer complications due to errors and oversights. For the physician, the technology can save time and support better decisions. For both hospitals and physicians, it can lead to fewer lawsuits for malpractice. For payers, the result can be lower medical expenses. Despite the potential benefits, EMRs exist in a minority of U.S. hospitals and physician offices. Some of the reasons will be examined later and include both the cost of the technology and disagreement on who should pay for it.

IMPROVING PATIENT SATISFACTION AND ACCESS TO CARE

Patients who visit a physician's office and the radiology and laboratory departments of a hospital are very likely to be asked for the same information (name, Social Security number, etc.) three times. Commonly, they will be asked for the same information if they return to that hospital at a later date. It would be hard to name another service in the United States that requires such redundant (and boring) requests for information.

> The ways in which health care organizations fail to use information technology to serve patients and improve operations grow more obvious all the time.

The ways in which health care organizations fail to use information technology to serve patients and improve operations grow more obvious all the time. Americans can track the progress of a package from FedEx or UPS hour by hour, but have absolutely no idea about the progress of their blood test once they've left their doctor's office. We can order movie tickets on the Internet, but have to wait on hold for a receptionist when we call to make a doctor's appointment.

But the problem goes beyond improving patient satisfaction. Technology can make it much easier for patients to communicate with providers. A patient who has a question about a medication may now have to make multiple phone calls to contact a physician. This information could be provided by e-mail or by accessing information on a Web site. Patients may not know whom to contact to provide a service they feel that they need; again, that information could be made available on the Internet. Thus, technology can improve access to care as well.

CONTROLLING COSTS

By improving the quality and timeliness of care, information technology can help control health care expenditures, whether for patients with chronic diseases, emergencies, or routine health care needs. Costly chronic conditions such as asthma must be carefully managed and assessed regularly. Patients must learn how to monitor their condition and to take appropriate action. Information technology can help in two ways: facilitating better tracking of patients' status and delivering information to them. For example, there are devices that asthma patients can breathe into that will transmit data on lung performance to a clinician, who then can provide better advice on medications. In emergency situations, personalized Web sites can provide access to past test results and records that can help critical care providers diagnose a condition faster and avoid complications. E-mail can be used to send messages from clinicians and health education materials that permit patients to manage their health and avoid acute episodes. All these applications can improve care and save time and money by avoiding problems that might lead to hospitalizations.

Information technology also can improve efficiency. Scheduling software can track the use of operating rooms and surgical equipment to assure that both are available when needed and neither is underutilized. Inventory management systems can control the use of drugs and other supplies. While the financial impact of technologies to improve clinical quality and patient satisfaction may be hard to measure, a range of information technologies is available that has been proved to control costs. Yet even these well-established technologies have not been widely adopted by hospitals and physicians.

The benefits for the patient are lower health care expenses as a result of avoiding more expensive treatment. The payer, both employer and insurer, can avoid medical expenses normally paid through insurance. To the extent that hospitals have signed agreements to assume the financial risk of providing care, they can also benefit. Physicians can benefit from technologies that improve the efficiency of care and save them time.

Improving Clinical Quality Through Information Technology

The Institute of Medicine's (1999, 2001) landmark reports documenting problems in U.S. health care quality focused attention on information technology's potential role in achieving improvements. "Much of the potential of IT to improve quality is predicated on the automation of at least some types of clinical data," the 2001 report stated (p. 170). The Institute of Medicine committee discussed four of the barriers to the automation of clinical information: privacy concerns, the need for standards, financial requirements, and human factor issues. The first two were partially addressed by the federal government through the Health Insurance Portability and Accountability Act of 1996 (HIPAA), which set standards for providers in maintaining the security and privacy of personal health information and insurance claims data.

A number of highly publicized breaches in security have emphasized that much remains to be done to assure the confidentiality of patient information. In most cases, these problems have resulted from employees' poor handling of data (especially taking it home with them), rather than the work of hackers or deliberate spying. For example, in 2006, the Veterans Administration (VA) reported that a laptop computer containing personal information on 26.5 million veterans was stolen from an employee's home; in January 2006, Providence Health & Services lost information on 365,000 patients after 10 backup tapes and disks were stolen from an employee's minivan.

While recognizing the efforts of a number of organizations to develop standards, the Institute of Medicine's 2001 report noted that "these efforts, as important as they are, amount to a patchwork of standards that address some areas and not others, and are not adhered to by all users" (p. 173). While the federal government has now focused attention on the issue and more standards have been created, the lack of standards and inconsistent use are still issues.

The 2001 Institute of Medicine report noted that providers may have a hard time justifying the expense of acquiring information technology systems, because "capital decisions are also being made in an environment in which benefits are difficult to quantify" (p. 174), and "current payment policies do not adequately reward improvements in quality" (p. 175). While quality improvement organizations such as the Leapfrog Group have begun to offer financial incentives for acquiring health care information technology, these incentives are available to a small number of hospitals and only for the adoption of specific information technologies. Most physicians must bear all of the cost of acquiring an electronic medical record system. The human factor issues include the highly variable HIT-related knowledge and experience of the health care work force and individuals' varying receptivity to learning these skills. Disruptions in patient care, while physicians and staff members are learning a new system, can result in lost revenues for clinicians. Physicians may worry that patients' much greater access to information—on drugs, diseases, and treatments—will alter the physician-patient relationship, or they may be threatened by patients' growing access to data on physician performance.

To address this range of problems, the Institute of Medicine committee called for a "comprehensive national health information infrastructure," defined as "a set of technologies, standards, applications, systems, values and laws that support all facets of individual health, health care and public health" and "offer a way to connect distributed health data in the framework of a secure network" (2001, p. 176). To do this requires the promulgation of national standards to protect data privacy and for the definition, collection, coding, and exchange of clinical data; changes in the legal and regulatory structures that impede the adoption of useful HIT applications; and greater effort to inform the U.S. public of the benefits and risks of automated clinical data and electronic communication.

In April 2004, President Bush established the Office of the National Coordinator for Health Information Technology to coordinate health information activities, standards development, and partnerships with the private sector. This step acknowledged that considerable progress still needs to be made in addressing the barriers identified by the Institute of Medicine and that federal leadership is required. Three years later, the major issues remain of how to accelerate the adoption of health information technology and deal with the remaining obstacles, particularly security (privacy and confidentiality) and interoperability (that enables one health records system to talk to another).

TECHNOLOGIES FOR IMPROVING CLINICAL QUALITY

Computers' roles in clinical decision support can be categorized as "tools for information management," "tools for focusing attention," and "tools for patient-specific consultation" (Shortliffe & Perreault, 1990, p. 469). Each category offers the opportunity to improve how care is provided. Systems that manage information can gather and display relevant information about the patient; systems that focus attention can alert the clinician to conditions that should be dealt with, such as abnormal laboratory values; and systems that provide consultation or advice combine patient-specific data with the latest information or judgments about appropriate care. For example, a consultation function might suggest what antibiotic to use, taking into account patient allergies, age, and other relevant factors.

> Sentara Norfolk General Hospital in Norfolk, Virginia, monitors patients in multiple intensive care units from a remote location. When intervention becomes necessary, the remote staff can communicate with on-site personnel through a video and audio connection. A study of Sentara's first year's experience with this set-up "showed faster intervention led to a 25 percent decrease in hospital mortality rates for ICU patients." Use of the system also meets the Leapfrog Group's standard for around-the-clock coverage by an intensive care specialist, making the hospital eligible for additional reimbursement. (Drazen & Fortin, 2003, p. 10)

REDUCING MEDICATION ERRORS

In hospitals, medications are a significant source of errors and adverse events, causing an estimated 7,000 deaths annually. Because many of the errors are process errors (unknown allergies, interactions among drugs, misread physician's order, wrong drug given to patient, and so on), they have been a prime target of efforts to improve clinical quality of care through better information systems. Unlike handwritten medication orders, computerized physician order entry with clinical decision support systems (CDSS) allows for interaction between the clinician and information stored in the computer:

> When a physician at the Weiler Hospital of Montefiore Medical Center in the Bronx orders a drug, its $100 million computerized medication management system checks whether the patient is already taking the drug, is allergic to it, whether it might interact with another drug the patient is taking, whether any laboratory tests indicate a danger, whether the dosage is correct given the patient's weight and age, and whether there is a cheaper alternative. When orders were handwritten, "12 percent of inpatient prescriptions led to some kind of error—wrong drug, wrong timing, wrong dose—though the patient was rarely harmed." The error rate is now 2.5%. (Perez-Pena, 2004, p. 6)

Computerized systems also can prevent errors at the patient's bedside, when busy nurses are administering medications:

> Danville Regional Medical Center in Virginia uses bar-codes attached to each medication dose and to the patient's wristband to assure that the right patient receives the right medication. The patient's nurse scans both bar-codes with a wireless scanner, and, if they match, is cleared to give the medication. The time the medication was administered is recorded automatically. Danville has documented an average of 84 to 264 potential medication errors prevented each week. (Sublett, 2002, p. 24)

A medication error may still occur if the patient has received medications the system isn't aware of—for example, from community physicians. This is a particular problem during the transition to and from a hospital or other facility. Rarely do Americans have a single medical record that covers all contacts with health care providers. Creation of a data repository for an entire health care system or the sharing of information among providers in a community would help resolve this problem (McDonald, Turisco, & Drazen, 2003).

Medication-management technologies like these are not used by very many hospitals. In 2004, only 125 of the nation's more than 5,000 hospitals used bar code systems for medication administration—in part because only about 35% of hospitals' drug suppliers included bar codes on drugs at that time. The FDA published a rule in February 2004 requiring bar codes on the labels of all drugs in hospitals within 2 years, predicting that it would prevent more than 550,000 adverse drug events within two decades. Reliable data are not available on the number of hospitals that have well designed CPOE-CDSSs, which have been shown to reduce the incidence of serious medication errors by as much as 55% (Bates et al., 1998; Teich et al., 1996). However, most hospitals still do not have them.

Fewer than 5% of hospitals had the technology to allow physicians to enter orders directly into the computer (Cutler et al., 2005; Jha et al., 2006). The Leapfrog Group requires that 75% of physicians use an online hospital system to order prescriptions and tests to win its approval, but only 40 hospitals in the United States met that standard in 2004 (Freudenheim, 2004).

ADHERENCE TO CLINICAL GUIDELINES AND PROTOCOLS

Donald Berwick (1999) has noted that, because important medical journals number in the hundreds, it is futile to rely on reading and memory as the means to assure that important changes work their way into care practices. To use evidence-based medicine, a fact base must be created and made accessible to clinicians at any time. From that fact base, clinical guidelines and protocols can be developed. These guides can become the decision support component of clinical information systems, merging the processes of looking for knowledge and applying it.

Clinical guidelines and protocols can be offered to physicians as part of a CPOE-CDSS. When an order is entered, the physician can be reminded that a particular test or procedure is suggested by a guideline. The physician can also be asked to provide a written justification for not following the guideline or even be asked to seek approval from a department head or medical director for ordering a test or drug not deemed necessary or appropriate. The absence of an order also can be noted and a reminder or alert sent to the physician or nurse when some standard procedure has been overlooked—for example, if the medication order log indicates that aspirin has not been ordered for a patient who has suffered a heart attack.

> University Health Network, a three-hospital system in Toronto, Ontario, Canada, has an HIT clinical advisory committee that recommends which lab tests should be ordered for which patient conditions, and why. Its recommendations are sent to a medical advisory committee for the entire system that has final approval on which evidence-based rules and alerts are programmed into its system of automatic reminders. The medical advisory committee measures the impact of each new rule after six months and often makes modifications. (Schuerenberg, 2003, p. 46)

AVAILABILITY AND ACCURACY OF PATIENT RECORDS

Storing patient records electronically opens up a number of possibilities for improving their availability and accuracy. While a paper record is available in only one location, computerized records can be accessed by authorized users from a single institution or, again with proper confidentiality safeguards and authentication protocols for people seeking access, by people outside the institution or system via the Internet. Such Web-enabled medical records systems give clinicians in remote rural areas the ability to consult with experts from major medical centers; they enable patients with a rare disorder to be "seen" electronically by the world's leading experts in their condition; and patients can have access to their own records, enabling them to examine and verify information or seek second opinions.

If clerks enter data from handwritten documents into a computer, the accuracy of that data could be worse than the paper record. A trained nurse will interpret a physician's handwriting or call to verify the information. Clerks are more likely to type what they believe they see. The great advance in accuracy from computerized records comes when clinicians enter information themselves or it is automatically sent directly to the patient's record from the laboratory, pharmacy, or other hospital department. Persuading clinicians to enter information directly has been difficult, because it involves a change in behavior. Technologies that can assist in data entry include wireless systems that connect the clinician to the computer from a patient's room or hallway and devices such as personal digital assistants and tablet computers.

> The great advance in accuracy from computerized records comes when clinicians enter information themselves or it is automatically sent directly to the patient's record from the laboratory, pharmacy, or other hospital department.

Whether a clerk, nurse, or physician is entering data, computer systems can check for missing data and logic errors. This can be as simple as checking the date of a lab test and rejecting entries that precede the date of hospital admission. Or it could be a more complex check that rejects a procedure inconsistent with other information, such as diagnosis. Such edit checks also are important for reimbursement, since insurance companies run similar checks and reject claims with illogical data, delaying payment.

Far less frequently, computer systems are used to look across the various places where patients receive care to validate the accuracy of data. More likely, a home care nurse who visits a patient after hospital discharge will carry a list of medications that doesn't match the one in the primary care physician's records or the bottles in the patient's home. Efforts are now being made within hospital systems and communities, through regional health information organizations to create ways to gather data from multiple sources about a single patient, either in a data repository or "on the fly."

> The Indiana Network for Patient Care (INPC), serving Indianapolis and surrounding counties in central Indiana, includes information from five major hospital systems (15 separate hospitals), the county and state public health departments, and Indiana Medicaid. It provides cross-institutional access to physicians in emergency rooms and hospitals. The network includes and delivers laboratory, radiology, dictation, and other documents to a majority of Indianapolis office practices. (McDonald et al., 2005, p. 1215)

ACCESS TO KNOWLEDGE

Information technology is available to assist clinicians, by presenting information when it is needed. The National Library of Medicine's digital archive, PubMed, houses more than 300 biomedical and life sciences journals, allowing clinicians to search for and retrieve journal articles from around the world (www.ncbi.nlm.nih.gov). But it remains up to clinicians to extract the information that would be useful for a particular decision.

Personal digital assistants (PDAs) have become popular devices for providing specific, up-to-date information when clinicians need it. Services such as ePocrates (www.epocrates.com) allow physicians to use a PDA to access a wide variety of clinical and drug information that is constantly updated (unlike a book on the shelf). Web sites such as the *Journal of Mobile Informatics* (www.rnpalm.com) and pdaMD. com (www.pdamd.com) offer reviews of PDA software for physicians and nurses.

Information from these sources is not specific to the institution where the clinician practices—or to a particular patient. Guidelines or protocols can be made available using computer systems in a hospital or physician practice. The information can be downloaded to a PDA or made accessible from a computer. Such knowledge can be provided passively or actively.

In *passive information systems,* the clinician simply asks for knowledge or advice. In *active information systems,* information is presented when a problem or diagnosis is entered, or a test, procedure, or medication is ordered, and this information could include citations from the latest medical journals. These are sometimes referred to as evidence-based systems, because the information comes from evidence obtained through clinical research. In the most sophisticated systems, information from the medical record is used to tailor the information that is provided. For example, if a patient were allergic to penicillin, the information system might return recommendations only for other antibiotics, or it could scan the institution's clinical data repositories to report the effectiveness of different antibiotics in treating specific infections seen in that particular hospital.

Information Technology's Benefits for Patients

A comparison of the experience of a bank customer and a patient who visits a physician's office suggests the extent to which health care providers have fallen behind in adopting information technology. Banks allow the retrieval of most information and many transactions using an automated teller. Many transactions that don't involve physical objects, such as cash or checks, can be carried out online using a secure Internet site. Customers can utilize interbank networks to conduct transactions at banks not their own, even in foreign countries. Most patients can transact very little health care business using a computer. They cannot retrieve personal information, make a request for services, such as the renewal of a prescription, or communicate with anyone in the physician's office. Records from a physician's office cannot be accessed even by emergency room physicians in a nearby hospital.

IMPROVING ACCESS TO INFORMATION AND SERVICES

Web sites are the most obvious way to provide online information for patients. Through personalization and two-way interaction, patients can customize the information they receive and carry out transactions, such as appointment scheduling or obtaining test results.

My HealtheVet (MHV) is a personal website for veterans, created by the U.S. Department of Veterans Affairs (VA), that provides access to health information, links to federal and VA benefits and resources, a Personal Health Journal, and online VA prescription refills. It keeps track of an individual's vital signs and health measurements, such as blood pressure and cholesterol. It also provides personalized information on VA treatment locations and physicians. (*www.myhealth.va.gov*)

Approximately 70,000 Cleveland Clinic patients "have access to their medical records 24/7," through the organization's MyChart system. From home, diabetic patients can go online and enter their daily blood glucose readings into their MyChart record. Software determines whether the readings are abnormal, and, if so, the patient's doctor receives an electronic alert, allowing quicker action to avert a potential health crisis. In 2007, Cleveland Clinic plans to add new MyChart functionality to meet the needs of patients with other chronic illnesses, including asthma and high blood pressure (McGee, 2006, p. 2).

ONLINE COMMUNICATION WITH CLINICIANS

Once a visit to a physician is over, most patients rely on the telephone for any additional communication needed. This is at best indirect and often frustrating, especially if the call is urgent. Patients are put on hold or asked to leave a callback number. Callbacks can be missed, leading to a game of "telephone tag" that frustrates all concerned. But phone calls and voicemail are no longer the only option for communication between physicians and patients.

Although some health systems have set up e-mail communication services for patients to use in contacting their physicians, most have not. Stepping into this void are commercial systems developed independently of a particular hospital or health system, including RelayHealth (www.relayhealth.com) and Medem (www.medem.com). Physicians anywhere in the country may participate by registering and paying a monthly fee. In return, the services provide a range of types of communication (clinical, scheduling, referrals), maintain message security, enable more structured messages, create an audit trail (something phone calls do not do), and integrate e-mail messages with the patient's electronic health record, if the practice uses them. Physicians can decide whether to charge patients for use of the system; the vendors also are seeking reimbursement from health insurers. Some commercial hospital and physician information systems include applications that allow access to medical information and the use of e-mail to communicate with other clinicians. Examples are Elysium Clinical Messaging (www.axolotl.com) and EpicWeb (www.epicsystems.com).

E-mail offers the same advantages in health care as it does in business and personal communication. It allows each party to communicate when they are available, avoiding inconvenient interruptions. It provides better documentation. It is legible. But it also has disadvantages. Communication is not in real time, so the provider can't engage in a question-and-answer conversation to obtain information the patient may have left out. The patient cannot follow up with additional questions without sending another message. Regular e-mail is not secure, so messages could be intercepted. Physicians are concerned about a possible flood of messages, which they are not paid to respond to, although a number of systems have found this is not a problem. They also are concerned about the legal implications of e-mail communication.

E-mail systems have been developed to address some of these concerns. The assumption that e-mail must be direct communication with the physician isn't necessarily correct. As in telephone communication, a physician office can develop a triage process that routes appropriate messages to the appropriate staff member for timely response.

MANAGING WAITING TIME

An obvious potential benefit of electronic communication with health care providers is to save patients' time. Saving patients' time is one of the quality of care goals promulgated by the Institute of Medicine in its *Crossing the Quality Chasm* (2001) reports.

> St. Jude's Children's Research Hospital in Memphis implemented a centralized scheduling system that allows one scheduler to make all the appointments for a patient. St. Jude's vision was to "integrate orders with scheduling without multiple phone calls to provide patient-centered schedules." The amount of time children had to wait was reduced, and the number of appointments that could be arranged to occur all on the same day was increased, resulting in fewer trips to the hospital. (Shepherd & Dotson, 2002, p. Session 39, p. 3)

> When patients at Candler Hospital in Georgia go to the ER for a minor problem, they are handed the same type of beeper you would see at a busy restaurant. It allows them to go to the snack bar and the nurse doesn't have to call out their name to find them. Candler uses PeopleAlert pagers made by Jtech Wireless Solutions (www.jtech.com) which vibrate and flash when alerted. While the pagers don't reduce waiting time, they can reduce the anxiety patients feel about missing a call when they leave the waiting room and can reduce the boredom of waiting. (Hart, 2003, p. 10)

Information Technology's Role in Controlling Health Care Costs

Providers have long believed that the return on investment (ROI) in information technologies is low or nonexistent. Although evidence suggests that some information technologies do lower costs, those savings are not always delivered to the organization that has to incur the expense.

For example, a hospital spends $500,000 on a system to reduce medication errors that uses bar codes. The result is a shorter length of stay for the patient. But if the hospital is being paid an all-inclusive per diem by the insurer, it receives no additional revenue. The savings accrue to the insurer. Nurses may spend less time administering medications, but that is likely to result in nurses' spending more time on other tasks rather than on nurse staff reductions that would lower hospital expenses. The hospital may also incur lower expenses related to litigation. That estimate is difficult to make and involves speculation on what might have happened. Lower malpractice insurance rates might also represent a savings, but not all insurers offer such reductions.

The professional journals, therefore, have begun to discuss ROI in terms of "soft savings" (uncertain or difficult to estimate in dollars) versus "hard savings" (certain and measurable in dollars). The former would include improved clinical decision making, resulting in improved patient outcomes. The latter would include a reduction in expenditures on paper and film. So far, many of the technologies reviewed in this chapter offer obvious soft savings (e.g., improvement in patient satisfaction), but any hard savings are difficult to document. However, if information technologies could be shown to contribute to controlling health care costs for the organizations that have to make the investment, investing in them might be easier to justify.

REDUCING HEALTH CARE COSTS THROUGH DISEASE MANAGEMENT

There are three categories of disease management tools. *Predictive modeling* applies sophisticated mathematical models and analysis to identify patients whose medical conditions or health status are most likely to require significant medical treatment or hospitalization; once identified, these patients' care is more closely managed. *Patient registries* are primarily database tools that track patients with certain conditions so that clinical interventions are completed as required and patients are kept healthier through preventive care. *Patient-focused disease management tools* include a wide range of devices that patients use in the home to monitor and manage their own condition; such devices increasingly are able to connect and communicate with the physician office or hospital clinic (McDonald et al., 2003). Disease management programs are currently popular among payers who believe they offer one of the best opportunities to simultaneously improve health care and reduce its costs. It's not surprising, then, that disease management programs are primarily undertaken by the payers, who would realize the savings in health care expenses, rather than by physicians or hospitals, who do not have financial responsibility for patients (unless they have accepted that responsibility in a contract with a managed care organization such as an HMO).

The Health Buddy is a device placed in the home and connected to a telephone line. Patients can be prompted to carry out and report specific activities that are important for health maintenance and improvement (www.healthhero.com), including providing reminders to take medications. A report is sent directly to the patient's clinician, who can evaluate the results. This is not only time-saving for patients, but also vastly more convenient for patients who are frail, elderly, or unable to drive. The system can prompt the clinician to make contact with a patient who hasn't used the device or carried out a particular action.

MORE EFFICIENT USE OF RESOURCES

Providers incur a significant cost when expensive resources are not used. When an operation is delayed because a microscope isn't available or because an instrument is broken, the hospital and surgeon lose revenue, but their overhead costs continue to accrue. When operating room (OR) scheduling is inefficient, ORs can stand empty at times and be flooded with cases at others, creating delays, cancelled procedures, frustration, and lost revenue. When patients do not appear for an appointment, the result again is lost revenue. All of these problems can be handled by scheduling systems that record the day and time of a procedure, verify that the needed resources are available, and optimize use of the surgical suites. They can also prompt staff to call patients in advance to remind them of the visit; these reminders can be automated and use the physician's voice.

Computerized resource management systems also can be used to track and control inventory.

The Louisiana State University Health Sciences Center adopted automated MedSelect drug-dispensing cabinets at nursing stations for narcotics and as-needed medications (drugs that are dispensed when a patient needs them rather than on a specific schedule). After the nurse entered a password, PIN number, and patient's name, a list of approved medications appeared. From this list, the nurse chose the needed drugs and the corresponding drawers in the cabinet would open. With this system, the hospital's emergency department saved approximately $20,000 per month due largely to better inventory control.

Digital acquisition and transmission of images from radiographic, magnetic resonance imaging (MRI), and computerized tomography equipment can permit radiologists to provide services to multiple facilities without traveling. The University of California at San Francisco Department of Radiology provides primary interpretations and second opinions of unusual or difficult cases, as well as second opinions for difficult modalities, such as cardiac (MRI) for images sent electronically or by courier (www.radiology.ucsf.edu/physicians). If a provider switches to digital images, the expense of film and chemicals is eliminated, as well as the cost of filing, delivering, and refiling films. Systems that collect, store, and retrieve digital images are called picture archiving and collection systems.

Speeding Adoption of Health Care Information Technology

A number of explanations are posited for why health care providers have not implemented technologies that are commonplace in banking, retail sales, and other consumer services. Often cited is the lack of funding and reimbursement. Purchase of such technologies competes with purchase of new diagnostic and treatment technologies that are not only reimbursable and potentially profitable, but also help an institution maintain its competitive position in the health care market. Faced with the choice of acquiring an improved MRI scanner or an electronic records system, the choice—in the past, at least—has most often been the former.

> Faced with the choice of acquiring an improved MRI scanner or an electronic records system, the choice—in the past, at least—has most often been the former.

Hospital decision makers have heard about or experienced system failures, including data systems that couldn't talk to each other or handle the volume of data required; they've also suffered from complicated commercial software that was disliked by staff or needed costly, constant upgrades. They know that installing a new system will be costly, time-consuming, and entail much training, taking physicians and staff away from their clinical duties. Constant upgrades and evolution of standards undermine their confidence that a new system is a good long-term investment. Clinicians may object to the increased transparency that electronic systems enable; in particular, they may question whether patient access to records is advisable (even though HIPAA makes that a patient right).

Although issues such as these can be formidable barriers, a final key factor is that, until recently, the demand for health information technology was low. Neither patients nor providers expected easier access to information and have not considered this an important factor in choosing a physician or hospital. A bank that failed to provide 24/7 access to cash and information would quickly lose customers. A physician's office or hospital that fails to offer online information can still be thriving. That situation is gradually changing, as the quality movement has emphasized the systems breakdowns that lead to adverse events, even deaths, many of which could be prevented by the wise adoption of health IT.

COST OF INFORMATION TECHNOLOGY

Investments in information technology must compete with investments in diagnostic and treatment technologies, for which they can be reimbursed or that may even be profitable. They also compete with other important budget line items—salary increases for nurses, facility renovation, and so on. Today's environment is one in which many hospitals face lower reimbursement, higher expenses for indigent care, and strong competition from other hospitals.

Estimates of the cost of CPOE have ranged from $3 million to $10 million depending on hospital size and level of existing IT infrastructure (Advisory Board Company, 2001). A report prepared by First Consulting Group (2003) for the American Hospital Association estimated one-time combined capital and operating costs from $6.3 million to $26 million, with an average of $12 million. Annual operating costs were estimated to be $370,000 to $3 million, with an average of $1.5 million.

The low level of HIT investment to date makes it harder for hospitals and physicians to catch up. A bank that has made recent investments in computers can consider only the cost of new software and training in deciding whether to install a new system. A hospital that doesn't have PCs at all nursing stations or computer cables connecting them will have to bear the cost of installing them before considering an electronic medical record system. Similarly, a physician's office with one PC in the office of the business manager faces hardware costs before implementing an EMR system. A hospital may have multiple homegrown systems created without an overall strategy—none of which can talk to each other. The cost of hardware and software is only the first hurdle and may not be the best estimate of the true cost of implementing a coordinated system.

In 2004, Baylor Health Care System in Dallas launched a $119 million initiative to transform clinical care using information technology. More than half of the expense of the 7-year project is attributable not to hardware and software, but to professionals' time to complete an internal reorganization emphasizing efficiency, evidence-based medicine, and patient safety. Rather than automating overly complex and poorly organized care processes, Baylor is first redesigning them.

WHO WILL PAY FOR IMPROVEMENTS?

If we accept the principle that those who benefit should pay, there isn't a clear answer to whether providers or payers or patients should bear the cost of IT. Those likely to improve quality do not necessarily result in higher net revenues for hospitals and physicians. For example, computerized physician order entry could result in fewer medication errors, lower expenses for care, and shorter patient stays. Shorter lengths of stay might cause hospitals to lose revenue for patients whose insurers pay on a per diem basis, while they would gain for patients whose insurers make a lump-sum payment for the entire stay (as with many Medicare patients).

So perhaps payers who might realize lower health care costs should be asked to pay part of IT's cost. In fact, some major employers, who have formed an organization called the Leapfrog Group (www.leapfroggroup.org) to attempt to leverage quality improvements, have offered to increase payments to hospitals that adopt specific information technologies.

In short, whether information technology is a cost of doing business that should be borne by providers regardless of whether it generates any financial benefits, or whether it is a cost of providing health services that should be borne by payers is an issue of continued debate. To speed the adoption rate, however, probably will require external funding, demonstrated return on investment, or a commitment to proceed resulting from values or external pressure, including actions by competitors. The immediate problem of how to obtain capital might be lessened by providing low- or no-cost revolving loans to provider organizations for the adoption of certain technologies.

THE POTENTIAL FEDERAL ROLE

The federal government is also a possible source of funds, either through grants or incentive payments to hospitals serving Medicare and Medicaid recipients (virtually every hospital in the country) that adopt specific information technology. The Bush administration has chosen instead to emphasize coordination, certification, and the development of standards.

In September 2005, the Department of Health and Human Services awarded the Certification Commission for Healthcare Information Technology (CCHIT) a 3-year contract to develop and evaluate certification criteria and create an inspection process for HIT in three areas:

● Ambulatory electronic health records for office-based physicians or providers
● Inpatient EHRs for hospitals and health systems
● The network components through which they interoperate and share information

The goals of CCHIT product certification are to:

● Reduce the risk of HIT investment by physicians and other providers.
● Ensure interoperability (compatibility) of HIT products.

- Assure payers and purchasers providing incentives for EHR adoption that the ROI will be improved quality.
- Protect the privacy of patients' personal health information.

CCHIT first certified ambulatory EHR products for office-based physicians and providers in 2006 and began certifying inpatient EHR products in 2007.

The Office of the National Coordinator for Health Information Technology also has awarded contracts to develop and evaluate prototypes for a nationwide health information network architecture that maximizes the use of existing resources such as the Internet to achieve widespread interoperability among software applications, particularly electronic health records. These contracts are intended to spur technical innovation for nationwide electronic sharing of health information in patient care and public health settings.

LACK OF STANDARDIZATION

A U.S. bank customer can obtain cash at an ATM in Europe because standards exist for the transmittal of data between banks. Such standards have not been widely adopted for the exchange of clinical data among U.S. physicians, hospitals, and other health care providers. HL7 (Health Level 7, www.hl7.org) is a 2,400-member, not-for-profit standards developing organization accredited by the American National Standards Institute, which is working toward a comprehensive framework and standards for exchanging, integrating, sharing, and retrieving electronic health information. However, its standards are voluntary, and many of the computer applications currently used by physicians and hospitals don't use HL7, either because they were developed before the standard was written or the vendor chose not to use it.

Progress in resolving this problem has been made, but complete standardization is unlikely very soon. The HL7 provider identification and billing standards under HIPAA and bar code standards for drugs are a beginning. The DICOM (digital imaging and communications in medicine) standard was developed to facilitate the transmission of medical images and their associated information.

BUILDING CLINICIAN ACCEPTANCE AND SUPPORT

Indifference or hostility on the part of physicians and nurses to clinical information systems is often attributed to age, prior training, or organizational culture. Many of the most experienced and politically powerful clinicians were trained without this technology, and they may be concerned about their ability to use it or may be unwilling to change their established work habits. Some may believe the technology could affect their ability to practice as they see fit—for example, by advising on what care to provide. In a 2002 survey, hospital leaders said that a primary barrier to adopting CPOE is physician resistance, because of the perception that it would take more of their time and reduce efficiency (Poon et al., 2004).

Based on the experience of hospitals and practices that have implemented HIT successfully—and those that have not—much has been written on how health care organizations can resolve clinicians' concerns. Physician (and other patient care staff) involvement in the design and implementation of new systems is critical. Influential physician and nurse "champions" should be identified to work with their respective professional groups. These are influential (but not necessarily the most knowledgeable) clinicians who could offer support once they are persuaded of the benefits. They would then be included on committees involved in selection and implementation.

Similarly, a full- or part-time paid position can be created for a physician and nurse who would provide advice to managers and a voice for clinicians within the information technology team. Such individuals could be recruited from the growing pool of younger clinicians who are well versed in HIT through their training, have a strong interest in it, and want opportunities to learn more. The Association of Medical Directors of Information Systems is an organization for physicians who have such a formal title and role (www.amdis.org).

Fine-tuning the process of implementation is also advocated. The experts suggest pilot tests that allow documentation of positive results and the rapid identification of problems. The pace of implementation needs to be monitored to assure that it is neither too fast nor too slow. Careful training is essential, as well as constant personal support. The systems need to be customized, as much as possible, to the needs of clinicians (Poon et al., 2004). Much can be done to help clinicians accept and use information technology. Successful implementation isn't guaranteed merely because the technology may have significant benefits for the patients, hospitals, or payers.

ASSURING CONFIDENTIALITY OF PATIENT INFORMATION

The continual flow of news stories about computer viruses and hackers would make anyone concerned about the confidentiality of medical information stored in computers. Concerns about privacy may delay passage of legislation to provide financial assistance for providers who want to implement electronic medical records in their facilities (Freudenheim & Pear, 2006).

However, to date, most of the major breaches have come not from these sources, nor from deliberate disclosure, but from careless handling of health information. The Department of Health and Human Services Office for Civil Rights, charged with enforcing the Health Insurance Portability and Accountability Act—the nation's strongest health information privacy law—received more than 22,000 complaints between 2003 and 2006. Allegations of "impermissible disclosure" have been among the most common complaints. But the office has filed only three criminal cases and imposed no civil fines. Instead, it has focused on educating violators about the law and encouraging them to obey it in the future (Freudenheim & Pear, 2006).

Several surveys have shown that Americans worry that information in their medical records might limit their job opportunities or cause them to lose their health insurance. If legislation is passed that requires the permission of each consumer for transmission of medical information, it could severely limit the extent to which information could be stored or transmitted among health care providers.

The fears about electronic medical records should be balanced by the less widely appreciated fact that medical information on paper is not secure either. Physicians and nurses and a wide array of hospital staff not involved in patients' care can examine paper charts. Staff who handle billing in hospitals and physician offices have access to medical information, as do workers in insurance companies, research teams, and others.

> Those who advocate computer storage of medical records must demonstrate that this information can be kept secure and private.

Still, those who advocate computer storage of medical records must demonstrate that this information can be kept secure and private. Measures can be taken. Computer systems with audit trails record the identity of each person who looks at a medical record. Patients can ask to see who has been reading their records, and they have that right under HIPAA. Employee education and a schedule of penalties help to deter inappropriate access.

Clearly, the privacy and security of electronic medical information depends as much on people as on technology. A hospital can require the use of passwords to access files, but if a medical resident gives that password to someone else, security and privacy are compromised. A physician may enjoy the convenience of working away from the office, but if she accesses patient records while others are nearby and able to view her computer screen, privacy is compromised. Clearly stated procedures, training on those procedures, and monitoring and enforcement are critically important.

Equally important is the use of specific technology for assuring privacy and security. This includes technology for *authorization*— that is, determining who has access to which parts of a record. Unlike paper files, access to specific elements of an electronic medical record can be restricted on a need-to-know basis. A clerk arranging for transportation to the radiology department needs to know the patient's room number and name but not the diagnoses. Technology is also available for *authentication*—that is, verifying the identity of those who attempt to access information. A common procedure requires the user to "know something and have something." They must know a password and user name and also possess a key or special card encoded with information on a magnetic strip or in a computer chip. The voluntary or involuntary sharing of passwords and user names is then no longer a threat to confidentiality. There is growing interest in devices that use fingerprints, the iris of the eye, and facial images to authenticate identity (International Biometric Group, www.biometricgroup.com).

Access to the information system outside of the health care facility raises additional security issues. Virtual private networks allow private, protected communication on the public Internet (Gillespie, 2003). Or access may be allowed only through secure Web sites. PDAs and laptops may be set to access information only on Web sites so that nothing is stored on the device itself.

Conclusion

Information technology that can improve the quality of health care, increase patient satisfaction, and help control health care costs is available. At present, it is effectively used by a relatively small number of hospitals and physicians in the United States. The obstacles are real, but concrete ways of overcoming them are being developed and debated by providers and payers, including the government. The demand for change will increase because of the growing gap between what consumers, government, and employers have come to expect—based on their experience with information technology used by other sectors of our economy—and what health care providers currently offer. An important unresolved issue is determining who will pay for information technology applications in a climate of rapidly rising health care expenditures.

References

Advisory Board Company. (2001). *Computerized physician order entry: Lessons from pioneering institutions.* Washington, DC: Author.

Bates, D. W., Leape, L. L., Cullen, D. J., Laird, N., Petersen, L. A., Teich, J. M., et al. (1998). Effect of computerized physician order entry and a team intervention on prevention of serious medication errors. *Journal of the American Medical Association, 280*(15), 1311–1316.

Berwick, D. (1999, September 27). Knowledge always on call. *Modern Healthcare,* 2–4.

Burt, C., Hing, E., & Woodwell, D. (2006). *Electronic medical record use by office-based physicians: United States, 2005.* Retrieved January 11, 2007, from http://www.cdc.gov/nchs/products/pubs/pubd/hestats/electronic/electronic.htm

Cutler, D., Feldman, N. & Horwitz, J. (2005). U.S. adoption of computerized physician order entry systems. *Health Affairs, 24*(6), 1654–1663.

Drazen, E., & Fortin, J. (2003). *Digital hospitals move off the drawing board.* Oakland, CA: California HealthCare Foundation.

First Consulting Group. (2003). *Computerized physician order entry: Cost, benefits and challenges.* Long Beach, CA: Author.

Freudenheim, M. (2004, April 6). Many hospitals resist computerized patient care. *New York Times,* Section C, p. 1.

Freudenheim, M., & Pear, R. (2006, December 3). Health hazard: Computers spilling your history. *New York Times,* Section 3, p. 1.

Gillespie, G. (2003, September). Are VPNs safe for the wild wild Web? *Health Data Management, 11*(9), 54–58, 60.

Hart, A. (2003, November 1). Patience lost, patients gained. *Savannah Morning News,* p. 10.

Institute of Medicine and Committee on Quality of Health Care in America. (1999). *To err is human: Building a safer health system.* Washington, DC: National Academy Press.

Institute of Medicine and Committee on Quality of Health Care in America. (2001). *Crossing the quality chasm: A new health system for the 21st century.* Washington, DC: National Academy Press.

Jha, A., Ferris, T., Donelan, K., DesRoches, C., Shields, A., Rosenbaum, S., et al. (2006). How common are electronic health records in the United States? A summary of the evidence. *Health Affairs, 25*(6), W496–W507.

McDonald, C., Overhage, J. M., Barnes, M., Schadow, G., Blevins, L., Dexter, P. R., et al. (2005). The Indiana network for patient care: A working local health information infrastructure. *Health Affairs, 24*(5), 1214–1220.

McDonald, K., Turisco, F., & Drazen, E. (2003). *Advanced technologies to lower health care costs and improve quality.* Westborough, MA: Massachusetts Technology Collaborative.

McGee, M. (2006, December 13). Insurers push patients toward e-health records. *InformationWeek.* Retrieved December 10, 2007, from http://www.informationweek.com/news/showArticle.jhtml?articleID=196603941

Perez-Pena, R. (2004, April 6). Bronx hospital embraces online technology that others avoid. *New York Times,* p. 6.

Poon, E. G., Blumenthal, D., Jaggi, T., Honour, M. M., Bates, D. W., & Kaushal, R. (2004). Overcoming barriers to adopting and implementing computerized physician order entry systems in U.S. hospitals. *Health Affairs, 23*(4), 184–190.

Schuerenberg, B. K. (2003, May). Clearing the hurdles to decision support. *Health Data Management,* 42–46, 48.

Shepherd, G., & Dotson, P. (2002). The design and implementation of an integrated scheduling application. In *Proceedings of the 2002 Annual HIMSS Conference.* Chicago: Healthcare Information and Management Systems Society.

Shortliffe, E. H., & Perreault, L. E. (Eds.). (1990). *Medical informatics: Computer applications in health care* (469, 475–480). Reading, MA: Addison-Wesley.

Sublett, P. (2002, November). Technology's impact on reducing medication errors. *Health Management Technology,* 24–26.

Teich, J. M., et al. (1996). Toward cost effective, quality care: The Brigham Integrated Computing System. In Computer-Based Records Institute Staff (Ed.), *Proceedings of the CPR Recognition Symposium: 2* (19–56). New York: McGraw-Hill.

PART THREE

System Performance

14

Key Words

accountability
benchmarking
board composition
structure and function
chief executive officer
competencies
environmental scanning
governance

governing boards
integrated delivery system
mission
organizational autonomy
and performance
managerial skills and
performance
not-for-profit

for-profit and governmental
ownership
political terrain
position description
product-line management

Governance, Management, and Accountability

Anthony R. Kovner

Learning Objectives

- Specify how governance and management contribute to health care organization (HCO) performance.
- Identify the pros and cons of for-profit, not-for-profit, and public ownership.
- Describe how performance is measured in health care organizations.
- Apply concepts of accountability to health care organizations.
- Identify ways to improve HCO governance, management, and accountability.

Topical Outline

- Governance as a process of decision making
- Measuring organizational performance
- Ownership of health care organizations
- Current governance issues
- Management
- Management work in health care organizations
- Current management issues
- Accountability

P

ut simply, *governance* is the system organizations use to make important decisions, such as about mission, goals, budget, capital financing, and quality improvement. *Management* is responsible for implementing these decisions. And *accountability* means being answerable for the decisions that an organization (or individuals and governments) make. Increasingly, in large organizations, governance is differentiated from management. In smaller organizations, the owner-managers often govern as well as manage. Organizations are constrained by the accountability mandates of government and by the autonomy of customers (including, in the case of health care organizations, physicians) who decide whether to use services. The mechanisms of accountability also create opportunities for organizations to manage the expectations and commitment of major stakeholders.

This chapter has three parts. The first, on governance, defines what governance is, describes the contribution of owners to measuring performance, reviews the advantages and disadvantages of different patterns of ownership, and discusses current governance issues. The second part, on management, describes what managers do and how managerial work is carried out in health care organizations and discusses current management issues. The third part, on accountability, describes how organizations are accountable to stakeholders and how their behavior is limited and focused by customers.

Governance as a Process for Decision Making

The governance system is how decisions are made in organizations. Those who govern or own the organization exercise ultimate direction, control, and authority. They are accountable to payers and users for the way the organization uses resources to provide care. The governance process in any organization may be dominated by a few individuals or by many; governance may be exercised in an authoritarian or in a participatory way.

Every organization has a set of stakeholders who have interests in organizational performance. For health care organizations (HCOs), the stakeholders include payers, users, clinicians and other employees, unions and professional organizations, accreditors, and regulators. Stakeholders often want the organization to perform differently from the way the organization is performing currently—for example, as to which services are provided by whom or how employees are to be compensated. HCOs depend on various resources—patients, clinicians, facilities, and legitimacy—to achieve their purposes and survive. Governance influences the supply of resources as well as their allocation.

GOVERNANCE CONTRASTED WITH MANAGEMENT

Although those who govern should make policy and those who manage should implement policy, unfortunately, the boundary between governance and management is not clear-cut. In practice, top managers are often key participants in governance, because they have the necessary time and information to define an issue or limit consideration among policy alternatives. In large part, this is what managers are paid to do. Yet, because they, at least potentially, have the power and will to do so, trustees or directors may carry out policy or manage as well. A more useful distinction between governance and management therefore concerns the nature of the decisions and their relative importance. Decisions about who governs, the mission of the organization, and major capital investments are governance—not management—decisions. Hiring, scheduling, and coordinating frontline providers of care are typically day-to-day management decisions.

> The boundary between governance and management is not clear-cut.

Griffith, Sahney, and Mohr (1995) specify four types of organizational decisions: what the mission/vision is, how resources are to be allocated, how the organization is designed, and how its programs are implemented. They point out that these decisions may be considered at a strategic (policy) or at a programmatic (operations) level. For example, at the strategic level, mission/vision can be considered as assessing the environment and developing a strategic plan; at the programmatic level, it might involve developing and carrying out a marketing plan or a joint venture with another organization. These are governance decisions, because they concern the scope of services and the generation of resources; or they are management decisions, as they relate to generating information and motivating workers to carry out policy decisions. Governance includes decisions about what services the organization provides to whom at what price. Management involves implementing those governance decisions through prioritizing objectives and strategies and reconsidering objectives and strategies as circumstances change. (See Griffith & White, 2007, for the contrast between functions of the governing board and the executive office in HCOs.)

Measuring Organizational Performance

One reason for attempting to document effective or acceptable organizational performance is to focus attention on who controls organizational decision making. If performance is acceptable to trustees, managers, and clinicians, does it matter what anyone else thinks? If it does matter, what are other stakeholders going to do if they find performance unacceptable?

A second reason for developing measures of performance concerns the distribution of organizational resources. To adjudicate claims on resources, performance goals must be clear. And they must track directly back to the organization's mission. When performance goals are clearly specified, they enable answers to questions such as, How is our HMO doing? How does what we do compare with what our physicians and nurses, accreditors and regulators, customers and potential customers think we ought to be doing?

Agreed-upon performance standards also facilitate performance evaluation and compensation. Statements such as, "The hospital made a $100,000 surplus this year, 1% of patients made formal complaints, and our turnover rate in nursing was 15%," may sound specific—and positive—but actually they are not very precise indicators of performance unless they can be tied to previously agreed-upon performance standards. In this case, the governing body may have expected that the surplus would be $250,000, that it would tolerate a complaint rate of 3%, and that a nursing retention program it authorized would reduce turnover to 9%. In this example, the managers failed on two important measures. The standards of performance for which the organization and its managers are to be held accountable must be made clear *in measurable terms* and *in advance*. Of course, as circumstances change, targets can be adjusted for fully explained reasons.

Examining the turnover rate in nursing more closely, a manager may want to know: (1) in which units is nurse turnover high or low; (2) how turnover compares with that of similar hospitals; (3) how to differentiate involuntary turnover (e.g., spousal moves) from voluntary turnover; and (4) whether there are different rates between nurses who have worked for this hospital less than 2 years and longer-term employees. Answers to such questions are essential to devising remediation strategies, setting realistic targets, and assessing the effectiveness of retention efforts.

Individuals or institutions that own HCOs are typically concerned with organizational performance. This includes defining standards;

specifying measures of acceptable and superior performance; and hiring, retaining, or firing the key managers who are responsible for achieving organizational objectives. Superior organizational performance is defined differently by different stakeholders. Employees want higher salaries, clinicians want the latest equipment, patients want more convenient and higher quality services, and payers want better cost containment.

A common way to evaluate HCO performance is in terms of market share or financial profitability. Those governing the organization must decide what is acceptable financial performance and how it is to be measured. If they do not formally decide this, judgments on performance outcomes will be based on the behavior of individuals and groups at lower organizational levels. Further, different parts of the same HCO obviously may operate at different levels of success relative to each other or to the organization as a whole. An example would be to compare the performance of a hospital's cardiac service with its cancer service. There may be large differences in financial as well as quality of care performance between these very different units, even though they are part of the same hospital or health system.

Ownership of Health Care Organizations

Different sponsors or owners of HCOs have different goals. HCO owners include physicians and nurses, cooperatives, government, religious organizations, investors, employers, unions, and philanthropists. Different categories of owners establish an HCO for different reasons, although their motives are often mixed. For example, a politician's goal in securing funding for a new public hospital may be to gain votes and create jobs as well as to improve health services. An archdiocese may seek to maintain ownership of a hospital in part to assure that Catholic doctrines are followed in the community (for example, with regard to abortions).

HCOs are commonly grouped as to whether they are for-profit, not-for-profit, or public. Which type of ownership makes the most sense varies according to the population being served, the nature of competing providers, and the interests of sponsoring stakeholders, including trustees and the attending physician staff. Ownership may change from one form to another. For example, a church may sell a nonprofit hospital to a for-profit corporation because the church officials decide that the monies gained from the sale can be used elsewhere to better serve the poor, while the for-profit corporation is better positioned to attract the capital required to upgrade and expand hospital facilities.

BOARDS OF DIRECTORS (TRUSTEES)

Most organizations have a governing body with legal responsibility for control of the organization. Corporations are required to designate membership of the governing body as a condition of incorporation by the state in which home offices are located.

Bylaws outline the purposes of the organization; the composition and duties of the governing board; the requirements for periodic meetings of the board and notice of meetings; the duties and nature of corporate officers and the method of their selection; the nature and purpose of board committees; and how the bylaws can be amended. A physician partnership agreement, for example, typically specifies the responsibilities of the partners, how net income is shared and losses are borne, disability provisions, termination of a partner's agreement, and the composition of the executive committee or board and its functions.

The legal powers of the governing board, as suggested in a model constitution and bylaws for nonprofit hospitals published by the American Hospital Association (1981), are as follows:

> The general powers of the corporation shall be vested in the governing board which shall have charge, control and management of the property, affairs, and funds of the corporation; shall fill vacancies among the officers for unexpired terms; and shall have the power and authority to do and perform all acts and functions not inconsistent with these bylaws or with any action taken by the corporation. (p. 11)

Although in theory the governing board has the responsibility for making policy, in practice the power and function of governing boards vary widely, depending on population served, financial strength, and local power structure. Policy for the HCO may be decided by different internal subgroups and by external organizations. For example, while allocating funds for a hospital's capital improvements may be decided by the board of the multiunit health system of which it is a part (in many states, major capital improvements also are subject to state and local government approval), the scope of services the hospital will provide is decided by the local governing board; the nature of its clinical education program is determined by the professional staff and accrediting organizations; and its initiatives in marketing and community relations are planned and implemented by management.

Board members of nonprofit organizations are often less clear about their responsibilities and functions than are their counterparts in for-profit entities. Nonprofit board members may not even be aware that they are (technically) the HCO owners. Board members serve for a variety of reasons: community service, contacts, compensation, status, access for their own medical care, or belief that their skills and experience will help the HCO attain its mission.

SELECTION OF BOARD MEMBERS

The functions and powers of a governing board are strongly influenced by its composition and its method of selecting members. At first, a governing board consists of the HCO's founders, who may be contributing the key resources to begin the enterprise. Officers are elected by members of the governing board. In investor-owned organizations, owners of shares elect the governing board. In nonprofits, board members usually elect themselves. Or board members may be chosen from superordinate nonprofit corporate bodies that, in effect, own the HCO. For example, an archdiocese may own several hospitals and appoint board members for each hospital. Or a hospital may be owned by members in a community who pay a fee to join the hospital corporation.

Boards of large HCOs typically are dominated by businessmen, bankers, and lawyers—essentially, White men ages 50 to 70—although board composition depends to some extent on the type of organization. Not surprisingly, government and religious hospitals have greater proportions of public officials and religious leaders on their respective boards. For-profit and osteopathic hospitals have greater proportions of physicians.

Board members may be insiders (managers or clinicians) or outsiders chosen for some special expertise, status, or access to resources. The type of person selected often depends on the functions and role of the board. If the primary purpose of the board is to raise money or give advice and counsel to the chief executive officer (CEO), then outsiders will be selected. If the primary function is policymaking, then the directors will need detailed knowledge of the business, and insiders may be preferred. Typically, nonprofit hospital boards are dominated by outsider "community influentials," and for-profit group practices are led by insider physicians.

According to Bowen (1994), the principal functions of a board of directors or trustees are:

- To select, encourage, advise, evaluate, and, if need be, replace the CEO.
- To review and adopt long-term strategic directions and to approve specific objectives, financial and otherwise.

- To ensure, to the extent possible, that the necessary resources, including human resources, will be available to pursue the organization's strategies and achieve its objectives.
- To monitor the performance of management.
- To ensure that the organization operates responsibly as well as effectively.
- To nominate suitable candidates for election to the board and to establish and carry out an effective system of governance at the board level, including evaluation of board performance.

Most board members, certainly of nonprofits, are not paid for their participation, yet active board service can require a great deal of time. Board members could be spending that time earning money. Payment to board members for their time might improve accountability or provide a more realistic opportunity for lower-income people to serve.

BOARD COMPOSITION, STRUCTURE AND FUNCTION

Governing boards vary in their makeup, structure, and function. According to an Ernst & Young study (1997), the average hospital board had 13 members, although some boards had fewer than 7 or more than 16. Boards usually meet monthly; some meet quarterly. Most boards have committees of two types: standing committees and special committees, which are discharged on completion of a task. Typical standing committees are long-range planning, finance, and nominating. Some boards will appoint non–board members to serve on committees. (Government HCOs are usually not run by boards but rather by executives, with oversight from the legislative branch.)

> The boards of a national for-profit nursing home corporation with facilities in 40 states and that of a nonprofit academic health center with one site should not have the same composition, structure, and function.

Appropriate composition, structure, and function of a board depend on organizational circumstances. The boards of a national for-profit nursing home corporation with facilities in 40 states and that of a nonprofit academic medical center with one site will not include the same types of individuals or have the same structure, because they face radically different issues. What constitutes the most effective board for a health care organization will depend on mission, strategy, resources, and the board's expected contribution to results.

THE CHANGING ROLE OF HCO BOARDS

Views differ and are changing regarding the role of the board of directors. More than 50 years ago, Burling, Lentz, and Wilson (1956) argued that a not-for-profit hospital governing board has a responsibility to provide and maintain the hospital to serve a community need according the wishes of the donor(s). To Umbdenstock (1987), the board must be the "organization's conscience, constantly assessing proposed directions . . . in light of what these steps mean for the implementation of a mission to serve and care for all" (p. 47).

According to Griffith and White (2007), the managerial functions of HCO governing boards include appointing the chief executive, establishing mission and vision, approving long-range plans and the annual budget, ensuring quality of care, and monitoring performance against plans and budget. As noted previously, it is easy to say that the board should be concerned with policy and oversight and that the staff should be responsible for management and administration (Bowen, 1994), but how this is best worked out in any organization depends on, among other factors, the skills, experience, and trust of the board chair and the CEO, the challenges the organization is facing at any particular time, and the expectations of major stakeholders.

The nonprofit form of ownership has been criticized as being less accountable than either the for-profit or public ownership form. Boards of for-profit hospitals are accountable to shareholders, and boards of public institutions are accountable to voters.

BOARD RELATIONSHIP TO INDEPENDENT MEDICAL STAFF

According to Griffith, Sahney, and Mohr (1995), in the nonprofit HCO, the governing board owns the organization but obviously cannot practice medicine. Instead, the board appoints independently practicing physicians to the medical staff—that is, gives them privileges to practice in the hospital. The CEO is the board's designee on site. The privileges agreement between attending physicians and the HCO grants this defined group of physicians permission not only to practice medicine, but also to collect private fees from patients in return for their commitment to abide by the hospital's rules and regulations. Especially important are the rules pertaining to the quality of medical care.

The medical staff has its own bylaws but also is in charge of making rules and regulations that affect the physicians who practice there, such as the procedures to follow when a patient is admitted or dies. The board (and there may be some physicians on the board) participates in implementing and revising the medical staff bylaws, as needed. The medical staff organization develops and enforces the rules as long as the board agrees that these are beneficial (in nonprofits, to the community; in for-profits, to the shareholders). Griffith specifies that the compact breaks down if the board does not act vigorously as trustees for community (or shareholder) interests. An example of the nonprofit hospital's compact with the community is a commitment to ensure that the area has enough specialists, even if physicians practicing at the hospital would prefer to restrict competition.

Current Governance Issues

PREFERABLE OWNERSHIP PATTERNS

Does it make any difference whether HCOs are owned by government or by for-profit or by nonprofit organizations? (For a review of the arguments for and against these three types of ownership for all organizations, see Hansmann, 1996.) Does it make enough of a difference to justify tax exemption for nonprofits? Currently, government is the primary owner of facilities that provide long-term mental health care and those that serve veterans. For-profits dominate in the health maintenance organization (HMO), nursing home, and physician practice sectors. Nonprofits are the form of ownership for most short-term community hospitals, particularly in the northeastern United States, principally for historical reasons. The first nonprofit hospitals were founded more than 200 years ago by local community leaders as institutions to care for the "deserving" poor. (The well-to-do were treated in their homes, and the "undeserving" poor were treated in almshouses.)

Nonprofit organizations reap numerous financial benefits: they are exempt from income, state, and local property taxes; they can attract donations, because these are tax-deductible for the donor; and they have access to tax-free bonds. Nonprofit organizations (hospitals, health plans) occasionally convert from nonprofit to for-profit status, primarily to attract capital so that the organization can be more profitable or gain greater future market share. The value of the nonprofit status is calculated by regulators—through a sometimes contentious process—and that value is returned to the community, often in the form of a foundation. (The California Endowment, the Archstone Foundation, the New York State Health Foundation, Denver's Rose Community Foundation, and many others began in this way.)

Unfortunately, there is insufficient evidence to make scientific conclusions regarding whether type of ownership affects the cost and quality of medical care an HCO provides or whether the performance of nonprofit HCOs justifies their continued preferential tax treatment. Nevertheless, advocates of each form of ownership make the as-yet unproved claim that it provides the best quality care.

Arguments against *for-profit ownership* are: First, for-profit organizations concentrate on providing only those services that are profitable—essentially raking off the most profitable activities (such as cardiovascular surgery) and leaving nonprofit and public HCOs with a less profitable service mix (such as psychiatry and obstetrics). Second, for-profits build facilities only in expanding high-income communities, leaving nonprofits and governmental HCOs to provide services to the poor and uninsured. Third, the monies allocated to the shareholders of for-profits can better be reinvested in the delivery of care for those lacking access. Arguments in favor of for-profit ownership counter that: first, even allowing for profit, these HCOs are more efficient, and they pay taxes. Second, consumers should be charged only for the costs of the services that they use, rather than be overcharged (in most cases, buffered by their third-party payers) to subsidize the costs of care for people who cannot pay, as nonprofits do. Third, for-profits respond more quickly and more flexibly in meeting market demand.

Arguments against *public ownership* are as follows: Primary emphasis in public HCOs is on keeping costs low, especially in this era of continual tax-cutting for the better-off, and government operations are inherently bureaucratic and inflexible. Arguments in favor are: first, total costs and unit costs are lower in government-owned HCOs, signifying greater efficiency, and second, every user is treated similarly, based on health care needs, regardless of income or insurance status.

Arguments against *nonprofit* ownership are: first, they have higher costs, and, second, in some or in many cases, the community service component is weak or nonexistent. Arguments in favor include their often long-standing ties to and traditions of service to the community.

To reach informed conclusions about what type of sponsorship is best, further research that relates ownership to performance (however defined) must be carried out. To properly do this, conditions other than ownership, such as organizational size, must be held constant.

IMPROVING NONPROFIT GOVERNING BOARD PERFORMANCE

What is the value added of the nonprofit governing board, and how can it be increased? Answering this question cogently assumes some agreement on the criteria for evaluating board performance. Boards represent an ownership interest that is different from management's, and different owners choose to maximize different values. Such values may include improving health care in a community at acceptable levels of cost and quality. In any case, nonprofit boards can add value by holding management accountable for results and by helping plan a future that will enable an organization to fulfill its mission and to meet the objectives and expectations of stakeholders. (For excellent recommendations as to how to improve HCO governance, see Pointer & Orlikoff, 2002.)

The goals of for-profits are usually clear-cut: to make more money now and in the future. Some of the critics of nonprofit boards point to the lack of agreement among board members as to mission and their roles as board members (Kovner, 2001), the length of time it takes for these boards to make policy decisions, the lack of usefulness of decisions when board members don't understand the business, and the time and effort it takes for management to educate boards and provide staff support.

An important issue is what stakeholders should do when nonprofit boards do not perform well. The federal government already sets some rules for governance (through IRS rules related to nonprofits and Centers for Medicare & Medicaid Services rules about financial performance) and should disclose information on the financial and managerial performance of health care organizations. Organizations that accredit HCOs have similar responsibilities. Setting the rules includes establishing personal liability for board members when they have committed a breach of fiduciary duty, as when they have a conflict of interest (for example, promoting use of a vendor in which they have a financial stake). Also needed is public disclosure of measures related to board performance—such as the limitation, if any, on terms of office; the presence or absence of measurable objectives for the board; and the numbers and types and value added of board committees. An argument can be made that government should set requirements for boards—such as who can serve, for how long, whether meetings should be open to the public, and how quality of care is monitored. A common suggestion is to extend the federal Sarbanes-Oxley legislation, intended to combat corruption in corporate boards, to nonprofit boards as well.

Management

Now we focus on managers in HCOs—what they do and how their work is organized. We also consider certain management issues, such as how management performance can be improved, how managers should be compensated, and how they should be trained.

WHAT MANAGERS DO

> Managers do, invariably, what they are supposed to do, what they are asked to do, what they want to do, and what they can do.

Managerial work can be viewed as occupying positions, carrying out functions, requiring competencies, and performing roles. Managers do, invariably, what they are supposed to do, what they are asked to do, what they want to do, and what they can do. Managerial work is characterized by choice or discretion after constraints are obeyed and demands are complied with.

Positions and Functions

A job or position description is one way of looking at the work that managers do. Longest (1980) views the basic managerial functions, which often are keywords in position descriptions, as:

- Planning, which involves the determination of goals and objectives.
- Organizing, which is the structuring of people and things to accomplish the work required to meet the objectives.
- Directing, which is the stimulation of members of the organization to meet the objectives.
- Coordinating, which is the conscious effort of assembling and synchronizing diverse activities and participants so that they work toward the attainment of objectives.
- Controlling, in which the manager compares actual results with objectives to provide a measure of success or failure.

Competencies

Boyatzis (1995) has developed a model that includes three groups of managerial competencies. These include, first, the primarily "people skills" of efficiency orientation, planning, initiative, attention to detail, self-control and flexibility (goals and action management), empathy, persuasiveness, networking, negotiating, self-confidence, group management, developing others, and oral communication; second, use of concepts, systems thinking, pattern recognition, theory building, technology, quantitative analysis, and social objectivity; and, third, written communication (analytic reasoning).

Goleman (1998) has found that the most effective leaders have a high degree of what he calls emotional intelligence, which is twice as important as are technical skills and IQ for managerial jobs at all levels. The five components of emotional intelligence in managerial work are self-awareness, self-regulation (e.g., the ability to think before acting), motivation, empathy, and social skills.

Managerial Roles

Roles are aspects of behavior that can be isolated for analytical purposes, such as leading or handling disturbances. Positions can be viewed as combinations of roles. Kovner (1984) has conceptualized managerial roles into four sets of activities: motivating others, scanning the environment, negotiating the political terrain, and generating and allocating resources.

Motivating Others. Managers spend a great deal of time recruiting and retaining their managerial and supervisory staff and in making decisions about rewards and promotions, work procedures, and development and training. To carry out these activities, they use communications and analytic skills. Managers facilitate the work of subordinates in doing what is required or desired, within organizational limits.

Managers motivate others through both personal characteristics—predictability, trustworthiness, empathy—and implementation of organizational policy around staff development (annual evaluations, learning contracts, and so on), pay level, and training. Managers must be developed, appropriately rewarded, and trained. Motivation is affected by a worker's self-image of job performance in any particular job. Managers can help improve performance by starting from where the worker is and using whichever strategies the worker will buy into to attain organizational goals and objectives. Worker performance also can be enhanced through improvement of systems and processes rather than by workers working harder and smarter; in fact, systems improvements are sometimes the most effective way to improve organizational performance. Finally, the organizational culture is important in improving the quality of work and the productivity of workers. For example, workers can be rewarded for treating patients as customers and meeting management's high expectations for quality and service, or merely paid as necessary complements to the physician's work.

Scanning the Environment. Effective managers scan or search the environment for potential problems and targets of opportunity. Scanning activities include long-range planning, market and product research, compensation monitoring, and quality benchmarking. The development of management information systems may be essential for effective scanning. In large HCOs, scanning activities are usually performed by special units for marketing, quality improvement, fundraising, human resources, and strategic planning. In smaller HCOs, managers scan the environment assisted by colleagues or consultants. Information about how similar organizations and managers perform is available from journals, books, the Internet, newsletters, and advertisements. Managers attend continuing education and trade association meetings and are part of online networks where colleagues and experts communicate. Managers visit similar organizations to learn firsthand about ways to improve effectiveness and efficiency. Openness to receiving such site visits has been a hallmark of public and nonprofit HCOs.

Negotiating the Political Terrain. Effective managers maintain trust and build alliances with groups and individuals. A positive political climate contributes to effective decision making and implementation. New managers must find out who is doing what to whom across a wide variety of organizational issues and problems. Put another way, managers must learn "what is the ballpark I'm really playing in, who are the players, and what are the rules?" Managers learn the informal power structure by looking and listening. The operative rules are not always easy to discover and may be quite different from any written management guides the organization has developed. Organizational cultures vary, and within organizations, different subcultures exist and come into play depending on the issue. Stakeholders involved in overhauling a management information system are different from those establishing a new renal dialysis unit, for example.

Activities that managers carry out when negotiating the political terrain include public relations, lobbying, labor relations, negotiating with governing boards and medical staffs, arbitrating among units and departments, and making alliances with other organizations.

Generating and Allocating Resources. Effective managers spend a great deal of time looking for ways to increase revenues and decrease expenses. In these analyses, managers consider past performance, performance in best practice organizations, and industry standards. For example, managers streamline buying procedures, secure long-term and working capital at low rates of interest, maintain buildings and equipment efficiently, set optimal prices, and sequence appropriately new construction and renovations. In managing stakeholder expectations, managers listen closely to what subordinates, clinicians, and customers say.

Effective managers make decisions about generating and using resources. This occurs as part of the budgetary process and in response to emergency or extraordinary requests. Less tangible resources, such as staff time, also must be allocated, as must resources that may be less amenable to negotiation, such as use of space.

Managerial Work in Health Care Organizations

The federal Bureau of Labor Statistics estimates that the demand for "medical and health services managers" will increase 16.4% between 2006 and 2016, to 305,000 such positions in 2016 (U.S. Department of Labor, 2007). Organizations that employ health services managers include hospitals and health systems, nursing homes, health maintenance organizations and other insurance companies, group practices, neighborhood health centers, home care agencies, ambulatory surgery centers, medical day care programs, durable equipment companies, home infusion agencies, and hospices.

In simple organizations, such as a solo physician's office, clinicians may perform managerial functions, such as billing patients or contracting with vendors to do so. In a group practice, the hiring, paying, and firing of physicians is done either by the whole group or (especially in larger groups) by a designated subset of physicians (who also see patients), while the billing function is supervised by nonphysician managers. In a large hospital or health maintenance organization, clinician and nonclinician general managers are supported by specialized managers in different functional areas: human resources, finance, information services, and marketing, among others.

The largest HCOs may cover whole regions of the country, and a few are national. Many are multiunit organizations (also called integrated delivery systems) that include hospitals, nursing homes, group practices, and HMOs. In these organizations, unit managers report to divisional managers for a geographic area, such as the northeastern United States. Divisional managers, in turn, report to managers in corporate headquarters who are accountable to the board of directors. Certain management functions are allocated among headquarters, divisions, and local HCOs. Headquarter functions commonly include legal affairs, construction, capital financing, and corporate public relations. Other functions, such as quality improvement and production standards, may be shared among the three organizational levels.

A newer development in the organization of managerial work in HCOs is product line management. A health system, large hospital, or group practice is reorganized into several divisions, such as women's health services, emergency care, cancer care, and rehabilitation services, each with its own manager and budget (see Herzlinger, 1997). The logic behind such reorganization is that these services can be more effectively managed as separate businesses than as part of a large HCO. Whether this is so is yet unproven.

As noted previously, accountability of health care organizations is uncertain unless there are measurable objectives set in advance and negotiated with stakeholders. Managers' contribution to organizational performance in health care has been criticized, because managerial costs are high per dollar of expenditures, and managerial salaries are often high. It has been difficult to isolate managers' contributions to organizational performance. For example, despite substantial managerial contributions, an HCO may be floundering because of a hostile environment or poor decisions by previous managers. Or the reverse situation may occur: Despite little or ineffective managerial contribution, an HCO may be growing rapidly and even improving the quality of service rendered due to lack of competitors, growth in demand for profitable services, excellent contributions by previous managers, and the performance of dedicated clinicians.

Current Management Issues

IMPROVING MANAGERIAL PERFORMANCE

To what extent does managerial performance in HCOs need to be improved? Why don't more HCOs have a greater capacity to change in a timely way? Why do they invest so little in training? Why is quality so uneven? Why is service to customers sometimes unfriendly? We might infer that at least some managers have learned answers to such questions, because they have successfully transformed organizational performance to reduce costs per unit of service, improve service quality, and increase market share. The Institute for Healthcare Improvement and others who have attempted to bring techniques from other industries (lean production, customer experience) into the health care sector have given managers new ways of analyzing and approaching issues in health care delivery.

Disclosure to customers and stakeholders of HCO objectives and the degree of their attainment relative to best practices is an excellent way to hold managers accountable for improving service, monitoring quality, cutting waste, and improving health status. It is the responsibility of stakeholders—government, owners, clinicians, and customers and payers—to expect improved performance and to act if expectations are not met. When the organization fails, the customers (not just patients, but physicians as well) either try to change performance or they seek services (or practice opportunities) elsewhere when they can, and the managers are fired or forced to resign. This has been the American way. It has been highly regarded by other developed nations, even as we are criticized as a society for the high preference given to organizational performance relative to community solidarity.

> Disclosure to customers and stakeholders of HCO objectives and attainment relative to best practice is an excellent way to hold managers accountable for improving service, monitoring quality, cutting waste, and improving health status.

HOW SHOULD MANAGERS BE COMPENSATED?

The median total compensation in 1999 for hospital administrators and chief executive officers, according to a survey by Hewitt Associates (Moore, 1999), was $210,000, and some health system CEOs make more than $1 million per year. Of course, managers get fringe benefits on top of that; in for-profit organizations, they may receive stock options as well. Some CEOs have bonus arrangements keyed to organizational performance, which allow them to make more money in any particular year. Is that too much or too little relative to their contribution to their organizations and relative to what comparable managers make in other sectors of the economy? Or relative to what physicians make? Once again, different stakeholders answer these questions differently.

Part of the answer on compensation relates to the contribution top managers make to organizational performance, and part relates to determinations of what are acceptable profits in a just society. Proponents of paying managers more money argue that health care is increasingly a competitive sector of the economy as patients are choosing lower-cost and higher-quality HCOs that are managed better. The management function contributes to keeping costs down and quality and revenues up, they argue, and the best managers must be attracted to work in health care rather than in other sectors of the economy. At the same time, managers should not be overcompensated when their organization is not doing well.

Opponents of higher managerial compensation argue that the monies going into high managers' salaries could be better spent on, for example, improving health care access for the uninsured. Of course, this is mostly a public relations argument, because the actual dollars would not go very far in redressing the needs of the uninsured. Based on their belief that health care is a right rather than a privilege, they also argue that HCOs should be competing not against each other for market share, but rather working cooperatively to improve population health. And they argue that health care managers should be paid like managers in other public service sectors, such as education, welfare, and religion.

Perhaps the most reasonable path out of this thicket is to pay managers based on performance relative to measurable objectives agreed to with stakeholders in advance and reported on regularly. Even if compensation (salary plus bonus) is set at lower levels, for managers who help their organizations do spectacularly well substantial additional bonuses could reward their contribution.

HOW SHOULD MANAGERS BE TRAINED?

How do people learn to be health care managers? Can health care management be taught? Is it a science, an art, a craft, or all three? What can best be learned at school and on the job?

Learning health care management is done either on the job or through continuing nondegree education in undergraduate programs or in graduate programs leading to a degree. But, despite the existence of large numbers of formal management education programs, much of what managers learn about what works in an organization and about how they can best work with clinicians and customers must be learned through experience. Most large HCOs have formal orientation programs and offer special training courses on site, as well. Managers can learn from others at work how to write what they mean, how not to always say what they are thinking, and how to influence others more effectively. Superiors, subordinates, and peers can assist managers in developing agendas and in forming and energizing networks through which to accomplish goals and objectives.

Continuing nondegree educational programs are of various lengths and cover various subjects, such as developing an efficient and sustainable physician compensation system or developing an integrated information system for an HCO. These programs are offered by universities, freestanding centers, professional associations, vendors, and large HCOs.

Undergraduate programs train managers for intermediate level positions in large HCOs and for higher level positions in smaller organizations. The curriculum is often similar in subject matter to that of graduate programs. Courses that are generally required include introduction to the health care field, economics, law, management, human resources, financial management, information, and quantitative methods.

More than 250 graduate programs in health care management operate in the United States today.[1] Programs are housed in schools of business, public health, public administration, allied health, and medicine. Curricula commonly cover:

- Structuring, marketing, positioning, and governance
- Financial management
- Leadership, interpersonal relations, and written and oral communications skills
- Managing human resources and health professionals
- Managing information
- Economic and financial analysis to support decision making
- Governmental health policy formation, regulation, and impact
- Assessment and understanding of the health status of populations, determinants of health and illness, and managing health risks and behavior
- Managing change
- Quality improvement (Accrediting Commission on Education for Health Services Administration, 2003).

Questions remain regarding where and how managers should be trained at various phases of their careers, what managerial competencies are required for which positions, what responsibility employers should take for management development, and how important clinical training is to management performance.

---

[1] For information about specific undergraduate and graduate programs, contact the Association of University Programs in Health Administration, 730 11th Street, NW, 4th Floor, Washington, DC, 20001; http://www.acehsa.org.

Accountability

Governance can be analyzed at various levels of the organization or with regard to an organization's accountability to various stakeholders: government, clinicians and other staff, patients, payers, and the public (see Table 14.1). Decisions made by government entities directly affect HCO governance. For example, the Medicare and Medicaid legislation of 1965 provided beneficiaries with better health coverage than many previously had and became a major source of provider revenue. However, the program was not designed by HCOs but by the elected representatives of the American people, who decided to have government collect and reimburse more uniformly for services provided to covered individuals. Decisions by frontline clinicians and by patients and consumers also affect an organization's management and performance. For example, registered nurses may leave the hospital to work in a home care agency or a nursing home; patients may choose to enroll in competing health plans that have different reimbursement rates and practices.

Government and consumers have to be accountable, too, for their behavior that affects the performance of HCOs. Legislation is often passed, particularly at the state level, requiring that insurance plans cover certain benefits, which drives the cost of insurance out of the range of affordability for smaller employers and individuals. Having more uninsured citizens greatly affects HCOs' bottom line. And many

Table 14.1	Stakeholders' Perspectives on Goals of Health Care Organization Governance
Stakeholder Group	**Goals**
Physicians and nurses	Autonomy for providers
Cooperatives	Service to membership
Government	Votes for politicians
Church	Service for coreligionists
Employers	Lower costs
Investors	Profit
Unions	Jobs for union members
Philanthropists	Prestige, advancing social goals

consumers lack basic health education; many graduate from high school without understanding much about health, staying healthy, or using the health care system appropriately.

THE EXTENT OF ORGANIZATIONAL AUTONOMY

To what extent do HCOs truly determine what services to provide to whom at what price? The autonomy of HCO governing boards has been shrinking since 1960. Federal and state governments have passed legislation, for example, forbidding discrimination against patients who seek admission or persons seeking employment, and invalidating a requirement that staff physicians of a non-profit hospital be graduates of a medical school approved by the Liaison Committee on Medical Education and be members of the county medical society. Government has made hospitals subject to state labor laws, specified licensure standards, and, in many states, required prior approval (a certificate of need) by state planners before hospitals, nursing homes, and related entities can build new facilities or make major renovations. Medicare and Medicaid limit payment for new technology; Medicare limits reimbursement to average length of stay regardless of cost; and some states enroll all Medicaid beneficiaries in managed care plans. Some states require that hospitals provide community service in order to retain their nonprofit status; West Virginia requires community representation on hospital boards; and some states cap hospital revenues. Some states require that managed care plans pay for hospital stays of 48 hours for normal deliveries, and some struck down HMO rules prohibiting physicians from discussing noncovered treatments with their patients.

> How free should health care organizations be to decide what services to offer, how much to charge for them, and whom to serve?

Different stakeholders in health care delivery have different responses to questions about the degree of autonomy that HCOs should have in deciding what services they offer, what prices they charge, and what populations they serve. The same stakeholders may answer these questions differently, depending on whether they are sick or well at the time. HCOs should have enough leeway to decide many issues, especially when they have better information than government does, as long as there are ways to intervene if the HCO falls unaccountably short of stakeholder expectations.

Too little autonomy for the HCO will prompt highly qualified individuals to withdraw from leadership positions—precisely the individuals who have helped it adapt to conditions in its local community. Excessive standardization and centralization of decision making in governmental bureaucracies stifle innovation and ultimately reduce productivity. At the same time, too much HCO autonomy may contribute to differences in age-adjusted mortality and morbidity rates by race and income, in overutilization of acute care and underutilization of preventive services and long-term care, uneven productivity across HCOs, poor quality service to customers, and high health care costs.

ACCOUNTABILITY TO THOSE SERVED

How should HCOs be accountable and to whom? Some advocate relatively formal accountability mechanisms, for example, insisting that HCO governing boards be controlled by consumer representatives. Others predict that strict controls would result in ineffective decision making by boards and eventual loss of community support, financial and otherwise, particularly since there is no evidence that consumers will be necessarily any more accountable to users and payers than typical hospital trustees.

At the same time, most stakeholders will agree on the value of having appeal mechanisms for major decisions that directly affect their interests. But to whom does the patient appeal if he or she is dissatisfied with the response of a patient advocate? Is the remedy adequate, given the time and energy it takes for a patient to pursue an appeal? Further, there are many aspects of care that consumers (and providers) find objectionable, but about which the HCO can do little, such as obtaining insurance reimbursement for uncovered services or adequate payment for services provided to the uninsured. Finally, appeal mechanisms may serve only as buffers that satisfy the occasional vocal complainant but do little to change institutional policies and systems that cause much unreported dissatisfaction. Other important accountability issues are the extent to which health care organizations appropriately manage the expectations of customers, whether these are patients or physicians, and whether they are ethical in their marketing and employment practices, not taking unfair advantage of either customers or employees.

In 2002, Congress enacted the Sarbanes-Oxley Act, which has reformed public company governance, finance, and accounting. The Act's requirements and standards now are viewed as best practices for both for-profit and nonprofit organizations. While the Act does not currently apply to nonprofits, leading HCOs have implemented many of its requirements on the role of independent directors and their representatives on audit and other key board committees; executive compensation and loan arrangements; new disclosure requirements for changes affecting the organization's financial status and adequacy of financial statements and controls; and detailed codes of ethics, business conduct, and comprehensive conflict-of-interest policies. For example, under the Act, a hospital's external auditor would be required to report directly to the board's audit committee, not to hospital management.

Conclusion

Governance and management are vitally important to the success of health care organizations and to the provision of accessible, efficient health care of high quality. Governance and management of HCOs have a cost and produce a benefit. Governance is a mechanism to focus accountability of HCOs for the stakeholders who provide these organizations with resources. And managers are the means through which the mission of health care organizations is articulated and accomplished. It is vitally important that patients, taxpayers, and the health care work force understand better how and why HCOs are governed and managed. It is only through understanding current governance and management behavior and processes, and the reasons for current functioning, that advocates can reasonably drive for changes that would improve HCO performance.

> There are reasons but no excuses why health care providers do not meet or manage patient and taxpayer expectations.

References

Accrediting Commission on Education for Health Services Administration. (2003). *Criteria for accreditation* (3rd rev. ed.). Arlington, VA: Author.

American Hospital Association. (1981). *Guide for preparation of constitution and bylaws for general hospitals.* Chicago: Author.

Bowen, W. G. (1994). *Inside the boardroom: Governance by directors and trustees.* New York: Wiley.

Boyatzis, R. E. (1995). Cornerstones of change: Building the path to self-directed learning. In R. E. Boyatzis, S. S. Cowen, D. A. Kolb, et al. (Eds.), *Innovation in professional education* (pp. 50–94). San Francisco: Jossey-Bass.

Burling, T., Lentz, E., & Wilson, R. (1956). *The give and take in hospitals.* New York: Putnam.

Ernst & Young. (1997). *Shining light on your board's passage to the future.* Cleveland, OH: Author.

Goleman, D. (1998). What makes a leader. *Harvard Business Review, 76*(6), 93–102.

Griffith, J. R., Sahney, V. K., & Mohr, R. A. (1995). *Reengineering health care: Building on CQI.* Ann Arbor, MI: Health Administration Press.

Griffith, J. R., & White, K. R. (2007). *The well managed health care organization* (6th ed.). Ann Arbor, MI: Health Administration Press.

Hansmann, H. (1996). *The ownership of enterprise.* Cambridge, MA: Belknap Press of Harvard University Press.

Herzlinger, R. (1997). *Market-driven health care.* Reading, MA: Addison-Wesley.

Kovner, A. R. (1984). *Really trying: A career guide for the health services manager.* Ann Arbor, MI: Health Administration Press.

Kovner, A. R. (2001). Better information for the board. *Journal of Healthcare Management, 46*(1), 53–66.

Longest, B. B. (1980). *Management practices for the health professional.* Reston, VA: Reston.

Moore, J. D., Jr. (1999, July 12). Holding the line (for you down there). *Modern Healthcare,* 43–48.

Pointer, D. D., & Orlikoff, J. E. (2002). *Getting to great: Principles of health care organization governance.* San Francisco: Jossey-Bass.

Umbdenstock, R. J. (1987). Refinement of board's role required. *Health Progress, 68*(1), 47.

U.S. Department of Labor, Bureau of Labor Statistics. Data search conducted 12/7/07 at http://www.bls.gov/home.htm

15

Key Words

complexity	**outcome**
quality	**risk adjustment**
structure	**outcome attribution**
process	**pay-for-performance (P4P)**

The Complexity of Health Care Quality

Douglas S. Wakefield and Bonnie J. Wakefield

Learning Objectives

- Describe and apply the concept of complex adaptive systems to health care quality.
- Describe how differing definitions of quality health care are influenced by the perspectives of different stakeholders.
- Describe and analyze alternative approaches for health care purchasers to implement pay-for-performance (P4P) quality improvement initiatives.
- Describe the importance of risk adjusting health care outcomes.
- Describe basic strategies for managing quality within the inherent complexity of health care organizations.

Topical Outline

- Health care
- Complexity and the health care quality challenge
- Defining quality of health care
- Pay for performance (P4P): helping to make the business case for quality
- Risk-adjusted quality outcomes
- Strategies for managing quality in the health care zone of complexity

Quality is neither mind nor matter. It is a third entity, independent of the two…Even though it cannot be defined, you know what Quality is!
—paraphrased from R. M. Pirsig, *Zen and the Art of Motorcycle Maintenance*, 1974

t the turn of the 21st century, two Institute of Medicine (IOM) reports galvanized national attention on problems with the quality and safety of U.S. health care. The first, *To Err Is Human: Building a Safer Health System* (2000), with its estimate that between 44,000 and 98,000 Americans die each year as a result of medical mistakes and that errors cost some $37 billion annually, captured the attention of policymakers, providers, payers, patients, and, importantly, the news media. Less sensational, but of groundbreaking importance, was the second report, *Crossing the Quality Chasm: A New Health System for the 21st Century* (IOM, 2001), which concluded, "Quality problems are everywhere, affecting many patients. Between the healthcare we have and the care we could have lies not just a gap, but a chasm" (p. 1). The report continues,

> The dominant finding of our review is that there are large gaps between the care people should receive and the care they do receive. This is true for preventive, acute, and chronic care, whether one goes for a checkup, a sore throat, or diabetic care. It is true whether one looks at overuse, under use, or misuse. It is true in different types of healthcare facilities and for different types of health insurance. It is true for all age groups, from children to the elderly. And it is true whether one is looking at the whole country or a single city. (p. 236)

In its call for major system changes, the report identified six commonsense aims for improvement, asserting that patient care should be:

1. *Safe:* Patients should not be injured from the very care processes designed to help them.
2. *Effective:* Scientific knowledge and evidence should be used to determine both what to do and what not to do to meet a patient's care needs.
3. *Patient-Centered:* Care should be provided in a respectful manner, honoring the patient's values, beliefs, and preferences.
4. *Timely:* Better care will come from reducing waits and untimely delays.
5. *Efficient:* Time, equipment, supplies, ideas, and people's energy should not be wasted because of poorly designed health care processes.

6. ***Equitable:*** Care quality should not vary as a function of geography, gender, ethnicity, or socioeconomic status.

One cannot readily disagree with the principles behind these six aims, and they have been transformed into continued demands for improved patient care quality and safety. Throughout the United States, health care providers, organizations, and systems have been put on notice that the quality and patient safety status quo is no longer acceptable. With increasing frequency, they are being required to show, and are being held accountable for, the quality and safety of the care they provide.

What does health care quality mean? How do we achieve it? This chapter explores these deceptively simple questions, starting with a discussion of complexity.

Health Care Quality:
Fundamentals

An historically important body of research by Donabedian framed the concept of quality assurance in terms of three types of measures: structure, process, and outcomes (see Figure 15.1). Donabedian (1980) noted that any efforts to improve quality needed to recognize that health care is embedded in, and greatly influenced by, the larger external environment. His model posits that health care providers and organizations draw patients being served as well as the resources necessary to care for these patients (e.g., funding, personnel, equipment, and supplies) from the external environment. From these resources

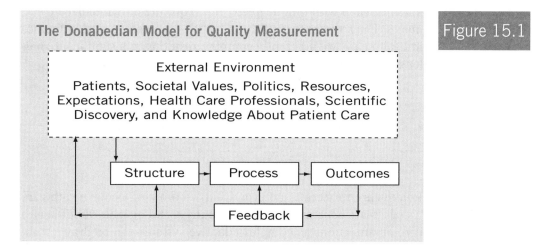

The Donabedian Model for Quality Measurement   Figure 15.1

External Environment

Patients, Societal Values, Politics, Resources, Expectations, Health Care Professionals, Scientific Discovery, and Knowledge About Patient Care

Structure — Process — Outcomes

Feedback

are created *structures* from which specific patient care *processes* can be developed and provided to patients. Patient *outcomes* are the direct result. Feedback about patient outcomes influences subsequent changes in the external environment, as well as the providers' patient care structures and processes.

In applying this model to a hospital, Donabedian would argue that structural aspects of the hospital (e.g., its physical plant, equipment, staffing levels and personnel mix, licensure and accreditation status, organizational culture) reflect both patient needs and the fiscal and other resources available to meet these needs. These structural elements, when combined with the needs of the patient population being served, directly influence the range and mix of diagnostic and treatment services (processes) offered. Outcomes (e.g., physiological status, mortality, morbidity, disability, functional status, satisfaction, quality of life, lost work days, costs) can be assessed for individuals and groups and used for feedback to influence subsequent changes in the external market (e.g., market share, payment levels), patient care structures and processes, as well as to assess the external environment from which patients and resources come.

Think of the complexity inherent in providing common medical procedures, such as double coronary artery bypass graft and aortic valve replacement surgery. The underlying patient-care process comprises a large number of sequential and parallel services and actions carried out by a large number of individuals with dozens of different job titles. Further, services commonly are carried out over several days, requiring extensive communication among all those involved across work shifts. The patterns of interaction developed across job specialties reflects a unique blend of services required to care for this general type of cardiovascular patient, plus the specific challenges that a particular patient may bring (comorbidities, language skills, allergies). In reality, hospitals care for many different types of patients, each with unique needs and requiring individualized treatments. Thus, the nature of the structures, processes, and outcomes in health care are inherently complex, resulting in a significant challenge to achieving quality.

Complexity and the Health Care Quality Challenge

Health care services—and even what we think of as our health care "needs"—are constantly changing. Many useful insights about health care organizations as complex adaptive systems can be drawn from complexity science (Plsek, 2001). Stacey (1996) argues that when there is a high degree of certainty about how specific actions can lead to specific outcomes, and if there is a high degree of agreement among those who carry out the actions, an organization can rely on mechanical systems (i.e., plan and control) to guide the work. But when there is little agreement about which actions lead to specific outcomes and little agreement among those acting, an organization is faced with what Stacey calls *chaos*. Between *plan and control* and *chaos* is what Stacey calls the *zone of complexity*. In health care, the size of the zone of complexity varies greatly, depending on what is known about the relative effectiveness of various treatment options, and it changes in size as new scientific knowledge accumulates, new diagnostic and treatment technologies are developed, the health care financing and regulatory environments alter, and new diseases or health threats emerge (see Figure 15.2).

When health care providers are in the plan and control zone, the probability of a specific patient care process yielding a given outcome is very high. For example, the clinical laboratory uses well-designed and highly standardized protocols when testing for a specific antibiotic-resistant organism. But when there is a low degree of agreement about whether various actions will produce the desired outcomes (that is, as one approaches the chaos zone), it is not possible to use probabilistic and mechanical approaches. Health care providers are closer to the chaos zone soon after the discovery of new diseases (e.g., HIV/AIDS, SARS) or when they have fresh scientific discoveries

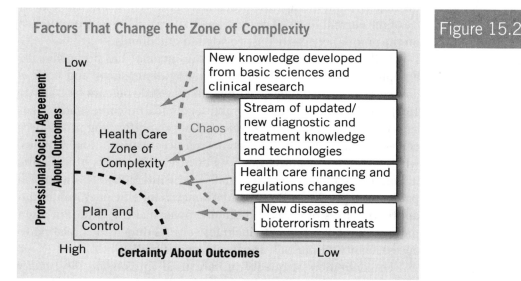

Figure 15.2

Factors That Change the Zone of Complexity

Note. Adapted from Stacey, R. D. (1996). *Strategic management and organizational dynamics.* Philadelphia: Trans-Atlantic Publications.

or new technologies. At these times, there is great confusion among patients, providers, payers/purchasers, and policymakers as to what care should be offered and what good quality of care would be.

In the zone of complexity, the probability that a given action will yield a specific outcome can vary greatly, depending on the many factors previously enumerated. Yet, the zone of complexity is where significant portions of health care occur. Clinicians' only choice is to take a probabilistic approach. A number of tools can help improve the quality of decision making in this zone, including evidence-based clinical guidelines and algorithms, computerized clinical data capture, real-time decision support systems, and continued investment in the education and development of the clinical work force. Despite all these strategies, the resulting variability in outcomes reflects the complexity of defining, measuring, and improving the inherently complex service of health care.

Defining Quality of Health Care:
Patients Versus Populations

INDIVIDUAL PATIENT LEVEL OF ANALYSIS

Health care quality at the individual patient level of analysis focuses on the provision and outcomes of personal health care services provided, based on the patient's unique care needs. The usual way of categorizing the enormous array of unique services is to group related services into categories, such as outpatient visits, inpatient admissions, diagnostic tests, and therapeutic procedures and treatments. The majority of the current focus of current health care quality improvement is on the unique services being provided to individuals.

At this level of analysis, health care "quality" has no universally accepted definition. Instead, it has many dimensions, and each is emphasized or de-emphasized by different stakeholders (see Figure 15.3). Providers, who are accountable for clinical outcomes and patient safety, tend to emphasize technical quality—performing procedures correctly and providing the correct services. Patients and families, who care about technical quality but rarely have ways of assessing it, emphasize touch or service quality—the interactions between the patient and providers. Payers add a concern for efficiency, value, and appropriateness of care. And, finally, policymakers—who are often payers, too—believe quality includes societal dimensions relating to access, equity, disparities, and legal responsibilities.

The definition of quality of care used in *Crossing the Quality Chasm* is "the degree to which health services for individuals and populations increase the likelihood of desired health outcomes and

Figure 15.3

Stakeholders' Differing Perspectives on Health Care Quality

- Providers: "Technical Quality"
  - "5 Rights": Providing the Technical Right Care, to the Right Patient in the Right Time, Right Way, and Right Amount

- Patients: "Touch Quality"
  - How Well the Patient Feels Treated (Satisfaction, Access to Care)
  - Communication, Coordination, Compassion, Respect, Personalization, and Time Spent With Patient Are Key

- Payers: "Technical and Touch Quality"
  - The Appropriateness, Timeliness, Cost Effectiveness, and Resulting Patient Satisfaction Are Key

- Policy makers: "Technical and Touch Quality"
  - Some Elements Shared With Payers Include Appropriateness, Timeliness, Cost, Cost Effectiveness, and Resulting Patient Satisfaction
  - Care Also Should Be Accessible and Meet the Needs of the Larger Population and Societal Needs

are consistent with current professional knowledge" (IOM, 2001, p. 232). Patient health outcome is then defined as

> The result that happens to a patient from performance (or nonperformance) of one or more processes, services, or activities carried out by healthcare providers. A patient health outcome represents the cumulative effect of one or more processes at a defined time, as in survival to discharge following a gunshot wound to the chest or an acute myocardial infarction. (p. 594)

Intuitively appealing and consistent with the Donabedian model, this definition has as its primary focus the result or outcome of the care process. However, a wide range of patient care outcomes is possible. For example, the Dartmouth Clinical Value Compass lists four primary outcome categories: (1) clinical outcomes; (2) functional status, risk status, and well-being; (3) satisfaction with care and perceived benefit; and (4) costs (Nelson, Mohr, Batalden, & Plume, 1996). Each dimension has quality indicators specific to the disease or condition of interest.

> Patient care outcomes are influenced by numerous factors that reside outside the control of a single physician or hospital.

Although a focus on outcomes in defining and measuring quality is reasonable, to what extent is it also reasonable to assume that a specific combination of health care services will actually lead to the outcome? In reality, patient care outcomes are influenced by two categories of factors that reside outside the control of a single health care provider. First, patients may receive services simultaneously from several, frequently independent, sources. For example, a patient with multiple chronic diseases may be under the care of a number of different specialists (who may not share a common medical record or information about the patients they treat in common), obtain prescribed medications from different pharmacies, and use self-prescribed, over-the-counter medications, complementary alternative medications, and dietary supplements unbeknownst to their physicians. As a result, while each provider, acting individually, might give the patient technically perfect treatment, the combination of different prescribed medications and patient self-treatments may thwart treatment or at least use health care resources ineffectively.

Second, outcomes are affected by differences in patients' individual characteristics, such as health status, genetic makeup, personal health habits (e.g., diet, exercise, smoking, excessive alcohol consumption, and drug abuse), personal wealth or health insurance coverage, educational status, language skills, home environment, social support systems, depression or other mental health problem, and attitudes toward and beliefs about the health care system.

Take, for example, two patients undergoing the exact same surgical procedure: Patient A is in very poor physical and nutritional health, with a long history of smoking and alcohol and drug abuse, and is too poor to buy prescribed medications; Patient B is just the opposite in all these regards. Patient A also has poor eyesight and has difficulty understanding his doctor's instructions, whereas Patient B is well educated, familiar with scientific terms, and has family members willing and able to help her follow her doctor's treatment regimen. Assuming that the technical aspects of the surgery are performed perfectly and in exactly the same manner for both patients, the differences in their personal characteristics will very likely affect the outcomes profoundly.

Other industries have improved the quality of their outputs by reducing variability in the quality of their inputs—the raw materials used in the production process. But health care providers generally do not have the luxury of caring for just the healthiest, wealthiest, and most compliant patients. In fact, if health care providers are caught "dumping" patients, the financial and legal repercussions can be enormous. Thus, the inherent variability among patients—the clinical process's raw material—adds significantly to the complexity of assessing the quality of care received, particularly as measured by patient outcomes.

Given these difficulties, perhaps evaluators should focus on assessing process measures of quality. This useful definition links outcomes to process: "Quality of care is that portion of a patient's outcome over which healthcare providers, whether individuals or organization, have control" (Chin & Muramatsu, 2003, p. 7). This definition focuses on outcomes for which there are reasonably well-known process-outcome relationships. With available resources (e.g., equipment, staff, supplies), providers have the most control over process—what is or is not done to and for the patient. This concept is further defined by the Five Rights of Patient Care.

- *Right Care.* Quality health care requires that physicians, nurses, and other health care providers be held responsible for accurately assessing and providing appropriate patient care interventions, given their knowledge about the underlying disease(s) or condition(s) being treated, and within the constraints of available resources.
- *Right Patient.* Quality health care requires that patients should only receive the care (e.g., diagnostic tests, medical, or surgical treatments) specifically planned for them. Just as replacing the radiator in a car that needs a new water pump represents poor quality, so does giving a patient the wrong treatment.
- *Right Way.* Quality health care requires that health care providers be held responsible for using the appropriate equipment and patient care protocols in the appropriate way and that patients be informed of and participate in decisions regarding treatment options and be treated in a respectful and considerate manner.
- *Right Time.* Quality health care must be provided in a timely manner, with no inappropriate or avoidable delays in care (e.g., surgery cancellations, failure to perform required tests, excessive clinical or emergency department wait times).
- *Right Amount.* Quality health care requires that both under- and overutilization of services be avoided. Quality is affected in the first instance, because patients do not receive the services they need. In the latter instance, quality is affected because, when they receive services they don't need, not only is there a risk of iatrogenic harm, but they and the system also incur unnecessary costs.

POPULATION LEVEL OF ANALYSIS

Population-level analyses of health care quality extend individual patient-level analyses by aggregating patient care process and outcome data across larger populations and geographic regions. These larger populations can be defined in terms of patients with similar characteristics, such as specific diseases or disease risks (e.g., diabetes, hypertension, cancer); age; gender; ethnicity or race; socioeconomic status (e.g., education, income, insurance); or some combination of these. Regional or geographical comparisons of quality can compare nations, states, counties, cities, or health care market service areas. Process analyses tend to focus on specific disease screening or preventive services (e.g., prenatal care, breast cancer screening), diagnostic procedures, or treatments. Outcome analyses have looked at issues such as lost work days, morbidity, potential years of lost life, and mortality.

Historically, population-level analyses of patient care quality have received comparatively little attention. While the reasons for this are many, two principal ones are the absence of meaningful population-level data and scanty funding for this type of research. The following discussion focuses on two types of population-level analyses: (1) service underuse, misuse, and overuse and (2) health care disparities.

UNDERUSE, MISUSE, AND OVERUSE OF HEALTH CARE SERVICES

The variability of population-based rates for the distribution and utilization of health care services across different market areas has great implications for health care policy. Building on Wennberg and Gittelsohn's (1982) small-area analyses, the Dartmouth Atlas Project has become instrumental in stimulating thinking about quality. Using health care claims data from more than 3,000 individual hospital service areas in the United States, Wennberg and colleagues have created 306 discrete hospital referral regions, defined in terms of where people living in a specific geographic area are generally hospitalized (http://www.dartmouthatlas.org). Identifying these regions has allowed researchers to pursue a number of important questions about quality that are related to underuse of effective care, misuse of preference-sensitive care, and overuse of supply-sensitive services across referral regions (for an example of the power of this method of analysis, see Figure 15.4, which shows a fourfold difference in number of physician visits near the end of life across the regions).

Underuse of Effective Care
Effective care is considered to be "services that are of proven value and have no significant tradeoffs—that is, the benefits of the services so far outweigh the risks that all patients with specific medical needs should receive them" (Center for the Evaluative Clinical Sciences [CECS], 2007a, p. 1). A commonly used example of effective care is the use of beta blockers for heart attack patients. Effective care is underused when this care is not provided. Underuse of effective care has been persuasively demonstrated. Asch, Sloss, Hogan, Brook, and Kravitz (2000) used a panel of clinical experts to identify services that were either "necessary care" or important for preventing negative outcomes for 15 common conditions. They examined administrative

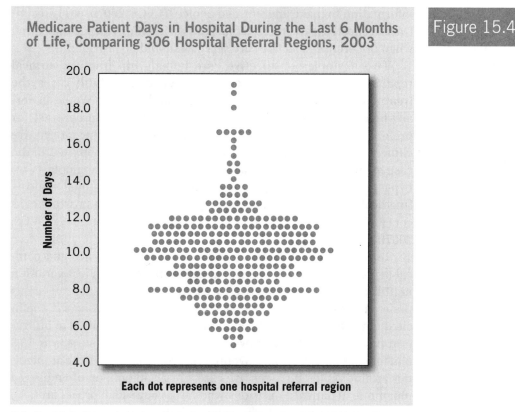

Figure 15.4

Medicare Patient Days in Hospital During the Last 6 Months of Life, Comparing 306 Hospital Referral Regions, 2003

Each dot represents one hospital referral region

Note. Reprinted with permission from the Dartmouth Atlas Project. Copyright 2007 by the Trustees of Dartmouth College.

(claims) data and found patients were receiving these services less than two-thirds of the time. African American patients received the services even less often. McGlynn and colleagues (2003) compiled a list of 439 patient care processes generally considered to represent effective care. Through an audit of patients' medical records, the researchers found that about 55% of patients actually received care that should have been provided. Another way of looking at this is as a "defect rate" of about 45% in providing the expected care. Such results have prompted third-party payers to consider how their leverage can be used to improve care, leading to development of the numerous pay-for-performance experiments now under way and discussed below.

Misuse of Preference-Sensitive Care

Preference-sensitive care is defined as "treatments that involve significant tradeoffs affecting the patient's quality and/or length of life. Decisions about these interventions—whether to have them or not, which ones to have—ought to reflect patients' personal values and preferences, and ought to be made only after patients have enough information to make an informed choice" (CECS, 2007b, p. 1). In contrast to effective care, there is much less scientific evidence indicating when preference-sensitive care services should be provided.

Two examples of effective care include hip fracture surgical repairs and colectomy for colorectal cancer. In both cases the treatment decisions are relatively clear and patients would generally be expected to receive a surgical intervention. In contrast for preference-sensitive care there is evidence for providing alternative clinical interventions for the same condition. This is apparent in the case of chronic stable angina (medical treatment vs. angioplasty vs. bypass surgery), back pain due to herniated disc or spinal stenosis (medical treatment vs. back surgery), and early-stage prostate cancer (watchful waiting vs. radiation vs. radical prostatectomy) (CECS, 2007b).

Because of the different degrees of scientific evidence and clinical agreement involved, one would expect to see much less variation in utilization rates for effective care (like hip fracture surgery) versus preference-specific care (like back surgery). Indeed, using the coefficient of variation as way of comparing the relative variation in utilization rates, the coefficient of variation for hip fracture surgery is 13.8 and for back surgery is 93.6 (Wennberg, 2007). Because of the ambiguities around preference-sensitive care, physician opinion often plays a major role in patients' decisions whether to have such procedures.

Research increasingly documents that, in some geographic areas (holding patient variables constant), there are much higher utilization rates of specific procedures, which raise interesting questions: Is more care better care? How can patients become more informed decision makers? Readers are encouraged to review the work of Fisher (2003) and O'Connor et al. (1999) as examples of work addressing issues related to the potential harm stemming from providing more care and the fact that similar patient care outcomes can be achieved with very different levels of service intensity and utilization (Ashton et al., 2003). The patient decision-making research and decision support tools developed by the Foundation for Informed Medical Decision Making (2007) represent some of the state-of-the-art work related to the second question.

> Fully half of U.S. medical spending may be related to supply-induced, rather than true patient care need, factors.

Overuse of Supply-Sensitive Care

Supply-sensitive care is care related "to an area's supply of hospital beds, physician specialists, etc. Where there is greater capacity, more care is delivered—whether or not it is warranted" (CECS, 2005, p. 1). Supply-sensitive care is directly related to the famous Roemer's law of health care demand, which identified the concept of supply-induced demand: in an insured population, where third-parties pay the bill, "a built bed tends to be a filled bed." After extensive research on the excessive variation in certain types of utilization, the Dartmouth Atlas group concludes: "Our research shows there are wide variations in what Medicare spends for services to treat chronically ill patients and that higher spending does not achieve better outcomes" (CECS, 2005, p. 1). Fully half of U.S. medical spending may be related to supply-induced, rather than true patient care need, factors (Wennberg, 2005).

A recently released CECS report exhaustively analyzes variations in the management of chronic illnesses—first comparing U.S. states and then academic medical centers—by looking at Medicare expenditures during decedents' last 6 months and last 2 years of life (Wennberg et al., 2006). The report provides a fascinating assessment of the health care system's varying responses to Medicare beneficiaries' end-of-life care needs.

During the last 6 months of life, Medicare beneficiaries nationwide spent an average of 11.7 days as hospital inpatients—with a range of from 7.3 days in Utah to 16.4 days in Hawaii. On average, they spent 3.2 days in the intensive care unit (ICU), with a range of from 1.5 days in North Dakota to 4.7 in Florida. Their average number of physician visits was about 29, with a range of from 17 in Utah to 41.5 in New Jersey. And, nationally, about 18.5% of deaths were associated with admission to an ICU—ranging from 11.7% in South Dakota to 25% in New Jersey.

Given that only care provided in the last 6 months of life was examined, differences in patient characteristics and clinical status can explain only a small part of the state-to-state variation. What accounted for much more of the variation were differences in the states' supply of hospital beds and medical specialists.

HEALTH DISPARITIES

Health disparities are population-specific differences in the prevalence of disease, outcomes of care, or access to health services. In an ideal society and all other things being equal, there would be no differences in health status, receipt of appropriate health care services, or health care outcomes—such as functional status, morbidity, and mortality— due to individual characteristics such as gender, race, ethnicity, or socioeconomic factors. Health care disparities reflect the interaction of health care access and utilization with broader societal issues related to racial and ethnic, socioeconomic, and gender differences (Williams, 2005). Non–health care factors include personal, socioeconomic, and environmental factors; these directly affect factors that help determine health care access, such as insurance, language, and health literacy. Unfortunately, in the United States, there is abundant evidence of disparities in health status, health care access, and health care quality that provides a useful way to assess the quality of care at a population or macro-systems level.

Discussions of health care disparities do not focus merely on whether there are differences between population subgroups, but rather on whether these differences are related to characteristics that define the subgroups. Clearly, some diseases—like Tay-Sachs disease in Ashkenazi Jews or sickle cell anemia in people of African heritage are related to ethnicity; disparities refer to differences that arise between populations where such inherent differences in disease susceptibility, not (yet) remediable by medical care, are not involved. Important issues to consider when attempting to measure health disparities include differentiating the use of relative versus absolute disparities, the effect of the subgroup or population size on the analysis, and choice of reference group.[1]

Disparities Based on Race and Ethnicity

The research literature (e.g., U.S. Department of Health and Human Services, for Healthcare Research and Quality, 2005) contains numerous examples of health care disparities based on patients' racial or ethnic backgrounds and the lack of progress in reducing them:

> If the mortality rates for Blacks and Whites were the same, there would be 83,570 fewer deaths among Blacks each year.

- Blacks are 10 times as likely as Whites to develop AIDS, Black children with asthma are 3.7 times as likely to be admitted to a hospital, and Blacks are nearly twice as likely to leave hospital emergency departments without being seen.
- Native Americans and Alaska Natives were about twice as likely to lack prenatal care in the first trimester than were Whites.
- Children of poor families were about half as likely to receive dental care or to seek care for illness or injury care as quickly as children of high-income families.
- An innovative study identified "eight Americas," defined in terms of race, county, population density, race-specific per capita income, and cumulative homicide rates. Comparing best-off and worst-off areas revealed substantial differences in both male and female life expectancy (a more than 20-year difference) and rates of AIDS, cardiovascular diseases, cancers, and other diseases (Murray et al., 2006);
- Finally, former U.S. Surgeon General David Satcher and colleagues, in a thought-provoking 2005 article, estimated that, if the

---

[1] Although it is beyond the scope of this chapter to address all of these issues, readers are encouraged to review a publicly available online/CD course that provides an excellent overview of many of the health disparities measurement issues: http://sitemaker.umich.edu/mhd/home

mortality rates for Blacks and Whites were the same, there would be 83,570 fewer deaths among Blacks each year (Satcher et al., 2005).

Pay for Performance (P4P):
Make the Business Case for Quality

Crossing the "quality chasm" requires fundamental changes in the way health care services are organized, provided, evaluated, and financed. But, given the complexities of health care, disagreement about what quality means, health care payment practices that sometimes militate against quality, and limited resources with which to purchase health care services, what can be done to effect these changes? One of the chief barriers to quality improvement has been the difficulty of specifying a clear and compelling "business case" for high-quality health care (Leatherman et al., 2003). The typical disconnect between quality improvement and third-party payer practices has been described eloquently:

> A hospital in the Midwest implemented a program to improve choices of initial antibiotics to treat pneumonia. Mortality rates went down, hospital days went down, and costs went down, but it cost the hospital money because these patients were less sick, their DRG categories were less serious, and the hospital received less money. The system itself is bizarre. If the system makes a mistake and produces kidney failure, this will put the patient into a higher-paying DRG. That is not aligning incentives with regard to quality. (Shine, 2001, p. 8)

Similarly, Leatherman and colleagues (2003) say:

> the misalignment of financial incentives creates a formidable obstacle to the adoption of quality interventions. . . . a healthcare organization may be reluctant to implement improvements if better quality is not accompanied by better payment or improved margins, or at least equal compensation. Without a business case for quality, we think it unlikely that the private sector will move quickly and reliably to widely adopt proven quality improvements. (pp. 17–18)

The U.S. health care system is in the early stages of attempts by third-party payers to more explicitly link payment to quality (Institute of Medicine, 2007). These so-called pay-for-performance or P4P quality improvement initiatives are experimenting with a variety of direct and indirect financial incentives targeted to different categories of providers—finally creating a business case for quality. The underlying assumption behind many of these programs is that health care providers require financial incentives and disincentives in order to provide care deemed to be effective. Three core issues must be considered in developing and implementing P4P strategies: whom to target with incentives, which incentive options to use, and what to focus the incentives on.

WHOM TO TARGET WITH INCENTIVES

The choice of whom to target for P4P quality improvement incentives has significant implications for what to target and the types of incentives that will be used. Choice options range from individual physicians, medical groups, hospitals, physician-hospital organizations, and integrated delivery systems. Focusing quality improvement incentives on individual physicians will have a very limited effect. Because of the extensive specialization within medical practice, patients are rarely cared for by only one physician, especially older patients who are the health system's greatest users. While aggregating a P4P initiative at the medical group level may partially address this limitation, some patients may not receive all of their care from the same group. Many medical groups are still relatively small and tend to be single-specialty or include only a few specialties.

Alternatively, a P4P approach could focus on hospitals, as the Centers for Medicare & Medicaid Services (CMS) are doing in the Voluntary Hospital Reporting Initiative and Premier Hospital Quality Demonstration Project (http://www.cms.hhs.gov/quality). The approach in both is to focus on common conditions for which there are generally agreed-upon standards for what should be done for the typical patient. CMS focuses on 10 specific "process of care indicators"—that is, 10 things that should be done for patients with acute myocardial infarction, heart failure, or pneumonia. Quality is then assessed in terms of the percentage of all patients for whom these steps are taken (unless contraindicated). In addition to the several limitations associated with focusing on process of care measures (discussed below), other potential limitations of a hospital focus include insufficient number of cases in small hospitals, absence of risk-adjusted patient groupings, wide variations in physician staffing patterns, and patients' receiving care in more than one hospital.

Further aggregation to the physician–hospital organization or to the integrated delivery system levels can solve some of these problems, providing a larger group of patients to work with and assuring that individual patients receive most or all of their care from a single organization. Unfortunately, such systems cover relatively few Americans.

WHAT KIND OF INCENTIVES TO USE

A second major issue to consider in implementing a P4P quality improvement incentive plan is what types of incentives might be used. Direct financial incentives are intended to flow to the provider and to be explicitly linked to specified actions or performance. Direct financial incentives include quality bonuses or incentives, performance-based fee schedules, quality improvement grants, payment for preventive services, and variable cost-sharing arrangements. Indirect financial incentives try to improve performance by providing information comparing clinicians' performance or helping physicians achieve a more manageable workload. Examples include provider performance profiling, publicizing provider performance, providing technical assistance for quality improvement, reducing administrative burdens imposed by third-party payers, and reducing the number of patients (panel) for whom a physician is responsible.

To the extent that incentives can be linked to specific provider behavior, there is great potential to improve health care quality. With all incentive schemes, a key challenge is to anticipate and mitigate the effect of unintended consequences. The Leapfrog Incentive and Reward Compendium (http://www.leapfroggroup.org/ircompendium. htm) documents the growing use of specific incentives within P4P quality and patient safety initiatives.

WHAT TO TARGET FOR QUALITY IMPROVEMENT

Potential quality improvement targets can be grouped into the three categories of structure, process, and outcomes. Examples of potential *P4P structure targets* include improvements in information technologies, staffing patterns, and volume-based referral practices. Specific P4P information technology targets include investment in and use of computerized physician order entry systems with real-time decision support, bedside bar coding systems, patient data warehousing, and enhanced clinical decision support systems. An example of a P4P staffing pattern target would be full-time intensivist coverage in intensive care units, either on site or remotely. With growing support from the medical literature, the Leapfrog Group has endorsed the concept of volume-based referral, meaning that, all other things being equal, hospitals and physicians that treat a higher number of cases of a particular disorder are more likely to produce better outcomes.

P4P process targets focus on the ways in which care is delivered. The primary goal is to standardize patient care processes whenever possible, based on the best available science. P4P process targets are being used in the CMS Consumer Assessment of Health Providers (CAHPS) initiatives targeting hospitals, nursing homes, and home health agencies (http://www.cms.hhs.gov/quality). Quality is measured by the extent to which patients receive appropriate, specified care processes. As a condition of Medicare participation, acute care hospitals must regularly submit these data. The CAHPS program has been expanded to include the Hospital CAHPS (HCAHPS) survey, which assesses patients' perspectives and satisfaction with their hospital care (http://www.cms.hhs.gov/HospitalQualityInits/30_HospitalHCAHPS.asp#TopOfPage).

A P4P quality improvement focus on patient care processes is useful only to the extent that good scientific evidence supports a particular process. Even when a proven process is implemented well, however, a patient still may not have a good clinical outcome, because of the personal factors described previously. A second potential limitation of a process-only approach is the uncertainty regarding exactly what and when specific care processes should be provided. Finally, creating incentives for health care providers to comply with specific processes rather than to improve patients' health may in the long run inhibit significant quality improvements.

The Holy Grail of P4P quality improvement initiatives is to improve patient care *outcome targets*. Unfortunately, outcome-focused quality improvement initiatives are relatively rare at this point due to several factors. First, the specific outcomes of interest must be determined—is it related to a disease, a combination of diseases, a specific patient, a cost reduction? This choice depends in part on whose perspective the outcome reflects. Patients may want to be symptom-free and able to return to work; insurers may seek cost-effectiveness; public policymakers may want to see undifferentiated access to care. Another issue to consider is whether the outcome being measured should reflect the specific services or intervention (e.g., a single hospitalization, surgical procedure, or office visit) or the combination of inpatient and outpatient services provided over a longer episode of illness. Likewise, should the analysis be disease-specific or address an individual's entire set of medical conditions? Finally, and perhaps of greatest importance to those seeking to "purchase" quality care, a P4P analysis should compare outcome quality for similar types of patients cared for by different providers. To do this requires valid, reliable, and meaningful risk-adjusted outcome data.

The Bridges to Excellence initiative (http://www.bridgestoexcellence.org), active in 18 states as of this writing, designs and implements condition-specific quality improvement programs focused on diabetes and cardiac care. California's Integrated Healthcare Association initiative includes patient satisfaction measures related to, for example, timely access to care, patient–physician communication, and overall care ratings (http://www.iha.org).

Deciding whether to focus on structures, processes, outcomes—or some combination of these—as quality improvement targets requires assessment of their respective strengths and limitations. Without the appropriate structures—such as physical plant, staff, equipment, and supplies—the ability to provide high-quality care is limited. Given the relatively primitive state of clinical information technology systems in many hospitals, P4P incentives that support investment in information technology are not surprising. However, simply having access to state-of-the-art technologies does not guarantee that the best or most appropriate patient care will actually be provided. Thus, health care structures can be thought of as necessary, but not sufficient, preconditions for high-quality care.

> Improved health care structures can be thought of as necessary, but not sufficient, preconditions for high-quality care.

In summary, P4P is still in an emergent phase with much learning yet to occur about how to most effectively align economic incentives to achieve the desired patient care outcomes (Epstein, 2007). The continued emergence of new P4P-related initiatives offers important learning opportunities to answer questions such as:

1. What is the underlying goal?
2. Are the measures adequate?
3. Is implementation feasible?
4. Will rewards be sufficient?
5. Could there be unintended consequences? (Fisher, 2006)

Risk-Adjusted Quality Outcomes

How can we assess the quality of care provided, given the large number and complexity of patient factors over which providers and health care organizations have no control? The answer in part is to risk-adjust the outcomes. Risk adjustment attempts to account for the differences that patients bring to the health care encounter so that outcomes can be compared across different patient groups, treatments, providers, health plans, or populations.

Several risk-adjustment methodologies have been developed. Two examples are the Acute Physiology and Chronic Health Evaluation (APACHE) and diagnosis-related groups (DRGs). These two methods define risks in relation to outcomes differently and use different populations. APACHE has three versions, two of which focus on in-hospital mortality in adult patients in intensive care units. DRGs focus on total hospital charges of all hospitalized patients.

Devising appropriate risk-adjustment strategies requires answers to these four questions:

1. ***What Outcomes Require Risk Adjustment?*** Historically, the outcome of most interest has been mortality. However, outcomes may include other clinical outcomes, functional status, complications, resource use (including charges for and length of hospital stay), patient satisfaction, and quality of life. As noted earlier, the Dartmouth Clinical Value Compass lists four primary outcomes categories: clinical, functional, satisfaction, and costs.
2. ***Over What Time Frames Should Risk-Adjustment Methodologies Be Applied?*** Selection of the time frame for risk adjustment is important, because different time frames provide different perspectives. For example, some risks—such as the complications of diabetes—occur over a life time, while others—such as postoperative or in-hospital mortality within 30 days of the procedure—are relatively short-term. The time frame selected can relate to, for example, a single surgical procedure or longer episodes of care that include the inpatient and outpatient care received prior to or after surgery.
3. ***For What Patient Populations Will the Risk-Adjustment Methodology Be Applied?*** Patient population characteristics must be specified carefully, especially demographic ones (e.g., age, income). Type of care previously received also may be of interest, given studies showing that both overall and ICU resource use are significantly higher for hospital patients transferred from other institutions.
4. ***For What Purpose(s) Will the Risk-Adjusted Outcomes Be Used?*** The purpose can be, for example, to compare providers or health plans, set payment levels, or encourage health plans to accept and treat high-risk, high-cost patients.

SOURCES OF DATA FOR RISK ADJUSTMENT

Administrative (claims) data, clinical data (patient record abstraction), and patient surveys are sources of information for risk adjustment, each of which has distinct advantages and disadvantages.

Risk adjustment is most often accomplished using administrative data, usually claims data. These data include large numbers of individuals, are generally representative of the community, make it possible to follow patients over time, have relatively standardized content, and are inexpensive for researchers to acquire. But, because they are primarily collected for financial purposes, many important variables needed for risk adjustment are not present, such as patients' functional status or health literacy. Further, they typically do not include data on people and services not covered by insurance.

A second source of data is clinical abstracts of patients' medical records. While these provide more detailed information about patients, information on key risk-adjustment variables may be absent or unreliable. In some cases, only the presence of abnormalities may be documented, records may be missing or unavailable, documentation practices may be inconsistent across clinicians or health care facilities. Clinical abstraction is a labor-intensive method of data collection, and federal and state privacy regulations may restrict access to individual medical records. Some of the problems of availability, standardization, and cost-effectiveness will be resolved as more providers adopt electronic medical records.

Patient surveys are a third source of data and probably the best way to assess patient preferences, satisfaction, and self-reports of health status (a good predictor of outcomes). Their disadvantage is potential bias due to low response rates overall or among specific groups of patients (such as sicker patients or those reluctant to complain) or due to surveys' being completed by someone other than the patient.

Trends in Quality Assessment

A number of emerging themes and trends in quality assessment and improvement merit close observation: the impact of health care technologies and computerized information systems (e.g., clinical decision support, regional health information data bases), growing demand for increased data transparency, the increasing complexity of external expectations, and efforts to implement systems approaches to providing care. In the remainder of this section, we will consider the last three of these.

DATA TRANSPARENCY

The public had access to data on nursing home quality before it had such information for acute care hospitals (see chapter 9 for details on the nursing home initiatives). Private groups, state governments, and the federal government are among those seeking public access to meaningful data for assessing and comparing the quality of patient care across hospitals. Because of the size and scope of the Medicare program, the Centers for Medicare & Medicaid Services have taken a national leadership role in this area through the Hospital Quality Initiatives program, a collaborative public-private partnership.

Beginning in 2005, with plans for future expansion, hospital-specific quality data have been made available at CMS's Hospital

Compare Web site for heart attacks (acute myocardial infarction)—eight indicators; heart failure—four indicators; pneumonia—seven indicators; and surgical infection prevention—two indicators (http://www.cms.hhs.gov/HospitalQualityInits/25_HospitalCompare.asp# TopOfPage). Beginning in June 2007, CMS and its partners began reporting 30-day, risk-adjusted mortality rates for acute myocardial infarction and heart failure patients discharged from acute and critical care hospitals. Also in 2007, the Hospital Consumer Assessment of Healthcare Providers and Systems survey began making available data on patients' perspectives on hospital care.

> Health care providers find themselves in an increasingly tenuous position of trying to decide which of these external demands for quality improvement they should and can respond to.

Clearly, the trend will be for increased data availability and transparency. Of course, for health care providers to collect and submit the increasing amounts of data required by the Minimum Data Set, CMS quality indicators, and HCAHPS will consume staff time and resources for which they are not reimbursed. We can expect to see a growing tension between health care providers and payers over the questions of how much data to collect, how often it needs to be updated, at what cost, and at whose expense?

COMPETING EXTERNAL EXPECTATIONS

Beyond data collection, health care providers and organizations must respond to the varying demands, expectations, and priorities of private, quasi-governmental and governmental regulators concerned with improving patient care quality and safety. Health care providers find themselves in an increasingly tenuous position of trying to decide which of these external demands they should and can respond to. Three major external regulators are described here.

The *Joint Commission* (until 2007, the Joint Commission on Accreditation of Healthcare Organizations [JCAHO]) was formed in 1951 with a mission to improve health care delivery through periodic evaluation and accreditation of health care organizations (originally, just hospitals). Because organizations gaining Joint Commission accreditation are deemed by CMS to meet the requirements necessary to bill Medicare (and many private payers), it is in reality a quasi-regulatory organization. As the nation's largest accreditor of health care organizations, it currently accredits nearly 15,000 hospitals and providers of ambulatory care, home care, laboratory services, and assisted living services, as well as networks. Since 2003, the Joint Commission has issued an annually updated list of national patient safety goals. The 2007 list includes 23 specific goals that must be met in addition to the accreditation requirements.

While Joint Commission requirements have been an impetus for much of the work on health care quality assessment and improvement (Wakefield, 1994), its role in actually improving quality is controversial. On one hand, the need to meet Joint Commission standards has provided incentives to improve care in important areas such as pain control (Gallagher, 2003) and care of patients with stroke (Stradling et al., 2007). On the other hand, a 2002 research project found no correlation between a hospital's outcome measures and Joint Commission accreditation scores (Griffith, Knutzen, & Alexander, 2002), and questions have been raised about the quality of care provided at accredited hospitals (Sloane, 2004).

Any organization with this much power over reimbursement is bound to come in for criticism. And, indeed, the Joint Commission's structure and processes have been faulted for having a board dominated by hospital and physician groups, inconsistencies among surveyors, establishing standards that increase providers' costs without sufficient evidence of benefit, and applying broad guidelines at the individual patient level.

More recently, an assortment of private-sector regional and national business coalitions have formed with the goal of improving health care quality. The *National Committee for Quality Assurance* (NCQA) is a not-for-profit organization offering a variety of accreditation, certification, and physician recognition programs in areas such as disease management, utilization management, and credentialing and for specific diseases such as diabetes and stroke (National Committee on Quality Assurance, 2007). Its Health Plan Employer Data and Information Set measuring patient care service elements is used by nearly all U.S. health plans. The NCQA standards have become another set of external expectations for providers.

The *National Quality Forum* (NQF) is a not-for-profit membership organization focusing on the development of a national strategy for measuring and reporting health care quality and on building the capacity for system-wide improvement (National Quality Forum, 2003). With a broad-based membership drawing from all types of health care organizations and professional associations, as well as public and private purchasers, the NQF uses a structured approach to developing consensus on quality and safety standards. Through 2006, more than 300 measures, indicators, events, and products designed to improve quality assessment have been endorsed by the NQF. The impact of the NQF consensus standards is demonstrated by its influence on the *Leapfrog Group* (2007)—a consortium of the nation's largest employers, health insurers, and governmental purchasers. Leapfrog promotes use of the various NQF standards, including those for "never events" (28 rare medical errors that should *never* happen to patients) and "safe practices for better healthcare"

(30 practices that protect patients and should *always* be employed when indicated). With the leadership provided by the Leapfrog Group and other employer-purchaser coalitions, many of the NQF consensus standards have moved from voluntary to required status. Because of their growing influence, both the NCQA and NQF may in time receive the same kinds of criticisms as the Joint Commission.

Looking at the specific quality and safety improvement expectations being put forth by the Joint Commission, NCQA, NQF, and others from the private sector, combined with the growing number of P4P and governmental initiatives intended to improve quality, two things are immediately apparent. First, there is little coordination and only modest commonality among all the competing external expectations. To some degree, each external group comes up with something different and unique simply to validate its existence. Second, enormous challenges—logistical and financial—face health care organizations attempting to determine whether and how to address these various external expectations, in addition to whatever quality improvement initiatives have been internally identified.

SYSTEMS REFORM: THE CHRONIC CARE MODEL

The Chronic Care Model (CCM) (see also chapter 8) was first developed in the early 1990s and was published in its current form in 1998. It is a primary care–based framework for improving care of patients with chronic illnesses. In partnership with the Institute for Healthcare Improvement (IHI) and using its collaborative approach, the CCM has been used to help organizations make system-level changes to improve care delivery. The IHI collaboratives have involved more than 1,000 health care systems to date, across a wide range of organizational sizes and sophistication. In addition, the NCQA and Joint Commission have developed accreditation and certification programs for chronic disease management based on the CCM (http://www.improvingchroniccare.org/change/model/components.html). The CCM comprises six elements:

- delivery system design (e.g., team practice, care coordination)
- patient self-management support (e.g., patient education and activation, resources and tools)
- decision support (e.g., guidelines, expert consultation)
- clinical information systems (e.g., patient registries, performance data feedback)
- community resources
- support for health care organization leadership (Bodenheimer, Wagner, & Grumbach, 2002a, 2002b).

To date, successful full-scale adoption of the CCM has been limited, despite evidence that adoption of its elements will improve care. For example, a meta-analysis of chronic care interventions found that those containing at least one element from the CCM improved outcomes across a range of conditions, including asthma, chronic heart failure, depression, and diabetes (Nutting et al., 2007; Tsai, Morton, Mangione, & Keeler, 2005). However, efforts to fully implement all six elements simultaneously have been less effective (Hroscikoski et al., 2006). The full model is intuitively appealing but requires broad changes in both the system and culture of health care. Given the aging of the U.S. population and the prevalence of multiple chronic conditions among older people, effective care for chronic illness is clearly an important quality issue.

Strategies for Managing Quality in the Health Care Zone of Complexity

Because a great deal of health care resides within the zone of complexity, strategies for managing and improving quality should center on ways of increasing the probability of achieving the desired outcomes. This section discusses five fundamental strategies, each building on the previous.

CREATE A QUALITY AND PATIENT SAFETY– DRIVEN ORGANIZATIONAL CULTURE: LEADERSHIP, VALUES, BELIEFS, BEHAVIOR, AND INCENTIVES

Every organization is made up of people who, through their shared experiences, values, and efforts, create a product or service. The glue holding everything together and serving as the "invisible hand" of internal control is the organizational culture in which they work. Terms used to discuss organizational culture include group norms, espoused values, formal philosophy, climate, and shared meanings. Establishing and maintaining a positive, productive culture is a key responsibility of leadership.

> Culture and leadership are two sides of the same coin in that leaders first create cultures when they create groups and organizations . . . if cultures become dysfunctional, it is the unique function of leadership to perceive the functional and dysfunctional elements of the existing culture and to manage culture evolution and change. . . . The bottom

line for leaders is that if they do not become conscious of the culture in which they are embedded, those cultures will manage them. (Schein, 1992, p. 15)

Health care provides many recent examples of the growing recognition of the importance of building and managing organizational cultures that facilitate the provision of high-quality and safe patient care. The first of NQF's 30 safety practices is to create an overall culture of safety. Many of its remaining practices are either directly related to or the result of that culture, including whether it engenders a sense of trust among staff:

> Accelerating improvement will require large shifts in attitudes toward and strategies for developing the healthcare workforce . . . [required is] a workforce capable of setting bold aims, measuring progress, finding alternative designs for the work itself, and testing changes rapidly and informatively. It also requires a high degree of trust in many forms, a bias toward teamwork, and a predilection toward shouldering the burden of improvement, rather than blaming external factors. (Berwick, 2003, p. i2)

High-risk industries promote safety practices through organizational cultures described as informed, wary, just, flexible, and learning (Hudson, 2003). A safety culture matures, Hudson suggests, through five stages:

- pathological (Who cares as long as we're not caught?)
- reactive (Safety is important; we do a lot every time we have an accident.)
- calculative (We have systems in place to manage all hazards.)
- proactive (We work on the problems that we still find.)
- generative (Safety is how we do business around here.)

With respect to reducing medication prescribing errors, many hospitals are still at the reactive or calculative stage rather than the proactive or generative stages. Some researchers have specifically argued for organizational cultures that emphasize "that prescribing is a complex, technical, act, and that it is important to get it right" (Barber, Rawlins, & Franklin, 2003, p. i29). In our work examining medication administration error reporting by nursing staff, we have found markedly different perceptions of the percentage of errors being reported. We have consistently found four reasons for *not* reporting that relate to organizational culture: disagreement over what constitutes an error; amount of effort it takes to report an error; fear of being perceived as incompetent by peers, physicians, or patients; and the nature of the administration's response when errors are reported (Wakefield, Uden-Holman, & Wakefield, 2005). To change these behaviors, institutional culture would have to change.

Many health care organizations (particularly hospitals) comprise several different cultures—that of the overall organization and those of its major subunits, specific patient care teams, and a host of different professions. In the best of all worlds, these cultures work in concert to define, assess, and make necessary adjustments as quickly as possible to ensure the provision of high-quality, safe patient care. At worst, they are in conflict over defining what high-quality and safe care is, how to assess it, and who is responsible for making appropriate and timely changes. Much remains to be done to align these cultures. Without understanding and managing the many organizational and professional cultures at play in health care organizations, it is impossible to make major improvements in quality and patient safety. Put another way, "An organization is a system, with a logic of its own, and all the weight of tradition and inertia. The deck is stacked in favor of the tried and proven way of doing things and against the taking of risks and striking out in new directions" (Rockefeller, 1973, p. 72).

PROVIDE THE NECESSARY DATA AND TOOLS: INVEST IN IT, ANALYTIC CAPACITY, AND DECISION SUPPORT

Improving health care quality is not just about collecting more data. Rather, it requires the ability to convert that data into something useful. Data become useful information only after they have been processed or analyzed in some way to derive meaning. In health care, data from several difference sources (e.g., lab values, patient history, and physical examination) are combined and processed to generate useful information: the diagnosis. The diagnosis then guides development of a specific treatment plan for a particular patient. A challenge faced by all health care providers and organizations is how to convert reams of individual patient information into more generalized knowledge that will be useful in treating similar patients, assessing clinician performance, or managing the organization.

To successfully achieve the transformation of data into information and information into knowledge requires a significant investment in health care organizations' information technologies (IT) and their analytic and decision-support capabilities. Today, health care institutions and organizations are working hard to develop comprehensive electronic medical records systems that include extensive amounts of data—not only on the specific services provided (e.g., diagnostic and therapeutic procedures, nursing care, pharmaceuticals), but also detailed clinical data (e.g., specific lab values, vital signs, risk factors).

Thus, in some situations, it is now possible to have automated, real-time clinical care monitoring and decision support services. For example, computerized physician order entry (CPOE) systems with decision support have been widely touted as a potential solution to most medication prescribing errors (see also chapter 13). True CPOE systems do more than enable a physician to use a computer to order a patient's medication. They simultaneously analyze a patient's discrete data elements from several different sources (e.g., laboratory, physician notes, pharmacy, and nursing notes, including the medication administration record) to evaluate the appropriateness of a physician's medication order and identify potential contraindications.

MEASURE WHAT YOU MANAGE: DISCIPLINED USE OF QUALITY IMPROVEMENT METHODOLOGY

With an organizational culture centered on providing high-quality and safe patient care, supported by an IT and analytic infrastructure, the stage is set to sharpen the focus of quality care efforts. Such a sharpened focus requires two things: prioritization of what is important to monitor and manage and the disciplined use of quality improvement (QI) approaches.

What to Measure

The choice of measurement indicators and metrics is critical. For example, managers could focus on specific processes of care for selected types of patients. Or they could have an outcomes orientation, tracking indicators such as mortality, functional status, patient satisfaction, or resources used for specific diseases or conditions. Or they could monitor error-related indicators for a hospital's total patient population, specific patient care service lines, or patient care units. Or they could focus on sentinel events—that is, unexpected death or serious physical or psychological injury, including patient suicides, wrong-site surgery, and medication errors.

In leading the national quality improvement and safety research agenda, the federal Agency for Healthcare Research and Quality (AHRQ) has identified and defined three primary categories of error-related indicators that might be used for ongoing monitoring:

- *Medical Errors*—Acts of omission or commission defined as "The failure[s] of a planned action to be completed as intended or the use of a wrong action to achieve an aim. . . . Errors can include problems in practice, products, procedures, and systems" (AHRQ, 2001, p. 5).
- *Adverse Events*—"Undesirable and unintended incidents in care that may result in adverse outcomes, or may require additional

care efforts to thwart an adverse outcome" (AHRQ, 2001, p. 5). Organizations must decide whether they will collect, analyze, and act on information about only those adverse events that actually harm patients. Ignoring the others risks losing critical information about potential weaknesses in the way care is currently being provided.

● *Near Misses*—Undesirable events prevented because a problem was identified and rectified before harm occurred. Such a recovery may occur because of a specific safety check or by careful observation.

Near-miss data raise the interesting question of whether, and to what extent, it is useful to track things that "almost happened." The value of near-miss data has been dramatically demonstrated in the aviation and nuclear power industries, and they potentially could be useful in other industries requiring high reliability. Several advantages of supplementing adverse event and error reporting with near-miss reporting are: (a) near misses are thought to occur much more often than actual adverse events or errors and thus enhance quantitative analysis; (b) people are more likely to report near misses, because they shift the focus from the negative (something bad occurred) to the positive (it was prevented); (c) the focus on prevention allows for systematic learning about how recovery from the potential error was achieved; and (d) near-miss reporting is less biased by hindsight. In health care, a growing number of studies have examined near misses in blood transfusions, anesthesia, and medication safety, for example. Existing adverse event and error reporting systems do have limitations. Most were designed to emphasize accountability at the expense of learning. This emphasis comes about because of: (a) a risk management orientation, which emphasizes reporting known major adverse events and errors rather than minor ones and near misses; (b) participation in comparative reporting systems required by external groups (i.e., JCAHO, purchaser groups, and state facility licensure agencies); (c) a failure to assess whether an organization's internal reporting culture is hindering reporting of adverse events and errors; and (d) use of these data for assessing individual performance rather than as opportunities to learn about reducing systems-related problems. In this way, ironically, punitive risk-management programs sometimes operate counter to quality and performance improvement.

In summary, basic questions to consider when evaluating the validity, reliability, and usefulness of the health care quality and patient safety indicators include:

● To what extent does an organization rely on automated systems to measure quality or detect and report patient safety problems?

- To what extent do the processes used to measure quality or report patient safety problems rely on individual physician, nurse, or other health care providers' decisions and actions?
- To what extent do an institution's organizational and professional cultures enhance or reduce the validity, reliability, and usability of the care quality and patient safety indicators?
- What percent of errors, adverse events, or near misses are to be reported?
- To what extent will quality and patient safety indicator information be used for establishing individual accountability rather than organizational learning?

Quality Improvement Methodologies

In conjunction with the decision about what to measure, health care organizations must adopt a consistent quality improvement methodology. These methodologies typically provide an iterative framework and tools for analyzing existing processes or problems, developing and testing interventions, and continued monitoring and evaluation for potential revisions. Examples of such methodologies range from the process-specific plan-do-study-act cycle to the more organization-wide Six Sigma, ISO-9000, and Baldridge National Quality Program approaches.

Each of these methods shares common features. They were widely used in industry prior to their adoption in health care settings; they rely on similar types of data collection and analytic tools; they use similar tools to design improvements; and each emphasizes the need for ongoing monitoring and intensified study if performance problems emerge.

CREATE LEARNING ORGANIZATIONS: INVEST IN STAFF KNOWLEDGE AND SKILLS

Health care organizations have a unique opportunity to improve patient safety and the quality of care by tapping into the knowledge of their workers and by studying near-miss data. In non–health care organizations, organizational development and learning strategies have sharpened the focus on ways to more effectively and efficiently extract and share what is already known or what might be learned about quality and safety. Central to this rapidly expanding body of literature is the basic question: how can organizational productivity—including the value, quality, and safety of health care services and products—be enhanced through the creation of learning organizations? Beyond the three approaches already discussed are the following additional strategies that can be helpful in building health care organizations that learn.

Patient Care Quality, Safety, and Value as Core Competencies

Whose job is it to ensure that patient care services are high quality, safe, and add value? Everyone's—from the chair of the governing board to the most recently hired housekeeper. Everyone must have the relevant quality, safety, and value improvement competencies specified in their position descriptions and recognized as part of their role within the organization. In addition to the specific technical competencies associated with a particular position, staff must know how to interpret and use quality and patient safety-related information and be ever-alert for potential unanticipated problems that may be outside their formal job description. Depending on the worker's level of supervisory or managerial responsibility, additional competencies might include conducting basic process analyses, leading quality/safety/value improvement teams, and helping to design, implement, and test interventions.

> Everyone must have the relevant quality, safety, and value improvement competencies specified in their position descriptions and recognized as part of their role within the organization.

Organizational and Professional Education as an Opportunity for Improvement

Each year health care providers and organizations invest significant resources in ongoing education. Most states require that licensed health care professionals complete a minimum amount of professional education each year. This continuing education is generally offered by outside organizations and frequently paid for by health care organizations. In addition, hospitals and other health care organizations provide a variety of in-house educational programs designed to improve their staff's knowledge of specific legal, administrative, and patient care–related processes and skills. Continuing education costs include not only the direct expenses of attending external educational programs (registration fees, travel, hotel) and internal programs (program preparation and delivery), but also paid time away (salary and benefits for participants and their temporary replacements). An organization's investment in continuing education programming can range from several thousands to millions of dollars each year. Ironically, few if any hospitals calculate their return on these sizeable investments, and, to date, they are far from maximized. Hospitals could make great strides in quality improvement if they targeted these investments on what matters most in improving quality and safety.

Quality Improvement as Fundamental to Every Organizational Initiative

An additional strategy to consider when creating learning organizations is to view every organizational initiative as an opportunity to improve quality—regardless of whether the initiative is focused on improving service excellence, reducing nosocomial infections, making new IT investments, or carrying out revenue and supply chain management initiatives.

PERSIST: QUALITY, SAFETY, AND VALUE IMPROVEMENT IS NOT A FAD

There are no quick quality improvement fixes in health care. The challenge of providing high-quality, individualized, appropriate, and effective services within dynamic internal and external environments is daunting. Daily crises—major and minor—stemming from uncertainty in dealing with myriad changing requirements can and do distract clinical and administrative leaders from efforts to improve quality. But if a commitment to quality is fully integrated into the organization's culture, there is much less risk that it will suffer when leaders' attention is elsewhere. Persistence in improving the quality, safety, and value of health care must become everyone's job, every day.

References

AHRQ (2001). *Improving patient safety: Health systems reporting, analysis and safety improvement research demonstrations.* Release date February 2, 2001, 1–26.

Asch, S. M., Sloss, E. M., Hogan, C., Brook, R. H., & Kravitz, R. L. (2000). Measuring underuse of necessary care among elderly Medicare beneficiaries using inpatient and outpatient claims. *Journal of the American Medical Association, 284,* 2325–2333.

Ashton, C. M., Souchek, J., Petersoen, J. N. J., Menke, T. J., Collins, T. C., Kizer, K. W., et al. (2003). Hospital use and survival among Veterans Affairs beneficiaries. *New England Journal of Medicine, 349,* 1637–1646.

Barber, N., Rawlins, M., & Franklin, B. D. (2003). Reducing prescribing error: Competence, control, and culture. *Quality & Safety in Health Care, 12*(Suppl. 1), i29–i31.

Berwick, D. M. (2003). Improvement, trust, and the health care workforce. *Quality & Safety in Health Care, 12*(Suppl. 1), i2–i6.

Bodenheimer, T., Wagner, E. H., & Grumbach, K. (2002a). Improving primary care for patients with chronic illness. *Journal of the American Medical Association, 288*(14), 1775–1779.

Bodenheimer, T., Wagner, E. H., & Grumbach, K. (2002b). Improving primary care for patients with chronic illness: The chronic care model, Part 2. *Journal of the American Medical Association, 288*(15), 1909–1914.

Center for the Evaluative Clinical Sciences. (2005). *Supply-sensitive care.* Hanover, NH: Dartmouth University. Retrieved March 10, 2007, from http://www.dartmouthatlas.org/topics/supply_sensitive.pdf

Center for the Evaluative Clinical Sciences. (2007a). *Effective care.* Hanover, NH: Dartmouth University. Retrieved March 10, 2007, from http://www.dartmouthatlas.org/topics/effective_care.pdf

Center for the Evaluative Clinical Sciences. (2007b). *Preference-sensitive care.* Hanover, NH: Dartmouth University. Retrieved March 10, 2007, from http://www.dart mouthatlas.org/topics/preference_sensitive.pdf

Chin, M. H., & Muramatsu, N. (2003). What is the quality of quality of medical care measures. Rashomon-like relativism and real-world applications. *Perspectives in Biology and Medicine, 46*(1), 5–20.

Donabedian, A. (1980). *Explorations in quality assessment and monitoring: The definition of quality and approaches to its assessment* (Vol. 1). Ann Arbor, MI: Health Administration Press.

Epstein, A. M. (2007). Pay for performance at the tipping point. *New England Journal of Medicine, 356,* 515–517.

Fisher, E. S. (2003). Medical care—Is more always better? *New England Journal of Medicine, 349,* 1665–1667.

Fisher, E. S. (2006). Paying for performance—Risks and recommendations. *New England Journal of Medicine, 355,* 1845–1847.

Foundation for Informed Medical Decision Making. (2007). Retrieved March 27, 2007, from http://www.fimdm.org

Gallagher, R. M. (2003). Physician variability in pain management: Are the JCAHO standards enough? *Pain Medicine, 4*(1), 1–3.

Griffith, J. R., Knutzen, S. R., and Alexander, J. A. (2002). Structural versus outcomes measures in hospitals: A comparison of Joint Commission and Medicare outcomes scores in hospitals. *Quality Management in Health Care, 10*(2), 29–38.

Hroscikoski, M. C., Solberg, L. I., Sperl-Hillen, J. M., Harper, P. G., McGrail, M. P., & Crabtree, B. F. (2006). Challenges of change: A qualitative study of Chronic Care Model implementation. *Annals of Family Medicine, 4,* 317–326.

Hudson, P. (2003). Applying the lessons of high risk industries to health care. *Quality & Safety in Health Care, 12,* i7.

Institute of Medicine & Committee on Redesigning Health Insurance Performance Measures, Payment, and Performance Improvement Programs. (2007). *Rewarding provider performance: Aligning incentives in Medicare.* Washington, DC: National Academy Press.

Institute of Medicine & Committee on Quality Health Care in America. (2000). *To err is human: Building a safer health system.* (L. T. Kohn et al., Eds.). Washington, DC: National Academy Press.

Institute of Medicine & Committee on Quality Health Care in America. (2001). *Crossing the quality chasm: A new health system for the 21st century.* Washington, DC: National Academy Press.

Leapfrog Group. (2007). Retrieved March 22, 2007, from http://www.leapfroggroup.org

Leatherman, S., et al. (2003). Making the business case for quality. *Health Affairs, 22*(2), 17–30.

McGlynn, E. A., Asch, S. M., Adams, J., Keesey, J., Hicks, J., DeCristofaro, A., et al. (2003). The quality of health care delivered to adults in the United States. *New England Journal of Medicine, 438,* 2635–2645.

Murray, C. J. L., Kulkarni, S. C., Michaud, C., Tomijima, N., Bulzacchelli, M. T., Iandiorio, T. J., et al. (2006). Eight Americas: Investigating mortality disparities across races, counties, and race-counties in the United States. *PLoS Medicine, 3*(9), e260. Retrieved from http://medicine.plosjournals.org/archive/1549-1676/3/9/pdf/10.1371_journal.pmed.0030260-S.pdf

National Committee on Quality Assurance. (2007). Retrieved March 22, 2007, from http://web.ncqa.org

National Quality Forum. (2003). *Safe practices for better health care.* Retrieved January 6, 2004, from http://www.qualityforum.org/projects/completed/safe_ practices

Nelson, G., Mohr, J., Batalden, P., & Plume, S. (1996). Improving health care, part 1: The clinical value compass. *Joint Commission Journal on Quality Improvement, 22*(4).

Nutting, P. A., Dickinson, W. P., Dickinson, L. M., et al. (2007). Use of Chronic Care Model elements is associated with higher quality care for diabetes. *Annals of Family Medicine, 5*(1), 14–20.

O'Connor, G. T., Quinton, H. B., Traven, N. D., Ramunno, L. D., Dodds, T. A & Marciniak, T. A., et al. (1999). Geographic variation in the treatment of acute myocardial infarction: The cooperative cardiovascular project. *JAMA 281.* pp. 627–633.

Plsek, P. (2001). Redesigning health care with insights from the science of complex adaptive systems. In Institute of Medicine (Ed.), *Crossing the quality chasm: A new health system for the 21st century* (pp. 322–355). Washington, DC: National Academy Press.

Rockefeller, J. D., 3rd. (1973). *The second American revolution: Some personal observations.* New York: Harper & Row.

Satcher, D. S., Fryer, G. E., McCann, J., Troutman, A., Woolf, S. H., Rust, G., et al. (2005). What if we were equal? A comparison of the Black-White mortality gap in 1960 and 2000. *Health Affairs, 24*(2), 459–464.

Schein, E. H. (1992). *Organizational culture and leadership* (2nd ed.). San Francisco: Jossey-Bass.

Shine, K. (2001). *2001 Robert H. Ebert Memorial Lecture: Health care quality and how to achieve it.* New York: Milbank Memorial Fund. Retrieved July 12, 2004, from http://www.milbank.org/reports/020130Ebert/020130Ebert.html

Sloane, T. (2004, August 2). A commission out of joint; another report adds evidence that JCAHO needs a total overhaul. *Modern Healthcare,* 20.

Stacey, R. D. (1996). *Complexity and creativity in organizations.* San Francisco: Berrett-Koehler.

Stradling, D., Yu, W., Langdorf, M. L., Tsai, F., Kostanian, V., Hasso, A. N., et al. (2007). Stroke care delivery before vs. after JCAHO stroke center certification. *Neurology, 68,* 469–470.

Tsai, A. C., Morton, S. C., Mangione, C. M., & Keeler, E. B. (2005). A meta-analysis of interventions to improve care for chronic illness. *American Journal of Managed Care, 11,* 478–488.

U.S. Department of Health & Human Services, Agency for Healthcare Research and Quality. (2005). *2005 national healthcare disparities report.* Retrieved from http://www.ahrq.gov/qual/nhdr05/nhdr05.pdf

Wakefield, B. (1994). The evolution of the Joint Commission's nursing standards. *Journal for Healthcare Quality, 16*(3), 15–21.

Wakefield, B. J., Uden-Holman, T., & Wakefield, D. S. (2005). Development and validation of the Medication Administration Error Reporting Survey. In K. Henriksen, J. B. Battles, E. Marks, & D. I. Lewin (Eds.), *Advances in patient safety: From research to implementation: Vol. 4. Programs, tools, and products.* AHRQ Publication No. 05-0021-4. Rockville, MD: Agency for Healthcare Research and Quality.

Wennberg, J. (2005). *Variation in the use of Medicare services among regions and selected academic medical centers: Is more better?* New York: Commonwealth Fund.

Wennberg, J. (2007). *Understanding high value care and reducing unwarranted variation in health care.* Dartmouth Hitchcock Medical Center Department of Medicine Grand Rounds, February 9, 2007. Retrieved March 10, 2007, from http://www.dartmouthatlas.org/index.shtm

Wennberg, J., Fisher, E. S., Sharp, S. M., et al. (2006). The care of patients with severe chronic illness: An online report on the Medicare program by the Dartmouth

Atlas Project. Retrieved March 10, 2007, from http://www.dartmouthatlas.org/atlases.shtm

Wennberg, J., & Gittelsohn, A. (1982).Variations in medical care among small areas. *Scientific American, 246*(4), 120–134.

Williams, D. R. (2005). Patterns and causes of disparities in health. In D. Mechanic, L. B. Rogut, D. C Colby, & J. R Knickman (Eds.), *Policy challenges in modern health care* (pp. 115–134). New Brunswick, NJ: Rutgers University Press.

16

Key Words

Access to Care

John Billings and Joel C. Cantor

Learning Objectives

- Understand the nature of the access problem.
- Understand the distinction between economic and noneconomic barriers to health care.
- Understand the characteristics of the uninsured and the policy implications of those characteristics.
- Understand how access barriers impinge on health.
- Understand how access barriers affect the health care delivery system.
- Understand the range and limitations of options for reform—increasing coverage and reducing barriers to care.

Topical Outline

- Economic barriers to care
- Noneconomic and quasi-economic barriers to care
- Health care reform: improving access
- The future: continuing and emerging issues

445

ince the early 20th century, the U.S. health care system has struggled to assure access to health care services for all Americans. Major steps forward include the growth of private, employer-based health insurance following World War II, the passage of the Medicare and Medicaid programs in 1965, and the growth of federal efforts in the 1970s to expand direct service programs, such as community health centers, for low-income patients. All these developments helped improve access for many Americans. But the debate surrounding the proposed Clinton Health Reform Plan of 1993 and its subsequent failure illustrate the difficulties in making further progress.

Access is often viewed as a one-dimensional problem: lack of health insurance coverage. By this measure, an estimated 45 million Americans were uninsured in 2005—15.3% of the nonelderly U.S. population (see Table 16.1) (U.S. Census Bureau, 2007). Moreover, the situation has deteriorated over the past 25 years, with the percentage of the population that is uninsured growing steadily, although there has been an increase in coverage levels for children (currently with 11.6% uninsured). The potential impact of lack of insurance on patients is obvious and well documented. Large numbers of uninsured patients also have deleterious effects on the health care delivery system, as providers struggle to have other payers subsidize the expenses incurred by patients without coverage. With the expansion of managed care and the emergence of stronger market forces, the situation is expected to get worse.

The problem of access, however, is enormously more complex than insurance coverage. An insurance card alone does not eliminate barriers to access. First, there are issues of the extent and adequacy of coverage. Are outpatient services covered as well as inpatient care? Are prescription drugs included? Mental health and substance abuse services? Long-term care? And what about the levels of co-payments and deductibles? Some 61 million adult Americans are estimated to be underinsured; their coverage is inadequate to assure financial access to care (Schoen, Doty, Collins, & Holmgren, 2005).

> An insurance card alone does not eliminate barriers to access.

Then there's the other side of the coin. How adequate are the insurer's payments to providers? For example, Medicaid's pattern of low physician payment rates have discouraged physicians from participating and thereby limited where Medicaid recipients can

Table 16.1	Who Are the Uninsured? 2005 Uninsurance Data by Race/Ethnicity	
Population Group	**Number Uninsured**	**Percent Uninsured**
All races	44,815,000	15.3
White	33,946,000	14.4
White, not Hispanic	20,909,000	10.7
Black	7,006,000	19.0
Asian	2,161,000	17.2
Hispanic (of any race)	13,954,000	32.3

Note. From U.S. Bureau of the Census. (2007). *Health insurance coverage by race and hispanic origin, 1999 to 2005.* Washington, DC: U.S. Bureau of the Census. Retrieved from http://www.census.gov/hhes/www/hlthins/usernote/schedule.html

receive care; managed care companies typically do not pay enough for mental health counseling, so that agencies lose money on every insured patient visit.

In addition, even insured patients can face serious noneconomic barriers to care that have a dramatic effect on access, service utilization, and health outcomes. The delivery of care remains largely fragmented and uncoordinated, making it difficult for many users to arrange for and obtain the services they need. To the extent that the health care delivery system fails to respond to differences in language, culture, health care beliefs, care-seeking behavior, or educational levels, it creates additional impediments to access. Such nonfinancial barriers are often worse for low-income patients. For example, obtaining timely care for a child may require that a parent take time off from work, forgo wages, arrange child care for siblings, or obtain transportation—all of which may be more difficult for families with limited resources or who are socially isolated.

This chapter examines the nature and extent of all of these barriers to care. In the next section, we explore economic barriers, including an overview of the characteristics of the uninsured, a discussion of problems in the extent and adequacy of coverage, and an examination of the consequences that lack of adequate insurance has on patients and providers. In the following section, we describe noneconomic barriers and document their impact. In the final section, we examine various reforms, discuss their potential impact and limitations, and explore future issues related to access.

Economic Barriers to Care

IDENTIFYING THE UNINSURED

The level of uninsurance among the elderly is very low (0.8%), reflecting the dramatic impact of the Medicare program, which provides almost universal coverage for Americans age 65 and over. Although the program has important limitations in coverage and some noneconomic barriers exist for this population, Medicare has done much to make health care services accessible for older Americans. Among the nonelderly, the highest rates of uninsurance are among young adults ages 18 to 34. The higher rates in this age group reflect two important factors: their dependence on employer-based coverage for private insurance and the impact of the federal-state Medicaid program. When U.S. employers fail to offer insurance to their workers, or when an individual becomes unemployed, the risk of becoming uninsured increases enormously. The cost of individual coverage is prohibitive for most uninsured people, especially low-income workers or the unemployed. Young adults have higher rates of unemployment, are more recent entrants to the workforce, and typically have lower-wage jobs or work only part-time.

Young adults also often have difficulty establishing Medicaid eligibility, although eligibility rules vary among states. Medicaid eligibility is limited to low-income individuals in certain age groups (children, the elderly) or who are blind/disabled, pregnant, single parents, or unemployed parents (in some states). Employed parents or childless adults generally are not eligible for Medicaid, regardless of income (unless they become blind, disabled, or pregnant), although some states provide coverage through state-financed programs (home relief, medically indigent, etc.) for some. The targeted nature of the Medicaid program also is reflected in the lower rates of uninsurance for children (who are categorically eligible) and women (who are more likely to be single parents or may become eligible through pregnancy).

Most uninsured Americans work at least part-time. About 85% live in households where the family head has been employed during the past year. Accordingly, the problem of uninsurance is typically due to the failure of an employer to offer insurance or to the employee's refusal of coverage. The highest rates of uninsurance are among nonprofessional or managerial occupations in the retail, service, construction, and agricultural sectors, with much higher rates of uninsurance among small employers and the self-employed. Low-wage earners (incomes less than 200% of the federal poverty level) represent more than half of the working uninsured and have rates of uninsurance more than six times greater than higher-income workers. The rising cost of health

care—and hence health insurance—has greatly outstripped both general inflation and workers' earnings (see Figure 16.1).

Rates of uninsurance also differ markedly among states (see
Figure 16.2). For example, in Iowa, Rhode Island, Minnesota, and
Wisconsin, less than 9% of the population is uninsured, while in
Texas and New Mexico, more than 20% is, according to the Census
Bureau. In addition to the categorical requirements noted above
(children, the aged, people who are blind/disabled, etc.), states set
minimum income standards for eligibility. Historically, these standards were tied to welfare payment levels, again with considerable differences among states. Recent federal reforms have broken this link
and have given states more flexibility in setting eligibility standards.

The profile of the typical uninsured person might be a young adult
in a low-wage job working for a small employer in the retail/services
sector. Any realistic solution to the problem of uninsurance cannot

Figure 16.1

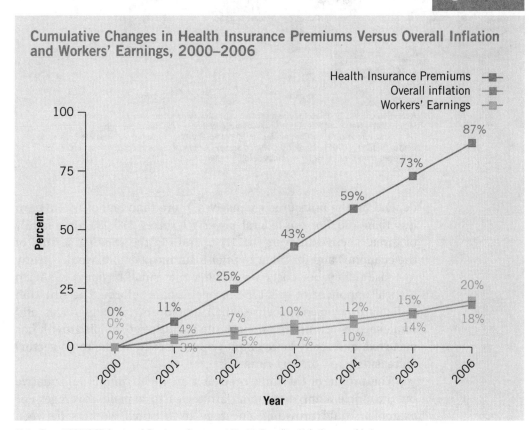

Cumulative Changes in Health Insurance Premiums Versus Overall Inflation and Workers' Earnings, 2000–2006

Note. From KFF/HRET Survey of Employer-Sponsored Health Benefits; U.S. Bureau of Labor
Statistics, Consumer Price Index, U.S. City Average of Annual Inflation; U.S. Bureau of Labor
Statistics, Seasonally Adjusted Data from the Current Employment Statistics Survey.

Figure 16.2

Health Insurance Coverage of Nonelderly Americans, by State, 2004–2005

United States 17%

Washington 14%
Oregon 18%
Idaho 16%
Montana 20%
North Dakota 12%
Minnesota 9%
New Hampshire 11%
Maine 11%
Vermont 13%
Massachusetts 12%
New York 14%
Rhode Island 12%
South Dakota 13%
Wisconsin 11%
Michigan 12%
Pennsylvania 12%
Connecticut 13%
New Jersey 16%
Wyoming 16%
Nevada 20%
Utah 16%
Colorado 18%
Nebraska 12%
Iowa 10%
Ohio 12%
Indiana 12%
Illinois 15%
West Virginia 19%
Virginia 15%
Delaware 15%
Maryland 15%
District of Columbia 14%
California 20%
Kansas 12%
Missouri 13%
Kentucky 15%
North Carolina 17%
Arizona 21%
New Mexico 23%
Oklahoma 22%
Arkansas 19%
Tennessee 15%
South Carolina 18%
Mississippi 19%
Alabama 15%
Georgia 19%
Texas 26%
Louisiana 19%
Florida 23%
Alaska 18%
Hawaii 10%

9 to 12%
13 to 16%
17 to 20%
>20%

Note. Percentages updated to reflect revised estimates released by the U.S. Census Bureau, March 2007. Retrieved from http://www.census.gov/hhes/www/hlthins/usernote/schedule.html Urban Institute and Kaiser Commission on Medicaid and the Uninsured estimates are based on Census Bureau. (2006). *Current population survey (Annual social and economic supplements).* Retrieved from http://www.kff.org/uninsured/index.cfm

depend on the uninsured themselves, more than half of whom earn less than 200% of the federal poverty level, or $30,000 for a family of three. Their employers mostly operate in the weakest sectors of the economy, and for them to offer insurance benefits would greatly increase their labor costs. No wonder that small business has been a vocal opponent of this type of health care reform. The situation is likely to worsen, because small employers in the services and retail sectors are where much of the nation's recent job growth has occurred, and many large employers (especially in the retail sector) increasingly rely on part-time workers.

The profile of the uninsured at a point in time is informative but insufficient for developing strategies to expand coverage. For example, would providing coverage to seasonal workers between jobs or the unemployed significantly reduce the percentage of the population without coverage? What about providing an extra 6 or

12 months of Medicaid or SCHIP coverage for individuals entering the workforce? To answer such questions, analysts turn to longitudinal studies that characterize individuals' transitions in and out of health coverage. Such studies show that many more individuals go without coverage over a period of time than appear in the annual statistics. One 4-year study found that nearly 85 million Americans are without coverage for at lease 1 month during the year—more than double the number identified in studies reporting on a single point in time (Short & Graefe, 2003). That same 4-year study showed that about 12% of people uninsured at some point during 1996–1999 were without coverage for the full 4 years. This suggests that, for many people, being uninsured is transitory, although for some it is a long-term proposition. The uninsured are a heterogeneous lot, and no single policy (short of universal government insurance) is likely to address all of their coverage needs.

UNDERINSURANCE AND OTHER LIMITATIONS OF COVERAGE

As stated previously, having an insurance card does not always assure financial access to the services a person needs. For example, private insurance often excludes mental health services, preventive care, and long-term care. Most plans have exclusions or waiting periods for conditions present at the time of enrollment (preexisting conditions). These limits affect people most in need of coverage and subject them to substantial financial risk if the policyholder changes jobs. Many plans cover catastrophic illnesses inadequately; their maximum lifetime benefit limits are too low to cover the costs of a serious illness or accident. Moreover, virtually all private insurance plans, even most managed care plans, require co-payments or deductibles that may discourage patients—especially lower-income patients most sensitive to out-of-pocket costs—from seeking needed preventive care.

While almost 97% of Americans over age 65 have Medicare coverage, the program has substantial patient cost-sharing provisions and serious gaps in coverage. The deductible is more than $992 for hospital care and $131 for outpatient care, with substantial co-payments (20%) required in many cases. Moreover, before 2006, Medicare provided virtually no coverage for outpatient prescription drugs, and the recent coverage expansion leaves large gaps for non–low-income patients ($250 deductible, 25% co-payment for first $2,250 in drug costs, and no coverage for drug expenses between $2,250 and $5,100, as described in chapters 3 and 5). Medicare has substantial restrictions on long-term care (only 2% of the elderly's nursing home costs are paid by Medicare). As a result of these provisions, Medicare probably pays less than 50% of the total costs of health care for the elderly. Many elderly

Americans have supplemental coverage for some of these expenses (medigap plans), either through their employer/retirement plan or by purchasing it directly. But more than 20% of the elderly (35% of low-income elderly) have no supplemental coverage and are exposed to serious financial risks and potentially substantial barriers to access.

Low-income elderly Americans qualify for Medicaid, which is generally very comprehensive, covering most services (including drugs and long-term care) with few restrictions or co-payments. However, a great many providers don't participate in Medicaid. While Medicaid payments to hospitals historically have been guaranteed at levels reasonably related to costs, payments to physicians are set by state administrative agencies that are facing staggering increases in program costs. Not surprisingly, payment levels for physicians and other noninstitutional providers have often been set below market rates. For example, until 2000, New York's Medicaid program would pay physicians $11 for an "intermediate office visit," an amount unchanged since 1985, with the amount now raised to a well-below-market rate of $27.50. In 2004–2005, more than 20% of physicians would not accept new Medicaid patients (Cunningham & May, 2006).

The most significant federal health coverage expansion since the enactment of the State Children's Health Insurance Program (SCHIP) addresses the problem of underinsurance for the elderly and disabled. The Medicare Prescription Drug, Improvement, and Modernization Act of 2003 contained a broad range of provisions, at the center of which is drug coverage under a new Medicare Part D.

THE IMPACT OF ECONOMIC BARRIERS TO CARE

Being uninsured has profound impacts (Hadley, 2003). Uninsured people are less likely than those with private insurance to have a usual source of care; in fact, 24% of the uninsured do not have a usual source of care, compared to 8% of people with private insurance. Among those with health problems, uninsured people are more likely to have had no physician visits during a 12-month period than are people with private insurance (22% vs. 9%) and to have had fewer physician contacts (9.1 vs. 14.8). These differences persist even after adjusting for socioeconomic status (Millman, 1993).

> Being uninsured has profound impacts on health and health care.

The impact of coinsurance on utilization also is significant, especially among lower-income patients. While one goal of coinsurance is to discourage frivolous use of services, it also discourages use of preventive services (such as immunizations or screening tests), which may lead to conditions that are costly to treat later on.

Lack of insurance affects hospital utilization. Uninsured people are more likely to be admitted for preventable or avoidable conditions, such as asthma, diabetes, cellulitis, or other infections (Billings & Teicholz, 1990). In one study, uninsured hospital patients were found to be substantially less likely to receive common diagnostic tests (colonoscopy, endoscopy, coronary arteriography, etc.) or costly surgical procedures (bypass surgery, joint replacement, eye surgery, etc.), even after controlling for sociodemographic and diagnostic case-mix factors (Hadley, Steinberg, & Feder, 1991). In other words, regardless of their condition or its seriousness, uninsured people were less likely to receive services that insured people received—even those whose insurance was Medicaid. Moreover, whether people had insurance—not their income or how sick they were—determined what services they received.

Documenting the effect of insurance status on health status and on health outcomes is difficult, because the lack of insurance tends to be somewhat episodic (with individuals going on and off of insurance periodically). Still, researchers have observed substantial differences for the uninsured, compared to individuals with insurance, especially private insurance. For example:

● Uninsured mothers begin prenatal care later and have fewer total visits (Braveman, Egerter, Bennett, & Showstack, 1991).
● Uninsured newborns have adverse outcomes more frequently (Braveman, Oliva, & Miller, 1989).
● Uninsured women present with later-stage breast cancer and have lower survival rates—in fact, a 49% higher risk of death (Ayanian, Kohlker, & Toshi, 1993).
● Most dramatically, uninsured patients have higher overall mortality. In a study of a national cohort of patients between 1971 and 1987, uninsured patients had a 25% greater risk of dying, even after adjusting for differences in sociodemographic characteristics, general health status, and health habits (Franks, Clancy, & Gold, 1993).

In all these examples, insurance made the vital difference.

Although the cost of uninsurance and underinsurance is high in human terms, its serious impact on the health care delivery system affects all patients. First, distortions in utilization patterns can increase total costs. While uninsurance promotes underutilization, it also has the effect of steering uninsured patients to places and providers that must provide care, regardless of the patient's ability to pay—typically, hospital outpatient departments, emergency rooms, and community-based clinics. Costs in these settings, especially emergency departments, are high and increase the nation's overall health care spending. To the extent that an emergency visit is for a preventable condition or costs more than treatment in a primary care setting, these are unnecessary costs.

Potentially worse is the financial disequilibrium these utilization patterns create. Providers serving large numbers of uninsured patients must somehow cover the costs of unreimbursed care. These same providers usually serve substantial numbers of Medicaid patients for whom costs of care often exceed reimbursement rates. These shortfalls can be cost-shifted to other payers (by raising charges sufficiently above actual costs to generate enough revenue to cover unreimbursed expenses), or providers can seek government or private subsidies. Although some states have established elaborate pooling systems to subsidize costs of uninsured patients (taxing some hospitals or insurers to support hospitals with high burdens of uninsured patients) and many publicly operated providers receive direct subsidies, in most jurisdictions providers are dependent on the cost-shift.

Today's market forces make cost-shifting increasingly less viable. For example, managed care plans encourage enrollees to use facilities with lower charges. The net result of these trends is that hospitals must further increase charges to a shrinking base of full-pay patients in order to cover rising, unreimbursed costs. The wholesale movement of Medicaid patients into managed care plans that has begun in most states will further undermine the financial stability of many providers.

Ultimately, if hospitals close and safety-net providers fail, low-income people's access to care will be serious jeopardized. The providers most at risk of financial failure are the very ones that provide the most care to vulnerable people. It isn't clear that the remaining providers who have been too far away or too unwilling to serve low-income patients previously will do so.

Noneconomic and Quasi-Economic Barriers to Care

MEDICAID COVERAGE DOESN'T ERASE ALL BARRIERS

On some measures, patients with Medicaid coverage fare better than the uninsured, but not on most:

- Medicaid recipients have fewer preventable hospitalizations than do uninsured patients, but almost 75% more than insured patients (Billings & Teicholz, 1990).
- Incidence of late detection of breast cancer and survival rates for cancer were comparable for the uninsured and for Medicaid patients (Ayanian et al., 1993).

● Pregnant women on Medicaid, like the uninsured, delayed prenatal care and had fewer prenatal care visit rates, compared to privately insured women (Braveman et al., 1991).

For such patients, Medicaid failed to eliminate the barriers to needed care. Vulnerable populations clearly face special problems in dealing with the complexities of our fragmented delivery system that create impediments to timely and effective care.

RACE/ETHNICITY

Large and persistent differences in health status, utilization, and outcomes among racial and ethnic groups are well documented. Americans who are Black or Hispanic/Latin American are less likely to have a usual source of primary care; they have fewer physician visits; they have higher rates of no or late prenatal care; they have lower rates of immunizations and screening tests; and they report worse health status. Large racial differences also have been documented in rates for infant mortality, low–birth weight, late-stage cancer diagnosis, and mortality from all causes (Council on Ethical and Judicial Affairs, 1990; Fiscella, Franks, Gold, & Clancy, 2000; Millman, 1993).

In U.S. society, socioeconomic status and race/ethnicity are intertwined, and research has attributed part, but not all, of these racial/ethnic disparities in health care and health status to socioeconomic conditions. A growing body of research that attempts to control for socioeconomic and other factors suggests that minority status in and of itself is an important factor in utilization and outcomes. For example, after researchers adjusted for differences in insurance coverage, minority adolescents still were less likely to have a usual source of primary care, had fewer annual physician contacts, and had less continuity of care (Lieu, Newacheck, & McManus, 1993). Among children enrolled in managed care plans, minority children used fewer services, even after controlling for differences in health status (Riley, Finney, & Mellits, 1993).

In other research that could adjust for insurance coverage differences, African Americans with end-stage renal disease have been found to be 50% less likely to receive kidney transplants, and, when they did, had been on waiting lists significantly longer than nonminority patients (Gaston, Ayres, Dooley, & Diethelm, 1993). Similarly, among patients with coronary artery disease, Black patients have fewer angiograms and coronary artery bypass surgeries, regardless of disease severity (Johnson, Lee, & Cook, 1993).

Similar differences in rates for invasive cardiac procedures have been observed for Hispanic/Latin American populations (Carlisle, Leake, Brook, & Shapiro, 1996). A study of patients visiting a trauma center emergency room with bone fractures found that non-Hispanic Whites were more than twice as likely to receive pain medication as were Hispanic patients, even after accounting for differences in injury severity, pain assessment, insurance status, gender, and language (Todd, Lee, & Hoffman, 1994; Todd, Samaroo, & Hoffman, 1993). Other studies have documented additional differences among Hispanic/Latin American subgroups, with Mexican American, Puerto Rican, and Cuban American populations experiencing different rates of having no usual source of care, preventive care, and physician visits compared to non-Hispanic Whites (Council on Scientific Affairs, 1991).

Large racial/ethnic disparities in utilization also occur within the Medicare program. African American beneficiaries have fewer physician visits and receive less preventive care, such as influenza immunizations. They also have lower rates for many diagnostic procedures (such as computerized tomography scans, barium enema X rays, mammography, etc.), surgical procedures (coronary bypass, prostatectomy, hysterectomy, orthopedic surgery, etc.), and other services (Friedman, 1994; Gornick et al., 1996). Even in Veterans Administration hospitals, White veterans are significantly more likely to receive coronary surgery than are Black veterans (Whittle, Conigliaro, & Good, 1993).

Of course, many potential explanations exist for these differences in utilization, outcomes, and health status. In research, controlling for factors such as socioeconomic status, education, disease incidence/prevalence, illness severity, resource availability, and insurance coverage can be extraordinarily difficult, and interpretation of these research findings must be tempered by recognition of these methodological limits. However, differences by race/ethnicity are substantial and persistent across numerous studies that use a variety of research designs. Even if race is the determining factor in these differences, we are left with many unknowns, although the possibility of overt or latent racial/cultural bias at all levels of the health care delivery system cannot be discounted. A landmark study in which a large sample of physicians were presented with computerized patient scenarios in which actors were interviewed about their hypothetical chest pain showed that race and gender were important independent determinants of physicians' decisions to refer patients for advanced diagnostic procedures. That study showed that referral rates for cardiac catheterization were lower for women and Blacks (84.7% of each group) compared to White men (90.6%) (Schulman et al., 1999). Further research is required to explain the factors that contribute to or mediate any bias and to identify how patient preferences (e.g., in weighing risks and benefits of medical intervention), care-seeking

> Differences in health care utilization, outcomes, and health status by race/ethnicity are substantial and persistent across numerous studies that use a variety of research designs.

behavior, and attitudes toward the health care delivery system affect utilization and outcomes.

Managed care offers the hope of establishing a "medical home" for all enrollees, but it may erect other barriers to appropriate care. In one national survey, African American, Asian, and Hispanic respondents with private coverage were up to twice as likely as their White counterparts to lack a usual source of care, but these differences were much smaller among members of managed care plans. Still, minority managed care members were much more likely to report dissatisfaction with their usual source of care, compared to minority members of traditional (non–managed care) health plans, while dissatisfaction among Whites was low regardless of whether they were in managed care (Phillips, Mayer, & Aday, 2000).

CULTURE/ACCULTURATION/LANGUAGE

The effect of culture and acculturation on health care use and outcomes is not well understood. It is hypothesized that cultural barriers may contribute to lower or less optimal utilization patterns by Hispanic/Latin American and Asian immigrant populations in the United States. These barriers can involve a broad range of potential problems, including social isolation, distrust of Western medicine, unfamiliarity with the U.S. health care delivery system, differences in concepts of disease and illness, alternative care-seeking, perceptions of provider disrespect, fears about immigration status, or language difficulties.

Several studies have attempted to evaluate how increased acculturation tends to resolve these impediments to access. This research is limited by the difficulty of assessing levels of acculturation. One of the better-designed studies suggests that language proficiency may be either the best indicator of acculturation or the most important component of these cultural factors in facilitating access. In that study, better language skills resulted in more use of preventive services such as physical exams, cancer screening, and dental checkups (Solis, Marks, Garcia, & Shelton, 1990).

Of course, acculturation itself may create new problems and new barriers. For example, many immigrant families have stable family structures, including strong intergenerational ties. To the extent that these relationships become more attenuated in urban America, it may become more difficult for families to cope with the requirements of managing a serious health condition or chronic disease.

GENDER

Little research has been conducted on gender-related barriers to health care. Differences in rates of procedures have been documented, for example, with female end-stage renal disease patients less likely than males to receive a kidney transplant (Held, Pauly, & Bovbjerg, 1988; Kjellstrand, 1988) or have cardiac surgery (Udvarhelyi, Gatsonis, & Epstein, 1992). However, these differences were not associated with higher mortality rates for women (raising an important issue about whether access to more surgical care is always beneficial).

Again, further study is needed to determine whether gender-related patient preferences or attitudes toward surgery's risks and benefits help account for these differences. Three emerging lines of research underscore the potential seriousness of gender-related impediments to health care for women. First, women have been systematically excluded from clinical trials for new drugs and procedures (Cotton, 1990a, 1990b). The potential bias is obvious. To the extent that medical practice is based on findings of medical research, many practitioners may be reluctant to prescribe medications or recommend procedures that have not been fully tested for women. Accordingly, access to new drugs and technologies may be delayed for women, and resource utilization patterns significantly affected. But the corollary also raises serious concerns: when care provided to women is based on research that has been generalized from gender-biased studies, it may not be optimal.

A second body of research has begun to document how physician gender can affect practice patterns and the service utilization rates of their patients. For example, one study of preventive care found that patients of female physicians were more than twice as likely to receive cervical cancer screening tests (Pap smears) and 40% more likely to receive mammograms than patients of male physicians (Lurie, Slater, & McGovern, 1993). Again, the full impact of how differences in physician gender can influence the care provided to female patients has not yet been determined. Although the number of female physicians is growing, the potential for serious barriers to needed health care services for female patients remains large.

Finally, many women do not have access to family planning, abortion counseling, or abortion services. There are explicit restrictions on use of Medicaid funds for these services, and many religiously affiliated providers simply do not offer them. Moreover, the aggressive tactics of many antiabortion groups have deterred providers from offering these services and discouraged women from seeking them. Restricted access tends to affect low-income patients disproportionately, because they are likely to have fewer alternatives, but the chilling effect of politicization of abortion-related care affects access for all women (Henshaw, 1995; Mathews, Ribar, & Wilhelm, 1997; Rosenblatt, Mattis, & Hart, 1995).

EDUCATION

As with other indirect barriers to health care, it is difficult to isolate and quantify the effect of education on health care utilization and outcomes. Parental education deficits, however, are associated with lower levels of well-baby and other preventive services (Short & Lefkowitz, 1992) and lower overall health care utilization by their children (Newacheck, 1992). Differences in education also have been linked to lower rates of breast cancer screening, even after adjusting for a broad range of economic and sociodemographic factors (Lantz, Weigers, & House, 1997). In another study, Medicaid patients with limited education were found to be less likely to use preventive services, have greater difficulty following medical regimens, miss more appointments, and seek care later in the course of an illness (Weiss, 1994).

A growing body of research has begun to document the impact of functional health literacy—the ability to use reading, writing, and computational skills in typical, everyday patient situations, such as reading prescription labels, following diagnostic test instructions, or understanding treatment directions. Because an estimated 40 million Americans are illiterate and another 50 million are marginally literate (Kirsch, Jungeblut, Jenkins, & Kolstad, 1993), the potential impediments to timely and effective care are serious. In a study conducted in two public hospitals, 42% of patients could not understand directions for taking medication on an empty stomach, 26% could not comprehend information on an appointment slip describing the scheduled follow-up visit, and more than 25% could not follow instructions for preparing for a gastrointestinal radiological exam. Overall, almost 30% of patients using the facilities were determined to have inadequate functional health literacy, and another 14% had only marginal levels (Williams, Parker, & Baker, 1995). Contributing to these problems are inadequate health education in schools and lack of computer literacy that might enable some self-education.

> A growing body of research has begun to document the impact of functional health literacy—the ability to use reading, writing, and computational skills in typical, everyday patient situations, such as reading prescription labels, following diagnostic test instructions, or understanding treatment directions.

RESOURCE AVAILABILITY/PERFORMANCE

The supply of health care resources has obvious implications for access. In remote rural areas, the absence of a primary care practitioner, an obstetrician/gynecologist, a dentist, or even a hospital can have a serious impact on the ability of area residents to obtain timely care. In urban areas, supply issues are often more complex. There are huge, well-documented differences in physician supply across and within communities, with some central cities having serious shortages of practitioners. (See also chapter 12.)

The issue for access, however, is the availability of providers, not the supply. Many large urban hospitals (and their associated medical office buildings) are located in or near lower-income neighborhoods, but this proximity does not assure access. While many hospital outpatient departments accept patients who cannot pay (or charge them on a sliding fee schedule), this is certainly not necessarily the case for the private practice physicians clustered nearby. Moreover, the low Medicaid reimbursement rates for physician visits noted previously discourage many from participating in the program.

Little is known about how the performance of the primary care delivery system affects access to care. Clearly, a highly efficient provider who can serve numerous patients can increase access. But, more importantly, providers also can organize their practices to reduce many indirect barriers to care discussed previously (e.g., eliminating language barriers, reducing wait times, developing a culturally sensitive environment, and developing more effective techniques to help chronic disease patients who have literacy problems).

Recently, patient satisfaction has become the focus of many health care delivery systems struggling to attract and maintain their middle-class patient base. These developments have spawned a mini-industry of researchers and consultants attempting to help providers become more responsive to patient needs and desires. A parallel effort should be targeted at understanding the indirect barriers to care for low-income patients and helping safety-net providers adapt their delivery approach to these patients' needs. This is not yet on the horizon.

Noneconomic and Quasi-Economic Barriers:
Preventable Hospitalizations

As illustrated in many of the studies described previously, the impact of noneconomic and quasi-economic barriers on utilization patterns and health status can be substantial. A growing body of analysis has begun to explore how barriers to primary care services can result in increased use of other health care services, such as more costly hospital care (see Table 16.2) (Billings, Anderson, & Newman, 1996; Billings, Zeitel, & Lukomnik, 1993; Bindman et al., 1995; Weissman, Gatsonis, & Epstein, 1992).

This research is based on the simple premise that timely and effective primary care can usually (a) prevent the onset of an illness

 **Access Problems Reported by Low-Income Patients Hospitalized for Preventable/Avoidable Conditions**

Access Problem	Percentage Who Reported Problem[a]		
	6 Months–17 Years	18–64 Years	All Ages
Not up to going	5.1	36.1	29.2
Too nervous or afraid	10.2	33.8	28.6
Unable to get free time to get care	8.1	27.2	22.9
Had to wait too long to get appointment	20.3	20.4	20.4
Problems with child care	32.8	14.3	18.2
Costs too much	13.8	18.1	17.2
Unable to keep medical appointment	7.4	20.2	17.1
Couldn't fill prescription	16.4	16.9	16.8
Transportation difficulties	19.3	15.8	16.5
Didn't know where to go to get care	8.6	13.8	12.7
Not sure provider would understand needs	22.4	9.1	12.2
Care not available when needed it	11.3	12.1	12.0
Denied care	13.4	9.7	10.6
Didn't like usual place to get care	17.2	7.9	9.9
Lose pay/trouble getting off work	12.1	6.0	7.3
Language problem	1.8	4.7	4.3

[a] Percentages total more than 100% because some patients indicated multiple problems.
Note. From Billings, J., Mijanovich, T., & Blank, A. (1997). *Barriers to care for patients with preventable hospital admissions.* New York: United Hospital Fund.

(e.g., congenital syphilis, pertussis, tetanus); (b) control a condition before it becomes more acute (e.g., ear infections in children, urinary tract infections, dehydration); and (c) manage a chronic disease or condition to help reduce the chances of a serious flare-up (e.g., asthma, diabetes, congestive heart disease, hypertension). To the extent that barriers exist for ambulatory care services, causing a patient to delay or be unable to obtain care, an illness or condition may deteriorate to the point that it cannot be controlled in an outpatient setting, and hospitalization becomes necessary.

Conditions that should be managed on an outpatient basis are called *ambulatory care sensitive (ACS) conditions.* Researchers have documented huge differences in hospitalization rates for ACS conditions in different geographic regions. Areas with high ACS hospitalization rates, not surprisingly, also have more self-reported barriers to access than do areas with low ACS hospitalization rates (Bindman et al., 1995). Moreover, these differences are strongly associated with the area's average income; indeed, in some communities, more than 80% of the variation in admission rates among ZIP codes is explained by the percentage of low-income persons living there (see Figure 16.3). Admission rates for ACS conditions in low-income areas are on average 2.5 to 3.5 times higher than in more affluent areas, and rates associated with some low-income neighborhoods are as much as 20 times higher than rates in higher-income areas of the same community.

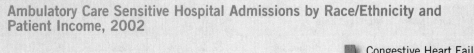

Figure 16.3

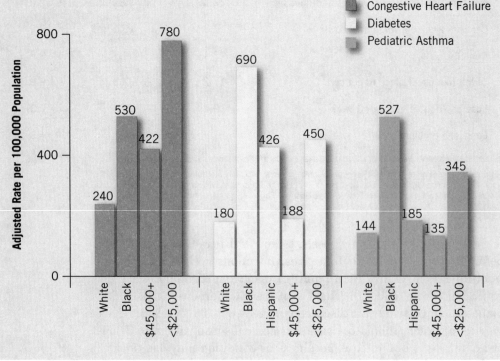

Note. From Commonwealth Fund National Scorecard on U.S. Health System Performance. (2006). Retrieved from http://www.meps.ahrq.gov/mepsweb/

Of course, not all admissions for ACS conditions are preventable. However, the strong association between ACS admissions and the prevalence of poverty in a given geographic area suggests significant barriers to primary care in these areas. Insurance coverage is undoubtedly an important factor: Differences in admission rates across urban areas in Canada, which has universal health insurance, are significantly smaller than in the United States (Billings et al., 1996). Lack of insurance coverage is nevertheless unlikely to be the sole or even the predominant cause for the disparities documented in U.S. urban areas, because the overwhelming majority of hospitalized low-income patients had Medicaid coverage. The impact of the noneconomic and quasi-economic barriers discussed above is undoubtedly substantial. A low-income patient who has no regular source of care, who is dissatisfied with available providers (because of long wait times, language difficulties, or lack of cultural sensitivity) or who has difficulties arranging child care, getting off work, or simply coping with problems associated with illness is clearly at significant risk of delaying or not getting needed care until hospitalization is necessary.

The potential relationships among these noneconomic factors and access are illustrated by an analysis of ACS admission rates in Miami, Florida. Although, like most U.S. urban areas, Miami has significant concentrations of poor and minority residents, the difference in ACS admissions rates between low- and high-income areas is relatively small (about 1.6 times higher in low-income areas), and the association between area ACS rates and income is weaker. This lack of a large income-related difference in ACS admission rates is particularly evident for ZIP codes where residents are mostly Cuban American. There, income did not affect hospitalization rates, but in other ZIP code areas the association between low-income and high ACS hospitalization rates was comparable to that of other U.S. metropolitan areas (Billings et al., 1996). These data suggest that noneconomic and quasi-economic barriers to care are not insurmountable. Further research is needed to sort out the influence of various factors, such as the family and social structure of the Cuban American population, their health status and care-seeking behavior, and the organization and performance of the primary care delivery system serving this population, which includes a substantial cadre of Cuban American physicians.

The extent and nature of indirect barriers to care are illustrated in a study of patients hospitalized for ACS conditions in New York City (Billings, Mijanovich, & Blank, 1997). In interviews after hospital admission and medical stabilization, 60.9% of low-income patients reported that they had received no care prior to the admission, and another 17.4% had received care only in the emergency room.

By contrast, among higher-income patients, 31.4% had received no prior care and 5.8% only emergency room care. More than half of low-income patients reported that they had delayed or not obtained needed care, compared with about one-fourth of higher-income patients. The leading explanations for delay or failure to obtain care among low-income patients were not directly related to the costs of care (the overwhelming majority had Medicaid coverage), but rather to a range of problems reflecting the difficulties encountered by low-income patients and their families in their daily lives and in negotiating the complexities of the health care delivery system. Over 25% of adult patients indicated they were "too nervous or afraid," "too busy with other things," or simply "not up to going," reflecting their serious ambivalence about the health care delivery system. Substantial numbers also reported difficulties arranging child care, problems with transportation, concern about having to wait too long, uncertainty about where to go, and apprehensions that providers wouldn't understand their needs.

Nonfinancial barriers to timely and effective care are substantial and serious. Clearly, successful access initiatives must go beyond simply providing an insurance card to the uninsured. Part of the solution must be to develop a health care delivery system that recognizes that low-income people are struggling with many aspects of their lives, as well as their health care problems. Longer clinic hours, home visits, and special outreach may be essential aspects of quality care for these groups, along with more responsive social service, education, and other programs.

Health Care Reform:
Improving Access

AT THE FEDERAL LEVEL: UNCERTAIN PATH TO REFORM

In 1992, 66% of Americans supported some form of national health insurance—a 40-year high. During the presidential election of that year, voters ranked health care as the third most important issue facing the nation after the economy and the federal budget deficit. By the time President Clinton took office in 1993, the issue had risen to second place, with 90% of Americans indicating they believed there was a crisis in health care (Blendon, Brodie, & Benson, 1995).

President Clinton responded by appointing a task force that developed a proposal for a Health Security Act in the fall of 1993. The plan assured coverage for a comprehensive benefits package for almost all Americans, but it was complex, and the debate was heated. As we all know, the plan failed to gain the necessary political support for enactment. Large employers ultimately did not support it, even though they were exempted from many of its requirements, and even though it promised to reduce their health insurance costs by eliminating their "hidden" financing of the cost-shift for uninsured patients and by reducing their liability for retiree coverage. Small employers strongly opposed the mandated coverage provisions, although many would have been insulated from some of the effects by federal premium subsidies. Insurance companies strongly resisted it, perhaps concerned that not all companies would survive in the competitive managed care environment the plan contemplated. Conservatives saw further encroachment of government into health care, with a complex system of quasi-governmental alliances and premium caps. Many liberals objected that the plan did not go far enough or disliked the concept of managed competition. The plan's failure virtually eliminated comprehensive health reform from national public policy debates. In the 1996 elections, only 5% of voters indicated that reforming health care should be a top issue for the new administration (Blendon, Benson, & Brodie, 1997).

The failure of the Clinton Health Security Act paved the way for a new willingness across the political spectrum to embrace incrementalism—modest legislative steps toward more accessible and affordable coverage for the uninsured. The political left saw the failure of the Clinton plan as taking comprehensive reform off the table for the foreseeable future, making them more willing to embrace small steps. The political right recognized the intensity of demand for reform by the public, and some saw the opportunity to advance a reform agenda that adhered to core conservative principles (e.g., greater role for market competition and a minimum role for government). Incrementalism was the new middle ground in the politics of health care.

> The failure of the Clinton Health Security Act paved the way for a new willingness across the political spectrum to embrace incrementalism—modest legislative steps toward more accessible and affordable coverage for the uninsured.

In 1996, passage of the Kennedy-Kassebaum Health Insurance Portability and Accountability Act (HIPAA) was one of the first consensus incremental reforms following the failure of the Clinton plan. HIPAA assured greater continuity of insurance coverage when a worker changes jobs—an important issue for the middle class, but one affecting the 45 million uninsured only marginally.

The 1995–1997 federal budget debates focused primarily on how much savings could be extracted from Medicare and Medicaid. In fact, the Balanced Budget Act of 1997 included Medicare and Medicaid reductions of almost $140 billion (mostly from reduced payments to providers). But the Balanced Budget Act also introduced one of the largest incremental expansions in access since the 1967 enactment of Medicaid and Medicare—the State Children's Health Insurance Program (SCHIP). The Balanced Budget Act included $40 billion over 10 years for SCHIP to provide coverage for many of the nation's estimated 10 million uninsured children. SCHIP supported state action and, unlike Medicaid and Medicare, it capped federal financial liability for expanded coverage, making it more acceptable to conservatives. Funds were to be distributed to states based on the number of low-income, uninsured children they have, adjusting for differences in wages and the cost of health care (see also chapters 3 and 5). As SCHIP has matured, states have encountered challenges in sustaining their progress. Federal SCHIP spending limits and state budgetary constraints led some states to freeze SCHIP enrollments and others to tighten eligibility rules (Cohen & Cox, 2004). In recent years, states have faced gaps between their SCHIP spending and federal allotments. In 2005, more than half of the states exceeded their federal funding allotment by 10% or more, causing stress on state budgets and pressure to limit SCHIP enrollment and program benefits (Lambrew, 2007).

In 2007, Congress is set to consider renewing the initial 10-year SCHIP authorization with a vigorous debate about its future. Advocates point to SCHIP's many accomplishments: more than 6 million children covered, lower rates of unmet health needs, and improved health outcomes. Indeed, even as uninsured rates for adults have risen, the percentage of low-income (defined in this instance as below twice the federal poverty line) uninsured children in the United States declined by nearly half, from 22.3% in 1997 to 14.9% in 2005 (Lambrew, 2007). The Bush administration has proposed levels of federal SCHIP funding that would require states to cut enrollment and would shift costs to the states with the most generous program eligibility rules (Kaiser Family Foundation, 2007b). Conservatives argue that expanding SCHIP beyond covering children in the low-income category is an inappropriate use of government funds and that it undermines private health insurance markets. The SCHIP reauthorization debate will play out in the waning days of the administration, and may be shaped by politicians' anticipation of the 2008 presidential election.

Despite advocating restraint in expanding the federal role in financing coverage for children, the Bush administration presided over another historically significant incremental expansion of the federal role in health care financing: the Medicare prescription drug benefit. To date, nearly 24 million Medicare beneficiaries have enrolled in Part D. Taking into account the additional 15 million with drug coverage from another source, only about 10% of Medicare beneficiaries do not have prescription coverage. Part D will cost Medicare about $50 billion in 2007.

The design features of SCHIP and Part D signal where there may be room for political compromise for future expansions in health care access. As noted, SCHIP caps federal financial liability. States are responsible for the design and management of their SCHIP programs and for any costs that exceed the federal cap. States have considerable latitude in how they design their SCHIP initiatives, latitude they do not have with Medicaid. Although Part D builds on the federally run Medicare program, states share in its financing (the so-called "claw-back" provision in which states pay to help finance Part D coverage for low-income beneficiaries covered by both Medicare and Medicaid). But unlike standard Medicare benefits, Part D is delivered by private prescription drug plans, which compete for enrollment. These two health care delivery platforms—state programs and private plans—are likely to figure prominently in any future federal health care reforms.

As in 1992, the run-up to the 2008 presidential election takes place in the context of public discontent with the status quo in health care. In 2006, surveys indicated that about three-fourths of the public viewed the U.S. health care system as in "a state of crisis" or with "major problems" (as opposed to minor or no problems), up from 65% in 2002 (Blendon, Hunt, Benson, Fleischfresser, & Buhr, 2006). In a spring 2007 poll, health care ranked second, after the war in Iraq, among issues that Americans would "like to hear the presidential candidates talk about," and half of the respondents supported a health reform plan that would cover nearly all uninsured, even if it would require an increasing in spending (Kaiser Family Foundation, 2007a). The stage may be set for the next president and Congress to address health care access.

STATE INITIATIVES TO IMPROVE ACCESS: INNOVATIONS AND LIMITATIONS

High voter interest in improving health care access, the troubling long-term decline in the number of people with employer-sponsored health coverage, and discord and delay in Washington over how to proceed with reform have stimulated debate and action at the state level. As states emerged from their fiscal slump of the late 1990s, a few took up the mantle of comprehensive reform (Burton, Friedenzohn, & Martinez-Vidal, 2007). Three New England states, in particular, have enacted bold new near-universal coverage strategies for their populations, and several have taken significant incremental steps. Interest among other states in health access reform runs deep.

Maine was the first of the latest wave of states to tackle comprehensive health reform with its 1993 Dirigo Health plan (*Dirigo,* the Maine state motto, is Latin for "I lead") (Rosenthal & Pernice, 2004).

Dirigo Health is a voluntary plan that offers new insurance products with sliding-scale state premium subsidies for people below three times the federal poverty rate. Part of the Dirigo coverage expansion is funded by Medicaid (partly with federal dollars), and some of the financing comes from employers and individuals. A controversial component of the Dirigo plan reduces payments to health care providers as more people gain coverage under the plan. The rationale is that, with most people insured, providers will incur less bad debt and charity care. Dirigo also includes significant quality improvement and cost-control features that policymakers hope will improve the cost-effectiveness and affordability of care over time. In the early phases of Dirigo's implementation, voluntary enrollment was slower than projected, but there is still time for Maine to meet its goal of affordable coverage for all by 2009.

In 2006, Massachusetts and Vermont followed Maine with even bolder reform strategies, each targeting coverage of at least 95% of state residents. Like Maine's, these states' plans are multifaceted and complex. Two strategies are at the center of the Massachusetts plan: a law requiring nearly every person in the state to have coverage and a new program for individuals and small-employer groups to purchase affordable coverage. The individual mandate—the boldest and most attention-getting part of the Massachusetts plan—was supported by conservatives (including then-governor, now Republican-presidential candidate, Mitt Romney) and liberals (including long-time, Democratic, national health insurance advocate Senator Edward Kennedy). To make coverage affordable, Massachusetts subsidizes individuals in families whose income is less than three times the federal poverty rate, using a blend of federal and state funds. The plan also requires employers with more than 10 workers to contribute to coverage. Residents who violate the individual mandate will face increasing financial penalties over time, and employers subject to contribution rules that do not help pay for coverage for their workers could also face penalties.

The second innovation in the Massachusetts plan is a new purchasing pool called the Commonwealth Health Insurance Connector. People eligible for state subsidies obtain their plans through the Connector, and it serves as a source of affordable coverage for other individuals and small businesses. The Connector also provides a vehicle for workers to use pretax dollars to buy coverage, and employers are required to offer this option. These so-called Section 125 plans (named for the governing provision in the federal Internal Revenue code) save workers roughly 25% on their premiums, because these payments are not taxed like other forms of income. In July 2007, implementation of the Massachusetts plan was on track, with implementation of plan options through the Connector and enrollment under the mandate progressing.

Vermont's Catamount Health plan, like the Maine and Massachusetts plans, provides a subsidized insurance product for those below three times the federal poverty line. It also requires employers to contribute to coverage for workers or pay an assessment to the state. Federal Medicaid matching dollars play a role in financing the Vermont plan, as does an increase in the state tobacco tax. A key feature of the Vermont plan is a concerted program to promote better management of chronic illnesses, such as diabetes and heart disease. These conditions often lead to expensive hospital care when not well controlled through lifestyle changes, adherence to prescription drug regimens, and strong ambulatory care management. To obtain approval for use of federal Medicaid dollars to fund the plan, Vermont has made the bet that chronic disease management and other plan features will control future health costs. Under a federal Global Commitment to Health Medicaid waiver, the federal government has given the state more flexibility in how it uses its dollars, in exchange for a cap on future federal Medicaid expenditure growth. It is too early to tell whether Vermont has made a wise bet, but implementation of Catamount Health is under way, with full implementation targeted for 2010.

The reforms in Maine, Massachusetts, and Vermont have some important elements in common (Burton et al., 2007). All three states started with the advantage of having low uninsured rates compared to other states and comparatively robust employer health insurance sectors. All three programs use subsidies to help pay premiums for families whose household income is less than three times the federal poverty rate—well above common Medicaid and SCHIP eligibility thresholds in most states. Each of the states brought new revenue to the table, and all three found ways to bring in federal new funding through Medicaid. The successes of SCHIP nationally suggest that federal financial participation may be key to the sustainability of these bold initiatives. The political culture of New England may have also played a role in bringing these plans to fruition, although, notably, these reforms all had bipartisan support, and in some cases, bipartisan leadership.

Whether comprehensive reform will spread beyond the Northeast is still to be seen. Three other states—Illinois, Pennsylvania, and Tennessee—enacted strategies to reach all uninsured children with affordable coverage options, and over a half-dozen diverse states have created new public-private partnerships to bolster their employer-sponsored coverage (see Burton et al., 2007; http://statecoverage. net/matrix/index.htm for more details). In addition, borrowing features from Massachusetts, Vermont, and other states, political leaders in California and Pennsylvania have proposed comprehensive reforms.

How far can state reform go toward universal coverage? In some ways, the bold legislative initiatives in the early 2000s are unprecedented, making it hard to predict how they will play out. But state-based reform initiatives from earlier decades have not fared well. Tennessee and Oregon, for instance, enacted and then repealed major coverage reforms (Hurley, 2006; Oberlander, 2006).

In some important ways, the reform deck is stacked against states. First, unlike the federal government, states are required to balance their budgets, so periods of economic downturn leave the financial sustainability of expensive programs in question. Indeed, economic downturns not only limit tax revenues available to pay for health coverage subsidies, but they increase demand for those very subsidies as more people lose jobs and coverage. Second, employer financing of coverage—a common source of revenue for state reforms—is constrained for two reasons. Imposing employer mandates and taxes works against states' economic development efforts to recruit and retain jobs within their boundaries, and federal laws restrict the degree to which states can regulate and tax employer benefit plans (see Butler, 2004). Finally, it is no accident that many of the states that have moved ahead with the boldest coverage reforms had comparatively low uninsured rates and high per-capita incomes. In fact, the states with the biggest access challenges are those with the least capacity to pay for new plans. This fact alone limits the degree to which the U.S. access problem can be solved by state reform. Still, it may take only a few comprehensive reform successes at the state level to show the nation that universal access is politically and fiscally feasible. Maine's name for its plan—*Dirigo*, "I lead"—may be prescient.

> In some important ways, the reform deck is stacked against states.

The Future:
Continuing and Emerging Issues

Fundamental problems related to access are likely to continue in the short and medium terms. Even with the SCHIP-sparked renewal of state initiatives to cover the uninsured, large numbers of Americans remain without coverage, and patients and providers continue to struggle to cope with the consequences of this reality. As of 2007, three new sets of access issues are emerging that will become increasingly important.

First, within the next few years, virtually all Medicaid patients (except the elderly in long-term care and some special needs populations) will be enrolled in managed care, and state SCHIP expansions will deliver coverage almost exclusively via managed care. Passage of the Balanced Budget Act of 1997 removes most restrictions on states wishing to expand mandatory Medicaid managed care enrollment.

On the positive side, capitated payments create strong financial incentives for managed care plans to solve some noneconomic or quasi-economic barriers to care. In particular, plans will want to provide effective disease management to reduce preventable hospital admissions (for example, better education of asthma patients on the use of inhalers, improved medication regimens, and nurse hot lines for care management advice during flare-ups). Similarly, they will want to develop more convenient ambulatory services to avoid emergency visits (longer clinic hours, shorter waits, child care services on site, and in-home visits). The solutions to these problems have historically eluded the fee-for-service world. How plans address these barriers should be tracked in order to inform new strategies to improve access as Medicaid and SCHIP managed care matures.

Publicly funded managed care also creates new enforcement mechanisms and opportunities for government agencies to assure better access for enrolled patients. For example, some states require plans to assure that patients with urgent care needs can obtain an appointment with their primary care provider within a specified period (e.g., 48 hours). In the past, Medicaid patients have adapted to long wait times for appointments at some clinics and outpatient departments (60 days or more in many cases) by using emergency rooms for routine care or by turning to costly "Medicaid mills" that churn large numbers of patients through their offices. Medicaid agencies had no effective means to compel providers to be more responsive because of the logistical problems of monitoring a huge number of care sites and because they did not want to penalize financially distressed providers. Moreover, since patients often used multiple providers, it was not possible to hold any single provider responsible for patient care—for example, when a newborn did not receive the requisite schedule of well-baby-care visits or appropriate immunizations.

In a managed care environment, a single health plan is responsible for each patient. Regulators can more effectively monitor the performance of the smaller number of plans (e.g., using mock patients who attempt to schedule appointments with the plan's providers by telephone; monitoring disenrollment rates; tracking performance indicators for immunizations, well-baby visits, or follow-up after hospitalization). They also have a realistic enforcement mechanism to assure accountability: they can close enrollment. The potential for assuring good service may exceed the reality, and a critical issue for the future concerns the extent and effectiveness of government oversight of Medicaid managed care, particularly since it is growing rapidly during a time of overall government cutbacks.

Medicaid managed care also could create a new set of barriers to care for low-income patients. The confusion associated with the enrollment process undoubtedly has negative consequences. For example, many patients may enroll in plans that require them to change providers; the new care sites may be inconveniently distant, but, even if they are not, continuity of care is disrupted. Other problems are likely to emerge, as well. Aggressive, entrepreneurial plans may enroll more patients than their primary care network can adequately serve. New providers brought in by managed care plans may underestimate the special needs of Medicaid populations. Requirements that patients use a gatekeeping primary care practitioner may discourage follow-up visits to specialists. And, of course, the most serious concern relates to the new set of incentives for providers: providing less care can mean higher profits.

Even though erecting barriers to care ultimately may lead to increased illness and costly hospitalization for some patients, in the short run, reduced utilization can be highly profitable. Since patients jump on and off Medicaid and from one plan to another, plans don't necessarily have a long-term financial interest in promoting patients' health. Therefore, policymakers must monitor these developments carefully and learn more about how these programs affect utilization and health outcomes. Until the Balanced Budget Act, states had to apply for waivers before they could require that Medicaid beneficiaries enroll in managed care. Waivers brought extra layers of scrutiny from the federal government, which are now gone.

> Even though erecting barriers to care ultimately may lead to increased illness and costly hospitalization for some patients, in the short run, reduced utilization can be highly profitable.

The second set of emerging access issues is the result of the changing health care marketplace. With the growth of managed care (in commercial, Medicare, and Medicaid markets) and the strengthening of market forces in the health care sector, the ability of traditional safety-net providers to survive remains under pressure. If they fail, the consequences are likely to be most dire for the uninsured and immigrant populations who will find it increasingly difficult to take advantage of public health insurance programs. Although the market-clearing effect of competition may reduce any system-wide overcapacity, the impact on patients who depend on these vulnerable providers may be serious. A critical issue in the next decade will be how well the financial imperative to reduce unneeded beds and services is balanced by efforts to assure the availability of services to vulnerable populations.

Finally, as efforts to cope with access problems continue to devolve to states and localities, policymakers need to consider the impact and limits of the various incremental reforms that they attempt. What are the most effective means of expanding coverage for children? How should insurance coverage be balanced with support or subsidies for providers for direct services to the uninsured? How do we meet the needs of uninsured adults, who use substantially more health resources than do children? Will people in similar economic circumstances but living in different states be treated the same? Is it possible to acquire more funds to improve access by eliminating the current waste in the system, which some experts say is enormous? How do states and locales strike the balance between what is politically feasible (programs for children and pregnant women) and where limited funds might be invested most effectively (adult immigrant populations, substance abuse programs, safety-net providers)? And, finally, what effects do all these initiatives have on people's health?

Clearly, serious access problems will remain for tens of millions of Americans for the foreseeable future. The ultimate question is when these problems—especially economic access—eventually reemerge as a major national policy concern, will national policymakers fail yet again to find a politically viable, financially affordable strategy to assure universal access to needed health care.

References

Ayanian, J. Z., Kohlker, B. B., & Toshi, A. (1993). The relationship between health insurance coverage and clinical outcomes among women with breast cancer. *New England Journal of Medicine, 329*(5), 326.

Billings, J., Anderson, G., & Newman, L. (1996). Recent findings on preventable hospitalizations. *Health Affairs, 15,* 239–249.

Billings, J., Mijanovich, T., & Blank, A. (1997). *Barriers to care for patients with preventable hospital admissions.* New York: United Hospital Fund.

Billings, J., & Teicholz, N. (1990). Uninsured patients in the District of Columbia. *Health Affairs, 9,* 158–165.

Billings, J., Zeitel, L., & Lukomnik, J. (1993). Impact of socioeconomic status on hospital use in New York City. *Health Affairs, 12,* 162–173.

Bindman, A., Grumbach, K., Osmond, D., Komaromy, M., Vranizan, K., Lurie, N., et al. (1995). Preventable hospitalizations and access to health care. *Journal of the American Medical Association, 274*(4), 305.

Blendon, R. J., Benson, J. M., & Brodie, M. (1997). Voters and health care in the 1996 election. *Journal of the American Medical Association, 277*(15), 1253.

Blendon, R. J., Brodie, M., & Benson, J. (1995). What happened to Americans' support for the Clinton health plan. *Health Affairs, 14,* 7–23.

Blendon, R. J., Hunt, K., Benson, J. M., Fleischfresser, C. & Buhr, T. (2006). Understanding the American public's health priorities: A 2006 perspective. *Health Affairs,* Web Exclusive, W508. Retrieved from http://content.healthaffairs.org/cgi/content/full/25/6/w508

Braveman, P. A., Egerter, S., Bennett, T., & Showstack, J. (1991). Differences in hospital resource allocation among sick newborns according to insurance coverage. *Journal of the American Medical Association, 266*(23), 3300.

Braveman, P. A., Oliva, G., & Miller, M. G. (1989). Adverse outcomes and lack of health insurance among newborns in an eight-county area of California, 1982–1986. *New England Journal of Medicine, 321*(8), 508.

Burton, A., Friedenzohn, I., & Martinez-Vidal, E. (2007). *State strategies to expand health insurance coverage: Trends and lessons for policymakers.* New York: Commonwealth Fund Commission on a High Performance Health System.

Butler, P. A. (2004). *ERISA update: The Supreme Court Texas decision and other recent developments.* Issue Brief. Washington, DC: Academy Health.

Carlisle, D. M., Leake, B. D., Brook, R. H., & Shapiro, M. F. (1996). The effect of race and ethnicity on the use of selected health care procedures: A comparison of south central Los Angeles and the remainder of Los Angeles County. *Journal of Health Care for the Poor and Underserved, 7*(4), 308.

Cohen, D. R., & Cox, L. (2004). *Out in the cold: Enrollment freezes in six State Children's Health Insurance Programs withhold coverage from eligible children.* Washington, DC: Kaiser Commission on Medicaid and the Uninsured.

Cotton, P. (1990a). Is there still too much extrapolation from data on middle-aged White men? *Journal of the American Medical Association, 263*(8), 1049.

Cotton, P. (1990b). Examples abound of gaps in medical knowledge because of groups excluded from scientific study. *Journal of the American Medical Association, 263*(8), 1051.

Council on Ethical and Judicial Affairs, American Medical Association. (1990). Black-White disparities in health care. *Journal of the American Medical Association, 263*(17), 2344.

Council on Scientific Affairs, American Medical Association. (1991). Hispanic health in the United States. *Journal of the American Medical Association, 265*(2), 248.

Cunningham, P. J., & May, J. H. (2006, August). Medicaid patients increasingly concentrated among physicians. *Tracking Report No. 16.* Washington, DC: Center for Studying Health System Change.

Fiscella, K., Franks, P., Gold, M. R., & Clancy, C. M. (2000). Inequality in quality, addressing socioeconomic, racial, and ethnic disparities in health care. *Journal of the American Medical Association, 283*, 2579.

Franks, P., Clancy, C. M., & Gold, M. R. (1993). Health insurance and mortality: Evidence from a national cohort. *Journal of the American Medical Association, 270*(6), 737.

Friedman, E. (1994). Money isn't everything: Nonfinancial barriers to access. *Journal of the American Medical Association, 271*(19), 1535.

Gaston, R. S., Ayres, I., Dooley, L. G., & Diethelm, A. G. (1993). Racial equity in renal transplantation: The disparate impact of HLA-based allocation. *Journal of the American Medical Association, 270*(11), 1352.

Gornick, M. E., Eggers, P. W., Reilly, T. W., Mentnech, R. M., Fitterman, L. K., Kucken, L. E., et al. (1996). Effects of race and income on mortality and use of services among Medicare beneficiaries. *New England Journal of Medicine, 335*, 791.

Hadley, J. (2003). Sicker and poorer—the consequences of being uninsured: A review of the research on the relationship between health insurance, medical care use, work, income and education. *Medical Care Research and Review, 60*(2), 3S.

Hadley, J., Steinberg, E. P., & Feder, J. (1991). Comparison of uninsured and privately insured hospital patients: Conditions on admission, resource use, and outcome. *Journal of the American Medical Association, 265*(3), 374.

Held, P. J., Pauly, M. V., & Bovbjerg, R. R. (1988). Access to kidney transplantation. *Archives of Internal Medicine, 148*, 2594.

Henshaw, S. K. (1995). Factors hindering access to abortion services. *Family Planning Perspectives, 27*(2), 54.

Hurley, R. E. (2006). TennCare—A failure of politics not policy: A conversation with Gordon Bonnyman. *Health Affairs,* Web exclusive, W217. Retrieved from http://content.healthaffairs.org/cgi/content/full/25/3/w217?maxtoshow=&HITS=10&hits=10&RESULTFORMAT=&author1=R.E.+Hurley&andorexactfulltext=and&searchid=1&FIRSTINDEX=0&resourcetype=HWCIT

Johnson, P. A., Lee, T. H., & Cook, E. F. (1993). Effect of race on the presentation and management of patients with acute chest pain. *Annals of Internal Medicine, 118*(8), 593.

Kaiser Family Foundation. (2007a). *Kaiser health tracking poll: Election 2008.* Menlo Park, CA: Author.

Kaiser Family Foundation. (2007b). *President's FY 2008 budget and the State Children's Health Insurance Program (SCHIP).* Menlo Park, CA: Author.

Kirsch, I., Jungeblut, A., Jenkins, L., & Kolstad, A. (1993). *Adult literacy in America: A first look at the results of the National Adult Literacy Survey.* Washington, DC: National Center for Education Statistics, U.S. Department of Education.

Kjellstrand, C. M. (1988). Age, sex, and race inequality in renal transplantation. *Archives of Internal Medicine, 148,* 1305.

Lambrew, J. M. (2007). *The State Children's Health Insurance Program: Past, present, and future.* New York: Commonwealth Fund Commission on a High Performance Health System.

Lantz, P. M., Weigers, M. E., & House, J. S. (1997). Education and income differentials in breast cancer and cervical cancer screening. *Medical Care, 35*(3), 219.

Lieu, T. A., Newacheck, P. W., & McManus, M. A. (1993). Race, ethnicity, and access to ambulatory care among U.S. adolescents. *American Journal of Public Health, 83*(7), 960.

Lurie, N., Slater, J., & McGovern, P. (1993). Preventive care for women: Does the sex of the physician matter? *New England Journal of Medicine, 329*(7), 478.

Mathews, S., Ribar, D., & Wilhelm, M. (1997). The effects of economic conditions and access to reproductive health services on state abortion rates and birthrates. *Family Planning Perspectives, 29*(2), 52.

Millman, M. (Ed.). (1993). *Access to health care in America.* Washington, DC: National Academy Press, Institute of Medicine.

Newacheck, P. W. (1992). Characteristics of children with high and low usage of physician services. *Medical Care, 30*(1), 30.

Oberlander, J. (2006). Health reform interrupted: The unraveling of the Oregon Health Plan. *Health Affairs,* Web exclusive, W96. Retrieved from http://content.healthaffairs.org/cgi/content/full/26/1/w96?maxtoshow=&HITS=10&hits=10&RESULTFORMAT=&author1=Oberlander&andorexactfulltext=and&searchid=1&FIRSTINDEX=0&resourcetype=HWCIT

Phillips, K. A., Mayer, M. L., & Aday, L. (2000). Barriers to care among racial/ethnic groups under managed care. *Health Affairs, 19,* 65–75.

Riley, A. W., Finney, J. W., & Mellits, E. D. (1993). Determinants of children's health care use. *Medical Care, 31*(9), 767.

Rosenblatt, R. A., Mattis, R., & Hart, L. G. (1995). Abortions in rural Idaho: Physicians' attitudes and practices. *American Journal of Public Health, 85*(10), 1423.

Rosenthal, J., & Pernice, C. (2004). *Dirigo Health Reform Act: Addressing health care costs, quality, and access in Maine.* Portland, ME: National Academy for State Health Policy.

Schoen, K., Doty, M., Collins S., & Holmgren, A. (2005, June 15). Insured but not protected: How many adults are uninsured? *Health Affairs,* Web exclusive, W5–289–302. Retrieved from http://content.healthaffairs.org/cgi/reprint/hlthaff.w5.289v1

Schulman, K. A., Berlin, J. A., Harless, W., Kerner, J. F., Sistrunk, S., Gersh, B. J., et al. (1999). The effect of race and sex on physicians' recommendations for cardiac catheterization. *New England Journal of Medicine, 340,* 618.

Short, P. F., & Graefe, D. R. (2003). Battery-powered health insurance? Stability in coverage of the uninsured. *Health Affairs, 22*(6), 244.

Short, P. F., & Lefkowitz, D. C. (1992). Encouraging preventive services for low-income children: The effect of expanding Medicaid. *Medical Care, 30*(9), 766.

Solis, J. M., Marks, G., Garcia, M., & Shelton, D. (1990). Acculturation, access to care, and use of preventive services by Hispanics: Findings from HHANES 1982–1984. *American Journal of Public Health, 80*(Suppl.), 11.

Todd, K. H., Lee, T., & Hoffman, J. R. (1994). The effect of ethnicity of physician estimates of pain severity in patients with isolated extremity trauma. *Journal of the American Medical Association, 271*(12), 925.

Todd, K. H., Samaroo, N., & Hoffman, J. R. (1993). Ethnicity as a risk factor for inadequate emergency department analgesia. *Journal of the American Medical Association, 269*(12), 1537.

Udvarhelyi, I. S., Gatsonis, C., & Epstein, A. M. (1992). Acute myocardial infarction in the Medicare population. *Journal of the American Medical Association, 268*(18), 2530.

U.S. Census Bureau. (2007, March 23). Census Bureau revises 2004 and 2005 health insurance coverage estimates. *News release.* Retrieved from http://www.census.gov/Press-Release/www/releases/archives/health_care_insurance/009789.html

Weiss, B. D. (1994). Illiteracy among Medicaid recipients and its relation to health care costs. *Journal of Health Care for the Poor and Underserved, 5*(2), 99.

Weissman, J., Gatsonis, C., & Epstein, A. (1992). Rates of avoidable hospitalizations by insurance status in Massachusetts and Maryland. *Journal of the American Medical Association, 268*, 2388–2394.

Whittle, J., Conigliaro, J., & Good, C. (1993). Racial differences in the use of cardiovascular procedures in the department of Veterans Affairs Medical System. *New England Journal of Medicine, 329*, 627.

Williams, M. V., Parker, R. M., & Baker, D. W. (1995). Inadequate functional health literacy among patients at two public hospitals. *Journal of the American Medical Association, 274*(21), 1677.

17

Key Words

health	malpractice	universal
hospital	tort	one-payer
cost	management	technology
nursing shortage	antitrust	evidence-based management
aging	Medicaid	cost-analysis
pharmaceuticals	Medicare	cost-effective

Costs and Value

Steven A. Finkler and Thomas E. Getzen

Learning Objectives

- Discuss the growth in health care costs over the last several decades.
- Explain some of the reasons for the rapid rise in health care costs.
- Describe some potential policy solutions to constrain the growth in health care costs.
- Describe some potential management solutions to constrain the growth in health care costs.
- Analyze whether available solutions are likely to be effective, and, if not, explain why not.

Topical Outline

- The problem: rising costs
- Why do costs rise?
- Cost to whom and for what?
- Potential solutions to rising costs
- Dilemmas: Spending is a political act
- Conclusion

F

or decades, health services policymakers and managers have struggled with rapidly rising health care costs. This chapter asks whether it has been worthwhile to spend so many billions of dollars on health care or whether a more efficient and productive medical system could have provided better results at lower costs. Briefly put, the answer is yes. Medical expenditures were very worthwhile—yet could have been much lower. Controlling costs is always problematic because it means that someone (doctors, hospitals, pharmaceutical companies) must accept less money—and that some patients are therefore likely to get less (or less convenient) services. Cost control is sufficiently difficult and unpopular with various powerful interest groups that many justifiable reductions are not likely to be enacted, for reasons explored later in this chapter. The discussion of solutions is divided into policy approaches and management initiatives. The chapter concludes with a brief discussion of some of the cost and value issues that still face the U.S. health care system.

The Problem:
Rising Costs

This chapter begins with the problem of cost containment in the U.S. health care system. Inherent in that statement is the assumption that there is a problem. What do we know about the growth of health care costs over time?

From 1960 to 2004, annual national health care spending rose from $27 billion to $1.9 trillion (see Table 17.1). Over that period, the U.S. population rose from 186 million to 299 million, and the gross domestic product (GDP) rose from $527 billion to $10.4 trillion. Clearly, health care spending grew at a much faster rate during this period than did population. In fact, per capita spending on health care rose from $148 per person in 1960 to $6,280 per person in 2004 (adjusted for inflation, the 1960 per capita spending would be $770 in 2004 dollars).

Health spending also grew faster than the GDP. Throughout the period from 1960 to 2004, the annual percentage increase in the GDP was always less than the percentage increase in health care expenditures. In 1960, health care spending was 5.1% of GDP, and by 2004 it had risen to 16.0%. This means that, although the GDP was increasing—creating a much bigger national economic pie—health

Calendar Year	2004	2000	1990	1980	1970	1960
National health expenditures						
Amount in billions of dollars	1,878	1,310	696	245.8	73.1	26.7
Per capita amount in dollars	6,280	4,672	2,738	1,067	348	143
Annual percent change						
Gross domestic product (GDP)	4.6	5.9	5.7	8.9	5.5	
National health expenditures	8.4	7.4	11.8	14.9	13.1	
U.S. population in millions[a]	299	280.4	254.2	230.4	210.2	186.2
Gross domestic product in billions of dollars	11,734	9,825	5,803	2,796	1,040	527
National health expenditures as a percentage of gross domestic product	16.0%	13.8%	12.4%	9.1%	7.2%	5.2%

[a] Resident population, less armed forces overseas and the population of overseas outlying areas.
Note. Abstracted from U.S. Bureau of the Census, Centers for Medicare & Medicaid Services, Office of the Actuary. (2003). *Table 1: National health expenditures aggregate, per capita, percent distribution and annual percent change by source of funds: Calendar years 1960–2001,* and from *Table 2: National health expenditures aggregate and per capita amounts, percent distribution, and average annual percent growth, by source of funds: Selected calendar years.* Data are from the National Health Statistics Group. Retrieved from http://www.cms.hhs.gov/statistics/nhe/historical/tables.pdf

care spending was an ever-larger slice of that pie. It also means that less of the pie is available for spending on all other goods and services.

If the current trend in health care spending were to continue indefinitely, eventually health care would squeeze out all other spending. But is it likely to continue? Federal estimates are that health care spending will more than double between 2004 and 2014, and by 2015 will consume 20% of the GDP (Borger et al., 2006).

The rate of cost increases varies substantially across the different parts of the health care sector. For example, in 2002, health care costs increased 9.3% overall. That year's increase in hospital spending of 9.5% and the physician increase of 7.7% were not substantially different from the overall rate. Meanwhile, nursing home costs rose 4.1%, but prescription drugs rose 15.3% (Centers for Medicare & Medicaid Services, undated).

So, let's start to answer the question, What do we know about the growth of health care costs over time? We know that they have grown substantially. We know that they have increased faster than either the population or the GDP. We know that they are projected to continue to grow rapidly. And we know that, if unchecked, health care spending will consume an ever-larger percentage of the GDP, squeezing out other spending. Since this last effect is generally viewed as undesirable, health care cost containment has been and continues to be an important national issue.

HOW DO WE KNOW THAT THE VALUE OF MEDICAL SPENDING EXCEEDS THE COST?

Every day, doctors and nurses experience the gratitude of patients who are thankful for what medicine has done for them and their families. With most regular purchases, the existence of happy customers is sufficient to indicate that the value of services received exceeded the costs. But in medicine, the bulk of the money (85%) comes from taxes, employer-paid health insurance premiums, philanthropy, and other third-party payments; therefore, it is necessary to use indirect measurements—what economists term *cost-benefit analysis.* The most evident benefit from medical spending in the United States is that Americans are healthier and living longer than ever before. In one influential study, Douglas Nordhaus (2002) of Yale University estimated that the gains in life expectancy over the last century (from 47 years to 78 years) were equal in value to all of the gains in market goods and services. If half of the true value of the U.S. economy is attributable to Americans' health, then, clearly, spending 5%, 15%, or even 25% of GDP is well worthwhile. From an economic point of view, the question can be posed as, Would the average American want to go back to a medical system where life expectancy at birth was 47 years, where one out of every five children died before the age of 10, and where there were no antibiotics or heart surgery, in order to have another $6,280 per year to spend at the mall? The answer, clearly, is no.

> With most regular purchases, the existence of happy customers is sufficient to indicate that the value of services received exceeded the costs.

HOW DO WE KNOW THAT MEDICAL SPENDING COULD HAVE BEEN REDUCED WHILE INCREASING THE VALUE PER DOLLAR?

Given that medical spending over the last hundred years is clearly worthwhile, should we just accept that medicine is expensive and stop worrying about spending so much? Not really, because the relevant question is not Should Americans do without medicine? but Should the country spend a bit less on medicine and perhaps more on education, housing, or defense? The relevant decision is not all-or-none but the incremental (marginal) effect of spending $10 billion more or less, or perhaps redirecting current spending to make it more effective.

A recent study (Cutler, Rosen, & Vijan, 2006) estimated that, on average, the cost per year of extra life added by medical care from 1960 to 2000 was about $19,900—which everyone would deem quite worthwhile. Yet the cost for extending life through cancer treatment among some groups was much higher—more than $100,000 per month and hence clearly unaffordable on a large scale. Thus, some economists argue that substantial cuts in spending could have been made without seriously harming the health of Americans by pointing out the following distinctions (discussed at length later in the chapter):

- The value of medicine lies in *care* as well as *cure*.
- Much of the benefit comes from medical science and public health as distinct from costly hospital days, doctor visits, and other medical care.
- We must distinguish between average (all-or-none) and marginal (do a bit more or less) benefits.

Why Do Costs Rise?

The rising costs of health care have long concerned managers and policymakers alike. One study concluded that the most significant causes of increased *hospital* spending were volume (more hospitalizations) and rising costs of goods and services. Increased volume results from both population growth and increased utilization per person. Labor costs account for the largest part of the increase in costs in the "goods and services" category. Combined, utilization per capita (34%), population growth (21%), and wages and benefits (39%) accounted for 94% of the increase in hospital spending from 1997 to 2001 (PricewaterhouseCoopers, 2003).

Part of the increase in hospital utilization is due to advances in health care technology; simply put, tests and treatments are available for more conditions today, and more highly technical and complex diagnostic procedures and treatments have been developed for many of them. Such advances are expected to continue. Utilization rates also are rising at least in part because of the aging of the U.S. population. That also will likely continue. However, some analysts believe a large share of utilization can be attributed to a health insurance system that is less generous in paying for prevention, nonphysician care, and nonhospital care and more generous in paying for procedures, hospitalizations, and physician services.

Labor costs are on the rise due to national shortages for key hospital personnel, for which there is little relief in sight. The well-documented shortages of nurses and other occupational groups—including technicians and pharmacists—will drive up the cost of these personnel. Other areas of concern are the rapidly rising cost of pharmaceuticals and malpractice insurance, as well as a reversal of the cost-constraining impact of managed care.

All of the foregoing elements may contribute to the nation's continued health care cost increases. However, if there is a single culprit to be named, then it is the American public; our health care costs so much because we live in an increasingly wealthy nation that is willing to pay more and more for the newest and most accessible medical care, even when it does not do all that much to improve the nation's health (see discussion of various factors below).

UTILIZATION AND VOLUME

The increase in utilization of medical care over time has, perhaps surprisingly, been quite small. The volume of services has increased as the U.S. population has grown, but the number of hospitalizations and doctor visits per person has not increased rapidly, and in fact has declined over the last 30 years (Getzen, 2007, p. 11). One major reason is that the U.S. population has become much healthier over time. Another is that medical care has become more intensive and efficient—more care is being packed into each visit or hospital day.

AGING

Even if the number of services did not increase, if patients were older and sicker, then the cost per service could be expected to rise for that reason. The aging of the U.S. population makes such an explanation seem plausible, but it does not hold together under closer inspection. International comparisons (see chapter 6) show that countries with older populations (such as Belgium, Germany, and the United Kingdom) do not have substantially higher health care costs. Also, the average 70-year-old person in 2007 is healthier than the 70-year-olds of 1907. Even more important (although perhaps harder to grasp), national spending depends mostly on national budgets and financing, not national rates of illness or mortality. Although a sick individual is apt to have much higher medical costs than a healthy one, a country with lots of illness (such as Sudan or Uganda) often has poorly funded health care and costs per person that are substantially lower than in a much healthier country (such as Sweden or the United States) (Getzen, 2006).

LABOR

Labor is the largest component (about 60 to 80%) of health care costs and has risen dramatically both in price and quantity. A natural consequence of a growing economy that becomes more technologically advanced and productive over time is that the cost per hour of labor will increase, and this will drive up the cost of labor-intensive services (landscaping, education, medical care) relative to manufactured goods. More wealth means that people must be paid more to give up an hour of their time to work for others. Increased efficiency may decrease the cost of computers or food or artificial joints (because it takes fewer and fewer minutes of labor to make each one), but the labor costs for programming, serving scampi, or surgery on a knee will continue to increase, because each hour of a professional's time becomes more and more valuable as per capita GDP increases. Other labor-intensive services that cannot be outsourced (such as legal advice or a university education) show similar rises due to labor cost increases.

Medical costs are growing more rapidly than legal or educational costs because the *number of hours per unit of service* is increasing as well as the cost per hour. Once upon a time, a hospital patient just got a bed, with very little care of the modern technologically advanced sort. Every nurse had to take care of many patients, and there were few other employees. Today, we have aides, therapists, pharmacists, and other workers—more than eight full-time-equivalent hospital employees per patient day (compared with 2.4 in 1965 and less than 0.5 in 1929).

> Medical costs are growing more rapidly than legal or educational costs because the *number of hours per unit of service* is increasing as well as the cost per hour.

Medical workers must have more and more training, and the expense of such extensive training must be built into the cost of their services. From time to time, shortages in various health care professions create pressure for salaries to rise, thus increasing health care costs (see chapter 12). At times, employment also becomes a political issue. For example, a city may desire to close a public hospital in a poor neighborhood. However, the hospital may be one of the community's few well-paying employers. Closure of the hospital would not only affect access to care, it would also mean layoffs of individuals whose wages pump money into the local economy. It can therefore become politically necessary to keep the hospital open, even if it is a higher-cost provider of care.

TECHNOLOGY AND THE DYNAMIC NATURE OF HEALTH CARE SERVICES

Some analysts believe that health care costs are rising partly because health care products are changing. Medical care offered today and medical care of yesterday are very different. Physicians apply new techniques, new technology, and new pharmaceuticals. Yes, we are paying more, but we are buying something different, so an important component of increases in per-patient health care costs are these significant product and service enhancements (Cutler, McClellan, & Newhouse, 1998).

Health care product change can be viewed in several ways. We now have better but more costly products, so some patients receive more expensive products in place of obsolete, less expensive ones. In addition, these new products and services can be sold to individuals who might not have been candidates for them in prior years. For example, with respect to treatment for heart attacks and ischemia, "the cost per surgical procedure has actually declined. Nevertheless, surgery is now deemed appropriate for an ever-larger percentage of patients" (Lee & Skinner, 1999, p. 131). We can save more people now, but that increases overall health care expenditures.

Another element of the changes in health care and health care products is that technology creates a potential for unlimited spending. Recent innovations such as total body magnetic resonance imaging (MRI) serve as a case in point (Queenan, 2002). As facilities start marketing this service directly to symptomless consumers, we open Pandora's box. Scans inevitably produce a certain number of false positive results. The potential cost of medical care services undertaken as a result is enormous. Is society willing and able to handle the potential explosion in health care costs that direct-to-consumer marketing campaigns for new technologies and drugs can generate?

Because there has not been much increase in the volume of medical services or in the severity of illness of patients treated, most of the cost increases must be embodied in extra labor and newer and more expensive technology (frequently termed "intensity"). However, extra labor and technology can be a *result* of additional spending, rather than a cause. For the most part, such increases in costs are funded by increasingly generous health insurance.

HEALTH INSURANCE

Whenever people are insured, the amount of services they use is apt to increase, because the money being spent is coming from an insurance company rather than their own pockets. In health care, such *moral hazard* (Pauly, 1968) is more likely to affect the quality of services rather than the quantity. An insured patient is more apt to use a sophisticated university hospital, the best surgeon, and the newest drug treatment—not seek more quantity by having three or four operations instead of one. For this reason, insurance reimbursement has had a profound influence over the development of costly new technology (Peden & Freeland, 1998). Without Medicare, there would be much less incentive to develop a treatment for Parkinson's disease or Alzheimer's or other diseases of aging. Consider what has happened with regard to malaria, leishmaniasis, and other tropical diseases that mostly affect poor countries without health financing systems—treatments for these diseases remain undeveloped or, if developed, undistributed, simply because the financing is not available that would make it worthwhile to providers.

MALPRACTICE INSURANCE COSTS

Cyclical increases in medical liability insurance costs have long been a concern to those interested in controlling overall health care spending. In particular, they are a concern because the current system is extremely wasteful. Ideally, a medical malpractice system would compensate people for injuries received at the hands of their medical providers, and it would deter providers from treating patients negligently. The current system is ineffective in achieving either of these goals.

As background, malpractice cases are supposed to include the element of negligence, but a great many patients are injured in the health care system not by negligence; these patients, in theory, have no remedy. Even patients injured negligently rarely are compensated, because, contrary to common belief, most do not sue, and, among those who do, many do not win their cases. Thus, only a very small percentage of negligently injured patients receive compensation. How much money they receive is generally in the hands of a jury made up not of scientists, who could weigh the medical evidence, or economists, who could assign economic valuations, but of average citizens. Not surprisingly, we occasionally learn through the news media about a multimillion-dollar jury award that seems out of proportion to the patient's injury. What the media does not report is how those rewards are usually substantially reduced in subsequent court proceedings.

In the early 2000s, there was an increasing focus on malpractice reform, as insurance costs for both hospitals and physicians underwent a rapid increase; in some cases, physicians had trouble obtaining insurance at any price (Mello, Studdert, & Brennan, 2003). Although the situation has now abated, tort reform remains a popular political issue.

Some experts believe malpractice concerns contribute to a cycle of ever-higher health care costs, not because of the absolute price of insurance, but because of how fear of lawsuits affects provider behavior. Health care providers, especially physicians, tend to greatly overestimate their chances of being sued and, as a result, may practice *defensive medicine,* erring on the side of caution by ordering extra tests and procedures, often unnecessarily—but driving up health care costs nonetheless.

What causes the cyclical increases in malpractice premiums? Physicians tend to blame the legal profession for having convinced the public that they are entitled to a payment if there is a bad outcome in health care, regardless of whether there was medical negligence, and trial attorneys contend that the problem is that there are too many medical errors (Mello et al., 2003).

In the early 2000s, the steep decline in the stock market caused insurers to lose a great deal of money in their investment portfolios, and they raised premiums. They contended that the increases were needed to cover higher administrative costs, higher average payouts for malpractice claims, and extremely large, high-end outlier awards.

Regardless of the underlying cause, malpractice premium increases are likely to be built into providers' fees, in which case they contribute to the overall costs of health care. Many experts believe that malpractice insurance rates cannot be controlled without fundamental tort reform that reins in the amount of malpractice awards. Newer approaches to dealing with medical injuries include "health courts" (see http://cgood.org/healthcare-events-62.html), which could more effectively provide compensation, deterrence, and corrective justice or establishing a highly structured system to determine the size of malpractice awards akin to the workers' compensation system to eliminate the current near-lottery system of jury decisions.

Finally, malpractice has proved a weak approach for deterring medical errors. Other types of quality assurance efforts or regulation might be a more efficient, and thereby less costly, means to this end. Deterrence is an essential philosophical component of the current system, because without it, malpractice is merely a way to compensate victims. Otherwise, there is little justification for compensating only the victims of negligence and not victims of nonnegligent medical mishaps.

Cost to Whom and for What?

Why are we so much more concerned about costs in health care than in energy or housing or education? For several reasons, health care is a unique commodity. Acquiring health care services can be an issue of life or death. Most of us are likely to need medical care at some point in our lives, yet those points are for most people few and far between, so that some form of financing is needed to spread out the costs. However, some of us are born with or develop a chronic illness that will require expensive care for decades.

Patients usually lack the knowledge or desire to make medical decisions; therefore, most of the important choices are made for them by doctors. Furthermore, payments for services are largely made from health insurance or taxes, so that the standard cost-benefit calculus does not occur. Whereas a usual transaction involves a buyer and a seller, in medicine the transactions almost always include a third party (insurance) and a context (current medical practice) that constrains decisions. The transactions that shape medicine occur when a new MRI is brought into the local hospital, or when Congress enacts part D of Medicare. The decisions that result are not the same as the choices made at point-of-sale in a mini-mart. The right to individual patient choice is legally maintained, but as a practical matter the type of medicine one receives for an illness depends mostly on community standards of care and perhaps on the type of insurance one has—not a considered evaluation of value and harm by the person receiving treatment.

WHAT DO PATIENTS WANT?

Patients want the best possible care for themselves and their families without worrying about the cost. They do not want to try to figure out what the best, or even reasonably good, medical care is or what it should cost. Most of all, they do not want to try to figure out whether they should request the steel rather than the titanium bone screw or the radiation rather than the pill in order to save Medicare $60 or $600 or $160,000. Most are quite willing to pay a little bit for better medical care—but not much, maybe 10% of what the actual cost might be. After all, they expect medical care to be there for them if they need it, not to be presented with a spreadsheet comparing possible cost levels for treatment patterns that they could not understand even if they were not sick and in pain.

WHAT DO PROVIDERS WANT?

Health care institutions want to provide excellent medical care and to do so by providing working conditions and incomes that will attract the best clinicians. For a hospital, this usually means trying to find a few million dollars to renovate the emergency room, purchase a spiral positron emission tomography scanner, or raise the wages of the nurses. For doctors, it means having the freedom to treat and prescribe in line with what they think is best for their patients—while also taking home a six-figure income. Providers do not want to cut costs, and, in many cases, rising medical costs make providers better off. If you were to ask hospital chief financial officers what they are trying to do, they would say they want to get hold of as much money as possible in order to provide more medical care for the community they serve, make life better for their workers, and provide some funding for charity and research. Figuring out how to take in less money is not part of their job description.

COST-SHIFTING VERSUS COST CONTAINMENT

So, if patients and providers do not want to cut costs, who does? Those who are responsible for organizing payment (and indirectly represent patients and providers)—that is, employers that provide health insurance, and the government(s) that provide Medicare, Medicaid, veterans health care, and other programs.

What everybody does seem to want is for somebody else to pay the bills. Thus, the patient has elective surgery paid for by the insurance company, the employer gets a tax break from the government, and the government permits private insurance to subsidize the cost of Medicaid for poor people. But, at the end of the day, all of the money must come from somewhere. Shifting bills from place to place simply moves the burden of one financing plan to another without making the burden any lighter—just more spread out and less visible. *Cost-shifting* is pervasive in medicine. Everyone believes that the poor deserve some care, even when they cannot afford it, so extra is added to all hospital charges to account for charity care. Similarly, the expense of trying out experimental treatments and innovative drug research is borne by adding a bit to charges across the board. It is far easier to shift costs than to cut them. Thus, the game of musical chairs that is our health care reimbursement system goes round and round without ever addressing the hard questions of who gets what and how much.

> The game of musical chairs that is our health care reimbursement system goes round and round without ever addressing the hard questions of who gets what and how much.

DISTRIBUTION: WHO GETS CARED FOR? WHO PAYS?

Health care financing inevitably involves redistribution from those who earn income to those who are sick. Pooling of funds through insurance is the main way of dealing with this problem but, as we have seen, creates problems of its own. No one disputes that we need a distributive mechanism for health care, but once we try to specify exactly how distribution will occur in terms of payments and service delivery, consensus breaks down. Suppose Americans collectively decide to contain the costs of medical care, who should get the benefits from such cost reductions? Taxpayers, corporations that provide health insurance, or individuals who are currently paying co-pays and deductibles out of pocket? Whose care should get cut—those who are taking a lot but not contributing much (the sick poor), those who are consuming marginal care that is expensive and promises to add little to total life expectancy (many cancer and stroke victims), or those whose demands on the health care system are currently low? Generally speaking, every group wants some other group to bear a disproportionate share of the burden. Persuading all the disparate factions to work together on a solution is the job of politics, and the job is more challenging than the best leadership of the last 30 years has been able to handle.

AN EXAMPLE: PHARMACEUTICALS

Consider the expenses and revenues of pharmaceuticals. Most drugs are actually very cheap to manufacture. The industry's greatest costs lie in drug development, testing, distribution, and marketing (see also chapter 11). Once a drug is launched, almost all of these costs are sunk costs. And it costs about the same to develop and test a new drug whether it can be used to treat 1,000 or 100 million patients. However, it is much easier to recover the cost of development by adding $6 to each of 100 million prescriptions than to add $600,000 to each prescription for the unfortunate 1,000. The usual balancing of marginal costs and marginal benefits is out of whack (or irrelevant) with most pharmaceuticals. Production cost and price bear no relationship to each other. And drug companies need to charge not only for the cost of developing the drug being sold, but also for all the development costs of drugs that, for various reasons, never reach the market. Similarly, the ability to charge a lot for a drug depends not so much on how effective a drug is, but how many reasonable substitutes are available. If a 10¢ antibiotic will cure a life-threatening infection within 3 days, then there is little reason to pay $750 for a new antibiotic that achieves the same cure in 2 days—unless, possibly, insurance is paying.

Potential Solutions to Rising Health Care Costs

Many authors approach the issue of cost containment from a policy perspective: What can government policymakers do to constrain the overall societal spending on health care while still making progress in the areas of access and quality? Equally important, however, is the management perspective: What can managers do in their institutions to control their costs? Government must assure that managers have appropriate incentives to constrain costs. But managers must proactively determine ways to minimize the costs of providing care without compromising outcomes. One physician argues,

> With our high standard of living, the public expects that we have skilled personnel, sophisticated new equipment, the latest pharmaceuticals, and modern technological advances. So medical costs will always be on the high side in developed countries. (Queenan, 2002, p. 629)

Certainly, there is truth to this statement, but it doesn't mean that we must allow health care costs to rise unchecked.

MANAGED CARE

Managed care has been one major attempt to control rising health care costs, as described elsewhere in this volume. By far the most important way in which managed care has cut medical costs has been the most direct: negotiating lower prices for physician and hospital services (Cutler, McClellan, & Newhouse, 2000). Managed care has also succeeded in reducing the utilization of some services by requiring prior authorization and concurrent review of appropriateness. In some cases, managed care has also reduced costs by substituting equally effective but less expensive therapies—outpatient instead of inpatient rehabilitation services, generic drugs instead of brand-name versions, or rapid transfer to a nursing home where the cost per day is less than in a hospital. Another important managed care technique is *disease management,* defined as

> a population-based, pro-active, and preventive strategy that identifies individuals at risk of developing costly diseases (e.g., hypertension, diabetes, cancer, or heart disease) *before* the disease appears and provides preventive, educational, and early detection and treatment services, thus minimizing or averting future health costs associated with disease consequences and complications. (Cohen, 1999, pp. 701–702)

That sounds pretty good. At their best, managed care organizations improve health and reduce costs. But at their worst, managed care organizations erect barriers to patients who are seeking necessary care in order to maximize profits (Thorpe, 1999). While costs may be constrained by preventing unnecessary (and in some cases, necessary) care, managed care plans also create another costly layer of marketing, administration, and profits.

Recent years have definitely seen a consumer backlash to perceived limits on appropriate care by managed care organizations. In response to both this backlash and the enactment of "any-willing-provider" laws, managed care organizations have relaxed some restrictions, with the result that health care costs have again started to grow at a faster rate (Lesser & Ginsburg, 2003). (Any-willing-provider laws require managed care plans to contract with any health care providers who are willing to conform to the plan's normal terms and rates.) Although one study has shown that any-willing-provider laws don't affect HMO profits (Carroll & Ambrose, 2002), they have the potential to drive up a plan's costs, when it must contract with providers who recommend unnecessary services for enrollees.

USING INFORMATION TECHNOLOGY TO CONSTRAIN COSTS

Technology is another major cost for health care managers, but some technologies also hold promise to be cost-saving (Mahoney, 2002). The two major types of technologies specific to health care are clinical technologies and information technologies, and, increasingly, new equipment and systems blend the two. Expensive new clinical equipment may be able to diagnose medical problems earlier and specify more accurate treatment, thereby saving the cost of unnecessary tests and treatments. Information technology has the capacity to move patient information faster, locate it instantly, deliver it to whomever needs it wherever they are, reduce errors, manage workflow better, and enable faster, more accurate billing.

Although the potential is there, health care organizations have spent millions of dollars on information technology that to date has never fulfilled its promise, either on the clinical order entry and medical records side or on the management and financial management side. In part, this is a cultural problem. Systems sometimes fail because technology experts develop them without sufficient input from clinical staff or because the ultimate users are not sufficiently trained in how to use the new system effectively. Some of the innovative ways health care technology could be cost-saving include the implementation of:

- in-home monitoring devices, which allow for shorter hospital stays or eliminate them entirely (Taylor, 2003). The devices can wirelessly transmit clinical readings to physicians' offices and, in some cases, start treatment when a problem is detected (for example, heart monitoring devices that can regulate heartbeat and deliver lifesaving shocks when necessary).
- nursing resource management information systems (Ruland & Ravn, 2003).
- computerized physician order entry, which, when combined with clinical decision support systems, has the potential to reduce errors (the problem of illegible physician handwriting is not a myth) and save costs (Foster & Antonelli, 2002).

We have just scratched the surface on this complex issue. Suffice it to say that the combination of computerization of records, networking via the Internet, and wireless transmission give managers real opportunities to innovate and save costs (*Health Data Management,* 2003).

EVIDENCE-BASED MANAGEMENT

Recently, a movement has started that is encouraging health services managers to increase their reliance on research evidence as they make decisions related to the operation of their organizations—in other words, to employ *evidence-based management* (Axelsson, 1998; Finkler & Ward, 2003; Kovner, Elton, & Billings, 2000). Typically, these managers do not know enough about the cost of goods and services used by their organizations, and, until they obtain that information, they cannot effectively manage them (Finkler, Henley, & Ward, 2003). Part of the problem is a lack of sufficient research that would provide evidence for managers to use, and part is because managers do not seek out the evidence that is available. Most clinicians have begun, however reluctantly, to accept that evidence-based medicine can significantly improve practice outcomes, but adoption of this concept by managers still lags (Kovner & Rundall, 2006).

If managers and researchers work together to generate and use evidence as a basis for management decisions, however, we may finally make progress in finding solutions to health care cost increases. For example, some might argue that we buy and pay for services that don't provide predictable value for patients. Rigorous clinical research could illuminate such questions, enabling providers to make better clinical decisions and insurers to make more cost-effective coverage decisions.

Of course, one of the difficulties in controlling health costs is that whenever insurers have tried to limit health care services because they are not cost-effective (the benefit to the patient doesn't justify the cost), consumer groups raise strong objections. Individual patients want insurance to pay for anything and everything that might possibly benefit them, no matter how remote the possibility. For example, should we spend $1,000 for a test that could save someone's life? Sounds good. What if the test will save one life out of a million people tested? The cost of that test is now $1 billion to save one life. Society probably has many ways that billion dollars can be spent (e.g., on safer roads, better housing, food safety, and so on) that could save many more lives than the test would. Insurance companies and policymakers would probably argue against paying for it. But if one person dies because coverage of the test was denied, the media will have a field day about how a ruthless, profit-mongering insurer allowed one of its members to die to save a lousy thousand dollars. Insurers may conclude that the bad press isn't

> Even logic and evidence cannot always prevail in the unique market for health care services.

worth it. They'll cover the test and pass the cost along in the form of higher premiums spread across millions of beneficiaries, but driving up overall health care costs even further. Even logic and evidence cannot always prevail in the unique market for health care services.

OTHER MANAGERIAL INITIATIVES TO CONSTRAIN COST INCREASES

An almost unlimited number of other management-related initiatives can help constrain cost increases in health care organizations. These are a few examples:

- *Outsourcing*—Many activities carried out by health care organizations might be less expensive if they were performed by outside contractors—food services, laundry, and bill collection are common outsourced activities. Even certain clinical services are being outsourced: radiologists in India read the day's X rays, providing their reports early the next morning; centrally located intensive care physicians use electronic connections and video cameras to remotely monitor ICU patients for several hospitals.
- *The revenue cycle*—The last few years have seen a growing focus on containing costs throughout the process of collecting patient revenues. However, managers have started to pay attention to the entire cycle, which runs from patient scheduling to registration, treatment, discharge, and collection. To a greater degree than ever before, managers are focusing on assuring that they have the information to collect all revenues due, rather than simply thinking of this as a process of collecting accounts receivable (LaForge & Tureaud, 2003).
- *Physician buy-in*—One critical element mentioned earlier is physician cooperation (*OR Manager*, 2002). Physicians hold an unusual position in health care organizations. They are responsible for ordering the consumption of resources, even though they may not be facility employees. To apply cost controls on the ordering of tests, procedures, and drugs, hospital managers must secure the cooperation of the staff physicians.
- *Nurse recruitment, retention, and substitution*—The nursing shortage is likely to result in pressure on health care labor costs. To control these costs, managers can develop effective recruitment and retention programs that reduce turnover. These include comprehensive efforts to improve the physical environment, work processes, and culture of hospitals and nursing homes—steps that improve the work environment for all employees. Simple recruitment drives—such as hiring bonuses—may help individual organizations but are unlikely to constrain overall societal costs unless they are aimed

at recruiting nurses from other countries, thereby increasing the overall supply of nurses in the United States (a strategy that creates its own problems). Alternatively, we are likely to see at least some efforts by managers to continue searching for ways to substitute less-costly labor for nurses while still maintaining high quality of care.

- *Product-line management*—Another way for organizations to save money is to specialize in high-volume services. High volumes allow fixed costs to be shared among many patients, lowering the cost per patient. To achieve this, managers can try to cull low-volume services from among those they offer, but historically it has been politically difficult to eliminate services, especially by hospitals that are the sole providers in their community.

Managers have struggled with cost control for a long time. Without their efforts at the institutional or organizational level, health care spending would undoubtedly have increased even more rapidly. Future management efforts are likely to be vigorous and, in many cases, effective at constraining cost increases, but management initiatives by themselves will not be sufficient to slow the growth in health costs so that it mirrors GDP growth.

CONTROLLING PRESCRIPTION DRUG COSTS

The most rapidly increasing component of health care costs over the last few decades has been pharmaceuticals, an area in which the role of federal policy historically has been limited. As Kane (1997) notes,

> there are no national price controls, no national drug formularies, no universal policies regarding consumer cost-sharing. Rather, the main role undertaken by the national government has been regulatory control over entry into the market. . . . While high regulatory barriers to entry discouraged the introduction of marginal drugs into the US market, stringent regulations also discouraged the entry of lower-priced generic substitutes. (p. S72)

Individual states have been more active in their efforts to control costs of prescription drugs within their Medicaid programs, but this has not constrained the overall rapid growth in spending.

With the new Medicare prescription drug coverage, the federal government has moved actively into this arena. Officials predict that the new law will not only reduce the direct costs paid by Medicare beneficiaries, but will also restrain the overall growth in drug costs. However, it is far too early to tell whether that cost reduction will actually occur. The nonpartisan Congressional Budget Office has estimated that provisions of the law that allow comparison shopping and health plan negotiations with pharmaceutical manufacturers will result in 25% initial reductions in drug prices. The law also encourages assessment of the comparative effectiveness of alternative drugs in an effort to ensure that Medicare gets the best value for its money (Frist, 2003). Especially for people with chronic diseases, more generous drug coverage may encourage use of prescribed drugs, preventing costly trips to the hospital. (Some employers are experimenting with reducing or eliminating drug co-payments for employees with chronic conditions, as part of multifaceted strategies to better manage these costly diseases.) However, some analysts fear that expanding drug coverage will lead to a new explosion in health costs.

Because many individuals are eligible for both Medicare and Medicaid, part of the drug benefit's increased cost to Medicare might be offset by decreased Medicaid costs (Dale & Verdier, 2003). Medicaid systems have instituted drug utilization review programs (Gencarelli, 2003; Moore, Gutermuth, & Pracht, 2000), but they have not had much success in stemming the rise in medication costs. Will Medicare's new plan fare better? Policymakers will likely spend a number of years evaluating its impact and proposing modifications aimed at obtaining the maximum clinical benefit at the lowest possible cost.

Policymakers will likely also continue to debate the issue of drug price controls, balancing the societal benefit of reasonably priced drugs with the desire for a robust drug research effort.

While the policy debate over high prescription drug costs often winds up as a discussion of possible governmental price controls, health care organizations have taken a different tack. The insurance industry has taken the lead in this area, although hospital and nursing home managers also carefully scrutinize their spending on drugs to assure that they are using the least costly efficacious drug. Insurers (traditional insurance companies, managed care organizations, or employer-sponsored plans) have proactively attempted to negotiate with pharmaceutical companies for the best prices.

Beyond that, much of their focus is on giving patients incentives to make choices that will help constrain costs. Insurers can require patients to make a flat co-payment (e.g., $10) per prescription filled to discourage the filling of unneeded prescriptions; the insurer can set a lower co-payment rate for generic drugs; or insurers can require coinsurance, in which case the consumer pays a percentage of the drug's price. For example, in a 20% coinsurance arrangement, prescription drugs with a negotiated price of $70 would cost the patient $14 (20% of $70 = $14).

A newer approach is the use of reference pricing (Kanavos & Reinhardt, 2003). While relatively new in this country, reference pricing has been used for a number of years in Europe. In this approach, the insurer might pay 80% of the negotiated price for a particular drug. The negotiated price is referred to as the *reference price*. Patients pay the remaining 20%. If they choose an alternative drug, they must pay the entire difference between the 80% the insurer would pay and the retail price of the drug selected. For example, for a generic drug that retails for $20, the insurer might negotiate a price of $14 and will pay 80% of $14, or $11.20. Patients who accept that drug pay $2.80 (20% of $14), but patients who instead choose a brand name drug with a retail price of $100 must pay the difference between $11.20 and $100. This $88.80 cost to the consumer is a much stronger financial incentive than co-payments or coinsurance alone.

Another, more common, cost-management approach is the use of a *formulary*—essentially a list of approved drugs. Pharmacy departments in hospitals and other institutions usually have formularies, and the physicians who practice there are encouraged—in some cases, required—to order drugs the hospital regularly carries.

Depending on state law, physician prescriptions either must be filled exactly as written (in which case, patients have no control over what version of a drug they receive at the pharmacy), or patients have latitude to select a generic product when the prescription was written for a brand name or vice versa. Their insurance plan's formulary may be open or closed. With an open formulary, there is no penalty if the patient selects a more expensive version of the prescribed drug. An open formulary is primarily an educational device showing the relative cost of drugs and making the case for the less expensive versions. In closed formularies, patients are charged higher co-payments or perhaps the full cost of drugs not included in the formulary (Kane, 1997).

MEDICARE AND MEDICAID REFORM

Experience has shown that Medicare has done a better job of constraining costs than have private insurers, because Medicare can set prices (Boccuti & Moon, 2003), and researchers continue to press the argument that a single-payer, universal coverage system would keep costs low (DeGrazia, 1996). The best illustration of the cost-containment power of Medicare is found in the Balanced Budget Act of 1997. By imposing stringent rules on reimbursement for home health, nursing homes, hospital stays, and physicians visits, the federal government cut the share of personal health expenditures paid for by Medicare from 21.3% in 1997 to 19.2% in 2004 (U.S. Department of Health and Human Services, Centers for Medicare & Medicaid Services, 2006). Indeed, Medicare spending fell by more than $4 billion in 1998, even before accounting for inflation. Of course, there were significant effects. Many costs were shifted to Medicaid and private employer-provided health insurance. Also, virtually all of the major nursing home chains lost millions of dollars and several went bankrupt due to lower reimbursements.

The Balanced Budget Act of 1997 put in place the sustainable growth rate (SGR) principle for physician reimbursement. According to the SGR provision, reimbursement for all physician services could rise only by the same percentage as GDP growth. However, such restraint proved easier in principle than in practice, because Congress has voted almost every year to bypass the SGR limit and provide extra Medicare physician payments.

States can cut Medicaid payments through several means. They can tighten eligibility requirements, making it harder to qualify for benefits. Or they can restructure benefits, eliminating coverage of certain services. Or they can pay providers less for the services that they do cover. Do such actions really constrain total health care costs? Perhaps they do, to some extent: some beneficiaries may no longer use health care services that are not covered; some providers, under financial pressure, may find less expensive ways to provide care or decline to take on Medicaid patients. However, it's just as likely that these approaches merely shift health care costs around. If Medicaid doesn't pay enough to cover the cost of providing services, the rates providers charge to other payers may rise to cover the shortfall. If recipients don't seek routine care because they cannot find a provider or the desired service isn't covered, their conditions may worsen and require more costly emergency or long-term care. Thus, cutting Medicaid payments may have little, if any, beneficial impact on overall costs, while posing a risk to beneficiaries' health. It's a good example of how policymakers must be careful to consider the multidimensional impact of "simple solutions" to controlling health care spending.

Variations in state initiatives to constrain Medicaid cost increases by enrolling recipients in managed care are dramatic. By 2000, Medicaid recipients' enrollment in managed care ranged from zero in Alaska and Wyoming to 100% in Tennessee. "Although eleven states had enrolled more than 80 percent of their Medicaid caseload in managed care, seven other states reported managed care enrollments of less than 20 percent" (Hackey, 2000, p. 757).

> Policymakers must be careful to consider the multidimensional impact of "simple solutions" to controlling health care spending.

The advantage of Medicaid managed care is that a state can set a single fixed budget for all care for all recipients. That is also its disadvantage. Medicaid patients have no choice; they must accept what the state provides as health insurance or do without. That said, the actual experience with state Medicaid HMOs has been quite favorable. They control costs, and, even though choices are constrained, most recipients are at least as happy with the HMO as with previous Medicaid systems, and more patients seem to receive routine diagnostic and preventive care. Having all of the Medicaid patients enrolled in a single HMO provides the state with bargaining power and reduces administrative costs.

The major lesson to be learned from examining Medicare and Medicaid cost containment is that setting a single fixed budget does cut costs—although it is painful, and it has side effects that are sometimes unpleasant and unfortunate.

USING COMPETITION TO CUT COSTS

Because providers vehemently oppose any cuts in Medicare, would it be easier to lift the heavy hand of government from health care and use the invisible hand of the market to control costs? If competition works for the computer industry, airlines, and automobiles, why not apply it to medical care? Several strategies are available to increase the forces of competition.

Maintaining Competition: Antitrust

Policymakers are sometimes concerned with health care industry mergers. In theory, as organizations merge, they might gain enough market power to be price-makers rather than the price-takers in the free-market economic model. That is, if there are too few providers in a geographic area, they may raise prices higher than they would if the situation were more competitive. Some research supports the belief that hospital mergers in the United States have, in fact, concentrated markets and produced higher prices (Young, Desai, & Hellinger, 2000). As a result, one way to constrain costs would be for policymakers to enact appropriate antitrust legislation and ensure that it is enforced.

Medical Savings Accounts and Consumer-Driven Health Care

The current champion of competitive strategies for controlling health care costs, consumer-driven health care, involves the use of tax-sheltered *medical savings accounts* (also called health savings accounts or individual health reimbursement accounts, depending on the applicable legislation) combined with a high-deductible ($1,000 to $5,000) indemnity health insurance plan. The theory is that patients, spending more of their own money, will act more like a smart shopping consumer, curtailing the use of low-value services, choosing cheaper alternatives, and becoming more involved in maintaining their own health. So far, only a small percentage of people eligible for employer-provided health insurance have chosen to enroll in these high-deductible plans (Rosenthal, Hsuan, & Milstein, 2005; Wilensky, 2006).

PREVENTING FRAUD

Everyone wants to get rid of fraud and waste. It is sometimes thought that doing so would solve—or at least much reduce—the financial problems of health care, but such is not the case (Stanton, 2001). It is not that there is no fraud in health care. On the contrary, Medicare has collected hundreds of millions of dollars from *qui tam* (suing on behalf of the government and oneself) whistleblower lawsuits by going after fraudulent billing practices. Yet even hundreds of millions of dollars is a drop in the bucket among trillions. Medical reimbursement is complicated. Much of the fraud represents honest (or at least gray-area) misunderstandings. Once a hospital loses millions in a fraud settlement, it needs to recoup by charging higher prices. Eliminating waste is similarly elusive as a cost-control method, although a new emphasis on lean operations as an important feature of quality initiatives bears watching. Even if a major reform effort eliminated waste and fraud and succeeded in cutting costs by 5%, that would only be a one-time savings; medical expenditures would continue to rise by 8% in each subsequent year.

PRICE CONTROLS AND OTHER INEFFECTIVE POLICIES

Research evidence suggests that state and federal policymakers have not had much impact at all on slowing the growth of health care costs through initiatives (described in chapter 3 and elsewhere) such as the introduction of diagnosis-related group (DRG) payment systems for hospitals, physician payment controls, and certificate-of-need laws to restrain facility construction. An estimated $200 billion in new hospital construction and renovation is expected in the next decade. As a result, health spending has been described as a balloon: when you squeeze it on one side, it simply bulges out somewhere else (Schroeder & Cantor, 1991). In part, this is the consequence of piecemeal efforts. For example, DRGs, which were aimed at reducing hospital costs by decreasing lengths of stay, prompted substantial increases in the volume and cost of outpatient care.

> The balloon metaphor seems to hold as long as we fail to get our hands entirely around its circumference. In other words, without an appropriately targeted, comprehensive, and coordinated policy strategy, the nation is unlikely to rein in systemwide health care costs. . . . And it should be evident from [other industrialized nations'] ability to deal effectively with cost pressures in their respective systems of care, while assuring universal coverage for their populations, that cost control and universal access are not only *compatible* goals but that a high degree of both pooled finance

and coordinated payment may actually represent a means of "squeezing the balloon" from all sides. (Cohen, 1999, p. 701)

President Nixon applied price controls to health care through the Economic Stabilization Program in 1971, and the prospective payment system created a form of price controls for hospital care through the DRG reimbursement system in 1983 and for physician services through the Resource-Based Relative Value Scale reimbursement system in 1990. More recently, the Ambulatory Payment Classification system has been put in place to control Medicare outpatient payments. Price controls always work in the short run and fail in the long run. Capitalism is creative. Accountants always find ways around price controls. The most common method is to unbundle services and increase volume. That is, to move from charging just for a day in the hospital to adding separate charges for each lab test, bandage, transport to the operating room, etc., until any shortfall from low prices has been made up.

Clinicians have also responded by increasing the frequencies of visits (that is, bring someone back for six, 3-minute visits rather than two, 20-minute visits). Medicine is such a technologically dynamic field that it is relatively easy to justify higher charges for the new and (possibly) better drugs, operations, scans, and so on that are developed each year—and thus escape the force of price controls, which are necessarily historical and backward-looking. The only effective way to control all the costs of medical care is to control the total, setting a fixed budget for all charges, regardless of prices or volume or case mix or technological change. Once adjustments are allowed, the continual adjustments will eventually make costs rise just as rapidly as if no controls had ever been imposed.

> The only effective way to control all the costs of medical care is to control the total, setting a fixed budget for all charges, regardless of prices or volume or case mix or technological change.

Dilemmas:
Spending Is a Political Act

The problem is not that we do not know how to control costs, but that controlling costs is painful. It involves rationing care and reducing provider incomes. If all the providers continue to earn as much as they did before, and drug companies, insurers, and others earn as large a profit as they did before, then costs cannot be reduced. If every patient can get all the care he or she wants or needs while someone else pays, then there will be very little real pressure to do much about it. Only in a crisis will we act—but the crisis may be getting closer than is comfortable.

In Philadelphia, home of the oldest hospital and medical school in the United States, there are too many hospitals. Every health care expert in Philadelphia knows this, and everyone wants some hospitals to close—just not *their* hospital. When the Medical College of Pennsylvania first went bankrupt, the governor (whose house is located nearby) and the city's mayor joined forces to make sure it would not close. Why? For one thing, closing the hospital would mean 2,800 people had to find new jobs, and housing prices in the neighborhood would decline. After several bail-outs and rescue attempts, the hospital is now mostly closed, yet it has been a long, slow death, and the pain is not yet over (several affiliated hospitals are effectively broke as well and are being shopped around by their current owners).

The grim reality of cost containment is that only two things actually reduce cost in labor-intensive service industries: cutting wages or cutting the number of employees. The math is that simple and that grim (it is not for nothing that economics is called the dismal science). Of course, we can cut medical costs the same way we could cut college tuitions or reduce defense spending (or raise taxes to spend more on all three). All we have to do is get people to agree to do it—and exactly how and to whom it gets done. Whose hospital gets downsized? Who has to wait before their injury gets treated?

Ultimately, the nation will probably have to resort to policy approaches, such as rationing, that limit access to care. We must learn which rationing approaches best balance cost, quality, and access (Dombovy, 2002). The current dilemma largely arises because, when we consider large populations, we are quick to laud cost-effective care. Rationing care to the population as a whole makes good sense. But when we consider a specific individual—a person with a face and a name—we have difficulty arguing that there should be any financial limit on care that might save that person's life. Until we can resolve that dilemma, the fight to constrain health care costs will always be difficult.

On second thought, it seems that most of us already wait for a long time in the emergency room before our injury is treated, unless it is very severe or we happen to be an important politician. Rationing health care is not new; what *is* new (and difficult) is talking about it openly. In most health care, the rationing takes place subtly, as physicians shift their recommendations from surgery to medication or from the newest brand-name drug to the generic version.

The simple answer to cost control is for us to accept a fixed annual budget for health care services. There is not much chance that this will be a reality in the next few years. As one analyst observed,

> because many Americans—and private stakeholders in the health care system—find the concept of pooled finance either unfathomable or

> The 30-year battle to enact Medicare is merely a warm-up for the next fight.

unpalatable, the United States is not likely to move in that direction in the near future. (Cohen, 1999, p. 701)

Many vested interest groups profit from the current system—insurance companies, technology companies, and others. The 30-year battle to enact Medicare is merely a warm-up for the next fight.

Conclusion

For decades, health services policymakers and managers have struggled with rapidly rising health care costs, due in part to the existence of health insurance, the lack of complete information on the part of patients, technological advances, the growing number of elderly, shortages of critical trained labor, increasing costs for drugs, increasing health insurance profits, malpractice insurance costs, and a reversal of the cost-constraining impact of managed care.

In recent years, policy efforts to constrain health care spending have focused on managing prescription drug costs, tort reform, antitrust, Medicaid reform, and universal health care coverage. Additionally, the introduction of DRGs, physician payment systems, and certificate-of-need laws to restrain facility construction are just a few of the many governmental policy initiatives aimed at slowing health care spending. Managers of health care organizations also play a critical role in constraining the growth of health care costs through their efforts to control drug costs and effectively employ clinical and information technology and evidence-based management.

Even with policymakers and managers both addressing this issue, cost containment remains a difficult challenge. Most difficult of all is accepting the political reality that cutting costs will make providers change the way they work and make patients change the way they obtain health care. Cost-shifting can only move around the blame; it can never reduce the total bill. New approaches will need to be added to current efforts if we are to successfully rein in the rapid rate of growth of health care costs over the long term.

References

Axelsson, R. (1998). Toward an evidence-based health care management. *International Journal of Health Planning and Management, 13*(4), 307–317.

Boccuti, C., & Moon, M. (2003). Comparing Medicare and private insurers: Growth rates in spending over three decades. *Health Affairs, 22*(2), 230–237.

Borger, C., Smith, S., Truffer, C., Keehan, S., Sisko, A., Poisal, J., et al. (2006). Health spending projections through 2015. *Health Affairs Web Exclusive 25*:w61–w73. Exhibit 1.

Carroll, A., & Ambrose, J. M. (2002). Any-willing-provider laws: Their financial effect on HMOs. *Journal of Health Politics, Policy and Law, 27*(6), 927–945.

Centers for Medicare & Medicaid Services. (undated). Table 2: National Health Expenditures Aggregate Amounts and Average Annual Percent Change, by Type of Expenditure: Selected Calendar Years 1980–2004. Retrieved from http://www.cms.hhs.gov/statics/nhe.historical/t2.asp

Cohen, A. B. (1999). Hitting the "target" in health care cost control. *Journal of Health Politics, Policy and Law, 24*(4), 697–703.

Cutler, D. M., McClellan, M., & Newhouse, J. P. (1998). What has increased medical-care spending bought? *AEA Papers and Proceedings, 88*(2), 132–136.

Cutler, D. M., McClellan, M., & Newhouse, J. P. (2000). How does managed care do it? *RAND Journal of Economics, 31*(3), 526–548.

Cutler, D. M., Rosen, A. B, & Vijan, S. (2006). The value of medical spending in the United States, 1960–2000. *New England Journal of Medicine, 355,* 920–927.

Dale, S. B., & Verdier, J. M. (2003, April). State Medicaid prescription drug expenditures for Medicare-Medicaid dual eligibles: Estimates of Medicaid savings and federal expenditures resulting from expanded Medicare prescription coverage. *Commonwealth Fund Issue Brief, 627,* 1–12.

DeGrazia, D. (1996). Why the United States should adopt a single-payer system of health care finance. *Kennedy Institute of Ethics Journal, 6*(2), 145–160.

Dombovy, M. L. (2002). U.S. health care in conflict—Part II: The challenges of balancing cost quality and access. *Physician Executive, 28*(5), 37–43.

Finkler, S. A., Henley, R. J., & Ward, D. M. (2003). Evidence-based financial management. *Healthcare Financial Management, 57,* 64–68.

Finkler, S. A., & Ward, D. M. (2003). The case for the use of evidence-based management research for the control of hospital costs. *Health Care Management Review, 28,* 348–365.

Foster, R. A., & Antonelli, P. J. (2002). Computerized physician-ordered entry: Are we there yet? *Otolaryngology Clinics of North America, 35,* 1237–1243.

Frist, W. H. (2003, December 15). *The Medicare Prescription Drug, Improvement and Modernization Act: Controlling rising prescription drug costs.* Washington, DC: U.S. Senate, Office of the Majority Leader.

Gencarelli, D. M. (2003, May 10). Medicaid prescription drug coverage: State efforts to control costs. *NHPF Issue Brief, 790,* 1–17.

Getzen, T. E. (2006). Aggregation and the measurement of health care costs. *HSR: Health Services Research, 41*(5), 1938–1954.

Getzen, T. E. (2007). *Health economics and financing* (3rd ed.). New York: Wiley.

Hackey, R. B. (2000). Review essay: Making sense of Medicaid reform. *Journal of Health Politics, Policy and Law, 25*(4), 751–759.

Health Data Management. (2003). Reader's perspectives: The Internet has proven to be a useful tool to cut health care costs and boost revenue. *Health Data Management, 11*(3), 72.

Kanavos, P., & Reinhardt, U. (2003). Reference pricing for drugs: Is it compatible with U.S. health care? *Health Affairs, 22*(3), 16–27.

Kane, N. M. (1997). Pharmaceutical cost containment and innovation in the United States. *Health Policy, 41*(Suppl.), S71–S89.

Kovner, A. R., Elton, J. J., & Billings, J. D. (2000). Evidence-based management. *Frontiers of Health Services Management, 16*(4), 3–24.

Kovner, A. R., & Rundall, T. G. (2006). The promise of evidence-based management. *Frontiers of Health Services Management, 22*(3), 3–22.

LaForge, R. W., & Tureaud, J. S. (2003). Revenue-cycle design: Honing the details. *Healthcare Financial Management, 57*(1), 64–71.

Lee, R. D., & Skinner, J. (1999). Will aging baby boomers bust the federal budget? *Journal of Economic Perspectives, 13*(1), 117–140.

Lesser, C. S., & Ginsburg, P. B. (2003, May). *Health care cost and access problems intensify.* Issue Brief No. 63. Washington, DC: Center for Studying Health System Change.

Mahoney, M. E. (2002). Transforming health information management through technology. *Topics in Health Information Management, 23*(1), 52–61.

Mello, M. M., Studdert, D. M., & Brennan, T. A. (2003). The new medical malpractice crisis. *New England Journal of Medicine, 348*(23), 2281–2284.

Moore, W. J., Gutermuth, K., & Pracht, E. E. (2000). Systemwide effects of Medicaid retrospective utilization review programs. *Journal of Health Politics, Policy and Law, 25*(4), 653–688.

Nordhaus, W. D. (2002, January). *The health of nations: The contribution of improved health to living standards.* NBER Working Paper 8818. Cambridge, MA: National Bureau of Economic Research.

OR Manager. (2002). Getting MD buy-in on cost management. *OR Manager, 18*(6), 20–22.

Pauly, M. V. (1968). The economics of moral hazard. *American Economic Review, 58*(3), 531–537.

Peden, E. A., & Freeland, M. (1998). Insurance effects on U.S. medical spending 1960–1993. *Health Economics, 7*(8), 671–687.

PricewaterhouseCoopers. (2003, February 19). *Cost of caring: Key drivers of growth in spending on hospital care.* Washington, DC: PricewaterhouseCoopers. Retrieved from http://www.aha.org/aha/press-release/2003/030219-pr-costofcaring.html

Queenan, J. T. (2002). The increasing cost of medical care. *Obstetrics & Gynecology, 100*(4), 629–630.

Rosenthal, M., Hsuan, C., & Milstein, A. (2005). A report card on the freshman class of consumer-directed health plans. *Health Affairs, 24*(6), 1592–1600.

Ruland, C. M., & Ravn, I. H. (2003). Usefulness and effects on costs and staff management of a nursing resource management information system. *Journal of Nursing Management, 11,* 208–215.

Schroeder, S. A., & Cantor, J. C. (1991). On squeezing balloons: Cost containment fails again. *New England Journal of Medicine, 325,* 15.

Stanton, T. H. (2001). Fraud-and-abuse enforcement in Medicare: Finding middle ground. *Health Affairs, 20*(4), 28–42.

Taylor, C. W. (2003). What works. Bridging the gap. In-home monitoring device reduces cost of treating underserved populations in rural Alabama. *Health Management Technology, 24*(4), 36–38.

Thorpe, K. E. (1999). Managed care as victim or villain? *Journal of Health Politics, Policy and Law, 24*(5), 949–956.

U.S. Department of Health and Human Services, Centers for Medicare & Medicaid Services. (2006). *National health expenditure accounts.* Retrieved from http://www.cms.hhs.gov/NationalHealthExpendData

Wilensky, G. R. (2006). Consumer-driven health plans: Early evidence and potential impact on hospitals. *Health Affairs, 25*(1), 174–185.

Young, G. J., Desai, K. R., & Hellinger, F. J. (2000). Community control and pricing patterns of nonprofit hospitals: An antitrust analysis. *Journal of Health Politics, Policy and Law, 25*(6), 1051–1081.

PART FOUR

The Future

Key Words

The Future of Health Care Delivery in the United States

James R. Knickman and Anthony R. Kovner

Learning Objectives

- Explain the rationale for futures planning.
- Describe approaches to planning.
- Analyze likely factors driving change in the health system.
- Predict changes likely to occur in the health system.

Topical Outline

- Definitions and approaches to forecasting
- Key drivers of change, 2007–2012
- Areas where change is likely to occur, 2007–2012

Forecasting:
Definition and Approaches

Forecasting is a hazardous business. For example, through eight editions and over 30 years, the editors of this textbook have been predicting the imminent implementation of national health insurance in the United States. But universal insurance still remains "just around the corner." While change often happens slower than we expect, it also can be sudden. Witness the rise of "homeland security" after 9/11, the tearing down of the Berlin Wall, and the integration of Internet-based technology into many aspects of our daily lives in the past 15 years.

A concern about change preoccupies most Americans. All stakeholders in health care—taxpayers, patients, providers, suppliers, employers, and government officials—suggest changes and respond to change proposals. Sometimes they seek to make change occur, while at other times they block it. Managing the change process is a key part of most high-level careers in the health sector. Strategic decisions about change can have very long-lasting impacts. For example, installation of a new regional information system or building a new children's hospital can affect the delivery of care for decades; and freezing wages during World War II gave rise to a tremendous increase in employer-based health insurance, because adding benefits was a way of increasing compensation without increasing wages. Without this wage freeze, health insurance in 2007 might have been based on citizenship rather than employment status.

What impact do forecasts have on those of us who work in health care? Can we work together to achieve a positive forecast or forestall a dismal one? We suggest that forecasts can be made in a way that helps us plan for the future. Forecasters can tell us, for example, how much insurance coverage for all children would cost, using different assumptions, and how increased coverage is likely to affect access to care and utilization of services. Of course, "the experts" don't always agree on such matters, because their analyses are inevitably based on less-than-perfect information and some amount of uncertainty. But, collectively, they may suggest a reasonable range of futures.

Forecasts should not dictate actual policy choices, however, which must take into account not just analysis, but also values. The citizenry, not just the experts, must decide whether we want universal coverage or electronic medical records and how much of our spending should be on priorities outside of the health sector—achieving energy independence or improving public education, for example.

Exercises in forecasting have a range of practical values. Most important, forecasting is a crucial step in strategic planning. Deciding where to focus attention depends on a sense of future trends and prospects. What new services must be designed? How large should a new hospital be? How many elderly will use Medicare services 20 years from now? Questions such as these guide current actions, and some approach to forecasting is crucial in order to provide tentative answers to these questions.

Forecasting forces us to look at history. Often, forecasting starts with a look at patterns of past trends to make predictions about future trends. In this sense, as Norman Cousins said, "history is a vast early warning system." Studying what caused what helps us create new solutions to current problems. Epidemiologists, for example, use the natural patterns of past behavior and events to sort out what types of behavior, environmental factors, and interventions are associated with good and bad health outcomes. This type of analysis then leads to ideas for how to achieve improvements. Most social scientists use the same basic approach in studying how the health system works and how it can be improved.

Finally, forecasting gives us a reference point that we can use in the future to assess our past logic. Some years ago, Kovner (1995) wrote a "Futures" chapter for a previous edition of this text that tells us how we thought about health care then and how our logic has evolved in the intervening 16 years. Some of Kovner's predictions have borne out. For example, he said that government increasingly will regulate the cost of, quality, and access to health care and that the power of physicians to shape and benefit from the delivery system will diminish relative to other providers and to consumers. And some of the changes he predicted have not come to pass: For example, he suggested that cost pressures would cause Americans to use less medical care. Reexamining earlier forecasts allows us to sharpen our analytic abilities, to make forecasts more accurate, and to link causes to effects. For example, what would cause Americans to use less medical care per capita on an age-adjusted basis? Would it take increased cost-sharing? Or price competition based on clinical outcomes? Or increased electronic communication between physicians and patients? Or single-payer national health insurance? What would be the intended and unintended consequences of using less medical care per capita? Lower employment of physicians or higher physician charges? Under any likely scenario, would Americans use less medical care, as long as new technology and drugs keep producing better outcomes? In 2000, one of us wrote:

> Imagine the future: I wake up, take a reading on my health monitor (connected to a health information system that tracks 300 aspects of my health status, including a list of specialized self-chosen health goals). I lean over to the monitor, make a few clicks, and quickly get key information on how my 105-year-old mother—who lives 800 miles away—did overnight and get a forecast about how she will feel during the coming day. As I get in my car to commute to work, I am comforted by its advanced anticollision system that makes life-threatening accidents a concern of the past. I do find the many billboards advertising health-enhancing services of every stripe a general nuisance and source of visual pollution. My grandchildren cannot believe the stories of how physicians used to work in small groups or by themselves and how there were thousands of hospitals, each one operating on its own rather than as a part of the four national chains of health plans that now compete vigorously in the health market. (Knickman, 2002, pp. 455–456)

While this seemed a bit far-fetched just a few years ago, many systems similar to those described are actually being implemented in 2007.

In 2007, a scenario such as the following may seem as unlikely as the monitoring scenario above:

Imagine the future: competition in health care is based primarily on quality of service—that is, the results a set of providers obtain for patients with a specific medical condition, such as heart attack, hip or spine operation, or diabetes. The price of their services is known in advance, and patients receive a single bill for all services related to their medical condition. Everyone has basic insurance. All Americans have their own health record on a wallet-sized card, and all providers can access this record when the patient shows up for care. To graduate from high school, children must demonstrate that they understand how their body works and how to keep it healthy, and all prospective parents are paid to attend child-rearing classes.

Will the future really look like this? When, if ever? In truth, it may be easier to specify the forces shaping the nation's future health care than the specific results of those forces. In the preceding 17 chapters, authors have examined many of these forces, as they explored key aspects of the health system. Understanding the present and being knowledgeable about the past are first steps in making relevant forecasts and adapting to predicted change: "If you don't know where you're going, you might wind up somewhere else."[1]

---

[1] This famous aphorism is from Yogi Berra. By contrast, the Greek playwright Euripides said, "What we look for does not come to pass. God finds a way for what none foresaw."

Forecasting Methods

Forecasting methods vary. Economists have developed highly quantitative forecasting approaches. They analyze past data to predict future economic events. Often they collect time-series data on a set of economic variables, then develop theories about how each variable influences the others, then test these theories with data from the past, and finally estimate how the variables will change events in the future, based on the estimated relationships established. This approach works only when extensive empirical data are available and is most useful for short-term forecasts.

The Delphi method, a more qualitative approach to forecasting, systematically obtains expert opinions, with an end goal of achieving consensus. Delphi administrators poll experts about their forecasts in three of four rounds of questionnaires. After each round, results are tabulated and disseminated to the group. The group completes a Delphi when it reaches a convergence of opinion. The Delphi method overcomes geographic barriers that plague many consensus-building exercises. Its flexibility allows it to apply to health and medicine as easily as to war and weapons, and to all levels of decision making. However, reliability, as well as the work required, increase as the number of rounds and experts increases. Poor questionnaire design also can limit the method's usefulness.

A third, less scientific, approach to forecasting is to rely on nationally recognized leaders in a field to apply their experience about the past and the dynamics of the present to make predictions about the future. This is the approach often used in the popular media, where forecasting is common, and it is the one we use in this chapter, drawing on the wide literature contributed by experts analyzing the present to predict the future and present our interpretation and inferences of what current patterns in the health system suggest for the future. Our analysis is shaped by our vantage points, working full-time at a philanthropy and a major university, and part-time on boards of hospitals and health systems in the greater New York City area.

Drivers of Change in the New Millennium

It is difficult to know whether a given period—as we live in it—is one of rapid change, but 1995 to 2005 was a time of fundamental change in how health care is organized and delivered and in how we think about maintaining health. It is often difficult, as well, to distinguish drivers of change from key aspects of change itself. Still, we see four fundamental forces shaping health care in 2007 and beyond:

- the preferences of consumers and the ideology of the citizenry
- demographic changes in the U.S. population—both aging and ethnic shifts
- the growing understanding that individual behavior and environmental factors affect health outcomes more than health services
- an increasing likelihood of serious and widespread natural and man-made catastrophes.

PEOPLE'S PREFERENCES AND IDEOLOGIES

Market forces are a key influence on health care, yet system change is driven (or constrained) by the preferences and ideology of the public. Perhaps most striking to peoples of the developed world is Americans' ongoing distrust in government, especially the federal government. Most Americans have been persuaded that the federal government cannot be trusted to sponsor or manage large social programs.

Of course, not all Americans view the government this way. African Americans, who look to the federal government to redress racial and ethnic inequalities, express higher-than-average trust. Those with lower incomes, as well as young adults, also view the government as more trustworthy. Regardless of whether Americans' distrust is justified, their attitudes sharply limit health system interventions that involve large public sector roles.

Another strong American preference is the importance placed on choice in any health care system. Choice consciousness drove the movement away from managed care (although some informed observers still believe that managed care, in the form of prepaid group practice, is the "least bad" way to reorganize health care delivery). Americans are accustomed to being able to pick and choose from various options when making purchases in most parts of the economy. Increased restrictions in health plans constrain these choices.

AGING AND ETHNIC CHANGES IN THE POPULATION

The continued aging of the U.S. population will certainly affect health policy over the next 10 years. Approximately half of hospital admissions are currently for Americans over age 65, who account for less than 15% of the population. The number of people over age 65 will double in the next 25 years, driving up the demand for health care, especially chronic illness care and support services for those over age 85—the greatest users of health and support services.

A second key population shift, the effect of which is difficult to predict, is growing ethnic diversity. According to the U.S. Census Bureau, by 2060, a majority of Americans will be ethnic "minorities." By 2050, the non-Hispanic White population will increase only moderately, to 213 million, non-Hispanic Blacks will increase to 54 million (from 36 million in 2000), and the Hispanic population will triple from 11 million in 2000 to 36 million. The diversity of the population varies widely across regions of the country.

The impact of this transformation on health care requirements depends on how quickly the growing ethnic groups assimilate into the economic mainstream of American life. Currently, Blacks and Latin Americans have greater-than-average health care needs principally related to lower income and behavior patterns. If population growth continues to occur mostly among the low-income part of the U.S. population, and if wealth continues to be concentrated in a smaller and smaller percentage of Americans, we can expect growing demands for public health care services.

Increasing numbers of immigrants do not have health insurance, which puts financial pressure on hospitals and other providers. Health care providers also must respond to patient diversity in how they deliver medical care. Many ethnic minorities prefer services delivered by providers who understand their culture, and care may be more effective in such cases. Creating a more diverse health care workforce will be a key challenge as the 21st century progresses.

HEALTH AND BEHAVIOR

Americans are beginning to understand that the real determinants of health have little to do with the trillions of dollars that are invested annually in the health system and more to do with the way we lead our lives and the environment in which we live. Perhaps half of all deaths in the United States can be attributed to individual behavioral and environmental factors, as reported several times in this volume. The most prominent contributors to these deaths are tobacco, diet, activity patterns, and alcohol.

Despite the established links between behavioral risk factors and illness and death, the Centers for Disease Control and Prevention have estimated that only about 3% of total U.S. health expenditures are spent on keeping people well. This investment pales in comparison with the more than $500 billion in direct health care costs for Americans with chronic conditions (many of which are preventable).

To improve population health would require public health programs that attach environmental risks to health and attempt to improve the way individuals maintain their own health. A recent public health initiative by the state of Arkansas, under Governor Michael Huckabee (2006), is interesting. The state is trying to reduce obesity and smoking and increase exercise by launching wellness initiatives where Arkansans live, work, and learn. For example, Huckabee is working through school districts to improve health education and increase regular physical activity, improve nutrition, engage parents about students' fitness levels, convene public forums to promote physical activity and healthy foods within schools, and encourage schools to work with local chefs and farmers to offer healthier, appealing foods.

A focus on behavior as a key determinant of health problems can lead to more research on behavior-change interventions. It also supports the idea that capitated payments should reward providers and health systems that intervene early in chronic health problems and prevent costly complications and flare-ups. A number of managed care organizations have found cost-effective approaches to behavioral risk factor management, but it is clear that additional incentives, such as pay for performance, will be needed in order to encourage investments in preventive care. When health plans do nothing to influence modifiable health risks, such as physical inactivity, obesity, or smoking, significant short-term costs result. In one study, health care costs for plan beneficiaries who smoked, were overweight, and inactive were almost 50% higher over an 18-month period than for those without these risk factors (Pronk, Goodman, O'Connor, & Martinson, 1999).

CATASTROPHES

Judging from the past 5 years, the rate of serious natural and man-made catastrophes is increasing faster than the health system's capability to deal with them. Earthquakes, hurricanes, terrorism and bioterrorism, dam and bridge collapses, or the potential for an avian flu pandemic have increased perceptions of the importance of disaster preparedness. The Institute of Medicine (2006) has concluded that the U.S. emergency care system is inadequately prepared to handle a major disaster. Emergency departments and trauma centers are already overcrowded, and many emergency personnel lack the necessary equipment, funds, and training to deal with catastrophic events.

Responsibility for emergency preparedness largely remains with the states. We can only predict that calls for improved preparedness will increase, as will calls for research and analysis. What actually occurs will probably depend on the nature of any next catastrophe and the response—locally, regionally, and nationally—to it. This is basically a political matter of fixing accountability and transparency, then raising the funds and training the personnel to deal with emergencies.

Where Change Is Likely to Occur

We suggest that, in the next 5 years, change is likely to occur in the following areas:

- health insurance
- cost containment
- services for the chronically ill
- accountability and transparency.

Five years ago, Knickman (2002) compiled a somewhat different list: serving the elderly and the chronically ill, genetics and technology, health system change, Medicare, information, and health promotion. Only one of these areas—serving the elderly and chronically ill—is the same in our new list. Information and health promotion from the 2002 list are now clustered under accountability and transparency. Health system change and Medicare, from the 2002 list, have been clustered as cost containment. We have omitted genetics and technology, even though change is expected to occur in these areas, because the results of such change seem to us too unpredictable.

The four areas we have selected for discussion below are interdependent. For example, improving services for the chronically ill depends on broadening insurance coverage, which, in turn, must be financed by success in containing costs and targeting services to those who can most benefit from them, as well as fixing accountability for providing these services, getting results, and making transactions increasingly transparent to prospective purchasers.

HEALTH INSURANCE

Over the past 5 years, the number of Americans lacking adequate health insurance has increased, and even Americans with adequate health insurance are paying much more for their health care through increasing coinsurance and deductibles. More providers are increasingly not accepting insurance or Medicare and Medicaid payments and insisting on being paid in cash, leaving consumers to negotiate with insurers (and generally to receive only partial reimbursement).

A key tipping point for national health insurance will occur when enough middle-class Americans—however many that may be—are so affected by loss of insurance and the increasing cost of medical care that they elect politicians who will do something about it. Politicians will attempt to extend Medicare and Medicaid to more people (a logical extension is for Medicare to cover children). Or they may try to mandate single-payer coverage or require all Americans to have basic medical insurance, such as with auto insurance. If they cannot afford to pay, their insurance bill will be paid from tax revenues, as is the case under a new plan in Massachusetts.

COST CONTAINMENT

Costs (and often prices) of the medical care we buy are too high, and we buy more than we need. Still, most stakeholders seem to prefer that the health system remain more or less as it is, and they do not wish to risk changing the health system in ways that have uncertain consequences.

Different stakeholders try to contain costs to themselves, but, meanwhile, costs overall continue to rise rapidly. Medicare contains its costs by limiting what it will pay for services, such as for hospital episodes of care. Employers contain their costs by increasing what employees have to pay. Consumers *could* help contain health costs by changing their health habits—eating sensibly, exercising, giving up smoking, reducing alcohol consumption, and controlling their weight—but could do a great deal more.

Because none of these efforts to date has been at all successful in overall cost containment, we clearly need fundamental changes. On one hand, new technology is helping to prolong life and improve health status for those who get to use it, but, on the other hand, the price tag for assuring that all Americans can do so becomes greater and greater. The social choice about who can have access to services and who pays for it is inherently political. Any efforts to reshape the delivery system or to make it more equitable or efficient will affect the incomes of many providers and the profits of many industries.

Judging from the last 5 years, health costs will not be contained effectively over the next 5 either (see Table 18.1). Yet, we remain cautiously optimistic. An increasing number of Americans see health care cost containment as a serious issue, and more policymakers want to do something about it. Given the tremendous waste in our health system and the potential for making significant changes without negative health consequences, improvements in effectiveness and efficiency may be quite doable.

Table 18.1	Projected National Health Expenditures, 2005–2016		
Year	Total Expenditures (In Billions of Dollars)	Dollars per Person	Percent Out-of-Pocket
2005 (actual)	$1,973.3	$6,649	12.5
2006 (actual)	$2,105.5	$7,026	12.0
2007	$2,262.3	$7,498	11.7
2008	$2,420.0	$7,957	11.6
2009	$2,596.0	$8,468	11.5
2010	$2,776.4	$8,985	11.4
2011	$2,966.4	$9,525	11.3
2012	$3,173.4	$10,110	11.1
2013	$3,395.8	$10,735	11.0
2014	$3,628.8	$11,383	10.9
2015	$3,874.6	$12,062	10.8
2016	$4,136.9	$12,782	10.7

Note. Actual 2005–2006 data from Catlin, A., Cowan, C., Hartman, M., Heffler, S., and the National Health Expenditure Accounts Team. (2008). National health spending in 2006: A year of change for prescription drugs. *Health Affairs 27:* 14–29. Projected data for 2007–2016 from U.S. Centers for Medicare and Medicaid Services. (undated). *National health expenditure projections.* Baltimore, MD. Retrieved February 3, 2008, from http://www.cms.hhs.gov/NationalHealthExpendData/downloads/proj2006.pdf

SERVING THE CHRONICALLY ILL AND ELDERLY

Five years ago, Knickman (2002) noted that the aging of the population will refocus the health system so that its primary concerns revolve around chronic disease management, geriatrics as a medical specialty, and the general field of services for the frail.

This refocusing obviously is not yet complete. But tremendous changes are occurring. Private chronic care insurance enrollments are growing, and, although public long-term care insurance has not been adopted in the United States, it has been implemented in many developed countries, such as Sweden and Japan, where the cost of insuring both acute and chronic care costs a lot less than the costs of insuring acute care alone in the United States.

In the United States, more sophisticated ways have been developed to pay managed care organizations for the care they deliver to the chronically ill. And physicians and other providers have tested new approaches to better manage chronic conditions, emphasizing four components: evidence-based care protocols; data management systems that track patient care; patient self-management and activation; and the use of coordinated, interdisciplinary provider teams.

Also under way are demonstration projects attempting better integration of services directed at both the medical problems of the chronically ill and their social support needs. Prospects have changed for better services integration, arising from state governments' interest in better coordinating resources coming from Medicare (which focuses mostly on medical care) and Medicaid (which pays for more support services). Ironically, as a result, service integration sometimes happens more quickly for the poor and near-poor than for the middle class.

A somewhat related aspect of change is the development of new industries catering to the various needs of an aging population. The next Microsoft or McDonald's will likely emerge in this market. New approaches to assisted living and management of retirement resources will be in great demand. Older Americans already prefer one-stop shopping to obtain medical, health promotion, support, and lifestyle services in a trusted, convenient environment. It is difficult to predict exactly what this new service sector will look like, but it will involve large resources and will likely be led by private corporations.

SERVING THE CUSTOMER

Competition in health care will increasingly focus on results achieved in caring for a medical condition over a full cycle of care—before and after surgery, for example—relative to the costs of providing that care, according to some experts (Porter & Teisberg, 2006). Comparing outcomes with costs would require determining accountability for the delivery of care and increasing information about the results achieved. The U.S. health system has a long way to go to achieve this level of customer service.

What gives us optimism are the results achieved in other parts of the U.S. economy that have made rapid improvements in effectiveness and efficiency, such as banking, food service, and computer services. In the health system, increasingly, some large organizations have made significant changes in the processes of care that benefit consumers. They then publicize their performance as part of their marketing efforts. For example, in many U.S. markets, although hospital services may not be increasing greatly overall, the market share of the larger system providers is increasing. We believe this is due to perceptions of quality based on performance measures, rather than on monopoly power.

Porter and Teisberg (2006) suggest that health care providers should narrow the scope of their services and widen the areas they serve. They cite the experience of an array of specialized hospitals that deliver superior value: M. D. Anderson Cancer Center in Houston, Bascom Palmer Eye Institute in Miami, and many others. They assert that strategic focus is not about narrow specialization, but about pursuit of excellence and deepening penetration in chosen fields. For example, in Minnesota, Fairview-University Children's Hospital's long-term commitment to excellence in the area of cystic fibrosis has made it the nation's top treatment facility for this condition, with a median survival age of 46, compared with the U.S. average of 32.

Recent developments in primary care practice organization include open-access scheduling, which lets patients be seen the next day rather than waiting several weeks for appointments, and concierge medical practices, such as MDVIP, in which patients pay a several-thousand-dollar annual fee, but gain almost immediate appointments and e-mail access to their clinician, an executive physical, and other benefits. At-home wireless telemetry devices can monitor patients' status and transmit the data to their health care provider, obviating the need for frequent in-office monitoring visits.

The lean thinking of the Toyota Motor Company also has found a place in some health care facilities (Bohmer & Ferlins, 2006)—for example, at Seattle's Virginia Mason Medical Center. "Lean" is an important dimension of quality; all work that doesn't add value for the customer is defined as waste (estimated at 50% of all health expenditures).

Purporting to represent customer interests, various independent groups rate health care. *U.S. News and World Report* ranks hospitals, the Baldrige Awards recognize quality, some hospitals are deemed "Most Wired," others are recognized as "Magnet Hospitals" for nurses. Providers advertise their rankings and Press-Ganey scores, attempting to establish that they meet criteria of value to the customer, ranging from time waiting to see a doctor in the emergency department to percentage of nursing time spent on direct patient care.

Increasingly, patients and families have available to them a wide array of information about the treatment of medical conditions. They use this information in subsequent conversation with providers. Accountability becomes fixed at the provider level, and consumers can confidently ask more detailed questions about treatment and services.

The growing awareness that healthy lifestyles have much more impact on long-range health than access to health care should translate into significant changes in Americans' approach to health maintenance (see Table 18.2). We forecast increasingly focused accountability and more effective health education in grades K–12.

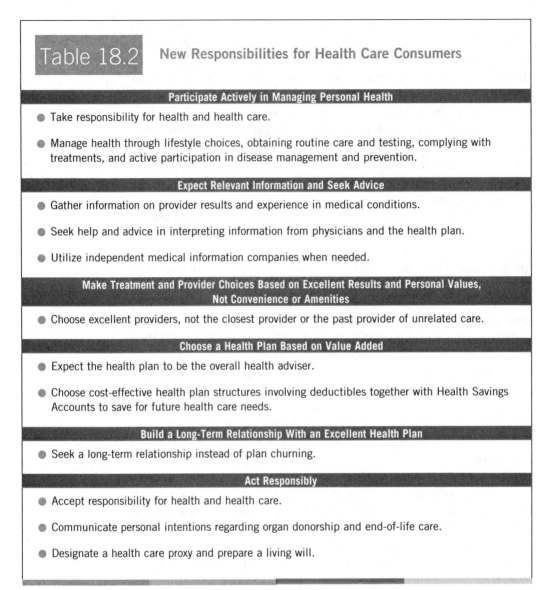

Table 18.2   New Responsibilities for Health Care Consumers

Participate Actively in Managing Personal Health

- Take responsibility for health and health care.

- Manage health through lifestyle choices, obtaining routine care and testing, complying with treatments, and active participation in disease management and prevention.

Expect Relevant Information and Seek Advice

- Gather information on provider results and experience in medical conditions.

- Seek help and advice in interpreting information from physicians and the health plan.

- Utilize independent medical information companies when needed.

Make Treatment and Provider Choices Based on Excellent Results and Personal Values, Not Convenience or Amenities

- Choose excellent providers, not the closest provider or the past provider of unrelated care.

Choose a Health Plan Based on Value Added

- Expect the health plan to be the overall health adviser.

- Choose cost-effective health plan structures involving deductibles together with Health Savings Accounts to save for future health care needs.

Build a Long-Term Relationship With an Excellent Health Plan

- Seek a long-term relationship instead of plan churning.

Act Responsibly

- Accept responsibility for health and health care.

- Communicate personal intentions regarding organ donorship and end-of-life care.

- Designate a health care proxy and prepare a living will.

Note. From Porter, M. E., & Teisberg, E. O. (2006). *Redefining health care: Creating value-based competition on results.* Boston: Harvard Business School Press.

This would include a use of results-based curricula that promote healthy behavior and an understanding of how the human body works and the leading preventable risks to health.

Conclusion

In chapter 1, we suggested that opinions differ as to why we have the health care delivery system we do and how we should go about changing it. We listed six groups of stakeholders in health care: taxpayers, patients, providers, vendors and suppliers, employers and payers, and regulators and government. In this chapter, we have tried to specify drivers of change and where change is likely to occur. We believe this is related to the growing and waning power of the six groups of stakeholders. We predict that the following groups will gain power over the next 5 years: taxpayers, patients, and regulators and government. The remainder may lose power. Readers should examine our assumptions and make their own forecasts.

A dozen years ago, Kovner (1995) concluded that it is important "to predict future directions in the American health care delivery system, not so much because of confidence that they will happen but rather to focus discussion on key issues, the constraints that surround them, and the opportunities for resolving them" (p. 552). We hope that the discussion of "futures" presented here will stimulate needed reflection and discussion of ways to bring about better health care—and better health—for Americans.

References

Bohmer, R., & Ferlins, E. M. (2006). Virginia Mason Medical Center. *Harvard Business School,* Case 9-606-044.

Huckabee, M. (2006). A vision for a healthier America states can do. *Health Affairs, 25,* 1005–1009.

Institute of Medicine. (2006). *The future of emergency care: Key findings and recommendations.* Washington, DC: National Academy Press.

Knickman, J. (2002). Futures. In A. R. Kovner & S. Jonas (Eds.), *Jonas and Kovner's health care delivery in the United States* (7th ed., pp. 455–475). New York: Springer Publishing.

Kovner, A. (1995). Futures. In A. R. Kovner (Ed.), *Jonas's health care delivery in the United States* (5th ed., pp. 532–553). New York: Springer Publishing.

Porter, M. E., & Teisberg, E. O. (2006). *Redefining health care: Creating value-based competition on results.* Boston: Harvard Business School Press.

Pronk, N. P., Goodman, M. J., O'Connor, P. J., & Martinson, B. C. (1999). Relationship between modifiable health risks and short-term health care changes. *Journal of the American Medical Association, 282,* 2235–2239.

PART FIVE

Appendices

Appendix A
Glossary

Anthony R. Kovner

access: An individual's ability to obtain medical services on a timely and financially acceptable basis. Factors determining ease of access also include availability of health care facilities and transportation to them and reasonable hours of operation.

accreditation: A decision made by a recognized organization that an institution substantially meets appropriate standards.

activities of daily living (ADLs): Tasks people can do that are required for normal functioning.

acute care: Medical care of a limited duration, provided in a hospital or outpatient setting, to treat an injury or short-term illness.

advanced practice nurse: Registered nurse such as a clinical nurse specialist, nurse practitioner, nurse anesthetist, and nurse midwife with a master's or doctoral degree concentrating on a specific area of practice.

adverse selection: Occurs when a population characteristic such as age (e.g., a larger number of persons age 65 or older in proportion to younger persons) increases the potential for higher utilization than budgeted, and increases costs above those of the capitation rate.

alliance: Organizational relationship for specific purposes.

ambulatory care: Health care services that patients receive when they are not an inpatient or home in bed.

Several of these definitions have been adapted from terms defined in *Healthcare Acronyms & Terms for Boards and Medical Leaders,* published by the Governance Institute, 6333 Greenwich Drive, Suite 200, San Diego, CA 92122, June 2004.

appropriate care: Care for which expected health benefits exceed negative consequences.

assisted living: Services provided to individuals who need assistance with activities of daily living.

attending physicians: Doctors who have the privilege of using the hospital for patient care.

average daily census: The average number of patients counted in a health care institution, usually over a 1-year period.

behavioral risk factor: An element of personal behavior—such as unbalanced nutrition, use of tobacco products, leading a secondary lifestyle, or the abuse of alcoholic beverages—that leads to an increased risk of developing one or more diseases or negative health conditions.

benchmark: The best known value for a specific measure, from any source.

beneficiary: Any person, either a subscriber or a dependent, eligible for service under a health plan contract.

benefits: Specific areas of plan coverage or services provided, such as outpatient visits and hospitalization, that make up the range of medical services marketed under a health plan.

biotechnology: The application of a technology such as computer science, mechanical engineering, economics, or electronic imaging to the prevention, diagnosis, evaluation, treatment, or management of a disease or negative health condition.

capitation: A payment method in which a physician or hospital is paid a fixed amount per patient, per year, regardless of the volume or cost of services each patient requires.

carrier: An insurer; an underwriter of risk that is engaged in providing, paying for, or reimbursing all or part of the cost of health services under group insurance policies or contracts, medical or hospital services agreements, membership or subscription contracts, or similar group arrangements in exchange for premiums or other periodic charges.

case management: Often utilized as part of a managed care system; a practitioner known as a gatekeeper makes decisions regarding the type and volume of services to which the patient may have access.

case manager: An individual who coordinates and oversees other health care workers in finding the most effective methods of caring for specific patients.

catastrophic coverage: A type of insurance that pays for high-cost health care, usually associated with accidents and chronic illnesses and diseases, such as cancer and AIDS.

census: In the United States, refers to the count of members of the national population and their demographic characteristics undertaken by the U.S. Census Bureau every 10 years on the 10th year; in the health care delivery system specifically, refers to the number of patients in a hospital or other health care institution at any one time.

Centers for Medicare & Medicaid Services (CMS): Administers Medicare, Medicaid, and the State Child Health Insurance Program (SCHIP). Formerly called the Health Care Financing Administration (HCFA).

certificates of need: Franchises for new services and construction or renovation of hospitals or related facilities, as issued by states.

charity care: Care given to needy patients without expectation of payment.

chronic care: Treatment or rehabilitative health services provided to individuals on a long-term basis (over 30 days), in both inpatient and ambulatory settings.

clinical nurse practitioner: Nurse with extra training who accepts additional clinical responsibility for medical diagnosis or treatment.

clinical trials: The testing on patients in a clinical setting of a diagnostic, preventive, or therapeutic intervention, using a study design that will provide for a valid estimation of safety and efficiency.

closed panel: A managed care plan that contracts with physicians on an exclusive basis for services and does not allow those physicians to see patients for another managed care organization.

coinsurance: A provision in a member's coverage that limits the amount of coverage by the plan to a certain percentage, commonly 80%. Any additional costs are paid out of pocket by the member.

community hospital: A hospital offering short-term general and other special services, owned by a corporation or agency other than the federal government.

community rating: The rating system by which a plan or an indemnity carrier takes the total experience of the subscribers or members within a given geographic area or "community" and uses these data to determine a reimbursement rate that is common for all groups regardless of the individual claims experience of any one group.

complementary and alternative medicine: Diagnostic and treatment interventions that fall outside of the realm of state-licensed medical practice as it is defined by the privileges to use certain restricted diagnostic regimens, prescribe drugs from a restricted list, and practice surgery. Such disciplines include chiropractic, acupuncture, homeopathy, herbal medicine, naturopathy, therapeutic touch, and others.

comprehensive coverage: A health insurance system that pays for a broad range of services.

Consolidated Omnibus Budget Reconciliation Act of 1985 (COBRA): A federal law (P.L. 99–272) that requires all employer-sponsored health plans to offer certain employees and their families the opportunity to continue, at their personal expense, health insurance coverage under the group plan for up to 18, 24, or 36 months, depending on the qualifying event, after their coverage normally would have ceased (e.g., due to the death or retirement of the employee, divorce or legal separation, resignation or termination of employment, or bankruptcy of the employer).

continuous quality improvement (CQI): A systematic approach to improve processes of health care, such as admission to the hospital or delivery of meals to a patient.

co-payment: A specified amount that an insured individual must pay for a specified service or procedure (e.g., $8 for an office visit).

cost sharing: A provision that requires individuals to cover some part of their medical expenses (e.g., co-payments, coinsurance, deductibles).

cost-shifting: Passing the cost of one group onto another group. For example, if the rate one group of health plan enrollees pays for services is less than the actual cost of those services, the difference can be made up based on charges higher than cost paid by another group.

credentialing: The most common use of the term refers to obtaining and reviewing the documentation of professional providers.

critical pathway: The mapping out of day-to-day recommendations for patient care based on best practices and scientific evidence.

data: In health, an event, condition, or disease occurrence that is counted. In health services, an episode of care, costs of care, expenditures, quantification of human resources and facilities and their characteristics, and the like.

deductible: The amount a patient must pay out of pocket, usually annually on a calendar-year basis, before insurance will begin to cover costs.

defined contribution plan: Benefits plan that gives employees a certain amount of total compensation to allocate among various benefits, rather than providing employees with the specific benefits, such as hospitalization.

demographic characteristics: Such characteristics of an individual or a population group (averages in the latter case) as age, sex, marital status, ethnicity, geographic location, occupation, and income.

denominator: For health care, the total number of people among whom numerator items are being counted (see *numerator*).

diagnosis-related groups (DRGs): Groups of inpatient discharges with final diagnoses that are similar clinically and in resource consumption; used as a basis of payment by the Medicare program and, as a result, widely accepted by others.

discharge planning: A part of the patient management guidelines and the nursing care plan that identifies the expected discharge date and coordinates the various services necessary to achieve the target.

disproportionate share hospital (DSH): A hospital that provides a large amount (or disproportionate share) of uncompensated care and/or care to Medicaid and low-income Medicare beneficiaries.

Emergency Medical Treatment and Labor Act (EMTALA): Federal law setting forth requirements for hospitals participating in Medicare to provide emergency care so that patients who cannot pay are not "dumped" to other hospitals.

Employee Retirement Income Security Act (ERISA): A 1974 federal law (P.L. 93–406) that set the standards of disclosure for employee benefit plans to ensure workers the right to at least part of their pensions. The law governs most private pensions and other employee benefits and overrides all state laws that concern employee benefits, including health benefits; therefore, ERISA preempts state laws in their application to self-funded, private employer-sponsored health insurance plans.

encounter: A patient visit to a provider. The term often refers to visits to providers by patients in capitated health plans.

enrollment: The process by which an individual and family become a subscriber(s) for coverage in a health plan. This may be done either through an actual signing up of the individual or through a collective bargaining agreement on the employer's conditions of employment. A result, therefore, is that the health plan is aware of its entire population of eligible beneficiaries. As a usual practice, individuals must notify the health plan of any changes in family status that affect the enrollment of dependents.

entitlements: Government benefits (e.g., Medicare, Medicaid, Social Security, food stamps) that are provided automatically to all qualified individuals, and are therefore part of mandatory spending programs.

evidence-based medicine (EBM): That portion of medical practice, estimated at much lower than 50%, that is based on established scientific findings.

experience rating: A method used to determine the cost of health insurance premiums, whereby the cost is based on the previous amount a certain group (e.g., all the employees of a particular business) paid for medical services.

Federal Employee Health Benefits Program (FEHBP): Also referred to as Federal Employee Plan or FEP. The health plans made available to federal employees as part of their employment benefits.

fee-for-service: A billing system in which a health care provider charges a patient a set amount for a specific service.

fee schedule: A listing of accepted fees or established allowances for specified medical procedures as used in health plans; it usually represents the maximum amounts the program will pay for the specified procedures.

fixed costs: Costs that do not change or vary with fluctuations in enrollment or in utilization of services.

formulary: A listing of drugs prepared by, for example, a hospital or a managed care company, that a physician may prescribe. The physician is requested or required to use only formulary drugs unless there is a valid medical reason to use a nonformulary drug.

for-profit hospitals: Those owned by private corporations that declare dividends or otherwise distribute profits to individuals. Also called investor-owned, many are also community hospitals.

full-time equivalent (FTE): Refers to the number of hours employees must work to be regarded as full time; thus two half-time employees working 20 hours a week equals one full-time equivalent.

gatekeeper: A health care practitioner who makes decisions regarding the type and volume of services to which a patient may have access; generally used by health maintenance organizations (HMOs) to control unnecessary utilization of services.

generic drug: A therapeutic drug, originally protected by a patent, the chemical composition of which meets the standards for that drug set by the Food and Drug Administration, made by a company other than the company that originally developed and patented the drug. Generics are usually not manufactured and made available until after the original patent has expired.

governance: The activity of an organization that monitors the outside environment, selects appropriate alternatives, and negotiates the implementation of these alternatives with others inside and outside the organization.

governing board: A group of individuals who, under state law, own an organization, regardless of whether they can obtain any financial advantage through such ownership.

graduate medical education: The education and training of physicians beyond the 4 years of medical school, in positions that may be termed internship, residency, fellowship, postgraduate year 1, 2, 3, and so on. Although one can enter medical school only with an undergraduate degree at the baccalaureate level, in the United States, the 4 years of medical school leading to the MD or DO (doctor of osteopathy) degrees are customarily referred to as undergraduate medical education.

group model: An HMO that contracts with a medical group for the provision of health care services. The relationship between the HMO and the medical group is generally very close, although there are wide variations in the relative independence of the group from the HMO; a form of closed panel health plan.

group practice: Three or more physicians who deliver patient care, make joint use of equipment and personnel, and divide income by a prearranged formula.

health care delivery: The provision of preventive treatment or rehabilitative health services, from short term to long term, to individuals as well as groups of people, by individual practitioners, institutions, or public health agencies.

Health Care Financing Administration (HCFA): The former name of the unit within the U.S. Department of Health and Human Services that manages Medicare and Medicaid, among other responsibilities. This unit is now the Centers for Medicare & Medicaid Services (CMS).

health care providers: Professional health service workers—physicians, dentists, psychologists—who are licensed to practice independently of any other health service worker.

health care work force: All of the people, professional and nonprofessional alike, who work in the health care services industry.

Health Insurance Portability and Accountability Act of 1996 (HIPAA): Key provisions of this federal law improve health coverage for workers and their families when they change or lose jobs and establish privacy standards for medical records, overseen by the Department of Health and Human Services Office of Civil Rights.

health maintenance organization (HMO): A managed care company that organizes and provides health care for its enrollees for a fixed prepaid premium.

Health Plan Employer Data and Information Set (HEDIS): A standard set of performance measures to measure the quality and performance of health plans, sponsored by the National Committee for Quality Assurance (NCQA).

health promotion (personal): Personal health promotion is the science and art of helping people change their life-style to move toward a state of optimal health. Optimal health is defined as a balance of physical, emotional, social, spiritual, and intellectual health.

health systems: Organizations that operate multiple service units under a single ownership.

Healthy People 2010: Formal goals and objectives for the nation's health status, updated every 10 years by the federal government.

home health care: Health services provided in an individual's home.

hospice care: Programs that operate in different settings to provide pain relief and comprehensive support services to dying patients, as well as counseling and bereavement support for their family members. Hospice care is reimbursable under Medicare and many state Medicaid programs, as well as private insurers.

hospitalists: Physicians, usually employed by hospitals, who practice only in acute care settings to provide inpatient care otherwise provided by attending physicians.

hospitalization: The admission of a patient to a hospital.

hospitalization coverage: A type of insurance coverage for most inpatient hospital costs (e.g., room and board), diagnostic and therapeutic services, care for emergency illnesses or injuries, laboratory and X ray services, and certain other specified procedures.

human genome: Projects to develop a draft of the human genetic code, involving billions of pairs of letters in the DNA sequence of 26,000 to 40,000 genes in the 23 human chromosomes.

incidence: The number of new events, disease cases, or conditions counted in a defined population during a defined period of time.

indemnity insurance: Benefits paid in a predetermined amount in the event of a covered loss; differs from reimbursement, which provides benefits based on actual expenses incurred. There are fewer restrictions on what a doctor may charge and what an insurer may pay for a treatment, and generally there are also fewer restrictions on a patient's ability to access specialty services.

independent practice association (IPA): Association of independent physicians formed as a separate legal entity for contracting purposes with health plans. Physicians see fee-for-service patients as well as those enrolled in HMOs.

infant mortality: The death of a child born alive before he or she reaches 1 year of age.

information technology: Electronic systems for communicating information. Health care organizations want information technology that is accessible—with privacy safeguards—to multiple users within an organization.

integrated delivery system (IDS): A group of health care organizations that collectively provides a full range of health-related services in a coordinated fashion to those using the system.

integration, horizontal: Affiliations among providers of the same type (e.g., a hospital forming relationships with other hospitals).

integration, vertical: Affiliations among providers of different types (e.g., a hospital, clinic, and nursing home forming an affiliation).

international medical school graduate: A U.S. citizen or noncitizen physician who has graduated from a medical school not located in the United States that is also not accredited by the U.S. medical school accrediting body, the Liaison Committee on Medical Education.

investor-owned hospital: A hospital owned by one or more private parties or a corporation for the purpose of generating a profitable return on investment.

Joint Commission: Formerly the Joint Commission on Accreditation of Healthcare Organizations (JCAHO), the Joint Commission is a national organization of representatives of health care providers: American College of Physicians, American College of Surgeons, American Hospital Association, American Medical Association, and consumer representatives. The Joint Commission inspects and accredits quality of operations for hospitals and other health care organizations.

length of stay: Days billed for a period of hospitalization.

licensure: A system established by a given state recognizing the achievement of a defined level of education, experience, and examination performance as qualifying the person or organization meeting those standards to work or operate in a defined area of practice, prohibited to any person or organization that has not met those standards.

life expectancy: The predicted average number of years of life remaining for a person at a given age.

long-term care: A general term for a range of services provided to chronically ill, physically disabled, and mentally disabled patients in a nursing home or long-term home health care setting.

loss ratio: A term used to describe the amount of money spent on health care. A company with a loss ratio of .85, for instance, spends 85 cents of every premium dollar on health care and the remaining 15 cents on administrative costs, such as marketing and profits.

major medical: A precursor of catastrophic coverage, it is coverage characterized by larger maximum limits, which is intended to cover the cost associated with a major illness or injury.

managed care: A system of health care delivery that influences or controls utilization of services and costs of services. The degree of influence depends on the model used. For example, a preferred provider organization charges patients lower rates if they use the providers in the preferred network. HMOs, on the other hand, may choose not to reimburse for health services received from providers with whom the HMO does not contract.

mandated benefits: Benefits that a health plan is required to provide by law. This term generally refers to benefits above and beyond routine insurance-type benefits, and it generally applies at the state level (where there is high variability from state to state). Common examples include in vitro fertilization, defined days of inpatient mental health or substance abuse treatment, and other special condition treatments. Self-funded plans are exempt from mandated benefits under the Employee Retirement Income Security Act (ERISA).

Medicaid: A joint federal/state/local program of health care for individuals whose income and resources are insufficient to pay for their care, governed by Title XIX of the federal Social Security Act and administered by the states. Medicaid is the major source of payment for nursing home care of the elderly.

medically indigent: Those who do not have and cannot afford medical insurance coverage and who are not eligible financially for Medicaid.

medical savings account: Accounts similar to individual retirement accounts (IRAs) into which employers and employees can make tax-deferred contributions and from which employees may withdraw funds to pay covered health care expenses.

Medicare: A federal entitlement program of medical and health care coverage for the elderly and disabled and persons with end-stage renal disease, governed by Title XVIII of the federal Social Security Act and consisting of several parts: Part A for institutional and home care; Part B for physician care; a managed care component (informally called Part C); and Part D, covering prescription drugs.

Medicare Prescription Drug, Improvement, and Modernization Act (MMA): Federal law signed in 2004 that offers a discount card at a nominal fee to Medicare beneficiaries for drugs and a prescription drug benefit starting in 2006 for those on Medicare who enroll and pay a premium.

medigap: Also known as Medicare supplement insurance, a type of private insurance coverage that may be purchased by an individual enrolled in Medicare to cover certain needed services that are not covered by Medicare Parts A and B (i.e., "gaps").

morbidity: An episode of sickness, as defined by a health professional. A morbidity rate is the number of such episodes occurring in a given population during a given period of time.

mortality: A death. A mortality rate is the number of deaths (either the crude rate, which is all deaths, or a specific rate, which is number of deaths by, for example, a specific cause, at a specific location, or within a specific age group) occurring during a given period of time.

natality: A live birth. The natality rate is the number of live births occurring in a given population during a given period of time.

national health insurance: A system for paying for one or more categories of health care service that is organized on a nationwide basis, established by law and usually operated by a government agency.

National Health Service (NHI): In the United States and Great Britain, NHI refers specifically to the comprehensive, government-funded and -operated system such as that found in Great Britain.

network: An arrangement of several delivery points (i.e., medical group practices affiliated with a managed care organization); an arrangement of HMOs (either autonomous and separate legal entities or subsidiaries of a larger corporation) using one common insuring mechanism such as Blue Cross Blue Shield; a broker organization (health plan) that arranges with physician groups, carriers, payer agencies, consumer groups, and others for services to be provided to enrollees.

nonprofit or not-for-profit plan: A term applied to a prepaid health plan under which no part of the net earnings accrues, or may lawfully accrue, to the benefit of any private shareholder or individual. An organization that has received 501-C-3 or 501-C-4 designation by the Internal Revenue Service.

numerator: For health care, a number of events, disease occurrences, or conditions that are counted over some defined period of time.

nurse practitioner (NP): Registered nurses who have been trained at the master's level in providing primary care services, expanded health care evaluations and decision making, and prescriptions under a physician's supervision.

office visit: A formal, face-to-face contact between a physician and a patient in a health center, office, or hospital outpatient department.

open enrollment period: A requirement that all possible customers for a particular health insurance policy be accepted at all times for coverage and, once accepted, not to be terminated by the insurer due to claims experience.

outcomes: Measures of treatments and effectiveness in terms of access, quality, and cost.

outlier: Under a DRG system of payment, additional per diem payments are made to the hospital for cases requiring a patient to stay in the hospital beyond a threshold length of stay. Such cases are referred to as long-stay outliers.

per diem payment: Reimbursement rates that are paid to providers for each day of services provided to a patient, based on the patient's illness or condition.

physician assistant (PA): A specially trained and licensed worker who performs certain medical procedures under the supervision of a physician. Physician assistants are usually not registered nurses.

point-of-service plan (POS): A managed care plan that offers enrollees the option of receiving services from participating or nonparticipating providers. The benefits package is designed to encourage the use of participating providers, through higher deductibles and/or partial reimbursement for services provided by nonparticipating providers.

policy: Guidelines adopted by organizations and governments that promote or constrain decision making and action and limit subsequent choices.

preexisting condition: A physical and/or mental condition of an insured that first manifests itself prior to issuance of a policy or that exists prior to issuance and for which treatment was received.

preferred provider organization (PPO): A limited group (panel) of providers (doctors and/or hospitals) who agree to provide health care to subscribers for a negotiated and usually discounted fee and who agree to utilization review. The arrangement created among the providers and others (employers, unions, commercial insurers, HMOs, etc.) is called a PPA or preferred provider arrangement.

premium: A periodic payment required to keep an insurance policy in force.

prepayment: A method of providing in advance for the cost of predetermined benefits for a population group through regular periodic payments in the form of premiums, dues, or contributions, including contributions that are made to a health and welfare fund by employers on behalf of their employees and payments to managed care organizations made by federal agencies for Medicare eligibles.

prescription: An order, usually made in writing, from a licensed physician or an authorized designee to a pharmacy, directing the latter to dispense a given drug, with written instructions for its use.

prevalence: The total number of events, disease cases, or conditions existing in a defined population, counted during a defined period of time or at a given point in time (known as point-prevalence).

primary care: The general health care that people receive on a routine basis that is not associated with an acute or chronic illness or disability and may be provided by a physician, nurse practitioner, or physician assistant. Definitions of primary care physicians usually include those who practice family medicine, pediatrics, and internal medicine; other physicians often included in this definition are obstetricians and gynecologists, as well as practitioners of preventive and emergency medicine.

primary care practitioners: Doctors in family practice, general internal medicine, or pediatrics; nurse practitioners and midwives; and may also include psychiatrists and emergency care physicians.

privileges: Rights granted annually to physicians and affiliate staff members to perform specified kinds of care in the hospital.

public hospital: A hospital operated by a government agency. In the United States, the most common are the federal government's Department of Veterans Affairs; state governments' mental hospitals; and local governments' general hospitals for the care of the poor and otherwise uninsured.

public psychiatric hospital: A hospital devoted to the treatment and management of mental illness and disorders, owned and operated by a government agency (in the United States, most commonly at the state level).

quality assurance: A formal set of activities to measure the quality of services provided; these may also include corrective measures.

quality of care: A measurement of the quality of health care provided to individuals or groups of patients, against a previously defined standard.

rates, crude and specific: A rate is a measure of some event, disease, or condition occurring in members of a defined population divided by the total number in that population. For crude rates, the whole population is the denominator. A specific rate defines the denominator by one or more demographic characteristics.

registered nurse: A nurse who is a graduate of an approved education program leading to diploma, an associate degree, or a bachelor's degree, who has also met the requirements of experience and exam passage to be licensed in a given state.

reinsurance: Insurance purchased by a health plan to protect it against extremely high-cost cases.

relative value system (RVS): A method of valuing medical services, especially physician services. The federal government changed to a resource-based relative value scale (RBRVS) physician payment system in early 1992, an RVS payment system for physician services to Medicare recipients. Each service is assigned a given number of relative value units based on, for example, how long it takes to do a procedure, which is multiplied by a national conversion factor to determine a dollar amount for payment of that service.

reserves: A fiscal method of withholding a certain percentage of premiums to provide a fund for committed but undelivered health care and such uncertainties as higher hospital utilization levels than expected, overutilization of referrals, and accidental catastrophes.

resource-based relative value scale (RBRVS): As of January 1, 1992, Medicare payments are based on a resource-based relative value scale, replacing the customary and prevailing charge mechanism for fee-for-service providers participating in the Medicare program. The objective is for physician fees to reflect the relative value of work performed, their practice expense, and malpractice insurance costs.

risk: Any chance of loss, or the possibility that revenues of the health plan will not be sufficient to cover expenditures incurred in the delivery of contractual services.

risk contract: A contract to provide services to beneficiaries under which the health plan receives a fixed monthly payment for enrolled members and then must provide all services on an at-risk basis.

risk management: Identification, evaluation, and corrective action against organizational behaviors that would otherwise result in financial loss or legal liability.

Sarbanes-Oxley Act (SOA): The 2002 federal legislation that affects corporate governance, financial disclosure, and the practice of public accounting.

self-insurance: A program for providing group insurance with benefits financed entirely through the internal means of the policyholder, in place of purchasing coverage from commercial carriers. By self-insuring, firms avoid paying state taxes on premiums and are largely exempt from state-imposed mandates.

skilled nursing facility (SNF): Facility providing care for patients who no longer require treatment in the hospital but who do require 24-hour medical care or rehabilitation services.

socialized health service: Usually an epithet used by opponents of any type of national government involvement in either the financing or operation of a health care delivery system on a nationwide basis to describe any such system, regardless of whether such a government could be defined as socialist.

solo practice: Individual practice of medicine by a physician who does not practice in a group or does not share personnel, facilities, or equipment with three or more physicians.

staff model: An HMO that employs providers, who see members in the HMO's own facilities. A form of closed-panel HMO.

stakeholders: Persons with an interest in the performance of an organization. Examples of hospital stakeholders are physicians and nurses, payers, managers, patients, and government.

Stark legislation: Federal laws (named after their sponsor, California Rep. Fortney "Pete" Stark) that place limits on physicians referring patients to facilities in which they have a financial interest.

strategic planning: A process reviewing the mission, environmental surveillance, and previous planning decisions used to establish major goals and nonrecurring resource allocation decisions.

surveillance: Ongoing observation of a population for rapid and accurate detection of events, conditions, or diseases.

teaching hospital: A hospital in which undergraduate and/or graduate medical education takes place.

tertiary care: Highly specialized medical care or procedures that are performed by specialized physicians in some, but not all, hospitals.

third-party administrator: An organization that acts as an intermediary between the provider and consumer of care but does not insure care.

underwriting: Bearing the risk for something (i.e., a policy is underwritten by an insurance company); also the analysis that is done for a group to determine rates or to determine whether the group should be offered coverage.

uninsured: In the United States, a person who is not the beneficiary of any third-party source of payment for health care services.

universal health insurance: A national health insurance system that provides for comprehensive coverage for all permanent residents of a country.

utilization: Quantity of services used by patients, such as hospital days, physician visits, or prescriptions.

utilization review: A system for measuring and evaluating the utilization by physicians for their patients of various health services ranging from diagnostic tests to admission to hospital, against a preestablished standard of "good" or "appropriate" utilization of such services.

vertical integration: The affiliation of organizations providing different kinds of service, such as hospital care, ambulatory care, long-term care, and social services.

vital statistics: Numbers and rates for births, deaths, abortions, fetal deaths, fertility, life expectancy, marriages, and divorces.

volunteers: People who are not paid for giving their time and service to a health care organization, their only compensation being the satisfaction they achieve from their work.

wraparound plan: Insurance or health plan coverage for co-payments and deductibles that are not covered under a member's base plan, such as Medicare.

Appendix B
A Guide to Sources of Data

Jennifer A. Nelson and Mary Ann Chiasson

This appendix is a guide to the principal sources of health and health services data for the United States as of 2007. It contains up-to-date descriptions of these sources, indicates how frequently each is published, lists the categories of data and other information they contain, and gives information for ordering and downloading. Also included is a brief introduction to sources of international data.

Almost all federal sources of data are available for purchase through the U.S. Government Printing Office (USGPO), Superintendent of Documents, PO Box 371954, Pittsburgh, PA 15250-7954; Web site: bookstore.gpo.gov; telephone (866) 512-1800; fax (202) 512-2104.

Health data are available not only in print form, but also on the Internet. Many of the publications listed in this appendix are available in whole or in part via the Internet; others may be ordered using the Internet. In fact, to reduce costs, many organizations and government agencies are producing fewer print versions of their publications than in the past, and some elect to produce only electronic reports.

Basic statistical tables are often included on government and organization Web sites, sometimes via an interactive database that allows users to design tables with variables of interest. In addition, many data sets are available for public use and can be downloaded from the Internet or ordered on CD. Most of the data available online, particularly data from federal sources, are free.

Comprehensive Guides to Data Sources

There are at least two comprehensive guides to sources of data that are published annually. The first appears in the *Statistical Abstract of the United States*. Its Appendix I, "Guide to Sources of Statistics, State Statistical Abstracts and Foreign Statistical Abstracts," contains an extensive listing of sources of health data (as well as the sources of all other data appearing in the *Statistical Abstract*). Appendix III, "Limitations of the Data," presents brief descriptions and analyses of the limitations of the major sources of data listed in Appendix I.

The second regularly published comprehensive guide to sources appears in *Health, United States*. Its Appendix I contains very useful, detailed descriptions of all the common health data sources published by the several branches of the federal government, the United Nations, and some private agencies.

In addition, the *AHA Guide*, published regularly by the American Hospital Association, lists in its Part C the major national, international, U.S. government, state and local government, and private "Health Organizations, Agencies, and Providers," with addresses, telephone numbers, and Web site addresses.

Using the Internet to Access Data

The Internet has changed the way that we seek and retrieve data. Information and statistics on almost any topic can be easily obtained with a few clicks of a computer mouse. However, the volume of information available can be overwhelming, and it can be difficult to know where to begin to look for the particular bit of information needed. The following suggestions are a few places to begin a search for health and health services data. Specific Internet addresses relating to the principal sources listed in the following sections are noted in those sections.

The federal government is a major source of health data. Each department of the U.S. government has an Internet address; some of them are listed in the sections below. All federal government department and agency Web sites can be accessed through **www.usa.gov** (formerly www.firstgov.gov). In addition, access to federal data produced by more than 100 agencies in the U.S. government can be obtained via **www.fedstats.gov.** Two agencies that are responsible for a large amount of population, health, and health services data are the U.S. Census Bureau (**www.census.gov**) and the Centers for Disease Control and Prevention (**www.cdc.gov**). Exploring their Web sites is a good way to become familiar with the data available.

Most states and professional organizations have Web sites as well. Links to state and local sites, which can be excellent sources of state and local data, are available at **www.statelocalgov.net** or through **www.firstgov.gov.** The Web sites of state departments of health and other agencies can also be reached via state homepages.

Internet search engines such as Yahoo and Google can also be used to locate the sites of government agencies and health organizations that have health and health care information and data.

Principal Sources of U.S. Health and Health Care Data

CENTERS FOR DISEASE CONTROL AND PREVENTION (CDC)

Web site: www.cdc.gov

The CDC has created a Web site—www.cdc.gov/DataStatistics—that serves as a portal to the wealth of data available, including the sources detailed below. A number of interactive tools allow users to query databases and create tables to meet their needs.

National Center for Health Statistics (NCHS)

Web site: www.cdc.gov/nchs

Part of the Centers for Disease Control and Prevention in the U.S. Department of Health and Human Services, the National Center for Health Statistics (NCHS) is the federal government's primary agency for vital and health statistics. Through its data systems, the NCHS collects data on health status, health behavior, and the use of health care; it also serves as the repository for data from the nation's vital statistics systems. Data are collected through national population surveys such as the National Health and Nutrition Examination Survey (NHANES), the National Health Interview Survey (NHIS), the National Survey of Family Growth (NSFG), and the National Immunization Survey (NIS). Health services data are collected through a family of surveys of health care providers, collectively known as the National Health Care Survey (NHCS), which includes the National Hospital Discharge Survey (NHDS), the National Ambulatory Medical Care Survey (NAMCS), the

National Hospital Ambulatory Medical Care Survey (NHAMCS), the National Survey of Ambulatory Surgery (NSAS), the National Nursing Home Survey (NNHS), the National Home and Hospice Care Survey (NHHCS), and the National Employer Health Insurance Survey (NEHIS). Data from the Vital Statistics System and the health surveys are published in a series of regular and periodic reports. The center's Web site serves as an entry to a great deal of information about these data systems and to data in tabular form, as well as publication lists and downloadable versions of many publications. In addition, many of these data sets are available for public use and can be downloaded from the Web site.

Health, United States. *Health, United States* is published annually. A wide variety of health and health care delivery systems data are presented, primarily in tabular form, under categories such as population, fertility and natality, mortality, determinants and measures of health, utilization of health resources, health care resources, health care expenditures, and health insurance. *Health, United States* also contains useful appendices describing sources and limitations of the data (described above), as well as a glossary (Appendix II: Definitions and Methods). It is a boon to students and researchers in health care delivery systems analysis because it provides one-stop shopping for the most important health and health care data.

To order: USGPO
To download: www.cdc.gov/nchs/hus.htm

National Vital Statistics Report (NVSR). The *NVSR* publishes several types of reports. "Provisional Data," published monthly, contains the most recent figures for the traditional vital statistics—births, deaths, marriages, and divorces. The *NVSR* publishes preliminary and final data on each of these vital statistics for each year. In addition, special analyses on related topics using vital statistics data appear periodically. These reports were formerly published as *Monthly Vital Statistics Reports.*

To order: USGPO
To download: www.cdc.gov/nchs/products/pubs/pubd/nvsr/nvsr.htm
www.cdc.gov/nchs/nvss.htm (entry page for vital statistics reports and data)

Vital Statistics of the United States (VSUS). These are the full, highly detailed annual reports on vital statistics from the NCHS, the summary versions of which are published in the supplements of the *NVSR.* Data are available for years from 1890 to the present.

To order: Reports for some years are available from USGPO.
To download: www.cdc.gov/nchs/products/pubs/pubd/vsus/vsus.htm

Vital and Health Statistics. These publications of the NCHS, distinct from the Vital Statistics reports described above, appear at irregular intervals. As of 2004, there were 18 series, not numbered consecutively. Most of them report data from ongoing studies and surveys that the NCHS carries out, such as NHIS, NSFG, and others listed above. Also published are *Advance Data From Vital and Health Statistics,* which provide early data from many of the surveys, detailed reports on which are often later published in the following 18 series: Series 1, Programs and Collection Procedures; Series 2, Data Evaluation and Methods Research; Series 3, Analytical and Epidemiological Studies; Series 4, Documents and Committee Reports; Series 5, International Vital and Health Statistics Reports; Series 6, Cognition and Survey Measurement; Series 10, Data From the National Health Interview Survey; Series 11, Data From the National Health Examination Survey, the National Health and Nutrition Examination Surveys, and the Hispanic Health and Nutrition Examination Survey; Series 12, Data From the Institutionalized Populations Surveys; Series 13, Data From the National Health Care Survey; Series 14, Data on Health Resources: Manpower and Facilities; Series 15, Data From Special Surveys; Series 16, Compilations of Advance Data From Vital and Health Statistics; Series 20, Data on Mortality; Series 21, Data on Natality, Marriage, and Divorce; Series 22, Data From the National Mortality and Mortality Natality Surveys; Series 23, Data From the National Survey of Family Growth; Series 24, Compilations of Data on Natality, Mortality, Marriage, and Divorce.

To order: USGPO
To download: www.cdc.gov/nchs/products/pubs/pubd/series/ser.htm

National Center for Chronic Disease Prevention and Health Promotion (NCCDPHP)

Web site: www.cdc.gov/nccdphp

Charged with preventing and controlling chronic disease and promoting healthy behaviors, the National Center for Chronic Disease Prevention and Health Promotion not only supports and administers programs, but also collects data to monitor the progress of those efforts and to measure the prevalence of health risk behaviors. The surveillance systems listed below are a major part of these efforts and are collaborations with state health and education departments and other agencies.

Behavioral Risk Factor Surveillance System (BRFSS)
Web site: www.cdc.gov/brfss

The Behavioral Risk Factor Surveillance System (BRFSS) is an ongoing data collection program designed to serve a dual purpose: to meet the need for behavioral health data, necessary for designing preventive programs to reduce morbidity and mortality, and to meet the need for that data at the state level, where the activities and targeting of resources generally occur. States use a CDC-developed standard core questionnaire to conduct telephone surveys collecting data on health risks and behaviors. BRFSS data files for 1984–2006 are available to download free in several formats. In addition, *BRFSS Summary Prevalence Reports* are available for 1997–2001. Topics covered include general health status; quality of life; health insurance; smoking status; alcohol consumption; immunization; HIV/AIDS; overweight/obesity; and screening for diabetes, cholesterol, hypertension, and colorectal, breast, and cervical cancer. These reports are available to download from the BRFSS Web site. Prevalence and trends data, much of it accessed through an interactive database, are also available directly from the Web site. In addition, the Web site includes searchable databases of published work that uses BRFSS data.

Youth Behavioral Risk Surveillance System (YBRSS)
Web site: www.cdc.gov/yrbss

The Youth Behavioral Risk Surveillance System was designed to monitor health risk behaviors, such as tobacco, alcohol, and drug use; unhealthy diet and inadequate physical activity; sexual risk behaviors; and behaviors related to unintentional injury and violence, among the nation's youth. The YBRSS includes a national survey conducted by CDC as well as state and local surveys conducted by local health and education departments, all directed toward 9th through 12th grade students. Representative samples of public and private high school students are surveyed every 2 years using a standard questionnaire. Data files (1991–2005), fact sheets, a bibliography, and data tables created through an interactive database are available on the YBRSS Web site.

Pregnancy Risk Assessment Monitoring System (PRAMS)
Web site: www.cdc.gov/prams

The Pregnancy Risk Assessment Monitoring System is a state-specific surveillance system surveying a population-based sample of women who have recently delivered a live infant about maternal attitudes and behaviors during and immediately following pregnancy. Thirty-seven states and New York City participate in PRAMS as of 2007. The

PRAMS Web site includes Surveillance Reports, which can be downloaded, as well as a list of publications that use PRAMS data. Outside researchers may submit proposals for use of PRAMS data sets.

Cancer Registries
Web sites: www.cdc.gov/cancer/npcr
            seer.cancer.gov

State cancer registries collect data on incidence, stage of disease at diagnosis, treatment, and outcomes for the different cancer types and body locations. The CDC supports these registries and promotes the use of data collected through its National Program of Cancer Registries (NPCR). In conjunction with the National Cancer Institute's Surveillance, Epidemiology, and End Results (SEER) Program, NPCR periodically produces *United States Cancer Statistics* (most recently in 2003), a compilation of data collected by the registries. Additional state and national data are available from the NPCR and SEER (seer.cancer.gov) Web sites.

Morbidity and Mortality Weekly Report (MMWR)
Web site: www.cdc.gov/mmwr

This is a weekly publication of the Centers for Disease Control and Prevention. It is available free via the Internet or e-mail subscription. It is also available by annual subscription from the USGPO. However, following a large subscription price increase in 1982, *MMWR,* in the public domain, has also been made available at a much lower cost by other organizations, such as the Massachusetts Medical Society. In the past, *MMWR* was concerned primarily with communicable disease reporting, and it continues to provide reports on infectious disease surveillance. However, *MMWR* now also regularly presents brief reports on chronic diseases and special studies of such diverse health topics as alcohol consumption among pregnant and childbearing-age women, human rabies, progress toward global poliomyelitis eradication, rubella syndrome in the United States, adult blood-lead epidemiology and surveillance, prevalence of arthritis, state-specific prevalence of cigarette smoking among adults, and many other topics. In addition to articles, *MMWR* publishes weekly the numbers by state of reported provisional cases of selected notifiable diseases (from the National Notifiable Disease Surveillance System), including (as of 2007) AIDS; chlamydia; coccidiodomycosis; cryptosporidiosis; encephalitis/meningitis; West Nile; *Escherichia coli;* giardiasis; gonorrhea; *H. influenzae* (invasive); viral hepatitis (acute, by type); Legionellosis; Listeriosis; Lyme disease; malaria; meningococcal disease; pertussis; animal rabies; Rocky Mountain spotted fever; salmonellosis; shigellosis; streptococcal disease (invasive, group A); *Streptococcus pneumoniae* (invasive); primary, secondary, and congenital syphilis; tuberculosis; typhoid fever; and varicella. *MMWR* also reports deaths in 122 U.S. cities on a weekly basis and periodically publishes "Recommendations and Reports" of various governmental and nongovernmental health agencies and organizations and the results of "CDC Surveillance Summaries" on various diseases, conditions, and procedures.

To order: www.cdc.gov/mmwr (e-mail); USGPO (print); Massachusetts Medical Society, CSPO Box 9120, Waltham, MA 02454-9120; telephone (800) 843-6356 (print)
To download: www.cdc.gov/mmwr (editions from 1982 to the present are available)

UNITED STATES CENSUS BUREAU
Web site: www.census.gov

Statistical Abstract of the United States
Web site: www.census.gov/compendia/statab

Published annually by the U.S. Census Bureau, the *Statistical Abstract* contains a vast collection of tables reporting information and data collected by many different government (and in certain cases nongovernment) agencies. The principal health and health services data are found under the headings Population, Vital Statistics, and Health and Nutrition.

To order: USGPO; www.ntis.gov/product/statistical-abstract.htm; a CD version is available from Customer Services Center, Census Bureau, telephone (301) 763-INFO (4636); fax (301) 457-3842
To download: www.census.gov/compendia/statab

U.S. Census of Population
Web site: www.census.gov/main/www/cen2000.html
(2000 census)

The U.S. Constitution requires that a census be taken every 10 years, at the beginning of each decade. The original purpose of the census was to apportion seats in the House of Representatives. Since it was first taken, the census and the voluminous amount of data it produces—going well beyond a simple count—have come to serve many other purposes as well. In addition to the decennial census, the Census Bureau conducts a multitude of other surveys each year. One of these, the relatively new American Community Survey collects each year from a sample of approximately three million households the population and housing information that previously was collected every

10 years. Many reports on the decennial censuses, as well as the interim surveys and analyses, are published by the Census Bureau (a part of the U.S. Department of Commerce). A good place to begin is in Section 1 of the *Statistical Abstract.* Also available are special analyses for a wide variety of geographical subdivisions of the country. In addition, many data products, including datasets, reports, and tables created through interactive databases, can be accessed through the Census Bureau Web site. Data access tools, including American FactFinder, can be found at www.census.gov/main/www.access.html.

To order: USGPO; Customer Services Center, Census Bureau, telephone (301) 763-INFO (4636); fax (301) 457-3842; Online Sales Catalog: census catalog.mso.census.gov/esales
To download: Data and publications may be downloaded from various parts of the Web site. Most reports can be accessed through www.census. gov/prod/cen2000/index.html or www.census.gov/prod/www/titles.html

Current Population Reports

Web site: www.census.gov/main/www/cprs.html

In addition to reports from the decennial censuses, the Census Bureau regularly publishes *Current Population Reports (CPRs),* based on data obtained through the Current Population Survey (CPS). They present estimates, projections, sample counts, and special studies of selected segments of the population. Reports in the following series are available: P-20, Population Characteristics; P-23, Special Studies; P-25, Population Estimates and Projections; P-60, Consumer Income; and P-70, Household Economic Studies. CDs with data files and reports can be ordered through the Census Bureau. In addition, data files, data tables, and technical information are available from www.census.gov/cps.

To order: USGPO; Customer Services Center, Census Bureau, telephone (301) 763-INFO (4636); fax (301) 457-3842
To download: www.census.gov/main/www/cprs.html

CENTERS FOR MEDICARE AND MEDICAID SERVICES (CMS)

Web site: www.cms.hhs.gov

Health Care Financing Review

Web site: www.cms.hhs.gov/HealthCareFinancingReview/

The *Health Care Financing Review* is a quarterly publication of the Centers for Medicare & Medicaid Services (CMS), formerly the Health

Care Financing Administration (HCFA), in the U.S. Department of Health and Human Services. It annually publishes the official CMS reports, "National Health Expenditures" and "Health Care Indicators." It also publishes an extensive and wide-ranging series of academic articles, reports, and studies. The emphasis is on Medicare/Medicaid (for which CMS is directly responsible), but "a broad range of health care financing and delivery issues" are also covered. CMS also publishes an annual Medicare & Medicaid Statistical Supplement to the Health Care Financing Review.

To order: USGPO (subscription)
To download: www.cms.hhs.gov/HealthCareFinancingReview

Other Data Available From CMS

CMS makes available additional data on health care financing, particularly Medicare and Medicaid. It publishes an annual *Data Compendium,* which includes historic, current, and projected data about these programs. This compendium and other CMS data and statistics, including data tables and data files from the Medicaid and Medicare systems, can be accessed at **www.cms.hhs.gov/home/ rsds.asp.**

AMERICAN HOSPITAL ASSOCIATION (AHA)

Web site: www.aha.org

American Hospital Association Guide to the Health Care Field

The *AHA Guide,* available in print or on CD, lists and profiles U.S. hospitals and health care organizations, including systems, networks, and alliances. It includes basic data on size, location, type, ownership, and services as well as information on utilization and expenses. It also contains the comprehensive lists of health and health care organizations referred to in an earlier section of this appendix.

To order: tel. (800) 242–2626; fax: (866) 516–5817; e-mail: aha-orders@ tbd.com; www.ahaonlinestore.com

Hospital Statistics

AHA also publishes *Hospital Statistics,* based on an annual survey of over 5,000 hospitals. It contains a great deal of summary descriptive, utilization, and financial data on U.S. hospitals, presented in many different cross-tabulations. It can also be purchased on a CD, which includes Microsoft Excel data tables and allows users to customize tables.

To order: telephone (800) 242-2626; fax (866) 516-5817; e-mail: aha-orders@tbd.com; www.ahaonlinestore.com
To download: Not available

PHYSICIAN AND NURSING ORGANIZATIONS

American Medical Association (AMA)

Web site: www.ama-assn.org

The AMA produces a variety of useful data on the physician work force and related subjects. The AMA regularly conducts surveys of physicians, medical groups, and residency programs. Titles appearing on a regular basis include *Physician Compensation and Production Survey Report, State Medical Licensure Requirements and Statistics,* and *Physician Characteristics and Distribution in the U.S.*

To order: telephone (800) 621-8335; catalog.ama-assn.org/Catalog/home.jsp
To download: Very little is available for free download

National Council of State Boards of Nursing

Web site: www.ncsbn.org

The National Council of State Boards of Nursing is a source of data about the licensing and employment of nurses. The Council regularly compiles *Licensure and Examination Statistics* and publishes a series of reports on findings from the Practice Analysis Studies. Information, abstracts, executive summaries, and limited data are available online, while these and other publications may be purchased.

To order: NCSBN Orders, PO Box 541, Mt. Morris, IL 61054-0541; telephone (800) 765-3944; ncsbn.k-online.biz
To download: Some research briefs are available for free download; others must be purchased: www.ncsbn.org/269.htm

International Health and Health Services Data

What follows is not a comprehensive guide to sources of international population and health data, but a description of several major sources, which are good places to begin. Many of the Web sites listed below also include links to other sites where international health data may be found, including foreign government Web sites and statistical and health agencies in countries around the world.

U.S. CENSUS BUREAU INTERNATIONAL PROGRAMS CENTER

Web site: www.census.gov/ipc/www

The International Programs Center (IPC) of the U.S. Census Bureau periodically produces a publication entitled *Global Population Profile* (formerly *World Population Profile*). It includes data on population growth, fertility, mortality, migration, population aging, and contraceptive use for the world, regions, development categories, and some specific countries. The International Programs Center also produces other reports on various related topics. In addition, it administers an online International Database that has statistical tables of demographic and socioeconomic data for all countries of the world.

To order: USGPO; Customer Services Center, Census Bureau, telephone (301) 763-INFO (4636); fax (301) 457-3842
To download: www.census.gov/ipc/www/publist.html

UNITED NATIONS (UN)

Web site: www.un.org

The United Nations system is comprised of a host of agencies and organizations devoted to a wide variety of topics of international relevance; many of these collect and compile population and health data.

Most UN publications can be ordered through the UN Publications Department (United Nations Publications, 2 UN Plaza, Room DC2-853, New York, NY 10017; telephone [800] 253-9646; [212] 963-8302; fax [212] 963-3489; e-mail: publications@un.org) or online at www.un.org/Pubs. An online catalog of UN publications is available through the publications Web site, or a copy can be requested via e-mail to publications@un.org. Specific ordering information for some publications can be found on individual agency Web sites. Many online UN databases can also be accessed through the publications Web page.

Links to the Web sites of all UN agencies can be found at **www. unsystem.org.** Some UN offices and agencies to consider when looking for international health data are World Health Organization (WHO), United Nations Population Fund (UNFPA), United Nations Statistics Division (UNSD), United Nations Children's Fund (UNICEF), Joint United Nations Program on HIV/AIDS (UNAIDS), and the Population Division of the United Nations Department of Economic and Social Affairs (UNPD).

World Health Organization (WHO)

Web site: www.who.int

The World Health Organization is the principal UN source for health and health care data. The WHO publishes an annual *World Health Report* that includes a number of population health indicators as well as a narrative discussion of world health, each year examining one additional topic in more depth. For example, the 2006 *Report* focuses on the global health care work force. Other publications include *World Health Statistics* and the *Weekly Epidemiological Record.* The WHO Statistical Information System (WHOSIS; www.who.int/whosis) includes core health indicators from the *Report* as well as links to a variety of other information and data, to other world health sites, and to the Department of Health or Statistical Bureau Web sites for many countries.

To order: www.who.int/publications/; WHO Publications Center USA, 5 Sand Creek Road, Albany, NY 12205-1400, telephone (518) 436-9686, fax (518) 436-7433; e-mail QCORP@compuserve.com
To download: www.who.int/publications;
www.who.int/whr (World Health Report)

United Nations Statistics Division (UNSD)

Web site: unstats.un.org/unsd

The United Nations Statistics Division provides statistics on numerous topics, including demographics and vital statistics. It publishes a *Monthly Bulletin of Statistics (MBS)* and a quarterly journal, *Population and Vital Statistics Report,* that reports population estimates, birth and mortality statistics for the world, regions, and 229 countries or areas. Both are available by subscription in online and print editions. The UNSD also publishes annually the *Demographic Yearbook* and two general statistical references: *Statistical Yearbook* and *World Statistics Pocketbook.* Limited data are freely available online and a number of data files are available for purchase on CD.

To order: UN Publications Department
To download: Not available

United Nations Population Fund (UNFPA)

Web site: www.unfpa.org

UNFPA produces an annual report entitled *The State of the World Population,* which includes statistics. It can be downloaded from

UNFPA or ordered through the UN Publications Department. Additional data and policy information are available in *Country Profiles for Population and Reproductive Health,* published biennially. Data from the report are also available online (www.unfpa.org/profile), where they are updated annually. This publication can be downloaded or requested directly from UNFPA.

To order: UN Publications Department
To download: www.unfpa.org/swp (State of the World Population)
www.unfpa.org/profile (Profiles)

United Nations Children's Fund (UNICEF)

Web site: www.unicef.org

Basic indicators related to child health, organized by country, can be accessed via the UNICEF Web site. In addition, information from UNICEF's key statistical databases can be accessed at **www.childinfo.org,** including data on child survival and health, nutrition, maternal health, and immunization, among other topics. UNICEF also produces an annual report, *The State of the World's Children,* which includes many child health statistics.

To order: UN Publications Department
To download: www.unicef.org/publications

United Nations Population Information Network (POPIN)

Web site: www.un.org/popin

The United Nations Population Information Network is a guide to population information on UN system Web sites. It provides links to statistics and publications on population-related data such as fertility, mortality, and migration produced by agencies and organizations throughout the UN system, including many of those listed above.

DEMOGRAPHIC AND HEALTH SURVEYS

Web site: www.measuredhs.com

The Demographic and Health Survey program, also known as MEASURE DHS, is funded by the United States Agency for International Development (USAID) and implemented by Macro International, Inc., and is a source of population and health data for developing countries. MEASURE DHS provides developing countries with assistance in undertaking surveys to collect data on population, family planning, maternal and child health, child survival, sexually transmitted infections, and reproductive health. These data are available for public use in a number of formats. Basic country statistics are available on the DHS Web site. Publications with comprehensive survey results for individual countries can be downloaded or ordered. Other publications available include comparative, analytic, and trend reports. Data sets are available to authorized researchers. The DHS STATcompiler (www.statcompiler.com) is an online database that allows users to create custom tables drawing on hundreds of surveys from numerous countries and including hundreds of indicators.

To order: www.measuredhs.com/pubs; telephone (301) 572-0958
To download: www.measuredhs.com/pubs

Appendix C
Useful Health Care Web Sites

Kelli A. Hurdle

Categories of Online Resources

1. Web site finders and links
2. Government Web site finders and links
3. Bibliographical search
4. Statistics and databases
5. Federal government agencies
6. Trade associations
7. Professional associations
8. Other health-related organizations
9. International health and health services data
10. Consulting firms
11. Online industry news
12. Magazines and journals online
13. Job search

This version of Appendix C builds on that of the previous edition, by Leslie Reis.

14. General information resources

15. Glossaries

WEB SITE FINDERS AND LINKS

www.aha.org/resources	American Hospital Association Resource Center; links to other health care–related Web sites
www.auburn.edu/~burnsma/ha.html	Auburn University's director of health administration and policy links
www.healthfinder.gov	Health Finder; search engine and links to other health sites
www.movingideas.com	Idea Central; health policy links
www.google.com	Google; generic Internet directory with hundreds of thousands of subject categories
medworld.stanford.edu	Independent Stanford Medical Student Web site; medical and health Web page search engine
www.medweb.emory.edu/medweb	MedWeb; Emory University's medical and health information search engine
www.health.gov.nhic	National Health Information Center; links to Web sites of 1,200 health organizations
www.understandinghealthcare.com	Understanding Healthcare; answers hundreds of key questions related to health and medical care, and provides links to other resources and Web sites

GOVERNMENT WEB SITE FINDERS AND LINKS

www.fedworld.gov	FedWorld; links and information search engine for the federal government
www.usa.gov	The U.S. government's official Web portal
www.statelocalgov.net/index.cfm	State and local government on the Internet; directory of official state, county, and city government Web sites
www.loc.gov/rr/news/stategov/stategov.html	Information on state and local governments as well as government documents; maintained by the Library of Congress
www.hhs.gov/agencies	U.S. Department of Health and Human Services (HHS); links to all HHS agencies

BIBLIOGRAPHICAL SEARCH

igm.nlm.nih.gov	Grateful Med; health care bibliographical search engine
www.ipl.org	Internet Public Library
lcweb.loc.gov	Library of Congress
www.medscape.com	Medscape; medical search engine; access to online journals and current news
www2.ari.net/chrc/oldchrc/nhirc	National Health Information Resources Center; clearinghouse and communications hub for health information
www.nlm.nih.gov	National Library of Medicine, National Institutes of Health
www.ncbi.nlm.nih.gov/pubmed	Pub Med; National Library of Medicine's search engine that accesses citations in MedLine and Pre-MedLine and other related databases
www.amedeo.com	Amedeo; Medical literature guide; links to Web sites on various health topics
www.ovid.com	Ovid; access to thousands of health journals, texts, and databases

STATISTICS AND DATABASES

www.ahcpr.gov/data	Agency for Healthcare Research and Quality; access to the Healthcare Cost and Utilization Project, the National Medical Expenditure Study, the Safety Net Monitoring Initiative, and other governmental data and studies
www.ahd.com	American Hospital Directory; online data for most U.S. hospitals constructed from claims data, cost reports, and other public use files obtained from the Centers for Medicare & Medicaid Services; includes hospital characteristics, financial data, inpatient utilization, outpatient utilization, and links to the hospitals' Web sites
stats.bls.gov/iif	Bureau of Labor Statistics; Injuries, Illnesses, and Fatality program data
oshpd.cahwnet.gov	California Office of Statewide Health Planning and Development; utilization and financial data for California hospitals and long-term care facilities

www.fedstats.gov	FedStats; links to federal data and statistics produced by government agencies
www.cms.hhs.gov	Centers for Medicare & Medicaid (formerly the Health Care Financing Administration); data and statistics, including utilization, financial, and monthly reports
www.hsls.pitt.edu/inters/guides/statcbw.html	Health Sciences Library System; guide to locating hospitals
www.health.gov/healthypeople	Healthy People; access to Healthy People 2010, of HHS, prevention agenda and national health objectives information
www.hospitallink.com	Hospital Link; provides basic information on all hospitals in the United States
www.healthgrades.com	Health Grades, The Healthcare Quality Experts; source of hospital quality ratings and advisory services
www.nahdo.org	National Association of Health Data Organizations; links to the sites of federal and state agencies, other health care associations, and nonprofit organizations that have health information and data
www.cdc.gov/nchs	National Center for Health Statistics; basic source of data in the health care field
www.nlm.nih.gov/databases	National Library of Medicine; affiliated with National Institutes of Health; databases and electronic information sources
www.census.gov/prod	*Statistical Abstract of the United States/Healthcare;* complete publications with over 1,000 tables and charts for years 2001–2003
www.census.gov/dmd	U.S. Census Bureau; Census 2000 data

FEDERAL GOVERNMENT AGENCIES

www.ahcpr.gov	Agency for Healthcare Research and Quality
stats.bls.gov	Bureau of Labor Statistics
www.census.gov	Census Bureau
www.cdc.gov	Centers for Disease Control and Prevention
www.cms.hhs.gov	Centers for Medicare & Medicaid Services (formerly HCFA)
www.cbo.gov	Congressional Budget Office
www.ha.osd.mil	Department of Defense, Health Affairs

www.ed.gov	Department of Education
www.dhhs.gov	Department of Health and Human Services
www.usdoj.gov	Department of Justice
www.dhs.gov/index.shtm	Department of Homeland Security
www.dol.gov	Department of Labor
www.va.gov	Department of Veterans Affairs
www.epa.gov	Environmental Protection Agency
www.uscourts.gov	Federal Judiciary
www.ftc.gov	Federal Trade Commission
www.fda.gov	Food and Drug Administration
www.gao.gov	Government Accountability Office
www.gpo.gov	Government Printing Office
www.hrsa.gov	Health Resources and Services Administration
www.house.gov	House of Representatives
www.ihs.gov	Indian Health Service
www.medpac.gov	Medicare Payment Advisory Commission
www.nih.gov	National Institutes of Health
www.nlm.nih.gov	National Library of Medicine
www.ophs.dhhs.gov/ophs	Office of Public Health and Science
www.senate.gov	Senate
www.ssa.gov	Social Security Administration
www.whitehouse.gov	White House

TRADE ASSOCIATIONS

www.advamed.org	Advanced Medical Technology Association; organizations that manufacture health care products and equipment
www.aahp.org	American Association of Health Plans; information and statistics regarding managed health care plan enrollment, benefits, utilization, and prices
www.aahc.net	American Association of Healthcare Consultants; consulting firms focusing on the health care industry
www.aaihds.org	American Association of Integrated Healthcare Delivery Systems

www.abms.org	American Board of Medical Specialties; medical specialty and subspecialty societies
www.ahca.org	American Health Care Association; assisted living, nursing facility, and subacute care providers
www.aha.org	American Hospital Association; hospital and health systems
www.abhw.org	Association of Behavioral Health and Wellness (formerly the American Managed Behavioral Healthcare Association); health plans focused exclusively on behavioral (mental) health and wellness
www.amia.org	American Medical Informatics Association; dedicated to the development and application of medical informatics in support of patient care, teaching research, and health care administration
www.aphanet.org	American Pharmacists Association; pharmacists, new practitioners, student pharmacists, and technicians
www.aslme.org	American Society of Law, Medicine and Ethics; provides information for professionals working with law, health care, policy and ethics; access to journals, newsletters, and research projects
www.aahcdc.org	Association of Academic Health Centers; medical and other health sciences schools in addition to their teaching hospitals
www.aamc.org	Association of American Medical Colleges; medical schools, academic societies, and teaching hospitals
www.aupha.org	Association of University Programs in Health Administration; graduate and undergraduate programs in health administration
www.chausa.org	Catholic Health Association; Catholic hospitals and health systems
www.fahs.com	Federation of American Health Systems; investor-owned hospitals and health systems
www.ahip.org	America's Health Insurance Plans; health insurance companies and managed care organizations
www.nahc.org	National Association for Home Care and Hospice; home care agencies, hospices, and home care aide organizations

www.nacds.org	National Association of Chain Drug Stores; represents views and policy positions of member drug chains
www.naph.org	National Association of Public Hospitals and Health Systems; provides legislative and public policy information publications
www.ncsbn.org	National Council of State Boards of Nursing; source of data about the licensing and employment of nurses; annual statistics and publications
www.nhpco.org	National Hospice and Palliative Care Organization; represents organizations that provide hospice and palliative care

PROFESSIONAL ASSOCIATIONS

www.aameda.org	American Academy of Medical Administrators; chief medical officers in hospitals and health systems
www.achca.org	American College of Health Care Administrators; managers of long-term care, assisted living, and subacute facilities
www.ache.org	American College of Health Care Executives; executives/managers in all types of health care organizations
www.acpe.org	American College of Physician Executives; physician executives in all segments of the health care industry
www.healthlawyers.org	American Health Lawyers Association
www.ama-assn.org	American Medical Association; physicians
www.ana.org	American Nurses' Association; registered nurses
www.osteopathic.org	American Osteopathic Association; osteopathic physicians
www.apha.org	American Public Health Association; public health professionals
www.aone.org	Association of Nurse Executives; nurse managers
www.aanp.org	American Academy of Nurse Practitioners
www.cmsa.org	Case Management Society of America; case managers
www.hfma.org	Health Care Financial Management Association; financial management professionals in health care organizations

www.mgma.com	Medical Group Management Association; physician practice and medical group managers
www.nahq.org	National Association for Healthcare Quality; quality management professionals
www.nahse.org	National Association of Health Services Executives; African American health care executives
www.nln.org	National League for Nursing; provides information on nursing education programs and publications
www.phrma.org	Pharmaceutical Researchers and Manufacturers of America; research-based pharmaceutical and biotechnology companies
www.nmha.org	National Mental Health Association
www.aapa.org	American Academy of Physician Assistants
www.naemt.org	National Association of Emergency Medical Technicians
www.apta.org	American Physical Therapy Association
www.certifieddoctor.org	American Board of Medical Specialties Public Education Program; verifies a doctor's certification status

OTHER HEALTH-RELATED ORGANIZATIONS: ASSOCIATIONS, ACCREDITING BODIES, CENTERS, INSTITUTES, AND FOUNDATIONS

www.aarp.org	American Association of Retired Persons
www.astho.org	Association of State and Territorial Health Officials; links to public health agencies in all states; state initiatives and publications; mission is to formulate and influence sound national public health policy and assist state health departments in the development and implementation of programs and policies to promote health and prevent disease
www.bluecares.com	Blue Cross and Blue Shield Association; represents Blue Cross and Blue Shield associations throughout the country
www.chcs.org	Center for Health Care Strategies; a health policy research and resource center affiliated with the Woodrow Wilson School of Public and International Affairs at Princeton University

www.futurehealth.ucsf.edu	Center for Health Professions; University of California, San Francisco–based health employment policy research center
www.hschange.com	Center for Studying Health System Change; Washington-based research organization dedicated to studying how the U.S. health care system is changing and how these changes are affecting communities
www.tcf.org	The Century Foundation; research foundation undertaking analyses of major economic, political, and social institutions and issues
www.cmwf.org	The Commonwealth Fund; a nonprofit foundation engaged in independent research on health and social policy issues; dedicated to improving health care coverage and quality
www.ebri.com	Employee Benefit Research Institute; conducts research on employee benefits provided by commercial corporations
www.iom.edu	Institute of Medicine; a component of the National Academy of Sciences that studies health policy issues
www.iha.org	Integrated Health Association; California-based group of health plans, physician groups, and health systems, plus academic, purchaser, and consumer representatives involved in policy development and special projects focused on integrated health care and managed care
www.ihi.org	Institute for Healthcare Improvement; a not-for-profit organization; aim is health care for all with no needless deaths, no needless pain or suffering, no helplessness in those served or serving, no unwanted waiting, no waste; Web site contains wealth of information and useful tools
www.jointcommission.org	The Joint Commission; "Helping Health Care Organizations Help Patients"; the accrediting body for health systems, hospitals, and other providers
www.kff.org	Kaiser Family Foundation; foundation supporting health services research and demonstration projects
www.markle.org	The Markle Foundation; addresses critical public needs, specifically in the areas of health and national safety

www.mathematica-mpr.com	Mathematica Policy Research; conducts health and social policy research
www.nashp.org	National Academy for State Health Policy; disseminates information designed to assist states in the development of practical, innovative solutions to complex health policy issues
www.nchc.org	National Coalition on Health Care; the nation's largest and most broadly representative alliance working to improve America's health care; research and education about emerging health trends and policy studies
www.ncsl.org/programs/health/ **forum/index.htm**	National Conference of State Legislatures; Forum for State Health Policy Leadership
www.ncqa.org	National Committee for Quality Assurance; accrediting body for managed health care plans and designers of HEDIS
www.soros.org	Open Society Institute and Soros Foundation Network; a private operating and grantmaking foundation that implements a range of initiatives to support the rule of law, education, public health, and independent media
www.projecthope.org	Project Hope; a nonprofit organization that conducts research and policy analysis on both U.S. and foreign health care systems
www.rand.org	RAND Corporation; a nonprofit institution that helps improve policy and decision making through research and analysis
www.rwjf.org	Robert Wood Johnson Foundation; nation's largest philanthropy focused on health care; funds health services, research, and demonstration projects
www.uhfnyc.org	United Hospital Fund; health services research and philanthropic organization that addresses issues affecting hospitals and health care in New York City
www.urban.org	Urban Institute; a nonprofit, nonpartisan economic and social policy research organization
www.wbgh.com	National Business Group on Health; national nonprofit organization devoted to the analysis of health policy and related

worksite issues from the perspective of large public-sector employers

www.wkkf.org

W. K. Kellogg Foundation; a foundation that funds health services research and demonstration projects

www.healthprivacy.org

Health Privacy Project; provides health care stakeholders with the information needed to work more effectively toward greater protection of health information through research studies, policy analyses, congressional testimony, extensive work with the media, and a Web site

www.wellspouse.org

Well Spouse Foundation; offers support to husbands, wives, and partners of people with chronic illnesses and disabilities

INTERNATIONAL HEALTH AND HEALTH SERVICES DATA

www.bls.gov/bls/other.htm

Bureau of Labor Statistics; national and international statistical agencies

www.census.gov/ipc/www

International Programs Center of the U.S. Census Bureau; *World Population Profile* last published in 2002; online international database

www.unsystem.org

United Nations; links to the Web sites of all UN agencies

www.unicef.org

United Nations Children's Fund; basic indicators related to child health; *The State of the World's Children,* published annually

www.un.org/popin

United Nations Population Information Network; a guide to population information on UN system Web sites

www.un.org/depts/unsd

United Nations Statistics Division; *Population and Vital Statistics Report* published quarterly

www.census.gov/main/www/ stat_int.html

U.S. Census Bureau; international statistics agencies

www.who.int/en

World Health Organization

www.who.int/whosis

World Health Organization Statistical Information System

www.measuredhs.com

Demographic and Health Survey Program; source of demographic and health data for developing countries

CONSULTING FIRMS

www.aahc.net	American Association of Healthcare Consultants
www.arthurandersen.com	Arthur Andersen, LLP
www.ey.com	Ernst and Young, LLP
www.gehealthcare.com/usen/index.html	GE Healthcare
www.kpmg.com	KPMG Consulting
www.lewin.com	The Lewin Group; health care and human service consulting firm
www.pwc.global.com	PricewaterhouseCoopers

ONLINE INDUSTRY NEWS: HEALTH NEWS UPDATED DAILY OR WEEKLY

www.ahanews.com	AHA News; daily reports for health care executives
www.cnn.com/health	CNN; health news updated daily
www.nytimes.com/pages/health/index.html	*New York Times;* health news updated daily
www.hhnmag.com	Health and Hospitals Network; health industry news updated daily
www.newsrx.net	News Rx Network; current news stories; reports on bioscience, biotech/pharma, health, and medicine
www.individual.com	Free customized news service; index of online news stories on a variety of topics; updated weekly; can select health care news page
kaisernetwork.org	Kaiser Network of the Kaiser Family Foundation; provides daily updates on health and health policy news, as well as Web casts, interviews, and public opinion

MAGAZINES AND JOURNALS ONLINE

www.apha.org/journal	*American Journal of Public Health* and *The Nation's Health;* published by the American Public Health Association; article archives
www.healthaffairs.org	*Health Affairs;* health policy articles and abstracts

www.cms.hhs.gov/review	*Health Care Financing Review;* source of Medicare and Medicaid data and national health statistics and expenditures
www.healthforum.com	*Health Forum Journal;* selected articles available for the past 5 years
www.jama.ama-assn.org	*Journal of the American Medical Association*
www.trusteemag.com	*Magazine for Health Care Governance;* article archive
www.managedcaremag.com	*Managed Care Magazine;* access to current articles and analyses
www.milbank.org/quarterly.html	*The Milbank Quarterly: Journal of Public Health and Health Care Policy;* access to current articles and archives
www.modernhealthcare.com	*Modern Healthcare;* weekly news journal for health care management professionals
www.cdc.gov/mmwr	*Morbidity and Mortality Weekly Report;* weekly publication of the Centers for Disease Control and Prevention
www.nejm.org	*New England Journal of Medicine*
www.jcrinc.com	*The Joint Commission Journal on Quality and Patient Safety*

JOB SEARCH

www.academyhealth.org/career/index.htm	Academy Health's career center; source for career advancement in the fields of health services research and health policy
www.ache.org/career.html	American College of Healthcare Executives; career page; employment opportunities listing
www.futurestep.com	Future Step, a Korn/Ferry Company; job search for employment in health administration
www.h-s.com	Heidrick and Struggles; executive search firm
www.kornferry.com	Korn/Ferry International; executive search firm
www.mcol.com/emp.htm	Managed Care On-Line; employment opportunities listing
www.tylerandco.com	Tyler and Company; executive search firm

GENERAL INFORMATION RESOURCES: REPOSITORIES OF GUIDES, STUDIES, PAPERS, INFORMATION, AND MORE

hippo.findlaw.com	Health Hippo; collection of policy and regulatory materials related to health care
www.healthhero.com	Health Hero Network; helps patients and providers communicate via the Web; involves patients in the management of their illnesses
www.healthweb.com	HealthWeb
www.medconnect.com	MedConnect; online resource for medical professionals
www.refdesk.com/health/html	Refdesk; virtual encyclopedia for health and medicine
www.hopkinsmedicine.com	Johns Hopkins Medicine; extensive online access to medical research and general health information
www.understandinghealthcare.com	Understanding Healthcare; answers hundreds of key questions related to health and medical care and provides links to other resources and Web sites; a virtual encyclopedia

GLOSSARIES

www.medterms.com	Medicine Net; online medical dictionary
medical-dictionary.com	Online medical dictionary
www.who.ch/pll/ter/dicfair.html	World Health Organization; medical terminology search engine and dictionary
www.webmd.com	Web MD; online medical information source

Index